# GENDER, SEX AND THE
# OF MODERN EUROPE

# GENDER, SEX AND THE SHAPING OF MODERN EUROPE

## A HISTORY FROM THE FRENCH REVOLUTION TO THE PRESENT DAY

### SECOND EDITION

*Annette F. Timm and Joshua A. Sanborn*

BLOOMSBURY ACADEMIC
LONDON · NEW YORK · OXFORD · NEW DELHI · SYDNEY

BLOOMSBURY ACADEMIC
Bloomsbury Publishing Plc
50 Bedford Square, London, WC1B 3DP, UK
1385 Broadway, New York, NY 10018, USA

BLOOMSBURY, BLOOMSBURY ACADEMIC and the Diana logo are trademarks of
Bloomsbury Publishing Plc

First edition published 2007 by Berg
Second edition first published 2016
Reprinted 2017 (twice), 2018, 2019

A catalogue record for this book is available from the British Library.

Library of Congress Cataloging-in-Publication Data
Names: Timm, Annette F., author. | Sanborn, Joshua A., author.
Title: Gender, sex and the shaping of modern Europe : a history from the
French Revolution to the present day / Annette F. Timm and Joshua A. Sanborn.
Description: Second edition. | London ; New York : Bloomsbury Academic, 2016. |
Includes bibliographical references and index.
Identifiers: LCCN 2015035975| ISBN 9781472583802 (pbk.) |
ISBN 9781472583819 (hardback)
Subjects: LCSH: Sex role–Europe–History. | Sex–Europe–History. |
Europe–Social conditions–1789-1900. | Europe–Social conditions–20th century. |
Europe–History. | Social history.
Classification: LCC HQ1075.5.E85 T56 2016 | DDC 305.3094–dc23
LC record available at http://lccn.loc.gov/2015035975

ISBN: HB: 978-1-4725-8381-9
PB: 978-1-4725-8380-2
ePDF: 978-1-4725-8382-6
ePub: 978-1-4725-8387-1

Typeset by Integra Software Services Pvt. Ltd.
Printed and bound in Great Britain

To find out more about our authors and books visit www.bloomsbury.com
and sign up for our newsletters.

# CONTENTS

# Contents

# LIST OF ILLUSTRATIONS

List of Illustrations

# PREFACE TO THE SECOND EDITION

Almost a decade has passed since the publication of the first edition of *Gender, Sex and the Shaping of Modern Europe*. These years have seen continued social change in the direction that we hinted at in the concluding passages of that first book, in some areas (particularly gay rights) far more change than we could have ever imagined. The field of gender history has continued to see healthy growth with the publication of a very large number of books on Europeans' experiences as gendered and sexual citizens in the twentieth century and beyond. We felt that it was time to provide an update, incorporating at least some of this excellent new scholarship and making sure that our pronouncements about Europe 'today' had kept up with these political, social, cultural and legal changes. An entirely new sixth chapter now takes the narrative into the twenty-first century and up to the present. In the process of updating, we also corrected many small errors and omissions, though as with the first edition we make no pretentions to being entirely comprehensive.

We were encouraged to undertake this second edition by the positive response to the first. The book has been successfully assigned in courses across the world, and we were pleased by the fact that our colleagues have recognized it as original and stimulating. We were thrilled, for instance, to be invited to take part in a workshop discussing the past and future of gendered approaches to European history under the auspices of one of the French National Research Agency's Laboratories of Excellence – *LABEX AXE 6: Une histoire genrée de l'Europe* (Axis 6: A gendered history of Europe) – in June 2013. These intense discussions made clear that our insistence on integrating the history of sexuality into the history of gender did not sit well with some of the pioneers of women's and gender history. But we have become more convinced of this than ever. Recent eruptions of controversy about sexual violence on university campuses, about the proliferation of violent pornography on the Internet, about sexual threats to women with a high degree of online visibility and about sexist verbal abuse of female and gay athletes have made it clear that few victories for gender rights can be won without attention to the ways that sex can be used as a weapon in public debate. As advocates of equal rights seek to understand this latest wave of resistance to treating all people with respect and dignity, another look at how we got to where we are seems in order.

In preparing this second edition, we remain aware of the debt we owe to those who helped us with the first. We would like to thank Rhodri Mogford at Bloomsbury for suggesting this second edition and for guiding it through the process of revision with patience and encouragement. He also solicited several excellent reader reviews, which provided us with thought-provoking and challenging feedback on both our proposal for this new edition and its revision. We fear that we have not entirely lived up to the hopes of these scholars, who spoke to us in direct and convincing ways about how they have used our book in their teaching, but we are extremely grateful for the time they took to help us correct at least some of our errors and omissions. In addition, we would like to thank Shawn Brackett and Christine Shanahan, who helped us to prepare the updated bibliography, and Mikkel Dack and John Woitkowitz, who helped compile the suggested readings and found many of the newly included images. Philippa Hetherington graciously sent us a copy of her dissertation when we were rushing to meet our deadline. And, finally, we again thank our families. Our spouses, Scott Anderson and Kimberly Babcock Sanborn, have been unfailingly supportive, and our children, Madeleine Sarah Timm Anderson, Clayton Babcock Sanborn and Grace Babcock Sanborn, remain our inspiration.

# PREFACE TO THE FIRST EDITION

The authors of this book met as graduate students in a seminar on gender history at the University of Chicago. An incident in that course guaranteed that we continued to remember each other, despite our differences in speciality and our various postgraduation wanderings. One steamy day in late spring, what had been a collegial, interdisciplinary atmosphere erupted into a dispute between students in the class about whether scholars could ever break free of their own gender and racial backgrounds and become thoughtful critics of others with different backgrounds. The debate quickly turned personal. Pointed questions were raised about the extent to which men could or should participate in certain areas of class discussion (and indeed in the class itself) and whether white, middle-class women and men could or should critique positions taken by women of colour. Both of us left that seminar with scars. The details of the incident are unimportant, and our memories of it differ. But the experience left a lasting impression of what it means to be an apprentice in a fledgling field fraught with political and personal tensions. It was no accident that emotions exploded on a day when the assigned readings dealt with extremely personal stories of gender and racial oppression. The politics and emotions of the present intertwined with these stories of the past, and the question of who had the right to speak for oppressed minorities provoked angst and indignation. The dispute revealed that the ground rules of studying gender in a scholarly way were not entirely clear to any of us. We were acutely aware that the older categories of women's history and women's studies were being challenged and revised. We were also aware that new perspectives from cultural history, the history and theory of race, post-colonial theory and theories about masculinity should inform our understanding of gender. But at least for the two of us, the explosion of that day proved that numerous scholarly currents had collided around the term 'gender' and that establishing our own identities as scholars would involve a very careful balancing act.

Scholarly discussions about the meaning of gender continue, of course. But the participants in that graduate seminar have gone on to employ 'gender as a category of analysis' (Joan Scott) with self-confidence and the support of a burgeoning theoretical and empirical body of literature. It is a category that we can, for the most part, take for granted in our daily lives as researchers. There are, of course, still theoretical disputes about how gender should be approached historically. But there is also a vibrant, interdisciplinary and international community of scholars, which has developed a common language of scholarly reference points. While there is certainly still resistance from some quarters – one hears the grumbling in the hallways at large multi-speciality and regional history conferences about how the 'trendy' panels have pushed out 'traditional' subjects – historians who 'do' gender can generally rely on a respectful reception from the larger discipline. But being tolerated and having found comfortable niches are not quite the same thing as having been entirely integrated into the master narratives of our respective historical sub-disciplines. Most of us have developed scholarly identities based primarily on our geographic specialities, and we are comfortable in these academic homes. But scholars trained in gender theory and research methods can still find themselves frustrated by a lack of understanding in the larger historical discipline about what 'doing gender' actually means.

The degree to which gender still operates as a sub-speciality of historical practice is perhaps most evident in the structure of undergraduate history surveys. Even historians very amenable to gender approaches to history find it difficult to integrate these perspectives into the overarching narratives of their national survey courses or their broader overviews of European history. Throwing in separate lectures on family or on women's rights (the 'add women and stir' approach) has proven unsatisfying both for instructors and for students. Many instructors, including the present authors, have even taken lectures focused directly on 'gender' themes back out of their repertoire because they proved unpersuasive and confusing to students. Either students could not understand how these 'episodes' fit into the larger subject matter of the course, or they expressed resentment at the apparent attempt to 'indoctrinate' them with a 'feminist agenda'. It is our conviction that finding a way of integrating gender perspectives into undergraduate education is a necessary step along the road towards integrating gender into the broader narrative of European history.

As a result, our imagined audience when writing this book was a reader who knew (or was concurrently learning) the standard outline of European history. We expected that readers would know something about imperialism, feminism, fascism and communism, for instance, but we did not expect a detailed knowledge of these or other developments over the past 250 years. We also assumed no knowledge of gender theory. If we have accomplished our aim, the book should be accessible and informative for interested readers of any age, for students in introductory classes in European history and for a wide range of classes in gender studies programmes. We hope, finally, that the text will also be of interest to specialists in the field of gender history. Though there is now a large specialized literature on gender in Europe, there is a shortage of compact, interpretive works, and we wrote this book to help fill in that gap. We are certain that specialists will find much to dispute in terms of our thematic choices, our case studies and our particular narrative lines. But we are also optimistic that the book will stimulate scholars to see connections where they had not been evident before and to think of European gender history as an integrated whole. That, in any event, is what happened for us as we wrote the text.

The challenge is to elucidate both the gendered nature of politics and the political nature of gender. Our goal in this book is not simply to find areas of European history where gender played a role. Readers looking for an encyclopaedic reference to the history of feminism, the family or the progress of knowledge about sex and sexual difference will be disappointed. We are not looking to recover stories untold, describe a history of oppression or trumpet a success story of progress in equality and rights. Instead, this book attempts to track key shifts in how the roles of men and women were understood in modern European history. The fact that these key shifts come under the headings that are to be found in many European history survey courses is no accident. We are explicitly arguing that the dramatic ruptures in the political life of Europe in the modern era are incomprehensible without some attention to gender. Political revolutions, economic change and ideas about race and human hierarchy all rely on culturally constructed understandings of gender roles both for justification and for modes of implementation. Our ultimate goal is to make a case for the necessity of including gender in any comprehensive survey of modern European (or any other) history. Our method of achieving this goal relies on the most powerful tool of the historian's trade: weaving a convincing story.

In choosing the elements of the story to be told, we relied on a theoretical understanding of gender that stresses its relational nature. In our view, gender describes both male and female actions and identities and is impossible to understand by studying either masculinity or femininity in isolation. We chose our case studies with this in mind, focusing on moments where the two sexes collided or where the separation of their social roles was particularly important for the formation of broader cultural identities, such as the angel of the household, the mother of the nation, the soldier-citizen or the heroic male conqueror of foreign territory. We were also guided by our conviction that although gender touches on (and is affected by) many areas of human experience and behaviour, it is always, in some way, intimately and centrally about sex. How sexual activity was controlled, defined, intertwined with social norms and scientifically understood had a dramatic effect on individuals' sense of self and their understanding of themselves as citizens. The challenge in a book of this sort is to show the ways that gender is about large-scale social abstraction and individual human desire at the same time, and, most importantly, the ways that these seemingly natural and static forces can change dramatically in a relatively short period of time.

This book contends that gender history is neither a 'women's history' nor a 'men's history' and that to understand the operation of gender in modern Europe one must historicize it rather than trying to find one progressive narrative that explains how life came to be as it is today. The changes that this book describes laid bare the deep historical contingency of European notions of society, sexuality and individual identity. These changes were radical and important, but they were not always 'progressive' or unidirectional. They did not affect every European country equally or at the same time. Telling a coherent narrative about change across Europe runs into problems of definition and comparison. In terms of definition, we understand Europe to include both the central continent and its outer reaches, from Scotland to Sicily, and from Portugal to Russia. Rather than attempting the immensely complex and confusing task of comparing how each shift reverberated across the diversity of European nations or constantly placing each country on some kind of timeline of gender progress, we chose to emphasize what we viewed as especially illustrative moments of gender transformation. This bears the risk of making it seem like a dramatic event that occurred in one country can stand as a symbolic representation of change everywhere. We have no intention of implying this. Our goal instead is to provide a narrative that gives enough detail for undergraduates to understand how gender is intertwined with political and social change. This is more easily achieved, we believe, by pausing longer to reflect upon the symbolic meaning of individual cases rather than providing a comprehensive comparative account. Many of the cases we chose are well-studied parts of the standard narrative of European history, like our investigation of gender in France in the revolutionary era. Others rarely appear in textbooks, like our study of Bulgaria after the First World War. Some readers will no doubt wonder why we ignore Bulgarians in the revolutionary era; others will be frustrated that more attention was not paid to France after the First World War. We tried to achieve some balance between East and West, North and South, famous and obscure, but we knew that a perfect balance was impossible to achieve. The choices made here were the result of a productive and extended conversation between two authors with different perspectives and specialities. We hope that the result will contribute to a broader conversation about how European historians can make constructive use of gender in their teaching.

# INTRODUCTION

The biology of sexual difference has been studied since the time of the ancient Greeks. Aristotle believed that women were imperfect men. Basing his understanding of human anatomy on the concept of a conservation of fluids and heat, he argued that women were cooler: their need to expend fluids in menstruation and in breastfeeding left them insufficient heat to develop exterior genitals and the personality traits associated with them. Galen, writing in the third century BCE, concurred, arguing that female genitals were male genitals turned inside out. This one-sex model, as Thomas Laqueur has called it, had significant consequences for the Western understanding of sexual response, and it prevailed into the eighteenth century, with lingering effects into the nineteenth century and beyond.[1] In the early modern period, the one-sex model seemed to explain anatomical anomalies, such as external genitalia that seemed neither entirely male nor entirely female. (At the time these individuals were called hermaphrodites. Today we refer to them as intersex.) The sixteenth-century surgeon Ambrose Paré, for instance, recorded cases where 'swift and violent movements' or sexual encounters had caused pubescent girls to spontaneously sprout penises. They had, in his view, generated enough heat to become men.

The one-sex model postulated a vertical hierarchy of sexual difference that emphasized male superiority while still implying a spectrum of biological and psychological variation. The belief that men and women were different versions of the same thing (and the lack of knowledge about the actual biological processes of fertilization) also made it reasonable to assume that the sexual act was analogous for each sex. If a man had to ejaculate to impregnate a woman, then it made sense that a woman also had to achieve orgasm, perhaps simultaneously with her partner, in order to create the heat necessary for conception. The fact that science linked the sexual response of both sexes to their ability to reproduce had significant social and political repercussions. Among other things, it fuelled interest in female sexual response and led men who wanted to become fathers to pay some attention to the sexual desires of their wives. But this understanding of reproductive biology also helped fuel the prejudice

---

[1] Thomas Laqueur, *Making Sex: Body and Gender from the Greeks to Freud* (Cambridge, MA and London: Harvard University Press, 1990). Laqueur's model has received some criticism. See Michael Stolberg, 'A Woman Down to Her Bones: The Anatomy of Sexual Difference in the Sixteenth and Early Seventeenth Centuries', *Isis* 94, no. 2 (2003): 274–9. Laqueur replies to this critique of *Making Sex* in Thomas W. Laqueur, 'Sex in the Flesh', *Isis* 94, no.2 (2003): 300–6. The one-sex model also looks somewhat different when viewed from the perspective of non-Western readings of the ancient Greeks. See Ahmed Ragab, 'One, Two, or Many Sexes: Sex Differentiation in Medieval Islamicate Medical Thought', *Journal of the History of Sexuality* 24, no. 3 (2015): 428–54. For a recent discussion of the one-sex model, see Katherine Crawford, *European Sexualities, 1400–1800* (Cambridge: Cambridge University Press, 2007), esp. 101–17.

that women were entirely sexed beings, so controlled by their desires that they could not be considered politically mature subjects.

Since we now know much more about how reproduction works and about the genetic basis of sexual difference, it would perhaps be logical to expect that a shift in understanding about what makes men and women biologically different was the result of a scientific discovery or some advance in medical or anatomical knowledge. This was not the case. Around 1800, the one-sex model increasingly came under attack, but the roots of this shift had very little to do with scientific knowledge of reproductive biology. The first indication that ovulation might occur without copulation arose from Theodor L. W. Bischoff's experiments on dogs in 1843. Extrapolating from this research to humans, medical researchers began to agree that women were 'spontaneous ovulators'.[2] In other words, it was only in the middle of the nineteenth century that there was scientific evidence refuting a one-sex model of simultaneous ejaculation. Female orgasm and conception were now conceptually separated. But arguments that the two sexes were incommensurable preceded these anatomical discoveries by almost half a century. In the absence of new 'scientific' explanations, it is clear that social and political thought drove science rather than the other way around. It was no accident that men and women were found to be biologically opposite creatures at the precise moment, just after the French Revolution, when most Europeans were reinforcing the exclusion of women from the public sphere.

While we focus here on the modern period, our purpose in venturing back to the ancient Greeks is to point out that sexual difference has a history. The fact that Europeans between Aristotle and the nineteenth century could look at a vagina and see a penis turned inside out might well strike moderns as odd. But to dismiss this view as simply ignorance would be a mistake. Bodies are not easily read. Whether male or female or somewhere in between, they harbour no self-evident truths and no obvious clues as to how we should translate their differences into the fabric of our social and political lives. As a result, all aspects of sexual difference – as read in the body and as manifested in society and politics – are subject to historical change. Over the past 250 years, that change has been dramatic. While ancient and early modern understandings of sexual anatomy may seem faintly ridiculous to us today, it is precisely this strangeness that allows us to recognize that all of the ways we define maleness and femaleness – socially, culturally and biologically – are historically constituted. The way that we interpret sexed bodies today is no less strange and no more stable. As Joan Scott has argued, 'gender is … not the assignment of roles to physically different bodies, but the attribution of meaning to something that always eludes definition'.[3] Understanding how definitions of sexual difference were translated into norms of behaviour for European men and women and how these norms changed over the course of the modern period is a vital task for

---

[2] Thomas Laqueur, 'Orgasm, Generation, and the Politics of Reproductive Biology', *Representations*, no. 14 (1986): 24–7.

[3] Joan Wallach Scott, *The Fantasy of Feminist History* (Durham: Duke University Press, 2012), 6.

any student of modern European history. To set the scene, we will begin with a brief overview of how key concepts governing political definitions of sexual difference have changed between the mid-eighteenth century and today.

In 1750, patriarchy was the main organizing principle of European life. The word 'patriarchy' derives from the Greek roots for 'father' and 'rule' and refers to those social and political systems in which fathers or father figures exercise ultimate authority.[4] No system of power is ever total, of course, but the conviction that fathers should rule saturated European life from Ireland to Russia and from Sweden to Italy. This conviction provided the glue that held together the hierarchies of authority across the continent.[5] How it played out in practice took many forms. In rural areas across most of the continent, but particularly in the South and East, it was a durable pyramid of power reaching from a male head of household up to male village elders, who in turn owed deference and obedience to local lords and notables, who then swore fealty to kings, who universally promised to govern in obedience to God, the greatest patriarch of them all. In areas where traditional village life was already breaking down, such as parts of Great Britain, greater mobility gave some people, including women, more choices in life. But even in these more robust societies, centuries of tradition, of religious practice and of the consistent application of political power had solidified the theory of father-rule to such a degree that even those who tried to avoid its grip accepted it in principle.

Patriarchy manifested itself broadly, affecting not only the dynamics of family life, but also broader socio-economic and cultural forms. Patriarchal structures were especially well suited to life in the small agricultural communities that predominated throughout the continent in various forms. Eastern Europe, where more than 90 per cent of the population lived outside of urban centres in 1750, was particularly rural in composition, but farming families dominated everywhere. In north-western Europe, 72.2 per cent lived in the countryside, and in central and Mediterranean regions the number was around 65 per cent.[6] Usually, these villages were small. Everyone knew everyone else and indeed could watch everyone else. This intense intimacy allowed for more comprehensive social and sexual control. There were few secrets, and no one thought that sexual behaviour was a private matter between two parties.

The economic organization of rural communities had profound effects on family life. In the East, country people were still most likely to be living on large estates, while in Western, Northern and Central Europe, eighteenth-century economic life had been slowly shifting from a system of large manors and estates to an agricultural economy in which small family-based households were the primary economic unit. Those who still lived on estates operated within a very hierarchical universe in which landlords determined the boundaries of work and family life, including whether or not one had the right to marry

---

[4] Some historians use the word 'patriarchy' simply to refer to a hierarchy of the sexes with men at the top. See for example: Merry E. Wiesner-Hanks, *Gender in History* (Malden, MA and Oxford: Blackwell Publishers, 2001), 12–13. We insist throughout this book on this more precise definition of the term.

[5] We use 'continent' in this book to refer to the geographical unit, which includes the British Isles.

[6] Jan de Vries, *European Urbanization, 1500–1800* (Cambridge, MA: Harvard University Press, 1984), 32.

at all. But in areas already entering the early stages of industrialization, the production of manufactured goods within the home had become more common. Families thus began to function more as independent units, and parents asserted exclusive responsibility for their children, which changed both family dynamics and the meaning of work.[7] These family units had much more autonomy, and their decisions were increasingly governed by the economic needs of the family as a whole. In all areas, a complementary division of gender roles and forms of work was the norm. In other words, all family members contributed their labours to the joint effort of achieving subsistence or sometimes even a family income. The division of labour between the genders was quite strict in some regions and more flexible in others. But women's contribution was crucial everywhere, even as the principle of their subordination to the will of the male head of household was clear and repeatedly articulated.[8]

Beyond the local level, society was structured by patriarchy as well, usually through a formal system of social estates. One's social identity was normally ascribed, not chosen, and it was based on male status passed from fathers to sons and from husbands to wives. One's estate position determined one's economic and political prospects and even, in many areas, the laws to which one was subject. Some especially fortunate individuals rose from one estate to another through marriage or entrepreneurial success.[9] In France, it was possible for wealthy commoners to enter the nobility by purchasing a royal office. In Britain, industrialization brought various opportunities for enterprising individuals to move up the social ranks. In most other areas, though, even these very limited opportunities for social mobility were distant dreams. A boy born to a serf family in Russia, for instance, would be a serf himself when he grew up. He could be sold by his lord and was forbidden from moving. Religion also determined both social and legal status in many parts of the continent. A Jewish boy born in a trading family in Salonika, a European port city in the Ottoman Empire, would be governed by laws specific to the Jewish community there and would normally aspire to assume control of the family business when his father thought it was time.

In general, social mobility was not unheard of, but its routes were open only to a select few, and the distance travelled was usually quite small. Even in regions of Northern and Western Europe where modest degrees of social mobility were possible, most individuals occupied the same social station (and often the exact same job) that their parents had. In one region of eighteenth-century Scandinavia, half the population

---

[7] Heide Wunder, *He Is the Sun, She Is the Moon: Women in Early Modern Germany*, trans. Thomas Dunlap (Cambridge, MA and London: Harvard University Press, 1998), 68–9. Sociologists refer to this new model of family life as 'neo-locality': once married, couples form their own households, which means that they become economically independent. This system was quite unique in the world when it arose in early modern Europe. See Göran Therborn, *Between Sex and Power* (New York: Routledge, 2004), 144–7.

[8] Anna Clark, *The Struggle for the Breeches: Gender and the Making of the British Working Class* (Berkeley: University of California Press, 1995), 14.

[9] For various examples of this, see Maria Agren and Amy Louise Erickson, eds, *The Marital Economy in Scandinavia and Britain 1400–1900* (Aldershot, England and Burlington, VT: Ashgate, 2005).

passed away in the same farmhouse in which they had been born, and fully 95 per cent died in their home parish. Any social mobility that was achieved was normally a shift from being a farm worker to a farm owner or vice versa – a significant difference for those involved, of course, but hardly the mark of a highly fluid society.[10] Even among a sample of individuals most likely to see social mobility in the period (English writers of autobiographies, who were generally literate and of the 'middling sort'), only 10 per cent saw significant upward mobility and 3 per cent downward mobility.[11] For women, social mobility was equally difficult to attain. A girl born in Europe at this time derived her status from her father up until her marriage, at which point she took on the status of her husband. At all times, she was expected to be obedient to the will of the man in her life. Lived experience was of course not this universal, and plenty of women found possibilities to exert their own will at certain times or on certain issues. They acted as trustees for their sons, for instance, or negotiated with governments in their husbands' absence, sometimes relying on local customs that contradicted written law.[12] To varying degrees in different regions of early modern Europe, certain groups of women (such as those who chose the convent instead of marriage and thereby owed obedience to church fathers or those older women who either had never been married or had been widowed) were able to maintain positions of independence from men. The marginality and unique position of these women sometimes afforded them greater opportunities, as it did for widowed noblewomen in Russia, who were allowed to own property and otherwise act in many ways as if they were male householders.[13] Some exceptional women even attained prominence as authors and scientists.[14] But marginal and exceptional women could also find themselves in danger, as the victims of early modern witch trials could attest.[15]

European cultural forms were also deeply patriarchal in nature. Religious teachings, primarily in the form of Christianity, Judaism and Islam, provided a reliable cultural bulwark for male dominance. The doctrinal traditions of all three of these religions were developed in deeply patriarchal societies, first in what is now called the Middle East and

---

[10] Beatrice Moring, 'Marriage and Social Change in Southwestern Finland, 1700–1870', *Continuity and Change* 11, no. 1 (1996): 91–113.

[11] Michael Mascuch, 'Continuity and Change in a Patronage Society: The Social Mobility of British Autobiographers, 1600–1750', *Journal of Historical Sociology* 7, no. 2 (June 1994): 177–97.

[12] Amy Louise Erickson, *Women and Property in Early Modern England* (London and New York: Routledge, 1993); Margaret Hunt, *The Middling Sort: Commerce, Gender, and the Family in England, 1680–1780* (Berkeley and Los Angeles: University of California Press, 1996); Beverly Lemire, *The Business of Everyday Life: Gender, Practice and Social Politics in England, c. 1600–1900* (Manchester: Manchester University Press, 2006).

[13] Michelle Lamarche Marrese, *A Woman's Kingdom: Noblewomen and the Control of Property in Russia, 1700–1861* (Ithaca, NY: Cornell University Press, 2002), 27.

[14] Judith P. Zinsser, ed., *Men, Women, and the Birthing of Modern Science* (DeKalb: Northern Illinois University Press, 2005).

[15] See for example: Lyndal Roper, *Oedipus and the Devil: Witchcraft, Religion and Sexuality in Early Modern Europe* (London and New York: Routledge, 1994); Sigrid Brauner, *Fearless Wives and Frightened Shrews: The Construction of the Witch in Early Modern Germany* (Amherst: University of Massachusetts Press, 1995); James A. Sharpe, *Instruments of Darkness: Witchcraft in Early Modern England* (Philadelphia: University of Pennsylvania Press, 1997).

later throughout the European continent itself. Religious leaders, as a result, reaffirmed that patriarchy was the natural order of mankind, imposed by God Himself. To take just the most obvious example, Christians across the continent memorized the 'Lord's Prayer', in which the power of God, of political lords and of family fathers was linked together and worshipped. It begins 'Our Father, who art in Heaven, hallowed be thy Name. Thy Kingdom come, thy will be done, on Earth as it is in Heaven. Give us this day our daily bread …'. Obedience to the Father's will, on earth as well as heaven, was connected to the father's gift of economic goods and the ability to survive. There is perhaps no clearer statement of the premises of early modern patriarchy.

Religion, however, could also serve a bulwark against the unlimited power of men over women. Sharia courts in the Ottoman Empire, which stretched well into the Balkans during the eighteenth century, protected married women's property rights and punished men who physically assaulted women to a much higher degree than laws in Protestant or Catholic regions of Europe. Given current perceptions of sharia law as regressive, it is perhaps ironic that in the eighteenth century, Christian and Jewish women in these regions often consciously chose sharia courts to take advantage of these protections. Indeed, early modern women were far more prone to taking their disputes about property, abuse, rape, debt and guild relationships to the courts than previous generations of historians have assumed.[16] To understand how the system of patriarchy affected individual lives, it is critical to investigate its various models and to understand it as an historically constructed system of beliefs, laws and practices.

Unlike laws, which leave behind clear archival traces, the impact of patriarchal principles on cultural institutions is harder to measure but was probably even more influential in the daily lives of Europeans. Courtship practices were structured around the fact that the consent of fathers was necessary before marriage, even though many Europeans also believed that affection between spouses was desirable. Patriarchy was sustained most clearly in traditions of arranged marriages, which persisted in many regions of Europe and which occurred not only among powerful elites seeking to build strong political bases, but also among modest peasants seeking good matches in terms of production and reproduction. In early modern Europe, Jewish marriages were typically arranged, though it was expected that love would follow.[17] Family pressures or the disapproval of the community could take precedence over the desires of the individuals being wed. While love was not unknown in early modern marriage, the choice of partner was vital to one's economic survival, and issues of economic security were at least as important as sexual passion or love in choosing a mate.[18] It is easy to underestimate the

---

[16] Margaret R. Hunt, *Women in Eighteenth-Century Europe* (Harlow: Pearson Longman, 2010), 4–5.

[17] Merry E. Wiesner, *Women and Gender in Early Modern Europe* (Cambridge and New York: Cambridge University Press, 2000), 72.

[18] Ibid. Most historians now reject Lawrence Stone's very pessimistic view of love in the early modern period. See Lawrence Stone, *The Family, Sex, and Marriage in England, 1500–1800* (New York: Harper & Row, 1977). For a more balanced view that takes both economic necessity and the presence of affection into account, see John R. Gillis, *For Better, For Worse: British Marriages, 1600 to the Present* (New York: Oxford University Press, 1985).

degree to which this is still true today. Nonetheless, early modern European societies were more likely to link marriage choice directly to the continuance of the family farm, of the village, of the country and of the monarchy. In most regions, dowries were a cultural necessity for daughters of respectable families, meaning that when a family's perceived social status conflicted with their inability to provide a dowry, women were entirely prevented from marrying. In eighteenth-century Milan, for example, 34 per cent of aristocratic women failed to marry – most went to convents.[19] Inheritance laws in most European countries were similarly geared towards preventing the excessive division of property and thus favoured the patriarchal structure. Economic considerations, enforced by fathers or communities, could easily bar couples from marrying, sometimes forcing them to emigrate if they wished to stay together.

The age at which people married dramatically affected family life and sexual behaviour in Europe. In the British Isles, Germany, Scandinavia, France and Germany couples did not marry until surprisingly late. In Britain, for instance, the average age of first marriage in the first half of the eighteenth century was 27.5 years for men and 26.2 years for women.[20] This age was only slightly older than in other places in Northern Europe, where the average for women was twenty-five years.[21] This was far different from the pattern in the South and the East, where either couples married as teenagers and lived in extended families with one set of parents until later in life or where there was a large age gap between the husband and the wife.[22] These different models of marriage were suited to the specific systems of agriculture and economics in these regions, since they ensured that family life would bring economic stability. Extended families could unite their resources to pay feudal dues in areas where these still existed. In areas where marriage was late, households were only founded when a man might reasonably expect to inherit the family enterprise and become economically independent. This late-marriage model, however, was incompatible with the sexual desires of youth. As a result, premarital sex was common, and many local customs developed to govern it. In most rural and working-class communities in north-western Europe, it was expected that a couple would start sleeping together once they were betrothed. If pregnancy resulted, marriage generally followed. There certainly were heated family struggles and assaults upon young men and women who chose to ignore family or community standards about what made a good match. Men who were reluctant to marry their pregnant lovers faced the community's wrath, at least until expanding opportunities in the cities provided them with an escape route. But the disciplining of premarital sex in the early modern period was much milder than measures taken against other forms of deviance from the marital norm. Both adultery and same-sex sexual acts, for instance, were punishable by death in

---

[19] Hunt, *Women in Eighteenth-Century Europe*, 50.
[20] Stanley D. Nash, 'Marriage', in *Britain in the Hanoverian Age, 1714–1837: An Encyclopedia*, ed. Gerald Newman (New York and London: Garland, 1997), 439.
[21] David Levine, 'The Population of Europe: Early Modern Demographic Patterns', in *Encyclopedia of European Social History from 1350–2000*, ed. Peter N. Stearns (New York: Charles Scribner's Sons, 2001), 2: 46.
[22] Wiesner, *Women and Gender in Early Modern Europe*, 71.

many European legal codes, though in practice adultery was more usually punished by fines or shaming.[23] In much of medieval and early modern Europe, individuals convicted of sodomy (a vaguely defined term at the time) could be burned at the stake or otherwise punished under laws against heresy. However, these laws were so harsh that rulers were reluctant to impose them, and private homosexual acts tended to be ignored unless they were accompanied by crimes such as rape or murder or openly offended religious sensibilities.[24] Still, early modern courts were kept quite busy policing sexuality. In Essex, England, population 40,000, there were more than 15,000 people charged with sexual offences between 1558 and 1603.[25]

The world of 1750 seems very far away now. Almost nothing we have described above corresponds to European life today. By the early twenty-first century, though male power remained vibrant and dominant throughout the continent, the pyramid of early modern patriarchal authority had been utterly destroyed. It was no longer taken for granted that men should rule women or that older men should exercise tyrannical authority over younger men. The tradition of one-man rule was also gone. Though powerful male presidents, prime ministers and corporate chief executives still populate the political and economic landscape of the continent, they now nearly always rely on election to their posts and must in any case answer to bodies of representatives in the form of parliaments or boards of directors. And, though powerful fathers still rule families in many places in Europe and compel other family members to bend to their wishes, they no longer have an entire cultural and political system to buttress that power. States will not return rebellious young adults or demoralized wives to the family home if they decide to walk out, and police forces now uphold the legal rights of women and children while restraining, if only imperfectly, would-be patriarchs from the violent assertion of their authority.[26]

To the extent that patriarchy still exists in Europe today, it is a mere shadow of its former self. Male power has been forced to assume other forms, female power is much greater, and nearly everyone agrees that, in principle, authority should be based on factors other than gender. While pockets of patriarchal practice still exist, many Europeans consider them 'normatively deviant'.[27] The status system that governed the functioning of European political and social systems in the eighteenth century has collapsed. The estate system is long gone, and citizens are now equal under the law

---

[23] Women were punished far more harshly than men, but death penalties were rarely carried out in either case. Hunt, *Women in Eighteenth-Century Europe*, 117–8.

[24] Peter N. Stearns, *Sexuality in World History* (New York: Routledge, 2009), 53–4. See also: Jan Sundin, 'Sinful Sex: Legal Prosecution of Extramarital Sex in Preindustrial Sweden', *Social Science History* 16, no. 1 (1992): 99–128. See also Michael David Sibalis, 'The Regulation of Male Homosexuality in Revolutionary and Napoleonic France, 1789–1815', in *Homosexuality in Modern France*, ed. Jeffrey Merrick and Bryant T. Ragan (New York: Oxford University Press, 1989), 80–101, esp. 81.

[25] Lawrence Stone, *The Family, Sex and Marriage*, 492, 519.

[26] Historical accounts of family violence are still remarkably rare. For an exception, see Eliza Earle Ferguson, *Gender and Justice: Violence, Intimacy and Community in Fin-de Siècle Paris* (Baltimore: Johns Hopkins University Press, 2010).

[27] Therborn, *Between Sex and Power*, 130.

throughout the continent, though sex-based distinctions continue to exist in legal practice and in family law. Europeans are no longer predominantly a rural people. Whereas about 20 per cent of Europeans had lived in towns or cities in 1750, now 73 per cent of Europeans do.[28] London, Europe's largest city in 1800, had 900,000 inhabitants. Moscow, Europe's largest city in 2014, is 14 times bigger (with 12,063,000 citizens). Indeed, London's population of 900,000 would today be in sixty-third place, just behind Voronezh, Russia, and barely ahead of Bordeaux, France.[29] It is quite easy to move to a city where few people know you and into an apartment block where no one does. The previous forms of social control, based on the surveillance of neighbours, now exist only in small pockets, in some remaining villages and in urban apartment buildings with particularly nosy neighbours. Individuals now have much more freedom to choose sexual practices, gender expression, spouses, careers, friends and leisure activities.

Similarly, as we noted above, the model of political power has been completely transformed. Monarchs exist largely for the pleasure of tabloid readers, lords seek significance as much in sponsoring strange hobbies as in politics and diplomacy and sovereign decisions are theoretically made by parliaments, which are understood as the direct representatives of the people. Though political and economic decisions continue to be made by a small group of elite men, political participation of both sexes is enshrined in law and is commonplace, and all residents have legal protections.

Alongside the decline of patriarchy and monarchy, the controlling role of religion in the lives of Europeans has also greatly diminished. Church attendance, once almost mandatory for believers (at least on big holidays), has fallen sharply, while the role of religion in public and political life has dramatically declined. In 1750, despite significant religious diversity across the continent, there was a general consensus that individual behaviour should be governed by the commandments of sacred texts and an expectation that these religious edicts should be reflected in public policy. That consensus no longer exists. There are still many Europeans whose lives are guided by their faith, and there are ongoing debates about the degree to which European states should tolerate religious prescriptions that conflict with the principles of individual freedom. But religions in Europe no longer have the capacity to discipline the behaviour of non-members.

Sexual and matrimonial practices have likewise seen a sea change. In 1750, economic considerations were at least as important as emotional ones when contracting a marriage. Now the balance has tipped towards emotion, in theory if not always in practice. Love was not absent from the calculation in the eighteenth century and money is far from unimportant even now, but marrying for money today is not widely respected. Most

---

[28] United Nations Department of Economic and Social Affairs (Population Division), *World Urbanization Prospects: The 2014 Revision* available at http://esa.un.org/unpd/wup/ (accessed 10 July 2015); and Christopher R. Friedrichs, 'The City: The Early Modern Period', in *Encyclopedia of European Social History from 1350–2000*, ed. Peter N. Stearns (New York: Charles Scribner's Sons, 2001), 252.
[29] Friedrichs, 'The City', 252.

young men and women are taught by parents and public culture alike to marry for love, and they are expected to find their own mates. Individuals no longer need the consent or the approval of their or their spouse's father, either socially or legally. European men who ask their potential bride's father for his daughter's hand in marriage are seen either as faintly old school, faintly ridiculous or both. A man who does so without consulting his girlfriend first can get himself into real trouble. There are, of course, more conservative families and cultures across the continent that wish to maintain traditions of arranged marriages and parental control. But their practices now result in significant social and legal tension, a fact that further highlights the magnitude of the shift that has occurred in the dominant cultures of Europe.

Sexual union is now regarded primarily as a means of personal expression rather than social reproduction. This shift, whereby sex has been separated from reproduction in much of the public discourse and in the daily practices of Europeans, has had profound implications.[30] On the one hand, exceedingly few people, married or not, expect or desire to conceive a child every time they have sex. On the other, new technologies of assisted fertilization have given new hope to couples who desire children but cannot conceive them through their own efforts alone. Reproduction still looms, dangerously or promisingly depending on one's viewpoint, over heterosexual intercourse, but most sexually active Europeans can conceptually separate the two processes and believe that they can exert a great deal of control over when and if sex will lead to conception.

This now mundane separation of sex from reproduction has also reduced some of the aura of deviance and pathology that has surrounded homosexual activity for much of the modern era in Europe. It is evident that deep antipathy towards homosexuals and unease with the thought of homosexual acts persist for some Europeans, but the shift towards the assertion of individual rights in legal codes and the increased acceptance of varieties of sexual practice have changed much, not only since 1750 but particularly since 1950. Homosexual acts are legal across the continent, and same-sex partners now have partial or full marriage rights in most European countries.

This book is about how and why attitudes towards gender and its social configuration changed so dramatically over the course of the modern period, and we contend that it is impossible to understand the shape of these transformations simply by tracing the state of the relations between the sexes over time. We agree with Joan Scott's influential definition of gender: 'The core of the definition rests on an integral connection between two propositions: gender is a constitutive element of social relationships based on perceived differences between the sexes, and gender is a primary way of signifying relationships of power.'[31] Scott's definition is important because it insists that gender is constitutive of society, deeply affected by culture, and indispensable for analysing not only sexual politics,

---

[30] There are, of course, exceptions. See for example Ursula Barry, 'Abortion in the Republic of Ireland', *Feminist Review* 29 (Summer, 1988): 57–63.

[31] Joan W. Scott, 'Gender: A Useful Category of Historical Analysis', *American Historical Review* 91, no. 5 (1986): 1067.

but also politics as traditionally understood. Since gender is integral to the construction of political life, it is counterproductive to treat gender and politics in isolation from each other. The large shifts in European political life in the modern period are not completely comprehensible without some attention to changing gender norms. Though a good deal of the change in European gender history was incremental, there were also periods of more visible and dramatic change. Not coincidentally, the five most important such periods we treat in the five core chapters of this book are also the ones that we take to be the major historical ruptures in the larger narrative of modern European history.

The first moment of rupture, which we will explore in Chapter 1, was the assault on inherited status that was initiated during the era of democratic revolutions in the last quarter of the eighteenth century. Though open rebellion against monarchies took place first in the colonial spaces of the Americas, the most significant revolution within Europe took place in France. These democratic revolutions presupposed that sovereignty belonged to the people as a whole, but from the beginning this begged the question of who 'the people' were. Modern notions of citizenship developed precisely in order to answer this question. The revolutionary theory of popular sovereignty derived from Enlightenment beliefs in universal humanity and basic human equality. This notion of equality directly conflicted with the patriarchal model of inequality, particularly between the sexes, that preceded it. Although the ideas of equality embedded in revolutionary discourse provided a language for various disaffected groups throughout Europe to assert claims for increased political and social rights, models of patriarchal inequality proved flexible enough to insinuate themselves into new, ostensibly democratic guises. Equality remained a dream for women and for most other ethnically, sexually and economically marginalized groups. Even in France, the revolutionary heartland, conservative ideals were able to make a comeback within a decade of the first assaults on the monarchy. The subsequent rise and fall of France's expanding empire in Europe then allowed conservatives throughout Europe to reassert their power following Napoleon's final defeat in 1815.

While the political outcomes of the democratic revolutions were ambiguous at the outset of the nineteenth century, the trajectory of economic change was becoming far clearer. In Chapter 2, we will discuss how throughout Europe, at differing speeds, economic life was transformed by the new practices, technologies and organizational forms that historians lump under the term 'Industrial Revolution'. Over the course of the eighteenth to the twentieth centuries, steam power, wage labour and modern corporate structures changed the relationship between Europe's rural and urban regions. This had a more immediate and direct effect on family life and sexual organization than any abstract discussion of political rights. As Marx and Engels put it in 1848, the new barons of the industrial age had 'put an end to all feudal, patriarchal, idyllic relations' and had 'pitilessly torn asunder the motley feudal ties that bound man to his "natural superiors"'.[32]

---

[32] [Karl] Marx and [Friedrich] Engels, *Manifesto of the Communist Party*, 2nd revised edition (Moscow: Progress Publishers, 1977), 38.

Improvements in agriculture and the spread of manufacturing, both within homes and in factories, produced waves of migration across the continent. Cities like London and Amsterdam, for a long time hubs of international trade, became even more vibrant cosmopolitan centres, which attracted both internal and foreign immigrants. Elsewhere the change was quicker and more dramatic. A provincial backwater at the beginning of the nineteenth century, Berlin grew very rapidly into a metropolis, attracting a large number of workers from the increasingly impoverished surrounding countryside. By 1875, only about 40 per cent of the city's one million residents had been born in the city, and the population grew fourfold by the first decade of the twentieth century.[33] Berlin and other new industrial centres of continental Europe struggled to house and integrate the new arrivals.

The emergence of these modern cities created the possibility for dramatic changes in social relations. A combination of industrialization and urbanization eroded patriarchal control by forcing many young Europeans to become dependent upon their bosses rather than their fathers. These changes took place over the course of many decades. In parts of Britain they were well under way before the end of the seventeenth century, while in many regions of Russia they would not take place until the 1930s. Still, all Europeans eventually had to adapt to these new economic and social realities. Standards of living increased, but many Europeans at all levels of the social hierarchy felt anxious and insecure in their new world. Those seeking to shore up traditional values often dealt with these insecurities through desperate attempts to stabilize the gender order. These often succeeded on the surface, but they only barely concealed the changes that the modern world had wrought.

The transformation of European economies gave added impetus for European states to transform the nature of the globalized economy they had done so much to create in the early modern era. That first global economy was centred around trade; with the support of superior naval and military strength, imperial powers gained profit and influence by creating unequal terms of trade with partners around the world. The Industrial Revolution, however, impelled economic actors to focus more fully on production. This shift of focus helped lead to a wave of European emigration, first to Asia and then to Africa, as trading posts were replaced by growing settler populations engaged both in production and in forcing native societies to restructure their own economic activities to better fit into the imperial system. Europeans in the colonies were thereby exposed to societies with different norms and practices. As we will demonstrate in Chapter 3, this more intensive sort of colonial encounter did two things. On the one hand, it provided a space for criticism of the European social order, including its gender relations and norms of sexual behaviour. On the other hand, the fact of conquest and domination solidified a sense of civilizational superiority present in the imperial venture from the beginning. Thus the expansion of European power and people brought about first a new interest in human difference that included an obsession with eroticized foreign lands and then

---

[33] Alexandra Richie, *Faust's Metropolis: A History of Berlin* (London: Harper Collins, 1998), 941, n. 15.

new ways of conceiving of human difference, most prominently race, that were heavily shaped by notions of sexual difference and inequality.

The European civilization that solidified in the imperial milieu of the late nineteenth century was haunted by the fear that some nations, like some species, would not survive in a competition of the fittest. Ironically, this anxiety only hastened that bloody struggle. The aggressiveness and expansion of all European imperial states eventually led to a collision between them. Chapter 4 will demonstrate that the First World War and the Second World War represented both transitional moments in the history of progression of gender equality and the locus of particularly fierce gender conflicts. The gender models inherited from the nineteenth century were challenged by the social mobilization for war. Men and women found themselves occupied with different tasks, in different places and with different people than in the pre-war period – experiences that could work to either challenge or reinforce their understandings of what it meant to be male or female. The largely male society at the front developed a new set of ethical codes and social practices, not all of which fit comfortably into traditional understandings of masculinity, while the rapid integration of women into new economic and social spheres transformed the way that both men and women thought about the 'natural' characteristics of the sexes.

Despite the endurance of many traditional conceptions of male and female roles, wartime transformations effectively crippled patriarchy. Old men were replaced by young men as the icons of European power. This new 'fraternal' system had its roots in the French Revolution, but it came to maturity during the First World War. The fact that this 'victory' of sons over their fathers occurred in wartime made fraternalism even more intensely militarized than it had been before. The fraternal order also relied quite heavily upon the state, which had stepped in to fill important paternal economic and social functions when the dislocations of life on the home front turned the European family 'inside out'.[34] This combination of militarization and increased state power found expression in a wide variety of political systems in the inter-war era, ranging from a left-wing dictatorship in the Soviet Union, to right-wing authoritarian regimes in much of Eastern and Central Europe, to the rise of fascist states in Germany and Italy. These states were aggressive in even more toxic ways than their imperial predecessors had been, and Europe soon found itself in the throes of an even more devastating total war than the one that had just concluded. The Second World War saw the destruction of entire cities and the mass murder of social populations like Jews and homosexuals. The war's unprecedented violence demonstrated the horrible potential of militarized masculinity. The post-war period would be marked both by attempts to save this model of masculinity from itself and, eventually, attempts to challenge the very notion of male dominance that underpinned both the new fraternal and the old patriarchal models.

The First World War and the Second World War seemed on the surface to have initiated revolutionary change in the gender order. In particular, the dislocated societies

---

[34] Maureen Healy, *Vienna and the Fall of the Habsburg Empire: Total War and Everyday Life in World War I* (Cambridge and New York: Cambridge University Press, 2004).

of wartime Europe saw a collapse of social control over sexual activity. The result was a simultaneous increase in individual freedom of sexual choice and a weakening of social protections preventing coerced sexual relations. Rape was a commonplace experience in war zones, and populations threatened by invasion universally feared the sexual violence associated with war. But sexual practices were transformed even in places far removed from the fighting as societies were restructured. On the home front, near the battlefield, and within occupied territories, completely new possibilities for the formation of relationships outside of traditional family controls arose. For some, the somewhat freer social environment during the wars provided a glimpse into a future in which individuals could exercise freedom of choice in the sexual realm rather than being controlled by the prescriptions of conservative societies.

While war helped to transform sexual mores by exposing millions of Europeans to dramatically changed social and physical circumstances, similar disruptions were shaking up the world of ideas and the scientific understanding of sex. Already in the late nineteenth century, experts on human anatomy and psychology had begun to develop the field of sexology, and social commentators began making much more explicit pronouncements about the political and social consequences of human sexuality. By the early twentieth century, sexologists had virtually convinced Europeans that sex and politics were permanent bedfellows. Psychologist Sigmund Freud, the discipline's most famous scholar, made this link clear when he argued that civilized political systems could only develop if individual sexual urges were at least partially suppressed. The concept of sexual identity – the insistence that one's sexual desires and behaviours are fundamental to a sense of self and critical in determining social roles – had been born. Chapter 5 will explore both the roots and the political manifestations of this relationship between sex and politics, placing the famous sexual revolution of the 1960s into the broader context of European modernity. Student activists like the ones on the cover of this book claimed to be the instigators of a sexual revolution in the 1960s, but they were in fact drawing on a century's worth of social turmoil in the sexual realm. Massive cultural and social change in the 1960s and 1970s did indeed change the way that many Europeans thought about and practised sex. But the historical roots of this transformation ran far deeper than 1960s activists shouting slogans like 'make love not war' were willing to admit.

As this brief description suggests, we see no clear boundary between a 'history of gender' in Europe and a 'gendered history' of Europe. Determining the relationship between the two is, indeed, the challenge. Gender history takes its power directly from the irresolvable tension between asking both how gender affects history and how history affects gender.[35]

If sex and gender have a political aspect, it stands to reason that they have a history as well. The historical study of gender also has a history. The development of a historical tradition that focused on sex roles and gender structures happened

---

[35] Joy Parr, 'Gender History and Historical Practice', in *Gender and History in Canada*, ed. Joy Parr and Mark Rosenfeld (Toronto: Copp Clark Ltd., 1996), 20.

only gradually. The main character of Virginia Woolf's 1929 novel, *A Room of One's Own*, famously gazed at 'the shelves for books that were not there' and mused about what would happen if female students were to 'rewrite history' or at least provide a supplement to it, 'calling it, of course, by some inconspicuous name so that women could figure there without impropriety'.[36] Woolf was not being very charitable to the hundreds of female historians in Europe and North America who had begun writing compelling histories of women in the nineteenth century.[37] But it was not until the 1970s that historians in universities began to develop a scholarly field of 'women's history'. Before long, women's historians were filling university bookshelves with a wide variety of scholarly explorations about women's lives in the past and present.

Many of these pioneers linked their scholarship to their simultaneous activity in campaigns for political and social equality. In 1973, Sheila Rowbotham wrote a book called *Hidden from History: 300 Years of Women's Oppression and the Fight against It*, and she explicitly stated in her introduction: 'This book comes very directly from a political movement'.[38] Historians and university women of the 1970s were involved in forms of 'consciousness raising', group exercises to increase women's awareness of how society had shaped their own behaviours and their understanding of gender roles. The idea that 'the personal is political' was crucial to these endeavours. Historians and other academic feminists linked personal experiences (such as abortion, rape and workplace harassment) to larger political structures and social systems. Applying these insights to history immediately opened up new vistas of historical research, bringing into view historical subjects that had previously been ignored. This work represented an invaluable contribution to our knowledge about past societies. It revealed the historical roots of present-day social questions and the connections between political oppression in the past and in the present.

By the late 1980s, however, historians were growing increasingly concerned about the shortcomings of a historical approach that assumed sexual identity to be a universal constant. Without allying themselves to factions in the discipline that remained hostile to women's history as a whole, some historians began to challenge narratives that depended upon trans-historical definitions of gender difference and oppression. The writer most associated with this shift is Joan W. Scott, whose 1986 definition of gender we outlined earlier. That definition was part of Scott's broader criticism that the path of feminist scholarship in the 1970s had tended to render both female identity and male domination as universal constants, underestimating the historical variation of social influences on gender roles.

---

[36] Virginia Woolf, *A Room of One's Own* (New York: Harcourt, Brace and Co., 1929), 68.
[37] See Julie Des Jardins, *Women in the Historical Enterprise in America: Gender, Race and the Politics of Memory, 1880–1945* (Chapel Hill: University of North Carolina Press, 2003), 13–51; and Bonnie G. Smith, *The Gender of History: Men, Women, and Historical Practice* (Cambridge, MA: Harvard University Press, 1998).
[38] Sheila Rowbotham, *Hidden from History: 300 Years of Women's Oppression and the Fight Against It* (London: Pluto Press, 1973), ix.

Scott, and those who followed in her footsteps, made it clear that the development of gender history represented a challenge to women's history as much as it did an extension of it.[39] It has been a very civil challenge, however. Both inside and outside of the academy, most observers still think that gender history and women's history are basically the same thing. It is true that, in sharp contrast to the participants of more acrimonious intellectual battles, the practitioners of gender history and women's history tend to frequent the same conferences and panels and generally offer each other mutual respect and support. But substantive differences remain. To take just the most obvious example, there is no widespread agreement even about the definition of the term 'patriarchy', one of the central organizing concepts for both women's history and gender history.[40] Those influenced by feminist theories that were developed in the 1960s and 1970s use the term to refer broadly to male power in all its manifestations, both within larger political systems and within the family.[41] Others, including the present authors, prefer to use patriarchy only to refer to social systems based on the authority of a literal or symbolic 'father' and husband.[42] When used in its most overarching and universal sense, the concept of patriarchy can lead historians to search backwards in history for evidence of male dominance and to present this evidence in a way that makes male power appear universal, almost natural. But gender history has precisely the opposite goal. It seeks to denaturalize the gender roles of any given historical period by revealing how gender relations have changed over time and how they have been influenced by family structure, demographic and social conditions, and the interrelations between society and politics. The specific power relationship between men and women in any given society is formed through a constant process of familial, social and political negotiation. Assuming the universal existence of patriarchy does little to explain how it came to be or what tensions, contradictions and ambivalent effects it has produced for both men and women.[43]

If the word 'patriarchy' is historically unstable, this is all the more true of any word ever used in a European (or any other) language to describe variations on the traditional model of the heterosexual marital couple. Those whose behaviour, self-definitions or

---

[39] For an extended investigation of these developments, see Laura Lee Downs, *Writing Gender History*, 2nd edn. (London and New York: Bloomsbury Academic, 2010).

[40] For summaries of the debates, see Pavla Miller, *Transformations of Patriarchy in the West, 1500–1900* (Bloomington: Indiana University Press, 1998); and Karin Hausen, 'Patriarchat: Vom Nutzen und Nachteil eines Konzepts für Frauengeschichte und Frauenpolitik', *Journal für Geschichte* 5 (1986): 12–21 and 58.

[41] This definition of the term gained particular currency with the popularity of Kate Millett's *Sexual Politics* (New York: Ballantine Books, 1969). A much more complex picture emerges in later accounts. See for example Lynn Hunt, *The Family Romance of the French Revolution* (Berkeley and Los Angeles: University of California Press, 1992).

[42] For an extremely wide-ranging discussion of family that also takes patriarchy to mean male family power rather than gender discrimination more broadly, see Therborn, *Between Sex and Power*, esp. 8. Therborn uses 'phallocracy' to describe 'sexual power without paternal significance'. It should also be noted that many historians use the broader definition of patriarchy while still carefully contextualizing its extremely varied historical forms. For an example of this usage, see Marlene LeGates, *In Their Time: A History of Feminism in Western Society* (New York and Abingdon: Routledge, 2001), esp. chp. 1.

[43] Hausen, 'Patriarchat', 19.

bodies have contradicted heteronormative expectations have had to endure a wide array of epithets and slurs – a fact that was (and remains) both a sign and a means of their marginalization. These terms, however, have dramatically changed over time and are extremely culturally specific. To stick only with English examples (and only to words similarly used across the English-speaking world), terms that were once slurs – particularly 'queer' but also 'fairy' and 'dyke' – have since been adopted as powerful and malleable terms of self-identification by the groups to whom they refer.[44] A further complication is that words deemed less offensive in the past (such as 'homosexual' and 'prostitute') have come to offend some within those communities today. While we are aware that many of our present-day readers (perhaps particularly those engaged in the study of queer theory and contemporary sexual politics) would prefer us to use 'gay and lesbian' rather than 'homosexual' and 'sex worker' rather than 'prostitute', with a couple of exceptions, we have chosen to maintain the usage that was most common in the periods that we are investigating as long as these words were also used by the individuals to whom they applied.[45] Our primary reason for this choice is that words in present-day usage are not simply replacements for historical words that can now somehow self-evidently be described as slurs; the new words have new meanings and reflect new social realities. To give just one example, it is easy to understand the pain that many people today still experience when their parents insist on calling them 'homosexual' with a disapproving sneer and refuse to acknowledge or adopt the terminology that their children prefer. But this cannot change the fact that embracing the term 'homosexual' was a politically empowering and self-actualizing act in many times and places, and that many of the political activists who helped bring about the legal and social changes that have vastly improved the lives of LGBTQI (lesbian, gay, bisexual, transsexual, queer and intersex) individuals still detest being called 'queer'. There is, in other words, a generational divide in the reaction to these terms, but as historians we feel equally responsible to the sensibilities of our historical subjects as we to do to the generation of students likely to read this book. We hope, therefore, that readers who are uncomfortable with the historically specific terminology will understand that their discomfort is part of the historical lesson we aim to provide. For those seeking continued progress in gender and sexual equality, stories like the ones we are about to tell contain more jarring discomforts than soothing sources of self-identification.

---

[44] For historical accounts of the history of the word 'queer', see Jeffrey Weeks, 'Queer(y)ing the "Modern Homosexual"', *Journal of British Studies* 51, no. 3 (2012): 523–39; and Laura Doan, *Disturbing Practices: History, Sexuality, and Women's Experience of Modern War* (Chicago & London: University of Chicago Press, 2013), 7–10.

[45] The primary exception is our care in the use of the word 'hermaphrodite' to describe individuals with genitalia that do not conform to expectations of a clear line between male and female bodies. Our justification for this exception is that this word has a long history of allusion to monsters and freaks, and it is anatomically misleading. As the Intersex Society of North America puts it on their web site, 'The terms fail to reflect modern scientific understandings of intersex conditions, confuse clinicians, harm patients, and panic parents.' See http://www.isna.org/faq/hermaphrodite (accessed 24 July 2015). For a discussion of the history of these debates, see Elizabeth Reis, 'Divergence or Disorder? The Politics of Naming Intersex', *Perspectives in Biology and Medicine* 50, no. 4 (2007): 535–43.

The need to make this kind of statement about terminology is itself a kind of victory for the forces of gender and sexual equality; it is a demonstration that a vast amount of scholarship has made it impossible to claim that any one ideological, religious or political viewpoint can dictate a trans-historical definition of what it means to be a gendered or sexual being. This is apparent in the most recent research on gender history and the history of sexuality, which reveals a growing consensus that gender history should extend not only beyond women's history, but also beyond a narrow focus on explicit discussions of sex roles and sexuality. The past twenty years have seen the development of an expansionist perspective on gender and a tendency to view it as a nearly universal (though not all-encompassing) presence in political and social life rather than as a discrete aspect of human experience. Our notes and bibliography include only a fraction of what is now a very substantive corpus of scholarly work, and our interpretations rely heavily on the vibrant dialogues carried on by recent historians of gender. But this book is not a summary of recent scholarship. Rather than seeking to include all the key discoveries made in the field of gender history, we instead tried to answer a relatively simple question: how does the concept of gender matter to the study of modern Europe? Part of our answer to this question took the form of an explicit investigation of gender norms and sexual politics, and part of our answer took the form of a demonstration of how a gender perspective can help us see familiar events (like the Industrial Revolution or the outbreak of the First World War) in new ways. Our simple question therefore has quite a complicated answer. We trust that readers will understand that writing a short book with such a broad scope necessitated leaving out a great deal of interesting and important material. We can offer no further apologies. Modern European gender history is an enormous topic. This book is rather small. It is meant as an introduction and not a conclusion.

# CHAPTER 1
## LIBERTY, EQUALITY AND FRATERNITY

As the year 1789 dawned, the most powerful person in Europe was a woman. Born a minor German princess in the town of Stettin in 1729, Sophia of Anhalt-Zerbst was sent to be married at the tender age of fifteen years to a distant and cruel man who lived far away. She left for a foreign country where she was expected to learn a new language and adopt a new religion. She would never see her father again. Her new husband held no attraction for her, and his refusal to consummate the marriage for years following the wedding ceremony indicated that the feeling was probably mutual. She had no friends, no family and almost no practical experience of any kind. Virtually abandoned by her husband, she consoled herself with reading everything she could get her hands on, from ancient classics like the *Annals* of Tacitus to recent political tracts of the French Enlightenment like Montesquieu's *Spirit of the Laws*. There was just one redeeming feature of her situation. Her husband Peter was the heir to the Russian throne.[1]

Upon her marriage and adoption of Russian Orthodoxy, Sophia took on a new name, Ekaterina (Catherine, in English), and she seemed destined to be the next in a long line of forgotten women who were wed to the autocrats of Russia. Russia was one of the most patriarchal countries in Europe, but when Catherine arrived in St Petersburg in 1744, the ruler was the Empress Elizabeth (1741–61), the daughter of Peter the Great (1689–1725), Russia's vigorously reformist and 'Westernizing' tsar. Elizabeth was continuing a curious trend of female rulers in Russia that had begun with the regency of Peter's half-sister Sophia (1682–89) and had continued with Peter's widow Catherine I (1725–27) and with his niece Empress Anna (1730–40). This was a remarkable string considering that just a few generations before most elite women lived in seclusion, away from the gaze of any men but their kin. The rather surprising development of female rule indicated, of course, that elite women in Russia were now visible in the public sphere in ways unthinkable a century before, but it did not mean that women were treated as equals. On the contrary, the choice of women as leaders had occurred precisely because the top Russian aristocrats wanted to prevent the emergence of a powerful autocrat of the type of Peter the Great, who had disrupted their lives and threatened their social position. They expected that women rulers would be dependent upon them and that they could be strong-armed into serving the interests of whichever aristocratic clique had sponsored them. These expectations had not been fully borne out, as both Empress Anna and

---

[1] Isabel de Madariaga, *Russia in the Age of Catherine the Great* (New Haven, CT and London: Yale University Press, 1981), 8–9.

Empress Elizabeth proved to have stronger backbones than the men who surrounded them had hoped (Catherine I was considerably less forceful). Still, by their very presence, female monarchs did encourage factionalism, and ambitious courtiers were continually tempted to plan coups by selecting politically weak (and thus often female) candidates whose ascent would allow them to be the strong hand directing the puppet ruler.

It was in this way that Catherine would seize the Russian throne. Her husband Peter III was crowned tsar in December 1761 and quickly became as odious to many elite Russians as he had long been to his wife. The marriage that had begun so badly grew even worse over the years. Peter was rumoured to have decided to put Catherine aside and marry a young Russian princess, while Catherine, for her part, was bearing a child fathered by her lover Grigory Orlov.[2] Soon after the delivery, in late April 1762, Peter publicly humiliated his wife by screaming at her at a banquet and even ordering her arrest before being talked down by his advisors. Peter could have easily recovered from a split from an unfaithful wife, but he had also made the more serious mistake of alienating his officer corps. Orlov and Catherine were well positioned to organize a coup with the support of the army, and they did so with remarkable ease in June 1762. When Peter left the capital briefly with his mistress, Catherine was declared the new empress, a seizure of power Peter only learned of when he appeared at one of his summer palaces for a party to discover it empty. He was soon arrested and then died in custody, almost certainly murdered by Orlov and his brothers. It is unclear whether Catherine knew of the plan to murder her husband, but she benefited from it and likely shed few tears.[3]

Catherine was now the empress of the largest empire on earth, which stretched from the coast of the Baltic Sea to the shores of the Pacific Ocean. Her power was in principle unlimited. She issued law by decree, appointed the people who executed those laws and was a one-person supreme court. She commanded an army that had just defeated Frederick II's Prussian forces on their home territory and would go on to other notable successes. Over the course of her reign, Russia would establish itself firmly on the Black Sea through a series of convincing defeats of the Ottoman Empire and would incorporate much of Poland into its fold, destroying its long-time rival in Eastern Europe. Catherine 'the Great' was probably the most competent ruler in Russian history. In addition to her military victories, she regularized Russian administration, set in motion a process of reforms guided by the latest Enlightenment theories, sponsored scholarly and artistic projects both at home and abroad and presided over what the Russian nobility (though not the Russian serf population) would long remember as a golden age.

When Catherine died thirty-six hours after suffering a massive stroke in November 1796, Europe was roiled by revolution, but Russia remained a conservative anchor in the East. After thirty-four years of rule, she bequeathed to her country a political and military system that proved able to withstand Napoleon's invasion in 1812 and that would establish itself as one of Europe's great powers for the next 200 years. One might

---

[2] Ibid., 27.
[3] Ibid., 32–7.

have thought that with this experience in mind, female rulership would have been even more welcome in Russia than it had been in the eighteenth century. But Catherine was the last woman to rule the Empire. Almost immediately after her death, her son Paul (another disastrous tsar, who would be killed five years into his reign) changed the Russian succession law to formally prevent a woman from coming to the throne.

Catherine's reputation, meanwhile, was subjected to a concerted smear campaign on the part of Russian conservatives. Catherine and the women who preceded her were charged with having corrupted the morals of the whole country through light-minded frivolity, conspicuous consumption and, most damning of all, unbridled sexual excess. Catherine in particular was accused of being unduly influenced by men who sexually pleased her and of being voracious in her acquisition of new 'favourites'. Like many wise female monarchs in patriarchal systems, she had never remarried after the murder of Peter, as the presence of a husband would have called into question her capacity to rule.[4] Women were expected to be obedient to their husbands, an expectation fully underpinned by all European Christian churches, and this made it very difficult to combine autocratic power with wifely subordination. Not desiring to take a vow of chastity, Catherine continued to engage in sexual and political relationships with members of the Russian elite for the rest of her life in a pattern we would today call 'serial monogamy'. Gossip surrounding her bedroom activities and the political implications of her new alliances was the constant fodder of Russian high society.

The most systematic critique of female rule in general and of Catherine's reign in particular came from one of her former servitors, Prince M. M. Shcherbatov, who wrote a treatise entitled *On the Corruption of Morals* in 1786–87.[5] The manuscript was read only by confidants and family members at first, as the author rightly feared arrest if his scathing criticism were made public, but his views were shared by other members of his set. Russia's moral fabric, Shcherbatov claimed, had been eaten away over the course of the eighteenth century. The original sin belonged to Peter the Great, who in his eagerness to open up the country to Western influence had actively desegregated public life in Russia, allowing women and men to mix freely and encouraging liaisons and marriages based on affection rather than paternal order. The ceaseless attempts to please the opposite sex ruined the familial bond and led to useless consumption of luxury goods. The whole elite had become focused upon individual gratification rather than duty and obedience. This desire for sensual pleasure was, Shcherbatov argued, the main reason for the decline in morals, for it

---

[4] There is speculation that she may in fact have married Grigory Potemkin, her most trusted advisor and greatest love, in a secret ceremony. But the desire for that secrecy just underlines Catherine's political need to remain unwed. On Potemkin and his relationship with Catherine, see Simon Sebag Montefiore, *Prince of Princes: The Life of Potemkin* (London and New York: St. Martin's Press, 2000). See also Douglas Smith, ed., *Love and Conquest: Personal Correspondence of Catherine the Great and Prince Grigory Potemkin* (DeKalb: Northern Illinois University Press, 2004).

[5] Prince M. M. Shcherbatov, *On the Corruption of Morals in Russia*, trans. A. Lentin (Cambridge: Cambridge University Press, 1969).

gives rise to various violent desires, and a man will often stop at nothing in order to attain their gratification. Indeed, a man entirely given over to his disorderly desires, and worshipping the reprehensible passions within his heart, thinks little of the Law of God, and still less of the laws of the country in which he lives.[6]

Though a man had initiated these changes, Shcherbatov continued, and though it was male morality that had been corrupted most of all, the key to the problem lay with women, who loved both 'luxury' and 'despotism' more than men did.[7] The string of female monarchs, from Catherine I to Anna to Elizabeth, finally culminated in the reign of Catherine II. Shcherbatov was not blind to Catherine's abilities, but he saw even her political aptitude as essentially corrupt because of her moral degradation:

It cannot be said that she is unqualified to rule so great an Empire, if indeed a woman can support this yoke, and if human qualities alone are sufficient for this supreme office. She is endowed with considerable beauty, clever, affable, magnanimous and compassionate on principle. She loves glory, and is assiduous in her pursuit of it. She is prudent, enterprising, and quite well-read. However, her moral outlook is based on the modern philosophers, that is to say, it is not fixed on the firm rock of God's law; and hence, being based on arbitrary worldly principles, it is liable to change with them. In addition, her faults are as follows: she is licentious, and trusts herself entirely to her favourites.[8]

In sum, then, it was female sexual excess, in violation of God's law and encouraged by secular Western influences, that was accountable for the state that Russia found itself in, for it encouraged political corruption, loose morals among other elite women and the endless search for private pleasure rather than public good on the part of Russian males. 'By such stages', Shcherbatov concluded, 'Russia has reached the ruination of all good morals.' He begged God to bless Russia with a new emperor, who would be firm and fair in his rule and 'gentle and constant in friendship, showing an example in himself by his domestic harmony with his wife, and banishing licentiousness'.[9] Shcherbatov's treatise linked together many of the main concerns of eighteenth-century European thinkers: the relationship between virtue and good governance, the model of the wise monarch and the relationship between proper familial order and the social order as a whole. In all these areas, the so-called 'woman question' loomed large.

This explicit connection between conservative politics and fears of feminine sexual excess helps to explain one more legacy of Catherine the Great: the outrageous slur circulated soon after her death and repeated ever since that she had died while having sex with a horse. Presumably she was so debauched and bestial that mere men could

---

[6] Ibid., 115.
[7] Ibid., 159, 247.
[8] Ibid., 235.
[9] Ibid., 259.

no longer please her. This accusation was obviously and demonstrably false, but the popularity and durability of these rumours, combined with the prohibition of female rule, demonstrates that Catherine's reign coincided with real changes in the ways that gender and politics were discussed in Russia.

Catherine's story was, of course, unusual, but her story of gender and power in one of the most patriarchal and conservative regions of Europe is all the more telling because of its setting. It shows in sharp relief the set of changes that rocked the continent as a whole. While such powerful women in Europe were certainly atypical, the discourses surrounding them reveal how gender norms helped shape political norms and vice versa. Over the course of the eighteenth century, new ideas about citizenship and individual honour emerged that had profound effects upon the public roles of men and women. Politics, philosophy and scientific ideas were intertwined in this process, and ideas about gender were both reinforced and, in some cases, transformed. The French Revolution (1789–99) represents a momentous turning point in the history of gender in Europe, since new political ideas that might have brought about a shift towards increased political rights for women instead justified a much more strict separation of male and female spheres. Explaining how this occurred requires an examination of how the philosophical flowering known as the Enlightenment (c. 1685–c. 1789) prompted European thinkers to place increased emphasis on self-control and the attainment of individual virtue. It also requires an exploration of how the concept of citizenship came to be linked to the glorification of the citizen-soldier and the male head of a conjugal unit over the course of the revolutionary period.

Tracking the interrelationship of gender norms and political ideals from the late eighteenth to the early nineteenth centuries reveals the degree to which understandings about appropriate political roles for men and women were integral to the debates about the distribution of political power. At the very moment when human equality was being forwarded as a revolutionary slogan, women were pointedly demonstrating their capacity to think and to be active participants in politics. Simultaneously, a counter-current of thought was being promulgated that suggested that women were incapable of self-possession and needed to be protected from the storms of modernity that were building in strength throughout Europe. Explaining not only how this seeming paradox operated, but also how in some respects the very notions of liberty, equality and fraternity depended on a more aggressive subordination of women will be the theme of this chapter.

## The Enlightenment

Prince Shcherbatov's dislike of Russia's female monarchs was part of a long tradition in European religious and social thought that saw passion as corrupting and women as too susceptible to the wild extremes of pleasure. The core of this tradition was the story of Adam and Eve in Genesis, in which Eve succumbed to the treats of the devil and then tempted Adam to do the same. Preventing sin and social disorder meant keeping women away from sources of power and firmly subordinated to male control, first in the form of the father and then in the form of the husband. Women, the Bible implied, had to be obedient for their own sakes. Only the surrender of wilfulness would keep them away from dangerous apples. Eve's weakness in the face of temptation stood as an enduring metaphor for what Shcherbatov described as the 'corruption of morals' – a danger to male souls that could only be thwarted if women were kept subordinate.

This moral outlook was evident throughout the continent in the middle of the eighteenth century. Indeed, in significant respects, the intellectual developments associated with the Enlightenment strengthened these concerns. The assault on traditional religion made by some of the scientific and secular trends of the period is easy to overstate. Instead, as Norman Davies has pointed out, it is more accurate to talk of an Enlightenment ethic against 'fanaticism' or, more broadly, 'enthusiasm'.[10] Put another way, the Enlightenment was largely about control, beginning with self-control and continuing through control of social systems and ultimately to the control of nature itself. The exercise of reason as a form of external discipline, a check against the ignorance of folk tradition, the self-interested teachings of church leaders and the dark continent of human nature itself was a key feature of this search for control.

It is important to note that 'reason' in the 'Age of Reason' was not disembodied. Rationality found its power only when it was applied to 'nature' broadly defined. This was especially evident in the dramatic changes in scientific thinking that occurred on the eve of the Enlightenment. In the astronomical observations of Kepler and Copernicus, the physical laws of Newton and the biological classifications of Linnaeus, scientists sought not only to apply reason and (often mathematical) logic to the natural world, but also to demonstrate that the natural world had its own internal logic. Planets moved in regular patterns, gravity exercised its influence everywhere in the universe and species existed around the globe, already differentiated from each other and awaiting only the proper mode of observation. Nature, in other words, had laws, and these natural laws provided the context for everything else, including the behaviour of human beings and the exercise of rationality itself.

This embodiment of reason and the inner rationality of nature helped to account for the dualities, even self-contradictions, of much Enlightened thought, including that of individual thinkers who combined the abstract and metaphysical operations of reason with the very concrete and physical observations of natural conditions. Indeed, many of the most heated intellectual debates dealt with questions of 'epistemology' – the study of how we know what we know. Some, like Francis Bacon and John Locke, argued that humans create knowledge by observing and sensing their surroundings and inferring patterns from the data they accumulate. Others, like René Descartes, started from the proposition that only a mind pre-equipped with the capacity to reason could create knowledge and meaning from the sensory stimuli provided by bodily organs.

---

[10] Norman Davies, *Europe: A History* (Oxford and New York: Oxford University Press, 1996), 596.

These philosophical developments had significant implications for the way that human beings studied themselves and understood gender difference. On the one hand, the presence of universal and rational laws led to expectations of a fundamental equality for all human beings. If everyone was a member of the same species and equally subject to the laws of physics, then it followed that at the most basic level all humans were equal. Descartes' philosophy of abstract reason provided for a separation of body and soul that worked in favour of ideas of sexual and other types of equality. If the body did not make any difference to thought, then neither sex could be said to have a greater capacity to reason.[11] On the other hand, the observation of human society revealed a condition of deep inequality. Women throughout Europe (and almost everywhere one looked outside of Europe as well) were subordinated to men, held to be unequal and treated unequally. They were physically different, dressed differently and, many argued, shared sex-based behavioural characteristics. Shcherbatov's claims, for instance, that women loved 'luxury' and 'despotism' more than men were not at all unusual.

The contradiction between equality in principle and inequality in practice was dealt with in two major ways, which roughly corresponded to the 'nature vs. nurture' debate that still rages in discussions of human inequality. Some argued that all humans were *not* created equal and that the observed inequality was the result of natural inequality between men and women. Others claimed that oppressive social systems had thwarted the development of the female sex and deformed the natural order. But discussions on the question of human nature were complicated by confusions regarding the term 'nature' itself. 'Natural' had two meanings that were only rarely differentiated by authors and readers. In the first instance it was descriptive – it described one's surroundings as they were observed. It was in this sense that gravity was a 'natural' law. In the second instance, however, it was normative; that is, it described how things *should be* rather than how they were. In this sense, male dominance was a 'natural' law. Authors appealed to nature, to history, to biology and to logic to defend it, but unlike gravity it was a law that could be broken. It was not that violations could not exist in nature, but that they should not. These were very different notions of 'natural law', but both were treated as if they were scientific propositions of the same order, a confusion that still exists today when politicians or activists argue that specific human behaviours (like same-sex relationships, for instance) should be forbidden because they are 'unnatural'.

This contrast between the descriptive and normative meanings of 'nature' was especially salient in discussions of the 'woman question' in elite European circles in the eighteenth century, most notably in France. Women were becoming ever more educated and visible in aristocratic circles. Social and sartorial fashion became ever more open, as plunging necklines combined with an ethos of flirting to convince social critics that

---

[11] Geneviève Fraisse, *Reason's Muse: Sexual Difference and the Birth of Democracy* (Chicago and London: University of Chicago Press, 1994), xiv.

sexual propriety had collapsed. Many condemned what they saw as a rise of adultery and perversion. Similarly, when several important women formed intellectual circles in their salons (gatherings of artists and intellectuals held in the homes of wealthy patrons), they discovered new realms of cultural freedom and influence. Julie de Lespinasse, for instance, hosted a popular salon in Paris that discussed the most important cultural, philosophical and political events of the day. These gatherings were more than merely sociable; they were important spheres of political debate where pre-revolutionary ideas were formulated.[12] Women played an important role in public life, a fact that led some contemporary observers like Rousseau to despair, while others proclaimed the eighteenth century the 'century of women'.[13] With some philosophers attacking the underpinnings of social inequality in other spheres and advancing the notion that it was a 'self-evident' truth that 'all men are created equal', this demonstration of individual autonomy and intellectual capacity on the part of women logically promised to extend the notion of the 'rights of man' to women as well.

The notion that women might gain equality and exercise independence troubled not only conservatives hostile to the emerging order, like Shcherbatov, but many of the men who were leading the transformation in social and political thought as 'enlightened' philosophers as well. Jean-Jacques Rousseau was easily the most influential commentator on gender and proper familial relationships in this respect. In 1761, he published an epistolary novel entitled *Julie, or the New Héloise: Letters of Two Lovers who Live in a Small Town at the Foot of the Alps* that became an immediate and persistent best-seller both in France and abroad in translation.[14] It was the story of a young woman who, in the early chapters of the work, succumbs to passion and finds both fulfilment and unhappiness. In the later chapters, she marries a man she respects but does not lust for and discovers contentment and happiness in domestic life. *Julie* was popular, but it was immediately controversial. On the one hand, it alienated women who sought equality, for Rousseau's explicit message was that women had to submit to the authority of a good man and focus their energies on the household in order to be happy. On the other, it offended conservatives by frankly discussing pleasure, by portraying complex women and by blaming conservative patriarchs rather than free thinkers or lustful women for the moral decline in France. Rousseau

---

[12] See Dena Goodman, *The Republic of Letters: A Cultural History of the French Enlightenment* (Ithaca, NY and London: Cornell University Press, 1994); and Daniel Gordon, *Citizens without Sovereignty: Equality and Sociability in French Thought, 1670–1789* (Princeton: Princeton University Press, 1994). Goodman argues that Rousseau had a lasting impact on later interpretations of the salons that underrated their influence in the mid-eighteenth century (pp. 62–3). The salons eventually did lose their power, however, and 'when the literary public sphere was transformed into the political public sphere in 1789, it had already become masculine' (p. 280).

[13] Lieselotte Steinbrügge, *The Moral Sex: Woman's Nature in the French Enlightenment*, trans. Pamela E. Selwyn (Oxford and New York: Oxford University Press, 1995), 3.

[14] The most modern translation is Jean-Jacques Rousseau, *The Collected Writings of Rousseau*, 9 vols, vol. 6, ed. Roger D. Masters and Christopher Kelly (Hanover, CT: Published for Dartmouth College by University Press of New England, 1990).

insisted that female behaviour had to be viewed as a response to their place within family and society. 'But let us be fair to wives', he argued,

> the cause of their disorder lies less in themselves than in our evil institutions. Ever since all the sentiments of nature have been stifled by extreme inequality, it is from the iniquitous despotism of fathers that the vices and misfortunes of children arise; it is in forced and ill-matched unions that young wives, victims of their parents' avarice or vanity, undo ... the scandal of their original honesty.[15]

Rousseau's assault both on coquettish adultery and patriarchal arranged marriages through the figure of a flawed but richly drawn and ultimately moral woman struck a chord throughout Europe, especially among women. Female readers identified with Rousseau's characters because so many of them chased the same dreams of loving relationships, meaningful motherhood and happiness in the home. Rousseau's new moral order also promised women more respect, since the place and behaviour of women was at its core.[16]

This new social vision, so attractive to Rousseau's women readers, rapidly became attractive to many men in the late Enlightenment as well. Increasingly concerned not only with the damaging effects of traditional patriarchy, but also with the dilemmas faced by 'new men' in a world of increasing economic, social and political competition, philosophers and social critics alike sought a moral anchor. They found it in the figure of the tamed woman. Women were on the one hand thought to be 'naturally' wild and passionate. Without the guiding hand of man, they were directionless and potentially destructive. On the other hand, when controlled and 'domesticated', they could find their true moral nature and become useful within the order of civilization. This notion had long been a feature of patriarchal thought. What distinguished Rousseau's vision was the idea that for this new order to be effective, women had to voluntarily choose this path of submission. They had to be moral actors prior to marriage in order to exercise a beneficial moral influence in the household afterwards. This moral core made women fully human and therefore in a sense equal.

This distinction may seem slight to present-day readers, who could note that both before and after this 'Enlightened' intervention, women were supposed to be obedient to men and to focus their attention on domestic affairs. But in fact the change was substantive. It transformed notions of female education, which now focused even more clearly on the need for a moral education for daughters, and it struck a blow against fathers. Daughters in 'Enlightened' families were now expected to choose their own mates, not on the basis of passion but on the basis of love and respect. By wresting control over sexual reproduction away from their elders, young men and women were also wresting control over a great deal of social power. In family life, the faint outlines

---

[15] Ibid., 17–18.
[16] Mary Seidman Trouille, *Sexual Politics in the Enlightenment: Women Writers Read Rousseau* (Albany: State University of New York Press, 1997), 4.

of 'liberty, equality and fraternity' were beginning to emerge from the background. As we shall see, all these notions would take on a masculine flavour in the era of revolution, but they also all depended in central ways on a female willingness to serve as obedient moral compasses. This new order was bolstered and replicated not only in sentimental novels, but also in social treatises like the massive *Encyclopedia* edited by the famous philosopher Denis Diderot, which focused its investigation of the social order on male productive labour in the workplace and on the bodily attributes of female reproduction in the domestic realm. Thus philosophical investigations came to an Enlightenment consensus: humans were equal, but men and women were fundamentally different. This was a formulation of 'separate but equal' that was founded on the proposition that it was nevertheless 'natural' for men to rule and women to obey. At the very moment that the concept of nature was being employed to argue for human equality and freedom, it was also being used to exclude women from the realm of the free.[17] As the 1780s dawned in France, then, an important revolution of moral sensibilities had already taken place, one that promised a new nation based on the principles of liberty and equality, but only if it was run by a fraternity.

## The French Revolution

Politically knowledgeable Europeans living at the end of the eighteenth century had many reasons for believing that a realignment of gender relations might be afoot. Women were more active in the public sphere than they ever had been before. While the women of the salons exercised political influence in private spaces, poor women were voicing political demands in the streets: they participated (and often led) bread riots across Europe, and in Paris they were actively involved in political associations and revolutionary movements. Meanwhile, Enlightenment thinkers like the Marquis de Condorcet were arguing that women, though physically weaker, were – like men – perfectible, particularly if they were provided with the education from which they had thus far been barred. While Condorcet agreed with his contemporaries that women were more suited to domestic than to political tasks, he left open the possibility that exceptional women who were provided with education and opportunity could excel and 'leave behind them the vast majority of the human race', including most men.[18] Enlightenment beliefs in the perfectibility of 'mankind' opened up the theoretical possibility of perfecting 'womankind' too. Condorcet argued:

> The rights of men derive entirely from their status as sentient beings, capable of acquiring moral ideas and reasoning about those ideas. So women having the same qualities necessarily have the same rights. Either no individual of the

---

[17] The argument in this paragraph is derived largely from Steinbrügge.
[18] Quoted in Fraisse, *Reason's Muse*, 51.

human race has any real rights, or all have the same. And one who votes against the rights of another, whatever their religion, colour or sex, has by so doing abjured his own.[19]

Condorcet's views were not entirely original. Debates about female learning had flourished in the Renaissance and had prompted the Cartesian philosopher François Poulain de la Barre to write the treatise *On the Equality of the Two Sexes: A Physical and Moral Discourse Which Shows the Importance of Getting Rid of One's Prejudices* in 1673. This was an example of the debates about the credibility of *savantes* – self-taught female intellectuals – that raged in seventeenth-century France and Italy, where a *savante*, Elena Lucrezia Cornara, was awarded a doctorate at the University of Padua in 1678.[20] Yet a century later, the subject remained marginal. In the course of the revolution, women's rights were ignored and, in the end, actively denied. Enlightened and revolutionary movements gave women the language to claim unprecedented rights, but the republic that was eventually created not only excluded them as political subjects, but was also 'forged into a myth against them'.[21] The ambivalence of this situation has prompted serious debate between historians about whether or not the French Revolution was an emancipatory moment for women or the beginning of a long period of subordination to the demands of the modern nation state.[22] Rather than taking sides in this debate, we will focus here on how the events of the French Revolution helped to entrench the belief that the genders could only be equal in the sense that they were confined to entirely separate political and social roles. When hopes that women would be included in the definition of universal rights were dashed, the symbolic force of male citizenship took on new power, affecting the lives of both women and men. Traditional forms of patriarchy collapsed in France with the downfall and execution of the king and were replaced with a fraternal order whose foundational concept of the citizen took on an increasingly gendered connotation as revolution turned to Terror and counter-revolution.

The absolutist French state was understood metaphorically as a family. After the reign of Louis XIV (the 'Sun King', r. 1643–1715) in the seventeenth century, the king was almost literally viewed as the father of the French people. Louis reigned over France as a patriarch reigns over his family: the royal family's private acts and their cultivation

---

[19] Quoted in Siân Reynolds, 'Marianne's Citizen? Women, the Republic and Universal Suffrage in France', in *Gender and History in Western Europe*, ed. Robert Shoemaker and Mary Vincent (London: Arnold, 1998), 310.

[20] Siep Stuurman, 'The Deconstruction of Gender: Seventeenth-Century Feminism and Modern Equality', in *Women, Gender, and Enlightenment*, ed. Sarah Knott and Barbara Taylor (New York: Palgrave Macmillan, 2005), 371–409: 380–3.

[21] Reynolds, 'Marianne's Citizen?', 308.

[22] Compare the rather optimistic view of Darline Gay Levy and Harriet B. Applewhite, 'A Political Revolution for Women? The Case of Paris', in *Becoming Visible: Women in European History*, 3rd edn., ed. Renate Bridenthal, Susan Mosher Stuard and Merry E. Wiesner (Boston and New York: Houghton Mifflin Co., 1998), 279 to Olwen H. Hufton, *Women and the Limits of Citizenship in the French Revolution* (Toronto: University of Toronto Press, 1992). An overview of the debate is provided in Karen Offen, 'The New Sexual Politics of French Revolutionary Historiography', *French Historical Studies* 16, no. 4 (1990): 909–22.

of personal relationships took on enormous public significance.[23] Taking the sun as his symbol to emphasize that he was anointed by God, the creator of all life, Louis presided over a household of intrigue, nepotism and partisanship. His body was sacred, since it represented the life of the community.[24] Even the objects in his household, the possessions of the royal family, had unique symbolic power.[25] Women in the king's family and social circle played key roles as facilitators of the personal networking that was essential to the attainment of power. Matchmaking and sexual intrigue often proved more important in attaining political posts than birth or merit. It was this type of Old Regime patriarchal power that created the space for the role of the women of the salons. The dominant political role of the absolutist monarch – his fatherhood of the entire nation – placed all others beneath him in a similar subordinate position, causing conservative nobles to worry that their own emasculation in this system might bring about the 'feminization' of the national body politic as a whole.[26] The system held together as long as military, political and social successes were attained. But those successes were costly in financial terms to a public stretched thin by population growth and a series of poor harvests. When Louis XVI (1774–92) took the dramatic step of supporting colonial rebels in North America in their war with Great Britain (1776–83), the corresponding expenditures led to deep fiscal crisis.[27]

French involvement in the American War of Independence also undermined the monarchy in another way, as the connection between liberty, patriotism and military service was strengthened among those who had fought with the American rebels.[28] The war of the American colonies against the British Empire was a crucial step in the transformation of Western ideas about the relationship between soldiering and the rights of citizenship. This was neither the first nor the last time that experiences outside of Europe dramatically influenced ideas about gender and became intertwined with the very definition of citizenship. The degree to which the ideals of citizenship, masculinity and soldiering were fused in the eighteenth century is hardly understandable without exploration of events in the colonies.

Beginning in 1775, the success of local militias against British monarchist troops helped strengthen the conviction that military service to protect the homeland was an integral component of citizenship; serving as a soldier became the duty of all

---

[23] Joan B. Landes, *Women in the Public Sphere in the Age of the French Revolution* (Ithaca, NY and London: Cornell University Press, 1988), 18–20.

[24] Joan B. Landes, *Visualizing the Nation: Gender, Representation, and Revolution in Eighteenth-Century France* (Ithaca, NY: Cornell University Press, 2001), 57. For an extended account of the importance of imagery of the body during and after the French Revolution, see Dorinda Outram, *The Body and the French Revolution: Sex, Class and Political Culture* (New Haven, CT: Yale University Press, 1989).

[25] Leora Auslander, *Taste and Power: Furnishing Modern France* (Berkeley: University of California Press, 1996), 1–34.

[26] Landes, *Women in the Public Sphere*, 21.

[27] Simon Schama, *Citizens: A Chronicle of the French Revolution*, reprint edition (New York: Vintage, 1990), 61–2.

[28] Ibid., 40.

virtuous men. With armed conflict looming across the colonies, the duty to protect local communities made abstract patriotic principles much more concrete.[29] But early successes were followed by a series of crushing defeats as the British repeatedly drove back revolutionary forces. With each loss, the volunteer Continental Army suffered a decline of morale and an increase in desertion. Revolutionary leaders finally allowed non-citizens (and presumably unvirtuous men) like transients and criminals to volunteer. The numbers were still too small, and the losses piled up. After a series of setbacks, George Washington, the army's commander, convinced Congress to approve a coercive draft in 1778. No one, Washington included, wanted this institution to become permanent. All saw it as a temporary expedient, and indeed it was abandoned at the end of the war. The idea that the new United States of America would have a full army only in times of war and would rely on state militias to train citizens in military affairs and masculine civic virtue was written into Article I of the Constitution, which prescribed that Congress could only appropriate money for an army for a two-year period and that the permanent military force of the country would be militias regulated by the states. It was further reaffirmed by the Second Amendment to the Constitution, which gave every citizen the right to be an armed member of his state militia.[30] The political system that emerged from war and revolution in the American colonies was one that depended upon the exercise of male martial virtue.

These initiatives in political emancipation were begun by European colonists, and they were part and parcel of the European political and military milieu. These were not exclusively American events. European observers followed the action with great interest, British and French armed forces were directly engaged in the conflict and eager revolutionaries from across the continent (notably from Poland and France) volunteered to be on the front lines of history. As a result, the ideological and institutional legacies of the American Revolution were easily and rapidly reimported back into Europe. In particular, the idea that martial virtue was inseparably linked to civic emancipation became central to the revolutionary process in France. The Marquis de Lafayette played an important role in this process. When he returned to France in 1779 (after escaping the French army at the age of nineteen and fleeing to 'fight for liberty' in the Americas), he was welcomed home by a quickly forgiving king and ecstatic French crowds. Lafayette had been an extraordinarily successful general in key battles of the revolutionary war and had become a close friend of Washington. Granted honorary American citizenship, Lafayette's exploits in America became famous in France and helped to popularize the American notion of 'liberty' and the 'citizen-soldier'. Benjamin Franklin, America's minister to France at the time of Lafayette's return, helped to orchestrate this fame and consciously fostered the symbolism of

---

[29] Meyer Kestnbaum, 'Citizenship and Compulsory Military Service: The Revolutionary Origins of Conscription in the United States', *Armed Forces and Society* 27, no. 1 (2000): 11.
[30] For a clear discussion of this process, see Ibid.

American men as the upholders of freedom, truth and natural innocence.[31] As the political crisis at home deepened, the French looked to American notions of liberty as a remedy for corruption and mismanagement. The founding of the American Republic 'captivated European minds and made a powerful contribution to preliminary steps towards social and political reform'.[32] French experience in the colonies was also an important impetus for the formation of new ideas about the relationship between duty, military service and republican citizenship. Martial citizens banding together in brotherhood seemed preferable to courtiers juggling deviously incurred national debts. The seeds of revolution had been sown.

Still, the biggest reason for the political crisis that precipitated the French Revolution was the disastrous state of the king's finances. Misery in the countryside also played a role, and at key moments demands for bread and lower prices would influence the nature of revolutionary violence and political demands. But it was the concern about looming economic collapse that prompted Louis XVI, in August 1788, to convoke the Estates General (an assembly of representatives from the three estates of French society: the clergy, the nobility and everyone else) for the first time since 1614. The meeting of the Estates General, convening in Versailles (the king's palace about 20 kilometres outside of Paris) on 5 May 1789, began with a drawn-out debate about voting that pitted the Third (lowest) Estate against the nobility and most of the clergy. Fed up with conflict and having invited the other two estates to join them, the Third Estate took independent action and named itself the National Assembly on 17 June 1789.

The National Assembly was suffused with the ideas of civic and masculine republicanism that had been so important for both Enlightened French thinkers and American revolutionaries. In its first meeting, the assembly swore an oath to defy its opponents until a constitution had been written. The president of the assembly, Jean-Sylvain Bailly, led the assembled delegates in their oath by placing one hand over his heart and thrusting his other arm outwards and upwards like a military commander. 'With right arms outstretched, fingers taut, six hundred deputies became new Romans, echoing the oath' in unison.[33] Having removed themselves from the spaces of royal (family) control, the delegates' appropriation of martial symbolism also helped them to reclaim the roles of men of action, no longer cowed by the supposedly feminizing influences of the court. Paris received the news immediately. On 15 July, Lafayette was appointed commander of the National Guard, a force of 48,000 male citizens charged with the task of fighting for political liberty and protecting the revolution from the king's army. Crowds in Paris rioted, and the royal fortress, the Bastille, was stormed on the fourteenth by a crowd of women and men who had seized royal muskets. Rebellion also

---

[31] Schama, *Citizens*, 43.
[32] Georges Lefebvre, *The French Revolution: From Its Origins to 1793*, trans. Elizabeth Moss Evanson (New York: Columbia University Press, 1962), 12.
[33] Ibid., 359.

raged across the countryside with the sacking of churches and castles and attacks on landlords and nobles.[34]

The king did his best to quell the fear and gain the trust of the rioting crowds, and by doing so he unwittingly opened the floodgates to the political participation of women as well as men. On 17 July 1789, he appeared in Paris wearing the revolutionary tricolour cockade to accept the lists of grievances that the Estates General had been gathering from around the country at his request. These grievances provided vast numbers of French men and women from the Third Estate with the feeling of directly participating in the creation of what Rousseau had called the 'general will'.[35] While not all of the written grievances have survived to the present, a few of the 60,000 that still exist were written by women, suggesting that the experience of hoping to become involved in new forms of political participation was not limited to men.[36]

As in grievances authored by men, women requested changes to their immediate social circumstances – female flower sellers, for instance, wanted a controlled market that would prohibit other women from underselling them – rather than a transformation of the political system. In January 1789, women of the Third Estate petitioned the king, asking:

> To be enlightened, to have work, not in order to usurp men's authority, but in order to be better esteemed by them, so that we might have the means of living safe from misfortune and so that poverty does not force the weakest among us, who are blinded by luxury and swept along by example, to join the crowd of unfortunate women who overpopulate the streets and whose debauched audacity disgraces our sex and the men who keep them company.[37]

The fact that the petitioners would use their concern about prostitutes in the city besmirching the honour of all women as a rallying cry to seek recognition from the king is an indication of the degree to which sexual honour had become a central political category. Despite calls for political reform, the women's language demonstrates that demands for change in this first phase of the revolution were generally made in the language of the Old Regime; they appealed to the king's moral sensibility and his duty to provide in a fatherly way for his people. This political restraint was short-lived. Newly energized female political activists soon took a leadership role in the deepening crisis. Outraged over skyrocketing food prices, activists staged daily processions, and market women repeatedly protested bread prices in Paris over the course of the summer of 1789.

---

[34] The classic account of the revolution in the countryside is Georges Lefebvre, *The Great Fear of 1789: Rural Panic in Revolutionary France*, trans. John Albert White (New York: Schocken Books, 1973).

[35] Landes, *Women in the Public Sphere*, 232, n. 10.

[36] Ibid., 107.

[37] 'Petition of Women of the Third Estate to the King' (1 January 1789) at Liberty, Equality, Fraternity: Exploring the French Revolution, City University of New York and George Mason University, available at https://chnm.gmu.edu/revolution/d/472/ (accessed 20 February 2015).

In October, a group of women marched to Versailles, killed some of the royal guards and forced the king and the queen to return to Paris with them. Upon their return, many of these women swarmed into the National Assembly as it was meeting on 5 October 1789. They interrupted debate with their demands and voted on legislation about grain distribution.[38] At all the key moments in 1789, women were very visible and active. The symbolism of the women's seizure of the king was not lost on a nation that idolized the 'father' of their nation. Women's violent incursions into public space and revolutionary rhetoric garnered them considerable respect; in actively seizing the rights of citizenship, they were forging their own identities as female citizens.

These same actions also caused concern among frightened men outside of France who believed that these 'harlots' and 'furies' were out of control. Conservative member of the British Parliament Edmund Burke epitomized these fears when he claimed in his *Reflections on the Revolution in France* (1790) that the queen had been forced to flee almost naked to her husband and had been sexually threatened by the invading marchers. His description of the marchers' return to Paris displays his general disdain for the revolutionary violence of these days and women's participation in it: 'The royal captives who followed in the train were slowly moved along, amidst the horrid yells, the shrilling screams, and frantic dances, and infamous contumelies, and all the unutterable abominations of the furies of hell, in the abused shape of the vilest of women.'[39] Perhaps influenced by the force of these words, philosophers like Hannah Arendt and present-day historians have described the women as apolitical rioters concerned only with issues of subsistence. As Arendt put it in *On Revolution*, 'It is indeed as though the forces of the earth were allied in benevolent conspiracy with this uprising, whose end is impotence, whose principle is rage, and whose conscious aim is not freedom but life and happiness.'[40] Arendt believed that abject hungry bodies could only be a threat to considered political action, and her analysis of the women's march on Versailles makes it difficult to escape the conclusion that even one of the twentieth century's most prominent female philosophers viewed female bodies as particularly close to nature and therefore apolitical.[41] But a closer look at the actions of the women as the revolution progressed reveals that they were aware of the political issues at stake and were motivated not only by hunger, but also by the desire to transform their country.[42] Indeed, the fact that male members of the National Assembly became increasingly concerned about the involvement of women in revolutionary violence suggests that these actions carried considerable political weight. They must also be understood with reference to ongoing debates about the very meaning of citizenship.

---

[38] Levy and Applewhite, 'A Political Revolution for Women?', 272.
[39] Quoted in Landes, *Women in the Public Sphere*, 112.
[40] Hannah Arendt, *On Revolution* (London: Penguin Books, 1963), 112–3.
[41] Norma Claire Moruzzi, *Speaking Through the Mask: Hannah Arendt and the Politics of Social Identity* (Ithaca, NY: Cornell University Press, 2000), 38.
[42] Dominique Godineau, *The Women of Paris and Their French Revolution* (Berkeley and Los Angeles: University of California Press, 1998).

On 4 August 1789, the National Assembly took the first step to establishing a nation of equal citizens by abolishing feudalism, revoking the nobility's rights over peasants and ending the church's right to collect tithes. On 26 August 1789 the assembly submitted the 'Declaration of the Rights of Man and Citizen' to the king.[43] Drafted by Lafayette, this statement of principles defined the individual and collective rights of French citizens and insisted on the fundamental equality of all men. Article VI of the French Declaration said, 'All citizens being equal in the eyes of the law, are equally eligible to all dignities and to all public positions and occupations, according to their abilities, and without distinction except that of their virtues and talents.' The implication of this article for female political rights thus hinged upon the interpretation of the word 'citizen'. Many women reasonably hoped that they would now be enfranchised. But the declaration used only the masculine form of the word 'citizen' – *citoyen* – and insisted that the 'security of the rights of man and of the citizen requires public military forces'. This made it clear that military service to the state would help define the citizen as male. The feminine form of the word 'citizen' – *citoyenne* – later appeared in revolutionary rhetoric, but only as a kind of afterthought.[44]

Male revolutionaries never seriously considered female suffrage. The Constitution of 1791, which created a short-lived liberal constitutional monarchy, extended the franchise to all men over the age of twenty-five who met certain property qualifications, but it marked the first time that women had been explicitly excluded from voting rights in France, since they had previously been able to vote for some governing bodies if they owned property. Now all women (and poor men) were decreed 'passive' citizens. 'Passive' citizens could not participate in political bodies or become members of the National Guard.[45] There was, however, a telling exception to this exclusion. In 1790, legislation was introduced to allow men who were too poor to pay taxes to gain membership in the National Guard (and thus the right to vote) if they bought their uniforms, which cost far more than a year's taxes. As Clifford Dale argues, this fact demonstrates the degree to which citizenship was still being defined through reactions to the short-term contingencies of revolutionary change.[46] Given the continuing centrality of armed violence to the course of these events, the exclusion of women from the definition of active citizenship was all but guaranteed. Indeed, when the definition of 'passive citizen' was dropped in 1792, the continued exclusion

---

[43] Available online at the Avalon Project at Yale Law School, available at http://avalon.law.yale.edu/18th _century/rightsof.asp (accessed 10 July 2015).

[44] William H. Sewell, 'Le Citoyen/La Citoyenne: Activity, Passivity, and the Revolutionary Concept of Citizenship', in *The French Revolution and the Creation of Modern Political Culture: The Political Culture of the Old Regime*, ed. Colin Lucas, *vol. 2. Political Culture of the French Revolution* (New York: Pergamon Press, 1987), 105–25, esp. 114.

[45] For an extended discussion of the meaning of these terms and the enduring legacies of the limits to universality inherent in these decisions, see Immanuel Wallerstein, 'Citizens All? Citizens Some! The Making of the Citizen', *Comparative Studies in Society and History* 45, no. 4 (October 2003): 650–79.

[46] Dale L. Clifford, 'Can the Uniform Make the Citizen?: Paris, 1789–1791', *Eighteenth-Century Studies* 34, no. 3 (2001): 363–82.

of women from voting rights helped to entrench a purely masculine definition of citizenship.[47]

This is not to say, however, that the *practice* of citizenship truly excluded women. Historical contingencies and social relationships also governed definitions of the *citoyenne*. If we follow those historians who are now defining citizenship much more broadly – as a socially operative concept that transcends a legal definition of rights – then it becomes clear that a concept of female citizenship did arise during these tumultuous years.[48] It is thus overstating the case to argue, as William Sewell did, that the word *citoyenne* never carried the political weight of rights.[49] In detailed investigations of women's role and the importance of the family in setting the terms of republican virtue, Annie Smart, Suzanne Desan and Jennifer Ngaire Heuer have all demonstrated that 'revolutionary citizenship was not defined exclusively by political rights'.[50] Aside from changes to marriage laws and contracts, women were expected to become active civic participants, primarily but not exclusively through the inculcation of civic virtues in their children. The 'passive' definition of female citizenship arose due to very contingent circumstances, and it did not go unchallenged.[51]

The new citizenship laws prompted considerable dissatisfaction, particularly in Paris, where the majority of the working-class and middle-class activists had now been declared 'passive' citizens. Political clubs and organizations proliferated, many of them accepting female members and some supporting female suffrage. In this atmosphere, the question of female citizenship became central to political debate. Olympe de Gouges, a playwright, responded to the gendered nature of the original declaration and the Constitution with her own 'Declaration of the Rights of Woman' in 1791. Addressing her appeal to the queen, de Gouges called for the creation of a separate National Assembly for women,

---

[47] Judith Surkis, *Sexing the Citizen: Morality and Masculinity in France, 1870–1920* (Ithaca, NY: Cornell University Press, 2006), 2. Male voting rights were later restricted again.

[48] For examples of this broader definition of citizenship, see Kathleen Canning, *Gender History in Practice: Historical Perspectives on Bodies, Class and Citizenship* (Ithaca: Cornell University Press, 2006), xii; and Andreas Fahrmeir, *Citizenship: The Rise and Fall of a Modern Concept* (New Haven and London: Yale University Press, 2007), 2–3. Historians, it must be noted, came rather late to the game. See also the philosophical discussion of rights in Claude Lefort, *The Political Forms of Modern Society: Bureaucracy, Democracy, Totalitarianism* (Cambridge: Polity, 1986).

[49] Sewell, 'Le Citoyen/La Citoyenne', 114. Not all historians agree. Judith Surkis insists, for example, that the exclusion of women from the right to vote meant that any reforms enacted in the interests of protecting their welfare 'were, for the most part, enacted not in the name of women as rights-bearing individuals, but as social goods, necessary for the health of families, and hence the moral and physical strength of the nation.' Surkis, *Sexing the Citizen*, 3.

[50] Annie K. Smart, *Citoyennes: Women and the Ideal of Citizenship in Eighteenth-Century France* (Newark: University of Delaware, 2011); Suzanne Desan, *The Family on Trial in Revolutionary France* (Berkeley: University of California Press, 2006); and Jennifer Ngaire Heuer, *The Family and the Nation: Gender and Citizenship in Revolutionary France, 1789–1830* (Ithaca, NY and London: Cornell University Press, 2005).

[51] The contingency of revolutionary attitudes towards women is underlined in Allyssa Goldstein Sepinwall's investigation of Maximilian Robespierre's early support for women's integration into institutions of higher learning. See Alyssa Goldstein Sepinwall, 'Robespierre, Old Regime Feminist? Gender, the Late Eighteenth Century, and the French Revolution Revisited', *Journal of Modern History* 82, no. 1 (2010): 1–29.

female suffrage, legal protection for illegitimate children and their mothers and a role for women in government administration. To draw attention to women's participation in the revolution, de Gouges alluded to the fact that women had already been executed for their political involvement. 'Woman has the right to mount the scaffold', she argued, 'she must equally have the right to mount the rostrum.'[52]

De Gouges acted on her political convictions by forming and joining revolutionary societies. But even this most vocal of representatives of women's rights blamed the 'nocturnal administration of women' in the Old Regime for its corruption and called for prostitutes to be confined to certain areas. Her desire for women's rights, in other words, was balanced by a conviction that traditional understandings of female honour and chastity needed to be maintained and specifically motherly values and behaviours fostered. She asked that men grant women these rights; she saw no possibility of women seizing them for themselves. Her words thus 'functioned to preserve difference and hence guarantee sexual inequality, even as they were yoked to a universalist, egalitarian protest'.[53] Like many other aristocratic French women, de Gouges was profoundly affected by the rumours of sexual impropriety that circled around the royal family (particularly the queen, Marie-Antoinette), and her political views were affected by the desire to inculcate the values of republican motherhood as an antidote to royal corruption.[54] This appeal to womanly virtues can thus also be viewed as an early example of maternalist or relational feminism – an insistence that women's essential difference was a justification for their political participation rather than a validation for their exclusion.[55] Her declaration, however, had a rather specific audience and did not necessarily speak to the majority of women in Paris, whose demands centred much more directly on the needs of everyday survival.

Many of de Gouges's concerns were echoed in a far more extensive analysis of the implications of the French Revolution for women's rights that was written by a woman observing events from Britain: Mary Wollstonecraft. In *A Vindication of the Rights of Woman* (1792), Wollstonecraft forcefully argued that women too could be virtuous in Rousseau's sense of the word – having the moral fortitude to act in the interest of the polity and to actively care for public affairs. If European women had thus far failed to demonstrate their virtue, it was only because, like those men who had been denied

---

[52] The declaration is reprinted in its entirety, including the letter to the queen, in Darline Gay Levy, Harriet Branson Applewhite and Mary Durham Johnson, eds., *Women in Revolutionary Paris, 1789-1795: Selected Documents* (Urbana: University of Illinois Press, 1979), 87–96, quotation p. 91.

[53] Landes, *Women in the Public Sphere*, 123.

[54] The concept of republican motherhood developed in dialogue with American feminists. See Linda Kerber, *Women of the Republic: Intellect and Ideology in Revolutionary America* (Chapel Hill: University of North Carolina Press, 1980); and Jane Rendall, *The Origins of Modern Feminism: Women in Britain, France, and the United States 1780–1860* (Basingstoke: Macmillan, 1985), esp. chp. 2.

[55] This seems to be the direction of Annie Smart's argument. She insists that de Gouges 'writes both as a woman, from a particularly feminine experience, and as an advocate for the public good. The intimate sphere of the home becomes the privileged space from which to speak "as a *citoyenne*," or as an advocate for revolutionary change'. Smart, *Citoyenne*, 17.

the full rights of citizenship, the paths of civic action had been closed to them. Like de Gouges, however, Wollstonecraft argued that it was their role as mothers that earned women the right to political participation, and she blamed the frivolous concerns of wealthy women for the poor reputation of the sex. Only a concentrated effort to return women to their primary duties – to motherhood – could prevent aristocratic excess from undermining political freedom. Wollstonecraft's stirring appeal to motherhood as a motivation and justification for women's political involvement assured the fame and enduring influence of her book. She argued that

> If children are to be educated to understand the true principle of patriotism, their mother must be a patriot; and the love of mankind, from which an orderly train of virtues spring, can only be produced by considering the moral and civil interest of mankind; but the education and situation of woman, at present, shuts her out from such investigations.[56]

Failure to grant women the conditions to make republican motherhood possible would 'render both men and themselves vicious'. Men should grant woman these rights and cease impugning and threatening her chastity, while women should exercise self-control.[57] In all these respects, de Gouges and Wollstonecraft shared the conviction of Shcherbatov and Rousseau that self-control and virtue were necessary for an orderly society and that women in the Old Regime had exercised neither. They disagreed mainly about the potential of women to develop their own special sort of civic virtue. The tumultuous events of 1792 and 1793 would put many of these ideas about the role of women in politics to the test.

During the summer of 1792, women tried to persuade the members of newly formed political clubs like the Jacobins and Girondins, which were becoming more and more like political parties, to pay more attention to social and economic issues in the capital. Women were particularly active in the Girondist Society of the Friends of Truth, a political organization seeking social reform and the end to patriarchal family relations.[58] In March 1791, the Dutch woman Etta Palm d'Aelders (1743–99) formed a women's section within the society. This group lobbied for both female political rights and welfare measures for poor families.[59] But Girondin tolerance for these activities left them open to charges from the Jacobins that Girondin ministers were being controlled by their wives. The Jacobins also charged politically active women with having morals as loose as those of their aristocratic predecessors. Sexual innuendo thus undercut the efforts of Girondist women to bring about gender equality in the law. While divorce was legalized in 1792,

---

[56] Ibid., 4.

[57] Landes argues that 'She ultimately fails to appreciate the contradictions resulting from the applications of masculine ideology to women.' See Landes, *Women in the Public Sphere*, 134.

[58] On the early development of this group, see Gary Kates, *The Cercle Social, the Girondins, and the French Revolution* (Princeton: Princeton University Press, 1985).

[59] For a detailed account, see Landes, *Women in the Public Sphere*, 118–21.

and the age of majority (the age at which one could marry without parental consent) was set at twenty-one years for both sexes, efforts to reform laws on adultery failed.

As the revolution radicalized, so too did revolutionary women. They took part in the arrest of the royal couple, in their execution in 1793 and in the creation and expansion of mechanisms of political terror between March 1793 and August 1794. This 'reign of terror' led to the execution of 16,594 people, while civil war in the West killed as many as 200,000.[60] That terror, carried out by a largely Jacobin 'Committee on Public Safety', was based on the idea that violence would be necessary to create a 'Republic of Virtue'. Under the Committee's leadership, denunciation became a civic responsibility. It was the duty of all citizens to display their vigilance of revolutionary values, their virtue and their purity by denouncing enemies of revolution.[61]

In this atmosphere, radical women revolutionaries seized the opportunities that the Terror offered them to demonstrate their worthiness as citizens. Pauline Léon (an unmarried chocolate maker) and Claire Lacombe (a provincial actress) formed the Society of Revolutionary Republican Women. The group wanted to be 'armed to rush to the defence of the fatherland' and participated in surveillance measures to help enforce the repressive laws of the Terror. In other words, they hoped to use the weapon of denunciation, now defined as an act of citizenship, to prove that they should be considered fully active citizens of the republic. But their public visibility (they walked through Paris in groups, sporting red bonnets, tricolour ribbons and trousers) irked the Jacobins, who reacted to the women's taunts about insufficient enforcement of the Terror with attacks on female honour. At a Jacobin meeting on 16 September, François Chabot railed: 'It is these counter-revolutionary sluts who cause all the riotous outbreaks, above all over bread. They make a revolution over coffee and sugar, and they will make others if we don't watch out.'[62] In October 1793, market women attacked republicans trying to enforce revolutionary dress codes and later stormed a meeting of the Revolutionary Republican Women, beating some of them. The spectacle of women fighting pushed the National Convention (the constitutional and legislative assembly formed in September 1792 and charged with drawing up a new constitution) towards the Jacobin view that women had to be banished from the public sphere and forcibly returned to their domestic duties. All female involvement in political and popular societies was henceforth banned.

The debate preceding this decree made it clear that the republican camp was deeply divided over the question of whether women should receive equal rights with men.[63]

---

[60] Marisa Linton, 'Robespierre and the Terror', *History Today* 56, no. 8 (August 2006): 26; and David Andress, *The Terror: The Merciless War for Freedom in Revolutionary France* (New York: Farrar, Straus and Giroux, 2005), 6. See also: Marisa Linton, *Choosing Terror: Virtue, Friendship, and Authenticity in the French Revolution* (Oxford and New York: Oxford University Press, 2013); and Timothy Tackett, *The Coming of the Terror in the French Revolution* (Cambridge: Belknap Press, 2015).

[61] Colin Lucas, 'The Theory and Practice of Denunciation in the French Revolution', *The Journal of Modern History* 68, no. 4 (December 1996): 774.

[62] Quoted in Landes, *Women in the Public Sphere*, 142.

[63] Levy and Applewhite, 'A Political Revolution for Women?', 285.

But another event carried far more significant symbolic value: the execution of Marie-Antoinette. The execution was justified in primarily sexual terms. Already before the revolution, pornographic literature and satirical songs about Marie-Antoinette's supposed sexual exploits, adultery and lesbianism had made it almost impossible for her to be seen in public. If she did venture to the theatre, she was often greeted with hisses.[64] When she came before the revolutionary tribunal, her supposed political intrigues (including alleged collusion with the Habsburg Emperor, her brother) were conflated with sexual sins. She was accused of the sexual abuse of her own son, the eleven-year-old Dauphin, who had been taken away from her in prison and would soon die of physical maltreatment. The president of the revolutionary Paris Commune charged that the queen and her conspirators had taught the Dauphin to masturbate in order to 'enervate the constitution of the child in order that they might acquire an ascendancy over his mind'. Marie-Antoinette refused to respond to this charge of sexual treachery, asking only: 'I appeal to all mothers who are present in this room – is such a crime possible?'[65] But her days of representing French motherhood were over, and on 16 October 1793 she calmly laid her head under the guillotine's blade to the joy of cheering and jeering crowds. Nothing better symbolized the degree to which women's sexual crimes had now become political crimes.[66]

To some degree this connection to the sexual was inherent in the idea of monarchy itself. As Marilyn Morris puts it, 'the hereditary principle allowed the monarch's sexual body to be a legitimate object of public scrutiny.'[67] Sexual intrigues had always been part of court life because they had direct bearing on the mechanisms of power in a system of personal rule. Rumours about sexual perversion and depravity were immediately associated with the corruption of political life, since both represented disorder and besmirched the honour that was central to noble privilege in the early modern period. Concern that sexual immoderation was contributing to the political corruption of European royal families and the aristocracy was by no means new.[68] But such innuendo reached a crescendo during the eighteenth century, when widespread literacy and the mass production of political cartoons vastly increased its reach. A widely circulated drawing from 1789, for instance, showed General Lafayette kneeling between Marie-Antoinette's splayed legs and fondling her naked 'res publica'.

---

[64] Schama, *Citizens*, 221.

[65] Ibid., 226–27.

[66] Bonnie G. Smith, *Changing Lives: Women in European History since 1700* (Boston: Houghton Mifflin, 1989), 93. Marilyn Morris has recently commented that the spectacle of the French king and queen's demise also encouraged the British royal family to present themselves as 'moral exemplars' in contrast. See Marilyn Morris, *Sex, Money and Personal Character in Eighteenth-Century British Politics* (New Haven: Yale University Press, 2014), ix.

[67] Ibid., 98.

[68] See for example Cynthia B. Herrup, *A House in Gross Disorder: Sex, Law, and the 2nd Earl of Castlehaven* (New York: Oxford University Press, 2001).

**Figure 1.1** An engraving entitled *Ma Constitution*, c. 1790. The words between the queen's legs read 'res publica'. Reproduced by permission of the Bibliothèque nationale de France.

The reference to 'res publica' was a homophonic play on the words 'pubic' and the Latin term for 'public affairs', and it was the same phrase that Lafayette had used to symbolize the American republic in a painting he had had commissioned of George Washington. The drawing thus deploys a pornographic allusion to make a deeply political statement about the corruption of the royal family in general and the queen in particular.[69] Sexual innuendo about the 'sapphism' of the queen and her sister Caroline, queen of Naples, also helped undermine the family model of monarchical rule. Although no concept of lesbian identity existed at the time, the word 'sapphism' alluded to same-sex intercourse between women and was in this case meant to undermine the women's standing as mothers and respectable members of royal families. Rumours of yet another kind of sexual perversion were part of the republican effort to discredit the patriarchal system upon which monarchical power was based and through which these aristocratic women also maintained their status. These rumours drew on the popularity of *Confessions d'une jeune fille*, a fictional description of a 'Society of Anandrynes' (literally women without men) that posed as a journalistic exposé and began circulating in 1778. Along with many other pamphlets decrying the dangers of 'tribade' societies seeking to undermine the political system, various tracts connected the queen and her sister to a lesbian plot against France from the mid-1780s on.[70] Charges of sexual perversion and rumours about an

---

[69] Laura Auricchio, *The Marquis: Lafayette Reconsidered* (New York: Knopf, 2014), 230–1.
[70] Susan S. Lanser, *The Sexuality of History: Modernity and the Sapphic, 1565–1830* (Chicago: University of Chicago Press, 2014), 201–4.

intimate relationship with the queen were also partly responsible for the brutality of the death of Princess de Lamballe, daughter of the prince of Savoie and 'Superintendent of the Queen's Household'. She was arrested with the royal family and brought before a tribunal of citizens on 3 September 1792, who demanded that she swear her hatred for the king and queen. When she refused to do so, she was immediately taken out to the street and viciously tortured, (possibly) sexually violated and murdered. Her primary crime had been to stand as a symbol of aristocratic femininity in a court surrounded by rumours of sexual deviance.[71] As in the case of the story about Catherine the Great and her horse, impugning the sexual propriety of these powerful women revealed itself to be a remarkably effective weapon. Given the relationship that all of these women had with the queen, the power of the slur was magnified by its combination with rumours of the king's impotence.[72]

Neither the queen's attempt to portray herself as a loving mother nor the revolutionary zeal of republican women sufficed to overcome the fundamental dilemma of female citizenship in this era. The virtually universal conviction of the pre-revolutionary era that female power rested on underhanded sexual manipulation presented any woman (or man) advocating full female citizenship with an insurmountable rhetorical barrier. To deny the existence of feminine intrigue at court would have been to undermine a key element in the revolutionary argument about the illegitimacy of monarchical rule. But when women like de Gouges and Wollstonecraft highlighted the frivolity and corruption of elite women in their attempts to define specifically female virtue, they only drew attention to it and left all women open to the charge of unseemly, immoral behaviour. Female political action remained synonymous with sexual desire and depravity. Constant references to the need to control and rehabilitate prostitutes did not help matters.

In the end, women seeking increased political rights had, as Joan Scott has argued, 'only paradoxes to offer'.[73] They emphasized their difference by extolling the virtues of motherhood even as they sought to establish equality by appealing to the categories of universal rights and civic virtue. This was an understandable strategy, but it created difficulties. It meant accepting the 'natural fact' of sexual difference even as one was trying to eliminate it as a justification for political exclusion. When they made claims on behalf of women, de Gouges, Wollstonecraft and their like-minded contemporaries helped to reinforce 'woman' as a natural and immutable category: 'To the extent that it acted for "women," feminism produced the "sexual difference" it sought to eliminate. This paradox – the need to both accept and refuse "sexual difference" – has been the constitutive condition of feminism as a political movement throughout its long history.'[74]

---

[71] Antoine de Baecque, *Glory and Terror: Seven Deaths under the French Revolution* (New York: Routledge, 2013), 71.

[72] For a comprehensive collection of these rumours, see Antoine de Baecque, *The Body Politic: Corporeal Metaphor in Revolutionary France, 1770–1800* (Stanford, CA: Stanford University Press, 1997).

[73] Joan Wallach Scott, *Only Paradoxes to Offer: French Feminists and the Rights of Man* (Cambridge, MA: Harvard University Press, 1996), 3.

[74] Ibid., 3–4. For an extended treatment of this dilemma, see Denise Riley, *Am I That Name? Feminism and the Category of 'Women' in History* (London and Minneapolis: Macmillan and University of Minnesota Press, 1988).

In the atmosphere of a revolutionary regime that strove to balance political change with the destruction of poverty – to achieve both political freedom and freedom from natural necessities – it was almost inevitable that women's insistence on being closer to nature would backfire. Stressing difference helped fuel the arguments that excluded them from politics.

Over the course of the revolution, women mounted an unprecedented challenge to the notion that only men should engage in politics, and they questioned emerging notions of citizenship.[75] While it is important to remember that some of the most radical female political actors – such as the market women of Paris – were not necessarily seeking a transformation of gender norms, their politicization of social issues and their insistence on making their specific concerns heard did in practice challenge that gender order. Elite women like de Gouges saw that hunger and illiteracy among urban women were political questions and hoped that the acquisition of political rights would improve the material well-being of those who received them. This seemed a rational argument to be making at a time when revolutionary events were intertwined with demands for social change. The king's acceptance of grievances from his subjects had been, after all, an important impetus for the growth of political activism. Female activists were thus acting in the spirit of the times when they linked demands for political rights and for social justice. But neither poor women in the streets nor their elite counterparts ever found the means to counter a growing resistance from revolutionary men towards the idea of allowing women a political voice. Since women were not included in the definition of active citizen, they were excluded from the increasingly important public sphere; their concerns were labelled 'social' rather than truly political.[76] Revolutionary masculinity was thus founded upon the political exclusion of women.[77] The new social contract of republicanism implied and became dependent upon a 'sexual contract' that depicted only men as truly complete human beings; women were portrayed as being completely governed by their bodily functions, while men were associated with independent action – both in the public sphere and in civil society, that realm of associational and economic action between the home and politics.[78] This set a precedent for arguments

---

[75] Offen, 'The New Sexual Politics', 910. As Offen points out, seventeenth-century England provides some parallels.

[76] On 'the social' as a category, see Hannah Arendt, *The Human Condition* (Chicago and London: University of Chicago Press, 1958). See also the discussion in Arendt, *On Revolution*, 29. For an extended debate on the relationship between gender and the emergence of the public sphere, see the contributions by Daniel Gordon, David A. Bell and Sarah Maza to 'Forum: The Public Sphere in the Eighteenth Century', *French Historical Studies* 17, no. 4 (1992): 882–956.

[77] The most influential articulation of the impact of this exclusion is Carol Pateman, *The Sexual Contract* (Stanford, CA: Stanford University Press, 1988).

[78] Martina Kessel, 'The "Whole Man": The Longing for a Masculine World in Nineteenth-Century Germany', *Gender & History* 15, no. 1 (2003): 3. For an extended discussion of the importance of the sexual contract to the creation of a notions of civil society, see Isabel V. Hull, *Sexuality, State, and Civil Society in Germany, 1700–1815* (Ithaca, NY: Cornell University Press, 1996). Laura Lee Downs provides a useful summary of Hull's argument in *Writing Gender History*, 2nd edn. (London: Bloomsbury, 2010), 150–61.

against women's active participation in the public sphere that would grow in strength throughout Europe in the nineteenth century. The public sphere became a masculine sphere in a much more formal way than it ever had been before.


## Echoes of the French Revolution

The discussion of women's rights and involvement in the public sphere that emerged in the French Revolution resonated across Europe. Some men of influence began to argue that the new democratic ideals should foster an improvement of women's political position. In Prussia, Theodor Gottlieb von Hippel wrote *On Improving the Status of Women* (1792) in reaction to hearing that women had not been granted the rights of full citizenship in France. 'Do I go too far', he asked, 'in asserting that the oppression of women is the cause of all the rest of the oppression in the world?'[79] But this was a rare voice. Most European philosophers of the period (like Immanuel Kant and Georg Wilhelm Friedrich Hegel) shared Rousseau's opinion about women's place in the home. They 'succeeded in writing women out of the state' in their political philosophy.[80]

Nevertheless, France was far from the only country where the place of women in politics was debated during the revolutionary era. Women also demanded political rights in Belgium, the Dutch Republic and various regions of Italy and Germany. The Dutch case is particularly instructive. Over the course of two revolutions in the Netherlands (the Dutch Patriotic Revolution of the 1780s and the Batavian Revolution of 1795) there was a fundamental transformation in the role of women in political life. As in the French case, this transformation ultimately ensured the triumph of a male-dominated public sphere.

In the early modern period, women had enormous influence over community life in urban neighbourhoods and villages.[81] Dutch society gave women responsibility for maintaining community bonds: women controlled household finances, governed relationships with friends and neighbours, organized neighbourhood welfare programmes and dominated public spaces as market women. Given these positions close to the community, they were prominent in all the riots and rebellions of the early modern period. The Dutch Patriotic Revolution threw the political model that reserved a place for women within the popular politics of the crowd into turmoil. Patriots, who were inspired both by Enlightenment ideas and by direct experience in the American Revolution, reacted to military defeat at the hands of the British in 1784 by joining with Old Regime forces to drastically curtail the powers of

---

[79] Quoted in Karen M. Offen, *European Feminisms, 1700–1950: A Political History* (Palo Alto, CA: Stanford University Press, 1999), 70.

[80] Ibid., 72.

[81] The account to follow relies on Wayne Ph. te Brake, Rudolf M. Dekker and Lotte C. van de Pol, 'Women and Political Culture in the Dutch Revolutions', in *Women and Politics in the Age of the Democratic Revolution*, ed. Harriet B. Applewhite and Darline G. Levy (Ann Arbor: University of Michigan Press, 1990), 109–46. Quotation from p. 130.

Prince William V. His battles on behalf of the American rebels had led his nation to defeat and economic turmoil. In response (and several years prior to their French counterparts), the Patriots began demanding the 'sovereignty of the people'. By 1787, they had gained considerable political ground in the provinces. Women played an important but subsidiary role both in the patriot and monarchist camps. Princess Wilhelmina van Pruisen (William's wife) used her relationship with her brother (the king of Prussia) to secure the services of the Prussian troops, who would end the revolution and restore the monarchy in 1787. At the other end of the social spectrum, a female mussel seller named Kaat Mossel was prominent among the monarchists, while patriot women like Betje Wolff wrote political pamphlets. But Wolff confined her agitation for women to demands for improved education for girls, and she did not advocate specific rights for women.[82]

A second revolution began in December 1794, when Dutch Patriots joined with French revolutionary forces to drive the monarchists from power and institute representative democracy. Revolutionaries proclaimed the Batavian Republic in January 1795. The new regime was closely allied to France, and went through several political transformations between 1795 and 1810, when the Northern Netherlands were annexed to Napoleon's empire. In the midst of these transformations, Etta Palm d'Aelders, who had been forced to leave France, began to take a prominent role in Dutch political discussions. Signalling a new era of female involvement in politics, she called for the formation of women-only political clubs. 'Batavian Maidens' appeared at revolutionary celebrations and planted liberty trees as symbols of the new republic. An anonymously authored Dutch tract, *A Demonstration that Women Should Take Part in the Governance of the Nation* (1795), argued that excluding women from politics was a kind of 'despotism' and that the Dutch could become an example to the world by achieving what the French had not: a true inclusion of women in a new democratic state.[83] The 1790s saw a proliferation of female voices in political periodicals. In the last years of the century, several revolutionary journals published pieces advocating women's rights, and Petronella Moens founded a journal for patriotic women that advocated better training and education for women.

But these women's attempts to transform female political roles from the leadership of neighbourhood crowds into a substantial contribution to political debate foundered upon the new political system that the Patriots were developing. In their desire for a rational, democratic system of government, the Patriots shunned the old model of popular protest and were openly hostile to community activism, which they saw as an expression of the 'rabble' or the 'mob'. They wanted to replace this form of popular politics with a more organized politics from above. Patriots organized local committees and, most importantly, militias on the American revolutionary model. These militias eventually became highly successful in replacing crowd politics with orderly, disciplined political structures that by their very martial definition excluded women. Since the

---

[82] Ibid., 116.
[83] Brake, Dekker and van de Pol, 'Women and Political Culture in the Dutch Revolutions', 119.

Patriots followed the American example in linking active citizenship and the right to bear arms, this political order was increasingly interpreted as a male enterprise.[84]

While the exclusion of women from politics in the new Batavian Republic was never openly declared, the success of the militia model of local governance and revolutionary action brought about a decisive shift in Dutch women's political position. Townswomen's role as active organizers of crowd protests disappeared as local dissatisfaction was channelled into organized political committees and through the militias. The informal influence and formal authority of aristocratic women, like Princess Wilhelmina, was curtailed by the replacement of royal privilege with representative government. While women did not disappear from political life – they continued on as journalists and pamphleteers, often writing anonymously – by the turn of the century women's political clubs and the most prominent female publicists had disappeared from Dutch public life. It is difficult to avoid the conclusion that the elimination of traditional female paths to political participation ensured that the revolution represented a decline rather than an advance for Dutch women's rights.[85] But it is most important for our purposes to note that in the Dutch case, as in the French, the demarcation of spheres of activity for men and women was increasingly influenced by the ideals of martial citizenship. The ability to serve as a soldier – as a member of the militias – guaranteed a man's access to the rights of citizenship, while traditional forms of political participation for women, which had been a key force in the life of early modern Dutch communities and had been centred around specific social and economic conflicts, disappeared.

### Revolutionary wars and revolutionary nations

Republican ideology was not an invention of the late eighteenth century. The study of classical republics, particularly in Athens and Rome, was part of any elite European's education, and the great political theorists of early modern Europe, like Machiavelli, had attempted to rearticulate these theories in the new civic conditions that emerged from the sixteenth century onwards. Both the classical and early modern experiences of non-monarchical forms of rule in Italy, Britain and the Netherlands had demonstrated that republics were particularly vulnerable forms of government. On the one hand, they were prone to the corruption of self-interest, as politicians and potentates jockeyed for power and access to public funds and public projects. On the other hand, the lack of a central, undisputed source of authority meant that it was difficult to organize the coercive measures necessary to raise taxes and soldiers to defend the republic from foreign invasion. It turned out that rule by the 'public' required citizens to repress their selves (or at least their self-interest) in order for the republic to survive. This form of

---

[84] Ibid., 136. The Batavian definition of citizenship also included a provision that active (enfranchised) citizens had to pay a minimum of direct tax. This also effectively excluded women, who were considered dependents.
[85] Ibid., 139.

public-spiritedness and enlightened self-control is what republican theorists called 'virtue', a quality that could emerge through the proper training of young men, but not one that could be coerced.[86] This civic virtue was of course seen as an exclusively male trait. While male virtue was understood as a requirement of ethical public life, female virtue was thought to operate only in the private realm – as a curb on private sexual passions.

It was this connection between male civic virtue and the survival of the republic that inspired republican thinkers to argue that a healthy republic required all citizens to be soldiers and all soldiers to be citizens. It also followed that the right to civic participation and to participation in the military should be limited to those capable of exercising virtue, which is to say men who had received proper moral training. In addition, influential Enlightenment figures like the prominent Scottish philosophers Adam Smith and Adam Ferguson felt that this service should not take place in a standing army, which both men despised as a tool of despotic monarchs and a dangerous temptation to conduct the sorts of foreign military adventures that had ruined earlier republics. They instead envisioned a militia of all able-bodied men, living and training at home, ready to take up arms *en masse* when the republic was endangered but fundamentally unwilling to wage wars of aggression that would take them far from their families and farms.[87]

If there was little disagreement about the principles of military service in a functioning republic, there was a great deal of confusion about how revolutionary republics could build the military force necessary to overthrow existing regimes and then defend themselves from the conservative counter-attacks that were sure to come. After all, training in republican virtue was very weak in monarchical states, so one could not expect masses of men to have the fortitude necessary to fight long battles for liberty and freedom. And masses would be necessary, for the fight would almost certainly take place in conditions in which the enemies of the republic would deploy well-trained troops led by seasoned officers against a very green revolutionary force. Bluntly put, republicans feared, with good cause, that pitting all the virtuous revolutionaries against all the soldiers of reaction on the battlefield would result in defeat.

In their concerns about how to build a loyal army, French revolutionaries were well aware of the American experience. As we have seen, Lafayette had served with American forces and corresponded with American politicians during the 1770s and 1780s. French republicans experienced the same theoretical dilemmas about building loyal volunteer armies, though they ultimately resolved them in an even more extreme way than the Americans had. In France too, coercive drafts were resisted at first because they reminded members of the National Assembly of the methods of the armies of the Old Regime. Only one representative suggested in 1789 that France should consider

---

[86] J. G. A. Pocock, *The Machiavellian Moment: Florentine Political Thought and the Atlantic Republican Tradition*, rev. edn. (Princeton: Princeton University Press, 1975).

[87] For a discussion of the question of military force in the context of the Scottish Enlightenment, see Richard B. Sher, 'Adam Ferguson, Adam Smith, and the Problem of National Defense', *Journal of Modern History* 61, no. 2 (1989): 240–68.

an equal and universal military levy, and his plan was rejected in favour of supporting local militias.[88] As the revolution deepened, however, the prospect of war became ever more likely, especially after Louis XVI was captured while attempting to flee abroad in 1791 to join counter-revolutionary forces in Austria. Still, the assembly continued to call for volunteers throughout 1791 and again during 1792, when the expected invasion from abroad finally occurred. The volunteer soldier movement reached its peak in 1792. That year saw both the writing of the French revolutionary (and later national) anthem *La Marseillaise* as an inspirational hymn for volunteers and then later the Battle of Valmy, at which a French force partly composed of old army regulars and partly of new volunteers defeated Prussian forces and delayed the foreign assault. Those two events played a significant role in the building of French nationalism over the ensuing centuries, but they could not hide the deficiencies of the volunteer levies.

In 1793, as the revolution radicalized and the Terror began, the French turned towards a compulsory draft, tentatively at first, with a call for 300,000 soldiers selected by local officials authorized to use force to meet their quotas. This draft led not only to outright rebellion in parts of the country, but also to widespread tension in virtually every French town and village, as local notables were accused of corruption and other unfair practices in the selection of the young men who were conscripted.[89] Rather than give up on the idea of the draft, the leaders in Paris radically widened it, decreeing the *levée en masse* in August of 1793, which proclaimed that the entire population would be called for national service:

> All French persons are placed in permanent requisition for the service of the armies. Young men will go off to battle; married men will forge arms and transport provisions; women will make tents and clothing and serve in the hospitals; the children shall turn old linen into lint; the old men shall repair to the public places to stimulate the courage of the warriors and preach the unity of the republic and hatred of kings.[90]

This was not simply a crash course in enlarging the army. It was also a deeply political edict, intended to address the unrest that the earlier levy had caused and to radicalize the process of nation building.[91] Above all, the *levée en masse* represented 'an essentially ideological measure',[92] since it was based on the recognition of the desirability of universal

---

[88] Alan Forrest, 'Conscription as Ideology: Revolutionary France and the Nation in Arms', in *The Comparative Study of Conscription in the Armed Forces*, ed. Lars Mjøset and Stephen van Holde (Bingley, UK: Emerald Group, 2002): 99.

[89] Clarence J. Munform, 'Conscription and the Peasants of the Morvan District of Chateau-Chinon, 1792–1794', *Canadian Journal of History/Annales candiennes d'histoire* 4, no. 2 (1969): 7–9.

[90] Cited in Forrest, 'Conscription as Ideology', 103.

[91] See the various contributions in Daniel Moran and Arthur Waldron, eds, *The People in Arms: Military Myth and National Mobilization since the French Revolution* (Cambridge: Cambridge University Press, 2006).

[92] Peter Paret, *Understanding War: Essays on Clausewitz and the History of Military Power* (Princeton: Princeton University Press, 1992), 62.

equality in the field of military service. Many of the problems with the earlier levy had stemmed from the perception that the draft had been unjustly implemented. The mass levy in the autumn went far better than the partial one in the spring.[93]

Universal mobilization can also be seen as ideological, because it was based on a fraternal understanding of the revolutionary nation. Fraternity (the principle that social and political authority should rest with 'brothers' or 'sons' rather than their 'fathers') is the least studied of the great principles of the French Revolution, but it is impossible to fully understand either modern gender history or modern nationalism without understanding how fraternity was 'revolutionary'.[94] Part of the problem in understanding the phenomenon stemmed from the decision of some practitioners of women's history to define patriarchy as the system of power in which men dominate women. As we argued in the introduction, however, this characterization is too crude, for it ignores the variety of gender orders based on male power. Patriarchy is a specific form of male dominance in which fathers exercise authority not only over women and children but over young men as well. Power and influence in this system increase with age. The gender 'revolution' in the late eighteenth century transformed this generational relationship more than the relationship between the sexes.

As a result, sex-based challenges to patriarchy, like those articulated by Olympe de Gouges and Mary Wollstonecraft, were doomed to failure. The patriarchy they attacked was already in the process of being replaced by a definition of equality linked to fraternity. The ideology of the post-revolutionary nation depended upon a belief in the fundamental equality of citizens. But as we have seen, these citizens were gendered citizens, and the brotherhood that was slowly beginning to replace traditional patriarchy excluded women by its very definition.[95] Nevertheless, patriarchs did not relinquish their authority without a fight. A fraternal gender order was constructed over the course of the nineteenth century, but it would take the experience of two world wars in the twentieth century for 'brothers' to achieve dominance over their 'fathers'.

Before fraternity would rise, it would fall. The *levée en masse* was proclaimed at the high-water mark of revolutionary fraternity, just months after the execution of Louis XVI, the 'father of France', in January 1793.[96] The decree, as we have seen, was insistent on separating adult males into three separate categories (young men, married men and old men) based on age and family status, but it was indifferent to similar distinctions among the adult female population. Furthermore, the decree was notable for placing the figure of the young, unmarried man at the centre of attention. Traditionally, young unmarried men were the ones who did the assisting, working under the authority of

---

[93] Munford, 'Conscription and the Peasants of the Morvan District of Chateau-Chinon, 1792–1794', 14.

[94] For a ground-breaking study of revolutionary fraternity, see Hunt, *The Family Romance of the French Revolution*.

[95] Pateman, *The Sexual Contract*; Fraisse, *Reason's Muse*.

[96] For an extended discussion of the proposition that what fraternity meant in the French Revolution was the younger generation of 'brothers' destroying their father-king, see Hunt, *The Family Romance of the French Revolution*.

older men in family farms or family businesses. Their needs were filled only after those of married men and fathers in the family. That situation was suddenly reversed, as their older married brothers would make their guns and carry their provisions, their fathers would sing their praises in the town square, and their women and children tended to their medical and personal concerns. Just as significantly, soldiering was now portrayed as an honourable profession rather than as a trade for social deviants or as the fulfilment of an onerous state obligation.

All this was an ideological proposition describing how the Jacobins hoped military service would be performed and perceived rather than how it actually was. Systems of familial authority do not change overnight, even if the king is killed and a republic is declared. Nor did the prospect of military service suddenly become attractive for young men and their families. The long tradition of hating soldiering and fearing soldiers was maintained in most areas of the country. But ideologies are not simply fantasies.[97] The constant reiteration of shared values, the demands of state institutions and the routines of social and bureaucratic life turn previously unimaginable social transformations into the new givens of everyday life. In the long run, the figure of the national citizen-soldier would help establish the new political form of the fraternal nation and would remain its most reliable bulwark.

In the short run, revolutionary fraternity met with setbacks. As the chaos and violence of revolutionary upheaval dragged on, increasing numbers of people sought stability. Social stability in particular seemed to depend on solid families, and traditionalists were able to make an effective case that all this new-fangled thinking had upset the natural balance within the household. Radicals too were increasingly inclined to look askance at expressions of female independence. As we have seen, the Jacobins themselves excluded women from politics after women's riots in Paris threatened their position. As the 1790s progressed, the trend to look longingly towards the traditional family and away from any stray revolutionary thoughts of female civic equality deepened considerably. Indeed, even fraternal measures were now looked on with some suspicion. Rejecting the proposition that individuals were the building blocks of the national order, some French politicians, like Charles Guiraudet, were persuaded by 1797 that it was a mistake to think of individuals as distinct units and of societies simply as a collection of those individuals. Rather, the building blocks of society were families, and all other divisions could be 'neither elementary nor natural ... only man in the family forms the element of society.'[98]

This domestic conservatism, indeed this widespread reversion to patriarchy, found its leading light in the figure of Napoleon Bonaparte. Napoleon openly portrayed himself as the new 'father' of the nation, and he reinstituted or reinforced patriarchal institutions in many different ways. He portrayed himself as the patriarch of France,

---

[97] As Joan Scott argues, the very instability of the categories of gender and sex has meant that the way we have organized our lives around their definition is essentially governed by fantasy. This fact, however, means that 'fantasy becomes a critically useful tool for historical analysis'. Scott, *The Fantasy of Feminist History*, 5.

[98] Cited in Heuer, *The Family and the Nation*, 77.

made peace with the Pope ('father') of the Catholic Church and personally saw to it that the new comprehensive legal code being compiled in the early years of his reign would ensure the unchallenged authority of the father in French households. The code prescribed that familial rather than individual property would determine the voting eligibility of male heads of household, and it firmly placed women under male control in the family. Although the authors of the code chose not to reverse the 1791 decision of the Constituent Assembly to abrogate anti-sodomy laws, Napoleonic officials often 'ignored the inconvenient fact that the law no longer penalized "crimes against nature"' and harshly repressed any public sexual acts that they viewed as morally threatening.[99] Divorce, which had been legal for only about a decade, was now made nearly impossible for women. It was somewhat easier for men to dissolve a marriage, however, since men were allowed to divorce unfaithful wives, but women could divorce only if infidelity occurred inside the 'conjugal home'. Fathers, moreover, recovered the right largely lost to them in the revolutionary era to assume judicial authority in many matters concerning minor children, and they could withhold marriage consent from sons under twenty-five years old and daughters under twenty-one.[100] Rule of the father had clearly been re-established. In 1801, the revolutionary journalist Sylvain Maréchal wrote – only somewhat tongue-in-cheek – a 'Proposed law prohibiting women from learning to read'. While clearly satirical, Maréchal's proposal came just at a 'turning point in the history of sexual equality ... following the appearance of revolutionary women as political subjects in the public arena'.[101] Several prominent intellectual women were prompted to respond, and the 'joke' revealed that some revolutionaries fantasized about shutting women out of the public sphere entirely by denying them the key tools of involvement in political debate: reading and writing. Patriarchy was back in style.

But it was a new and modified patriarchy, because Napoleon remained a revolutionary in some respects, most notably in military affairs. Like his revolutionary predecessors, Napoleon's definition of citizenship was gendered male partly because it was inextricably linked to military service. France had established regular, annual male conscription in 1798 as a means of preserving the ideological basis of the popular, national army and of replenishing the troops raised five years earlier in the *levée en masse*. Napoleon had no desire to overturn the fraternal institution of conscription upon coming to power in 1799. He had built his reputation and career on the backs of the military that radical revolutionaries had created, and he intended to deploy armed force liberally in the years to come. Indeed, the Napoleonic era saw the routinization of military service as a passage to manhood rather than as a devastating imposition. Acceptance of army service as a duty grew, and draft evasion declined.[102] Temporary setbacks did nothing to change this trajectory, though the ruinous

---

[99] David Sibalis, 'The Regulation of Male Homosexuality in Revolutionary and Napoleonic France, 1789–1815', 80.

[100] Ibid., 129–30.

[101] Fraisse, *Reason's Muse*, 3.

[102] Forrest, 'Conscription as Ideology', 104; Isser Woloch, *The New Regime: Transformations of the French Civic Order, 1789–1820s* (New York and London: W. W. Norton & Company, 1994), 418.

losses and desperate levies that were occasioned by Napoleon's final campaigns, especially his disastrous invasion of Russia, finally did lead to another small increase in evasion and a short-lived abolition of conscription in 1815. In 1818, the draft was reinstated, and in conditions of peacetime, military service was linked even more inextricably to masculinity and the place of the young man in the civic order than it had been before. By mid-century, the popular image of the conscript had been transformed from that of a boy ripped from his weeping mother and stern father to that of a dashing youth whose return as a real man was eagerly awaited by fresh-faced available maidens.[103] This shift of focus from the emotions of the parents to the emotions of the lover was just another sign of the ways that conscription moved social attention to the younger generation.

Napoleon's military success, and then his military failure, did much to export this fraternal model. Virtually everywhere French troops went, they defeated old-style armies, occupied part or all of the conquered country and then struggled to deal with insurgencies that drew, ironically enough, on the revolutionary ideals of the nation, the people in arms and the citizen-soldier. The specific form of the response to Napoleon varied from place to place – ranging from an increased sympathy for 'regular guy' war heroes like Admiral Nelson in Britain to cautiously formed and quickly disbanded popular militias in Russia – but the influence of revolutionary nationalism was visible everywhere.

Perhaps the most dramatic and lasting responses to Napoleon's incursions occurred in Prussia and Spain. Prussia succumbed to France first. In 1806, Napoleon's forces routed the Prussian army at the Battles of Jena and Auerstadt, resulting in a peace treaty the following year that cut the size of the Prussian state nearly in half and mandated that the French had rights of occupation until a large war indemnity was paid. The impact of the defeat was enormous. It led to soul-searching across the country, especially among Prussia's proud military elite. Some, like the future military theorist Carl von Clausewitz, left the country to volunteer with the Russian army, the last intact fighting force on the continent. Others took advantage of the forced dismantling of the old Prussian army to suggest that when the time came to rebuild the military, they should do it on a popular basis. When the moment came for the army to be resurrected in the so-called 'Wars of Liberation' of 1813–14, visions of nations, citizens and the 'people in arms' held sway, leading eventually to the establishment of universal conscription in 1814.[104] The new Prussian 'bands of brothers' were a smashing success not only against Napoleon's weakened forces but against an array of other enemies over the course of the nineteenth century as well.

The same patriotic and national visions that structured the interaction of young Prussian men with the state opened up a temporary space for Prussian women to engage with the authorities too. Female activists from all classes formed a variety of patriotic associations to assist in the national war effort, and they sprang up in 414

---

[103] David M. Hopkin, 'Sons and Lovers: Popular Images of the Conscript, 1798–1870', *Modern & Contemporary France* 9, no. 1 (2001): 19–36.
[104] Paret, *Understanding War*, 66–72.

towns around the country. This effort was sanctioned by the state, as one such public appeal in 1813 made clear:

> The fatherland is in peril! Thus spoke the king to his loyal and affectionate subjects, and all hurried to remove it from this danger. Men grasp the sword ... But we women, too, must participate, and must help to promote victory. We, too, must unite with the men and boys to save our fatherland. Thus let us found an association with the name of Women's Association for the Good of the Fatherland.[105]

Women's activities were crucial to the war effort, and these civic groups provided many of the necessary auxiliary services, such as nursing, that Prussian troops required in the final spasm of the Napoleonic Wars. By 1815, in direct contradiction to the emerging notion that women could not and should not participate in the public sphere, women's patriotic associations were some of the most extensive and most numerous networks of civic organizations in all of Prussia.[106] In times of brotherhood, there was no logical or practical reason that systems of sisterhood could not emerge to play a visible and public role in civic and national life.

A similar phenomenon occurred in Spain, which came under French occupation in 1808. In contrast to Prussia, however, an anti-Napoleonic insurgency quickly gained an armed following, and the guerrilla war that ensued relied heavily on female participation. As would be the case in virtually all future partisan campaigns (in particular those during the Second World War), the rebels came to rely heavily on women comrades. Women were more effective at smuggling goods and information to partisan units precisely because they were women and raised less suspicion among occupying forces. They were the ones who provided food, animals and even safe houses for the guerrillas.[107]

Nor did some Spanish women refrain from taking direct military action when the opportunity arose. The most famous such warrior was Agustina Zaragoza, who rallied decimated defenders in one besieged town by firing a cannon into advancing French troops while wounded men lay prostrate and defenceless around it. The Spanish held the town for several more months before surrendering. Though Agustina and her four-year-old child were so ill that they were in hospital when the occupiers arrived, the French knew of her fame and ordered her sent as a prisoner back to France, a trip that killed her son. This maternal suffering only increased her popularity at home, and her celebrity reached such heights that she was eventually commissioned as an officer after her escape from French captivity.[108] Nor was she the only active female participant, as other women also took up arms during

---

[105] Cited in Karen Hagemann, 'Female Patriots: Women, War and the Nation in the Period of the Prussian-German Anti-Napoleonic Wars', *Gender & History* 16, no. 2 (2004): 403.
[106] Ibid.
[107] John Lawrence Tone, 'Spanish Women in the Resistance to Napoleon, 1808–1814', in *Constructing Spanish Womanhood: Female Identity in Modern Spain*, ed. Victoria Lorée Enders and Pamela Beth Radcliff (Albany, NY: State University of New York Press, 1999), 276.
[108] John Lawrence Tone, 'A Dangerous Amazon: Agustina Zaragoza and the Spanish Revolutionary War, 1808–1814', *European History Quarterly* 37 no. 4 (2007): 548–561.

the siege and many more attacked Napoleon's soldiers when they strayed too far into the countryside. As one French officer remembered, they were 'fighting the entire population; all the inhabitants, men, women, children, old folks and priests, were in arms, the villages abandoned'.[109] In Spain too, women were active and visible in the national struggle.

As politics were transformed across Europe in response to the revolutionary ideas and revolutionary wars, the political form of the nation emerged, based on the idea that all participants (citizens) in the nation should be equal and that they should feel the bond of brotherhood between them. Military action did much to strengthen these inclinations, though the upheavals of both revolution and war left many desiring a return to the relative stability of the past. As was the case in France, the assault on patriarchy left open the question of the position of women in the new political communities forming across the continent in places like Prussia and Spain. Would ideas of sisterhood create the possibility for an alliance between public-spirited young women and young men devoted to challenging the traditional authority of their elders? Would the logic of equality persuade politicians to extend civic equality to women? Would the repeated demonstrations that mass warfare required female participation allow this new ideology, seasoned by the violence of the Napoleonic era, to envision women and men alike as full actors in even the masculine arena of armed struggle?

The short answer to all these questions in all the countries of Europe was 'no'. In every case, these new nations followed the French model, which endorsed male dominance and female passivity and promoted male civic action and female domestic care as both politically necessary and 'natural'. This gender consensus became a fundamental plank of European nationalism. In Prussia, the wartime valorization of female patriotic action ended abruptly, with the remembrances and histories of the wars of liberation focusing on male action. Nearly all the women's associations shut down, with only 10 per cent remaining as charitable organizations. Within a generation, they were mostly forgotten, consigned to historical oblivion.[110]

In Spain too, women mostly disappeared from the narrative of the national uprising. Even in the case of Agustina, a peculiar but telling twist developed. When José Palafox, a Spanish commander, recounted Agustina's feat in his post-war account, he claimed that Agustina had leapt to the cannon after watching her fiancé being killed by a French bullet and that she had fired the gun with the words 'I am here to avenge you!' Agustina, in this account, was acting out her private passions rather than taking up the public and civic duty of defending her city and her country. She was acting, in other words, as women should and naturally did. But Palafox's story was a total fabrication. Agustina was already married and, as we have seen, already had a child. Her husband was not by her side. Palafox's account also contradicted Agustina's own report of her actions. Nevertheless, historians throughout the nineteenth century, and many much later on, believed Palafox.[111] As usual, myths proved more convenient than history in the accounts that nations liked to tell themselves.

---

[109] Cited in Tone, 'Spanish Women in the Resistance to Napoleon, 1808–1814', 263.
[110] Hagemann, 'Female Patriots', 408–9.
[111] Tone, 'A Dangerous Amazon'.

## Duelling and the nineteenth-century fraternity

The degree to which norms of masculine behaviour became ever more intertwined with militaristic action, physical vigour and notions of male honour is illustrated by the transformation of the practice of duelling. Having spread across Europe (and particularly Spain, Italy and France) in the sixteenth century, duelling became an important way for middle- and upper-class men to establish their honour in the revolutionary and Napoleonic eras.[112] Norbert Elias famously argued that the duel was a means of containing violent human tendencies through ritual and that it arose from the aristocracy's desire to establish codes of honour to distance themselves from the lower classes. 'The difference between the kind of act of violence minutely formalized in a duel and the comparatively informal brawling between people of the simpler strata', Elias wrote, '… can serve as a criterion of the social distance between the respective strata.'[113] European men fought duels to remove the taint of an insult that had besmirched their reputations, for trivial slights arising from a game of cards or an ill-timed joke, to protect the honour of their women, to avenge an adulterous act and ultimately to establish a firm hold over a position of social standing. The social rules governing this practice and its political significance changed over time, and those changes reveal important shifts in the meaning of masculinity from the eighteenth to the nineteenth centuries. Rulers across Europe tried to ban the practice in the late seventeenth and early eighteenth centuries, and by the time of the French Revolution it had become increasingly ritualized and less deadly.[114] In England, pistols had begun to replace swords as the primary weapon in these battles of honour, primarily because it was rarely possible to actually follow the ethos of pitting two equally matched combatants against each other, and the blade was more likely to inflict grievous wounds on the weaker fighter.[115] Duelling increasingly became a public spectacle as these rules developed, and the more public they became, the more they were considered an affront to the ruler's authority to settle disputes through the mechanisms of the law.

Perhaps the most striking example of the public and gendered nature of duelling in the revolutionary period is the case of the Chevalier d'Eon, a cross-dressing French aristocrat who became famous in late eighteenth-century England for engaging in fencing duels while dressed in female clothing. While in no sense representative, d'Eon's complicated story provides a fascinating example of how the duel had become a primary venue for the performance of gender by the late eighteenth century.

---

[112] France was the 'leading dueling nation' by the seventeenth century with 10,000 deaths by duel between 1589 and 1610 alone. Wolfgang Schivelbusch, *The Culture of Defeat: On National Trauma, Mourning and Recovery* (New York: Picador, 2003), 131.

[113] Norbert Elias. *The Germans: Power Struggles and the Development of Habitus in the Nineteenth and Twentieth Centuries* (Cambridge: Polity Press, 1996), 72.

[114] Ute Frevert, 'The Taming of the Nobel Ruffian: Male Violence and Dueling in Early Modern and Modern Germany', in *Men and Violence: Gender, Honor, and Rituals in Modern Europe and America*, ed. Pieter Spierenburg (Columbus: Ohio State University Press, 1998), 44.

[115] Robert B. Shoemaker, 'The Taming of the Duel: Masculinity, Honor and Ritual Violence in London, 1660–1800', *Historical Journal* 45, no. 3 (2002): 528.

**Figure 1.2** The Chevalier d'Eon in a fencing match. Reprinted by permission of Bridgeman Images.

Born into an impoverished aristocrat family in a small town in Burgundy in 1728, Charles Geneviève Louis Auguste André Timothée d'Eon de Beaumont had made his way in the world as a diplomat and spy for the French king Louis XV. After serving as a soldier in the Seven Years' War, he was sent to France to help negotiate a peace with England but was later replaced as ambassador and started to look for ways of re-establishing his position. Having instigated various diplomatic scandals in the 1760s (including making the charge that the new ambassador, the comte de Guerny, had tried to drug him), and having won many friends and public support in London, d'Eon blackmailed a pension out of Louis XV by claiming to possess secret documents detailing plans for an invasion of England. Meanwhile, d'Eon's fame spread in London, and rumours about his sexual identity spread. In 1771, bets were taken about his true sex on the London Stock Exchange, and he began defending his honour by challenging detractors outside of London's coffee houses to duels with the sword. After Louix XV's death in May 1774, the new king made a deal with the chevalier, who was allowed to return to France on the condition that he henceforth dress as a woman. The wording of this agreement suggested that d'Eon's diminutive stature and feminine voice, not to mention his alleged use of a female disguise when he was a spy in Empress Elizabeth's court in Russia, were evidence that he had in fact been assigned the female sex at birth but had been posing as a man.[116] After an extensive toilette d'Eon was presented to Louis XVI and Marie-Antoinette as a woman on 21 November 1777.

When the French Revolution put an end to Louis XVI's pension, d'Eon began earning money by touring Britain and fencing in female garb. A well-attended match at Vauxhall Gardens near London in 1791 was commemorated with the minting of a medal with an image of d'Eon as the cross-dressing Roman goddess Minerva. But Mademoiselle de Chevalière d'Eon de Beaumont's most famous match was against Monsieur de Saint Georges on 9 April 1787 in the presence of the Prince of Wales. The chevalière's victory was immortalized in a painting by Charles Jean Robineau that was bought by George IV and remains in the Royal Collection. The chevalière's own self-identification as a woman justifies using the female pronoun to describe her.[117] But the fact remains that it was her transgendered performance while fencing that gained her fame and thus acceptance as a female person. Having quit duelling after an injury in 1796, d'Eon continued to live as a woman, completely convincing the widow with whom she shared a humble apartment. It was only after her death in 1810 that an examination of the body definitely proved that the chevalière had indeed been born a chevalier. Whether or not we use the word transsexual to describe d'Eon's public presentation as a woman (a question upon which historians disagree), it is unlikely that she would have chosen duelling as a path to public recognition had she been born a few decades later. After the French Revolution, duelling became far more closely associated with specific political projects and less open to the kind of self-fashioning that d'Eon's appropriation of the public spectacle achieved.

Over the course of the nineteenth century, duelling became associated with the bodily demonstration of masculine strength and social rank and became more and more highly ritualized and specialized.[118] It persisted in aristocratic classes, but it

---

[116] Jonathan Conlin, 'The Strange Case of the Chevalier d'Eon', *History Today* 60, no. 4 (2010): 49. The details of d'Eon's life are extremely complex and reach back earlier than our focus here. For a rich collection of investigations of this fascinating historical character, see Simon Burrows et al., eds., *The Chevalier d'Eon and His Worlds: Gender, Espionage and Politics in the Eighteenth Century* (London and New York: Bloomsbury, 2010).

[117] Marilyn Morris also follows this practice, going against the trend among historians who have written about d'Eon. See her 'Identity, Gender, Genre and Truth in The Maiden of Tonnerre: The Vicissitudes of the Chevalier and Chevalière d'Eon' in Burrows, *The Chevalier d'Eon and His Worlds*, 147–60. The chevalier was actually not consistent, switching back and forth between male and female pronouns. See the autobiographical fragments in Roland A. Champagne, Nina Ekstein, and Gary Kates, eds., *Monsieur d'Eon Is a Woman: A Tale of Political Intrigue and Sexual Masquerade* (Baltimore: Hopkins Fulfillment Service, 2001).

[118] The literature on duelling has grown apace in recent years. To provide just a brief selection: Robert A. Nye, *Masculinity and Male Codes of Honor in Modern France* (New York: Oxford University Press, 1993); Peter Gay, 'Mensur – The Cherished Scar', in *The Bourgeois Experience, Victoria to Freud*, III: The Cultivation of Hatred (New York and London: W. W. Norton & Company, 1993), 9–33; James Kelly, 'That Damn'd Thing Called Honour': Duelling in Ireland, 1570–1860 (Cork: Cork University Press, 1995); Istvan Deak, 'Latter-Day Knights: Officers' Honor and Duelling in the Austro-Hungarian Army', *Oesterreichische Ostheft* 28, no. 3 (1986): 311–27; Irina Reyfman, *Ritualized Violence Russian Style: The Duel in Russian Culture and Literature* (Palo Alto, CA: Stanford University Press, 1999); Shoemaker, 'The Taming of the Duel'; Ute Frevert, *Men of Honour: A Social and Cultural History of the Duel* (Cambridge: Polity Press, 1995); Kevin McAleer, *Dueling: The Cult of Honor in Fin-de-Siècle Germany* (Princeton: Princeton University Press, 1994); and Steven C. Hughes, *Politics of the Sword: Dueling, Honor, and Masculinity in Modern Italy* (Columbus: Ohio State University Press, 2007).

grew in popularity particularly among those who saw the growth of republics and the demise of old political systems as an opportunity for their own advancement. The ancient chivalric code of honour was held up as a defence against the corruption and decay of the republican ideal under Napoleon. Elsewhere in Europe, it acted as a ritual to unite those who sought national unification, particularly in Germany and Italy.[119] Duelling was a way for bourgeois men to establish their honour as citizens through bodily performance, thus legitimating their right to hold the advanced positions that the decline of the aristocracy had opened up for them. It was an act that demonstrated individual skills (the ability to shoot straight or fence well) while still adhering to strict rules of engagement agreed upon by a fraternity, fencing club or honour code. For those who advocated it, duelling thus encapsulated the republican ideal of the individual's ability to act in his own self-interest while still upholding the values of the society as a whole. This was, in other words, a fraternal act. Establishing courage and physical

**Figure 1.3** Duel with swords between Boulanger and Floquet, 1888. Reprinted by permission of Mary Evans Picture Library.

---

[119] Robert A. Nye, 'Fencing, the Duel and Republican Manhood in the Third Republic', *Journal of Contemporary History* 25, no. 2/3 (1990): 366–67.

fortitude through duels with pistol, sword and sabre allowed men not only to defend their honour, but also to accrue it, unlike women, whose honour was confined to sexual chastity and fidelity and could only be lost.[120] From famous military generals like the Duke of Wellington to literary figures like the Russian poet Aleksandr Pushkin and several French prime ministers like Georges Clemenceau (who fought twenty-two duels), duelling struck most famous and not-so-famous men of standing in Europe as a necessary defence of their political and social honour. Since duelling had been prohibited by the pre-revolutionary French monarchs, it also held the attraction of defying royal prohibitions and fostering individual liberty.[121]

In post-Napoleonic Germany, duelling became an essential aspect of university life. Some German student fraternities or *Corps* continued to be dominated by aristocrats and aristocratic traditions. But the *Burschenschaften* (literally associations of lads or guys) were formed out of frustration with the fact that the defeat of Napoleon had not resulted in the unification of Germany. While some of the *Burschenschaften* scorned duelling, many of them encouraged it, transforming an aristocratic practice into an avenue for instilling honourable behaviour and the values of brotherhood in a generation that sought social advancement.[122] Members sparred in ritual fencing matches on the flimsiest of pretexts in hopes of garnering the cherished *Mensur* – a scar slashed across the cheek that would thereafter stand as evidence of both their willingness to fight and their involvement in nationalist university fraternities that were seeking German unification.[123] Like Diederich in Heinrich Mann's novel *Man of Straw*, most members of *Burschenschaften* viewed their participation in a duel as the defining moment of their lives: a coming-of-age ritual that ensured their acceptance by the fraternity and provided physical evidence of their devotion to the nation. Along with other kinds of initiation rituals, duelling was a codified and ritualized practice that helped to keep the fraternities exclusive. By literally marking their members with facial scars, the fraternities established networks of influence that lasted well past the members' university years.

German duelling fraternities saw themselves as preparing their members for the fight that they foresaw ahead of them to unify Germany as a liberal state. This 'exercise in aggression checked by accepted rules' was accompanied by the type of behaviours that are still familiar in male-only environments: initiation rituals, alcohol abuse and nepotism. Though German fraternities would eventually become sites of much more conservative (and even fascist) rituals,[124] they initially justified their existence with recourse to the ideals of political republicanism. Fraternities as a site of opposition to autocratic rule

---

[120] Nye, *Masculinity and Male Codes of Honor*, 9–11.

[121] Schivelbusch, *Culture of Defeat*, 131.

[122] Rolland Ray Lutz, 'The Burschenschaft: Reformist Movement or Conformist Movement?', *Consortium on Revolutionary Europe 1750–1850* 19, part 1 (1989): 357–77; Gary D. Stark, 'The Ideology of the German Buschenschaft Generation', *European History Quarterly* 8, no. 3 (1978): 323–48.

[123] Gay, 'Mensur – The Cherished Scar', 11 and 21.

[124] Hitler did not approve of the duel, but its culture was so engrained that even high-ranking SS members engaged in it. See William Combs, 'Fatal Attraction: Duelling and the SS', *History Today* 47, no. 6 (June 1997): 11–16.

were also evident elsewhere in Europe. The Russian Decembrists (a secret society that launched an unsuccessful uprising against Tsar Nicholas I in 1825) also viewed duelling as a way of establishing a form of honour distinct from monarchical rituals. By the late nineteenth century, and particularly in St Petersburg, university fraternities in Russia were following the German example in setting up strict honour codes of behaviour with disputes settled in ritualized duels. These societies provided venues for enduring friendships while also fostering opposition to the monarchical regime.[125]

For the middle classes, then, fraternities and duelling offered arenas where valour and worthiness could be demonstrated. The wars of the revolutionary era (which we did not have the space to describe in detail here) convinced many that nationhood could only be gained and maintained through the exertions of mass armies, and they created new roles for ambitious middle-class men to prove themselves as defenders of the nation. Duelling might be seen, then, as an arena to play out these roles in times of peace and in the face of republican frustrations. Perhaps this is best understood as a reaction to the fact that the political process put in motion by the French Revolution had held out the promise of 'universal' rights but had then quickly retracted this universality; as we have seen, even men's right to vote was restricted to those wealthy enough to pay taxes or to be able to afford their own military uniform. It was necessary, in other words, to prove that one was worthy of being equal. Duelling was a dramatic way of demonstrating one's willingness to stand and die as an honourable citizen. Simply being a member of an organization where the practice could be honourably conducted in accordance with strict duelling codes was already an indication of having been accepted into a self-regulating and powerful group. Women were by definition excluded from these groups. But it is perhaps even more important to notice that duelling and fraternities were the quintessential cultural expressions of a new martial definition of masculinity. The aggressive exclusion of women that had arisen out of the French Revolution was routinized further over the course of the nineteenth century through these male arenas of elite citizenship.

## Conclusion

Democratic activists across Europe in the revolutionary era proclaimed 'Liberty, Equality and Fraternity' as their main political goals. In each case, their victories were temporary, but they were not meaningless. The seeds of future change had been sown.

The concept of liberty that was developed in the American and French Revolutions had a lasting impact on the politics of Europe. It did not immediately or permanently transform political systems everywhere, but it provided a new language – a set of concepts and rhetorical weapons – that could not henceforth be banished from the vocabulary of those seeking political change. Even the new autocrat Napoleon

---

[125] Rebecca Friedman, *Masculinity, Autocracy and the Russian University, 1804–1863* (Basingstoke and New York: Palgrave Macmillan, 2005), 12. See also pp. 53ff.

described his quest for European hegemony in terms of liberty and encouraged the use of the word in the statutes and constitutions of the European states that fell under his yoke. The relationship between the individual and the state had changed, and all European nations were affected by the shift in terminology. From the French Revolution forward, to be declared a loyal citizen meant more than simply obeying the will of rulers above; it required individual commitment to the state and personal choice. Rousseau's prescriptions to women were exemplary of this new ideal of liberty. In granting women just enough rationality to make the choice to be subordinated to man's will, Rousseau perfectly described the limitations that were built into the concept of liberty from the start. As radical as the concept may have appeared when it was first uttered, Alexis de Tocqueville knew at the time that the 'real object of the [French] Revolution was less a new form of government than a new form of society; less the achievement of political rights than the destruction of privileges'.[126] Liberty had less to do with democracy than it had to do with building a new kind of political consensus. This consensus depended upon the existence of free will in the population, but it did not require absolute equality.

'Equality' stood as an unassailable tower in the rhetoric of the revolution. The Declaration of the Rights of Man and Citizen insisted: 'All citizens being equal in the eyes of the law, are equally eligible to all dignities and to all public positions and occupations, according to their abilities, and without distinction except that of their virtues and talents.' But as we have seen, 'equal' never applied to women and 'virtues and talents' could be used in such a way as to exclude many men from key civic roles and responsibilities. Neither the revolutionaries nor their successors were immune to the pressures of economic competition and social disruption, and they were quick to temper their political promises when social turmoil and violence threatened. The fact that the revolution had initially held out the promise of improved social conditions (the king had promised bread to the female marchers on Versailles and accepted grievances from the population) empowered the hungry masses to assume they too could use the language of equality to seize what they needed to survive. But the chaos and violence that resulted sent the new republic in search of moral certainties. One convenient path to stability appeared to be the taming of women, whose involvement in bread riots and other public disturbances was particularly disruptive of the traditional sense of order. Women, it seemed clear, needed to be domesticated. Following Rousseau, advocates of women's rights like de Gouges and Wollstonecraft insisted that this domestication should occur only through women's individual and educated choice. But as the events of the Terror proved, removing this choice from them and imposing a ban on their political participation proved a convenient way of demonstrating that a society wracked by violence could be returned to a semblance of order. Inequality quickly became the preferred path to orderly, rational politics.

---

[126] Quoted in Arno J. Mayer, *The Furies: Violence and Terror in the French and Russian Revolutions* (Princeton: Princeton University Press, 2000), 38.

To the extent that liberty and equality had been achieved, they had emerged through violence that was, if not unprecedented, then certainly of a particularly public nature. The guillotine's blade spilled blood in the streets of Paris in the name of 'public safety' and the good of the collective. When men sought sole control over this violence, declaring female participation illegitimate, they were codifying gender relations in the name of the public good. 'Fraternity' appeared to be the only guarantee of liberty and equality. Controlled masculine violence was the antidote to the chaos of the uncontrolled (feminized) mob and became the path to social advancement for the middle-class citizen. The debates over conscription in the Napoleonic state and in the nations trying to defend themselves from French invasion, along with the popularity of duelling in nineteenth-century Europe, made the centrality of disciplined male violence especially clear. As war consumed the continent, this connection between the martial code and citizenship was only further reinforced.

## Suggested readings

Fraisse, Geneviève. *Reason's Muse: Sexual Difference and the Birth of Democracy*. Trans. Jane Marie Todd. Chicago: University of Chicago Press, 1994.

Godineau, Dominique. *The Women of Paris and Their French Revolution*. Berkeley: University of California Press, 1998.

Heuer, Jennifer Ngaire. *The Family and the Nation: Gender and Citizenship in Revolutionary France, 1789–1830*. Ithaca, NY: Cornell University Press, 2005.

Hufton, Olwen H. *Women and the Limits of Citizenship in the French Revolution*. Toronto: University of Toronto Press, 1992.

Hunt, Lynn. *The Family Romance of the French Revolution*. Berkeley: University of California Press, 1992.

Landes, Joan. *Women in the Public Sphere in the Age of the French Revolution*. Ithaca, NY: Cornell University Press, 1988.

Nye, Robert A. *Masculinity and Male Codes of Honor in Modern France*. New York: Oxford University Press, 1993.

Offen, Karen M. *European Feminisms, 1700–1950: A Political History*. Palo Alto: Stanford University Press, 1999.

Pateman, Carol. *The Sexual Contract*. Stanford, CA: Stanford University Press, 1988.

Schama, Simon. *Citizens: A Chronicle of the French Revolution*. Toronto: Vintage Canada, 1990.

Scott, Joan Wallach. *Only Paradoxes to Offer: French Feminists and the Rights of Man*. Cambridge, MA: Harvard University Press, 1996.

Sewell, William H. 'Le Citoyen/La Citoyenne: Activity, Passivity, and the Revolutionary Concept of Citizenship'. In *The French Revolution and the Creation of Modern Political Culture: The Political Culture of the Old Regime*. New York: Pergamon Press, 1987.

Surkis, Judith. *Sexing the Citizen: Morality and Masculinity in France, 1870–1920*. Ithaca, NY: Cornell University Press, 2011.

# CHAPTER 2
## GENDERED CAPITALISM AND ITS DISCONTENTS

The political revolutions of the late eighteenth century transformed discourses about gender and sexuality in intellectual, political and scientific circles. But abstract notions of 'rights' or theories of sexual difference had very little impact on the everyday lives of the vast majority of Europeans, who had little or no access to this realm of sophisticated discourse or to social or political power. While the French Revolution marked a political and intellectual transition of enormous significance and therefore also affected conceptions of gender and sexuality, the economic transformations of the nineteenth century had a much more immediate effect on public attitudes towards gender roles, on patterns of family life and on the actual conditions of sexual behaviour in Europe. Industrialization and new technologies brought many changes to European society over the course of the nineteenth century. But nowhere were the changes more deeply transformative of everyday relationships and the patterns of daily life than in the sphere of labour. Industrialization changed not only how people worked and how they earned money, but also how they related to others socially and sexually. As European countries industrialized, transformations in labour changed the norms and practices of family life. In some cases (as in the South and the East) these changes took place very gradually, sometimes even imperceptibly. In Central and Northern Europe, the changes were much more sudden, dramatic and socially disruptive. But wherever the Industrial Revolution took hold, wage labour entrenched a new separation of the working lives of men and women.

It must be admitted at the outset that the term 'Industrial Revolution' is contested.[1] The word 'revolution' generally applies to a hectic and quickly completed process, and it often has connotations of positive progress. Europeans often did perceive industrialization in these terms. Norman Davies has described the nineteenth century as an era in which 'Europe vibrated with power as never before: with technical power, economic power, cultural power, intercontinental power'.[2] But Davies also argues that this was the perspective only of the minority of Europeans who were involved in or benefited from technological innovations. For a majority of the population in industrializing

---

[1] The causes of the Industrial Revolution are also contested. A classic argument, which continues to prompt debate, is provided in David S. Landes, *The Unbound Prometheus: Technological Change and Industrial Development in Western Europe from 1750 to the Present*, 2nd edn. (Cambridge: Cambridge University Press, 1969).

[2] Davies, *Europe*, 759.

countries, the process of transformation from agrarian to industrial societies was drawn out, uneven and filled with social disruption, turmoil and suffering. Industrialization also accelerated international competition and created many losers, especially among peasants, artisans and colonized peoples.

The technological aspect of industrialization was only one component of a larger process of social, cultural and economic modernization.[3] It took more than technology for European societies to transition from economic systems in which most people directly worked the land and clothed themselves to a society in which most people worked for wages that could then be used to buy food and clothing. It was necessary for norms of family life and social interaction to change before the factory system could take hold, and resistance to industrialized production was often justified with reference to the desire to preserve traditional family structures. This was a complex and long-term process. Nevertheless, the term 'Industrial Revolution' remains a powerful historical metaphor, because it suggests how important economic changes were in driving social and political change and hints at the ruptures that industrialization produced in the lives of Europeans.

As the struggles of developing nations today still demonstrate, industrialization is most likely and most rapid when conditions permit a stable political system, a sophisticated system of education and training, and the accumulation of capital. These conditions were present in Britain by the latter half of the eighteenth century, and British industry had rocketed ahead of all competitors by 1840. Germany industrialized later but did so at breakneck speed after unification and the creation of the German Empire in 1871. In France, industrialization progressed more gradually over the course of the nineteenth century. Industrialization did not, however, affect all regions of these countries equally. Life in cities like Paris, Vienna, Berlin and London, or in Rotterdam, Marseilles and Manchester, looked nothing like it did in rural, traditional Ireland, Sicily or Galicia. Life on the margins of Europe remained relatively untouched by these processes; a growing gap emerged between the industrializing North and West and the rural South and East. Even in the more dynamic West and North, the early phases of industrialization rarely increased people's wages, and the rising price of goods often offset any gains. Productivity (the amount of 'product' able to be created in a given time period) increased, but workers still struggled to survive.

Even when wages rose, standards of living could stagnate. Although real wages in Great Britain increased after 1815, levels of food consumption were lower in 1840 than they were in 1760.[4] Historians who explore the economic transitions from early modern to modern Europe must rely on insufficient and spotty statistical data, and there is heated debate about whether or not industrialization improved living conditions over the short and long terms.[5] There is very little debate, however, that for the people who

---

[3] Ibid., 764.

[4] Robert Lee, 'Demography, Urbanization, and Migration', in *A Companion to Nineteenth-Century Europe, 1789–1914*, ed. Stefan Berger (Malden, MA and Oxford: Blackwell Publishing, 2006), 64.

[5] For an overview of some of these debates, see John Komlos, 'Stature and Nutrition in the Habsburg Monarchy: The Standard of Living and Economic Development in the Eighteenth Century', *American Historical Review* 90, no. 5 (1985): 1,149–61. See also Lee, 'Demography, Urbanization, and Migration', 64.

lived through these tumultuous economic times anxieties produced by the shift to wage labour overshadowed the limited financial gains they saw. Infant mortality can be taken as a measure of this psychological suffering. Wherever there was a large influx of poor people into cities, infant mortality soared, primarily because working mothers could no longer breastfeed their infants, but also because poverty forced many city dwellers to live in extremely crowded conditions with poor sanitation.[6] Nevertheless, improvements in agriculture (first in the Netherlands, then in Great Britain and elsewhere) curtailed the cycle of famine that had long kept the growth of populations in check. In north-western Europe, population density doubled over the course of the eighteenth century.[7]

These changes affected men and women in different ways but ultimately combined to transform family life for all Europeans. The Industrial Revolution created new patterns of marriage and new relationships between community, family, the individual and the state. This chapter will outline these changes, pointing to the intersection of labour patterns, gender roles and the boundaries that economic organization and structure can set on sexual behaviour. On the one hand, the transformation of labour and the emerging system of capitalism provided the social conditions and the ideological justification for the argument that male and female life should be viewed as operating in separate spheres. But the reverse is also true. Gender norms and understandings of appropriate forms of work for men and women also had an impact on the form that capitalism took in Europe and on the tripartite relationship between the individual, the family and the state.[8]

## The transformation of labour and the family

In 1919, Alice Clark, a Quaker activist for women's rights, wrote a book entitled *The Working Life of Women in the Seventeenth Century*. Clark's path-breaking book was perhaps the best example of a flowering of extremely accomplished women's history being written outside of universities in late nineteenth- and early twentieth-century Britain and North America. She argued that before the Industrial Revolution women and men worked together cooperatively as part of a family unit. '*Family Industry*,' she wrote, 'is the form in which the family becomes the unit for the production of goods to be sold or exchanged.'[9] Tasks were divided into gender-specific categories (women spun the wool for weaving and men worked the looms, for instance), but it was the sum total of work performed by all members of the family that guaranteed its material and social survival. This system was transformed when factories tempted individual

---

[6] Lee, 'Demography, Urbanization, and Migration', 65.

[7] Ivan T. Berend, *History Derailed: Central and Eastern Europe in the Long Nineteenth Century* (Berkeley: University of California Press, 2003), 9.

[8] For a summary of the debates among historians about the proper role of gendered analysis in labour history, see Laura L. Frader, 'Labor History after the Gender Turn: Transatlantic Cross Currents and Research Agendas', *International Labor and Working Class History* 63 (2003): 21–31.

[9] Alice Clark, *The Working Life of Women in the Seventeenth Century*, new edn. (London: Routledge, 1992), 6.

family members away from family industry with the lure of higher, individualized wages. Women's contributions to family income were diminished by this turn to wage labour, Clark argued, since their domestic (or later industrial) work no longer functioned as a crucial cog in the wheel, but only as a supplement to the husband's income.[10] Sixty years later, and now from the security of university positions, Joan Scott and Louise Tilly supported Clark's assessment, supplementing it with demographic and social data that provided much richer detail about women's lives in the pre-industrial era.[11] Tilly and Scott argued against the notion that women only gained access to work after modern cultural values changed and women's rights became integral to 'modern individualist ideology'. Women had always worked.[12] Only if one restricted one's view to the history of urban middle-class women, they insisted, and excluded the vast majority of the population who lived in the countryside or who were working class, could one come to the conclusion that the history of women's work was a process of evolution from the home to the workplace spurred on purely by a shift in cultural values. Tilly and Scott (and many historians after them) emphasized that work in pre-industrial Europe centred around the family as the main unit of production. Individuals worked or earned money not for themselves alone but to ensure the survival and maintenance of their families.

The impact of the Industrial Revolution on gender relations must therefore be understood – in part – as a progressive dismantling of what Bonnie Smith has called the 'complementarity of the subsistence family'.[13] This transition from a social structure where most families worked together as a unit on farms to societies in which each individual member earned wages and worked in separate locations irrevocably transformed gender relations in Europe. In some cases, the independence of wage labour gave women the confidence to act in more self-confident and autonomous ways. As Barbara Engel's study of marriage in late Imperial Russia demonstrates, earning a wage gave women the confidence to petition the government for change; it gave them the power to 'act in [their] own world even as [they were] acted on' by social and legal structures that still excluded them from political power.[14] Yet newfound independence came with new challenges, and the social changes wrought by industrialization had vastly different effects for people of different social and economic class. For most women workers, wage labour was not a choice rooted in desires for autonomy; it was absolutely necessary for their own and their children's survival.[15] Codes of behaviour for men who were the new owners of industrial enterprises were, for instance, quite different from those for their

---

[10] Ibid., 307–8.

[11] Louise Tilly and Joan W. Scott, *Women, Work and Family* (New York: Holt, Rinehart and Winston, 1978).

[12] Louise Tilly and Joan W. Scott, 'Women's Work and the Family in Nineteenth-Century Europe', *Comparative Studies in Society and History* 17, no. 1 (1975): 36–64.

[13] Bonnie G. Smith, *Changing Lives*, 141.

[14] Barbara Alpern Engel, *Breaking the Ties That Bound: The Politics of Marital Strife in Late Imperial Russia* (Ithaca: Cornell University Press, 2011), 144.

[15] Susan Kingsley Kent, *Gender and Power in Britain, 1640–1990* (New York: Routledge, 1999), 181.

male employees.[16] Numerous factors both close to home (on the farms and in the cities) and farther away (in the seats of political power and on the routes of international trade) combined to bring about these far-reaching social changes, but for the moment we will concentrate on how changes in work patterns affected the relationship between family members.

What did pre-industrial families look like? In a Europe still largely rural, all family members worked, either on the farm, within the household or in nearby towns. In many cases, farm households were multi-generational, though the extent to which this was true varied in different regions. That family members were dependent upon one another for survival, however, was universal. Individuals who were left alone (after the death of a spouse, for instance) quickly remarried, since the work required to feed and clothe oneself while still bringing in some income for incidental needs was too much for any one person to manage. As David Sabean has so vividly demonstrated in his micro-history of the German town of Neckarhausen, quarrelling married couples who separated often found a way of reconciling when the reality of economic survival apart from the family unit sunk in.[17] Decisions about when to marry, whom to marry and whether to continue to live within a difficult marriage generally depended not only on bonds of affection, but also (particularly in times of economic insecurity) on the desire to survive or to preserve one's economic and social status.

The struggle to survive shaped family life long after marriage. Extremely high rates of maternal and infant mortality necessitated reconfigurations and complex childcare arrangements. During the late nineteenth century (before which statistics are difficult to come by) rates of infant death ranged between 100 per 1,000 live births in Scandinavia and 250 per 1,000 in Germany, Austria and Russia.[18] Similarly, pregnancy and childbirth were particularly life-threatening experiences in an era before knowledge of the spread of germs. Puerperal fever and other infections – generally lumped together under the label childbed fever – were common even for women with access to medical care, like Mary Wollstonecraft. A few days after giving birth to her daughter Mary (who lived to marry the poet Percy Bysshe Shelley and to author the novel *Frankenstein*) in 1897, Wollstonecraft was struck with chills, a racing pulse and an intense fever. She died a few days later, likely having contracted the infection from a medical procedure to remove an adhered placenta. Urbanization and the construction of large hospitals actually increased the number of these deaths, because by the middle of the century they had vastly increased the number of medical interventions (caesareans, episiotomies and forcep deliveries)

---

[16] As Karen Harvey and Alexandra Shepard argue in their introduction to a forum on the history of masculinity in the *Journal of British Studies*, 'it is important that historians of masculinity are attentive to the contribution of class to male identities.' Karen Harvey and Alexandra Shepard, 'What Have Historians Done with Masculinity? Reflections on Five Centuries of British History, circa 1500–1950', *Journal of British Studies* 44, no. 2 (1 April 2005): 277.

[17] David Warren Sabean, *Property, Production, and Family in Neckarhausen, 1700–1870* (Cambridge: Cambridge University Press, 1991).

[18] Carlo A. Corsini and Pier Paolo Viazzo, *The Decline of Infant and Child Mortality: The European Experience, 1750–1990* (The Hague: Kluwer Law International (UNICEF), 1997), xiii.

associated with birth. In 1847, Ignaz Phillip Semmelweis demonstrated why this was the case. He noticed that the high rates of puerperal fever at the Vienna General Hospital were being caused by doctors who were handling cadavers and then moving directly to the delivery room without disinfecting their hands. For those afflicted immediately after birth, death followed in 85 per cent of the cases, leading to rates of maternal mortality in Europe of between two and three per thousand births.[19] Like Wollstonecraft's husband, William Godwin, the fathers of half-orphaned infants often resorted to calling upon the mercies of next-door neighbours or family members to help them raise their children. Others quickly remarried in circumstances of considerable stress, thus decreasing the chances of a loving union.

It would be wrong, however, to suggest that these circumstances necessarily produced households devoid of love. Historians have recently begun to explore the history of emotions in much more nuanced detail, and it is now increasingly common to describe non-traditional families and households as emotionally cohesive and supportive units. For example, Carolyn Steedman's *Master and Servant: Love and Labour in the English Industrial Age* describes the relationship between an English single mother and the elderly clergyman who took her in when the father of her child refused to marry her in 1802. Threatened with social ostracism and destitution for her sexual transgression, Phoebe Beatson instead found refuge with a man who clearly felt great affection for his former servant and her child and left them a sizeable inheritance.[20] For upper-class Europeans, love relationships were further complicated by considerations of inheritance and status that often prevented young lovers from marrying partners of their choice. But even in this world of semi-arranged marriages, where nobles and upper-class Europeans would often marry their cousins to prevent any dissipation of family wealth, the idea of love was not absent. This is apparent in the degree to which love and romance were central to the novels of the eighteenth and nineteenth centuries. The Swiss author and Swedish ambassador's wife Madame de Staël married for the status her husband's position would afford her rather than for love. But her novel *Corinne ou L'Italie* (Corinne: or Italy, 1807) played to her readers' fascination with romance by sympathetically telling the tragic story of the beautiful English-Italian poet Corinne and her doomed love affair with Oswald, the British Lord Nelvil. Although duty triumphs over love when Nelvil abandons Corinne in order to live up to a promise to his dead father, it was clearly the novel's emphasis on true love that made it a huge success across Europe; it was translated into German, English, Dutch, Italian, Polish and partially into Russian and Spanish.[21]

Outside pressures on one's choice of marriage partner affected all classes. Individual towns and cities often prevented the poor from marrying in order to avoid increasing their

---

[19] Irvine Loudon, *The Tragedy of Childbed Fever* (Oxford and New York: Oxford University Press, 2000), 5–6. Loudon begins his book with a detailed description of Wollstonecraft's death.

[20] Carolyn Steedman, *Master and Servant: Love and Labour in the English Industrial Age* (Cambridge and New York: Cambridge University Press, 2007).

[21] Edith Saurer, *Liebe und Arbeit: Geschlechterbeziehungen im 19. und 20. Jahrhundert* (Wien: Böhlau Wien, 2014), 22–23.

numbers. But restrictions on marriage were also common for the gainfully employed, especially for members of guilds. Guilds were predominantly (though not exclusively) male organizations that controlled access to individual trades (carpentry, shoemaking, cabinet-making, stonemasonry, etc.) and established and protected the rights and privileges of their members.[22] Unlike unions today, they were less interested in increasing wages than they were in ensuring an equitable distribution of work between members. Guild membership was therefore something that had to be earned and was a carefully protected privilege. But guilds also determined the social lives of their members, setting rules and restrictions on marriage and providing the site for community celebrations, rituals and charitable support.[23] The 'familial' relationship between the master and his apprentice could produce warm bonds of belonging, but this did not change the fact that guilds were part of a broader system of control over the marriage and sexual practices of young adults.

Along with many other small-scale institutions of social discipline in early modern towns and villages, guilds slowly weakened and disappeared with industrialization. Many historians have described this process as an effect of the dramatic scale of economic change transforming family and sexual life in modern Europe. In the late 1960s, historians influenced by modernization theory (such as Edward Shorter and William Goode) argued that industrialization transformed marriage patterns by breaking down traditional pressures on couples to marry for economic reasons.[24] Shorter postulated an early 'sexual revolution' that followed industrialization, which, he argued, brought young people independence, the desire to be free from traditional structures and the ability to rely on their own wage labour to choose partners more independently.

These theories have since been soundly criticized by historians eager to demonstrate that, despite pressures from local communities, pre-industrial European family patterns had long allowed for individual choice.[25] The practice of 'bundling' (ritualized overnight visits from boys in girls' bedrooms) was common in Scandinavia and Central Europe, and it provided young couples with some control over the choice of future mates. These sleepovers were carefully monitored by the peer group and only partially controlled by parents. Any resulting premarital pregnancy was considered scandalous only if the

---

[22] For a useful case study of women's participation and eventual exclusion from guilds, see Jean Quataert, 'The Shaping of Women's Work in Manufacturing: Guilds, Households, and the State in Central Europe, 1648–1870', *American Historical Review* 90, no. 5 (1985): 1, 122–48. Quataert argues that women were increasingly excluded from guilds in the mid-seventeenth century as part of the process of guilds trying to defend their monopolies in a period of early industrialization.

[23] James J. Sheehan, *German History, 1770–1866* (Oxford: Oxford University Press, 1989), 108.

[24] William Joshiah Goode, *The Family* (Englewood Cliffs, NJ: Prentice Hall, 1964), 108–9; Edward Shorter, *The Making of the Modern Family* (New York: Basic Books, 1975), esp. 19–20.

[25] For an overview of these historiographical debates, see Christopher Lasch, 'The Family and History', *The New York Review of Books*, 13 November 1975, available at http://www.nybooks.com/articles/archives/1975/nov/13/the-family-and-history/ (accessed 10 July 2015). An historian of medicine, Shorter has more recently authored histories of desire and sadomasochism that have been even more critically received. See, for example, Richard Davenport-Hines, 'Review of *Written in the Flesh: A History of Desire* by Edward Shorter', *The English Historical Review* CXXI, no. 494 (1 December 2006): 1570–1.

couple did not follow through by getting married.[26] By the same token, as one study of Sweden has demonstrated, the decline of these practices and the increased opportunities for finding mates outside the village in the nineteenth century did not entail an end to parental control or a sudden 'burst of sexual energy and romantic love blast[ing] the walls of tradition defended by elders and parents'.[27] So even though marriage was crucially important to individuals' material well-being and survival in the early modern period, love was not a creation of the Industrial Revolution. Historians relying on the records of marital complaint are now uncovering considerable evidence that the hope for love was always present in early modern marriage, and that material interests were generally pragmatically balanced with the desires of each partner to fulfil emotional needs.[28]

Nonetheless, changing economic circumstances and the need to move away from an exclusively agricultural and rural existence greatly complicated married and family life. Families found it necessary to diversify their means of bringing in income, because a slow transition in agricultural production began to affect most of Europe in the mid-eighteenth century. Ironically, the impoverishment of many rural families was a result of agricultural innovations that spread across Western and Central Europe (we will return to the East and the South shortly) between the 1760s and the mid-nineteenth century. New strategies of crop rotation and organic fertilization increased crop yields. Many European regions also followed the lead of Frederick the Great of Prussia, who imported the potato from South America and eventually convinced (and sometimes forced) his peasants to cultivate it to guard against famine. Beginning in 1746, Frederick issued several 'potato decrees', ordered the free distribution of seed potatoes and even went on personal inspection tours to enforce new agricultural practices, though the new food stuff only really caught on after his death. Potatoes, turnips and beets proved much more resilient to unpredictable European weather patterns than wheat, while legumes added an important nutritional component to European diets. All this helped to break cycles of famine that had plagued Europe since the Middle Ages. But these new crops also changed the division of labour in the countryside, because they were most often worked by women, who were given the time-consuming tasks of hoeing, weeding and staking.

Agricultural productivity gains were generally not passed on to agricultural workers. Rather than paying farmhands more or allowing them to work less, landlords on the large estates tended to extract the same amount of labour from fewer individuals, pocketing

---

[26] For a detailed description of these rituals in rural Sweden, see Marco H. D. Leeuwen and Ineke Maas, 'Partner Choice and Homogamy in the Nineteenth Century: Was There a Sexual Revolution in Europe?', *Journal of Social History* 36, no. 1 (2002): 105–7.

[27] Ibid., 119.

[28] See for example: Sauer, *Liebe und Arbeit*; Joanne Bailey, *Unquiet Lives: Marriage and Marriage Breakdown in England, 1660–1800* (Cambridge: Cambridge University Press, 2003); Carolyn Steedman, *An Everyday Life of the English Working Class: Work, Self and Sociability in the Early Nineteenth Century* (Cambridge and New York: Cambridge University Press, 2014); and Andrew R. L. Cayton, *Love in the Time of Revolution: Transatlantic Literary Radicalism and Historical Change, 1793–1818* (Chapel Hill: University of North Carolina Press, 2013), which provides, among other things, a detailed account of the love between Wollstonecraft and Godwin.

the increased financial rewards or reinvesting them in industry. This both spurred on industrialization (since it created new sources of capital) and produced an oversupply of agricultural labour across large swathes of rural Europe by the nineteenth century. The first areas to industrialize were those where structural changes in agriculture coincided with a general growth in the population. Between 1700 and 1800, the population of Great Britain rose from six million to nine million, with most of the increase occurring in the second half of the eighteenth century.[29] This oversupply was exacerbated by specific policy decisions and systems of land ownership.

In the United Kingdom, agriculture was progressively transformed by the process of enclosures, which began in the sixteenth century and accelerated in the nineteenth. Enclosure was the process of consolidating strips of agricultural land that had previously been farmed separately (originally by serfs who owed service to the lord and later by peasants who paid a landlord rent) into larger, continuous units of land, controlled directly by the landlord. The process was initially resisted by the early modern monarchy, since dispossessing peasants of their land and livelihood created great social disorder. But the success of the larger estates eventually quelled this resistance, and by 1700, Acts of Parliament were used to legally regulate the process of enclosure.[30] Legislation now also made it possible for landlords to control what had previously been common lands, whose use was governed by local custom. New enclosure acts in 1801, 1836 and 1845 further rationalized and accelerated the process, with special government commissioners overseeing the transition and reporting back to Parliament. By the early 1800s, the percentage of Britons employed in agriculture had decreased to 33 per cent (compared to 60 per cent in the late seventeenth century), and enclosure had forced a growing number of rural families to become dependent upon wage labour.[31] There were, however, various transitional stages.

Families reacted to the pressure of an oversupply of rural labour in various ways. The first response was often to supplement agricultural income with small-scale manufacturing in the home or with itinerant labour outside of the home. Rural families in economic hard times sent their older children to work as itinerant farm labourers or domestic servants. The experiences of Tess in Thomas Hardy's novel *Tess of the D'Urbervilles* (1891) vividly symbolized the choices available to young rural women and the harsh conditions under which they laboured in the fields and in the homes of the upper classes. At various points, Tess works as a keeper of hens, a milkmaid and a labourer on a beet farm. The young lord of an estate takes advantage of her, she returns to her parents' house and gives birth to a baby, who soon dies. Later, her true love discovers the secret of Tess's girlhood indiscretion and abandons her, setting the stage for her ultimate downfall. Tess's tragedy

---

[29] David Landes, *The Unbound Prometheus*, 46.

[30] The exact periodization of these developments is the subject of some dispute among economic historians. See Robert C. Allen, 'Tracking the Agricultural Revolution in England', *Economic History Review* 52, no. 2 (1999): 209–35.

[31] Berend, *History Derailed*, 11; and Paul Carter, 'Enclosure, Waged Labour and the Formation of Class Consciousness: Rural Middlesex *c.* 1700–1835', *Labour History Review* 66, no. 3 (2001): 269–93.

was so powerful as a novel because it symbolized the experiences of scores of young women, whose tenuous economic and social existence left them vulnerable to sexual exploitation. Rural poverty also often forced men (both fathers and sons) into itinerant work away from home, though their choices were more diverse. Expanding cities meant a demand for labour in construction, railway and road building. These jobs separated men from their families and left women home alone to tend garden plots and animals. Since work outside of the household was paid in cash, it could be tracked in economic statistics and was understood as a vital part of the national economy. Domestic chores, on the other hand, were not quantified in this way, and they were thereby rendered virtually invisible as a form of economic production. Much of women's labour, in other words, was not part of the 'wealth of nations'; it was not taken into account in new investigations of national economic systems being written by philosophers like Adam Smith.

Not all rural families moved directly from agriculture to wage labour. Many also reacted to the agricultural revolution and the pressures that it put on rural life by resorting to cottage industry of various kinds. 'Cottage industry' and 'the putting-out system' were terms used to describe small manufacturing enterprises within the home. As capitalism developed in eighteenth-century towns, merchant capitalists wishing to expand their markets and increase their profits began to understand that they could circumvent the high wages of guild members by farming out small-scale manufacturing to rural families.[32] The best-known form of cottage industry was weaving. During times when agricultural work was lighter, families took in wool and divided up the tasks of washing, spinning and weaving it. Families purchased or rented equipment like the spinning jenny (invented by James Hargreaves in 1764) and sold their finished products (often under contract) to middlemen. Many areas of Europe had specialized forms of cottage industry. Handmade lace often supplemented or constituted the sole income of rural families, particularly in parts of France, Spain and Italy. In the early nineteenth century, lace machines were developed in Nottingham, England, and cottage industries of machine-made lace sprang up in the St Gall area of Switzerland, Plauen in Saxony and Calais in France. These complicated and expensive machines required considerable skill and investment, so more complex hierarchies of family labour developed, with the head of the household (the father) performing the most complex tasks and all other family members being assigned jobs according to their age and gender. Similar divisions of labour occurred in the homes of artisans, such as glassmakers in Bohemia.

The example of rural weavers demonstrates that the transition of labour from a predominance of household-based rural agriculture to a more urban, industrialized and wage-labour-oriented economy was by no means immediate or uniform across Europe, nor did it instantaneously transform social norms concerning marriage. There were long periods in each European country during which family life was characterized by what Olwen Hufton has called the 'economy of makeshift' – a combination of agricultural work

---

[32] William H. Sewell, 'Artisans and Factory Workers, 1789–1848', in *Working Class Formation*, ed. Ira Katznelson and Aristide R. Zolberg (Princeton: Princeton University Press, 1986), 50.

with various forms of manufacturing (including cottage industry), building or itinerant labour for wages that pieced together a meagre survival for early modern families.[33] The 'complementarity of the subsistence family' was thus already disappearing in the eighteenth century and was being replaced with a phase of 'proto-industrialization'.[34] In Neckarhausen, a German town of only eighty adult males, thirty were engaged in handicrafts of goods for sale in a larger market.[35] Historians have tended to assume that men's more frequent access to income from crafts or work outside of the village increased the likelihood that they would abandon their families in times of economic distress. But newer research has shown that divorce was most often provoked by women and that women were not averse to using the various laws describing the duties of husbands and wives to their advantage.[36] In Britain, for instance, laws of coverture gave women the right to make purchases 'suitable to the couple's situation in life' and provided women with a sense of entitlement to support from their husbands. Although these laws were premised on the idea that a woman's rights were simply subsumed under and secondary to those of her husband, the complementary nature of the subsistence family gave women some room for manoeuvre within these boundaries. Even though men generally owned the property and produced most of the cash income in the early modern family, they were dependent upon wives, who kept the family household running smoothly.[37] We can speak therefore of relationships of co-dependency in which the husband's patriarchal authority was kept in check by community standards and specific laws that defined his duty to his family.

Changes in how goods were produced and how individuals earned their living inevitably placed strains upon and transformed patterns of marriage. 'Marriage is, after all', Sabean writes, 'an exchange relationship, composed of, if not reducible to, a property settlement, a labor contract, sexual privileges and duties, and reproductive claims and responsibilities. All of these elements are under constant renegotiation as conditions change.'[38] As increasing percentages of the European population moved from agricultural production to manufacturing (or found ways of combining these two modes of making a living) the division of labour within families and the relative value placed on each family member's work inevitably changed. The work of rural European women had generally centred on the home. But in farming communities, these activities (which in many regions of Europe included the management of the household or shop's finances) were so essential to the family's survival that it is extremely misleading to categorize them as housework. It makes more sense to think about these women as contributors to 'smallholdings': rural farming households, practising diversified agriculture and other forms of income generation (including sale in markets, cottage industries and work in

---

[33] Olwen Hufton, *The Poor of Eighteenth-Century France, 1750–1789* (Oxford: Clarendon Press, 1974), 69ff., 25–43 and 108–9.

[34] For an overview of this transition, see Maxine Berg, *The Age of Manufactures: Industry, Innovation, and Work in Britain, 1700–1820* (Oxford: Basil Blackwell Ltd., 1985), esp. 69–77.

[35] Sabean, *Property, Production, and Family in Neckarhausen*, 156.

[36] On divorce, see Ibid., 157.

[37] Bailey, *Unquiet Lives*, 57 and 83.

[38] Sabean, *Property, Production, and Family in Neckarhausen*, 161–2.

rural or urban factories) in areas of dense population.[39] But the more common it became for individual family members to find work in factories, the more separate the daily experiences of men and women became. It is important to remember that smallholders often continued to maintain their farms even as family members began earning money in industry or other forms of wage labour. In some cases, such as on the dairy farms in the Swiss alps, this coexistence of smallholding and work in industry or the tourist trade persists to this day.[40] The separation between men's work and women's work therefore occurred quite gradually. We will return to this process of urbanization shortly. First, however, it is necessary to contrast the Western patterns of work and family that we have described above with circumstances in other parts of Europe.

## Family and work in Eastern Europe

The patterns of work and family life that we have described for the industrializing western areas of Europe bear little relationship to the experiences of Eastern and Southern Europeans. A description of life on an estate near the Baltic Sea will demonstrate the degree to which a different economic system and pattern of work could provide dramatically different boundaries for family life and the relationship between the genders.

Andrejs Plakans's description of life on an estate in Kurland (a Russian Baltic province now part of Latvia) in the 1790s provides a graphic illustration of the variety of conditions under which European families laboured in the early modern period. Peasants, who made up about 85–90 per cent of the region's population, were tied to the land under a system of serfdom that included the obligation to provide unpaid labour to the lords who owned the grand estates of this region. Central governments and their policies played very little role in life on the estates, which was governed by the landowner. While the peasants were Latvian and Estonian, the upper classes (landowners) were the descendants of the Teutonic Order that had conquered this region in the thirteenth and fourteenth centuries. These nobles still considered themselves German. This system of land ownership stayed in place until well into the mid-nineteenth century. As the estate owners faced international competition and decreasing profits, they increased the dues that peasants owed to their lords. On the estates, peasants lived in extended households that included several generations and some non-family members. These units were somewhat like the *zadruga* of the Balkan lands, where fathers lived together with their married sons and their families. Plakans provides a detailed description of how this system worked in the Daudzwas estate, a large agricultural estate with a population of 924.[41]

---

[39] Robert McC. Netting, *Smallholders, Householders: Farm Families and the Ecology of Intensive, Sustainable Agriculture* (Stanford, CA: Stanford University Press, 1993), 2.

[40] Ibid., 10. It is, in other words, incorrect to assume that these smallholdings are a phenomenon that disappeared with industrialization.

[41] Andrejs Plakans, 'Peasant Farmsteads and Households in the Baltic Littoral, 1797', *Comparative Studies in Society and History* 17, no. 1 (1975): 2–35.

The owner of Daudzwas did not live on the estate itself, which was managed by an unmarried male overseer. The estate housed one doctor, six German-speaking managers and several artisans, tradesmen and innkeepers, who provided their services to all those living on the estate. Each artisan hired a farmhand to work his household's land. Almost 72 per cent of the population on the estate were serfs, meaning they were tied to the land, were considered the landowner's property and were obligated to perform agricultural and other services for the landowner. Those whom the landlord considered suitable headed their own farms, while the others worked on yearly contracts for a *Wirth* (a peasant manager of a portion of the lord's land). A large percentage of landless peasants roamed from job to job within the estate. Their family lives were never stable, and their children seldom stayed with them past the age of ten. All this meant that people's daily lives were not governed by a family unit but by a farmstead (or commune), headed by a *Wirth* who might or might not be related to his underlings. Only the *Wirth* and his wife, and perhaps some older relatives, had a room of their own in the farmhouse. Others shared cramped quarters with makeshift sleeping arrangements or, when the weather was warmer, they slept out in the haylofts and barns. This farmstead worked as a unit to provide food for its inhabitants and the demesne labour service required by the lord.

The agricultural estates of the Baltic Littoral provide only one example of the organization of agricultural life in Eastern Europe. Nonetheless, the stark conditions of life on the Daudzwas estate are symbolic of the struggles that Eastern European families faced in the transition towards industrialization. The multi-generation household was typical of pre-industrialized Eastern Europe.[42] Even after serfs were emancipated during the nineteenth century (1816–19 in Russia's Baltic provinces, 1848 in Austria and the Habsburg Empire, 1853 in Hungary and 1861 in Russia proper), impoverished rural individuals had few alternatives but to continue working on the estates, since they either did not have the means to own property or were heavily indebted for its purchase. The opportunities for wage labour in the cities grew only slowly and unpredictably. In many cases the obligatory labour was simply renamed 'rent'.[43] These developments contrasted with the process that Max Weber observed on Prussian estates, where the Junker class's preference for cheap, seasonal wage labour and the lure of more rapidly growing German cities led to a depopulation of the East Elbian countryside. Indeed, many impoverished peasants from Baltic and Russian lands came to work for these meagre wages on Prussian estates.[44] Nonetheless, the freedom to move off the estate meant that younger brothers could go in search of their own headship rather than be forced to live as a subordinate in an older brother's household. In many areas of the Russian Empire, however, the freedom to leave could only be granted by a decision of the commune, which was collectively

---

[42] Andrejs Plakans, 'Agrarian Reform and the Family in Eastern Europe', in *The History of the European Family*, ed. David I. Kertzer and Marzio Barbagli, *vol. 2: Family Life in the Long Nineteenth Century, 1789–1913* (New Haven: Yale University Press, 2002), 77.

[43] Ibid., 86

[44] Max Weber, 'National Character and the Junkers', in *From Max Weber: Essays in Sociology*, ed. H. H. Gerth and C. Wright Mills (Oxford and New York: Oxford University Press, 1946), 386–95.

indebted for the purchase of land from the lord after emancipation. Given that the loss of a debtor meant an increase in everyone else's debt, requests for permission to move were not always granted. Emancipation also removed the lord's right to control the marital choices of peasants, but commune elders managed to take over authority in these matters for a time. Emancipation, in other words, did not immediately increase individual freedom. But it did provide for a dramatic transformation in individual identity. Peasants – who were now expected to sign contracts with landowners – were given surnames for the first time.

## Industrialized labour and gender conflict

European countries industrialized at different times and followed quite different patterns. Great Britain capitalized on a strong banking system, abundant natural resources, agricultural reorganization and access to foreign markets acquired through colonial possessions in North America, India and Africa, to be the first country to achieve the level of investment necessary to build large factories and raw-material processing plants. In France, the process was slowed by an agricultural system dominated by small landholders and (by the mid-nineteenth century) a declining birth rate, both of which diminished the supply of labour to new industry. A weak banking system and the damage to investor confidence wreaked by the Revolutionary and Napoleonic wars of the late eighteenth and mid-nineteenth century also thwarted investment in capital industry. Cottage industry thus prevailed far longer than in Britain. Meanwhile, German industrialists had to contend with many different tariffs, at least until the creation of the *Zollverein* (a free-trade zone encompassing most of the future German Empire) in 1834. Industrialization, particularly in coal and steel, began in earnest after German unification in 1871, but cottage industries remained prominent there much longer than in Britain. Despite these differences, the process of industrialization across Europe affected the gendered division of work in similar ways. Wherever industrial production grew, cottage industry and factories transformed the rhythms of work, the kind of work performed and the forms of work discipline for both men and women.[45]

Home manufacturing had allowed families to work together, but under factory conditions, parents worked separately from their children (at least after legislation banned child labour around mid-century) and from each other. The daily rhythms of family life were now governed by the factory whistle, and the clock replaced the rooster and the sun as the family's temporal point of reference. 'Those who are employed experience a distinction between their employer's time and their "own" time ... Time is now currency; it is not passed but spent.'[46] This division of life between family time and work time and the geographical separation of work and home (workers often had to travel considerable

---

[45] Laura L. Frader, 'Doing Capitalism's Work: Women in the Western European Industrial Economy', in *Becoming Visible: Women in European History*, 3rd edn., ed. Renate Bridenthal, Susan Mosher Stuard and Merry E. Wiesner (Boston and New York: Houghton Mifflin Co., 1998), 298–9.

[46] E. P. Thompson, 'Time, Work-Discipline, and Industrial Capitalism', *Past and Present* 38 (1967): 61.

distances to get to their jobs) had a significant impact on gender relations and was 'by and large, experienced as a calamity' by individuals more accustomed to the flexibility and cooperative possibilities of work within the home.[47] Skilled artisans were more able to resist stringent forms of discipline than unskilled workers and women. In specific crafts, they successfully organized, resisted moving to factories or maintained some independence within the factory system. Those who did move to factories were eventually forced to succumb to stricter time management and control of their communication with each other. The strongly patriarchal attitudes of most factory managers were particularly onerous for women, who endured various forms of harassment.[48] At the same time, male workers and male factory managers increasingly defined manliness in terms of skill, reinforcing a gender division of labour and a hierarchy between working men.[49] Factory work became increasingly gendered, with the more highly skilled and lucrative jobs being reserved for men. A specific monetary value was now placed on each family member's contribution to the household income. The task of raising children and performing housework fell to women, who inevitably earned less than men, even if they worked long hours outside of the home. These untenable circumstances led to various conflicts within the family and on the shop floor.

In some areas of Europe, the industrialization of production was contested precisely because of its dramatic influence on family life. In the 1840s, the handloom weavers of the Pays des Mauges (also known as the Choletais) in France successfully resisted the efforts of local mill owners to mechanize production.[50] After the 1860s, power looms eventually triumphed, but for a time the handloom weavers protected their identities as individual artisans in control of their own working lives and the destinies of their families. Given that handloom weaving was increasingly becoming less lucrative, the practice survived only because wives and daughters supplemented family incomes with underpaid factory jobs. Men protected their status as independent heads of households only with the help of female income. The resulting source of cheap female labour helped spur on new industries in the region, particularly in the shoe and garment industry. But the weavers clung to their trade as being vital to their identities as men and fathers, resorting to living off food 'pilfered from farmers by moonlight' rather than accepting jobs in the shoe industry.[51] As poverty eventually forced at least some of the weavers into

---

[47] Jürgen Kocka, 'Problems of Working-Class Formation in Germany: The Early Years, 1800–1875', in *Working Class Formation: Nineteenth-Century Patterns in Western Europe and the United States*, ed. Ira Katznelson and Aristide R. Zolberg (Princeton: Princeton University Press, 1986), 319.

[48] Daniel E. Bender has argued that late nineteenth- and early twentieth-century female American garment workers were subjected to harassment as a form of enforcing the sexual segregation of work and the women's lower pay scale. See Daniel E. Bender, '"Too much of Distasteful Masculinity": Historicizing Sexual Harassment in the Garment Sweatshop and Factory', *Journal of Women's History* 15, no. 4 (2004): 91–116.

[49] Anne Phillips and Barbara Taylor, 'Sex and Skill: Notes Towards a Feminist Economics', in *Feminism and History*, ed. Joan W. Scott (New York: Oxford University Press, 1996), 317–30.

[50] Tessie P. Liu, 'What Price a Weaver's Dignity? Gender Inequality and the Survival of Home-Based Production in Industrial France', in *Gender and Class in Modern Europe*, ed. Laura L. Frader and Sonya O. Rose (Ithaca, NY and London: Cornell University Press, 1996), 57–76.

[51] Ibid., 61–2.

the factories, the weavers, like their daughters before them, fed an industry that relied on cheap labour. Having hung onto their dignity so long by forcing their daughters into cheap labour, they had set off a 'negative spiral' that drove wages down and eventually exacted its price on both sexes.[52]

The British example shows how the gendering of work and skill continued on the factory floor. As steam-driven looms replaced handlooms in the 1840s, highly skilled male weavers were driven out of their jobs. They were often replaced by women, who were believed to possess more dexterous hands that could better operate the often dangerous spinning frames, but who were paid considerably less than men.[53] By the 1830s, this process of 'deskilling' (the replacement of 'skilled' artisans with 'unskilled' wage labourers using industrial forms of production) had produced an unsustainable social and economic situation, since families who had lost the income of an artisan head of household could now no longer make enough money to survive. An emerging trade union movement started to place pressure on government, and in 1847 the Ten-Hours Act limited the working day to ten hours for women and younger workers.

Factory legislation, though explicitly targeted at the concerns of the working class, was also an expression of middle-class values. Bourgeois commentators had become increasingly scandalized by the fact that men and women were working together on the same factory floor and had begun pushing for a clearer separation of men's and women's work. The ultimate effect was to further exclude women from the more skilled trades.[54] The more mechanized that industrial production became, the more 'skill' came to be defined in terms of gender rather than ability or training.[55] As disparity between women's and men's wages increased, women's double burden of work and domestic chores (including child-rearing) became more onerous and apparent. But most women did not protest the disparity in wages. On the contrary, by the late nineteenth century, female labour leaders in Britain were arguing that a 'woman's job' should get a 'woman's wage' and that improvements of conditions for working women could not come at the expense of working men.[56] The idea of a family wage (where the man alone could earn enough money to support the entire family) looked increasingly attractive to both sexes. Men hitched their sense of masculine identity to their roles as primary wage earners, and women sought relief from the double burden of work and domestic chores.[57] The move to the family wage not only further separated the labour of men and women, but

---

[52] Ibid., 76.

[53] Frader, 'Doing Capitalism's Work', 299.

[54] Michele Barrett and Mary McIntosh, 'The "Family Wage": Some Problems for Socialists and Feminists', *Capital and Class* 11 (1980): 51–72.

[55] See Gerjan de Groot and Marlou Schrover, 'Between Men and Machines: Women Workers in New Industries, 1870–1940', *Social History* 20, no. 3 (1995): 279–96; and Phillips and Taylor.

[56] Jane Lewis, 'The Working-Class Wife and Mother and State Intervention 1870–1940', in *Labour and Love: Women's Experience of Home and Family 1850–1940*, ed. Jane Lewis (London and New York: Basil Blackwell, 1986), 105.

[57] Sonya O. Rose, 'Gender Antagonism and Class Conflict: Exclusionary Strategies of Male Trade Unionists in Nineteenth-Century Britain', *Social History* 13, no. 2 (1988): 191–208 esp. 202.

it also provided an even stronger justification for male dominance within the family. As Friedrich Engels commented in 1891: 'In the great majority of cases today, at least in the possessing classes, the husband is obliged to earn a living and support his family, and that itself gives him a position of supremacy, without any need for special titles and privileges.'[58] The ideal of the family wage ensured that women continued to be excluded from the higher-skilled and higher-paid jobs, as they had been under the guilds, since they otherwise represented competition for male 'breadwinners'.[59]

## Utopian responses

The pressures that wage labour placed on families prompted some Europeans to think up radical solutions to the social and familial consequences of industrialization. In France, a group of social radicals formed a new church around the ideas of Charles Fourier and Claude Henri de Rouvroy, Comte de Saint-Simon. Fourier was a rather mystical self-taught philosopher who advocated the creation of self-contained communal societies that would end the dehumanization of labour by organizing production through interdependent work groups called phalanxes. This new organization, he argued, would balance out human passions and skills. Fourier believed that society could only progress if full sexual freedom were attained and the slavery of women ended. In 1808, he famously declared that 'the extension of the privileges of women is the general principle of all social progress', thus winning him a place in the hearts of future socialist feminists like Flora Tristan.[60] Saint-Simon was a Romantic philosopher who had written utopian pamphlets on the need to reorganize economic life around moral values. On Christmas Day 1829, his followers, the 'Saint-Simonians', named Prosper Enfantin (the son of a bankrupt banker) one of their two 'popes'. The group sought harmony between the classes, the equal valuation of all work and a peaceful process towards progressive social change. They believed that this could only be achieved through a religion where men and women were equally valued, and Enfantin promised that a female messiah would come to take the position of the second pope in the movement. He argued that social harmony could only be produced if male and female principles were brought into balance. In theory, he praised female emotion over male reason, but the movement continued to be governed by men despite the increased involvement of the movement's 'mother', Claire Bazard, who began to officiate at ceremonies in 1833. The Saint-Simonians also

---

[58] Excerpted from Friedrich Engels, 'The Origin of the Family. Private Property and the State in the Light of the Researches of Lewis H. Morgan (A Translation of the 1891 Edition of the Original German Text)' in *Women, the Family and Freedom: The Debate in Documents*, ed. Susan Groag Bell and Karen Offen (Stanford, CA: Stanford University Press, 1983), 81.

[59] Deborah Simonton, 'Women Workers; Working Women', in *The Routledge History of Women in Europe since 1700*, ed. Deborah Simonton (London and New York: Routledge, 2006), 157–8.

[60] Quoted in Charles Sowerwine, 'Socialism, Feminism, and the Socialist Women's Movement from the French Revolutionary to World War II', in *Becoming Visible: Women in European History*, 3rd edn., ed. Renate Bridenthal, Susan Mosher Stuard and Merry E. Wiesener (Boston: Houghton Mifflin Co., 1998), 359.

advocated free love and argued that sexual relationships should occur only on the basis of love, rather than with reference to considerations of family, class or socio-political needs. As Claire Moses has shown, however, these ideals provided only a thin cloak for what remained a sexual double standard that tolerated male promiscuity while tending to portray women as sexual temptresses.[61]

Although the Saint-Simonians ran into legal problems and faced charges that their philosophies endangered public morals, they provided the inspiration for early French feminism.[62] In 1832, a group of Saint-Simonian women under the leadership of the working-class feminist Suzanne Voilquin founded the newspaper *Tribune des femmes*. The paper was meant to represent a wide range of female experience and covered topics such as religion, work, sexual morality, marriage, economics and politics. To a far greater extent than Enfantin's mystical religion, the women of the *Tribune* attempted to blend 'sex consciousness' with 'class consciousness'.[63] While drawing inspiration from the communal living projects and the socialist critique of the early Saint-Simonian movement, these women recognized that Enfantin's preaching of sexual freedom made no sense to women who could be impoverished by single motherhood under the conditions of early capitalism. 'Saint-Simonian women emancipated themselves from male tutelage and created an independent women's movement, the first in history.'[64] They tried to convince women that they had a collective interest in fighting against masculine dominance and in bringing about far-reaching social changes that would ensure women's material and emotional well-being.

The conflict between the interests of men and women, and the ability of early socialist movements to generate ideas about female emancipation, was also apparent in British Utopian Socialism. After 1829, groups inspired by the thinking of factory reformer Robert Owen began forming Communities of Mutual Association, utopian communities that promised to create a 'world turned upside down' by giving the 'productive classes a complete dominion over the fruits of their own industry' and eliminating all relationships of power and subordination.[65] The capitalist should no longer dominate the worker, the parent the child or the man the woman. The Owenites argued that capitalists had purposely intensified gender conflict in order to further subdue the working classes and thwart their struggle against exploitation. Only a change in the material circumstances

---

[61] Claire Moses, 'Saint Simonian Men/Saint Simonian Women: The Transformation of Feminist Thought in 1830s' France', *Journal of Modern History* 54, no. 2 (1982): 240–67.

[62] Although the word 'feminism' only began to be used to describe female emancipation projects in the 1890s, we will follow common practice and use it to describe earlier movements. See Karen Offen, 'Defining Feminism: A Comparative Historical Approach', *Signs* 14, no. 1 (1988): 119–57. For a discussion of debates about the use of the word, see Sylvia Paletschek and Bianca Pietrow-Ennker, 'Concepts and Issues', in *Women's Emancipation Movements in the Nineteenth Century: A European Perspective*, ed. Sylvia Paletschek and Bianka Pietrow-Enker (Stanford: Stanford University Press, 2004), 7–8.

[63] Moses, 'Saint Simonian Men', 255.

[64] Ibid., 265.

[65] Barbara Taylor, '"The Men Are as Bad as Their Masters…": Socialism, Feminism and Sexual Antagonism in the London Tailoring Trade in the Early 1830s', *Feminist Studies* 5, no. 1 (1979): 9.

of European society, they insisted, could alter the subordinated status of women. 'Under the withering influence of competition for wealth, mammon worship and an aristocracy of birth', wrote an Owenite woman in 1839, 'very little progress can be made in the attainment of true liberty for women ... The only way left ... is to organize small societies on a better system, as examples and patterns to the rest of the world.'[66] The Owenites published hundreds of books, tracts and newspaper articles and travelled the country giving lectures in support of this new collective, egalitarian society. By the 1840s, London groups were delivering three lectures a week on 'women's rights' to large audiences.[67]

Owen believed that society could only be transformed if the 'human character' itself could be encouraged to nourish more harmonious relations. This meant reshaping sexual relations that subordinated women and creating a system of collectivized (though still exclusively female) housework and childcare. In his 1835 tract *Lectures on the Marriages of the Priesthood in the Old Immoral World*, Owen called for 'marriages of nature', formed out of affection rather than economic need. Owen's advocacy for 'free love' prompted one detractor to lament that his ideas would lead to the creation of 'one vast brothel' in every Owenite community. Women members of the movement also pointed out that free love could only benefit women if they had already achieved economic, social and political equality. Nonetheless, his ideas were extremely influential. They inspired Catherine Barmby and her husband Goodwyn to co-found the short-lived 'Communist Church' in 1841, which preached the doctrine of the coming of a 'Female Messiah' who would bring Owenite ideas on female equality to fruition.[68]

In February 1834, individual Owenite cooperatives merged to form a 'General Union of all Trades'. Although this organization was rent by conflicts between the different trades and lasted only seven months, it was feared by governments and attracted considerable female participation. Gender tension within this movement illustrated the larger tensions created by deskilling. Male workers protested against factory owners when they hired (cheaper) female labour, while women workers felt compelled to form their own unions to protect their own positions on the shop floor.[69] While this direct conflict between male and female unionists was only a brief flare-up in the short-lived history of the General Union, it displayed underlying gender tensions of the capitalist system. As soon as Owen and his followers began suggesting a universal commitment to eliminating divisions between workers and accepting the principles of sexual egalitarianism, the distinctly gendered nature of early capitalism was exposed.[70] As the

---

[66] Quoted in Ibid., from W. W. P. (pseudo.), 'Woman as She Is and as She Ought to Be', *New Moral World* 5, no. 13 (26 January 1839): 210.

[67] Ibid., 12.

[68] Citations and summary from Joy Dixon, *Gender, Politics, and Culture in Modern Europe* (Vancouver: Access Guided Independent Study, University of British Columbia, n.d.), 55–6.

[69] Barbara Taylor, *Eve and the New Jerusalem: Socialism and Feminism in the Nineteenth Century* (New York: Pantheon Books, 1983), 92–3.

[70] Ibid., 95.

emergence of these utopian projects demonstrates, the twin disruptions of political revolution and massive economic change were creating the possibility for novel visions of social order and political practices. Those possibilities became even clearer in the middle of the nineteenth century when a new wave of unrest crashed across the continent.

## Revolution and new political ideas

As the historian James Sheehan has written, 'Revolutions are rare because they require an unusual conjunction of suffering and hope, a sense of outrage and an act of faith.'[71] Just such a situation prevailed in several European countries in the spring of 1848. Poor harvests since 1845 had fuelled an economic recession and financial panics, particularly where banks were still weak (as they were virtually everywhere outside of Britain). The Irish Potato Famine of the late 1840s, which caused a million deaths, was the most extreme case among many across Europe. A string of bankruptcies threw workers into the streets, and soldiers were frequently dispatched to quell urban riots. Fears were heightened by the Swiss Civil War (1847–48) and insurrections in Milan, Palermo and Naples in early 1848. But once again, the spark of pan-European revolution was ignited in Paris, where rioting had prompted soldiers to construct barricades and King Louis-Philippe was forced to abdicate. A new French Republic was declared on 24 February 1848. The unrest spread eastward right up to the Russian border, and it fuelled patriotic efforts in Hungary and Italy to establish independence from the Habsburg Empire. Milanese patriots drove Marshal Radetzky's Austrian troops out of the city in five days of heavy fighting beginning on 15 March 1848. Although the Milanese were later forced to surrender, the spark of a national movement that would later lead to the unification of Italy had been lit. Nationalistic fervour was intertwined with demands for political reform in almost every case, and the revolutionary atmosphere across the continent prompted many critiques of existing social, economic and political structures. In Germany, liberal student groups met at banquets and proclaimed the need to unify the nation. In Austria too, intellectuals signed petitions and demanded an end to repressive censorship laws. But the driving force behind the growing violence came from below.

Romantic political ideas about nationhood were not particularly relevant to the masses of hungry Europeans who gathered in the major cities in 1848 to protest their destitute state. Skyrocketing food prices sent people – often crowds of women – into the streets to scream at merchants who had upped their prices yet again or to storm potato stands (as in Prussia in 1847) to steal what they could not afford to buy. As news of events in Paris spread, workers and even domestic servants organized themselves into unions and began to demand higher wages and other improvements to their working conditions. Women were almost always involved in the strikes and political protests and were particularly active in food riots. In Paris in the spring of 1848, the Parisian seamstress Julia Jacquier

---

[71] Sheehan, *German History*, 656.

wrote to the provisional government to demand that the promise of a right to work be upheld. Following her lead, women joined street demonstrations in June and began to articulate demands for social change to make it possible for women to support their families.[72] In Germany, the experience led women like Louise Aston, Mathilde Anneke and Louise Otto-Peters to found women's newspapers and set up clubs and organizations dedicated to improving the plight of women in general and the plight of female workers in particular. The radicalizing experience of the 1848 revolution also spurred women like Anna Skimborowicz, Kazimiera Ziemięcka and Wincentyna Zabłocka in Poland to form political organizations and publish reformist pamphlets and newspapers. In Britain, female members of the Chartist movement were active in the campaign for electoral reform. The Chartists fought for universal manhood suffrage and the removal of property requirements for elected officials. By the time the Chartists' third petition to Parliament was rejected in 1848, female membership had grown into the thousands, and there were over 100 separate female-only Chartist groups. While they made some demands for women's rights, these groups mostly lobbied for working-class male political representation and a decent 'family wage' to sustain families without female and child labour. Nevertheless, activism within Chartism was a training ground for women who would later form their own organizations.[73] Others, like the Saint-Simonian women in France, broke away from their larger organization and used the revolutionary violence to underline the need for attention to specifically female concerns.[74] In April 1849, Jeanne Deroin, editor of a feminist newspaper, made history by standing as a candidate in a by-election, though she and Pauline Roland were later arrested and spent six months in a prostitutes' prison for organizing a teachers' union.[75]

These organized efforts to seize the opportunity of the revolution to advance the cause of women's rights have been described as the beginning of an internationally connected women's movement.[76] Although most of these early groups of advocates for women's rights were intertwined with male organizations or were pushing for advances for women only in the sphere of education, the revolutionary fervour that swept Europe in the middle of the century certainly created new venues for women to engage in public debate. For instance, on 29 April 1848, a group of women published

---

[72] Judith DeGroat, 'Working-Class Women and Republicanism in the French Revolution of 1848', *History of European Ideas* 38, no. 3 (1 September 2012): 399–400.
[73] Dorothy Thompson, 'Women and Nineteenth-Century Radical Politics: A Lost Dimension', in *The Rights and Wrongs of Women*, ed. Juliet Mitchell and Ann Oakley (London: Penguin Books, 1976).
[74] For an overview of various women's groups during the 1848 revolutions, see John Chastain's excellent website, *Encyclopedia of 1848 Revolutions*, available at http://www.ohio.edu/chastain/index.htm (accessed 10 July 2015), particularly the following contributions: Ruth-Ellen B. Joeres, 'Frauen-Zeitung' and 'Otto-Peters, Louise'; Peter McPhee, 'Roland, Pauline'; Karen Offen, 'D'Hericourt, Jenny P.'; S. Joan Moon, 'Women's Rights in France'; Leszek Kuk, 'Women in Poland during the 1848 Revolution'; Isabelle Naginski, 'Sand, George'; Dorothy Thompson, 'Women Chartists'; and Robert B. Carlisle, 'Saint-Simonians'; Rüdiger Hachtmann 'Journeymen (Germany)'.
[75] Sowerwine, 'Socialism, Feminism, and the Socialist Women's Movement', 364.
[76] Bonnie S. Anderson, 'The Lid Comes Off: International Radical Feminism and the Revolutions of 1848', *NWSA Journal* 10, no. 2 (1 July 1998): 1–12.

'Demands of the Radical Hungarian' in a patriotic Hungarian-language newspaper in Pest. While demanding improvements to female education and the freedom of women to 'take part in public affairs as much as possible', these 'radical women' also insisted that women should only 'speak modestly as befits a female' and see their primary role as motherhood. It was not through their essential equality, then, that women should have access to the political realm, but primarily by virtue of 'the woman's realm and responsibilities'.[77] With the exception of a few women, like Louise Dittmar in Germany and Jeanne Deroin in France, most feminists of this era formulated principles that historians now call relational feminism. Their demands for female influence were formulated on the basis of a woman's unique role within the family and her motherly virtues.[78]

The revolutions brought some tangible political changes: the Second Republic was declared in France; limited constitutional reforms and tentative steps towards parliamentary government were achieved in the German and Habsburg lands; and the Hungarians, under Lajos Kossuth, were granted more independence and their own constitution within the Habsburg Empire. New constitutions were written in Naples, Piedmont-Sardinia, Tuscany and the Papal states. But the revolutions of 1848 left many regions virtually untouched, and political changes in Central Europe were quickly reversed. The Hungarian revolutionaries were eventually defeated by the combined imperial forces of Austria and Russia. By 1851, soldiers loyal to their monarchs had defeated revolutionary aspirations in Austria, Prussia, Italy and France. Though monarchies were faltering and definitions of citizenship and soldierly duty were transforming in the middle of the nineteenth century, older forms of loyalty had not yet been replaced by broad-based class consciousness or bonds of solidarity that stretched beyond rather immediate and local concerns. As Eric Hobsbawm has argued, middle-class theorists of democratic revolution were careful to avoid unleashing the full fury of the masses, since doing so threatened their own property and livelihoods. Meanwhile, the labouring poor were 'strong enough to make the prospect of social revolution look real and menacing, [but] they were too weak to do more than frighten their enemies'.[79] Nevertheless, the experience of revolution fuelled the search for unifying ideologies of social change that went beyond Chartism or Saint-Simonianism.

Above all, the revolution provided a venue for younger men to voice their concerns about new forms of patriarchy that were changing the social hierarchy and making it more difficult for them to establish themselves as heads of households. Journeymen were particularly numerous on the barricades in Berlin and Vienna, and they protested the growing gap in wages between various trades and their steadily decreasing chances of becoming a master. These arguments had a long history, particularly in France, where

---

[77] Robert Nemes, 'Women in the 1848–1849 Hungarian Revolution', *Journal of Women's History* 13, no. 3 (2001): 199–201.

[78] LeGates, *In Their Time*, 373.

[79] E. J. Hobsbawm, *The Age of Capital 1848–1875* (New York: Charles Scribner's Sons, 1975), 17.

journeymen's complaints had led to special laws to protect the familial relationship between apprentices and their masters during the First Republic.[80] In the early nineteenth century, the pressures of the transition to wage labour and the disruption that this caused to patterns of family organization provided a significant impetus for the formation of radical democratic organizations based on the ideals of fraternalism.[81]

In France Pierre-Joseph Proudhon (1809–65) developed a brand of socialism that sought the return of male dignity damaged by the factory work of women and the diminishing role of artisans. 'Women's place is in the home [*la femme au foyer*]', Proudhon proclaimed, receiving support from socialists in other countries, like Ferdinand Lassalle in Germany.[82] The initial inspiration for socialist ideology in the mid-nineteenth century was thus the goal to create a brotherhood of male workers to revolt against patriarchy in the workplace.

This particular brand of fraternity – one that placed less emphasis on soldiering and more upon male roles as heads of households – took on particular force after France's defeat in the Franco-Prussian War of 1870. The newly proclaimed Third Republic instituted universal male suffrage, which inspired a new wave of discussion about the qualities of a good citizen. Key thinkers of the day, such as the sociologist Émile Durkheim, now argued that the conjugal family was a particularly modern phenomenon that needed to be understood as a critical ethical unit at the core of the nation state. Durkheim was struck by the 'contraction of the paternal family'. By the late nineteenth century, the extended paternal or patriarchal family had withered away, and the conjugal family consisting of only 'the husband, the wife, and unmarried children' had become the organizational unit of society.

> But there is one fact which, better than any other, demonstrates how great a transformation the family is subjected to in these conditions. The conjugal family could have arisen neither from the patriarchal family nor from the paternal family, nor even from a combination of the two types of family, without the intervention of this new factor, the state.

Durkheim insisted that marriage had become a public act, since 'there is no moral society in which the members do not have obligations toward one another.'[83] For Judith Surkis arguments like this are indicative of a shift towards the 'sexed citizen'. A new emphasis on the family unit began to overlap with martial masculinity in the late nineteenth century; 'conjugal complementarity [the insistence that men and women have different but complementary social roles] became one way to organize and explain men and women's

---

[80] Auslander, *Taste and Power*, 152.
[81] Rüdiger Hachtmann, 'Journeymen (Germany)', in *Encyclopedia of 1848 Revolutions*. See also: Jonathan Sperber, *The European Revolutions, 1848–1851* (Cambridge: Cambridge University Press, 1984), 43–47.
[82] Quoted in Sowerwine, 'Socialism, Feminism, and the Socialist Women's Movement', 365.
[83] Emile Durkheim, 'The Conjugal Family [1892]', in *Emile Durkheim on Institutional Analysis*, ed. Mark Traugott (Chicago: University of Chicago Press, 1994), 229, 237 and 239.

sexual difference, not just as a natural principle, but also as a socially necessary one, as in fact, generative of sociality itself.' This had implications for both sexes, but the primary concern was 'the social and sexual regulation of men' through the auspices of moral training for citizenship within the family.[84] This was not an exclusively French idea. In Germany, philosopher Georg Wilhelm Friedrich Hegel made the family central to his theory of the state and civil society.[85] The ultimate effect was to even more firmly entrench male political supremacy, since women were integrated into the state only in their 'complementary' role as caregivers and moral guardians of the family.

Karl Marx (1818–83) directly responded to all of these political trends (French utopian socialism, republican liberalism and Hegelianism). He developed an analysis of mid-century European capitalism directly out of his experiences as a political radical during the revolutionary years before and after 1848. Unlike the socialist utopians before him, Marx argued that true social progress could not be achieved by setting up isolated communities. Instead, he sought to demonstrate to European workers that they had to transform the exploitative property relations that stood at the heart of the capitalist system.

In 1859, Marx argued that the economic system under which goods in any society are produced determines how the members of that society perceive the world. 'The mode of production of material life', he argued, 'determines the general character of the social, political and spiritual processes of life.'[86] It followed from this that modern European societies depended upon a specific type of property relations (private property being held by the wealthy, who also owned the means of production – the factories), which also determined the types of social interaction and created a social hierarchy of classes. For those who laboured in the factory, this system of production and property ownership created new fetters – new types of oppression that the strikes and social revolutions of the mid-nineteenth century were beginning to fight against. Under capitalist conditions as Marx observed them at mid-century, workers were 'alienated' from their labour since both how they worked and what they produced were now completely controlled by the employer. It was the bourgeoisie – the owners of the factories – who reaped the financial and material rewards of the workers' labours rather than the workers themselves. Despite any reservations we might now have about the workability of the communist political systems that others later created on the basis of Marx's ideas, the descriptive force of his critique of the economic system of nineteenth-century Europe has never lost its power. As Jonathan Sperber has convincingly reminded us, to understand the long-term impact of Marx's ideas, it is critical that we appreciate the fact that he was a man of his time – 'a mortal human being, and not a wizard' – whose words had impact not because they

---

[84] Surkis, *Sexing the Citizen*, 3.

[85] For an introduction, see John Keane, *Civil Society and the State: New European Perspectives* (London & New York: Verso, 1988), 50–65.

[86] Karl Marx, *Selected Writings in Sociology and Social Philosophy*, trans. T. B. Bottomore (London: McGraw-Hill, 1964), 51.

predicted the future but because they mercilessly analysed the exploitative economic relationships of his present.[87]

Together with his long-time collaborator Friedrich Engels (1820–95), Marx also insisted that marriage represented a similar kind of exploitative property relationship. Relying on Marx's notes after his death, Engels concluded in *The Origin of the Family* that 'Within the family [the husband] is the bourgeois and the wife represents the proletariat.'[88] Both Marx and Engels believed that this oppressive power of men over women would only end when capitalist relations of production were destroyed. Only the revolution of the proletariat (the urban working class) and the abolition of private property relations could end women's slavery. Nevertheless, Marx and Engels acknowledged that women's lot in nineteenth-century capitalism was more dire than men's. Women were subjected to a 'double oppression', because they received half the wages of men. Employers justified this lower pay with the argument that women were supported by their husbands, yet lower wages also kept women dependent upon a male primary wage-earner.[89] Marx and Engels argued that in a capitalist system women could only create a political space outside of the domestic sphere by engaging in wage labour. Economic equity would have to come before political equality.[90]

The intervention of Marx and Engels definitively transformed socialist discussions of gender relations. In 1891, the German socialist August Bebel revised his previously published book *Woman and Socialism* to reflect Engels's arguments. Bebel argued for women's rights to vote, to own property, to dress comfortably and to achieve personal sexual satisfaction. Bebel in turn inspired a generation of socialist feminists in Germany, the most prominent of whom – Clara Zetkin (1857–1933) – went on to become a founder of the German Communist Party in 1918 and a delegate to the German parliament in 1920. Marxism also inspired feminists in France, such as Hubertine Auclert (1848–1914) and Madeleine Pelletier (1874–1939), and in Russia, particularly Aleksandra Kollontai (1873–1952), who in 1917 was appointed Commissar for Social Welfare in the Soviet government.

All over Europe, socialist feminists grappled with the problem of how to achieve both sexual equality and a proletarian revolution. No dilemma better demonstrates how gendered oppression was intertwined with and often inseparable from class oppression in the era of industrialization.[91] Having aligned themselves with the socialist movement,

---

[87] Jonathan Sperber, *Karl Marx: A Nineteenth-Century Life* (New York: Liveright Pub. Corp., 2013), xiii.

[88] Friedrich Engels, *The Origin of the Family*, excerpted in Bell and Offen, *Women, the Family and Freedom*, 81.

[89] Marx and Engels's argument is summarized in Sowerwine, 'Socialism, Feminism, and the Socialist Women's Movement', 366.

[90] Quoted in Ibid.

[91] Biographies of key socialist feminists and historical accounts of their movements testify to the difficulty of balancing these two convictions. See Alfred G. Meyer, *The Feminism and Socialism of Lily Braun* (Bloomington: Indiana University Press, 1985); Taylor, *Eve and the New Jerusalem*; Jean H. Quataert, 'Unequal Partners in an Uneasy Alliance: Women and the Working Class in Imperial Germany', in *Socialist Women: European Socialist Feminism in Nineteenth and Early Twentieth Century Europe*, ed. Marilyn Boxer and Jean Quataert (New York: Elsevier, 1978); Karen Honeycutt, 'Clara Zetkin a Socialist Approach to the Problem of Women's Oppression', *Signs* 3, no. 3/4 (1976): 131–44; Charles Sowerwine, *Sisters or Citizens?: Women and Socialism in France Since 1876* (Cambridge and New York: Cambridge University Press, 1982).

feminists adopted an identity – that of the worker – whose imagery ran counter to the dominant imagery of womanhood, which continued to be linked to motherhood in all European societies. Despite the fact that women had worked as wage labourers since the very beginning of industrialization, they were always marginal to the symbolic language of workers' movements. In fact, women's involvement in socialist movements often provided rhetorical fuel to conservatives, who took it as a sign of danger and decadence. 'L'Ouvrière [female worker]!', French historian Jules Michelet (1798–1874) sputtered, 'impious, sordid word that no language has ever known, that no age ever understood before this age of iron, and that holds in the balance all our supposed progress!'[92] In cases where groups of female workers did manage to assert a specific public identity, they had to operate within the framework of existing cultural stereotypes and were rarely granted a public voice to assert identities of their own making. For instance, when 5,000 female tobacco workers created a media sensation by rioting in Seville in 1896, their communications with journalists were coloured by the image of the strong-willed yet intensely feminine *cigarrera* (female tobacco worker) made famous by Georges Bizet's opera *Carmen* (1875). Journalists, in other words, relied on stereotypes of fiery country girls and tended not to take women seriously as political actors.[93]

The imagery of the worker as male became even more ubiquitous as socialist movements gained momentum across Europe, and particularly after the Russian Revolution in 1917. Communism became closely identified with masculine strength; both the armed soldier and the muscular worker provided the iconic symbols of a movement that hoped to bring about world revolution.[94] Socialist feminists like Clara Zetkin in Germany did hope that socialism would bring about equal rights for women when she argued that 'the liberation struggle of the proletarian woman … must be a joint struggle with the male of her class against the entire class of capitalists'.[95] But the strength of masculine imagery in communist propaganda greatly complicated efforts to rhetorically link the struggle of the worker with the struggle for women's rights. In practice, feminist priorities generally took a back seat to socialist priorities, and socialist feminists were influenced and constrained by the common argument that socialist revolution had to precede the granting of equal rights to the sexes. Socialist

[92] Quoted in Judith F. Stone, 'Republican Ideology, Gender and Class: France, 1860s–1914', in *Gender and Class in Modern Europe*, ed. Laura L. Frader and Sonya O. Rose (Ithaca, NY and London: Cornell University Press, 1996), 239.

[93] D. J. O'Conner, 'Representations of Women Workers: Tobacco Strikers in the 1890s', in *Constructing Spanish Womanhood: Female Identity in Modern Spain*, ed. Victoria Lorée Enders and Pamela Beth Radcliff (Albany, NY: State University of New York Press, 1999), 151–72.

[94] Eric D. Weitz, 'The Heroic Man and the Ever-Changing Woman: Gender and Politics in European Communism, 1917–1950', in, *Gender and Class in Modern Europe*, ed. Laura L. Frader and Sonya O. Rose (Ithaca, NY and London: Cornell University Press, 1996), 313.

[95] From a speech given to the Party Congress of the Social Democratic Party of Germany, 16 October 1896. Clara Zetkin, 'Only in Conjunction with the Proletarian Woman Will Socialism Be Victorious', in *Clara Zetkin Selected Writings*, ed. Philip Foner, trans. Kai Schoenhals (New York: International Publishers, 1984), available at https://www.marxists.org/archive/zetkin/1896/10/women.htm (accessed 10 July 2015).

feminists who campaigned too single-mindedly for women's rights were often accused by their ideological brethren of being counterproductive or even of seeking to delay the proletarian revolution.

Liberal feminists – in other words those whose arguments were based on the belief in the rights of the individual, a democratic voting system and the rule of law – had an easier time reconciling their politics with their feminism. Despite the failures of the revolutionary era to instil the conviction that 'human rights' also implied 'women's rights', liberals who sought the improvement of women's political position in European society could appeal directly to the most basic tenets of liberal belief. The most influential liberal to do so was John Stuart Mill (1806–73). In close cooperation with his wife, Harriet Taylor Mill (1807–58), Mill built on the liberal theories outlined in *Principles of Political Economy* (1848) and *On Liberty* (1859) to advocate the inclusion of women in the liberal definition of rights. Mill (a member of parliament) brought petitions in favour of women's suffrage before the British House of Commons, though they were voted down in 1867. In 1869, Mill wrote his *On the Subjection of Women*, in which he argued that many of society's social problems could be traced back to the unequal treatment of men and women.[96] The essay was immediately translated into many languages (including Danish, Polish, French and Spanish) and helped to inspire liberal feminists across Europe. But most nineteenth-century (and many twentieth-century) liberals continued to believe that the right to participate in politics should be tied to the right to own property. Since European women rarely owned property or were legally excluded from the right to do so, liberal arguments about equal rights also came up against economic and social realities. It was not only the working classes, in other words, whose gender relations were structured by economic change and industrialization.

## Separation of spheres

We have already taken note of the separation of home and working lives among the working classes of industrializing Europe. This separation was perhaps even more pronounced among the middle classes – the property owners, civil servants, professionals and managers of the new capitalist economy. As these classes benefited from their role in driving industrialization and urbanization, their homes ceased being sites of production (such as the making of clothes, which could now be bought) and became places of relaxation and contemplation. Improvements in public transportation also made it possible for the wealthy to remove themselves from increasingly crowded and filthy industrial cities and to build comfortable homes on the outskirts of town.

This separation of work and home reinforced and was made possible by class distinctions. Middle- and upper-class families relied on domestic servants to perform

---

[96] For an excellent critical edition of Mill's key texts, including *On Liberty* and *On the Subjection of Women*, see John Stuart Mill, *Mill: Texts, Commentaries*, ed. Alan Ryan (New York: W. W. Norton, 1997).

any dirty, demeaning or laborious domestic chores. The 'unhygienic' homes of the lower classes were looked down upon, which intensified class prejudice. Cleanliness was thus a marker of middle-class values and the lack of it an 'obstacle to equality and improvement'.[97] The homes of the wealthy (and those striving to improve their social standing) were thus consciously organized to contrast with lower-class mayhem and mess. Houses were divided into 'living' areas for the primary inhabitants and 'domestic' areas for the servants. Doors and individual bedrooms, a luxury previously only enjoyed by the aristocracy, became a standard feature of bourgeois homes in the nineteenth century, thus vastly increasing individual privacy and the ability to withdraw in solitude.[98] The middle classes treated bodily functions of any kind as vulgar and unmentionable, and they used their class prerogatives and economic power to pass these nasty tasks to the lower classes whenever possible. Even nursing one's own baby was considered a job better suited to a lower-class wet nurse. The term 'back passages' came to refer both to the halls and doorways used only by servants in the mansions of the rich and to 'unmentionable' parts of the anatomy associated with waste.[99]

For some, the association between servants and bodily functions provided titillation. Middle-class men often sought out lower-class women for casual sexual liaisons. Lingering memories of physical warmth from lower-class nannies and nursemaids explain part of the attraction. Sigmund Freud was certainly not alone in remembering that his first sexual feelings had been for his nursemaid. But, as Leonore Davidoff has persuasively argued in her account of the relationship between Arthur J. Munby (a minor poet, writer and civil servant, who was supported mostly by his wealthy family) and Hannah Cullwick (a scullery maid), crossing the class boundary provided a thrill in itself.[100] Munby spent most of his time between 1859 and 1898 studying the lives of women who toiled at the most physically demanding forms of labour (in homes, mines and factories). He sketched them, took dozens of pictures of them and recorded his thoughts about their lives in his diaries. He eventually married Cullwick, with whom he had had a decades-long secret affair. Davidoff argues that the fact that he was completely uninterested in women of his own class and instead equated 'dirt and degradation with female strength and love' reveals a fundamental contradiction of Victorian society. 'The sheltered lives that middle-class ladies were supposed to lead depended directly on the labor of working-class girls and women, who through their service created the material conditions necessary to maintain a middle-class life-style for men and women alike.'[101]

---

[97] Jonas Fryman and Orvar Löfgren, *Culture Builders: A Historical Anthropology of Middle-Class Life* (New Brunswick, NJ: Rutgers University Press, 1987), 175. Fryman and Löfgren concentrate on conditions in Sweden, but their arguments hold true for other areas of Europe.

[98] Ibid., 127.

[99] Leonore Davidoff, 'Class and Gender in Victorian England: The Diaries of Arthur J. Munby and Hannah Cullwick', *Feminist Studies* 5, no. 1 (1979): 130.

[100] Ibid., esp. 130.

[101] Ibid., 130.

Middle-class women, unlike working-class women, could generally afford to stay out of the paid labour force. Indeed, having a 'woman of leisure' at home was one of the most important defining features of middle-class status.[102] In late nineteenth-century Germany, families scrambling their way up the social ladder (or those fearing that they were falling down it) often scrimped on groceries to avoid having to give up their domestic servant. Even with this domestic help, the woman was expected to spend the majority of her time caring for her family within the home. Images of the 'angel of the house' who protected the safe haven of the home from the harshness of the outside world proliferated in the novels, advice manuals and political rhetoric of late nineteenth-century Europe.[103] An 1877 Spanish pedagogical pamphlet defined the woman's role as being 'an angel of love, consolation to our afflictions, defender of our merits, patient sufferer of our faults, faithful guardian of our secrets, and jealous depository of our honor'.[104] An 1889 Swedish housekeeping manual preached a similar ideology to its readers when it observed that

> A man who spends his day away from the family, who has to work outside the home, counts on finding a restful and refreshing atmosphere when he returns home, and sometimes even a little merriment and surprise. A good man who ... provides for his family ... has the right to expect this, and it is his wife's duty to ensure that he is not disappointed in his expectation ... [S]he can thus continue to keep her influence over him and retain his affection undiminished.[105]

This 'domestic ideology' was part of a conscious effort to set middle-class values apart from both working-class mores and the 'immoral' values of the aristocracy. While the argument that women were predestined for domestic duties was certainly not new (Aristotle had argued that 'A good wife should be the mistress of her home' and had insisted that her only goal should be 'to obey her husband; giving no heed to public affairs'), the ideology of separate spheres was a particularly forceful organizing concept in the lives of middle-class families in the nineteenth century.[106] Domestic ideology drew on Enlightenment thinkers like Rousseau and was further reinforced by critics like John Ruskin. Ruskin insisted that men and women were entirely different, though infinitely

---

[102] Bonnie G. Smith, *Ladies of the Leisure Class: The Bourgeoises of Northern France in the Nineteenth Century* (Princeton: Princeton University Press, 1981).

[103] Catherine Hall, 'The Early Formation of Victorian Domestic Ideology', in *Gender and History in Western Europe*, ed. Robert Shoemaker and Mary Vincent (New York and London: Arnold, 1998), 181.

[104] Quoted in Mary Nash, 'Un/Contested Identities: Motherhood, Sex Reform and the Modernization of Gender Identity in Early Twentieth-Century Spain', in *Constructing Spanish Womanhood: Female Identity in Modern Spain*, ed. Victoria Lorée Enders and Pamela Beth Radcliff (Albany: State University of New York Press, 1999), 28.

[105] Quoted in Fryman and Löfgren, *Culture Builders*, 134.

[106] Amanda Vickery, 'Golden Age to Separate Spheres? A Review of the Categories and Chronology of English Women's History', in *Gender and History in Western Europe*, ed. Robert Shoemaker and Mary Vincent (New York and London: Arnold, 1998), 197. The quotation is from Aristotle, *The Politics & Economics of Aristotle*, trans. Edward English Walford and John Gillies (London: G. Bell & Sons, 1908). It is also available online at Paul Halsall's *Ancient History Sourcebook*, 'Aristotle: On a Good Wife, from Oikonomikos, c. 330 BCE', available at http://legacy.fordham.edu/halsall/ancient/greek-wives.asp (accessed 10 July 2015).

compatible: 'Each has what the other has not: each completes the other, and is completed by the other: they are nothing alike, and the happiness and perfection of both depends on each asking and receiving from the other what the other only can give.'[107]

Women were also responsible for navigating the increasingly complex selection of consumer goods, selecting clothing and home decorations that would best signal the bourgeois status of the family.[108] In large metropolitan centres, this often meant navigating the new consumer world of large department stores. Rather than relying upon the sage advice of trusted local merchants, it became fashionable in the late nineteenth and early twentieth century to frequent new shopping meccas like the Le Bon Marché in Paris, Selfridge's in London or Kaufhof des Westens (Department Store of the West, or KaDeWe) in Berlin. Department stores prompted new forms of advertising, new promotional models (including exotic displays and widely advertised seasonal sales) and new employer/employee relationships, which sometimes included live-in arrangements and uniforms for a new sales force of primarily lower-class women. As Émile Zola's 1883 novel *Au Bonheur des Dames* (translated as *The Ladies' Delight* or *The Ladies' Paradise*) so vividly depicts, this model of consumerism had a dramatic impact on traditional models of shopping and on the small family-owned businesses that department stores often forced out of business.[109]

Zola's novel tracks the story of Denise Baudu, who is forced by her parents' death to leave her small village and seek employment in her uncle's small shop in Paris to support herself and her two younger brothers. Having not received a warm welcome from her uncle Baudu, whose business is struggling in face of the competition from the glitzy new department stores, Denise seeks employment at The Ladies' Paradise. Although she suffers many indignities there and falls into destitution after being fired for taking in outside work, she is later reinstated, and Zola closes his novel with an uncharacteristically happy ending: Denise's marriage to the owner of The Ladies' Paradise, Octave Mouret. More interesting than the plot (which does not reflect Zola's otherwise superb story-telling talent) is the characterization of the massive social transformation that the department stores represented. Having replaced the patriarchal figure of the independent shop owner with a hierarchical (and no less patriarchal) structure of a massive business operation, the department store itself is really the main character of this novel. It represents a new gendering of consumption and an attempt to overwhelm the senses in a way directly targeted at female sensibilities. Zola expertly describes the artificially generated excitement of the seasonal sales, and he plays close attention to the exploitation of the salesgirls, who are desperate to support themselves but also eager to become part of a

---

[107] John Ruskin, *Sesame and Lilies*, ed. Deborah Epstein Nord (New Haven, CT: Yale University Press, 2002 [1865]), 77.

[108] Auslander, *Taste and Power*, 145.

[109] For a recent translation, see Émile Zola, *The Ladies' Paradise*, trans. Brian Nelson (Berkeley: University of California Press, 1992). An early translation by Ernest Alfred Vizetelly is available at Project Gutenberg, available at http://gutenberg.net.au/ebooks14/1400561h.html (accessed 24 July 2015). Zola's novel was the inspiration for a 2012 miniseries called *The Paradise* that was produced by BBC Worldwide America and Masterpiece Theatre. Demonstrating the pan-European relevance of the story, the series relocates the action to a department store in north-east England.

more fashionable world. Their world stands in stark contrast with the business-minded decisions of their employers, be they small shop keepers or the prosperous department owners, who are keen to devise entirely new ways of selling goods to customers who are primarily female. It is impossible to read this novel without gaining an appreciation of how new business models and methods of marketing reinforced a binary view of gender difference while disrupting certain traditional structures of class and family control.

The insistence upon a separation of male and female spheres was reinforced by the growth of new forms of Christianity across Europe. Evangelical movements in Great Britain, pietism in Germany and a revival of Catholicism in France reinforced a strict code of moral values within the middle classes and sought to instil a self-reflective moral code into everyday behaviour. Groups like the Clapham sect (a group that wanted to reform the Church of England from within) sought to encourage a new national morality through pamphlets, sermons, manuals and travelling preachers. Influential preachers of this message, like William Wilberforce and Hannah More, insisted that God's will could only be carried out by Christians who subjected themselves to constant self-criticism and who interpreted the political and social questions of the day in moral, Christian terms. Sin, they argued, was a grave threat to the family that could only be combated if women stood steadfast as the protectors of the private sphere.[110] Hannah More directly countered Mary Wollstonecraft's idea that education would elevate women so that they could demonstrate that they deserved legal and political equality with men. For evangelicals, the 'natural' division between the sexes was a rule of nature that had to be reinforced rather than undermined if the family was to survive the social changes of industrialization. While followers of such beliefs remained in the minority, their influence cannot be underestimated. By the 1830s and 1840s, the language of these evangelical preachers had begun to colour government reports and made it easier for middle-class commentators to preach a mode of living that only the wealthy could attain.[111]

Separate spheres ideology affected not only European working practices and religious sensibilities, but the practice of politics as well. As political life expanded in the wake of democratic revolutions, theorists and politicians alike began to see the 'public sphere' or what Jürgen Habermas has defined as the space 'made up of private people gathered together as a public and articulating the needs of society with the state' as a central political arena in which political opinions could be formulated and political progress achieved.[112] European women's exclusion from clubs and associations that were the venues of social discussion and places of debate limited their abilities to influence the shape of politics and society even after they had achieved the right to vote over the course of the twentieth century.[113] And they

---

[110] Hall, 'The Early Formation of Victorian Domestic Ideology', 183.

[111] Ibid., 195.

[112] Jürgen Habermas, *The Structural Transformation of the Public Sphere: An Inquiry into a Category of Bourgeois Society* (Cambridge: MIT Press, 1991 [1989]), 176.

[113] On the gendering of public spaces and the division between male/public and female/domestic identities see Leonore Davidoff and Catherine Hall, *Family Fortunes: Men and Women of the English Middle Class, 1780–1850* (Chicago: University of Chicago Press, 1987), esp. 13, 211, 229 and 409.

were not the only ones excluded. Even John Stuart Mill believed that anyone too poor to pay taxes could not be trusted to act in rational ways and should thus be denied the vote.[114] Working-class men thus fought to carve out their own public forms of communication by engaging in riots, marches and festivals that masqueraded as private ritual while in fact carrying political messages of protest against their employers and the political system. Workers' organizations across Europe were acutely aware that the impression of the poor as being solely guided by bodily needs and thus trapped in the private sphere had to be counteracted if their political goals were to be achieved. Swedish workers' organizers, for example, explicitly educated their members about the dangers of seeing themselves only as 'work-animals' and harshly punished them for disorderly conduct in public that might damage the image of the worker as a rational public actor.[115] The dramatic rise of unions across the continent in the nineteenth century has to be understood in part as a reaction to the idea that only the propertied heads of households could be truly independent and influence political life. The idea of separate spheres, in other words, could also be quite oppressive for many men.

But we must point out that domestic ideology, like any ideology, had its cracks and could never entirely describe or control lived reality. The vision of the home as a haven hid the fact that for many it was the site of abuse, mistrust and unhappiness.[116] 'The sweetness of home depended upon the drudgery of numerous servants',[117] and when budgets did not allow for them, middle-class wives and daughters toiled to live up to the exacting standards of bourgeois etiquette and decorum. Along with these servants, many women and men chose not to marry or were prevented from doing so for financial or other reasons; they spent their days without the lived experience, though still under the social influence, of domestic ideology. Some percentage of men and women who never married were more interested in pursuing same-sex liaisons.[118]

---

[114] John Stuart Mill, 'Representative Government', in ed. G.Williams *Utilitarianism; On Liberty; Considerations on Representative Government; Remarks on Bentham's Philosophy* (London: Everyman Paperback Classics), 291, 303–5, 308–9, cited in Madeleine Hurd, 'Class, Masculinity, Manners, and Mores: Public Space and Public Sphere in Nineteenth-Century Europe', *Social Science History* 24, no. 1 (2000): 78.

[115] Ibid., 80–5.

[116] Statistics on this are notoriously difficult to come by, but it is instructive that incest did not come to be thought of as a form of child abuse in England until the late 1880s. After a Royal Commission study in 1906 found that incest between men and young girls in their family was common, the Punishment of Incest Act was passed in 1908. See Adam Kuper, 'Incest, Cousin Marriage, and the Origin of the Human Sciences in Nineteenth-Century England', *Past & Present* 174 (2002): 159–83, esp. 180–1.

[117] Fryman and Löfgren, *Culture Builders*, 127.

[118] There is considerable debate about the extent of same-sex sexual activity. Lillian Faderman prefers to document 'romantic friendship' between women without exploring in detail whether these friendships involved sexual contact or not. See Lillian Faderman, *Surpassing the Love of Men: Romantic Friendship and Love between Women from the Renaissance to the Present* (New York: William Morrow and Company, Inc., 1981). Others, such as George Chauncey Jr. in *Gay New York: Gender, Urban Culture, and the Making of the Gay Male World, 1890–1940* (New York: Basic Books, 1994), 12–13, insist that self-definition is crucial. For an overview of the debate, see Martin Bauml Duberman, 'Reclaiming the Gay Past', *Reviews in American History* 16, no. 4 (1988): 515–25. Unmarried celibacy was, however, also common, particularly in regions with high emigration, such as Ireland. See Timothy Guinnane, 'Coming of Age in Rural Ireland at the Turn of the Twentieth Century', *Continuity and Change* 5, no. 3 (1990): 443–72.

The formal prescription of separation did not mean that female oppression was universal or that all men were disinterested in the family. While formally excluded from political life, some women had access to the public sphere through their activities as writers, charity organizers and – particularly in Britain – Methodist preachers and Anglican deaconesses.[119] Women often used domestic ideology and the bonds that they had formed with other women to buttress their case for the importance of female influence both within the home and outside of it. As Linda Kerber argues for the American case, historians have been unconsciously lured by Marxist analysis into assuming a much clearer break between family and work life than was always the case.[120] Individual historical studies have also demonstrated that many men were intimately involved in the day-to-day affairs of the family and played a larger role in the rearing of their children than the term 'separation of spheres' implies.[121]

As we have seen in our discussion of working life in Eastern Europe, the model of wage labour in factories far from home was also far from universal across the continent. Even in industrialized cities like Hamburg and Leipzig, factory owners built housing complexes right next to the job site.[122] But perhaps the most misleading aspect of the 'separation of spheres' as a description of gender norms in the nineteenth century is that it obscures the reality that male power rested upon a definition of masculinity as essentially whole. As Martina Kessel persuasively argues, prescriptive literature targeting middle-class Germans from the eighteenth century onwards relied on an essential paradox of the modern gender order. While the 'polarised gender hierarchy' that depicted men as essentially rational and women as essentially emotional pervaded all discussions of gender difference, it 'dovetailed' with an insistence upon male wholeness – on the image of a 'man, who was not only educated but also passionate and sensitive, who lived out his sexuality within the orderly context of the family, and drew his strength for morally correct behaviour from the balance between mind, heart and body.'[123] A closer

---

[119] See Robert B. Shoemaker's balanced conclusions on the usefulness of 'separate spheres' in *Gender in English Society, 1650-1850: The Emergence of Separate Spheres* (London and New York: Longman, 1998), esp. 305-18. On female preachers, see Susie Steinbach, *Women in England, 1760-1914: A Social History* (New York: Palgrave Macmillan, 2004), 154-8; and Deborah Valenze, *Prophetic Sons and Daughters: Female Preaching and Popular Religion in Industrial England* (Princeton: Princeton University Press, 1985).

[120] For an overview, see Linda K. Kerber, 'Separate Spheres, Female Worlds, Woman's Place: The Rhetoric of Women's History', in *Toward an Intellectual History of Women: Essays by Linda K. Kerber* (Chapel Hill: University of North Carolina Press, 2002), 159–199 esp. 164–5.

[121] See for example John Tosh's extended investigation of the family of Edward Benson, a teacher at Rugby School and Wellington College in the mid-nineteenth century. John Tosh, 'Domesticity and Manliness in the Victorian Middle Class: The Family of Edward White Benson', in *Manful Assertions: Masculinities in Britain since 1800*, ed. Michael Roper and John Tosh (London and New York: Routledge, 1991), 44–77.

[122] Robert Beachy, 'Business Was a Family Affair: Women of Commerce in Central Europe, 1650–1880', *Histoire Sociale/Social History* 34, no. 68 (2001): 313.

[123] Kessel, 'The "Whole Man"', 6.

reading of things like advice literature and the publications of student organizations has led historians to argue that gender roles were not quite as polarized as 'separate spheres' ideology might presume.[124] While male self-definition certainly rested on the exclusion of the feminine, the image of enlightened humanity forged through several phases of revolutionary movements also encouraged the integration of stereotypically feminine qualities into male behaviour. This helps to explain the rise of Masonic lodges and other male-only clubs in this period: They provided a space where men could act out their emotions and personal ties with other men in spaces that were safe from both the competitive pressures of the public world and the dangers of comparison to women.[125] The possibilities for homosocial emotional fulfilment only grew with the increasing vibrancy of social life in European cities.

## Urbanization, sexual danger and the creation of sexual identities

The late nineteenth and early twentieth centuries witnessed the transformation of many towns into cities and many cities into full-scale metropolitan areas. In 1800, London was the only city in Europe close to a population of one million. By 1900, five more cities gained the status of metropolis: Paris, Vienna, Berlin, Moscow and St Petersburg. Whereas only twenty-two European cities had populations of more than 100,000 before 1800, by 1900 there were eighty cities with populations over 100,000.[126]

Industrialization and urbanization provided Europeans with unprecedented possibilities for social and physical mobility. By 1902, London, Budapest, Glasgow, Paris and Berlin all had systems of rapid transportation with some underground railway lines. Also by the turn of the century, advances in metallurgy had helped make possible the mass production of bicycles, which provided women in particular with a socially acceptable means of transporting themselves unchaperoned across urban and rural spaces.[127] The spectacle of women racing across towns on mechanized vehicles wearing modified and 'masculine' clothing greatly worried conservative observers. Doctors and hygienists in France and elsewhere launched campaigns to try to restrict women's access to cycling on the grounds of protecting their reproductive health and social propriety.[128]

---

[124] Karin Breuer, 'Competing Masculinities: Fraternities, Gender and Nationality in the German Confederation, 1815–30', *Gender & History* 20, no. 2 (1 August 2008): 270–87, esp. 271; and Anne-Charlott Trepp, *Sanfte Männlichkeit und selbständige Weiblichkeit* (Göttingen: Vandenhoeck & Ruprecht, 1996).

[125] Ibid., 17; and Stefan-Ludwig Hoffmann, 'Civility, Male Friendship, and Masonic Sociability in Nineteenth-Century Germany', *Gender & History* 13, no. 2 (2001): 224–48; see also Amy Milne-Smith, *London Clubland: A Cultural History of Gender and Class in Late-Victorian Britain* (Basingstoke: Palgrave MacMillan, 2011).

[126] Robin W. Winks and R. J. Q. Adams, *Europe, 1890–1945: Crisis and Conflict* (New York: Oxford University Press, 2003), 2.

[127] Bicycle riding for women was controversial. See Patricia Vertinsky, *The Eternally Wounded Woman: Women, Exercise and Doctors in the Late Nineteenth Century* (Manchester: Manchester University Press, 1990), 76–83.

[128] Christopher Thompson, 'Un Troisième sexe? Les bourgeoises et la bicyclette dans la France fin de siècle', *Mouvement Social* 192, no. 3 (2000): 9–39.

But bicycles (and women on them) became an accepted feature of modern cities, and, along with the growth of bus and street-car systems, they allowed everyone to move across urban spaces much more quickly and relatively anonymously.

Cities provided an escape from the constraints of kinship networks and tight-knit communities that had carefully regulated sexual behaviour and courtship rituals. People with similar interests and sensibilities could more easily gather in spaces outside of the control of disapproving family members and other upholders of traditional norms. In cities like London and Berlin, networks of 'inverts', 'Uranians' and 'mannish' women were established. As we will see in Chapter 5, early debates about what to call these individuals involved discussions between self-identified homosexuals (who often called themselves 'inverts') and scientists and doctors interested in categorizing them. On both sides of this discussion most of the participants were initially male.[129] It was only in the 1920s and only in the largest urban centres that women identifying themselves as inverts started writing, producing art and dressing in recognizable styles – a form of identity creation that Laura Doan has called sapphic modernism. Before this, women who were attracted to other women were unlikely to categorize themselves in any particular way, though they might have thought of themselves as rather masculine women.[130] Because women were excluded from the rights of citizenship in nineteenth-century Europe, and because most legal codes only explicitly prohibited sex between men, lesbianism was often an afterthought even for those who were actively campaigning for homosexual rights. The German lawyer and activist Karl Heinrich Ulrichs, for instance, began focusing his attention on repealing laws against male same-sex acts in the 1860s. It was Ulrichs who had coined the word 'inversion', and he believed that homosexual men had 'a female soul confined in a male body'. While he theoretically acknowledged that the reverse was possible for women, he focused his attention primarily upon the fight to obtain legal protections for male citizens in the era of German unification, and he rarely commented on the condition or identities of lesbians.[131] This tendency to marginalize lesbians in discourses about homosexuality was by no means unusual, and it explains why male networks had far more influence upon both public perceptions and scientific definitions of homosexuality.

---

[129] Lucy Bland, *Banishing the Beast: English Feminism and Sexual Morality, 1885–1914* (London: Penquin, 1995), 257.

[130] Laura Doan, *Fashioning Sapphism: The Origins of a Modern Lesbian Culture* (New York: Columbia University Press, 2000).

[131] Heike Bauer, 'Theorizing Female Inversion: Sexology, Discipline, and Gender at the Fin de Siècle', *Journal of the History of Sexuality* 18, no. 1 (2009): 86 and 90. Quotation is from: Karl Heinrich Ulrichs, *Prometheus* (Leipzig: Gerbe'sche Verlagsbuchhandlung, 1870), 19. For a description of Ulrichs's legal campaign, see Karl Heinrich Ulrichs, 'The Urning and His Rights', in *Sodomites and Urnings: Homosexual Representations in Classic German Journals*, ed. Michael A. Lombardi-Nash (Binghamton, NY: Harrington Park Press, 2006), 21–24.

Stories about these early movements became visible thanks to the labours of scholars inspired by the lesbian and gay rights movements of the 1970s and 1980s.[132] In the early days of this research it was common to search for traces of 'authentic' sexualities of the past that had been repressed by political policy and social taboo and suppressed by traditional histories that relegated these stories to the margins or discussed them only in terms of perversity. But viewing the past as providing 'legitimating antecedents to the present' has its pitfalls, as Ludmilla Jordanova has convincingly pointed out.[133] It assumes, for one thing, that our current definitions of sexual identity are somehow stable and enduring, a belief that even the most cursory glance at the sexual identity politics of the present would quickly dispel. While it is undeniably true that cities provided space for alternative sexual expression that was simply not possible in claustrophobic villages, it would be misleading to presume that what we are finding are 'authentic' sexualities, released from their closets. A closer look at these sexual subcultures reveals that gay and lesbian identities were created in a symbiotic relationship with the larger culture. These subcultures and the very identity of being 'homosexual' or 'lesbian' (modern words for a vast array of historical terms which modern readers would no longer recognize) surfaced at different times across Europe. Randolph Trumbach has argued that identifiable homosexual subcultures arose in the larger European cities (Paris, Amsterdam and London) around 1700.[134] But other historians have pointed out that the existence of a community of men who wanted to have sex with other men is not identical to the existence of a particular sexual identity, whether we call it homosexual, as was common in the twentieth century, or gay or queer, as is more common today. The idea that one is either innately and unchangeably homosexual or heterosexual seems to have solidified in Europe and North America only in the late nineteenth and early twentieth centuries,[135] and it has been challenged many times since. Although many forces coincided to produce the idea of the homosexual, urbanization certainly played an important role. As Jens Ryström points out for the Swedish case, in rural areas of Europe, same-sex activity was still viewed primarily through the lens of the sin of sodomy – a crime that was associated with the act of penetration and thus included

---

[132] Martin Duberman, Martha Vicinus and George Chauncey Jr., eds, *Hidden from History: Reclaiming the Gay and Lesbian Past* (New York: Meridian, 1989); Matt Houlbrook, 'Toward a Historical Geography of Sexuality', *Journal of Urban History* 27, no. 4 (1 May 2001): 497–504.

[133] Ludmilla Jordanova, *Sexual Visions: Images of Gender in Science and Medicine between the Eighteenth and Twentieth Centuries* (Madison: University of Wisconsin Press, 1989), 11.

[134] See Randolph Trumbach, 'The Birth of the Queen: Sodomy and the Emergence of Gender Equality in Modern Culture 1660–1750', in Duberman, *Hidden from History*, 129–40. Before 1700, Trumbach argues, men who had sex with other men did not risk their reputations as masculine as long as they were the penetrative partner in the sexual act and as long as they also married and had children with a woman. More recently, Trumbach has asserted that 'no one at the present moment has any satisfactory explanation as to why this transformation occurred.' See Randolph Trumbach, 'Modern Sodomy: The Origins of Homosexuality, 1700–1800', in *A Gay History of Britain: Love and Sex Between Men Since the Middle Ages*, ed. Matt Cook et al. (Oxford and Westport, Conn: Praeger, 2007), 77–106, quote on 78.

[135] George Chauncey, *Gay New York*, 12–13. See also Véronique Mottier, *Sexuality: A Very Short Introduction* (Oxford and New York: Oxford University Press, 2008), 37.

bestiality. (Referring to the pre-modern period, Katherine Crawford has argued that sodomy 'meant masturbation, several forms of same-sex sexual behaviour, bestiality, non-procreative sex (oral or anal most commonly) between a man and a woman, or any form of sex in which conception was impossible'.)[136] As European nations industrialized, 'this paradigm rapidly gave way to a modern, urban homosexuality paradigm, which concentrated on the homo/hetero dichotomy' and which now pulled lesbianism into its purview.[137] At different times in different parts of Europe, homosexuality came to be thought of less as an act (of penetration) and more as an identity. Nevertheless, even after middle-class inverts started thinking of themselves as homosexuals, many working-class men were still viewing their sexual activities with other men in a more pragmatic way.

Jeffrey Weeks's exploration of male homosexual prostitution in late nineteenth-century Britain demonstrates that homosexual identities did not inevitably emerge from homosexual behaviours in this period. As early as the 1720s, a homosexual subculture was developing in Britain's larger cities that centred around 'Molly houses', pubs, public parks and lavatories. These centres of sexual exchange were known as 'markets'. All classes came together in these spaces, and the 'cash nexus' dominated – in other words, sex took place after an exchange or a promise of money or 'gifts'. By the last decades of the nineteenth century, the word 'trade' was in common use to describe any male homosexual act, whether or not a cash exchange took place.[138] The upper-class participants in this subculture, most of whom led 'respectable' family lives and sought out the markets in secret, were often searching for the thrill of crossing the class divide by having sex with lower-class men. Neither they nor the 'rough trade' recipients of their gifts, however, considered themselves to be homosexuals and often both were likely to understand prostitution as a form of entertainment and an expedient means of survival. While men certainly went to molly houses for sex, they also enjoyed various forms of sexually adventurous entertainment, including drag balls there.[139] Thus what we would today call a homosexual subculture actually depended upon and was nurtured by the economic inequalities produced by the industrializing city.

The most famous example of how this kind of cross-class relationship could lead to ruin was the case of the playwright Oscar Wilde. Wilde pushed the boundaries of public decorum, subtly (and later openly) calling attention to his sexual predilections. In 1892, he and several associates wore green carnations to the opening of his play, *Lady Windermere's Fan*. He insisted that this was simply a symbol of 'subtle artistic temperament', but others noted that the wearers of the green carnation all had the same

---

[136] Katherine Crawford, *The Sexual Culture of the French Renaissance* (Cambridge University Press, 2010), 4.
[137] Ryström is referring to Sweden, which urbanized in the early twentieth century, but his model applies well to other European areas during an earlier time period. Jens Rydström, 'From Sodomy to Homosexuality: Rural Sex and the Inclusion of Lesbians in Criminal Discourse', *NORA – Nordic Journal of Feminist and Gender Research* 13, no. 1 (2005): 31. On the impact of urbanization on homosexual identities, see also various contributions in Robert Aldrich, ed., *Gay Life & Culture: A World History* (New York, NY: Universe, 2006).
[138] Jeffrey Weeks, 'Inverts, Perverts, and Mary-Annes: Male Prostitution and the Regulation of Homosexuality in England in the Nineteenth and Early Twentieth Centuries', in Duberman, *Hidden From History*, 202.
[139] Cross-dressing in molly houses had long been coming. See Alan Bray, *Homosexuality in Renaissance England*, 2nd edn. (New York: Columbia University Press, 1996).

'waggle' – an affectation that had come to be taken as an emblem of homosexuality.[140] In 1895, Wilde took the Marquess of Queensbury (the father of his lover Lord Alfred Douglas) to court on libel charges for having called him a 'Somdomite' (*sic*). At the trial in April, the defence named several boys whom Wilde had solicited, and Wilde's case collapsed. Soon after, he was arrested for gross indecency under Section 11 of the Criminal Law Amendment Act of 1885. Two criminal trials eventually led to Wilde's conviction. He died of meningitis in November 1900, having sustained an ear infection while serving a two-year prison sentence. Wilde's fame, and even his witty rejoinders at his trials, guaranteed a new appreciation of the presence of homosexual subcultures in Europe. Having made use of the new public spaces and opportunities for sexual adventure that the modern metropolis afforded, Wilde was undone by the glaring light that this new public sphere shed upon private behaviours.

Far less visible were individuals who believed that they had been born into the wrong body – people we would today call transsexuals. As we saw with the story of the Chevalier d'Eon, this was not an entirely new phenomenon. What was new is that doctors were beginning to take individuals' own gendered self-perceptions seriously as unchangeable conditions rather than as pathologies or attempts at public deception. The anonymity offered by Europe's growing metropolitan centres made it more possible to transform oneself from one sex to another, and the growth of medical science provided access to psychological and medical assessments. We will discuss the science and political implications of sexology in more detail in Chapter 5. But it is important to remember that in investigating historical cases of transsexualism, we often only have evidence for a change of clothing and comportment; the anatomical or chromosomal circumstances of individuals' lives, particularly before the twentieth century, are often lost to us. Deciding which sex to assign a baby with ambiguous genitalia was generally the result of quick and furtive conversations between parents and doctors or midwives, and once made the decision was very difficult for the individual in question to change. In either case – whether individuals felt that the sex they had been assigned was primarily a physical misreading of their bodies or an emotional misreading of their souls – taking steps to change one's gender took enormous courage. A particularly striking image of such of an individual is provided on the next page.

This image is signed by Hermann Freiherr von Teschenberg, and it was first printed in a sexological journal in 1902. Teschenberg was one of the founders (in 1897) of the Scientific Humanitarian Committee in Berlin, the world's first gay rights organization. He was the only member of this organization to openly declare his homosexual tendencies, and his inscription – aimed at the sexologist Magnus Hirschfeld – makes his intentions with this image clear: 'Inspired by the integrity and the value of your efforts, and not out of vanity or other impure motives, I happily give you this image, which reveals my true nature, along with my name for the purposes of publication.'[141] This was a courageous act, even or perhaps especially for an aristocrat whose father had been an

---

[140] George Mosse, 'Masculinity and Decadence', in *Sexual Knowledge: Sexual Science: The History of Attitudes to Sexuality*, ed. Roy Porter and Mikulas Teich (Cambridge and New York: Cambridge University Press, 1994), 257.
[141] Quoted from Magnus Hirschfeld, *Geschlechtskunde*, vol. 4. Bilderteil (Stuttgart: Julius Puttmann, 1930).

**Figure 2.1** Hermann Freiherr von Teschenberg. Courtesy of the Magnus-Hirschfeld-Gesellschaft, Berlin. (Original Source: Magnus Hirschfeld, *Geschlechtskunde*, vol. 4. Bilderteil (Stuttgart: Julius Puttmann, 1930), p. 624.)

Austrian government minister; von Teschenberg, in other words, had much to lose. The experience for women who sought to adopt male identities was different, since in this case successfully passing in social settings or achieving a medically certified reassignment of gender could bring about a massive increase in social or political freedom.

**Figure 2.2** 'Female Transvestites.' Courtesy of the Magnus-Hirschfeld-Gesellschaft. (Original Source: Hans Abraham, 'Der Weibliche Transvestisumus' Med. Diss. (Institut für Sexualwissenschaft, 1921.))

In either case, however, cross-dressing could lead to harassment or even arrest, since police officers were likely to assume that the 'disguise' was an attempt to pursue nefarious purposes. Only those who could have a medical doctor certify that there were anatomical justifications for a legal change of sex (a topic we will explore further in Chapter 5) could change their identification and legal status. But even when this was not possible, individuals exploring various aspects of their sexual identity were more easily able to find each other in the growing metropolitan centres of industrialized Europe, and they could count on support from some medical authorities and from sympathetic portrayals in modern literature. More conservative observers, of course, took the visibility of such individuals as a sign that cities like Berlin were centres of sexual experimentation, sin and deviance.

By the 1920s, the big cities of Europe were increasingly looked upon as dens of sexual vice. The Austrian essayist Stefan Zweig described the scene in Berlin:

All values were changed, and … Berlin was transformed into the Babylon of the world. Bars, amusement parks, honky-tonks sprang up like mushrooms … along the Kurfürstendamm powdered and rouged young men sauntered and they were not all professionals; every high school boy wanted to earn some money and in the dimly lit bars one might see government officials and men of the world of finance tenderly courting drunken sailors without any shame. Even the Rome of Suetonius had never known such orgies as the pervert balls of Berlin, where hundreds of men costumed as women and hundreds of women as men danced under the benevolent eyes of the police. In the collapse of all values a kind of madness gained hold particularly in the bourgeois circles which until then had been unshakeable in their probity.[142]

Urban lesbian subcultures sprang up in Berlin and Paris. Unlike their male counterparts, lesbians could rely on a tolerance for female 'romantic friendships' that had been widespread in Europe for centuries.[143] In the early twentieth century they could also rely on the cloak of fashion to obscure their activities. With 'mannish' clothes all the rage in the roaring twenties, sartorial choices did not immediately mark women as having same-sex desires.[144] Prominent actresses like Marlene Dietrich played with the new possibilities for individual expression offered by the image of the 'new woman' with her boyish dress and hairstyles. Radclyffe Hall's semi-autobiographical novel *The Well of Loneliness* (1928) described the life of a female 'invert' who dressed and acted like a man. Hall was somewhat successful in gaining sympathy for lesbians by describing their condition as congenital.[145] Her novel was banned soon after publication but became an underground success. Films of the

---

[142] Quoted in Otto Friedrich, *Before the Deluge: A Portrait of Berlin in the 1920s* (New York: Harper Perennial, 1995 [1963]), 128–9.

[143] See Faderman, *Surpassing the Love of Men.*

[144] Laura Doan, 'Passing Fashions: Reading Female Masculinities in the 1920s', *Feminist Studies* 24, no. 3 (1998): 663–700.

[145] Faderman, *Surpassing the Love of Men*, 320.

1920s also helped to publicize the gender-bending of metropolitan culture, while generally emphasizing its dangers.[146]

The new public spaces that the city afforded created new venues for enacting gendered identities. The most iconic representative of the modern male urbanite was the flâneur, a character made famous by the French lyric poet Charles Baudelaire. Resembling the British dandy, the flâneur strolled through the newly built arcades of Paris and other metropolitan cities, seeing and being seen in the new public spaces of the modern city. This cosmopolitanism was 'a bourgeois male pleasure' not open to women (who could not walk so freely without danger to their reputations or their physical well-being) or to the underprivileged (who would not have been socially accepted in all spaces).[147] In their great attention to clothing and decoration, dandies and flâneurs set themselves apart from 'masculine' men and from those who could not afford their attention to style. 'They made a morality of the aesthetic of the everyday.'[148] Only men of privilege had the means to observe the city from a safe place and record its dangers and allures. The eye of the journalist recording sensational scandals, Arthur Munby's prurient interest in the lives of working women and Baudelaire's flâneur all had something in common: the city for them was a venue for voyeurism.

Baudelaire described the flâneur in his famous 1863 essay 'The Painter of Modern Life': 'The crowd is his domain, just as the air is the bird's, and water that of the fish. His passion and his profession is to merge with the crowd.'[149] The practice became fashionable after Louis Napoleon put Baron Georges Hausmann in charge of modernizing Paris. Hausmann reorganized the city: he straightened out roads, created long thoroughfares, tore down slums and began installing gas lamps in the 1850s. The goal was to modernize and make the city less susceptible to rebellions and revolution. But the reconstruction displaced thousands and further separated the poor from the areas, lit by gas lamps, where those with means could comfortably stroll. Baudelaire's 1857 collection of poems *Les Fleurs du Mal* described the possibilities for decadence and eroticism that this new city offered. The book was censored by the French government: six poems were removed on 'moral' grounds, and Baudelaire and his publisher were fined. But the obscenity trial only served to increase Baudelaire's fame. The collection contained several poems dedicated to the theme of lesbian love. His

[146] Richard W. McCormick, 'From Caligari to Dietrich: Sexual, Social, and Cinematic Discourses in Weimar Film', *Signs* 18, no. 3 (1993): 640–68.

[147] Judith R. Walkowitz, *City of Dreadful Delight: Narratives of Sexual Danger in Late-Victorian London* (Chicago: Chicago University Press, 1992), 16. Of course many middle-class women resisted these restrictions. See for example Deborah Cherry, 'Going Places: Women Artists in Central London in the Mid-Nineteenth Century', *London Journal* 28, no. 1 (2003): 73–96; Leslie Choquette, 'Paris-Lesbos: Lesbian Social Space in the Modern City, 1870–1940', *Proceedings of the Western Society for French History* 26 (1999): 122–32.

[148] Auslander, *Taste and Power*, 248–9.

[149] Quoted in Keith Tester, ed., *The Flâneur* (London and New York: Routledge, 1994), 2.

poem 'Lesbos', which incorrectly associated a Greek island with sex between women (in reality the island was famous for the practice of oral sex in general), helped bring the word 'lesbian' into European languages.

Walter Benjamin, the famous German philosopher and social critic, recognized that Baudelaire's poems presented 'woman as allegory of the modern'. On the one hand, the urban prostitute was modern because she represented the ultimate commodification of the female sex, whose specific characteristics had already been blurred by wage labour and work in industrial factories.[150] Lesbians, on the other hand, represented both a protest against modernity through their unwillingness to be commodified, and a testament to the new social conditions created in large urban areas.[151] Baudelaire's association between lesbians and the modern city would continue to influence French ideas about female same-sex love. In the 1920s, the tendencies of flâneurs to use the public spaces of the city to flaunt their sexuality were often juxtaposed against lesbians' more secretive practices.[152] But both flâneurs and lesbians showed how the modern city created spaces for alternative sexualities.

The image of the metropolis as a place of sexual sin was accentuated by the increasingly visible presence of prostitution. Prostitution was, of course, nothing new. But urbanization in the era of industrialization produced social conditions that were particularly conducive to the growth of commodified sex. Rural women who sought domestic service in the homes of the urban middle classes proved to be in a particularly vulnerable situation. If they continued to follow the courtship rituals of their rural villages, they could easily be left pregnant and abandoned by their suitors, who were now no longer acting under the watchful eyes of a small community. Employers often presented another danger, since the man of the house could rely on his unquestioned authority and his maid's innocence and vulnerability to assert 'rights' to sexual access. If these acts resulted in pregnancy or were discovered by the lady of the house, the girl was inevitably fired and left to fend for herself in the harsh city. Having 'fallen' she was likely to avoid the shame of returning to her rural home. Under these circumstances, prostitution often provided the only means of survival. Victor Hugo's character Fantine in Les Misérables and her descent into prostitution has come to stand as an enduring symbol of the immiseration that often befell single mothers during this period.[153] Some women, however, also resorted to prostitution only 'unprofessionally' as a way of attaining some small luxuries or as a supplement to wages that were too

---

[150] Christine Buci-Glucksmann, 'Catastrophic Utopia: The Feminine as Allegory of the Modern', Representations, no. 14 (Spring 1986): 220, 222.

[151] On the juxtaposition of images of prostitutes and lesbians, see Leslie Choquette, 'Degenerate or Degendered? Images of Prostitution and Homosexuality in the French Third Republic', Historical Reflections/Réflexions historiques 23, no. 2 (1997): 205–28.

[152] Carolyn J. Dean, 'Lesbian Sexuality in Interwar France', in Connecting Spheres: European Women in a Globalizing World, 1500 to the Present, ed. Marilyn J. Boxer and Jean H. Quataert, 2nd edn. (New York and Oxford: Oxford University Press, 1999), 290.

[153] Victor Hugo, Les Misérables, trans. Norman Denny, Reprint edn. (London: Penguin Classics, 1982 [1862]).

low for subsistence.[154] It is important to note that the line between professional and casual prostitution is difficult to draw. In Paris, for instance, entrepreneurial owners of institutions known as *brasseries à femmes* (literally 'cafés of women') carefully chose waitresses who were willing to tease customers with their apparent (and sometimes real) sexual availability in order to increase business.[155] Similar techniques were used by bar owners in London's Soho district, which became famous for its nightlife in the late nineteenth century and which moral purity crusaders decried as the 'center of cosmopolitan vice'.[156] Whether these women were prostitutes was as ambiguous to nineteenth-century customers as it is to us today. What is clear, however, is that to understand who the prostitutes of turn-of-the-century Europe were and why they resorted to renting their bodies, one must understand all the aspects of prostitution as a social institution. This also means understanding that the *demand* for prostitution was growing at this time. The Victorian ideology of sexual restraint (which we will discuss in more detail in Chapter 5) encouraged men of the upper classes to believe that sexual satisfaction (as opposed to the sober production of children) could not be found in the home and that any woman who surrendered herself before marriage was by definition unmarriageable. These beliefs combined with late marriage age to make the brothel visit a rite of passage for the middle-class male.[157]

The growth of prostitution prompted a feminist response, particularly in Great Britain and Germany. After 1869, Josephine Butler's Ladies National Association fought single-mindedly against the Contagious Diseases Acts passed by the Parliament of the United Kingdom in 1864, 1866 and 1869. The 'Acts' were originally motivated by the desire to protect soldiers from venereal infection. They called for the mandatory examination of prostitutes while leaving male customers entirely uncontrolled.[158] They followed a pattern already established by French authorities, who had drawn on the theories of Alexandre Jean-Baptiste Parent-Duchatelet's 1836 book *De la Prostitution dans la ville de Paris* to create a system of regulation for the prostitutes of the city of Paris.[159] Similar systems of

---

[154] The literature on the history of prostitution is quite substantial. See for example Lynn Abrams, 'Prostitutes in Imperial Germany, 1870–1918: Working Girls or Social Outcasts?', in *The German Underworld: Deviants and Outcasts in German History*, ed. Richard Evans (London and New York: Routledge, 1991), 189–209; Alain Corbin, *Women for Hire: Prostitution and Sexuality in France after 1850* (Cambridge, MA: Harvard University Press, 1990); Mary Gibson, *Prostitution and the State in Italy, 1860–1915*, 2nd edn. (Columbus: Ohio State University Press, 2000); Linda Mahood, *The Magdalenes. Prostitution in the Nineteenth Century* (New York: Routledge, 1990).

[155] Andrew Israel Ross, 'Serving Sex: Playing with Prostitution in the *Brasseries à femmes* of Late Nineteenth-Century Paris', *Journal of the History of Sexuality* 24, no. 2 (2015): 288–313.

[156] Judith R. Walkowitz, *Nights Out – Life in Cosmopolitan London* (Yale University Press, 2012), 12.

[157] Konrad H. Jarausch, 'Students, Sex and Politics in Imperial Germany', *Journal of Contemporary History* 17 (1982): 285–303.

[158] For an overview of recent historical literature on prostitution and extensive citations to scholarly work, see Timothy J. Gilfoyle, 'Prostitutes in History: From Parables of Pornography to Metaphors of Modernity', *American Historical Review* 104, no. 1 (February 1999): 117–41.

[159] Although Parent-Duchatelet's book was only published after his death, he was considered the foremost authority on prostitution all over Europe. See Jill Harsin, *Policing Prostitution in Nineteenth Century Paris* (Princeton: Princeton University Press, 1985), esp. 97–129; and Corbin, *Women for Hire*, 1–29.

regulation were implemented in the Russian Empire in 1843 and the Habsburg Empire in 1850.[160] Butler and her followers were outraged at the double standard implied by regulation. Worse, after being 'registered' by authorities, women had a much harder time leaving a life of prostitution for more respectable work. The abolitionists – or 'repealers' as they were known in Britain – sought to protect 'fallen' women by campaigning for the repeal of the Acts.[161] They inspired similar movements across Europe and North America, particularly in Germany.[162] But the repealers' tactics often produced unintended consequences. Playing up the imagery of under-age girls being entrapped and forced into prostitution, the repealers consistently represented women involved in prostitution as 'innocent victims of male lust'. They downplayed the agency of the prostitutes themselves and reinforced patriarchal values by calling on working-class men to protect 'their' women.[163] Although they succeeded in getting the Acts suspended in 1883, Butler and her followers also helped to reinforce the prevalent gender stereotypes of the day: the passive, asexual and vulnerable female and the lustful, powerful and patriarchal male. They inspired a string of sensationalistic newspaper articles in the *Pall Mall Gazette* (William T. Stead's 'Maiden Tribute of Modern Babylon series') that detailed 'true' accounts of girls being sold into sexual slavery. The Maiden Tribute essays prompted the passage in 1885 of the Criminal Law Amendment Act (mentioned above), which raised the age of consent for girls from thirteen to sixteen but also gave police far-reaching controls and made consenting sexual acts between men a crime.[164] In trying to combat the sexual dangers of the cities, Butler and other abolitionists reinforced gender norms that further restricted the possibilities for individual sexual choice.

The paradox of anti-prostitution activism – the fact that it often stigmatized individuals' sexual choices in the name of protecting them – is perhaps more comprehensible if placed in the context of more general attitudes towards class at the time. Sensationalist articles like the 'Maiden Tribute' exposé arose out of the practice of 'slumming', a British middle- and upper-class tradition of touring poor neighbourhoods with a mixture of benevolent and voyeuristic intent. As Seth Koven has argued, 'the widely shared imperative among well-to-do men and women to traverse class boundaries and befriend their outcast brothers and sisters in the slums was somehow bound up in their insistent eroticization of poverty and their quest to understand their own sexual subjectivities.'[165] Campaigns to

---

[160] Since what had been Poland was divided between the Russian, Prussian and Habsburg Empires in 1795, the Polish case provides a particularly useful comparison. See Keely Stauter-Halsted, 'The Physician and the Fallen Woman: Medicalizing Prostitution in the Polish Lands', *Journal of the History of Sexuality* 20, no. 2 (May 2011): 270–90.

[161] For a general account, see Frank Mort, *Dangerous Sexualities: Medico-Moral Politics in England since 1830* (London and New York: Routledge and Kegan Paul, 1987), 65–99.

[162] See Richard J. Evans, 'Prostitution, State, and Society in Imperial Germany', *Past and Present* 70 (1976): 106–209.

[163] Judith R. Walkowitz, 'Male Vice and Female Virtue: Feminism and the Politics of Prostitution in Nineteenth Century Britain', in *Powers of Desire: The Politics of Sexuality*, ed. Ann Snitow, Christine Stansell and Sharon Thompson (New York: Monthly Review Press, 1983), 423–4. Walkowitz gives a fuller account of the Maiden Tribute affair in *City of Dreadful Delight*, where she also details the panic surrounding Jack the Ripper.

[164] Ibid., 427.

[165] Seth Koven, *Slumming: Sexual and Social Politics in Victorian London* (Princeton: Princeton University Press, 2004), 4.

save the sexually violated were thus in some sense always bound up in an effort to police the boundaries of acceptable sexual behaviour.

Similar concerns motivated activists across the continent to launch concerted campaigns against what they called 'white slavery' or, in German, 'the trafficking in girls' (*Mädchenhandel*). Although abuse and trafficking certainly occurred, the attention that it garnered was primarily fuelled by fears of the effects that the anonymous, cosmopolitan and increasingly capitalist metropolitan centres of Europe would have on the morality of women and young girls. In the Habsburg Empire, campaigns to fight 'white slavery' were very often tinged with anti-Semitism and other forms of racism. The stereotypical white slavers depicted in the campaign literature of organizations like the Austrian League to Combat Traffic in Women were 'eastern European Jewish "Others" who kidnapped and even "enslaved" girls and took them to racially different faraway places to ply the sex trade'.[166] An International Abolitionist Federation (IAF) was founded in Geneva in 1877, and Butler's associate William A. Coote helped to found national committees across Europe and in Egypt, South America, South Africa and North America. The fears of these activists were not unfounded. For instance, in the late nineteenth century, Hungarian women were falling victim to criminals who promised them marriage partners in Argentina and then sold them to brothel keepers in Buenos Aires.[167] The panic about these activities came to a head in the fall of 1892, when twenty-seven people (ten of them women) were put on trial for trafficking in the multi-ethnic town of Lemberg, Galicia. The fact that all of these people were Jews and that they were all declared guilty fanned the flames of hysteria about both the 'white slave trade' and its Jewish roots.[168]

The rhetoric about 'white slavery' was equally heated in the Russian Empire, where the presence of anti-Semitism was also a crucial aspect of the debate. There too the phenomenon of migrant sex work was framed simply as the coercion of innocent young girls by (Jewish) organized crime syndicates. But, as Philippa Hetherington points out, a discourse that appeared to be all about sex had much broader implications. The Russian state (and many of the liberal professionals who opposed it) used the figure of the trafficked woman as a means to develop 'new techniques of biopolitics'.[169] The crusade against 'white slavery', in other words, was about more than prostitution; it was about creating new modes of supervision over women and over state borders as well. Focusing on trafficking victims also allowed state officials to enable 'statist projects to look like (and meld with) humanitarian ones'. Indeed, she concludes, this melding of 'state' and 'humanitarian' impulses allowed the 'international itself' to be produced as a 'field ripe for statist interventions'.[170] These various cases all demonstrate that prostitution served as

---

[166] Nancy M. Wingfield, 'Destination: Alexandria, Buenos Aires, Constantinople; "White Slavers" in Late Imperial Austria', *Journal of the History of Sexuality* 20, no. 2 (May 2011): 291–311, quote from 292.

[167] Ibid., 294.

[168] Ibid.

[169] Hetherington usefully defines 'biopolitics' earlier in her work as 'the production of state legitimacy through the use of the human body, and not just territory, as a critical site of control'. Philippa Leslie Hetherington, 'Victims of the Social Temperament: Migration and the Traffic in Women from Late Imperial Russia and the Soviet Union, 1870–1935' (PhD Diss., Harvard University, 2014), 23. Many thanks to Dr Hetherington for sending us a copy of her dissertation during our revision process.

[170] Ibid., 418.

a symbol for various fears about the speed with which social and economic life was changing in industrializing Europe. Campaigns to save fallen girls were very often also about preserving the presumed purity of a traditional moral order threatened by the big city and about the growing power of interventionist nation states at a time of rapid globalization.

Nonetheless, anti-vice campaigns were enormously successful in raising questions about sexual violence and unequal power relations between the genders. They helped to inspire more broad-based feminist movements everywhere in Europe. A vast network of women's organizations sprang up across Europe at the close of the nineteenth century. While some were engaged in active political campaigns to gain women equal political rights with men, most were primarily occupied with the search for social policies that would allow urban women to live more secure and fulfilling lives within industrial society. The word 'feminist' is often attributed to Charles Fourier but was in fact first used in French medical textbooks of the 1870s and popularized by the novelist Alexandre Dumas. In its original medical form, 'feminism' referred to a feminization of the male body. In Dumas's anti-feminist usage it described the 'virilization of women' or women who acted like men. In both cases, the word connoted a confusion between the sexes: 'Feminism is the appearance of man in woman or of woman in man.'[171] The word spread into other European languages in the 1890s and unsurprisingly found little favour with activist women, particularly in German-speaking lands, where the term *Feminismus* had (and still has, for many) an unpleasant ring.

Middle-class activists in particular took the word 'feminism' (and sometimes used it) as a slur, feeling that it did not describe their efforts to better the lot of women of various classes through reform rather than revolution.[172] Rather than concentrating on achieving equality with men (as the current usage of the word usually implies) liberal feminist movements on the continent (particularly in Germany and France) tended to devote themselves primarily to welfare work with the underprivileged or to the promotion of education for middle-class girls. These movements arose, in other words, as a reaction to the pressures of industrialization, its social dangers and new challenges. Leaders of the bourgeois movements, like Helene Lange (1848–1930) and Gertrud Bäumer (1873–1954) in Germany, or Maria Deraismes (1828–94) in France, were intent upon working within their respective political systems to improve social conditions for women. Bäumer openly rejected the word 'feminist', and long after women had gained the right to vote in Germany in 1918, she kept insisting that the true goal of the women's movement had never been formal equality or the outward trappings of political power, but rather to engender 'feminine-civil responsibility … for the preservation and improvement of the biological substance of her people.'[173] Like their socialist counterparts, bourgeois feminists in Europe were often more focused on economic

---

[171] Fraisse, *Reason's Muse*, 194.

[172] The German word *Feminismus* was, up until the 1960s, used to describe men who displayed female qualities. See Richard J. Evans, 'The Concept of Feminism', in *German Women in the Eighteenth and Nineteenth Centuries*, ed. Ruth-Ellen B. Joeres and Mary Jo Maynes (Bloomington: Indiana University Press, 1986), 247–8.

[173] Cited from Gertrud Bäumer, *Die Frau im deutschen Staat* (Berlin: Junker & Dünnhaupt, 1932) in Reinhard Opitz, *Der Deutsche Sozial-Liberalismus 1917–1933* (Cologne: Pahl-Rugenstein, 1973), 256.

and social conditions – the negative consequences of rapid industrialization – than on abstract principles and rights. They tended to remain closely wedded to male political parties (particularly in France, where they feared for the survival of the fragile liberal republic), and they dreaded being viewed as unpatriotic or lacking in propriety.[174]

There were, of course, exceptions. Hubertine Auclert was prepared to be declared unladylike when she began overturning voting urns and making radical speeches that made her more moderate feminist colleagues blanch. After the 1890s, Millicent Garrett Fawcett's National Union of Women's Suffrage Societies (NUWSS) set out to use constitutional means and steady, but non-violent, tactics to achieve the vote for British women. In Germany, Anita Augsburg and Lida Gustava Heymann formed the German Union for Women's Suffrage in 1902, organized a meeting of the International Woman Suffrage Alliance meeting in Berlin in 1904 and continued to work tirelessly for women's political rights up to the Nazi era. But by far the most visible campaign to achieve female suffrage was waged by British members of the Women's Social and Political Union (WSPU). Members of the WSPU were by no means typical of other European feminists in terms of their strategies and convictions.[175] But the publicity accorded to their struggle produced such strong reactions across Europe that this particular moment in the history of feminism can be taken as evidence of a striking shift in European discourse about women's relationship to the public sphere.

The WSPU was founded in 1903 by Emmeline Pankhurst (1858–1928) and her daughters Christabel (1880–1958) and Sylvia (1882–1960). Having been forced to provide for herself and her daughters after her husband's early death, Emmeline was moved by the plight of working women and found other feminist groups too timid and compliant with male wishes. She became disillusioned with the socialist movement and its continued exclusion of women. Inspired particularly by the ideas of Christabel, she began to insist that men only understood violence. She and her daughters set about bringing attention to the cause of women's suffrage in extremely public ways. They certainly succeeded. Through various acts of violence and public protest (firebombing, breaking windows, chaining themselves to railings, disrupting political meetings and hunger strikes) the 'suffragettes' – as the press soon dubbed members of the WSPU – drew attention to their cause and created public furore. In a brilliant public relations move later emulated by other activist groups, the women seized a word used to demean them – 'suffragette' – and made it their own, turning a slur into an identity. After Herbert Asquith, who was adamantly against women's suffrage, became Prime Minister in 1908, Emmeline and her followers led seven processions to Hyde Park in London, where they attracted crowds of up to 300,000.[176] When jailed and force-fed for their

---

[174] Stephen Hause and Anne R. Kenney, *Women's Suffrage and Social Politics in the French Third Republic* (Princeton: Princeton University Press, 1984); Stephen C. Hause and Anne R. Kenney, 'The Limits of Suffragist Behavior: Legalism and Militancy in France, 1876–1922', *American Historical Review* 86, no. 4 (1981): 781–806.

[175] The literature on feminist movements in Europe is too extensive to cite here. For an overview, see Offen, *European Feminisms*.

[176] A good summary of the activities of the suffragettes can be found in June Purvis, 'Deeds Not Words', *History Today* 52, no. 5 (2005): 56–63. For useful primary sources, see Cheryl R. Jorgensen-Earp, ed., *Speeches and Trials of the Militant Suffragettes: The Women's Social and Political Union, 1903–18* (Madison, NJ: Fairleigh Dickinson University Press, 1999).

hunger strikes in 1909, the suffragettes made sure that their depiction of this indignity as a kind of sexual assault made it into the press. On 18 November 1910 (a day later called Black Friday), police stopped a group of 300 suffragists from marching to Parliament. The women faced physical assault: their arms were twisted, their throats were grabbed, their breasts were pinched and they were thrown to the ground and kicked. The authorities made it very clear that these women, by taking charge of public space, had overstepped the boundaries of their gender. In return, they were treated like 'public' women – a euphemism for prostitutes.[177] On 4 June 1913, Emily Wilding Davison (1872–1913) drew attention to the suffragette cause by attempting to grab the reins of the king's horse, Anmer, at the Epsom Derby. She was trampled and died a few days later of a fractured skull. While it was unclear whether she had meant to commit suicide, and while she was viewed by the WSPU leadership as a reckless militant, fellow suffragettes decided to turn her rash act into a martyrdom, and at her funeral they marched in white dresses in front of large crowds, giving the coffin a

**Figure 2.3** Suffragette at Buckingham Palace. A struggle with police at the railings. Reprinted by permission of Mary Evans Picture Library.

---

[177] Susan Kingsley Kent, *Sex and Suffrage in Great Britain* (Princeton: Princeton University Press, 1987), 200.

military salute.[178] The suffragettes only gave up their militant tactics when the First World War made such violent protest seem unpatriotic and self-defeating.[179]

The suffragettes epitomized the new possibilities for political organization that urbanization and mass communication provided. Their extremely public protests were attempts to turn the public spaces of densely populated cities into a battleground of the sexes. It is tempting to view their strategies as publicity stunts. But theirs was an original insight. They recognized that modern cities provided new venues for gender conflict and for the manipulation of gender stereotypes. In forcing men (policemen) to assert masculine rights through physical violence and in refusing to portray 'respectable' ladies who demurely ceded public spaces to male power, the suffragettes both exposed the physical violence that lurked behind separate spheres ideology and challenged the confinement of women to the private sphere. They relied on society's understandings of proper male and female behaviour in order to tear down these categories. They performed gender roles in order to subvert them.[180] Davison's dramatic protest was immortalized on film and shown in newsreels across the country.[181] A new era of publicity had arrived.

## Conclusion

We have seen throughout this chapter that the transformation of labour and the processes of urbanization wrought by the Industrial Revolution fundamentally changed gender relations and discourse about the public roles of men and women. The introduction of wage labour destroyed the traditional family economy, leading to the massive disruption of traditional patterns of family and community life. It placed a premium on forms of labour that directly earned a wage and devalued women's work done in the home. The harsh conditions of early capitalism, the oversupply of labour in industrializing areas and the social vulnerability and isolation of country folk who had only recently made their way to the cities, all helped fuel arguments that a single 'family wage' earned by a male head of the household was the best way to protect the interests of wives and children, who were increasingly viewed as dependents. Class distinctions were intensified as middle-class women sought to establish social status and shield themselves from dirt by employing domestic servants. Religious revivals across the continent helped reinforce the image of woman as the angel of the household, whose primary role was to provide emotional support for her family. Unlike the various 'domestic goddesses' who would succeed her, however, this nineteenth-century homemaker was primarily a phenomenon

---

[178] June Purvis, *Emmeline Pankhurst: A Biography*. Revised edition (London and New York: Routledge, 2002), 223.

[179] Susan Kingsley Kent, *Gender and Power in Britain, 1640–1990* (New York: Routledge, 1999), 269.

[180] For a theoretical exploration of gender as performance, see Judith Butler, *Gender Trouble: Feminism and the Subversion of Identity* (New York: Routledge, 1990).

[181] See 'Vintage Video: Death of Suffragette at Epsom Derby, 1913'. FirstWorldWar.com. Available at http://www.firstworldwar.com/video/epsomsuffragette.htm (accessed 10 July 2015).

of the wealthier classes. The vast majority of women toiled – either in wage labour, in the shops and small businesses of their husbands, on the streets and in the bawdy houses of the urban centres or in the homes of the wealthy – simply to ensure their survival. Their working lives became more complex than they had been in small rural communities, since they were often removed from family networks and community cooperatives that could help to raise children or pool resources for the preparation of food and clothing. For these women, the Industrial Revolution could hardly have seemed like progress.

And yet the city did extend opportunities to women and marginalized men. Wage labour could lead to independence from strict family control, and the cities provided unprecedented possibilities for mobility, entertainment and individual choice. Despite the dangers of anonymity, cities also provided spaces for the development of new subcultures. Individuals interested in same-sex relationships could find each other in cities and remain relatively free from the intervention of their families and tight community norms. For these individuals, public space among the masses in urban centres provided a welcome respite from the strictures of tradition, even if – as Oscar Wilde found to his pain – it also created the conditions for much more public scandal and opprobrium.

The effects of industrialization and urbanization on individual men and women and their family and career choices can only be described as ambivalent. The city both reinforced and contradicted separate spheres ideology. Industrial wage labour brought about a gendering of women's and men's work that was at times stricter than traditional models of labour and the old ideal of complementarity within the family. At the same time, mechanization destroyed artisanal production and the guild system, thus undermining traditional assumptions about who could produce different types of goods. Politicians, religious authorities and social commentators scrambled to cope with the confusing changes, and they developed complex philosophies and scientific theories to buttress arguments meant to preserve the gender status quo. As we shall see in the next chapter, they were aided in this task by racial and economic theories that encouraged the projection of European power abroad. Imperialism and industrialism both worked to produce the new gender system of the nineteenth century.

## Suggested readings

Auslander, Leora. *Taste and Power: Furnishing Modern France: Studies on the History of Society and Culture*. Berkeley: University of California Press, 1996.

Berend, Ivan T. *History Derailed: Central and Eastern Europe in the Long Nineteenth Century*. Berkeley: University of California Press, 2005.

Clark, Anna. *The Struggle for the Breeches: Gender and the Making of the British Working Class*. Berkeley: University of California Press, 1995.

Davidoff, Leonore and Catherine Hall. *Family Fortunes: Men and Women of the English Middle Class, 1780–1850*. Chicago: University of Chicago Press, 1987.

Frykman, Jonas, and Orvar Lofgren. *Culture Builders: A Historical Anthropology of Middle-Class Life*. Trans. John Crozier. New Brunswick: Rutgers University Press, 1987.

Kent, Susan Kingsley. *Gender and Power in Britain, 1640–1990*. London: Routledge, 1999.

Sabean, David Warren. *Property, Production, and Family in Neckarhausen, 1700–1870*. Cambridge: Cambridge University Press, 1991.

Scott, Joan. *Gender and the Politics of History*. New York: Columbia University Press, 1999.

Shoemaker, Robert B. *Gender in English Society, 1650–1850: The Emergence of Separate Spheres*. London: Longman, 1998.

Steedman, Carolyn. *An Everyday Life of the English Working Class: Work, Self and Sociability in the Early Nineteenth Century*. Cambridge: Cambridge University Press, 2014.

Steinbach, Susie. *Women in England 1760–1914: A Social History*. New York: Palgrave Macmillan, 2004.

Surkis, Judith. *Sexing the Citizen: Morality and Masculinity in France, 1870–1920*. Ithaca, NY: Cornell University Press, 2011.

Tilly, Louise, and Joan A. Scott. *Women, Work and Family*. New York: Holt Rinehart and Winston, 1978.

Tosh, John. *A Man's Place: Masculinity and the Middle-Class Home in Victorian England*. New Haven, CT: Yale University Press, 2007.

Valenze, Deborah M. *Prophetic Sons and Daughters: Popular Religion and Social Change in England 1790–1850*. Princeton, NJ: Princeton University Press, 1985.

# CHAPTER 3
# THE IMPERIAL DRIVE AND THE
# COLONIAL WORLD

On the face of it, the developments of the Age of Revolution seemed to augur badly for European empires. The political upheavals of the era had begun with the revolt of a remarkably large coalition of thirteen American colonies against a British Empire that had just won the Seven Years' War against France (1756–63) and seemed to have cemented its place as the premier global empire. The victory of those colonies emboldened a generation of the politically dissatisfied. In addition to the dramatic events of the French Revolution that were discussed in Chapter 1, Haiti saw a successful slave revolt and independence movement between 1791 and 1803, and the Spanish Empire succumbed to the pressures of colonial uprisings and military defeat at home. By 1825, only Canada and a few island and coastal territories remained as European territories in the Western Hemisphere.

In Africa, though European influence had increased in the Mediterranean territories north of the Sahara Desert during the Napoleonic era, the presence south of the Sahara still mostly consisted of strips along the ocean that were fortified for defence of the trading activities that Europeans had been conducting with relish since the fifteenth century. In Asia, China loomed large as the dominant imperial power in the region, though European incursions in the early modern period had established European commercial and military influence in many of the most strategic areas of the continent. In India, the East India Company (the chartered company granted both economic rights and the responsibility for governing Indian dependencies from 1757 to 1857) had established itself as a political and military power to be contended with, and the Seven Years' War had removed French power from the equation on the subcontinent. Dutch and Portuguese traders and sailors had established themselves in Indonesia; French merchants and colonists continued to deepen their involvement in South-east Asia; British explorers had claimed Australia and New Zealand and Russian soldiers, explorers and officials continued to acquire prestige and territory throughout Central and Northern Asia.

Still, the vast majority of people living in Africa, Asia and the Pacific had no contact with either European traders or the representatives of European states. The web of early modern imperialism had transformed economic production and relations in many areas of the world, but most people were still governed by indigenous elites and maintained traditional social and cultural practices. The great empires and kingdoms in central Africa ruled unchecked, the early modern Islamic empires that stretched from North Africa to India still retained a significant amount of power and the massive Chinese Empire remained relatively unimpressed by the arrival of seaborne Europeans into the political ecosystem of East Asia. It was very much an open question whether European imperialism would strengthen or whether the great anti-imperial revolts and revolutions of the late eighteenth and early nineteenth centuries had shaken the ideological basis of European expansion.[1] Meanwhile, the economic changes associated with the Industrial Revolution had undermined the very basis of colonial economic policy. The mercantilist policies that had stressed the importance of the imperial state's regulation of commerce had come under severe attack (most famously in the Scottish political economist Adam Smith's 1776 *Wealth of Nations*), and new economic entrepreneurs now began to stress the slogan of 'Free Trade' in their dealings with the state. Even in the realm of the globalizing economy, the imperial state appeared to have lost its justification.

It turned out, however, that the era of empires had not yet passed. As the events of the next century would demonstrate, the imperial decline that many thought they were witnessing in the first years of the nineteenth century was illusory. In fact, those very same revolutionary forces that challenged the form of the early modern empire made possible a much stronger, more expansive and ultimately more destructive form of modern empire. By the end of the nineteenth century, virtually the whole world had been conquered or reduced to dependence by the great European empires. The only states that seemed able to resist were those very settler states in North and South America that had been so successful in breaking free during the Age of Revolution. By 1900, the chance that one would find a white man sitting in the governor's chair of virtually any province on the face of the earth was very good. Indeed, the global face of power was so white and so male that scientists and politicians alike came to believe that this manifestation of racial and gender superiority was natural rather than circumstantial.

Nor was this a thin layer of control, as it had been earlier. The wave of European emigration to the rest of the world crested in the nineteenth century, as the adventurers, the ideologues, the opportunists, the dispossessed and the disaffected sought their fame and fortune. Great Britain alone saw 22.6 million people emigrate to the colonies over the course of the century between the Congress of Vienna in 1815 and the outbreak of the First World War in 1914.[2] The percentage of ethnic Europeans living outside of Europe jumped from about 4 per cent to over 20 per cent over the course of the same century.[3]

---

[1] Anthony Pagden, *Lords of All the World: Ideologies of Empire in Spain, Britain and France c. 1500–c. 1850* (New Haven, CT: Yale University Press, 1995).

[2] Marjory Harper, 'British Migration and the Peopling of the Empire', in *The Nineteenth Century*, ed. Andrew Porter, vol. 3, *The Oxford History of the British Empire* (Oxford and New York: Oxford University Press, 1999), 75.

[3] B. R. Tomlinson, 'Economics and Empire: The Periphery and the Imperial Economy', in *The Nineteenth Century*, ed. Andrew Porter, vol. 3, *The Oxford History of the British Empire* (Oxford and New York: Oxford University Press, 1999), 68.

Economically too, the intrusion of European power was much more significant. The new form of empire was increasingly geared towards changing the way export goods were produced rather than towards simply extracting goods through unequal trade. Hunter-gatherers and nomadic pastoralists were forced into land cultivation, while new European enterprises expanded dramatically enough to push indigenous peoples into wage labour in many areas. The extraction of rubber expanded exponentially in many tropical regions, scarce minerals were systematically mined in Africa and enormous cotton plantations with extensive irrigation systems flowered from Uzbekistan to Egypt, destroying pastureland and traditional economies in the space of a few short years.

The increased presence of European demographic and economic forces in the colonial world was enough to justify greater intervention on the part of European imperial states. As land was fenced off and tilled, and as mines began churning out wealth, European colonists rushed to introduce their forms of law and the primacy of private property in the regions they controlled. Much to the dismay of local peoples, these institutional importations, though clothed in the language of the law, had little to do with justice. White newcomers usurped property worked by local people who had laid claim to it for generations, and the colonists then insisted that this form of property arrangement was both fair and part of a superior civilization that indigenous peoples were simply too ignorant to comprehend fully. When natives rebelled or protested against the colonial order, the Europeans brought out their guns. So, as European diplomats scrambled for new territories, local peoples scrambled to adjust to this much more intrusive new order, which came not only to rule and to profit, but also to legislate, to instruct and to lecture these new subjects on why they should learn to love their new positions. These powerful new men (and at the outset nearly all of the colonists were male), previously on the distant periphery of the lives of most Asians and Africans, were now much more intimate and much more present.

Our argument in this chapter is that the impact of this intimacy ran both ways. Just as local societies were forever transformed by the European invasions, so too were European societies deeply affected by their imperial ventures. When nineteenth-century Europeans thought about their own civilization, those musings were comparative in nature. Europeans were only 'civilized' because there was a world full of the 'uncivilized'. These comparisons were not value-neutral; one form of social order was considered better than the other. Needless to say, most Europeans saw their 'civilization' as superior to the 'barbarism' that existed in wilder societies, but this was always a judgement that was tinged with anxiety. Civilization meant in part the ability to objectify nature so as to better control it, a process that was most clearly seen in the rise of man-made urban centres throughout Europe that further distanced city dwellers from 'nature'. This creation of a civilized artifice troubled men and women who suspected that important things had been lost when 'natural' ties had been severed. The colonies served a paradoxical purpose in this regard. On the one hand, they were the arena for the daily demonstration of the superiority of the European way of life, a superiority felt not only in the smug quarters of colonial governors, but perhaps even more deeply and importantly among people who had never left the home country. On the other hand, the colonies were also the space to which those frustrated or troubled by domestic social norms and practices fled. In a sense, Europeans sent their 'savages' to perform the 'civilizing' mission.

These notions of superiority and feelings of anxiety were evident in the realm of gender and sex. Indeed, imperial relationships between Europe and the rest of the world provide a striking example of how political change was both predicated upon and helped to transform norms and relations of gender in Europe. The imperial project exposed Europeans to new forms of family relationships and to new expressions of sexuality. This exposure forced them to understand their own practices in a comparative light and eventually to construct an entire cultural, scientific, military and political edifice to codify and to justify their gendered visions, their sexual fantasies and their understanding of a proper social order. The engine that drove this process forward was the growing sense that there was a contradiction between one's primal sexual urges and the needs of an orderly, civilized society. As we have seen, this was a contradiction that had been explored earlier by figures like Rousseau in their discussions of proper gendered behaviour of upstanding men and women. Over the course of the nineteenth century, this question of the relationship between passion and control grew ever more important, finally culminating in the work of Sigmund Freud, who argued in *Civilization and Its Discontents* (1930) that the development of civilization from its earliest stages was based on the control of sexual urges.[4] In order to develop civilization, and with it global power, women had to control their urges by submitting obediently to their husbands, and men had to exercise iron self-control. Few individuals actually lived up to these ideals, but hardened and restrictive gender norms had an enormous impact on the ways in which Europeans thought about their world.

## Gender and the culture of empire

European explorers, social commentators and general publics were deeply fascinated by the places and peoples that the process of empire building opened up to them. This attraction to the exotic was present from the beginning of the age of exploration straight through to the present day, as readers, music fans and museumgoers picked up hints of cultural difference and let their imaginations run wild. Those imaginations did not run free, however, for they were bounded by the constraints of European cultures and by the concerns of individual lives. All human beings develop certain mental and behavioural patterns that condition the ways that they think and act in the world, and even the most novel experiences must be understood within those dynamic and changing patterns that we call 'cultures'. As a result, when Europeans described and imagined encounters with the foreign, they were reflecting as much upon themselves as upon the 'exotic' people they purported to describe.

---

[4] Sigmund Freud, *Civilization and Its Discontents*, trans. James Strachey (New York: W. W. Norton, 2005).

Michel de Montaigne's essay 'On Cannibals' (1580) was an early example of this sort of colonial encounter. Montaigne was a well-informed and highly placed French nobleman who kept abreast of news from the Americas and made sure to interrogate three Native Americans who had been taken back to Europe for a tour and a meeting with the French king. His essay described the culture of one of the peoples living in what is now Brazil. Montaigne had learned that these people killed and ate the prisoners they took in war, that they liked to dance nearly naked and that men took many wives. Nevertheless, Montaigne contended that these native Brazilians had much to teach his French compatriots. 'I do not believe', he argued, 'that there is anything barbarous or savage about them, except that we all call barbarous anything that is contrary to our own habits.' They were only barbarous 'in the sense that they have received very little moulding from the human intelligence, and are still very close to their original simplicity. They are still governed by natural laws and very little corrupted by our own.' This was a people, he continued, 'in which there is no kind of commerce, no knowledge of letters, no science of numbers … The very words denoting lying, treason, deceit, greed, envy, slander, and forgiveness have never been heard.'[5]

One might see in this idealized description of American 'savages' an ethic of cultural tolerance, as indeed there was, but we should also note that this was a stance as surely based upon fantasies of the exotic as the simultaneous condemnations of barbarous cannibals. The figure of the 'uncivilized' native, closer to nature and natural desires for sex and violence, held certain attractions for writers like Montaigne (and many more who would follow), but it portended visceral danger to many others. As a result, priests, soldiers and state officials frequently demanded that this danger be erased through forced assimilation via religious conversion, educational programmes, land settlement and other markers of European civilization. Montaigne's essay was not really 'on cannibals' at all; it was a critique of his own society, a critique that he shrewdly made through the voice of the colonized, who even explained in the conclusion of the essay (at Montaigne's urging) what they found strange about sixteenth-century France.

There are two important points to make about this debate between Montaigne and those who urged the mass conversion of cannibal tribes. The first is that this was a debate *within* Europe and *about* Europe. The natives themselves are barely known and serve only as surrogates for European positions (Montaigne, for instance, admits that he grew frustrated with the interpreter, that little real communication took place and that he could only remember two of the Brazilian observations of France). This is not to say that the colonized people had no historical agency; as we shall see shortly, they did. But it is to stress that the dynamics of exotic fantasies and imperial projects were part of the core of European identities, policies and practices in the modern era. Empires and colonies were not something external to Europe. They were constitutive of it. There was, as a result, a complicated interaction between fantasies of the colonial world and those actual places

---

[5] Michel de Montaigne, *Essays*, trans. J. M. Cohen (New York and London: Penguin, 1958), 108–10.

and peoples. As Edward Said has argued, the imperial project as a whole depended to a very large extent on the creation of an 'Orient' (an 'East' that stretched from Europe's border with the Ottoman Empire to Japan). This Orient, which was constructed both by cultural and by political figures, was necessary in order for the 'West' to define itself and to assert its political dominance and cultural superiority. With so much at stake, there was considerable pressure to maintain the internal consistency of European fantasies about the Islamic world, regardless of what facts emerged from the actual study of and interaction with those people and places. It was 'finally Western ignorance which [became] more refined and complex, not some body of positive Western knowledge which [increased] in size and accuracy. For fictions have their own logic and their own dialectic of growth or decline.'[6]

The second thing to note is that exposure to different peoples and different cultures created an opportunity for Europeans to see their own institutions and practices in new ways. Frequently, this cultural comparison led to proclamations of superiority and dreams of civilizing missions. Many, for instance, thought it better that Europeans did not eat their prisoners of war and believed it was their responsibility to prevent others from doing so as well. But the imperial nature of European states in the modern era also meant that there was a permanent source of social criticism always waiting to be tapped. For Montesquieu, Rousseau, Flaubert, Tolstoy, Conrad and many others, engagement with the colonial world allowed critics to condemn everything from European monarchies to European fashions.

One of the most prominent themes of these probing criticisms and the response of the conservative defenders of European civilization was the question of desire and the regulation of desire. What attracted and repelled European commentators on foreign societies was the perceived lack of restraint shown by colonial peoples. This lack of self-control, they observed, was manifested in violent cycles of blood vengeance, thoughtless crime and wanton expressions of sexuality. These images of savages following their 'natural' instincts were constantly condemned, and yet Europeans could not seem to look away, in part because so many longed to be free, at least temporarily, from the self-discipline that they felt marked their own lives. Put another way, the colonial encounter came to stand in for a tension that many Europeans felt within themselves between their 'lustful' desires and their desire for social order and civilization.[7] Since constructions of gender lie precisely at this intersection between desire and order, gender ideas in Europe both inflected the imperial project as a whole and were transformed by it. But this was no straightforward process. Instead, there was always a deep ambivalence about the colonial

---

[6] Edward W. Said, *Orientalism* (New York: Vintage Books, 1979), 62.
[7] We should not assume that this was a phenomenon only of the nineteenth century. It was really only in the 1980s that historical investigations of Africa started to eschew the 'stereotypical oversexualization of black women by whites' that had characterized European historiography up until that time. See Claire Robertson, 'Putting the Political in Economy: African Women's and Gender History, 1992–2010', in *Making Women's Histories: Beyond National Perspectives*, ed. Pamela Susan Nadell and Kate Haulman (New York and London: New York University Press, 2013), 61.

project, precisely because there was a deep ambivalence about European gender upon which imperialism shone a bright light.

These dualities of attraction and repulsion, freedom and anarchy, passivity and vigour were always present. The 'oriental' woman, for instance, was often portrayed by European authors as submissive, sensual and available, outside of the sexual and moral restraints placed upon European women. But this picture was always complicated by the simultaneous picture of the colonial woman as a source of treachery and manipulation. This was particularly the case when Europeans considered the place of the Muslim woman, who was viewed as completely subordinated to a patriarchal system that was condemned as despotic even by the grey patriarchs of Europe, but who was also the subject of eroticized fantasies. There were ways in which these two images could be partially reconciled, most notably through the sexual fetishization of the markers of Islamic patriarchal domination such as the harem and the veil, but this reconciliation was never total, either for authors or for colonists.

In a similar fashion, colonized men were seen as both emasculated and hyper-masculine. On the one hand, the very fact of European military victory and imperial domination suggested that colonized men had been stripped of core aspects of their masculinity. Unable to defend their lands and their families successfully, they were now forced into rituals of humiliating submission to foreign invaders, and this very humility suggested to European observers that they were somehow unmanly, weak and impotent. On the other hand, the same notion that natives were closer to nature meant that indigenous men were often portrayed as being somewhat more 'pure' in their sexuality and in their violence. This unchecked virility was thought to account for many of the 'barbarous' practices that repelled and fascinated European interlopers, but it also held a great deal of attraction. The thought that these pure men were manlier than the men who had conquered them troubled European masculine consciousness. The thought that European women might feel the same way and seek out the strong embrace of the colonized man drove European men to distraction. What if conquest had merely been the result of better tools? What if the men abroad were, man for man, better fighters and better lovers?

It is perhaps useful to examine this dynamic at play in the realm of literature. The revolutionary era was in some ways a culmination of Enlightenment trends that stressed the orderliness of the world and the usefulness of reason in understanding human behaviour and human progress, but it also witnessed a challenge to this sort of systematic approach. The last years of the eighteenth century and the first years of the nineteenth century saw a variety of new approaches to humanistic investigation that historians and art critics have subsequently grouped under the label of Romanticism. Naturally, an impulse rooted in the rejection of system-building was not expressed in a fully coherent and unified movement. Still, there was a group of artists and associated thinkers who liked reading each other's work and shared many outlooks and principles of behaviour. Romantic icons like Britain's Lord Byron and Russia's Aleksandr Pushkin liked to flaunt the vibrancy and pathos of their lives, and they tended to die young and dramatically. Their 'natural' vitality was heedless and ostentatiously unconventional. They flouted the principles of monogamy and took daring risks for their ideals that both surprised and titillated their rather more cautious and prudent compatriots. In addition, a valorization of the natural world played an important role in the movement throughout Europe, and the wilder the nature the better. This impulse drove British poets like William Wordsworth to the fields around Tintern Abbey for inspiration just as, in the United States, it drove Henry David Thoreau to the woods of Walden. Painters like the Swiss Arnold Böcklin turned to landscapes; ethnographers like the German Grimm brothers paid close attention to tales of big, bad wolves; and musicians like the Czech Antonín Dvořák sought folk themes and exotic melodies.

In this important way, Romantic artists, if not themselves 'savages', were at least interested in tapping into the attraction of the 'natural' men and women in the wilds of the European countryside, the European past and the colonial present for their own personal and literary purposes. As a result, Romantics were among the most important and visible commentators on the cultural and political issues that imperial expansion raised for Europeans in the first half of the nineteenth century. One such figure was Mikhail Lermontov (1814–41). Lermontov was one of Russia's premier Romantic writers, and he had been exposed to the colonial world through military service in the Caucasus Mountains, the imposing range that separates the Russian steppe from what is now a string of small countries (Georgia, Armenia and Azerbaijan) and a ring of much larger ones (Turkey, Iraq and Iran). Throughout the nineteenth century, the Russian Empire was actively engaged in conquering Islamic mountain peoples like the Chechens and Dagestanis and attempted to press its influence ever further into the Islamic world. This point of contact with the 'Orient' served as a formative experience for many Russian artists and intellectuals, including both Pushkin (b. 1799) and the slightly younger Leo Tolstoy (b. 1828). Like Pushkin, Lermontov acquired a reputation for his sexual escapades as well as his poetry, and both poets died young in duels.

Lermontov's most famous work was a short collection of stories entitled *A Hero of Our Time* set in the Caucasus and largely concerned with the critical examination of the contrast between 'civilized' Europeans and the 'savage' mountain dwellers.[8] The protagonist of the work was a disaffected Russian army officer named Pechorin whose destructive exploits deeply offended both the other characters in the book and his readers. Over the course of the story, Pechorin steals a native woman named Bela from her tribe and seduces her, only to abandon her in every sense of the word and consign her to a grisly fate. For sport, he also seduces and discards a young Russian debutante named Mary, encourages a fellow officer to attempt suicide in order to win a bet and treats old friends with cold indifference. He does not seem much like a 'hero' of his time, and this apparent contradiction has served as the main spur to literary commentary on the work ever since. Clearly, he was not intended to be a hero in the sense of a model character, and early furious criticism along these lines exasperated

---

[8] Mikhail Lermontov, *A Hero of Our Time*, trans. Vladimir Nabokov and Dmitri Nabokov (Ann Arbor, MI: Ardis, 1988).

Lermontov to no end.[9] The more sensible reading of Pechorin as an anti-hero and his outrages as a critique of Russian society has dominated ever since. Still, Lermontov cast significant doubt on the proposition that Pechorin was thoroughly reprehensible in an authorial aside in the text itself: 'Perhaps some readers will want to know my opinion of Pechorin's character. My answer is the title of this book. "But this is wicked irony!" they will say. I wonder.'[10]

If we examine Pechorin's character solely from within the context of domestic Russian society and dominant Russian masculine norms, it is difficult to see what Lermontov might be wondering. Either cynical callousness, the dishonourable treatment of women and an utter disregard for human life and the norms of respectable society are heroic or they are not. Vladimir Nabokov, a noted author in his own right and a sensitive commentator, touched on this issue but was unable to resolve it:

> Lermontov was singularly inept in his descriptions of women. Mary is the generalized young thing of novelettes, with no attempt at individualization except perhaps her 'velvety' eyes, which however are forgotten in the course of the story … Bela, an Oriental beauty on the lid of a box of Turkish delight. What then makes for the everlasting charm of this book?[11]

Nabokov has two answers. First, he says, the text has an energy and beauty despite Lermontov's choice of hackneyed phrases and cardboard characters. Second, readers have sensed that Lermontov somehow identifies deeply with Pechorin. These sharp observations are deeply suggestive but also troubling. How can it be that the text holds lasting interest if the descriptions of place are orientalist clichés and if the treatment of women, so central to the work as a whole, relies on stereotype of the crudest sort?

One reason is that many readers *liked* oriental clichés and continue to do so. As a result, the formulaic treatment of Chechens and of women was probably the key to the commercial success of the work. The first story, 'Bela', begins with Russian officers admiring the beauty of the natural setting, disparaging the natives for being both 'robbers and paupers' and sermonizing that the mountain tribes 'don't know how to do anything and are incapable of education'. The native men are portrayed as hot-headed, reckless and murderous figures who treat women as chattels to be traded for horses or slaughtered in fits of jealous rage. Native women, as Nabokov pointed out, are oriental cut-outs. Bela is stunningly beautiful, fully passive and the object of the struggle in the story rather than a subject. The same pattern recurs in the other tales in the book. In 'Taman', the lead figure (other than Pechorin) is a wild teenage girl who entices Pechorin to the sea with the prospect of some sex on the beach but in fact simply wants to lure him to his death so that her smuggling activities would not be discovered. The 'Orientals'

---

[9] Ibid., 1–2.
[10] Ibid., 64.
[11] Ibid., xviii.

in the text are savage, treacherous, lustful, beautiful and fully attached to nature. The beach girl, who falls out of a boat to what seems to be a sure death at sea, instead swims swiftly and surreptitiously to the shore, while Bela's refusal to remain within the fortress and her desire to be in nature leads to her final abduction. Sexy, available and natural, it turned out, proved to be as powerful an aphrodisiac for Pechorin as it was for so many European colonists. For this reason, some scholars writing in the feminist tradition have contended that, just as Lermontov drank from the cup of imperial superiority, so too did he exploit misogynistic themes in order to titillate his male readers. They agreed with Nabokov that Lermontov was 'inept' in his treatment of women.[12]

At this level, *A Hero of Our Time* was no different from any of the other pulp exotic tales that flooded European book markets. European readers clearly liked tales of savages, of wild countrysides and military adventure and of dusky men and gorgeous, available women.[13] This attraction to the core orientalist themes on the part of mass reading publics was not politically innocent, for these artistic representations were a key, constitutive part of a broader understanding of colonized peoples and places.[14] It was only in the context of seeing the rest of the world as uncivilized that a civilizing mission of empire could be systematically forwarded and pursued. One might, therefore, see Lermontov's work as just one more prop of imperialism and argue that Europeans of his era did not, indeed could not, sense the deeply inhuman and dehumanizing consequences of their orientalist literary projects and associated schemes of imperial expansion.

But here is a case where a sustained examination of the relationship between gender and empire pays off. Scholarship focusing on gender and empire in the Russian literary context convincingly demonstrates that the misogynistic and imperial attitudes of Lermontov's characters are presented not to valorize them but to criticize them. Peter Scotto argues perceptively that Lermontov sets up many of the moral dilemmas in 'Bela' to reflect on the inhumanity of imperial ideology and that the tragedy of the story unfolds not because Pechorin is corrupt but because the colonial context encourages precisely this devaluation of native lives.[15] Susan Layton, in the same vein, uses Lermontov's earlier poetry to demonstrate that his views of Caucasian masculinity in particular ran against the grain of the accepted imperial discourse, an observation that calls into question the thesis that Lermontov depicted the relationship between the sexes and his female characters 'ineptly' because he didn't know any better.[16] Indeed, Jane Costlow argues in line with Scotto that women were not presented as clichés simply to entertain but

---

[12] For a brief discussion of feminist criticism on the novel, see Robert Reid, *Lermontov's A Hero of Our Time* (London: Bristol Classical Press, 1997), 7.

[13] For a fine discussion of both the Russian oriental exotica and the response by writers like Lermontov, see Susan Layton, *Russian Literature and Empire: Conquest of the Caucasus from Pushkin to Tolstoy* (Cambridge and New York: Cambridge University Press, 1994).

[14] Said, *Orientalism*.

[15] Peter Scotto, 'Prisoners of the Caucasus: Ideologies of Imperialism in Lermontov's "Bela"', *PMLA* 107, no. 2 (1992): 246–60.

[16] Layton, *Russian Literature and Empire*, 141.

to criticize: like the natives, the female characters present the Russian male characters with moral tests that they fail precisely because they follow the dictates of the dominant imperial ideology.[17] All these authors agree that by the end of his life Lermontov was engaged in a project of challenging Russian imperial expansion and the orientalist ideology that underpinned it.

We can go further and argue that *A Hero of Our Time* precociously and systematically condemned the despotism of both colonial relations and gender relations. Those two despotisms, moreover, were linked in a fundamental way. What distinguishes *A Hero of Our Time* is that though Lermontov entices his readers into his oriental fantasy world by deploying tired stereotypes and utterly conventional adventure plots, he then attempts to demonstrate the inhumane destructiveness of both colonial relations and normative Russian gender relations. The result is complex – a criticism of colonialism in the form of a thrilling exotic adventure in the Orient and a devastating indictment of gender relations accomplished through cardboard women.

*A Hero of Our Time* highlights three important facets of the way that gender intersected with imperial culture in the nineteenth century. The first is that the colonial world was of great interest to Europeans. Orientalist themes were not relegated to niche markets. Instead, virtually every notable European author tackled them at some point or another, and many long-forgotten authors made their careers peddling exotic and erotic tales of the East. The second point is that conceptions of the imperial order were tightly bound to conceptions of the European gender order. The connection drawn in literature and in political metaphor between men as conquerors and women as the conquered does not take especially intrepid research to uncover. It was everywhere, and it had deep consequences not only for life in the colonies, where many unfortunate aspects of European masculinity were grotesquely overplayed and where the notion of what we would call today 'sex tourism' inflected colonial relations in many unhealthy ways, but also within Europe itself. The third point is that, though the bulk of colonial literature served to buttress the ideology of empire, there was criticism not just of imperial policy, but also of imperialism as such, even as expansion was going on. Put another way, what we today call 'post-colonial' criticism in fact emerged alongside colonialism, not after the fact.[18] The Haitian anthropologist Anténeor Firmin, for instance, began writing against European racial theories in 1885.[19] Taken together, these three observations add up to an additional conclusion: the gendered nature of imperial expansion served both to solidify the (unequal) gender order of Europe in the short term and to lay the groundwork for a form of opposition to the colonial order that was deeply imbued with feminism as well

---

[17] Jane Costlow, 'Compassion and the Hero: Women in *a Hero of Our Time*', in *Lermontov's a Hero of Our Time: A Critical Companion*, ed. Lewis Bagby (Evanston, IL: Northwestern University Press, 2002), 101.

[18] For another argument along this line in the American case, see Geoffrey Sanborn, *The Sign of the Cannibal: Melville and the Making of a Postcolonial Reader* (Durham, NC: Duke University Press, 1998).

[19] Firmin's book *De l'égalité des races humaines* (On the Equality of Human Races) was a direct rebuttal of Arthur de Gobineau's *Essai sur l'inégalité des races humaines* (Essay on the Inequality of Human Races), which we will discuss in more detail below.

as anti-racism. This convergence of feminist and anti-racist thought was a precocious form of 'intersectional' politics and it was driven by the 'intersectionality' of colonial oppression itself. Though it would take some time for this movement to develop fully, the sorts of criticisms of patriarchy and colonialism hinted at by Lermontov would enter the political realm soon enough. Within a decade of the publication of *A Hero of Our Time* in 1840 and Lermontov's death in 1841, Karl Marx and Friedrich Engels would link gender inequality and colonial inequality with what was, for them, the foundational inequality of class. They further argued in the *Communist Manifesto* that each ruling order inevitably sowed the seeds of its own destruction. While this was not necessarily universally true, it would soon prove to be the case for the great nineteenth-century European empires.

## Race and sex in the colonies

As we have seen, the metropolitan culture of empire was deeply tied to the entire imperial project. From its earliest phases, the colonial encounter was suffused with European erotic fantasies about other races; perceptions of racial difference were suffused with sexual meaning from the beginning. By the nineteenth century, depictions of sexually available colonized women had become a commonplace of European art and literature. Eugène Delacroix's 1834 painting, *Femmes d'Algers dans leur appartement* (Women of Algiers in Their Apartment), was but one example of how Orientalist art tended to eroticize colonial subjects.[20] Still, we should not imagine that there was any sort of direct correspondence between European fantasies (literary or not) and the actual interaction between colonizers and colonized on the ground. Though Europeans came to the colonies with scripts in their heads derived from the imperial culture 'at home', they then interacted with large numbers of people whose voices and actions were systematically excluded from domestic aesthetic cultures and political discourses. These interactions took many forms, ranging from economic to political to social, but the one that will concern us most here is the dynamic of sexual relationships in the expanding and deepening European colonies.

Until the late eighteenth century, statesmen in the European metropoles looked upon sexual contact between native women and European traders, frontiersmen, officials and other itinerants of the early modern empires with benevolence. Most of the Europeans abroad during the first centuries of empire were men, even in those parts of the empire (notably in North America) where full-scale colonization with large numbers of settlers was taking place, and few expected that the rough and ready men of the frontier would observe monastic celibacy. Indeed, there was even some tolerance for homosexual

---

[20] Sandra Ponzanesi, 'Beyond the Black Venus: Colonial Sexual Politics and Contemporary Visual Practices', in *Italian Colonialism: Legacy and Memory*, ed. Jacqueline Andall and Derek Duncan (Bern and New York: Peter Lang, 2005), 167.

relationships between the men inhabiting these male-only settings. Some of the most famous British imperialists, such as Cecil Rhodes, Henry Morton Stanley and Lawrence of Arabia, left behind evidence that they had formed intimate connections with young men on their travels.[21] The Islamic world in particular was associated with proclivities towards male homosexuality that both titillated and repulsed the European imagination.[22] French novelist Gustave Flaubert visited bathhouses in Cairo and caught syphilis from a fourteen-year-old boy in Beirut in 1850.[23] Even more famously, André Gide met up with Oscar Wilde in Algiers in 1895 and went on to write *The Immoralist* (1902), which drew on his own experiences in Algeria to positively portray homosexual love for the first time in European literature.[24] That the French associated male homosexuality with their North African colonies is demonstrated by the fact that the slang term *'faire passer son brevet colonial'* (literally, to pass a test and receive one's colonial certificate) was used as a code to mean initiating a young man into the practice of anal sex.

Gide and Flaubert were unusual. For the most part, Europeans looked upon homosexual practices in colonial spaces with deep fear and concern.[25] In some cases, such as during the sixteenth-century Spanish conquests in North and South America, the discovery of same-sex sexual practices among indigenous peoples were used as a justification for violent subjugation.[26] 'To justify imperial conquest', Anna Clark argues, '[Spanish] colonizers [in the new world] portrayed their victims as racially different, barbaric, and sexually immoral ... as sodomitic cannibals.'[27] More commonly, Europeans were simply baffled or bemused by the sight of individuals (usually men) who were clearly living the gender role of the opposite sex, and they tended to refer to them as 'male prostitutes', 'sodomites', hermaphrodites or, eventually, *berdaches*, a now controversial term that comes from a Persian word for captive or slave.[28] That these effeminate men would make sexual advances towards Europeans while still engaging in battle – as prized warriors with supernatural powers – perplexed colonist men

---

[21] Robert Aldrich, *Colonialism and Homosexuality* (London and New York: Routledge, 2002), 1.

[22] For an extended description of the cultural impact of these fantasies, see Joseph A. Boone, *The Homoerotics of Orientalism* (New York: Columbia University Press, 2014).

[23] Laurence M. Porter, ed., *A Gustave Flaubert Encyclopedia* (Westport, CT: Greenwood Publishing Group, 2001), 172.

[24] For a discussion of Gide's impact on ideas about homosexuality in France, see Florence Tamagne, *A History of Homosexuality in Europe, Vol. I: Berlin, London, Paris, 1919–1939* (New York: Algora Publishing, 2004), 130–40.

[25] Philippa Levine, 'Sexuality, Gender and Empire', in *Gender and Empire*, ed. Philippa Levine, (Oxford and New York: Oxford University Press, 2004), 151. Kenneth Ballhatchet, *Race, Sex and Class under the Raj: Imperial Attitudes and Policies and Their Critics, 1793–1905* (New York: St. Martin's Press, 1980), 10.

[26] Richard C. Trexler, *Sex and Conquest: Gendered Violence, Political Order, and the European Conquest of the Americas* (Ithaca, NY: Cornell University Press, 1999).

[27] Anna Clark, *Desire: A History of European Sexuality* (New York: Routledge, 2008), 100.

[28] Roger M. Carpenter, 'Womanish Men and Manlike Women: The Native American Two-Spirit as Warrior', in *Gender and Sexuality in Indigenous North America, 1400–1850*, ed. Sandra Slater and Fay A. Yarbrough (Columbia: University of South Carolina Press, 2011), 148.

with strict understandings of the division of gender roles.[29] Displaying their ignorance of native cultures and their biases about male sexual desire, settlers often blamed the existence of male homosexuality on native women, who supposedly withheld themselves from their men. Even this, however, was a more charitable explanation for non-conforming sexual practices than the one developed to explain why European colonists engaged in same-sex practices. In 1911, a French doctor argued that 'pederasty' resulted from a combination of a shortage of European women and the undesirability of the natives:

> The uprooted colonial easily becomes a sodomite ... [but] true homosexuality is seldom found ... The lack of women or the presence of Arab or black dirty and malodorous shrews, infested with vermin, prompts the uprooted colonial to seek the company of ephebes and to prefer them. These are occasional homosexuals who go back to normal once they return to the North.[30]

Ultimately, in other words, the encounter with seemingly less rigid codes of sexual conduct in faraway lands led Europeans to find creative ways of assimilating these 'natural' facts of human behaviour into their newly developing models of sexual science. For example, when Europeans encountered male same-sex behaviour in Polynesia, they at first simply described how common it was between all ages and social ranks. But, as Rudi Bleys argues, by the mid-nineteenth century, accounts of these practices by missionaries and colonialists tended to categorize everything in terms of a gendered hierarchy, where a passive and weaker male assumed a feminine role. This view was easier to assimilate into a growing scientific tendency of classifying homosexual behaviour as a kind of 'third sex' and of 'connecting sex and gender to one another in a way that was far more coercive than before.'[31]

Another threat to European sensibilities was what Europeans perceived as the less inhibited sexuality of colonized women. As Adele Perry and Sarah Carter have argued, settler men's perceptions of First Nations women in Western Canada were a mixture of awe and fear in the face of what was perceived as unbridled sensuality and a 'savage' lack of modesty. Unknowledgeable about the complex moral codes of these societies, which each had their own systems of sexual control, colonists read differences in clothing and comportment as a complete lack of inhibitions. As one Englishman observed upon his visit to Victoria in the mid-nineteenth century: 'among the Females

---

[29] That at least some tribes also had female *berdaches* – women who lived as men – was even more troubling. Unlike their originally male counterparts, these individuals gave up all gender fluidity and lived their lives exclusively as men. Ibid., 158.

[30] Chantal Zabus, *Out in Africa: Same-Sex Desire in Sub-Saharan Literatures & Cultures* (Woodbridge, Suffolk: James Currey, 2013), 33.

[31] Rudi C. Bleys, *The Geography of Perversion: Male-To-Male Sexual Behavior Outside the West and the Ethnographic Imagination, 1750–1918* (New York: New York University Press, 1995), 2 and 139.

there is a *painful* and *provoking* scarcity of petticoats.'[32] In the early days of European colonization in North America, this struggle between European propriety and lust was complicated by European men's reliance on native women for survival, since in harsh and unfamiliar climates this was the only source of information about how to survive on 'country food'.[33] During this largely male phase of colonialism, before permanent settlements lured European women to join the men, the notion that sexual restraint would strengthen the self-control of colonizers and thereby their control over native peoples was thus weakly developed. Indeed, although observers in the metropole were often concerned that regularized relationships would blur the line between colonizers and colonized, those more engaged in day-to-day survival in faraway lands were more likely to see the enormous usefulness of the intimate cultural exchange that occurred in such cases. Virtually everywhere, a select cadre of local women served as cultural and linguistic 'translators' between the probing explorers and cautious local political leaders. In conditions of general mutual unintelligibility there was an important and powerful space for such cultural brokers, a space that was occupied not only by the women, but also by the men who teamed up with them. These couples, who were engaged in mutual linguistic and cultural immersion programmes while those around them remained rooted in their own cultural worlds, became the transmission belts and information filters for economic, cultural and political exchange.[34]

These were 'marriages' based on the principle of cultural diplomacy,[35] and the women were not always consulted about their participation in the process. More than a few younger daughters of local elites found themselves packed off by their fathers to cohabit with strange-looking, pale and hairy men who did not speak their language. These were obviously unions based on inequality. European men had no legal obligations to their colonial wives or offspring. Many native families were abandoned when the men departed for home and were left to cope with local societies that often considered them ruined or, worse still, traitorous spies. Still, bonds of true affection did often arise, not only because of growing intimacy in their personal relationships and the joys and responsibilities of child-rearing, but also because both parties were isolated from their own societies and living on the margins of another.[36]

---

[32] Adele Perry, *On the Edge of Empire: Gender, Race, and the Making of British Columbia, 1849–1871* (Toronto: University of Toronto Press, 2001), 51. See also Sarah Carter, *Capturing Women: The Manipulation of Cultural Imagery in Canada's Prairie West* (Montreal and Buffalo: McGill Queens University Press, 1997).

[33] See George W. Colpitts, *Game in the Garden: A Human History of Wildlife in Western Canada to 1940* (Vancouver, BC: UBC Press, 2003), introduction.

[34] For an excellent discussion of this process in an area where neither colonizer nor colonized was European, see Paul D. Barclay, 'Cultural Brokerage and Interethnic Marriage in Colonial Taiwan: Japanese Subalterns and Their Aborigine Wives, 1895–1930', *Journal of Asian Studies* 64, no. 2 (2005): 323–60.

[35] Few of the unions entered into on the frontier were either blessed by religious authorities or formally recognized as marriage by metropolitan states and legal systems. This system of informal sexual and social partnership was known as 'concubinage', and it allowed many European men to maintain a concubine in the colonies and a wife in the 'homeland'.

[36] For an especially sensitive consideration of the affections and power potentials in play, see Maya Jasanoff, *Edge of Empire: Lives, Culture and Conquest in the East, 1750–1850* (New York: Alfred A. Knopf, 2005), 64–71.

Not all local societies encouraged or forced their young women to become cultural brokers through concubinage. Many had sexual or cultural concerns about this intermixing, and as the danger of associating too closely with the intruders became more clear, some tried to create distance rather than intimacy with ethnic Europeans. But the lure of wealth and power was significant, and sexual relationships between the colonized and the colonizers were difficult for indigenous elites to prevent. From the European perspective, this system of concubinage made a great deal of sense politically, economically and sexually, and it was very widely practised throughout the early modern period.

This makes it all the more surprising that it was not the native response that destroyed the system of inter-ethnic unions but policy initiatives taken by Europeans. This shift in colonial sexual norms occurred at different times in different places, but in the British Empire the changes began in the last quarter of the eighteenth century. In 1770, it was still common for high-ranking officials in the East India Company to have a whole Indian family.[37] By the turn of the century, the practice was socially unacceptable, and within only a couple more decades the East India Company formally prohibited it.[38] When the British government asserted direct control over Indian territories, it too first frowned on concubinage and then reiterated the ban in 1910.[39] In French Cambodia, the same process occurred in a more compressed period. On the eve of the twentieth century, relationships between French men and Cambodian women were commonplace. By 1920, they were considered nearly treasonous.[40] Not surprisingly, as concubinage decreased, prostitution tended to increase, since there was always a preponderance of men in colonized areas. This presented colonial governments with new concerns (since prostitution helped the spread of venereal diseases) and with new motivations to control the sexual choices of colonized peoples.[41]

There were many reasons why such a major shift in the patterns of cultural and sexual interaction took place. The shift from early modern imperialism, marked by thin presence and thin control, to high modern imperialism, marked by thorough colonization and more ambitious state projects, really began in the revolutionary era that we described in the first two chapters. The process of social unmixing that the sanctions against inter-ethnic marriage represented happened as part of this shift and occurred simultaneously with the great 'modernizing' developments like the creation of industrial economies and the expansion of the aims and means of state power. Put another way, one can see

---

[37] Kathleen Wilson, 'Empire, Gender, and Modernity in the Eighteenth Century', in *Gender and Empire*, ed. Philippa Levine (Oxford and New York: Oxford University Press, 2004), 36.

[38] Ballhatchet, *Race, Sex and Class under the Raj*, 2.

[39] Levine, 'Sexuality, Gender and Empire', 138; Ann Laura Stoler, *Carnal Knowledge and Imperial Power: Race and the Intimate in Colonial Rule* (Berkeley and Los Angeles: University of California Press, 2002), 49.

[40] Penny Edwards, 'Womanizing Indochina: Fiction, Nation and Cohabitation in Cambodia, 1890–1930', in *Domesticating the Empire: Race, Gender and Family Life in French and Dutch Colonialism*, ed. Julia Ann Clancy-Smith and Frances Gouda (Charlottesville, NC and London: University Press of Virginia, 1998), 117.

[41] Philippa Levine, *Prostitution, Race and Politics: Policing Venereal Disease in the British Empire* (New York: Routledge, 2003).

the rise of modern capitalism, modern nationalism, modern imperialism, modern state practices and modern racism at exactly the same time.

This simultaneous explosion of a new way of viewing and operating within the world was no coincidence. Instead, these seemingly independent phenomena were deeply interrelated. 'Modernity', the term used to describe the new order and new aspirations produced by these revolutionary shifts, was internally contradictory and thus instantly controversial. The appeal of the new vistas of wealth and power easily crossed cultural barriers. Many colonized people liked the new goods, admired the capacities of European states and European visitors and aspired to enter the circuits of power that these imperialists had opened up. At the same time, there was also resistance on the part of many natives, who challenged both the fact of foreign rule and 'European' values.

This same split was present within European societies as well. As our discussion of Lermontov demonstrated, there were many who saw the brave new world of European acquisitiveness and European liberty as inherently morally degrading. With earlier moral and social systems in ruins, they feared that 'modern' men and women would be prone to shallow and destructive behaviour. The immediate victims of imperial and industrial destruction would be nature, tradition and the native peoples bound by that nature and tradition. Indeed, one might see the very rise of the Romantic movement as an expression of this ambivalence towards the modern world and as a crucial way that Europeans could work through the power and peril of the new system they were creating. It was no accident, in other words, that European Romantics were obsessed with pre-modern peoples in the form of historical investigations, European folk studies or Oriental tales.[42] This Romantic urge is part and parcel of 'modernity' itself. As long as there are glowing descriptions of the wonders of capitalism and technology and the historical gift that the West gave the rest of the world by bringing those wonders to them, there will be idealized nostalgia for the pure, uncorrupted and natural world that supposedly existed before the wholesale exportation of smokestacks and white bureaucrats.

This deep ambivalence concerning the relative benefits and costs associated with the world we think we have and the world we imagine we lost is the defining feature of our 'modern' era, and it is crucial to observe that it has played itself out largely in gendered terms. The worlds of the past, of nature, of the colonized, were all marked definitively as feminine, while the worlds of progress, capitalism and civic liberty were marked as masculine. This did not mean, of course, that all men were progressive industrialists or that all women were basket-weaving, illiterate repositories of tradition. Instead, it meant that imperial and industrial policies were often framed in the 'masculine' terms of profit and power and challenged in the 'feminine' ones of morality and the pre-eminence of domesticity. And despite the fact that virtually all European policy-makers were men, we should not assume that 'masculine' priorities were consistently and ruthlessly followed.

---

[42] Saree Makdisi, *Romantic Imperialism: Universal Empire and the Culture of Modernity* (Cambridge: Cambridge University Press, 1998), 10.

Instead, and much like today, the revolutionary era ushered in a constant tug of war between advocates of progress and those who wished to preserve tradition, between those who built the factories and those who wished to preserve the countryside, and between those who wished to conquer and regularize the world and those who honoured its diversity.

If Romanticism was the attempt to represent and contain modernity culturally, nationalism was the effort to do so politically. On the one hand, as we saw in Chapter 1, the nation was construed as masculine and progressive, forged in battle, forward-looking and virile. On the other hand, it appealed to the past and to tradition. The modern study of history emerged to construct narratives that could express both the inherited legitimacy and youthful vigour of the national community and to clearly demarcate the cultural and territorial borders that set it off from other nations. Nationalism became a familial narrative that encompassed a tale of multiple generations and focused on the productive and reproductive union of male and female. Nations were unimaginable without masculinity and femininity, men and women. Men pushed forward and acquired, while women conserved those gains and reproduced them. In this respect, the Napoleonic conservative consensus we explored in Chapter 1 became the basis for the new model of nineteenth-century politics that saw the rise of the nation state and the expansion of European empire.

We are now in a position to understand better why mixed marriages fell from grace when they did. At the most basic level, as Europeans became more deeply entangled with the colonial world, their rather simplistic confidence in the power of their superior culture to transform local peoples was shaken. As a result, some colonial officials both on the ground and back in the metropole began to fear that in frontier conditions, intermarriage would be more likely to result in the European man 'going native' than in the native woman becoming civilized. This rather persistent imperial anxiety appeared as early as the seventeenth century in the French colonies in North America, and it encouraged colonists and colonial officials to articulate their superiority in terms of 'race' as well as of 'culture'.[43] The logical solution to this moral, sexual and political dilemma was to bring civilized white women to the frontier. They would stiffen the self-control of male settlers, provide a model of orderly domesticity and direct the primal urges of white men away from the natives and towards upstanding Christian matrimonial sexual practices. After the great revolutions and the birth of nationalism, the pressure to reduce interracial sex gained even greater political importance. European men on their own might imperially produce, but they could not nationally reproduce. Settler colonies would require white women if the European colonial presence was to be maintained. As one French official succinctly put it: female migration was desirable because 'a man remains a man as long as he stays under the gaze of a woman of his race'.[44]

---

[43] On this see Saliha Belmessous, 'Assimilation and Racialism in Seventeenth- and Eighteenth-Century French Colonial Policy', *American Historical Review* 110, no. 2 (2005): 322–49.
[44] Cited in Stoler, *Carnal Knowledge*, 1.

Thus the intent of this female migration was to civilize frontier men, to reproduce 'European' civilization both physically and culturally and finally to enforce racial separation by placing white female bodies and disapproval between European men and local women. Needless to say, these goals were never fully attained, but the intent and effect were sufficient to transform the culture of the colonial world. More than one European man would ruefully note the change that had occurred and blame the female migrants not only for the more restrictive sexual climate, but also for the noticeably more segregated ethnic conditions. This tendency to blame European women for the intensification of racism was adopted by many imperial historians. Subsequent scholarship has challenged the notion that female attitudes were the primary factor by demonstrating that there was racism in the colonies prior to the mass female migrations and by noting that it was odd for earlier historians to neglect women in their stories up to the point when it came time to apportion blame for colonial racism. But if women migrants did not invent racism, they did serve as the social enforcers of racial segregation in the realm of colonial sex, and they strove to create other segregated spaces in the colonies as well.[45]

The expanding population of white women did not logically have to reinforce sexual and racial segregationist tendencies. On the contrary, the arrival of female colonizers had the potential to call into question the gendered nature of colonialism. As we have seen, colonial ideology feminized conquered spaces and people while deeply masculinizing the figure of the white adventurer. Now the colonizers had a feminine side. Just as importantly, given the material discomforts and dangers of long-distance travel and of life in foreign climes, it was difficult to sustain the notion that all women were naturally passive, risk-averse and vulnerable. European expansion and imperialism had long served the purpose of providing enhanced opportunities for men who desired to take active part in the country's affairs and who loved novelty and the thrill of danger. It clearly contained the same possibilities for women seeking not only excitement but also relief from the constraints of domesticity.

A growing number of European women took up these new challenges, not only by personally travelling to the edges of the empire, but also by taking part in reform movements that concerned colonial issues. The most prominent early movement of this sort was the concerted campaign in Great Britain to abolish slavery, a reform effort that had its first success with the decision to forbid holding slaves on British soil in 1772 and which succeeded in extending that ban to colonial territories in 1838. Many groups had a hand in the movement, including liberals and religious organizations like the Quakers. But women activists were prominent; indeed the period of greatest abolitionist fervour coincided with the rise of modern British feminism. Women took active part in a movement that included both male and female activists and sought to free both male and female slaves.[46] There was a good reason why women were especially active in this

---

[45] Stoler, *Carnal Knowledge*, 34.

[46] Clare Midgley, 'Anti-Slavery and the Roots of "Imperial Feminism"', in *Gender and Imperialism*, ed. Clare Midgley (Manchester and New York: Manchester University Press, 1998), 162–3. The same close connection between abolitionism and feminism was present in the United States in the same period.

campaign and why they were, for the most part, welcome in it: abolitionism was above all a moral issue. As we have seen, morality was part of the female 'sphere', so women could become active in anti-slavery campaigns without challenging the established gender order. This fact gave political cover to those women who desired a public voice and who wanted eventually to obtain equal rights with men in this regard. Early feminist abolitionists would not live to see that day, however. Their very deployment of the notion that women had a special responsibility to comment on moral issues instead reinforced the system of separate spheres.

The mixture of gender politics and colonial politics resulted not in a joined movement of 'liberation of the oppressed' but in a movement in which energetic women were allowed to take prominent roles so long as they concentrated their efforts on correcting abuses abroad and on becoming the moral protectors of native women in the colonies. In part, this took the form of protecting them from the depredations of lonely white men through moral campaigns aimed at wild colonists. Increasingly, however, women activists in the colonies focused on the abuses that native women suffered at the hands of native men. Particularly important in this regard were the efforts in Africa to end the widespread practice of performing clitoridectomies on pubescent girls (the removal of the clitoris and much of the labia, and the narrowing of the vagina, now more often called female genital mutilation) and the effort in India to end *sati*, the custom of widows burning themselves on (or being cast into) the flaming funeral pyres of their husbands.[47] In short, women could be feminists as long as they were doing it as colonialists.

This acceptance of imperial and moral missions by active women was most obvious among female missionaries. Religious work had long been an arena in which many European women were welcome, and the expansion of empire dramatically enlarged the number of possible positions and the roles women might play in them. Many went abroad as 'missionary wives'. They were expected to model not only proper Christian behaviour but also proper (i.e. European) family norms. Missionary wives were to show obedience, of course, but they also were very active and visible in their own right. Few sat in their huts all day.[48] But even non-missionary women were expected to perform a certain 'civilizing' role – a role that was crucial not only ideologically but practically as well.

We have seen this already in the very reasons why women were encouraged to go to the colonies in the first place. Colonial planners in fact intended the intensified racial

---

[47] On clitoridectomy see Susan Pedersen, 'National Bodies, Unspeakable Acts: The Sexual Politics of Colonial Policy-Making', *Journal of Modern History* 63, no. 4 (1991): 647–80; Bodil Folke Frederiksen, 'Jomo Kenyatta, Marie Bonaparte and Bronislaw Malinowski on Clitoridectomy and Female Sexuality', in *The History of Sexuality in Europe: A Sourcebook and Reader*, ed. Anna Clark (New York: Routledge, 2011), 236–7. On *sati* see Gayatri Chakravorty Spivak, 'Can the Subaltern Speak?', in *Marxism and the Interpretation of Culture*, ed. Cary Nelson and Lawrence Grossberg (Urbana: University of Illinois Press, 1988), 271–313; Lata Mani, *Contentious Traditions: The Debate on Sati in Colonial India* (Berkeley: University of California Press, 1998).

[48] Catherine Hall, 'Of Gender and Empire: Reflections on the Nineteenth Century', in *Gender and Empire*, ed. Philippa Levine (Oxford and New York: Oxford University Press, 2004), 60.

segregation that followed the arrival of white women. As Ann Laura Stoler puts it, 'ratios of men to women *followed* from how sexuality was managed and how racial categories were produced rather than the other way around.'[49] Women were urged to reproduce a domestic environment that looked and felt European, from the furniture to the food, and in most places they did so willingly. As biological notions of race and civilization grew ever more important, this segregation extended even to practices that had long brought colonizer and colonized together, such as child-rearing. It had been commonplace for European women of a certain station to hire lower-class nursemaids and nannies. In the colonies, these servants were at first native, but the practice was increasingly curtailed, as whites feared the outcome of allowing their babes and children to drink native milk, to eat native food and to learn their first lessons from native women.[50]

Though the women who packed up and got on boats clearly had at least a little spirit of adventure and the ability to take care of themselves, their arrival also occasioned a rise of masculine protectiveness. In part this was an expression of the male anxieties described earlier. Many colonial men feared that their ability to protect themselves and their own was insufficient, and they especially feared that dark men might be enticing to white women. There is abundant evidence that this anxiety, for the British at least, intensified after the large rebellion (the so-called Sepoy Mutiny) in India in 1857, but it was also present elsewhere at other times.[51] By the twentieth century, these fears of interracial sexual liaisons between white women and colonized men had become something of a 'panic', leading, among other things, to assaults on black sailors in east London in 1917 and a series of race riots in 1919 in nine British port cities that had hosted colonial soldiers and mariners during the First World War.[52] These racial overreactions were nearly always based not on female complaints but on male suspicions. As one case study from Africa confirms, 'on the question of European women fearing the "sexually threatening African male," all the evidence from Nigeria throughout the colonial period points in the other direction, that women felt confident in remaining in an isolated camp for the day without any European male protection and in travelling freely on their own to remote parts of the interior'.[53] The outrage about 'black on white' sex and the proclamations of the need to defend the persons and honour of white women, in other

---

[49] Stoler, *Carnal Knowledge*, 2. Emphasis in original.

[50] Nancy Rose Hunt, 'Le Bébé en Brousse: European Women, African Birth Spacing, and Colonial Intervention in Breast Feeding in the Belgian Congo', in *Tensions of Empire: Colonial Cultures in a Bourgeois World*, ed. Frederick Cooper and Ann Laura Stoler (Berkeley: University of California Press, 1997), 296; Stoler, *Carnal Knowledge*, 133.

[51] Penelope Tuson, 'Mutiny Narratives and the Imperial Feminine: European Women's Accounts of the Rebellion in India in 1857', *Women's Studies International Forum* 21, no. 3 (1998): 291–303; Stoler, *Carnal Knowledge*, 58; Mrinalini Sinha, *Colonial Masculinity: The 'Manly Englishman' and the 'Effeminate Bengali' in the Late Nineteenth Century* (Manchester: Manchester University Press, 1995).

[52] Laura Tabili, 'Empire Is the Enemy of Love: Edith Noor's Progress and Other Stories', *Gender & History* 17, no. 1 (2005): 5–28; and Lucy Bland, 'White Women and Men of Colour: Miscegenation Fears in Britain After the Great War', *Gender & History* 17, no. 1 (2005): 29–61.

[53] Helen Callaway, *Gender, Culture and Empire: European Women in Colonial Nigeria* (Urbana and Chicago: University of Illinois Press, 1987), 235.

words, came not from the women to be protected but from colonial men and from men and women at home whose imaginations tended to overheat. It served to protect the gender order and the racial order, not actual women.

In sum, the figure of the white woman in the process of imperialism is a complex one. On the one hand, imperialism certainly opened up political and personal vistas for a great many European women over the course of the nineteenth and twentieth centuries. On the other, the condition of participating in the colonial enterprise was the acceptance of dominant gender and racial norms. As a result, women on the frontier adopted, and indeed did much to reinforce, the stereotypes that underpinned the notions of separate spheres and segregated colonies that structured European empire building in the modern era. Women had become quite politically active, often for causes that many modern readers would sympathize with. But they also played an active role in building and enforcing the structures of colonial racism that would do so much to poison the modern world.

## Gender and the science of empire

In early modern Europe, most discussions of ethnic difference centred on questions of civilizational difference rather than biological difference. We saw this in Montaigne, and it is present in innumerable other sources well into the nineteenth century. The dominant view of human genesis and difference was based in an interpretation of the Bible that posited that all humans belonged to a single family. All had descended from Adam and Eve, and though the dramatic events of the Old Testament gave sufficient explanation for why human beings had scattered and separated culturally over the years, there was an underlying unity to the human race.[54] This biblical vision did not necessarily entail ethnic tolerance. It also provided rhetorical justification for the massive and often forcible attempts at religious conversion that accompanied the spread of European empire throughout the imperial era. Nevertheless, in contrast with what came later, a fundamental baseline of humanity was preserved. Other ethnic groups might be murdered, displaced and enslaved, but their membership in the species was rarely challenged.

That view was to change in the wake of the revolutionary era. Again it is both impossible and undesirable to find a single cause for the rise of a more exclusive sense of race over the course of the nineteenth century. The eighteenth century had seen a great deal of systematization in both state policy and scientific practice as scientists and bureaucrats labelled, differentiated and acted upon the objects of their enquiry. Carl Linnaeus (1707–78) sought to place all living beings within a single taxonomic system, while biologists and anthropologists like Johann Friedrich Blumenbach (1752–1840) attempted to define the constituent features of human races. Drawing on science, state

---

[54] George W. Stocking, *Victorian Anthropology* (New York: The Free Press, 1987), 17.

officials devised methods of statistical collection and analysis in order to categorize their subjects. Having placed these groups into grids of their own making, it was easy for systematizers to ascribe essential and natural behaviours and attributes to each subgroup. Indeed, the whole point of the exercise was to create these multiple stereotypes in order to act upon diverse populations. As political action and scientific ambition became more totalizing in the modern era, some method was required that would allow both for broad vision and for detailed examination. The method of subdividing and stereotyping fit the bill perfectly.

Imperialism powerfully inflected the systematization of European knowledge. In the first place, it gave a sense of urgency to the process. As new peoples were encountered, scientists and state officials alike rushed to categorize them. Without this sense of order, the breathtaking diversity of humanity would have quickly overwhelmed even the most intellectually facile and curious scholars and politicians of the day. The result, however, was that earlier notions of humanity as a terribly large and unwieldy but single family and of nature as a single 'Chain of Being' created by a single God were discarded. They were replaced by theories that stressed diversity, but diversity of an irreconcilable sort. There were now sharp dividing lines between wolves and dogs, between 'Caucasians' and 'Negroes', between Jews and Turks, between workers and peasants. Whereas previous thinkers had of course noticed and attempted to make sense of human difference, they conceptualized rather fuzzier and more permeable dividing lines. In the nineteenth century, a vast expansion of the field of scientific and social knowledge occurred, but the boundaries hardened between the cells of knowledge that these new forms of investigation produced.

Much the same process occurred in terms of gender and sexuality. As we saw in the introduction, anatomists and biologists in eighteenth-century Europe subscribed to a one-sex theory, in which men and women were simply variations on a single theme. There were theories that the clitoris was a smaller version of the penis and that testicles were ovaries that had migrated to the outside of the body.[55] Over the course of the latter part of the eighteenth century and then with gusto in the nineteenth century, this single-sex notion, which stressed that social distinctions were fundamental and biological ones peripheral, was replaced by one that posited radical biological difference and argued that social effects flowed from the biological facts.[56]

What proved toxic was that the new political technologies of state officials and the new scientific technologies of European scholars, which might have proceeded in parallel ways, became deeply intermeshed. Concerted efforts were made to link the behaviour of individuals and the attributes of entire societies to biological factors. All this was done under a cloak of scientific authority. Energetic scholars fanned out to the colonies and

---

[55] Laqueur, *Making Sex*, 92–93.

[56] Nancy Leys Stepan, 'Race, Gender, Science and Citizenship', in *Cultures of Empire: Colonizers in Britain and the Empire in the Nineteenth and Twentieth Centuries, a Reader*, ed. Catherine Hall (New York: Routledge, 2000), 77.

to the slums of their own cities to measure skulls and noses, to observe bone lengths, to comment on genitalia and then to correlate the differences they discovered with the evident social and political inequalities of the era. And the fact of inequality was an important one. As we shall see, much of the classificatory project was determined to challenge the revolutionary ideals of equality. It was not just that skulls and skin were different; one type was superior to the other. Thus science and imperialism developed a symbiotic relationship: the expansion of the empire opened up new vistas, new projects and new data for scientists, while the findings of those scientists served to justify the imperial project.

The most iconic of the effects of this scientific classification of human species upon individual lives is the story of Sarah Bartmann (or Saartjie Baartman), a Khoikhoi woman who came to be known as the 'Hottentot Venus'. After her father and lover were killed in an attack on her village in the Gamtoos valley of South Africa, Sarah worked for a time as a servant and wet nurse in Cape Town. Her employer, Hendrick Cesars, and Alexander Dunlop, an army surgeon, then duped her into travelling to London. Their plan was to pay off their debts by displaying Sarah as a freak, because they knew that her anatomy would fascinate Londoners; she had protruding buttocks and prominent genitalia. When they arrived in London, Dunlop and Cesars placed an ad in *The Morning Post*: 'Just arrived: the Hottentot Venus. Two Shillings per Head. Piccadilly Street.' Sarah stood naked as the paying customers ogled and prodded her. After a month, anti-slavery campaigners had Sarah's employers charged with slavery, but a judge came to the verdict that she had agreed to her exhibition willingly in the hopes of making her own fortune.[57] In 1814, Cesars then sold Sarah to a French businessman connected to the Museum for National History in Paris, where scientists wanted to study her unusual anatomy. Sarah refused to allow the men to examine her, but when she died a year later, at the age of twenty-five, laws restricting the examination of corpses were ignored, and prominent scientist George Cuvier eagerly took charge of her body. He dissected the corpse, made a plaster cast of it, and published a detailed description of Sarah's physical attributes.[58] Thereafter, Sarah became an enduring symbol of the animalistic nature of black female sexuality in Europe. Pictures of her proliferated, notably at the Universal Exhibition in Paris, and her cast was exhibited as late as 1937. As Sander Gilman has argued, Cuvier succeeded in convincing the European public that they were seeing evidence of how the '"lowest" human species [resembled] the highest ape (the orangutan)', and his presentation of Sarah's 'organ of generation' influenced all future presentations of black female bodies as suffused with pathological sexual power.[59] The 'Hottentot Venus' (as but one example of the 'Black

---

[57] Rosemarie Buikema, 'The Arena of Imaginings: Sarah Bartmann and the Ethics of Representation', in *Doing Gender in Media, Art and Culture*, ed. Iris van der Tuin (London and New York: Routledge, 2009), 70–84: 74.

[58] Ibid., 75; and Clifton Crais and Pamela Scully, *Sara Bartman and the Hottentot Venus: A Ghost Story and a Biography*, reprint edn. (Princeton, NJ: Princeton University Press, 2010), 2.

[59] Sander L. Gilman, 'Black Bodies, White Bodies: Toward an Iconography of Female Sexuality in Late Nineteenth-Century Art, Medicine and Literature', *Critical Inquiry* 12, no. 1 (1985): 215–16.

Venus') stood as a symbol of the sexual dangers involved in close contact with subject peoples. How enduring this trope of female black sexual danger and titillation was in Europe, and particularly in France, is perhaps best exemplified by the enormous popularity of performer Josephine Baker in interwar Paris. Although an American, Baker's highly sexualized dances, which she premiered in Paris as *La Revue Nègre* on 2 October 1925, were performed virtually naked. They had titles like the 'savage's dance' and consciously drew on fantasies of the colonized African woman. Baker became one of the best-known French performers of the interwar period and was called, among other things, the 'Bronze Venus'.[60] Although her international tours eventually convinced her to retreat from this reliance on colonial stereotypes, Baker's popularity cannot be understood without reference to the long history of sexualized blackness and racialized sexual knowledge that began with Sarah Bartmann's enslavement and exploitation.

**Figure 3.1** The Hottentot Venus in the Salon of the Duchess of Berry, 1830. Artist: Sebastien Coere. Reprinted by permission of Bridgman Images.

---

[60] Baker herself was a controversial figure whose later support for Benito Mussolini led to her rejection by progressive black Parisians. See Jennifer Anne Boittin, *Colonial Metropolis: The Urban Grounds of Anti-Imperialism and Feminism in Interwar Paris* (Lincoln: University of Nebraska Press, 2010), 1–36.

The story of the transformation of Sarah Bartmann into the 'Hottentot Venus' reveals how important gender was in mediating all these disparate scientific investigations and political programmes. Gender, as we have already noted, is the social representation of sexual difference, and it provided a readily understandable model of the ways that biological difference might be deployed to justify a social system based both on inequality and complementarity. So too was sex brought to the foreground of investigation, as it represented the paradigmatic instance of the intersection between 'natural' biological practices and social structures.

Two examples might help us understand these developments a bit more clearly. In the middle of the 1850s, two important works were written that both consolidated the confusing proliferation of post-Enlightenment scholarship and served as new jumping-off points for future discussions of race, sexuality, gender and human progress. The first book, *Essay on the Inequality of the Human Races*, was published in instalments between 1853 and 1855 by Joseph-Arthur de Gobineau (1816–82), a French thinker interested in bringing together new trends in historical studies and new trends in anthropology and biology. De Gobineau focused his attention on the big picture of world history and asked why civilizations rose and fell. This had been a core historical question for most of the previous century, in large part because of the process of imperial expansion that had marked that era. The late eighteenth century was a period in which European statesmen were filled with anxiety about whether their conquests would weaken their states and about how and why previous empires and civilizations had declined.[61] Edward Gibbon (1737–94) best expressed this anxiety and the scholarly approach to this sort of macro-historical question in his famous six-volume *The History of the Decline and Fall of the Roman Empire*, published between 1776 and 1788 (precisely the period, of course, when the British Empire was rocked by the American rebellion). Gibbon's work stressed that the decline of the Roman Empire and its civilization was linked to the corruption of its morals and the corresponding weakening of its leaders and government.[62] In this respect Gibbon was firmly within the Enlightenment tradition we discussed in Chapter 1, which stressed political belonging and personal virtue far above ethnic group or biological attributes when considering forms of societies and governments.

De Gobineau rejected this argument about moral failure and started down an explicitly anti-Enlightenment road that would prove attractive to later fascists and racists. It was not, he wrote,

> generally true to say that in states on the point of death the corruption of morals is any more virulent than in those just born. It is equally doubtful whether this corruption brings about their fall; for some states, far from dying of their perversity, have lived and grown fat on it.[63]

---

[61] On this see Pagden, *Lords of All the World*.

[62] Edward Gibbon, *The History of the Decline and Fall of the Roman Empire* (London and New York: Penguin, 1994 [1776–88]).

[63] Joseph Gobineau, 'Essay on the Inequality of the Human Races (1853–5)', in *Gobineau: Selected Political Writings*, ed. Michael D. Biddiss (New York and Evanston, IL: Harper and Row, 1970), 51.

Nor did he think that government had much to do with the rise and fall of civilizations. 'People are convinced', he wrote, 'that the good administration of good laws has a direct and powerful influence on the health of a people, and this conviction is so strong, that they attribute to such administration the mere fact that a human society goes on living at all. Here they are wrong.'[64] Instead, he argued, racial strength and racial strength alone determined the vigour and viability of any given society:

> Societies perish because they are degenerate, and for no other reason ... The word degenerate, when applied to a people, means (as it ought to mean) that the people has no longer the same intrinsic value as it had before, because it has no longer the same blood in its veins, continual adulterations having gradually affected the quality of that blood. In other words, though the nation bears the name given by its founders, the name no longer connotes the same race ... He, and his civilization with him, will certainly die on the day when the primordial race-unit is so broken up and swamped by the foreign elements, that its effective qualities have no longer a sufficient freedom of action.[65]

As this passage indicates, de Gobineau linked historical progress and social survival with the purity of the racial 'stock'. A civilization could survive corrupt leaders, social anarchy and military misadventure, but it could not survive miscegenation.

This racial interpretation of history, of course, placed an enormous burden on women, who were responsible for preserving the purity of the race. Men who had sex with women of other races were wasting their racial contributions, but so long as they did not import these women into their home societies, their own race would not be affected. Women who had sex with men of other races, on the other hand, were poisoning national blood lines. For people concerned with the effects of miscegenation, sexual purity (and therefore continuing social vigilance about that purity) was absolutely necessary. For strict racialists, sex was more important than any other social act that individuals could perform. Though de Gobineau himself did not spend much time discussing sex (he preferred to talk about blood), the implications were clear to later thinkers and politicians. He influenced the theories of most racist thinkers in the twentieth century, from the Nazis to present-day right-wing extremists in Europe and North America.[66]

The second writer was the British naturalist Charles Darwin (1809–82). Darwin is, of course, famous for the theory of evolution through natural selection that he outlined in detail in his 1859 work *The Origin of Species By Means of Natural Selection or the*

---

[64] Ibid., 54.

[65] Ibid., 58–9.

[66] On European influence, see George L. Mosse, *Toward the Final Solution: A History of European Racism* (New York: Howard Fertig, 1978). He also generated contemporary critiques of the 'post-colonial' sort described earlier in this chapter. See in particular the work of the Haitian anthropologist Anténor Firmin, *The Equality of the Human Races*, trans. Asselin Charles (Urbana: University of Illinois Press, 2002 [1885]).

*Preservation of Favoured Races in the Struggle for Life.*[67] Darwin was fully a man of the imperial age. As the title of the work indicates, he thought about biodiversity on the planet in terms of racial and species classification. His insights derived from his ability to travel far beyond Europe to collect specimens and to think about the state of the globe, and his thinking about how human diversity and natural diversity were never far apart. Indeed, zoology and anthropology were pursuits that he would follow simultaneously during his trip away from 'civilization'. On the voyage to the Western Hemisphere that would provide the data for his theories, he wrote to a friend that his adventures near Cape Horn had given him 'an excellent opportunity of geologising and seeing much of the Savages'. After observing that the natives were in a 'miserable state of barbarism' and that their houses looked like houses built by children, he went on to note

> I do not think any spectacle can be more interesting, than the first sight of Man in his primitive wildness. It is an interest which cannot well be imagined, untill [sic] it is experienced … they threw their arms wildly round their heads and their long hair streaming they seemed the troubled spirits of another world.[68]

He observed the other locals he encountered with a similarly scholarly eye, commenting that in Tahiti 'the kind simple manners of the half-civilized natives are in harmony with the wild, and beautiful scenery',[69] but that the Maori in New Zealand were still savage, despite the beneficial impact of European missionaries, who 'have done much in improving their moral character and still more in teaching them the arts of civilization'.[70]

Similar categorizations were to be found regarding women, both in Britain and abroad. He was repelled and fascinated by the peoples he encountered in the Americas and, in a letter home, he openly admitted his attraction to the women of Lima, saying he 'could not keep his eyes off' these 'nice round mermaids'. In Australia, however, he found the female servants who waited on him 'abhorrent', and he observed that their 'vilest expressions' hid their 'equally vile ideas'.[71] As for women at home, he seems to have been less concerned with sexual possibilities than with the need for discipline; upon hearing of a recent wedding, he commented that he hoped his colleague would 'teach his wife to sit upright'.[72] His fantasies of British ladies appear to have consisted of dreams of a woman who was 'angelic and good' – a type that he had 'almost forgotten' about since leaving the bosom of Britain.[73]

---

[67] Charles Darwin, *The Origin of Species By Means of Natural Selection or the Preservation of Favoured Races in the Struggle for Life* (New York: Penguin, 1958).

[68] Charles Darwin, 'Letter to J. S. Henslow (11 April 1833)', in *Charles Darwin's Letters: A Selection, 1825–1859*, ed. Frederick Burkhardt (Cambridge and New York: Cambridge University Press, 1996), 27–8.

[69] Charles Darwin, 'Letter to Caroline Darwin (27 December 1835)', in Ibid., 48.

[70] Ibid., 49.

[71] Cited in Adrian J. Desmond and James Moore, *Darwin*, reprint edn. (London: Michael Joseph, 1991), 167, 179.

[72] Charles Darwin, 'Letter to Susan Darwin (23 April 1835)', in *Charles Darwin's Letters*, 45.

[73] Adrian Desmond and James Moore, *Darwin* (London: Michael Joseph, 1991), 168.

**Figure 3.2** 'Really, Mr. Darwin', *Fun* London, 1872. Reprinted by permission of the British Library.

As these selections from his correspondence indicate, Darwin was a scientist who made sense of the world by classifying it, and this habit was present in his social thought as surely as it was in his biological thought. In this sense, the Darwin who went to the wilds of the world went armed with the mindset of an educated imperialist, sure of his

143

ability to create a taxonomy of women and of races and to be able to generate knowledge from this process of labelling. His revolutionary scientific insights in many ways proceeded from this starting point. Without the grid of species in his mind, his notion of evolutionary progress would have been impossible; without the capacity as a scientist of the British Empire to be carried safely to the far side of the earth to study remote islands, the data that transformed his thinking would have been missing.

Darwin was at great pains to insist that the division of the animal world into species was a natural, and not human, phenomenon. 'From the most remote period in the history of the world', he wrote, 'organic beings have been found to resemble each other in descending degrees, so that they can be classed in groups under groups. This classification is not arbitrary like the grouping of the stars in constellations.'[74] The differences between species were more than cosmetic. Drawing on his predecessors of scientific classification, he argued that

> Expressions such as that famous one by Linnaeus, which we often meet with in a more or less concealed form, namely, that the characters do not make the genus, but that the genus gives the characters, seem to imply that some deeper bond is included in our classifications than mere resemblance. I believe that this is the case.[75]

Biology determined behaviour for both Darwin and de Gobineau, as indeed it had for Linnaeus.

The impact of racial thinking on Darwin's work is clear in *The Origin of the Species*. In the first pages of the work, he discussed an 1818 paper by Dr W. C. Wells that claimed that a form of natural selection took place among human beings. 'Negroes', Wells claimed, had developed resistance to tropical diseases and therefore flourished in tropical climes, and a similar process had happened with whites in the north.[76] Still, the impact on racial thinking came not so much from the content of the text itself, which dealt primarily with the diversity of plants and animals, as from the method of classification and the insistence on the primacy of biology in the behaviour of living beings. What Darwin provided was not the theory of classification itself, but 'plausible and dynamic explanations for the long recognised affinities already enshrined in taxonomic categories'.[77] Immediately, Darwin's theories were taken up by other commentators to explain human diversity in identical terms. A group of so-called Social Darwinists, led by the British sociologist Herbert Spencer (1820–1903), maintained that human races were analogous to animal species. Human

---

[74] Darwin, *The Origin of Species By Means of Natural Selection or the Preservation of Favoured Races in the Struggle for Life*, 385.

[75] Ibid., 387.

[76] Ibid., 19.

[77] Harriet Ritvo, 'Classification and Continuity in The Origin of Species', in *Charles Darwin's The Origin of Species: New Interdisciplinary Essays*, ed. David Amigoni and Jeff Wallace (Manchester and New York: Manchester University Press, 1995), 52.

behaviour was determined by racial belonging, those races were in continuous competition, the fittest would survive and this racial victory would be both 'natural' and progressive. In other words, the European (now 'white') conquest of the world was natural, inevitable and all for the good. At the same time, Social Darwinists argued that this dominance was in perpetual peril and that the danger came primarily from racial degeneration. Sexual policies, therefore, were literally matters of racial or national life and death.[78]

Just as Darwin provided a justification for the continuance of racial stereotypes and inequality, so too did he provide support for the sustenance of gender stereotypes and inequality. Here the connection was perhaps less obvious, but it played an important role in the theory of natural selection as a whole. This was his theory of sexual selection:

> This form of selection depends not on a struggle for existence in relation to other organic beings or to external conditions, but on a struggle between the individuals of one sex, generally the males, for the possession of the other sex. The result is not death to the unsuccessful competitor, but few or no offspring.[79]

The theory of sexual selection was based upon the premise that sexuality was rooted in vigorous male competition for the possession of passive females. As with race, Darwin did not focus on humans, and he argued in any case that sexual selection was secondary to the more important process of natural selection. But again, the applicability of these ideas to human societies was evident, and those ideas served to reinforce the dominant gender norms of the era:

> The *Origin*, seen in the wider context of Darwin's views on women, implies female subordination. The central focus on sexual reproduction, and the female's role as a vessel for the development of the next generation, meant that success in that role took on primary importance. Sexual selection forced males to become ever stronger and fitter, whilst making females progressively more passive. The female was akin to the infantile form, so different from the male as to be regarded in the light of separate species.[80]

Again, other commentators explicitly and quickly developed these implications, and Darwin later confirmed his view that sexual inequality was both natural and progressive for mankind.[81] Over the next 150 years, this model that privileged the biological roots

---

[78] J. W. Burrow, *The Crisis of Reason: European Thought, 1848-1914* (New Haven, CT and London: Yale University Press, 2000), 92–6.

[79] Darwin, *The Origin of Species By Means of Natural Selection or the Preservation of Favoured Races in the Struggle for Life*, 94.

[80] Fiona Erskine, '*The Origin of Species* and the Science of Female Inferiority', in *Charles Darwin's The Origin of Species: New Interdisciplinary Essays*, ed. David Amigoni and Jeff Wallace (Manchester and New York: Manchester University Press, 1995), 101.

[81] Charles Darwin, *The Descent of Man and Selection in Relation to Sex* (New York: D. Appleton, 1902).

of behaviours and stressed difference and inequality would be challenged from within the scientific community again and again, just as it would be in the political realm, but it continues to exert a powerful influence today.

In science as well as in politics, the issues of sex and race were central in the Victorian era, and the trend in both was to highlight essential difference *and* fundamental inequality. These processes were deeply inflected by the experience of empire, in particular the urgency of dealing with the issue of human diversity, the desire to justify European dominance and the intense interest in primal sexuality, exotic races and, of course, primal sex with members of exotic races. All these concerns were tied together in the notion of 'civilization', that bundle of practices and outlooks that allowed Europeans to exert dominance but also repressed many of their deepest desires.

## Gender and the politics of empire

The concept of civilization as a higher form of social order based in the proper alignment of gender roles had tremendous implications, as it justified both the process of imperial conquest and the increasing intrusion into the daily lives of non-Europeans. That expansionist tendency had its limits, as the expense of conquering and maintaining empires called into question the economic profitability of the enterprise, and as the different European powers rapidly came into conflict with one another outside of Europe. These imperial dangers were very visible. At virtually every step of the way, politicians in the capital cities of Europe questioned whether ultra-competitive global conquest was really in anyone's best interest, and these questions became more pressing as time went on. As the British Foreign Office put it, when the ambitious explorer Lovett Cameron claimed the mouth of the Congo River for the British Crown in 1875 without consulting London first, 'the last thing Great Britain needs is more jungles and more savages'.[82] The dominant political figure in Germany during the latter half of the nineteenth century, Chancellor Otto von Bismarck (1815–98), had a similarly cautious view about German interests in the Balkans at the same time, claiming that German interest in the region was 'so slight as to not be worth the bones of a Pomeranian musketeer'.[83] Similarly, when Europeans expanded into the domains of older empires like the Ottoman or the Qing, the dominant note was one of caution. This has led many historians to argue that the great European imperial conquests, far from being driven by greed or reckless militarism, were accomplished not willingly but, in the memorable phrase of Sir John Robert Seeley, 'in a fit of absence of mind'.[84]

---

[82] Cited in H. L. Wesseling, *Divide and Rule: The Partition of Africa, 1880–1914* (Westport, CT: Praeger, 1996), 81.
[83] Cited in Louis Leo Snyder, *The Blood and Iron Chancellor; A Documentary-Biography of Otto Von Bismarck* (Princeton: Van Nostrand, 1967), 1.
[84] John Robert Seeley, *The Expansion of England* (Chicago: University of Chicago Press, 1971), 12.

There was indeed a certain momentum of events that individual leaders and states felt unable to check, but it is going too far to suggest that there was no human agency on the part of powerful European diplomats. The question thus arises: if European statesmen increasingly doubted the financial or political gains from imperial expansion, why did they take the decision to expand? The answer is complicated, and it transcends the question of gender, but one important aspect of the decision-making process was certainly the model of white masculinity that all European politicians shared. They believed that they had a duty to protect the interests of their children and therefore did not want to lose out in the struggle for land, even if that struggle was costly in the short term. They had a duty to civilize the yellow, brown and black races of the world, to rid them of their horrid customs, to teach them the delights of property and to train them in the masculine self-control necessary for colonial obedience and future self-governance. Finally, they were firmly convinced that they had the unbreakable duty to protect what was already theirs and to allow no encroachment on the territory, property, honour or prestige that their forebears had sweated, bled and died for.

This final duty was, of course, deeply and self-consciously conservative, and it could not be upheld indefinitely in a competitive, multi-actor struggle. Not only was the potential for expansion rapidly shrinking, but new forces were also emerging to challenge the nineteenth-century imperial order. Politically speaking, three of these challenges deserve special mention here. The first challenge was the one most noted at the time and by later historians: the sudden shift in the balance of power within the club of 'Great Powers'. The new German Empire, formed in 1871 after the Prussian army thrashed French forces in the Franco-Prussian War, was proving to be a dynamic and destabilizing force in global affairs. In economic terms, in political influence, in territorial acquisition and in naval strength, Germany was threatening to establish itself as the pre-eminent power in Europe, a prospect looked on with horror by most of its neighbours and by Great Britain. The second challenge, which was clearer in hindsight than it was at the time, was that the forces of decolonization were organizing in the colonial world. By 1910, the movement for home rule in India had acquired such significant dimensions that Gandhi was able to suggest that 'all our countrymen appear to be pining for National Independence'.[85]

The third challenge was that decolonizing movements had come of age in many places in Europe itself. These movements, which universally declared themselves to be 'nationalist' and deployed the familiar rhetoric of the French Revolution as the justification for their desires for independence, were threatening to destroy the imperial order from within. They were maturing all over the continent, from Ireland to Poland, but the most significant developments were occurring in the place where imperial control had collapsed the most: in the Balkans. The standard-bearer of nationalist statehood in the region was Serbia, and it was on a collision course with the Habsburg Empire, which could not tolerate such an ambitious neighbour and such a dangerous precedent.

---

[85] Mohandas Gandhi, *Hind Swaraj and Other Writings* (Cambridge and New York: Cambridge University Press, 1997), 13.

All three of these challenges to the Victorian system had one thing in common: they declared themselves to be young and masculine. Serbia, having only recently gained independence, was of course eager to stress its youth, but even Gandhi, who liked to stress the ancient roots of Indian civilization, called the newspaper he edited from 1919 to 1931 *Young India*.[86] German propagandists were equally fond of describing their nation as young and vigorous. Heinrich von Treitschke, one of Germany's great historians, argued that Germany had proved successful in creating a unified state and empire in the nineteenth century because 'it is, as a rule, only the virile formative energy of youthful peoples that achieves success in the fierce struggle for the beginnings of national unity'.[87] The maleness was even less in doubt. Prussia's leadership in the unification process was because of their 'vigorous will':

> There, in the marches beyond the Elbe, a new North German tribe had come into existence … Hard were they, and weather-proof, steeled by toil on a niggardly land, fortified too by the unceasing combats of a frontier life, able and independent after the manner of colonists, accustomed to regard their Slav neighbors with the contempt of a dominant race, as rugged and incisive as was compatible with the genial and jovial solidity of the Low German character.[88]

This focus on muscular vigour was evident throughout Europe in the last decade before the Great War. It was no accident that the first years of the twentieth century saw much more intense attention paid to adolescent boys than ever before. Every hint of national or imperial decline across the continent, whether it was the British embarrassment in the Anglo-Boer War (1899–1902) or the Russian humiliation in the Russo-Japanese War (1904–5), occasioned a bout of handwringing about the 'feminizing' forces of modern urban culture and the need to develop harder, manlier and healthier boys. The desperate fear of going soft was occasioned not only by specific defeats, but also by the more general sense of crisis and threat that pervaded European culture at the turn of the century.

The response to this fear was articulate and concrete. Throughout the continent, there was a wave of militarization that focused on the bodies and sentiments of boys. Programmes of gymnastics and other physical education, usually heavily nationalist and directed by military men, mushroomed in Germany, in the Czech lands and in Russia. Anxieties about the 'effeminate' decline of the nation led Robert Baden-Powell to form the Boy Scouts in a similar spirit in Britain in 1908, and Scouting took off almost immediately across Europe and North America. The Scout motto perfectly reflected this ethic of masculine defensiveness: 'Be Prepared!' The watchword of preparedness extended to industrial policy as well. The economies of the Great Powers, long geared to the low-intensity conflict and high-intensity foreign trade of colonialism, began the

---

[86] Ibid., 14.
[87] Heinrich von Treitschke, *Treitschke's History of Germany in the Nineteenth Century*, vol. 1, ed. Eden Paul and Cedar Paul (New York: McBride Nast & Company, 1915), 8.
[88] Ibid., 28–9.

process of preparing for the high-intensity conflict and much lower intensity of trade that a European total war would produce.

This trajectory of economic and masculine escalation had a rather obvious logical conclusion: a devastating total war that would bleed the continent dry both in terms of human and economic power. Many European thinkers found it difficult to believe that such a comfortable continent would trade relative peace and prosperity for death and destruction. Jan Bloch, a Polish subject of the Russian Crown and wealthy railway magnate, thought that such a war was 'impossible'. As he noted in an interview with a British journalist:

> The very development that has taken place in the mechanism of war has rendered war an impracticable operation … we should find the inevitable result in a catastrophe which would destroy all existing political organizations. Thus, the great war cannot be made, and any attempt to make it would result in suicide.[89]

Norman Angell quite agreed in his influential book *The Great Illusion*, in which he argued that military action, far from preserving domestic capital and allowing for its expansion abroad, so disrupted global trade that war was no longer economically feasible. It was now an 'economic impossibility for one nation to seize or destroy the wealth of another or for one nation to enrich itself by subjecting another'.[90]

These were sensible and logical conclusions, but they presupposed that material concerns were weightier than masculine ones. This was a great illusion that the Great War would do much to dispel, but even before the outbreak of war many citizens understood that a large part of the problem was the sudden rise to dominance of a particular model of military masculinity. Three groups of people recognized the danger and scrambled to avoid the looming collision by challenging the new, virulent form of European masculinity. The first group was that of feminist pacifists, who presumed along with the militarists that war came naturally to men and peace naturally to women. They argued that the only way to derail the train of war was to counterbalance the political strength of military masculinism with the political force of pacifist feminism. As Jane Addams, the internationally renowned American peace activist and feminist put it, feminism and militarism were in 'eternal opposition' and the only way to defeat militarism was to grant a political voice to women, who valued life as a result of their maternal instincts.[91] This position was extremely influential among European feminists involved in the international peace movement.[92]

---

[89] Ivan Stanislavovich Bloch and R. C. Long, *The Future of War in Its Technical, Economic, and Political Relations: Is War Now Impossible?*, trans. R. C. Long (New York: Garland Publishing, 1899; reprint, 1972), xi.

[90] Norman Angell, *The Great Illusion: A Study of the Relation of Military Power in Nations to Their Economic and Social Advantage* (New York: Putnam, 1910), vii.

[91] Jean Bethke Elshtain, *Women and War* (Chicago: University of Chicago Press, 1987), 234.

[92] Richard J. Evans, ed., *Comrades & Sisters: Feminism, Socialism & Pacifism in Europe, 1870-1945* (New York: St. Martin's Press, 1987).

The second group of people challenged the notion that war and aggression were natural parts of masculinity and sought to redefine the notion of what a 'real man' was. This group faced an uphill struggle, as the weight of scientific expertise at the time suggested that male aggression and violence were not only natural but also biologically necessary for survival. This was both a Darwinist argument that killing was genetically embedded in every man and a Social Darwinist argument that projected a species imperative onto human races, societies and nations. The emerging canon of secular historical studies argued along similar lines that warfare was endemic to human society and that it proved to be a force for progress. It was perhaps therefore not surprising that the dominant challenge to these powerful secular modernist discourses came from rather traditional, indeed fundamentalist, religious sources. The most prominent figure on the continent arguing that men were naturally peaceable was Leo Tolstoy, the famous Russian novelist and former army officer who underwent a religious conversion at the height of his literary fame and devoted the rest of his career to the cause of peace and of Christianity. His Christian radicalism earned him scorn from the established churches of the day. He was in fact eventually excommunicated from the Russian Orthodox Church for constantly arguing that true Christians must oppose modern states and modern armies. But he was enormously influential; the educated elite of Europe knew him and his work, and peace activists from around the world sought to correspond with him or meet him personally.[93]

Finally, there was a group of people convinced both that martial masculinity was natural and that peace was necessary. This was an international group that included a collective of Heidelberg professors who wrote to the German government just before the outbreak of the First World War urging it to create an 'army of public peace' which would unite different classes of German men in the spirit of shared national service while backing away from armed conflict with other states.[94] The most widely read articulation of this position came from the Harvard philosopher William James, who sought to contest military masculinism within the bounds of the dominant scientific and historical discourses.[95] He freely admitted that 'our ancestors have bred pugnacity into our bone and marrow, and thousands of years of peace won't breed it out of us.' He

---

[93] See especially: Leo Tolstoy, *Writings on Civil Disobedience and Nonviolence* (Philadelphia: New Society Publishers, 1987).

[94] Kenneth Holland, 'The European Labor Service', *Annals of the American Academy of Political and Social Science* 194 (November 1937): 152–64.

[95] James had an international reputation largely connected with his theories of pragmatism, and his essay on war had a similar scope. The German theologian Adolf Deissmann, for instance, wrote an essay in 1913 urging Europeans not to adopt Social Darwinism as a guide to political practice and suggested adopting James's views as an alternative. On Deissmann see Charles E. Bailey, 'The British Protestant Theologians in the First World War: Germanophobia Unleashed', *The Harvard Theological Review* 77, no. 2 (April 1984): 199. James's ideas appealed not only to pacifists but to fascists like Mussolini as well. William Kilborne Stewart, 'The Mentors of Mussolini', *The American Political Science Review* 29, no. 4 (November 1928): 843–69.

further conceded that the position of 'reflective apologists for war' had merit, that no 'healthy minded person' could help agreeing at least in part that the horrors of war

> are a cheap price to pay for rescue from the only alternative supposed, of a world of clerks and teachers, of co-education and zoophily, of 'consumer's leagues' and 'associated charities,' of industrialism unlimited, and feminism unabashed. No scorn, no hardness, no valor any more! Fie upon such a cattleyard of a planet!

Yet James also agreed with Angell and Bloch that war had become 'absurd and impossible from its own monstrosity'. His solution was to redirect the aggression and to maintain military virtues in a different war by conscripting all young men into an 'army enlisted against Nature', where they would serve a tour of duty in difficult conditions, in mines, on trains or on 'fishing fleets in December'.[96]

These three counter-models of masculinity stood little chance. James was in no position to create the sort of institutions he proposed, and Tolstoy, though often admired, was seen as dangerously naïve. The feminists, from the perspective of their opponents, were much more dangerous. They were more numerous, they were building an organizational base, and they were forwarding the popular notion of equality. The fear of 'feminism unabashed' led to delusions that a mass 'sex war' was in the offing, especially in Great Britain. There were genuine concerns that increased female political activism would make the nation 'effeminate' and therefore vulnerable to exploitation or conquest. But the frightened masculinists need not have worried so much. Behind the military model of masculinity stood science, the state, the entire educational establishment, the organized churches of the day and a deep attractiveness that reached down to all levels of European society. The new model of fraternal, militarized manhood had become embedded in high politics, in colonial policy, in industrial production and in the sphere of social relations. It would come to the forefront of political life in the years of the Great War, just as it had briefly during the years of revolution more than a century before. But this time, it would retain its pre-eminence and would colour gender relations until the present day.

## Conclusion

At the turn of the twentieth century, Britain's most famous imperial writer was Rudyard Kipling (1865–1936), the author of *The Jungle Book* and many other thrilling tales about life in India. One of his most famous poems, however, had little obvious connection to overseas exploits, despite the fact that it was inspired by the pluck of British officers in the 1895 'Jameson Raid' in South Africa. It was an anthem to stoic manhood entitled 'If'.

---

[96] William James, 'The Moral Equivalent of War', in *The Moral Equivalent of War and Other Essays*, ed. John K. Roth (New York: Harper and Row, 1971).

If you can keep your head when all about you
Are losing theirs and blaming it on you
If you can trust yourself when all men doubt you,
But make allowance for their doubting too;
If you can wait and not be tired by waiting,
Or, being lied about, don't deal in lies,
Or, being hated, don't give way to hating,
And yet don't look too good, nor talk too wise;

If you can dream – and not make dreams your master;
If you can think – and not make thoughts your aim;
If you can meet with Triumph and Disaster
And treat those two imposters just the same;
If you can bear to hear the truth you've spoken
Twisted by knaves to make a trap for fools,
Or watch the things you gave your life to broken,
And stoop and build 'em up with wornout tools;

If you can make one heap of all your winnings
And risk it on one turn of pitch-and-toss,
And lose, and start again at your beginnings
And never breathe a word about your loss;
If you can force your heart and nerve and sinew
To serve your turn long after they are gone,
And so hold on when there is nothing in you
Except the Will which says to them: 'Hold on';

If you can talk with crowds and keep your virtue,
Or walk with Kings – nor lose the common touch;
If neither foes nor loving friends can hurt you;
If all men count with you, but none too much;
If you can fill the unforgiving minute
With sixty seconds' worth of distance run –
Yours is the Earth and everything that's in it,
And – which is more – you'll be a Man my son![97]

We cite this poem in full because it provides a sharp description of imperial masculinity. Kipling's masculinity was a disciplined one. It encompassed cool rationality, a rejection of emotional extremes, a combination of inner confidence and humility, and above all

---

[97] Rudyard Kipling, 'If', in *Rudyard Kipling's Verse: Definitive Edition* (Garden City, NY: Doubleday and Co., 1946), 578.

a power of will that could overcome both physical unpleasantness and social anxieties. This set of virtues could be expressed simply: self-control is necessary before one can rule others. When that process of self-discipline was successful, immense power would be joined to strong notions of duty, and then the world would be yours, and everything that's in it. And which was 'more', both for Kipling and for his readers, one would be a man. The road to power and to a stable gender identity led through self-control.

Not every European with power was as keen on discipline and proud insularity as Kipling, a fact that our investigation of sex during this chapter demonstrated. The wild world that opened up before European colonists and adventurers was simultaneously attractive and repulsive, and it was often chaotic, escaping knowledge, representation and control. Sex was always right on the border of order and chaos. Where male dominance, restraint and religious virtue could be asserted, sex provided the basis for racial regeneration, colonial reproduction and imperial stability. But not all sex was in this, shall we say, missionary position. And as Europeans fanned out across the world – sometimes precisely to avoid this sexual repression – discipline and order in sexual affairs could and did break down. That freedom from restraint took many forms. For some it was a frankly exploitative form of what is today called sex tourism. Others took the opportunity to engage in sexual activities that were considered exotic at home (as the continuing fascination with the Kama Sutra and Tantric sex demonstrates) or were illegal (like homosexuality). The concerted effort of colonial states to rein in this disruptive sexuality by sending European women in to police the sexual interface in the colonies did much to cement certain sorts of femininity and masculinity in place. It did not, however, erase the association of sexual liberty with the colonial world, something amply attested to by the fact that Westerners are still prone to describing tired women stripping in windowless hovels as 'exotic dancing'.

Still, European men know what they *should* do. It remains much more respectable to have a stiff upper lip on the battlefield than other sorts of stiffness in an 'exotic' dance club, just as it was better for colonials to be buttoned up in the English club rather than unbuttoned with the natives throughout the later imperial era. And as the imperial age continued and deepened, the colonial interface was increasingly envisioned in martial terms. This imperial masculinity, rooted in racial notions of natural superiority and the duties as well as privileges of rule, owed a lot to the experience of colonial warfare, where Europeans were consistently outnumbered by local troops but continually prevailed due not only to superior weapons technology, but also to superior organizational technology.[98] Colonial troops, like colonial settlers, were formed into social organizations devoted to conquest and domination, and these ethics and practices of organization migrated back and forth between the colonial world and the European homelands.[99]

---

[98] For discussions of the early development of these weapons and organizational technologies, see Geoffrey Parker, *The Military Revolution: Military Innovation and the Rise of the West*, 2nd edn. (Cambridge: Cambridge University Press, 1996).

[99] See here: Isabel V. Hull, *Absolute Destruction: Military Culture and the Practices of War in Imperial Germany* (Ithaca, NY: Cornell University Press, 2005).

The common imperial masculinity so succinctly encapsulated by Kipling bound this discipline and violence together, and it depended fundamentally on the opportunity to conquer first oneself and then others. These rituals of dominance and discipline were practised in different geographical and social settings, most commonly in relation to women, but also in relation to lower-class subjects of their own realms and to colonized peoples. It was a masculinity that relied upon aggression and which demanded continuous contests with other men to prove one's worth. These contests might be channelled into sporting activities, which blossomed in the late imperial era, but mortal combat remained the true test, the final exam of masculinity, throughout the continent. As the twentieth century dawned, so many adolescents were girding for this battle, and so many states were eager to provide them with weapons, that war began to be seen not as a necessary evil, but as a necessary process without which boys could never find out whether they were really men.

Kipling's son John was one of those young men with 'If' in the back of their minds as they sought to unravel the mysteries of manhood through the practice of war. John was only sixteen when the First World War broke out, and though his youth and poor eyesight disqualified him from service, he entreated his father to pull strings to get him enlisted in the army. Kipling did so proudly. Within only a few weeks after his arrival in the lines, in the autumn of 1915, John disappeared, last seen attempting to limp away from a failed charge into a position defended by machine guns. At first, Kipling hoped he had been taken prisoner, but as time dragged on he became reconciled to the fact that his son was dead (John's battlefield remains were finally identified in 1992). Kipling continued to write patriotic verse to buck up the morale of the nation, but he was grieving deeply. He put on a good face in public, but privately he was working through the pain in verse: 'My son died laughing at some jest, I would I knew/What it were, and it might serve me at a time when jests are few.'[100]

In 1917, Kipling publicly attempted to reconcile his patriotism and his grief in a lament entitled 'The Children':

These were our children who died for our lands: they were dear in our sight.
We have only the memory left of their home-treasured sayings and laughter.
The price of our loss shall be paid to our hands, not another's hereafter.
Neither the Alien nor Priest shall decide on it. That is our right.
But who shall return us the children?

At the hour the Barbarian chose to disclose his pretences,
And raged against Man, they engaged, on the breasts that they bared for us,
The first felon-stroke of the sword he had long-time prepared for us—
Their bodies were all our defense while we wrought our defences.

---

[100] Cited in Lord Birkenhead, *Rudyard Kipling* (New York: Random House, 1978), 269.

They bought us anew with their blood, forbearing to blame us,
Those hours which we had not made good when the judgment o'ercame us.
They believed us and perished for it. Our statecraft, our learning
Delivered them bound to the Pit and alive to the burning
Whither they mirthfully hastened as jostling for honour –
Not since her birth has our Earth seen such worth loosed upon her.

Nor was their agony brief, or once only imposed on them.
The wounded, the war-spent, the sick received no exemption
Being cured they returned and endured and achieved our redemption,
Hopeless themselves of relief, till Death, marvelling, closed on them.

That flesh we had nursed from the first in all cleanness was given
To corruption unveiled and assailed by the malice of Heaven –
By the heart-shaking jests of Decay where it lolled on the wires –
To be blanched or gay-painted by fumes – to be cindered by fires –
To be senselessly tossed and retossed in stale mutilation
From crater to crater. For this we shall take expiation.
But who shall return us our children?[101]

Kipling clearly had not given up believing in the aims of British power that he had identified with throughout his life. Indeed, like many of his compatriots he was if anything even more desperate to reconfirm them in the years that followed the war. But a note of doubt had crept into his work, as it had throughout Europe. That increased uncertainty, and the wars that provoked it, is the theme of the next chapter.

## Suggested readings

Aldrich, Robert. *Colonialism and Homosexuality*. London: Routledge, 2002.
Ballhatchet, Kenneth. *Race, Sex and Class Under the Raj: Imperial Attitudes and Policies and Their Critics, 1793–1905*. London: Weidenfeld and Nicolson, 1980.
Callaway, Helen. *Gender, Culture, and Empire: European Women in Colonial Nigeria*. Urbana: University of Illinois Press, 1987.
Hall, Catherine. *Civilising Subjects: Metropole and Colony in the English Imagination 1830–1867*. Chicago: The University of Chicago Press, 2002.
Hull, Isabel V. *Absolute Destruction: Military Culture and the Practices of War in Imperial Germany*. Ithaca, NY: Cornell University Press, 2005.
Jasanoff, Maya. *Edge of Empire: Lives, Culture, and Conquest in the East, 1750–1850*. New York: Alfred A. Knopf, 2005.
Levine, Philippa, ed. *Gender and Empire*. Oxford: Oxford University Press, 2007.

---

[101] Rudyard Kipling, 'The Children', in *Rudyard Kipling's Verse: Definitive Edition* (Garden City, NY: Doubleday and Co., 1946), 522.

Mani, Lata. *Contentious Traditions: The Debate on Sati in Colonial India*. Berkeley: University of California Press, 1998.

Midgley, Clare. *Gender and Imperialism*. Manchester: Manchester University Press, 1998.

Mosse, George L. *Toward the Final Solution: A History of European Racism*. New York: Howard Fertig, 1978.

Pedersen, Susan. 'National Bodies, Unspeakable Acts: The Sexual Politics of Colonial Policy-Making'. *The Journal of Modern History* 63: 4 (1991): 647–80.

Said, Edward W. *Orientalism*. New York: Vintage Books, 1979.

Sinha, Mrinalini. *Colonial Masculinity: The 'Manly Englishman' and the 'Effeminate Bengali' in the Late Nineteenth Century*. Manchester: Manchester University Press, 1995.

Stoler, Ann Laura. *Carnal Knowledge and Imperial Power: Race and the Intimate in Colonial Rule*. Berkeley: University of California Press, 2002.

Trexler, Richard C. *Sex and Conquest: Gendered Violence, Political Order and the European Conquest of the Americas*. Ithaca, NY: Cornell University Press, 1999.

# CHAPTER 4
# BROTHERS AND SISTERS AT WAR

In the immediate wake of the Second World War (1939–45), it was hard to escape the impression that the great wars of the twentieth century had done more to change gender relationships in Europe than all of the political lobbying, modernist and feminist provocations, and economic changes in peacetime combined. Most European countries granted women the right to vote after the Great War (the First World War, 1914–18). Russian women, for instance, voted in 1917, British women over the age of thirty who met certain property requirements were granted suffrage in 1918, and German and Austrian women balloted in 1919. Many other states followed suit, and the other holdouts granted women the vote at the end of the Second World War. Indeed, in both France and Italy, the vote was granted even before the end of hostilities, and in Greece, where full suffrage would not come until 1952, areas controlled by resistance fighters gave women the vote in the midst of the war as well. The social changes were just as evident. Throughout the continent women had been enlisted into industry in large numbers, had spent time alone with men they were nursing, had donned uniforms and had generally rushed en masse into the public sphere from which they had largely been excluded in the nineteenth century. By the 1970s, there was a consensus among historians and social scientists that the wars had fundamentally transformed the gender landscape of the continent.

The reason for this transformation was also seemingly clear: the active role that women had played in the war effort had challenged the deeply ingrained nineteenth-century stereotypes about female capacities and had proved that they deserved political and social equality with men. In 1914, those hostile to equal rights for women could write that the 'full power of citizenship cannot be given to a sex which is by nature debarred from fulfilling some of the crucial duties of citizenship – enforcement of law, of treaties and of national rights, national defence, and all the rougher work of Empire'.[1] The participation of women in war industries, in the rough work of nursing and sanitation near combat zones and in the more hostile spheres of combat and espionage during the war called into question how 'natural' political and social discrimination was. Suffrage was thus presented as a gift to the women of Europe for exemplary service in one of the century's two world wars. As the Greek resistance fighters put it in 1944, 'the women of Greece participated so actively in the struggle against fascism, and so by their own efforts they won the right to

---

[1] *Anti-Suffrage Review*, cited in Jenny Gould, 'Women's Military Services in First World War Britain', in *Behind the Lines: Gender and the Two World Wars*, ed. Margaret Randolph Higonnet et al. (New Haven, CT and London: Yale University Press, 1987), 117.

debate and manage communal affairs.'[2] The importance of the wars in spurring on female suffrage is perhaps best demonstrated by the fact that neutral Switzerland only granted universal female suffrage in 1971, the last European nation to do so.[3]

The model of proclaiming that women's liberation had been achieved through total war came under serious attack beginning in the 1970s with a new wave of feminist scholarship that saw – with perhaps greater clarity than the previous generation had seen – how incomplete the wartime moves towards equality had been. These historians pointed out that the wartime economic situations were extraordinary and short-lived and that women lost their new jobs as soon as veterans returned to reclaim them. Indeed, in many countries the post-war situation was bleaker than it had been before the war, as women formed a smaller part of the industrial workforce than they had before it began. In Great Britain, for instance, a smaller percentage of women worked in factories in 1921 than had done so in 1911.[4] In cultural terms too, the wars had valorized men and aggressive masculinity in ways that called into question the triumphal narratives of female emancipation. Far from being liberated by the wars, this literature argued, women had suffered during them. They worked long hours in the war economy while still fully engaged in domestic economies, they bore the brunt of brutal occupation policies, they cowered in bomb shelters, and they received smaller food rations than their male counterparts. When the war ended, their men victimized them in other ways. They were fired from their jobs, questioned about their wartime behaviour by jealous husbands and forced out of the public sphere. Whatever had changed during the war, the fact of male dominance and female subordination had not. Indeed, if anything, these historians argued, the situation had become even more polarized in highly militarized societies where war, in the form of the Cold War, still loomed darkly.[5]

These two positions may seem irreconcilable – either the wars served the cause of women's liberation or they did not. In fact, both accounts are basically right. History does not move in a single direction. It is no contradiction to argue both that the era of total war brought about massive transformation in European gender relations and that those transformations were not all 'progressive'. We strive in this chapter to describe the gender changes that occurred over the course of the war years and that may have been missed by those mainly concerned with whether war had really furthered the cause of women. One important aspect that has been largely overlooked in the tendency to draw up a score sheet of liberty and equality for women is the extent to which all gender relations were affected by the dramatic

---

[2] Cited in Tasoula Vervenioti, 'The Adventure of Women's Suffrage in Greece', in *When the War Was Over: Women, War and Peace in Europe, 1940–1956*, ed. Claire Duchen and Irene Bandhauer-Schöffmann (London and New York: Leicester University Press, 2000), 105.

[3] Although Sweden, Portugal, Iceland, Ireland and Spain also remained officially neutral throughout the Second World War (Denmark, Norway, Belgium, the Netherlands and Luxumbourg began as neutrals but were later invaded by Nazi Germany), all of these countries had previously granted female suffrage at least to a limited extent. For a recent overview of female suffrage in Europe, which unfortunately does not include Switzerland, see Blanca Rodriguez Ruiz, ed., *The Struggle for Female Suffrage in Europe: Voting to Become Citizens* (Leiden: Brill, 2012).

[4] Susan Pyecroft, 'British Working Women and the First World War', *The Historian* 56, no. 4 (1994): 708.

[5] This line of reasoning is particularly pronounced in Higonnet et al., *Behind the Lines*. This volume has been very influential in the field and remains so today.

'victory' of fraternity in the first half of the twentieth century. As we argued in Chapter 1, the revolutionary era had challenged patriarchy not so much because women challenged men as because brothers challenged their fathers. Both fraternal and patriarchal systems are based on male domination, but that does not make them the same. The way that men thought about themselves and their social roles was definitively transformed, so too was the social and cultural relationship between men and women, not to mention the political and rhetorical conditions under which women had to state their claims for equality. The nationalistic and warlike manifestations of fraternity set the tone for gender relations in the twentieth century.

As we have seen, the fraternal model of masculinity recovered from the post-revolutionary backlash by attaching itself to the common European project of empire. Bellicose manliness was also present in many of the organizations that challenged the large European empires at the start of the twentieth century, certainly within the working-class socialist and communist movements, but also within the nationalist independence movements that were developing both within Europe and outside of it. There was simply too big a surplus of fighting spirit among statesmen, revolutionaries and nationalist warriors to imagine that war could be avoided indefinitely. It was not the outbreak of a global war in 1914 that was so surprising; it was the fact that it had not happened sooner.

## The great explosion

Broad, long-term historical pressures rarely converge precisely. On 28 June 1914, however, they did. The young, fraternal, nationalist and decolonizing forces in Europe attacked the old, patriarchal, imperial and recolonizing forces with the first of what would be many shots in a long war. Gavrilo Princip was nineteen years old and a member of a fraternal revolutionary organization named 'Young Bosnia'. The members of Young Bosnia were deeply aggrieved by the recent annexation of Bosnia to the Austro-Hungarian Empire. Prior to 1878, Bosnia had been a part of the Ottoman Empire, but as that collapsed, a fierce struggle for control in the region ensued between two old empires (the Austro-Hungarian and Russian) and the newly emerging national states throughout the Balkans. In 1878, Habsburg troops occupied the territory, and in 1908 Emperor Franz Joseph announced that he was annexing it outright from the Ottoman Empire. This was a blow to the Russian Empire, which had hopes of being the dominant Great Power in Balkan affairs, but it was also intended as a show of strength to intimidate the Serbian government, which the Habsburgs felt had become far too uppity. Uncomfortable with an independent young state on their borders, the Austro-Hungarian Empire had attempted in 1906 to force Serbia to become 'economically and politically dependent' upon them by imposing trade sanctions. This policy had failed.[6]

The turn from sanctions to military action on the part of Vienna prompted many Serb nationalists to seek violent solutions to the Bosnian question. Large crowds protested

---

[6] Cited in Misha Glenny, *The Balkans: Nationalism, War and the Great Powers, 1804–1999* (New York: Penguin Books, 1999), 282.

in the streets of Belgrade shouting 'Down with Austria!' and the Serbian government ordered a mobilization of the army before the other Great Powers successfully convinced them to adopt a course of moderation.[7] Moderation was the last thing that the volatile members of Young Bosnia wanted. Instead, they believed that Bosnia, with its large Serb population, properly belonged in an expanded Serbian state. The battlefield successes of the Serbian army against the Ottoman Empire and then Bulgaria in the first two Balkan Wars (1912–13), which led to significant territorial expansion for Serbia, only seemed to further demonstrate the viability of violence in resolving the territorial and political questions that decolonization in the Balkans had occasioned.

There was also a strong undertone of generational conflict within the revolutionary movement. Many older and more prosperous members of the Serbian elite welcomed Vienna's annexation of Bosnia, which promised greater prosperity and stability. Indeed, Evgenije Letica, the head of Sarajevo's Orthodox Church, had even arranged a public prayer for Franz Joseph in 1908 to demonstrate the loyalty of the local population. When the congregation knelt to intone the prayer, only a group of high-school boys refused to bow for the dynasty, providing a rather visual demonstration of the divide between sons and fathers. Nor was this generational divide peaceable: the outraged members of Young Bosnia resolved to assassinate Letica and three other Serb notables in Sarajevo for their collaboration with the enemy.[8]

First, however, they had larger patriarchs to attack. The Habsburg dynasty was the oldest in Europe. In 1914, it had a seventy-three-year-old emperor who had been sitting on the throne for sixty-six years. Even the heir to the throne, the emperor's nephew Franz Ferdinand, was old enough at fifty to be the father of nearly every member of Young Bosnia. And Franz Ferdinand had resolved to come to Sarajevo in the summer of 1914 to observe military exercises in the new Bosnian territory of the empire. On 28 June, the arrogance of age collided with the incompetence of youth. Only a series of foolish security lapses allowed the six assassins to succeed in killing Franz Ferdinand, as the first attempts to bomb or shoot the archduke failed for lack of expertise (the bombing attempt failed when the hand-thrown bomb bounced off the rear of the car) or lack of nerve (four of the young men did not fire at the archduke as he passed). It was only because Franz Ferdinand's driver literally stopped in front of a surprised Gavrilo Princip after missing a turn and stalling his car that the boy's shaking hand was able to fire the shot that would trigger the continental catastrophe.

Still, there was a moment's hesitation before war was declared. In every government across the continent, sober statesmen urged caution and restraint even as others beat the drums of war. Indeed, in most governments, the faction of caution seemed dominant throughout the month of July. Shelves of books have been written assigning various amounts of blame to the key actors in the crisis who tipped the scales for war, but the factor most important in our context is the role that masculinity played in the diplomatic decision-making process. Throughout Europe, officers and politicians alike paid close attention to their personal honour and prestige during debates; similar concern for

---

[7] Bernadotte Everly Schmitt, *The Annexation of Bosnia, 1908–1909* (New York: H. Fertig, 1970), 46–7.
[8] Glenny, *The Balkans*, 297.

the honour and prestige of their nations was constantly voiced. But this still does not fully explain why war was declared. After all, smaller crises had threatened war over the previous decade, and diplomatic solutions that allowed for peace with honour had been reached. This time, however, no exit strategy was found, in part because neither Austria-Hungary nor Germany was willing to countenance a diplomatic solution that did not envisage a humiliation of Serbia. The direct assault on an old Great Power by a small young country appeared to have touched a particularly sensitive nerve.

But even in countries that far preferred peace to war in 1914, such as Russia, the factor of masculinity was decisive. When Russian cabinet ministers met to discuss the implications of mobilizing the army, all of them knew that such a move could very well mean war, and all of them also understood what one member called the 'grave danger which Russia would run in case of hostilities'. They were right to see these possibilities. The mobilization did in the end tip the scales for war, and the empire would collapse in revolution and anarchy as a result only a few years later. But they decided to mobilize both because they felt that 'the honour, dignity and authority of Russia were at stake' and because they convinced themselves that a show of strength might actually bring about a peaceful end to the crisis. As one noted, 'if we remained passive, we would not attain our object … All factors tended to prove that the most judicious policy Russia could follow in present circumstances was a return to a firmer and more energetic attitude towards the unreasonable claims of the Central European powers.'[9]

This adoption of youthful, even reckless, masculine vigour ('firm and more energetic' rather than 'passive') by the old men of Europe led in short order not to peace but to the declaration of war. Every army on the continent had prepared for such a contingency, and they pulled their mobilization schedules off the shelves. Men were packed onto trains and hurled against one another. Russians hurried to the Polish and Ukrainian fronts; Austrians deployed to Serbia and Ukraine; Germans hustled mainly to Belgium and France, though defensive forces were left in Poland and East Prussia. Serbs, Frenchmen and Belgians dug in to defend their homelands, often in vain. In due time, most of the rest of the continent would follow down the road to war.

European society instantly changed. Over the course of the war 59,471,000 men were called up from the reserves, conscripted or volunteered for the armed forces.[10] These troop deployments produced the largest sexual separation in European history to that date. Unsurprisingly, mass mobilization recast the gendered spatial schemes of nineteenth-century Europe as well. Instead of the male/female divide mapping onto the public/private spheres, it now mapped onto front/home front. Just as that earlier gendered division of space was never fully reflective of reality, so too did the wartime gender division obscure the variety of ways that men and women moved, acted and lived during the war. Plenty of men remained at home because of age, disability or other reasons, and thousands of women streamed to the front in official or unofficial capacities.

---

[9] All cited in D. C. B. Lieven, *Russia and the Origins of the First World War* (New York: St. Martin's Press, 1983), 143.
[10] John Ellis and Michael Cox, *The World War I Databook: The Essential Facts and Figures for All the Combatants* (London: Aurum, 2001), 245.

Still, these varieties of experience did almost nothing to change the notion that the front was masculine territory and that 'home' was feminine. The transformation was most evident and immediate for soldiers. In contrast to the situation behind the lines, a single-gender community did form in combat regions. This was a welcome development for many nationalist ideologues and military men, who cultivated an ethic of unsullied masculinity and frankly preferred the company of men to the company of women. The fantasy of a community of men pre-dated the war, but the scope of the European conflict allowed for its creation on a scale previously undreamed of. For those who valued hardness, vigour and solidity, this was better than any service in a fishing fleet in December.

These masculine communities were, of course, intentional constructs. Military leaders throughout the ages have recognized the importance of social cohesiveness to combat effectiveness, and the training techniques of every European army reflected this concern. Soldiers were taught to build small communities of trust that could be extended in concentric circles outwards as far as the entire nation in arms. The most intense small-scale socialization exercises tended to take place at the level of the company (a group of roughly 100 men), though in combat practice, the platoon (about 10–20 men) was usually the group one most relied upon. As the circle of trust expanded, the ties relied more on symbolic strength and less upon personal social cohesiveness. Thus, when soldiers were taught about connections to their regiment (about 2,000 men) as much weight was placed on regimental history as on developing social ties between men of different companies or battalions. By the time one reached the identification with the armed forces as a whole (millions of men for most combatants), the procedures were almost entirely symbolic.

Within the confines of military structures, these were truly male communities, and this maleness was crucial to the way that soldiers understood their war experiences. Love between men was both encouraged and expected. These male experiences of love were quite often deeply affectionate. They were based on daily cohabitation, shared burdens, communal victories and mutual sacrifice. Thomas Kühne has explored how these bonds of affection and comradeship under great duress could blur gender boundaries. His reading of German soldiers' letters led him to argue that relationships between men at the front also included many 'soft' female emotions along with the 'hard' emotions of the masculine warrior. 'Motherly' tenderness in the treatment of the wounded and strong bonds of community that helped soldiers cope with the violence they were experiencing and perpetrating do not entirely conform to military definitions of masculine heroism.[11] As Allen Frantzen has demonstrated, this was a love with deep roots in Christian notions of chivalry that combined Christ's own self-sacrifice with a rather less Christian warrior ethos based in vengeance and other forms of violent self-defence.[12]

---

[11] Thomas Kühne, *Kameradschaft: Die Soldaten des Nationalsozialistischen Krieg und das 20. Jahrhundert* (Göttingen: Vandenhoeck & Ruprecht, 2006); and Thomas Kühne, 'Comradeship: Gender Confusion and Gender Order in the German Military, 1918–1945', in *Home/Front: The Military, War and Gender in Twentieth-Century Germany*, ed. Karen Hagemann and Stefanie Schüler-Springorum (Oxford: Berg Publishers, 2002), 233–54. See also Robert L. Nelson, *German Soldier Newspapers of the First World War* (Cambridge and New York: Cambridge University Press, 2011), esp. 88–102.

[12] Allen J. Frantzen, *Bloody Good: Chivalry, Sacrifice, and the Great War* (Chicago: University of Chicago Press, 2004).

**Figure 4.1** German soldiers spending an enjoyable evening in the dugouts during the First World War. Reprinted by permission of Mary Evans Picture Library.

Not all this male affection was quite as Christian as the chivalric model might suggest, however. There was a real strand of homoeroticism in the literature of the war, as men spent a good deal of time observing (and admiring) male bodies and feeling tragic loss when those bodies were mutilated or destroyed. There were also a good many 'crushes' that developed within the ranks, often within the context of the stylized authority relationship that was present between an officer and his men. Paul Fussell believed that most of this erotic tension was a 'sublimated (i.e. "chaste") form of temporary homosexuality' and that there was not much of the 'active unsublimated kind',[13] but it is in fact difficult to know how widespread sexual relationships were within the ranks. At least 230 British soldiers were convicted for homosexual practices during the war, but this is surely only a small percentage of the number of homosexual liaisons that occurred. It is, however, impossible to know with any degree of certainty how small.[14] Jason Crouthamel argues, for instance, that the German military concentrated prosecution efforts on sexual assaults and generally looked the other way for consensual acts, in part to avoid attracting public

---

[13] Paul Fussell, *The Great War and Modern Memory* (New York: Oxford University Press, 1975), 272.
[14] A. D. Harvey, 'Homosexuality and the British Army during the First World War', *Journal for the Society of Army Historical Research* 79 (2001): 313–19.

attention to the prevalence of homosexuality in the military.[15] There was a prevailing assumption that sexual acts between men resulted from the sexual deprivation of their isolation on the front; it was, in other words, opportunistic.[16] Although our understanding of the prevalence of homosexuality today suggests that this was not always the case, the precise cultural influences of front culture certainly created specific conditions for homoerotic contact and likely led some to experiment in ways that they did not later repeat. For others, however, the war experience encouraged the search for similar bonds of comradeship on the home front. In Germany homosexual men could join a growing and diverse homosexual rights movement, which was primarily based in Berlin. For some this meant accepting their more feminine natures and seeing themselves as a 'third sex', somewhere in between male and female.[17] Others, such as Elisar Kupffer, attacked the notion of a 'third sex', viewing it simply as feminization and extolling the virtues of models of male love from ancient Greece. Those who took the male bonding experiences of the war as the guiding principle of their existence found a congenial home in Adolf Brand's organization, the *Gemeinschaft der Eigenen* (Community of the Self-Owned, founded in 1903), which advocated a muscular kind of homosexuality that hearkened back to a Greek ideal and eschewed all aspects of femininity.[18] Other German masculinists, such as Hans Blüher and Benedict Friedländer, advocated various versions of a *Männerbund* – a community of men – that praised the supremely virile and heroic figure of the soldier and thus encouraged those who had their first homosexual experiences on the front to see them in a positive light.[19] The fact that Berlin had become an epicentre of gay life did not go unnoticed in the rest of Europe. As Matt Cook has demonstrated, British commentators made constant references to 'the connection between sodomy, Germany and treachery' throughout the war.[20]

---

[15] Jason Crouthamel, *An Intimate History of the Front: Masculinity, Sexuality, and German Soldiers in the First World War* (New York: Palgrave Macmillan, 2014), 124–5.

[16] Ibid., 59.

[17] This term was coined, along with many other descriptions of human sexuality, by Magnus Hirschfeld. See his *Berlins Drittes Geschlecht* (Berlin: Verlag rosa Winkel, 1991 [1901]). For a summary of the debate between theorists of the 'third sex' and masculinists who rejected all forms of male femininity, see Glenn Ramsey, 'The Rites of Artgenossen: Contesting Homosexual Political Culture in Weimar Germany', *Journal of the History of Sexuality* 17, no. 1 (2008): 85–109.

[18] For descriptions of Brand's organization see Robert Beachy, *Gay Berlin: Birthplace of a Modern Identity* (New York: Knopf, 2014), 101–18; Harry Oosterhuis, 'General Introduction: Homosexual Emancipation in Germany Before 1933: Two Traditions', in *Homosexuality and Male Bonding in Pre-Nazi Germany: The Youth Movement, the Gay Movement, and Male Bonding Before Hitler's Rise: Original Transcripts from* Der Eigene, the First Gay Journal in the World, ed. Harry Oosterhuis and Hubert Kennedy (Binghamton, NY: Harrington Park Press, 1991), 1–27; Clayton Whisnant, 'Gay German History: Future Directions?', *Journal of the History of Sexuality* 17, no. 1 (2008): 1–10; and Claudia Bruns, 'The Politics of Masculinity in the (Homo-)Sexual Discourse (1880 to 1920)', *German History* 23, no. 3 (2005): 306–20.

[19] Rainer Herrn, 'Magnus Hirschfeld (1868–1935)', in *Personenlexikon der Sexualwissenschaft*, ed. Volkmar Sigusch and Günter Grau (Frankfurt: Campus, 2009), 284–94; and Claudia Bruns, *Politik der Eros: der Männerbund in Wissenschaft, Politik und Jugendkultur (1880–1934)* (Cologne: Böhlau, 2008).

[20] Matt Cook, 'Queer Conflicts: Love, Sex and War, 1914–1967', in *A Gay History of Britain: Love and Sex between Men Since the Middle Ages*, ed. Matt Cook et al. (Oxford and Westport, Conn: Praeger, 2007), 145.

To varying degrees in different European countries, the war also afforded opportunities for women to function in close cooperation with one another and in previously unheard-of roles. Aside from the iconic image of the female munitions worker, women could also be seen in paramilitary units, front nursing, ambulance corps and various war-related voluntary organizations. Radclyffe Hall (author of *The Well of Loneliness* (1928), which is often regarded as the first lesbian novel) later stated that it was particularly 'inverted' women who benefited from these opportunities. Indeed, as Laura Doan notes, many women later famous for their lesbianism worked as ambulance drivers during the Great War: Gertrude Stein, Dolly Wilde (Oscar's niece), and the suffragettes Vera 'Jack' Holme and Evelina Haverfield.[21] But unlike in the case of male homosexuality, these women had no collective organizations that might have encouraged them to translate their emotional and/or physical experiences into an identity. In her investigation of British women's involvement in the two world wars, Doan finds that most 'had little sense of sexual selfhood or subjectivity' and certainly did not identify as lesbians – a term that did not really describe any women's self-perceptions until the interwar period.[22] Although commentators at the time might have been taken aback by the male dress and independent comportment of these 'mannish' women, and although close and even romantic relationships might have formed, the link between 'gender deviance and sexual deviance' was never that clear and 'female mannishness was not always a challenge to the sexual order, nor did it possess one simple meaning.'[23] Nonetheless, as for homosexual men, the war presented an unprecedented opportunity for developing same-sex bonds completely divorced from the realm of home and family.

Taking both homosexual and heterosexual experiences together, it is tempting to view the gender relations on the front in the Great War as a world of two solitudes: a monstrous pre-adolescent tree fort from which women were forcefully excluded on the one side and a girls club of adventure on the other. But the situation was far more complicated. Women, with only a very few exceptions, were not allowed to serve in combat units, but as we shall see shortly, this did not mean that there was no contact between men and women during the war. Still, combat units were male fraternities. It was not simply war that built cohesion in these masculine communities, but the very fact of female exclusion. Women were seen as real dangers by military authorities charged with maintaining morale. They warned their soldiers that women were unreliable, likely to gossip and betray military secrets, and that the women they would meet would be loose at best or prostitutes at worst and therefore likely to carry venereal disease. These steps were taken both because state and military leaders genuinely believed that individual women could pose serious intelligence and health risks and because the war effort required a depersonification of women and their intense symbolization.

Rightly or wrongly (probably rightly), propagandists and officers believed that the best way to motivate soldiers to risk death, to endure awful living conditions and to do so for extended periods of time was to make soldiering identical to the fulfilment of masculine duty. They equated national defence (of territory, power or honour) with the masculine

---

[21] Doan, *Disturbing Practices*, viii.

[22] Ibid., 140.

[23] Paul R. Deslanes, 'Exposing, Adorning, and Dressing the Body in the Modern Era', in *The Routledge History of Sex and the Body, 1500 to the Present*, ed. Sarah Toulalan and Kate Fisher (New York: Routledge, 2013), 179–203: 197.

defence of hearth and home, of women and children and indeed the motherland itself. Even German masculinists often claimed that lacking families made them more able to devote their energies to the protection of the home front.[24] In this respect, the ideologies of the nation and of the community of men, which were converging upon each other with alarming speed during the war years, valued women quite highly. The purpose of the war became the defence of Woman with a capital W. They were the nurturing, passive bearers of the nation, and they were threatened by the enemy.

As this brief description of martial sexuality suggests, however, the positive and idealized symbolization of women depended in its daily practice upon sexual segregation. Women could be protected by their men only if their men could be insulated from feminine contact. Military regulations were explicit on this point in most armies of the era. In Russia, military officials at the highest levels concerned themselves with remarkably mundane questions regarding contact between their soldiers and women. They tried to prevent female members of the Red Cross and other nursing units from entering combat areas, they believed that female personnel in the rear negatively affected the morale of wounded soldiers in military hospitals, and they were positively paranoid about local civilian women.

Combined with this fear and suspicion was a widespread belief that virile young men required outlets for their sexual energy. The war represented, in a way, an end to (or at least a hiatus in) the 'civilized' repression of primal urges we discussed in previous chapters. Instead, it not only made possible, but also seemed to require a new relationship between 'natural' desires and male behaviour. It was reasonable for officials to presume that unleashing the instinct to kill would probably unleash sexual instincts as well. Many officers hoped that blocking access to sex might increase the potential for violence even more. But others believed that their boys would both need and deserve sexual release. Thus, across the armies, there was ambivalence about consorting with prostitutes. Despite official fears of venereal disease and espionage, soldiers of the Great War found ample opportunity to pay for sex with local women or camp followers. As the war dragged on, army and state officials in many combatant countries got directly involved in the sex trade by regulating the brothels that their soldiers visited. In most cases, official intervention took the form of 'authorizing' certain establishments that agreed to medical testing of their employees and that allowed officials to impose military discipline upon providers and clients alike. In a few locations, armies even operated their own brothels, taking over the positions previously held by madams or pimps.[25] In France,

---

[24] See, for example, Adolf Brand, 'What We Want (1925)', in *Homosexuality and Male Bonding in Pre-Nazi Germany: The Youth Movement, the Gay Movement, and Male Bonding Before Hitler's Rise: Original Transcripts from Der Eigene, the First Gay Journal in the World*, ed. Harry Oosterhuis and Hubert Kennedy (New York: Haworth Press, 1991), 155–66.

[25] It is still unclear just how many of these army brothels existed and in which armies. It appears that they were most common in the German army, but much research remains to be done. See Lutz Sauerteig, 'Militär, Medizin und Moral: Sexualität im Ersten Weltkrieg', in *Die Medizin und der Erste Weltkrieg*, ed. Wolfgang U. Eckart and Christoph Gradmann (Pfaffenweiler: Centaurus-Verlagsgesellschaft, 1996), 197–226; Elisabeth Domansky, 'Militarization and Reproduction in World War I Germany', in *Society, Culture, and the State in Germany, 1870–1930*, ed. Geoff Eley (Ann Arbor, MI: University of Michigan Press, 1996), 427–63; and Joshua S. Goldstein, *War and Gender: How Gender Shapes the War System and Vice Versa* (Cambridge: Cambridge University Press, 2001), 343–4.

these institutions were called *maisons tolérées* (tolerated houses) and were hierarchically organized to serve men of different ranks, with a blue light outside marking those for officers and a red for the other ranks.[26] Though many soldiers appreciated this access to easy sex, it would be misleading to assume that all did. As Belgian singer Jacques Brel made clear in his anti-war song 'Au Suivant', some were instead traumatized by the coldness and inhumanity of being obliged to wait in a long line at the doors for such a deeply impersonal experience. Regardless of whether the experience was positive or negative, the proximity of assembly line sex to assembly line death in the war zone led many veterans to connect sex and violence in memories of the war experience.

But there was an even darker, more hostile form of military misogyny, one that quickly came to dominate the discussion of wartime sex. As in many previous wars, soldiers raped women in territories they crossed and occupied. The extent of this behaviour is difficult to gauge for two reasons. First, both the attackers and the victims had good reasons for remaining silent about the crime, so most sources based on personal narratives systematically ignored the issue. Official records are little better, for though military justice systems would occasionally prosecute soldiers for their depredations, there is no way of telling what percentage of offences they brought to trial. Second, though we see only the tip of the iceberg at the micro-level, the issue of rape at the symbolic macro-level came into special prominence during the war years. As soon as the war began, rape became an important propaganda issue. The German invasion of neutral Belgium was instantly portrayed as a violent sexual act. The 'Rape of Belgium' became a staple of wartime mobilization for everyone who opposed the Central Powers. Posters in Great Britain decried the crime and hinted that the barbaric Germans might not stop in Belgium, patriotic directors in Russia made films on the issue, and those sympathetic to the Entente in neutral America made much of the despoiling of the innocent as they lobbied their way towards eventual entry into the war.

Describing the invasion of a country as a 'rape' was metaphoric, but journalists and state officials also argued that actual rapes were accompanying the military incursions. German officials protested that the lurid stories of predatory sex were propaganda devices of their opponents and that their troops were in fact disciplined. If anything, they argued, they were the real victims, as the savage, 'Asian' Cossacks of the Russian army were responsible for widespread sexual abuse during their short occupation of East Prussia in 1914 and their rather longer occupation of Austrian Galicia over the course of the war. Neutral observers had difficulty determining the merits of these claims and counterclaims during the war, and dispassionate neutrality became nearly impossible after the war, when war crimes and the question of war guilt became an obsession among European politicians and for generations of European historians. The most recent

---

[26] Clare Makepeace, 'Male Heterosexuality and Prostitution during the Great War: British Soldiers' Encounters with Maisons Tolérées', *Cultural and Social History* 9, no. 1 (2012): 71. See also Craig Gibson, *Behind the Front: British Soldiers and French Civilians, 1914–1918* (Cambridge and New York: Cambridge University Press, 2014), 309–45.

scholarship suggests that though the public outrage surrounding rape was less focused on the personal suffering of the women involved than it was with broader questions of the nation and the war effort, rapes did in fact occur. Belgian women were raped, French women were raped, German women were raped and Galician women were raped.[27] Some soldiers were court-martialled and executed for their violation of the laws of war and their own military discipline, but an unknown number of men went unpunished, often because their own commanders chose to look the other way and to treat rape as part and parcel of soldiering. We should not see these sexual assaults as accidental or natural, or even as part of the 'heat of battle'. Rapes almost never occurred when bullets were flying. They were instead the expression of the peculiar sexual culture of the society of men and the expression of the violent quest for dominance that was the life of the soldier. It is also important to understand that these acts of violence against women were not in opposition to the symbolic idealization of women or the motherland. On the contrary, the enemy acts of misogyny stimulated one's own masculine desire to protect mothers and the motherland, and vice versa. All the armies raped, and all promised to protect their own women. Paradoxically, the defence of civilization and the practice of rape were dependent upon one another.

Still, it is possible to make too much of this phenomenon. However widespread rape was during the war, it is clear that the vast majority of soldiers never assaulted a single woman or child. And despite the organized misogyny at the front, most soldiers also had healthier and kinder relationships with women. More than a few soldiers sought girlfriends instead of prostitutes or victims in the occupied lands, though this search generally resulted in a combined effort by military authorities and local communities to prevent such a destabilizing relationship. There were also, of course, the women that men had left behind. In armies in which home leaves were provided, it was understood that the soldier on leave would make full use of his temporary respite from the men on the front to seek sexual gratification from his wives, girlfriends or any other willing women behind the lines. Finally, and perhaps most importantly, women were present through their letters. The Great War was marked by the literacy of its soldiers. Even in countries like Russia and Serbia, in which literacy had grown much more slowly and recently than in the countries of Western Europe, the majority of soldiers could read. At home, even though female literacy lagged behind male literacy, women who could not write would often get a literate friend or relative to do so. The letters, photos and mementoes from home were important parts of army existence, and though they did not replace physical presence, the communication between men and women meant that despite the fantasies of a purely male society, the actual army was in fact a society that included women, though mostly through the marks of their absence.

---

[27] The model example of a historical work that seeks both to document wartime atrocities and to account for the power of atrocity propaganda is John N. Horne and Alan Kramer, *German Atrocities, 1914: A History of Denial* (New Haven: Yale University Press, 2001). On Russian atrocities in East Prussia, see Alexander Watson, '"Unheard-of Brutality": Russian Atrocities against Civilians in East Prussia, 1914–1915', *Journal of Modern History* 86, no. 4 (2014): 780–825.

The gender situation on the 'home front' was, if anything, even more complicated. The term 'home front' itself was developed in Britain during the First World War, and it betrayed both the desire to distinguish the male and female spheres of the war and the inability to stabilize the boundary between the two.[28] On the one hand, the declaration that this was 'home' marked it as a female space, a connotation that was only strengthened by the eviction of so many men from that space during mobilization. On the other hand, it was declared a 'front', with all the military and masculine connotations that implied. The combination of the two terms raised an important but largely unarticulated question: was there such a thing as martial femininity?

The answer to this question is quite difficult. Everyone knew that women had assumed special duties during wartime throughout the course of European history, but the traditional role they played was one of support for male family members. This had meant temporary husbandry at the homestead during campaigns, taking care of the male jobs as well as the female ones on the farm. More importantly, it meant moral support. Women were expected to reassure anxious men, to remind them of their masculine and patriotic duties as warriors and to promise continued obedience and fidelity in their absence. The sexual aspects of this particular contract were present even in ancient Greece, as the memorable sexual strike waged by the Athenian women in Aristophanes' play *Lysistrata* (411 BCE) to end the Peloponnesian War attests. But even this precocious (and fictional) peace protest only reinforced the notion that the social organization through which women were expected to work was the family. The more common phenomenon of the so-called Spartan Women who told their sons to come home either 'with their shield or on it' became part of European mythology, and it too stressed the role of women within the family in times of war.

The same situation prevailed all over Europe at the beginning of the war. It was only in two neutral countries (Norway and Finland) that European women had the vote in 1914, and the explicit reason for their exclusion elsewhere was that the fundamental social unit throughout the continent remained the patriarchal family, not the individual. Women were represented by their men at the ballot box; so too would they be represented by men at the front while women tended to domestic affairs. It was therefore no surprise that belligerent states across the continent used the family as one of the devices to mobilize soldiers and the main device to mobilize non-soldiers throughout the war.

The only other institution through which women could reasonably expect to contribute to the war effort in large numbers in 1914 was the church. Christian charity work had been one of the few areas in which women visibly acted in the public sphere in patriarchal Europe, and it seemed only natural that women eager to participate in the war effort would do so under the aegis of the cross. The cross that most chose during the war was the Red Cross, an institution that blended the Christian, the national and the feminine in a socially acceptable way. But nursing was far from the only outlet for

---

[28] Susan R. Grayzel, *Women's Identities at War: Gender, Motherhood, and Politics in Britain and France during the First World War* (Chapel Hill, NC: University of North Carolina Press, 1999), 7.

charity that the war promised to provide. As events would show, families deprived of breadwinners would slip into poverty, refugees would fill the roads and city streets begging for assistance, and children adrift in the war-torn world would need guidance. Women would be expected to care in public ways for non-family members, and the long history of women's charitable activities within Christian churches would structure and legitimate that activity without posing any threat to the established social order.

This attempt to find a way to mobilize women in a socially conservative way found its most pure expression in the attempts of female members of Europe's royal families to take visible leadership roles in charitable fund-raising and work. In Russia, Empress Alexandra participated in caring for the war-wounded from the very first winter of the war, and the tsar's second daughter served as the patron of one of the most important social relief organizations of the war, the 'Tatiana Committee for the Relief of War Victims', which began its work in September 1914 to care for war widows and children but then added care for refugees to its portfolio in 1915. In Austria, Empress Zita made public stops at soup kitchens and lent her name to important charity organizations.[29] At the start, the social conservatism of these organizations even led some, like the Russian Red Cross, to insist that only educated, upper-class ladies could serve in them.[30]

The conservative dream that a state could wage a massive war without significant alteration in the social order did not come true, as the fate of Alexandra's and Zita's charity work demonstrates. Both Alexandra and Zita had been members of the multinational European elite prior to their marriages. Alexandra came from Hesse-Darmstadt and spoke Russian with a strong German accent. Zita was from the house of Bourbon-Parma and thus carried the taint of a French and Italian background. These international marriages had long been the norm for the great European dynasties, as few ruling houses wished to disrupt the local aristocratic order by raising native noble families to royal status, and as each sought political gain from the wedding of their offspring. In previous conflicts, national background had not mattered very much, as monarchical political systems stressed personal fealty above ethnic loyalty. But this was a new war waged in new political circumstances. Instead of receiving love and praise for their visible wartime relief work, Alexandra and Zita were vilified for being too cosmopolitan and were rumoured to have committed treason. It turned out that the subjects of the Habsburgs and Romanovs believed that ethnic belonging counted for far more than marriage into a powerful dynasty.

This shift may seem relatively insignificant; it was not. In patriarchal systems, women were expected to assume a new social position and identity upon their marriage. When the father handed his daughter to her husband at the wedding, this entailed a shift of duties, of loyalties and of subjectivities that was understood to be complete and irrevocable.

---

[29] Peter Gatrell, *A Whole Empire Walking: Refugees in Russia during World War I* (Bloomington: Indiana University Press, 1999), 40–1; Healy, *Vienna and the Fall of the Habsburg Empire*, 187.

[30] Joshua A. Sanborn, *Drafting the Russian Nation: Military Conscription, Total War, and Mass Politics, 1905–1925* (DeKalb: Northern Illinois University Press, 2003), 148.

By law, a woman automatically took on the citizenship status of her husband rather than her father at the moment she traded her father's last name for her husband's. This absolute shift reflected the principle of absolute control of women that was the bedrock of patriarchal ideology, and it presumed that whatever political sentiment or cultural affinity a woman might have was, like a dowry, objective and fully transferable. Given this theory of the effects of marriage on women, one might have expected Alexandra to have become totally Russian and Zita to have become totally Austrian at the moment the church bells chimed.

Despite the popular rumours to the contrary, all available evidence suggests that both did: there seems to have been little ambivalence on the part of either woman during the war. Each was a hearty patriot. But the fact that there were widespread doubts is significant. The suspicion that a woman might secretly hold onto the political beliefs of her youth and wait for the moment when she might act accordingly implied that though women might lack political rights, they did not lack political subjectivity. This was, of course, the argument that feminists had been making for years, and the very existence of feminist movements should have demonstrated that this was the case. But, more effectively in some places than others, those movements had been marginalized prior to the war. During the war, it became clear that feminine political subjectivity was a universal condition, one that extended beyond the aberrant suffragettes all the way up to the royals.

It would be easy to conclude, having seen the shift in female political subjectivity, the rapid expansion of female volunteer and paid work outside of the home, the family and the church, and the acquisition of the vote in so many countries at the end of the war, that an extremely durable patriarchal bulwark had been shattered and that a new female gender role based upon autonomy instead of dependence had now emerged. Indeed, such a transformation did happen, but the new gender archetype was not unchallenged. The spectre of the independent woman, a staple of conservative nightmares for centuries, was now more tangible, and the old patriarchal model was now fatally weakened, but a third model, which we might call the 'fraternal' model of femininity, also appeared and quickly became normative.

This model, largely developed during the First World War, was based not on the destruction of the family as the context of feminine behaviour but the reconfiguration of that family. As Maureen Healy has acutely observed, one of the key dimensions of the Great War was the fact that 'the family was turned "inside out" for the purposes of war-making.'[31] Two aspects of this transformation were especially important. First, women and children became very public figures whose daily lives and daily choices were understood to be deeply political and crucial for the war effort. Second, the erasure of the civilian man from the iconography of the nation led to a real crisis of masculinity for men out of uniform. The war occasioned both of these transformations, and the main outcome was the increased visibility of the state, which was actively

---

[31] Healy, *Vienna and the Fall of the Habsburg Empire*, 26.

transforming the old patriarchal order into one of state paternalism. In the long run, this change had dramatic effects upon the family. Just as the debates over a 'single wage' focused attention on the economic institution of the family at the very moment that industrialization was undermining the model of familial complementarity, so too did the increased visibility of state 'family policies' during and after the First World War indicate that the patriarchal family was actually losing power as an autonomous political institution. As the state loomed over the economic, social and (increasingly) sexual relationships within the home, the family became above all a community of sentiment. The family was very visible in the national political ideologies, but the power of householders speaking on behalf of the family unit had actually declined as states dealt directly with individual citizens without the pesky intermediary institutions of community, caste or family.

The reconfiguration of the family during the First World War opened up new possibilities for female activity. Many European women saw the transformation of gender roles that occurred during the war as a moment of liberation. Despite the tragedies of the period, some of them even expressed a certain joy in being able to participate meaningfully in what most Europeans understood to be the defining moment of their generation.[32] Taking on 'men's' work in defence industries demonstrated their capacity to work, and tending broken soldiers as nurses showed that they could help the war effort from a position of relative power over bedridden and dependent men.

In Russia, this desire to be an active part of the war effort extended to combat participation. Several women petitioned the tsar to allow them to become soldiers during the first three years of the war; much to everyone's surprise, the tsar granted some of these requests, probably hoping that every bit of patriotic energy that his subjects could provide would strengthen the war effort and his own precarious position. The most famous of these women, Maria Bochkareva, noted in her memoir both how difficult the position of the woman soldier was and how exciting it was. Coming from a very dark corner of Europe's patriarchal world, Bochkareva had been abused by her father and her husband and latched rather forcefully onto patriotism as a positive and defining cause for her life. In some respects, her journey from Siberian peasant woman to soldier was a flight from the traditional world, but she portrayed and understood it as a reaffirmation of traditional Russia and as a submission to the authority and unquestioned will of the father-tsar and then to the officers who would command her.[33]

When the tsar fell in March 1917, Bochkareva sought to invigorate this quasi-traditional, quasi-modern sentiment among other women by successfully lobbying for the creation of an all-woman 'Battalion of Death' that would fight for the Provisional Government (the government that sought to rule Russia between Nicholas's abdication

---

[32] Sandra M. Gilbert, 'Soldier's Heart: Literary Men, Literary Women, and the Great War', in *Behind the Lines*, ed. Higonnet et al., 216.

[33] Maria Bochkareva, *Yashka: My Life as Peasant Officer and Exile* as set down by Isaac Don Levine (New York: Frederick A. Stokes Co., 1919).

in March and the successful seizure of power by radical communists in October). This women's unit was sanctioned by the government as a way to 'shame' the men of Russia by demonstrating that many women were more ready to fight for their country than were draft dodgers, rebellious soldiers or deserters. Bochkareva's battalion saw combat action in the middle of 1917, but it had no more success than the rest of the Russian army, which fell apart with alarming speed after a failed offensive in June of that year. In October, the traditional aspects of the women's soldier movement became even clearer. Seeing the collapse of discipline and obedience in the army as a plague, and blaming socialists for the mess, Bochkareva and her women tried to defend the Winter Palace in Petrograd when the Bolsheviks moved in to arrest the ministers of the Provisional Government and complete their coup. They were quickly defeated, Bochkareva was arrested and her battalion was disbanded.

Bochkareva's unusual rise and fall showed both the potential and limits of 'liberation' for European women. For most, however, the war was far more burdensome than liberating. Women had new opportunities, to be sure, but there was a reason that these opportunities were pitched as duties rather than benefits. Virtually everywhere, the work that women had traditionally performed got more difficult, and the work that mobilized men had done was shifted to them as well. For every childless, excitable young lady who welcomed the war and exulted in its challenges, there were several women who worked much longer and harder in the paid sector of the economy, only to return home to deal with issues of childcare, cooking and cleaning. Women tolerated these onerous burdens out of feelings of 'sacrifice' and 'duty' to the war effort, but the effort required was often barely sustainable.

A European-wide food crisis from 1916 to 1918 worsened conditions even further. One of the key features of the First World War was a mutual economic blockade between the warring parties. That blockade, combined with difficulties in providing enough transportation capacity for civilian interests in many regions of the continent, led to increasingly dire food shortages. Hunger appeared in many regions, from Vienna to Berlin to Petrograd. Social breakdown loomed long before outright starvation, however, because the straw that broke the camel's back was the added burden of having to wait in line every day just for the chance to purchase basic necessities at increasingly ruinous prices. There were simply not enough hours in the day for women to add several more in breadlines, and the failure of wages to keep up with inflation angered them further. The response was one of bitterness and desperate protest. Citizens blamed the state, the rich and each other. Stories of how the wealthy dined warranted press coverage, and rumours of speculation, of hoarding and of abuse of the food system led to acute social tension between consumers and merchants, between urban residents and local farmers, between poor and rich and between citizens and their states. Again the most notable instance of this was in Russia, where the 300-year Romanov dynasty, which had survived rebellions, coup attempts, assassinations and revolutions in its recent past, succumbed in a matter of days in late February and early March 1917 to mass demonstrations in the streets of the capital begun by outraged women standing in breadlines. But much the same was occurring elsewhere. In Berlin and Vienna in particular, the social, political and economic structure of total war fractured first among exhausted urban women.[34] Even in Britain, where the hunger was less severe, women were involved in community-based Citizens Committees that pressured the government to reform food supply strategies, and they engaged in various boycotts and consumer actions to protest the rising prices of staple goods like milk and potatoes.[35] In this way, even women who had eschewed politics and the public sphere in the past became openly politicized in ways that the conservative order could not effectively manage.

Remarkably little has been written about the gender transformation of home-front men during the war. As we noted earlier, the spatial order of the war made the front masculine territory and the home-front feminine territory, but most men were not in fact enlisted in the armed forces, much less sent into combat.[36] This combination of forces decisively transformed European masculinity. In the first place, it normalized healthy men in their teens, twenties and thirties, and marginalized all the rest. Men not at the front were not real men. They might be boys waiting to be men, or they might have been real men in the past, or they might simply have something wrong with them. Young, old, blind, disabled or diseased, certain males were coded as dependent, perhaps even partially feminine, by the war. The situation was even less secure for those men who were not visibly dependent. The implications for healthy, hale men over forty but well short of elderly were significant. These were the sort of men who had been masculine icons of power in traditional Europe, at the peak of their working years, budding or actual patriarchs in their own right. Now, however, the masculine focus was elsewhere, with younger men away from home. Young, muscular men were visibly powerful in war propaganda, but they also exerted an invisible influence on the hearts and minds of the women and children they had left behind. The question of generational power, which we highlighted at the outset of this chapter, became ever more acute.

For men who were of fighting age and had no visible disabilities, the war years were uncomfortable ones. There were a variety of legitimate and illegitimate reasons why such men stayed in civilian life. On the continent, where conscript armies were the norm (of the major European combatants, only Britain lacked a draft at the start of the war; it would institute one in 1916), one was simply told when and where to appear. It was often difficult for military officials to even deal with volunteers in these circumstances. In addition, most states allowed for occupational exemptions of one sort or another. Though the list of reserved jobs varied from place to place, skilled workers in defence industries often got to stay at the bench, and policemen, firemen,

---

[34] Belinda Davis, *Home Fires Burning: Food, Politics, and Everyday Life in World War I Berlin* (Chapel Hill: University of North Carolina Press, 2000); Healy, *Vienna and the Fall of the Habsburg Empire*.

[35] Karen Hunt, 'The Politics of Food and Women's Neighborhood Activism in First World War Britain', *International Labor and Working Class History* 77, no. 1 (Spring 2010): 8–26. esp. 13 and 18.

[36] In a development that few civilians or politicians fully understood, the more 'total' war became, the lower the proportion of uniformed men in combat became, since the enormous need for military supplies and basic necessities required an equally large logistical support system. As long as the supply system functioned, a relatively small number of combat troops could launch massive amounts of metal at the enemy lines. Given that the enemy could do the same, it made sense to keep the number of front-line troops to a minimum as well.

many government bureaucrats, clerics and students were among the other groups freed from military service (depending on the country in question). In addition, not all health defects were visible to the naked eye. Medical examinations at induction points checked for a wide range of ailments from infectious disease, to heart irregularities, to simple 'weakness'. Finally, there were men who simply dodged the draft, resisted the recruiter or deserted soon after induction. It is only a slight exaggeration to say that these varied and very numerous reasons why a young man might not be in the army were streamlined to only three in the public imagination: one was either 'connected' by virtue of social station or fortunate job circumstances, one was physically defective or one was a coward. Many of the men who remained home performed essential tasks (a fact hinted at by the severe problems caused by home-front labour shortages in all combatant countries) but this did little to change the social stigma of being a male non-combatant. Across the British Empire, for instance, women dispensed white feathers to men they suspected of being too fearful to fight,[37] and citizens rapidly came to despise and envy privilege of all sorts. In any case, men at home were perceived to have something wrong with them, and a masculine gap emerged within civilian society. If the real men were away, and only weak men remained, who would provide for and protect the women and the children?

The answer was the state, which sought to fill the absent shoes of men by promising order, justice and social benefits to 'helpless' women and children. The rise of this state paternalism had enormous consequences. In the short term, states across the continent became much more intimately involved with their citizens. *Laissez-faire* principles were abandoned as quickly in the social realm as they were in the economic policies of the warring states. The enormous social dislocation and the demands of absent soldiers made either new or much enhanced social welfare policies an essential part of virtually every wartime social system. In most combatant states, soldiers' wives received supplements, widows got death benefits and the state took on the responsibility for paying these and other welfare bills. And, while both soldiers and their families wanted this money distributed with no strings attached, the state insisted that those who received this aid be 'worthy', normally by virtue of being dependent upon an absent man and free from moral vice. In Britain the benefits women received were linked to their status as wives, so the government thought it perfectly appropriate to cease payments if women neglected their wifely duties by cheating on their husbands. The Russian state, for its part, stopped paying young wives if their husbands deserted or committed some other significant crime at the front, further reinforcing the idea that these benefits flowed through the social contract that the state had made with its men. As Susan Pedersen has argued for the cases of Britain and France, the war introduced 'a particular logic of welfare and new institutional structures' and further 'enhanced the appeal and power of particular

---

[37] Nicoletta Gullace notes that although 'female patriotism … gave women a powerful language with which to lay claim to the war' those who were disturbed by women's more public roles used the white-feather campaign to 'lay the responsibility for male deaths at the feet of women'. Nicoletta F. Gullace, '*The Blood of Our Sons*': *Men, Women, and the Renegotiation of British Citizenship during the Great War* (New York: Palgrave Macmillan, 2004), 3.

ideologies and political groups and enabled these groups to capture the issue of family policy in the inter-war period'.[38]

In simple human terms, this rise of the paternal state and of aggressive, familial propaganda for the nation is indicative of one of the most important human aspects of the war. For people all over Europe, intimacy was lost at the expense of institutions.[39] Hungry women interacted with bureaucratic states, and soldiers fought for idealized women. But the social fact of large-scale human separation defined the war years. This is evident in the poems of the war, the memoirs of the war and above all the letters of the war, which were filled with mutual expressions of loneliness between husbands and wives, between sons and parents and between good friends. Loneliness quickly led to alienation. Those at the front felt they could not communicate their experience to those who had not shared their burdens, and those at home in many instances felt the same way. By the war's end, there was a need for everyone to stress how he or she had been victimized. Hungry civilians believed they had suffered for the sake of the soldiers at the front, and soldiers believed they had suffered for the sake of those at home. No one could actually bear to receive these sacrificial gifts. As a result, the language of unredeemed hurt and loss dominated the post-war landscape.

When the war ended, then, the gender landscape of the continent had been deeply changed. First, a generational shift had occurred. The iconic male was now much younger than he had been before. Second, the sexual separation of the war led to fundamental change as well. The idea of the community of men as the basis of political and (in some respects) intimate life had merged extensively with the national idea, and this only strengthened the fraternal overtones of the generational change. The successful assault on patriarchy changed the place of women as well. This new military fraternal gender order was paradoxically both more inclusive and exclusive of women than had been the case in the traditional patriarchal world. There was a deep undercurrent of sexual alienation at the heart of this new order that sometimes led to unrealistic idealization and sometimes to outright misogyny, but this alienation was always rooted in a rupture of intimacy. That said, the massive institutionalization of the war years, produced in part by the fact of social alienation, did much to incorporate women into national life. Not only were they on propaganda posters and serving as symbols of the nation, but they were also active politically on the newly created 'home front' through their daily action. Indeed, state paternalism required formal female political participation in order to exist at all. Simply put, the new European welfare states required female citizens.

### 'Uniform politics' and the post-war order

We are now in a position to understand the paradox we introduced at the beginning of the chapter. The fraternal rise to dominance meant the creation of a more aggressive

---

[38] Susan Pedersen, *Family, Dependence, and the Origins of the Welfare State: Britain and France, 1914–1945* (New York: Cambridge University Press, 1993), 130–1.
[39] See here Domansky, 'Militarization and Reproduction'.

and violent masculinity based, ironically enough, on an ever greater stress on male affection. This often had negative effects upon women, as we shall see. On the other hand, the overt politicization of women during this total war led to the widespread acknowledgement of female political subjectivity and the formal incorporation of female citizens in the ever more intrusive and ever more inclusive institutions of the paternal state. These twin expressions of the fraternal order, born of the sexual separation and totalization of the Great War, reconstituted the European gender order in deeply ambiguous ways.

The post-war story of gender begins with homecoming. This was a protracted and often difficult process. In the first place, many did not come home at all, and many who did found those homes empty, abandoned by families who had fled the war, had migrated to cities or had died of disease. In most cases, though, people were reunited. These reunions were often difficult. However much men and women might have hoped that they could pick up their lives and their relationships where they had left off, the fact remained that the war had changed individuals in profound ways. In some respects, these were more reintroductions than reunions. There were, of course, personal traumas and joys that had not been shared together and could not now be fully shared. Just as importantly, however, the whole context of personal relationships had been changed as a result of the shift in gender order and the rupture of intimacy that the war had produced.

The first expression of these fractures was sexual jealousy. The long absences had produced deep anxiety about fidelity on the part of spouses virtually everywhere. Some of this anxiety was expressed in letters; much more of it must have remained unsaid during the separation itself. Given that lurid stories of overheated soldiers and randy villagers and of lonely housewives seduced by wealthy shirkers ran rampant through oral networks during the war, suspicion must have at least flitted through the minds of most separated Europeans. At some point in those first few nights home together, that doubt must have flickered across faces and through hearts as well. Some relationships survived doubt (and of course the actual infidelities that did occur). Others simply did not. More permissive divorce laws came into force in some areas, and divorce rose quickly. In Russia and Germany in particular, divorce rates in the 1920s were four or five times higher than they had been before the war.[40]

Homecoming also meant a restructuring of economic life. Most men believed that the wartime flood of women into the industrial workforce was meant to be temporary, but not all women who enjoyed a regular pay cheque and a measure of economic independence from their husbands wanted to leave the jobs they had taken. In the end, the public and private pressure to abandon work and give returning veterans their jobs

---

[40] Marcelline J. Hutton, *Russian and West European Women, 1860–1939: Dreams, Struggles and Nightmares* (Lanham, MD: Rowman & Littlefield Publishers, 2001), 148. The divorce rate was also no doubt higher because of the many 'quickie' marriages that occurred in wartime, as couples in the trial period of courtship rushed to wed (and bed) before military deployments occurred.

back was too great. By late 1919 in Great Britain, for instance, nearly 750,000 women had lost their jobs, and the retraining sessions they were offered focused on domestic work.[41] The reassertion of male dominance in the economic realm did not mean that European culture reverted to what had existed prior to the war. As Chapter 5 will show, deep changes were taking place in sexual practices and sexual identities, changes that were marked by new clothing fashions, by new standards of proper behaviour in public and above all by the continued visibility of the independent and intelligent 'modern woman'.

In many ways, the most interesting gender developments in the interwar years were political. As we have seen, there had been deep anxieties even prior to the war that had focused on changes in the gender order. The upheaval of the war dwarfed those earlier hints of instability. Throughout the continent, as politicians and citizens cast about for an anchor to calm their storm-tossed lives, Europeans sought to bring order and predictability to gender relations. There were some, of course, who wanted to resurrect the past and 'return to normality', but the changes the war brought made that a futile desire. The imperial patriarchs would not be coming back. Austria's Franz Joseph had died during the war, and his successor, Karl, ruled only briefly before military defeat and the dismemberment of the Habsburg Empire brought an end to the dynasty. Tsar Nicholas II had been arrested in 1917 and executed in 1918, replaced by an aggressively fraternal band of communist brothers in the lands of the Russian Empire. Kaiser Wilhelm had abdicated and was forced into exile. In states where electoral politics dominated, veterans returned to win ballot after ballot. Now fraternal nationalism was the norm throughout the continent. The task of gender stabilization, therefore, was to find a way to take account of the wartime changes but still to construct a reliable and comfortable gender order. The road to stability varied depending on the political heritage of the region in question, but gender questions proved central nearly everywhere.

In Great Britain, the long battle for suffrage finally peaked with the passage of a compromise bill in 1918 that expanded the previously limited franchise to all men of twenty-one years of age and to women who had reached thirty and met certain property requirements (or were married to men who met them). In 1928, both the age differential and the property qualifications were eliminated, and all women and men gained the vote upon their twenty-first birthday. Two important aspects of this suffrage victory need to be highlighted here. In the first place, as we have already pointed out, granting women the vote was presented as a gift for noble wartime service. Ideologically, this stressed both the importance of the war to politics and the continued pre-eminence of men (who after all remained the dispensers of this gift of the vote). But we should also note that more pragmatic political concerns were at play as well. One of the reasons that conservative parties and politicians were either more muted in their opposition to suffrage or dropped it completely was that opposing suffrage now carried a significant political risk. Female political activism during the war had made eventual suffrage more

---

[41] Pyecroft, 'British Working Women and the First World War', 707.

likely, and no party wanted to oppose women voters only to face their wrath at the next election. In addition, now that the range of female political activity had expanded, there was reason to expect that any party could court women voters. There were also hopes that limiting the vote to older women would make electoral returns much less radical than they might otherwise be. Just as importantly, however, suffrage was grudgingly accepted by conservatives in order to pre-empt the possibility of a 'sex war' that had seemed imminent in Britain before the war and now seemed ready to re-erupt on the basis of accumulated wartime grievances.[42]

This desire for unity was also visible in other contexts. Nationalists stressed the idea that nations at war needed to be unified. In Germany and France, conservatives reached a consensus even with socialists and feminists that a temporary political peace – *Burgfrieden* (castle truce) in German and *union sacrée* (sacred union) in French – needed to be declared in the interests of achieving victory. As we have seen, British suffragettes also laid down their firebombs and rallied to the nationalist cause. This rejection of dissent and other forms of political or ethnic pluralism was the result, in large part, of the militarization of national politics that had developed in the early twentieth century and had intensified during the war years. When the war ended, this militarization subsided only among select groups in select places. While many European intellectuals, especially in Britain and France, had indeed blanched at the horror of the war and rededicated themselves to explicitly pacifist causes, the more common post-war experience was one of conflict and constant preparation for the next war. The armistice that ended the Great War in November 1918 had not ended combat in Europe. Civil war washed over most of Central and Eastern Europe for varying lengths of time, and these wars further honed the violent practices and martial form of masculinity while establishing the new political contours of the continent. The success of the communist revolution in Russia raised the spectre not only of international war, but also of continuing class-based civil wars. While communist uprisings failed or petered out in regions outside of the Soviet Union, the 'red menace' remained a constant part of European thought throughout the 1920s and 1930s, and the fear of Bolshevism contributed decisively to the rise of fascism in Germany and Italy. The antidote to communism was sought in civic solidarity, in the valorization of obedience and duty and in the suppression of individuality. This search for unity and uniformity informed the political developments in many places during the interwar period.

Bulgaria is a case in point. Even before the Great War, Bulgaria had been consumed with violent conflict as it fought first the Ottoman Empire and then its Balkan neighbours in a failed bid for regional dominance. This aggressive foreign policy was costly in treasure and blood and aroused domestic opposition, most notably from Alexander Stamboliiski's Agrarian Party. Stamboliiski felt that continuing conflict and a militarized state only served to impoverish and oppress the peasant Bulgarians he

---

[42] Susan Kingsley Kent, *Making Peace: The Reconstruction of Gender in Interwar Britain* (Princeton: Princeton University Press, 1993).

sought to represent. As a result, he called upon Bulgarians to reject 'war-lovers'[43] and campaigned against entry into the Balkan Wars of 1912–13 and into the First World War. He failed each time, though Bulgaria joined the Central Powers relatively late, in 1915.

The war effort was disastrous. Bulgaria lost a higher percentage of its troops than any other non-Balkan state during the war, runaway inflation destroyed the economy and military defeat brought about the abdication of Tsar Ferdinand in favour of his son Boris, who assumed the throne in October 1918. Less than a year later, the Agrarian Party won national elections and Stamboliiski took control of the government. Given the consistency of his anti-war stance, one might have expected a rather thorough demilitarization of Bulgarian politics. The years of war, however, had left a deep imprint. Stamboliiski did attempt to rein in the military by demobilizing many of its soldiers and officers, but other than that he did little to challenge the fundamental core of the fraternal and military nation. In the first place, the leaders were young. There were nine cabinet members in Stamboliiski's government in 1920. Five were in their thirties, and Stamboliiski was only forty-one.[44] Second, the leadership proclaimed its commitment to military virtues even as it cut the size of the army.

Most significantly, the signature initiative of Stamboliiski's government was a militarization of the economic sphere. 'Drafting' people to work was a practice that many states used during the war, and it appealed to many leaders seeking economic growth in the post-war period as well. If coercion and discipline worked in the organization of violence, the thinking went, why should it not work in the organization of the economy? The Law for Compulsory Labour Service was implemented in June 1920, and it envisioned the conscription of all men at the age of twenty for one year of service and all women at the age of sixteen for six months of service. It was a scheme not unlike the one we saw earlier from William James; like the James plan, it was as much about promoting unity and social cohesion as it was economic growth. The notion of militarized young people in uniform fulfilling their duty to the nation seemed attractive to him and his supporters in a way that would have been nearly inconceivable a decade before.

Women were part of this vision too, as Stamboliiski dearly wanted to integrate women into civic life. Stamboliiski hoped that women would eventually become voting citizens, but the Compulsory Labour Service was seen as a first, halting step towards the emergence of women into the public sphere. In practice, there were many gaps in the universality of female service. Married women were exempt; so too was Bulgaria's large Muslim population. Even those eligible were not always called, and the experiment was mostly limited to urban areas and to occupations like cooking and laundering that were already gendered as female.[45]

---

[43] John D. Bell, *Peasants in Power: Alexander Stamboliski and the Bulgarian Agrarian National Union, 1899–1923* (Princeton: Princeton University Press, 1977), 105.

[44] Ibid., 153.

[45] Ibid., 175–6.

One can see a certain sort of 'progressive' nationalism in Stamboliiski's regime. It sought the economic advancement of the poor, envisioned the eventual abolition of sex-based legal discrimination and sought to avoid needless military confrontation. But the militarized fraternalism was just as clear. Military virtues were upheld, cross-class comradeship on the basis of masculinity was valorized, and radical changes in family life or the social position of women were barely contemplated. This sort of complex political system, structured around the militarized nation but moderate in its policies, was vulnerable. Many contemporaries feared that the explicit concern for the oppressed and the distrust of capitalism embedded in the peasant populist ideology meant that Bulgarian politics would shift to the left as a result.

As it turned out, the real threat was from radicals on the right. Many officers and veterans, seeing even Stamboliiski's mild populism as a communist provocation and a threat to tradition, plotted against him from the very first days of his rule. They urged the formation of 'parties of order' who would pursue policies of 'social harmony' and mimicked the fascist experiments that Benito Mussolini was pioneering in Italy at the same time by forming youth organizations, sporting clubs and other militarized organizations.[46] In response, Stamboliiski, now obviously very far removed from whatever pacifist inclinations he might have held before the war, resolved to strengthen the paramilitary organizations of his own party, the so-called Orange Guard.

These developments soon reached their logical conclusion. Political street fighting intensified, and the officers finally launched their coup in June 1923. Stamboliiski was captured, tortured and killed as a way of starting a wave of right-wing terror that would result in the murder of about 16,000 members of left-wing parties.[47] Bulgaria became a right-wing authoritarian state, as so many other European countries would in the years between the First World War and the Second World War.

In Britain and Bulgaria alike, politicians believed that the communist threat required the pre-emption of sex war and training in masculine values through mechanisms that reaffirmed male supremacy and male virtues. In the Soviet Union, by contrast, revolutionaries who had proclaimed themselves crusaders for women's equality had come to power. This commitment to the 'emancipation' and the 'enlightenment' of women was taken very seriously by Bolshevik leaders, a fact reflected in the wave of legislation that dramatically transformed the legal position of Russia's women in the space of a few short months. Women had been enfranchised during the brief period of the Provisional Government in 1917 and had cast ballots in the important elections and plebiscites of that year. With the accession of the communists to power they were, in addition, granted full civic equality, promised extensive benefits for maternity and childcare, urged to join the ranks of the Communist Party and generally exhorted to help destroy the patriarchal core of Russian society. These initiatives had mixed results. The legal changes proved lasting and important, but the efforts to transform the gendered

---

[46] Ibid., 212–13.
[47] Ibid., 245.

social, economic and cultural patterns met with more difficulty. Communal kitchens and nurseries failed to materialize on a mass scale because of the lack of resources, and the domestic economy changed very little. Few men, revolutionaries or not, cleaned the house, did the shopping, cared for the children or cooked dinner. As a result, the new economic and political opportunities offered to women quickly turned into exhausting duties, and Soviet women would labour under this 'double burden' for the rest of the communist period.[48]

The double burden emerged because Russian progressives and radicals understood the oppression of women to be the result of the patriarchal structure of capitalism. This was the core of what they called the 'woman question' in the pre-revolutionary era. They assumed that the destruction of capitalism implied the destruction of all forms of patriarchy, and they believed that the establishment of legal equality set the stage for the eventual liberation of women. What was left virtually unasked was the 'man question'. This was a serious omission. Convinced that the communist revolution had destroyed the old world, revolutionaries largely failed to notice how similar Soviet post-war masculinity was to that in the 'bourgeois' European states and how both had emerged from the same wartime springs. Both before and during the Great War, Russian youths had undergone the same militarization as their counterparts to the West. Veterans came home feeling the same isolation, alienation and mix of deep longing and deep suspicion for women. These veterans made up the core of the Communist Party cadres after the Russian Civil War concluded in 1921. Ideals of masculine behaviour for these men hardly differed from those in other parts of Europe. The body type they were to emulate was the same, and so too was the moral code they were supposed to practise. As a result, despite a period of time in the 1920s when it looked like a new socialist masculinity was emerging, one that would explicitly reject the notion of male supremacy and traditional ideas about monogamous heterosexual sex within families, the fraternal, martial masculinity that dominated Europe held firm in the Soviet Union as well.[49] This brief period of gender uncertainty came unceremoniously to an end in the mid-1930s, when the Stalinist regime changed the family code to outlaw abortion, recriminalize sodomy and make divorce more difficult while reaffirming martial masculinity as the norm.

The right-wing army leaders in Bulgaria and the left-wing communist leaders in the Soviet Union were different in many ways. Still, scholars of both groups have stressed a key similarity between these government officials in the 1930s. Both turned towards 'neo-traditional' policies in the years leading up to the Second World War.[50]

---

[48] Wendy Z. Goldman, *Women, the State, and Revolution: Soviet Family Policy and Social Life, 1917–1936* (Cambridge: Cambridge University Press, 1993).

[49] See here: Sanborn, *Drafting the Russian Nation*, esp. chp. 4, 'The Nationalization of Masculinity'.

[50] Krassimira Daskalova, 'Bulgarian Women in Movements, Laws, Discourses (1840s–1940s)', *Bulgarian Historical Review* 27, no. 1 (1999): 180–96; Terry Martin, 'Modernization or Neo-Traditionalism? Ascribed Nationality and Soviet Primordialism', in *Stalinism: New Directions*, ed. Sheila Fitzpatrick (London and New York: Routledge, 2000), 348–67.

As Krassimira Daskalova notes, the neo-traditional discourse in Bulgaria was different from older brands of traditionalism because of 'the different style and argumentation of this discourse – more aggressive, pseudoscientific, consciously ideological and manipulative'.[51] Neo-traditionalism was, in essence, an anchor thrown out by European radicals of both the left and the right. The appeals to 'traditional' beliefs and identities were intended to stabilize, to unify and to give social support to the rather ambitious military and economic plans of the leaders of the interwar period.

But we should not see these programmes as purely 'manipulative'. This term implies that neo-traditionalists did not believe what they were saying. Quite the opposite is the case, especially when it came to the scientific underpinnings of neo-traditional thought. What Daskalova calls 'pseudoscience' was, of course, just called 'science' in the 1930s. Biology was especially crucial in this regard, as it served as the justification for social orders based upon sexual and racial differences. The principles of equality and social peace came into sharp contrast once more with the Social Darwinist view of difference and warfare. This ideological conflict produced a certain amount of tension within most states, as we saw in the brief treatments of Britain, Bulgaria and the Soviet Union. It was possible, however, that radicals on one side of this ideological divide would successfully destroy the other ideological position within a given state. Given the experience of the war, it was especially likely that a movement would join the aggressive and misogynistic aspects of wartime masculinity with the biological justifications for sexual and/or racial dominance and would create a system that would promote unity on the basis of the ideas of radical masculinity and the practices of violent male bonding. We have a name for this system: fascism.

It is important to recognize that fascism was not a strange, exotic disease that simply afflicted Italians and Germans who fell under the spell of Mussolini and Hitler. It might be comforting for us to believe that these modern Europeans had been brainwashed or forced by circumstance to accede to the evil wishes of their dictators, since it would allow us to distance ourselves from their experience. But the historical record shows a great deal more conscious support for fascist movements not only in Italy and Germany, but across Europe as a whole as well.[52] Explaining the attraction of fascism is a book in itself; for our purposes, however, what must be stressed is how appealing this martial, neo-traditional gender order was to so many men and more than a few women as well.

The origins of fascism are intimately connected to the Great War and to the glorification of masculine violence that it engendered. Benito Mussolini began his political life as a socialist journalist and pacifist, but the war stirred something entirely new in him, and he soon abandoned his socialist roots in favour of strident support for Italian intervention in the war. Nationalist fervour and the hope of territorial

---

[51] Daskalova, 'Bulgarian Women', 193.
[52] Michael Mann has a thoughtful discussion of the geographical and social dimensions of fascism in interwar Europe. See Michael Mann, *Fascists* (Cambridge and New York: Cambridge University Press, 2004).

expansion encouraged an ineffective leadership concerned about its legitimacy to enter the war on the side of the Western Allies in May 1915, but the results were disastrous. A poorly led army almost completely collapsed in October 1917, and by the end of the war 600,000 soldiers had been lost with virtually no territorial gain. The Battle of Caporetto in October 1917, where Austro-Hungarian and German forces routed Italian troops causing 40,000 casualties and taking 280,000 prisoners, was particularly humiliating. From this day on the expression 'it was a Caporetto' in Italian meant complete disaster, a fact that forged a permanent link between military prowess (or lack thereof) and national pride upon which Mussolini and other nationalists drew. Particularly after the Italians failed to receive all of the spoils of war that they had been promised in the 1915 Treaty of London, various radical factions sought ways of overthrowing the government. The charismatic romantic poet Gabriele D'Annunzio led a troop of volunteers to seize power in Fiume. Although this effort eventually failed, Mussolini was inspired and formed his own squad of nationalist paramilitary units, which he called the *fasci di combattimento* – literally 'bundles of combat'. Mussolini was inspired to coin the word 'fascism' by the weapons that guards of Roman politicians had carried in ancient times: a bundle of rods wrapped around an axe. Mussolini's new movement, in other words, was conceived in the ashes of the First World War but drew on the experience of brotherly togetherness – for which he coined the word 'trenchocracy' – that its combatants had shared, even in the face of what was for Italians primarily an experience of military defeat. Motivated by a combination of nationalism, socialism and a belief in the purifying effects of violence, the *squadristi* or 'Black Shirts' roamed the countryside and towns to fight communists while 'squeezing the rich' and protecting landlords. By 1921, Mussolini had gathered together 250,000 followers, and in November of that year he formed his movement into a political party, the *Partito Nazionale Fascista*, or National Fascist Party.[53] A frightened liberal government and the baffled King Victor Emmanuel III proved the effectiveness of this militaristic approach to politics when they named Mussolini prime minister in October 1922 in reaction to the rather unimpressive 'March on Rome' of mostly unarmed Black Shirts. Nationalists across Europe took note, particularly a certain Adolf Hitler in Germany.

Adolf Hitler had become the leader of the National Socialist German Workers' Party in 1921. He was inspired by Mussolini and copied many of his tactics, eventually gaining power through a similar combination of electoral success and appointment by conservative politicians who thought they could harness his growing popularity to their own ends. From the beginning, and particularly as chancellor from 1933 to 1945, Hitler insisted that all public power should be aggressively male, indeed that it should rely on the type of soldierly community of men that he fondly recalled from the years of the First World War. Nazi women did not have to be barefoot, but it was certainly best

---

[53] John Whittam, *Fascist Italy* (Manchester, UK; New York, NY: Manchester University Press, 1995).

if they were pregnant. As Hitler put it in a speech to the National Socialist Women's Organization in 1934:

> If the man's world is said to be the State, his struggle, his readiness to devote his powers to the service of the community, then it may perhaps be said that the woman's is a smaller world. For her world is her husband, her family, her children, and her home ... The two worlds are not antagonistic. They complement each other, they belong together just as man and woman belong together. We do not consider it correct for the woman to interfere in the world of the man, in his main sphere. We consider it natural if these two worlds remain distinct.[54]

In December 1938, Hitler initiated a programme to grant the mothers of many 'racially fit' children with the 'Cross of Honour of the German Mother' – bronze for four or five children, silver for six or seven children and gold for eight or more children. The medals required extensive investigations into the racial origins of the families and genetic health of the children, and they were awarded in elaborate ceremonies on Mother's Day.

**Figure 4.2** A Nazi party member awards the Cross of Honour of the German Mother as League of German Girls members watch. Reprinted by permission of the Bundesarchiv Berlin.

---

[54] Adolf Hitler, 'Hitler's Speech to the National Socialist Women's League, 8 September 1934', in *Nazism 1919–1945. Volume 2: State, Economy and Society 1933–39: A Documentary Reader*, ed. Jeremy Noakes and Geoffrey Pridham (Exeter: University of Exeter Press, 2000), 255–6.

These policies were not entirely original. Mussolini had instituted a national holiday to honour mothers and their infants in 1932, and he had established various tax incentives and subsidies to reward those who had many children in the 1920s.[55]

Hitler was not alone in his hope that German women would stay at home and produce as many little soldiers as possible. Joseph Goebbels, the director of Nazi propaganda, once declared that 'the mission of women is to be beautiful and to bring children into the world.' He also prevented women from serving on juries because 'they cannot think logically or reason objectively, since they are ruled only by emotion.'[56] This was a view of women that was shared by early historians of Nazism, who drew on the interpretation of self-serving eyewitnesses like Hermann Rauschning, who had described 'the rapturously rolling, moist, veiled eyes of [Hitler's] female listeners' in his since discredited book about his 'conversations' with Hitler.[57] This interpretation was swallowed with little critical reflection by prominent male historians of the 1970s, who wrote of women's responsibility for the 'over-excited, distinctly hysterical tone' of Hitler's early rallies (Joachim C. Fest) and the 'sexual hysteria' of 'spinsters' who projected their 'repressed yearnings' onto the Führer (Richard Grunberger).[58] Despite later claims that women had elected Hitler,[59] in early 1933, even as the Nazi electoral fortunes were rising dramatically, only 5 per cent of women had joined the party.[60] Nevertheless, the neo-traditional Nazi message of stable, healthy 'Aryan' families with a gendered division of labour struck a chord with many women and men in a country that had seen its share of upheaval in recent years. After the Nazis secured power and began vigorously promoting the traditional child-raising family, even more women accepted the programme. There is some dispute among historians as to the amount of voluntary adoption of Nazi tenets among women and the degree of enthusiasm they brought to the Nazi project. Some argue that women, by facilitating the activity of the Nazis, were complicit in the Nazi project even if they never directed policy.[61] Others maintain that women were primarily victims of a suffocating, misogynistic

---

[55] Carl Ipsen, *Dictating Demography: The Problem of Population in Fascist Italy* (Cambridge and New York: Cambridge University Press, 1996), 157–9; Patrizia Albanese, *Mothers of the Nation: Women, Families, and Nationalism in Twentieth-Century Europe* (Toronto: University of Toronto Press, 2006), 52–7. For a general account of fascist policies towards mothers, see Elizabeth Dixon Whitaker, *Measuring Mamma's Milk: Fascism and the Medicalization of Maternity in Italy* (Ann Arbor: University of Michigan Press, 2000).

[56] Both quotes in Klaus P. Fischer, *Nazi Germany: A New History* (New York: Continuum, 1995), 355.

[57] Quoted from Hermann Rauschning, *Hitler Speaks: A Series of Political Conversations with Adolf Hitler on His Real Aims* (London: Thornton Butterworth, 1939), 259 in R. J. Evans, 'German Women and the Triumph of Hitler', *Journal of Modern History* 48, no. 1 (1976): 123–175.

[58] Quoted from Joachim C. Fest, *The Face of the Third Reich* (Harmondsworth: Penguin, 1972), 401; and Richard Grunberger, *A Social History of the Third Reich* (Harmondsworth: Penguin, 1974), 117 in Evans, 'German Women', 125–6. For a description of how feminist historians reacted to these arguments, see Annette F. Timm, 'Mothers, Whores or Sentimental Dupes? Emotion and Race in Historiographical Debates about Women in the Third Reich', in *Beyond the Racial State*, ed. Mark Roseman, Devin Pendas and Richard F. Wetzell (Princeton, NJ: Princeton University Press, forthcoming).

[59] As Julia Sneeringer demonstrates, the picture is much murkier than this. See Julia Sneeringer, *Winning Women's Votes: Propaganda and Politics in Weimar Germany* (Chapel Hill: University of North Carolina Press, 2002).

[60] Michael H. Kater, *Hitler Youth* (Cambridge, MA and London: Harvard University Press, 2004), 74.

[61] Claudia Koonz, *Mothers in the Fatherland: Women, the Family, and Nazi Politics* (New York: St. Martin's Press, 1987).

regime.[62] Like most viable historical debates, this one derives vitality from the fact that there is evidence to support both sides, but this is in part because the question is posed so broadly.[63] We cannot expect to make precise claims about the activities and attitudes of fully half of the population. Any determination of complicity or victimhood should be made when considering rather smaller groups of people, and historians have begun to do just that. Particularly in Germany, historians have begun to focus much more attention on women who were active supporters of the regime and even perpetrators of racial crimes.[64]

Still, if individual women and individual men had different degrees of entanglement with the Nazi project, there can be no denying that the Nazis forwarded a gendered vision that privileged men and masculinity. From the beginning, Nazi Party leaders had appealed to young men inclined towards violence and comradeship, and that remained their power base during the entire course of the Third Reich. Soldiers and veterans of course played a significant role in both forming the social base and the mythology of the movement, but the appeal was broader. The teenage boys who entered the Hitler Youth, for instance, joined a prestigious organization that promoted ideals of self-sacrifice, fraternal care and belligerence. Through shooting drills, physical education, sports and explicit political training they were prepared for a future as fighting men in Hitler's cause. As one historian has remarked, the 'hallmark of HJ [*Hitler Jugend* or Hitler Youth] socialization was militarization, with a view to a war of territorial expansion and, as its predetermined goal, the neutralization of Europe's Jews'.[65] For girls who joined the female version of the Hitler Youth – the League of German Girls (*Bund Deutscher Mädel* or BDM) – militarization meant learning how to cultivate an aura of passivity and obedience towards men and preparing oneself for motherhood. Despite these stated goals, however, the BDM also held quite different attractions for young girls. Being able to leave home to go to meetings, camps and other activities provided them with opportunities of which they could previously only dream. While instilling obedience, the BDM also gave girls an enormous sense of social and political engagement and, not

---

[62] Gisela Bock, 'Racism and Sexism in Nazi Germany: Motherhood, Compulsory Sterilization, and the State', *Signs* 8, no. 3 (1983): 400–21. For her direct response to Koonz, see Gisela Bock, 'Die Frauen und Der Nationalsozialismus: Bemerkungen zu einem Buch von Claudia Koonz', *Geschichte und Gesellschaft* 15, no. 4 (1989): 563–79.

[63] For general accounts of the debate, see Adelheid von Saldern, 'Victims or Perpetrators? Controversies About the Role of Women in the Nazi State', in *Nazism and German Society, 1933–1945*, ed. David F. Crew (London and New York: Routledge, 1994), 141–65; Ralph M. Leck, 'Conservative Empowerment and the Gender of Nazism: Paradigms of Power and Complicity in German Women's History', *Journal of Women's History* 12, no. 2 (2000): 147–69; and Claudia Koonz, 'A Tributary and a Mainstream: Gender, Public Memory, and Historiography of Nazi Germany', in *Gendering Modern German History: Rewriting Historiography*, ed. Karen Hagemann and Jean H. Quataert (New York and Oxford: Berghahn Books, 2007), 147–68.

[64] The literature here has already become vast. For representative examples, see Elizabeth Harvey, *Women and the Nazi East: Agents and Witnesses of Germanization* (New Haven: Yale University Press, 2003); Elissa Mailänder, *Female SS Guards and Workaday Violence: The Majdanek Concentration Camp, 1942–1944*, trans. Patricia Szobar (East Lansing, Michigan: Michigan State University Press, 2015); Sybille Steinbacher, ed., *Volksgenossinnen: Frauen in der NS-Volksgemeinschaft* (Göttingen: Wallstein Verlag, 2007); Franka Maubach, *Die Stellung Halten: Kriegserfahrungen und Lebensgeschichten von Wehrmachtshelferinnen* (Göttingen: Vandenhoeck & Ruprecht, 2009).

[65] Kater, *Hitler Youth*, 28–9.

least, the chance to exercise power over other girls.[66] Power for girls would prove to be an illusion, but the feelings of inclusion instilled in these youth organizations were equally strong for both genders. Emotional attachments to a political system can be as important as ideological or political ones in establishing a political culture.[67] Through carefully orchestrated recreational activities, both male and female branches of the Hitler Youth made it fun to participate in the creation of gendered citizenship. Already counting an impressive 100,000 members in early 1933, the Hitler Youth grew rapidly, counting 5.4 million boys and girls by the end of 1936.[68] The future seemed to belong to a gender order that promised the stability of the strict gender binaries of the past in the guise of a 'new racial order' that provided insiders new excitement and new forms of power.

Fascist movements combined masculine aggressiveness and expansiveness with firmly bounded ethnocentrism, and fascist leaders were often able to exploit the confusion among other European leaders about which of these strands was more central. This confusion came to a head in 1938, during the crisis over the Sudetenland, when Hitler insisted that the German Reich had the right to take this territory away from Czechoslovakia because it was heavily populated by ethnic Germans. Many European leaders saw Germany's growth in the mid-1930s for what it was: the expression of the core values and practices of a regime that loved martial uniformity, praised combativeness and sought imperial expansion. Others took Hitler's ethnic politics as central and believed that Germany would cease its adventures after it annexed the 'German' areas of Europe (and drove out the non-Germans). The anti-Semitic outrages of the Nazis may have been distasteful and the truncation of Czechoslovakia unfortunate, but British, French and American politicians were willing to pay this price in order to preserve what British Prime Minister Neville Chamberlain described as 'peace in our time'. The Czechs were rather less sanguine about these developments. So too was the Soviet Union, which pressed the European powers to go to war with Nazi Germany in 1938, in no small part because the communist leadership believed, rightly as it turned out, that fascism was fundamentally aggressive and expansionist. Hitler proved more than able to split these two camps, and he did so by meeting only with the politicians who were inclined to believe that Germany would be peaceful once it became ethnically homogeneous. No representatives from Czechoslovakia or the Soviet Union attended the infamous meetings in Munich in 1938 at which Hitler was supposedly 'appeased'.

The Soviets, suspicious that the real deal at Munich had been to lay the groundwork for a Nazi assault upon the Reich's communist enemies, immediately sought to turn the

---

[66] Nori Möding, "'Ich muß irgendwo engagiert sein – fragen Sie mich bloß nicht, warum." Überlegungen zu Sozialisationserfahrungen von Mädchen in NS- Organisationen', in '*Wir kriegen jetzt andere Zeiten': Auf der Suche nach der Erfahrung des Volkes in nachfaschistischen Ländern*, ed. Lutz Niethammer and Alexander von Plato (Bonn: J. H. W. Dietz Nachf., 1985), 256–304; Dagmar Reese, 'Bund Deutscher Mädel – Zur Geschichte der weiblichen deutschen Jugend im Dritten Reich', in *Mutterkreuz und Arbeitsbuch: Zur Geschichte der Frauen in der Weimarer Republik und im Nationalsozialismus*, ed. Frauengruppe Faschismusforschung (Frankfurt am Main: Fischer, 1981), 163–83.
[67] Raphael Gross, "'Loyalty" in National Socialism: A Contribution to the Moral History of the National Socialist Period', *History of European Ideas* 33, no. 4 (2007): 488–503. For a philosophical perspective, see Martha C. Nussbaum, *Political Emotions: Why Love Matters for Justice* (Cambridge: Belknap Press, 2013).
[68] Kater, *Hitler Youth*, 19.

**Figure 4.3** 'To the Führer [belongs] the Youth.' Nazi propaganda poster for the Hitler Youth. Reprinted by permission of the Deutsches Historisches Museum, Berlin.

tables by redirecting the inevitable Nazi aggression to the West rather than the East. This they accomplished in August 1939, with the signing of a Nazi–Soviet non-aggression pact. The promise not to attack one another and to abstain from alliances 'directly or indirectly aimed at the other party' was supposed to be in force for ten years. Neither Hitler nor Stalin really believed that the pact would last quite that long. Both knew that the immediate impact of the agreement would be to start a European war by laying the basis for a joint invasion of Poland and the Baltic States, and both suspected that the establishment of a joint border between the two empires would be unlikely to promote long-term peace between these hostile and heavily armed parties.

## 'Women and children first'

The attack on Poland proceeded as planned. The Nazis attacked on 1 September 1939, and the Soviets invaded on 17 September. It was immediately clear that this new war was different from the last. The violent tactics towards civilian populations that had been gradually and in some cases unwillingly used by army officials during the First World War had been honed and made part of strategic planning in the Second World War. In Eastern Poland, the Soviets deployed the policies of mass deportation and political terror that the tsarist army had used sporadically in the First World War and that the Bolsheviks had been using regularly within the Soviet Union itself over the past decade. It turned out that practice had made perfect. Lavrentii Beria, Stalin's chief of the secret police, instructed his minions to deport as many as a million Poles eastwards to the interior of the Soviet Union and ordered the execution of tens of thousands of men whom the Soviets believed to be security risks. These operations proceeded ruthlessly. Deportees were locked in incredibly cramped train cars that lacked toilets, windows and heat. Many children and elderly Poles perished en route, the bodies taken away from grieving family members in bags. It was a classic case of ethnic cleansing.[69]

In Western Poland, German forces demonstrated from the first days of the war that they had taken the most toxic aspects of martial masculinity to their most extreme conclusion. Not only were civilian men to be assaulted, but, in contrast to the ethos of the earlier age, women and children were to be expressly targeted as well. European military figures in the modern age had long accepted the deaths of women and children as what is today (controversially) called 'collateral damage', and they were not above killing them intentionally as an extreme punitive measure either. But the Nazis made the murder of civilians a normal part of their strategy. On the eve of the invasion of Poland, Hitler instructed his commanders to 'kill without pity all men, women, and children of Polish race or language. Only in such a way will we win the vital space we need.'[70] Though

---

[69] Katherine R. Jolluck, *Exile and Identity: Polish Women in the Soviet Union during World War II* (Pittsburgh, PA: University of Pittsburgh Press, 2002), 9–20.

[70] Cited in Richard C. Lukas, *Did the Children Cry?: Hitler's War against Jewish and Polish Children, 1939–1945* (New York: Hippocrene Books, 1994), 16.

this full extermination of ethnic Poles never came to fruition, witnesses recorded that even early in September 1939 it was common to see mounds of dead children and their parents in villages and along roadsides.

There was a definite gendered aspect to the Nazi war on civilians on the Eastern Front. The Nazis drew heavily upon the most aggressive and misogynistic strands of modern militarized masculinity. The war in the East was explicitly conceived of as one of racial extermination. Since women and children represented the future of the races under assault, they were not only acceptable but in many cases primary targets. Total extermination was not envisioned at first, however. The economics of warfare made it unfeasible to murder all the civilians one encountered. In the first place, such organized massacres took time and resources that the army high command wanted to use against the military forces that opposed them. In the second place, every army needs local civilian populations to provide them with goods and an economic infrastructure. This economic calculus made the labour potential of any given civilian in occupied territory the most important factor in determining his or her worth to the occupying army. These calculations disadvantaged women and children, whose prospects for labour in support of the German war effort were much less significant. Thus, in contrast to the situation in the First World War, in which young males were the most likely to be targeted for deportation, execution or other coercive practices, those males were now strangely privileged. But women made up about a third of those, mostly from the Soviet Union, Poland and Ukraine, who were rounded up and sent into slavery in factories within the German Reich.[71]

The situation was made worse by the sexual dynamic of the war zone. Sex was one of the few areas of 'labour' in which local women were seen to have more potential than local men. Sexual contact is a feature of all war zones, where it can run the gamut of levels of coercion, from voluntary to rape.[72] Sometimes this was straight prostitution, but local women also exchanged sex for other economic and social favours (such as protection, access to scarce goods or the chance for mobility) and these motivations were even more important in the dire conditions of the Second World War. In all theatres of the war, troops were very sexually active. In Paris, German commanders appropriated brothels when they occupied the city in 1940, and the US army took control of the same buildings and women when they took the city in 1944. In occupied Italy, about 75 per cent of American soldiers admitted to having had sex with local women on an average of once or twice per month. Most paid cash in exchange, though some paid in rationed food. Some did not pay at all.[73] On the Eastern Front, German soldiers both paid for sex and acquired local 'mistresses', but they engaged in more

---

[71] 'Forced Labor – Background', 7 May 2008, on *Forced Labor 1939–1945: Memory and History*, available at http://www.zwangsarbeit-archiv.de/en/zwangsarbeit/zwangsarbeit/zwangsarbeit-2/index.html (accessed 10 July 2015). This web site project, directed by Prof Dr Nicolas Apostolopoulos at the Free University of Berlin, houses 590 interviews with survivors of Nazi forced labour.
[72] Shani D'Cruze, 'Sexual Violence Since 1750', in *The Routledge History of Sex and the Body, 1500 to the Present*, ed. Sarah Toulalan and Kate Fisher (Abingdon, Oxon and New York: Routledge, 2013), 444–59.
[73] Goldstein, *War and Gender*, 337.

rape than either they or their enemies did on the Western Front.[74] Part of the reason for this was the very misogyny we discussed during our account of the First World War. As in the previous war, German commanders warned troops that Russian women were nearly universally infected with venereal disease and that they were all spies. The special Nazi touch was to remind soldiers that sex with inferior peoples endangered racial purity and constituted a 'moral offense'.[75] These formal injunctions did little to stop sex in the East. For one thing, despite laws against miscegenation, military orders specific to this front freed soldiers from punishment for crimes against civilians, and punishments for rape were rare.[76] As Timothy Snyder writes, soldiers 'would also rape Jewish women, casually, as though this were not an offense for which they could be punished. When they were caught, they were reminded of the German laws against racial mixing'.[77] As Doris Bergen has argued, 'ideology … did not constitute a barrier to violence of a sexual nature … Instead ideology shaped the forms that sexual violence took … Nazi ideology determined the kinds of violence that furthered the goals of the Third Reich'.[78] Rape in Soviet lands was not treated as an obstacle to the enslavement of the Slavic race, and it was very widespread. The German government itself estimated that Germans had fathered 10,000 children in Ukraine during the war, a large percentage of which would have been the result of non-consensual sexual acts, whether rape or enforced concubinage.[79] These were relationships governed by both a logic of brutal occupation and racial subjugation. Just because rape seems to be a universal feature of war does not mean that it has the same causes or means the same thing in every historical setting. This is an area of historical research that has perhaps seen more expansion than any other since we wrote the first edition of this book. A subject that was largely taboo is now being explored in significant detail and with particular attention to the dynamics of war and occupation. 'Up until recently,' Pascale Bos writes:

---

[74] Birgit Beck, *Wehrmacht und sexuelle Gewalt: Sexualverbrechen Vor Deutschen Militärgerichten 1939–1945* (Paderborn: Ferdinand Schöningh, 2004); and Regina Mühlhäuser, *Eroberungen. Sexuelle Gewalttaten und intime Beziehungen deutscher Soldaten in der Sowjetunion 1941–1945* (Hamburg: Hamburger Edition, 2010).

[75] Omer Bartov, *The Eastern Front, 1941–45: German Troops and the Barbarisation of Warfare* (New York: St. Martin's Press, 1986), 128.

[76] Wolfram Wette, *The Wehrmacht. History, Myth, Reality* (Cambridge, MA: Harvard University Press, 2006), 93–100.

[77] Timothy Snyder, *Bloodlands: Europe between Hitler and Stalin* (New York: Basic Books, 2010), 123. The waves of sexual violence had a large impact on the politics of the Cold War. See Norman M. Naimark, 'The Russians and Germans: Rape during the War and Post-Soviet Memories', in *Rape in Wartime*, ed. Raphaelle Branche and Fabrice Virgili (London and New York: Palgrave Macmillan, 2012), 201–19.

[78] Doris L. Bergen, 'Sexual Violence in the Holocaust: Unique and Typical?', in *Lessons and Legacies VII: The Holocaust in International Perspective*, ed. Peter Hayes and Dagmar Herzog (Evanston, IL: Northwestern University Press, 2006), 179. See also: Regina Mühlhäuser, 'The Unquestioned Crime: Sexual Violence by German Soldiers during the War of Annihilation in the Soviet Union, 1941–45', in Branche, *Rape in Wartime*, 34–46.

[79] Karel C. Berkhoff, *Harvest of Despair: Life and Death in Ukraine under Nazi Rule* (Cambridge, MA: Belknap Press of Harvard University Press, 2004), 182.

wartime rape often was seen as either merely accidental (and incidental, the act by a renegade individual soldier committed in the heat of the moment) or, conversely, as so common as to make it almost universal. In either case, wartime rape was not considered to be in need of further analysis.[80]

But the racially motivated policies that made mass rapes on the Eastern Front possible do require further analysis.

Though some Germans simply ignored the commands from above (largely with impunity), others took a darker lesson and resolved that no witnesses should be left alive after the racial 'crime' they were committing. Rape-murder, after all, left no possibility for long-term racial pollution, and it could be portrayed as an act of race extermination, on the one hand, and of intimidation of the men who often had to witness the violence upon their loved ones, on the other. Indeed, rape-murder represented the pinnacle of aggressive misogyny. It destroyed women, demonstrated one's own dominance and virility and emasculated enemy men. Thus, as Omer Bartov notes, it 'was possible for at least a significant part of the German troops to fraternize with individual Russians for a while, and then to "eliminate" them and burn down their houses as part of a mass of dangerous and contemptible "*Untermenschen*" ["inferior people"] the moment this or that "security" situation called for such actions.'[81]

Rape and slaughter had thus marked life in Eastern Europe since 1939, with the advancing German forces, the main perpetrators. In 1943, however, the tide of war changed. At the Battle of Stalingrad, the Soviet forces finally stopped the German conquest and began rolling them back. By 1944 they had crossed pre-war borders, having reconquered their country kilometre by kilometre and having seen the devastation the Nazi invasion had wrought. When they moved into Eastern and Central Europe, they attacked civilians with a furore. Soviet soldiers also used sexual violence as a form of revenge. Though much research remains to be done to establish the extent and motivations of the atrocities, it is clear that the lurid tales of the Soviet army's penchant for rape were based in fact.[82] In those regions that later became part of the Soviet bloc, stories about these rapes have been particularly taboo. Mark James estimates that 50,000 women were raped in Budapest during the Red Army's invasion of Hungary. The integration of Hungary into the Soviet sphere of interest, however, meant that while memories of this violence burned fiercely for some, it was actively denied and repressed by others.[83] But German women suffered even more

---

[80] Pascale R. Bos, 'Feminists Interpreting the Politics of Wartime Rape: Berlin, 1945; Yugoslavia, 1992–1993', *Signs: Journal of Women in Culture & Society* 31, no. 4 (Summer 2006): 995.

[81] Bartov, *The Eastern Front*, 129.

[82] Norman Naimark, *The Russians in Germany: A History of the Soviet Zone of Occupation, 1945–1949* (Cambridge, MA and London: Belknap Press of Harvard University Press, 1995); Atina Grossmann, 'A Question of Silence: The Rape of German Women by Occupation Soldiers', in *West Germany under Construction: Politics, Society, & Culture in the Adenauer Era*, ed. Robert G. Moeller (Ann Arbor, MI: University of Michigan Press, 1997), 33–52. See also Anonymous, *A Woman in Berlin: Eight Weeks in the Conquered City* (New York: Metropolitan Books, 2005).

[83] James Mark, 'Remembering Rape: Divided Social Memory and the Red Army in Hungary 1944–1945', *Past & Present* 188, no. 1 (1 August 2005): 133–61.

during the almost literal rape of the German capital in the final days of the war. Atina Grossmann has estimated that one in three of the approximately 1.5 million female residents of Berlin were raped, many more than once.[84] The screams of violated women echoed throughout the city for days on end. Estimates from local hospitals indicated that somewhere between 95,000 and 135,000 women had been raped, many by multiple attackers, in the days just before and after Hitler's suicide and the final capitulation of the German army in May 1945.[85] Thus did the gruesome war end in a gruesome way on the streets and in the shattered apartments of Berlin.

The apotheosis of this gendered race war against civilians was of course the Holocaust. The groups that the Nazis targeted for destruction – homosexuals, Roma (Gypsies), the disabled, and above all the Jews – were all identified and abused in very gendered ways. Nazi propaganda painted Jewish men as sexual predators, constantly plotting to defile German women. But Jewish men were also feminized; the image of the Jew promoted by the Nazi state was that of the anti-male, cowardly instead of brave, weak instead of strong, duplicitous rather than forthright. In the Nazi mind, Jewish women lacked the necessary attributes of femininity as well, especially after the Holocaust began. Stripped of their clothes and dignity, starved and beaten, and subjected to various kinds of sexual torment, forced prostitution, and violation,[86] women became less 'feminine', not only to their tormentors, but also to themselves and their loved ones. As one survivor remembered, she had pictured throughout her captivity how beautiful her reunion with her daughter would be if they both survived the war. Instead, her child screamed 'My mommy is the one in the picture, this ugly woman isn't my mommy!' when they finally found one another back home in Austria.[87] In the camps themselves, the same dynamic in which women and children were disproportionally targeted for immediate extermination, and often made to suffer sexual assault and torture as well, was present.[88] Sex was a form of barter in the camps, both for men and women. Dr Gisella Perl, survivor of Auschwitz-Birkenau, described the sexual practices that thrived in conditions of extreme hunger and the constant threat of death:

> The latrine also served as a 'love nest'. It was here that male and female prisoners met for a furtive moment of joyless sexual intercourse in which the body was used

---

[84] Atina Grossmann, 'The "Big Rape": Sex and Sexual Violence, War, and Occupation in German Post World War II Memory and Imagination', in *Gender and the Long Postwar: The United States and the Two Germanys, 1945-1989*, ed. Karen Hagemann and Sonya Michel (Washington, DC and Balitmore: Woodrow Wilson Center Press and Johns Hopkins University Press, 2014), 32.

[85] Antony Beevor, *The Fall of Berlin, 1945* (New York: Viking, 2002), 410.

[86] Na'ama Shik, 'Sexual Abuse of Jewish Women in Auschwitz-Birkenau', in *Brutality and Desire: War and Sexuality in Europe's Twentieth Century*, ed. Dagmar Herzog (London and New York: Palgrave Macmillan, 2011), 221–46.

[87] Helga Embacher, 'Unwelcome in Austria: Returnees and Concentration Camp Survivors', in *When the War Was Over: Women, War and Peace in Europe, 1940-1956*, ed. Claire Duchen and Irene Bandhauer-Schöffmann (London and New York: Leicester University Press, 2000), 197.

[88] While the extent of sexual violence in the course of the Holocaust is still under-researched, there is a growing consensus that the laws prohibiting German men from sexual contact with Jewish women were honoured more often in the breach. See for example Sonja M. Hedgepeth and Rochelle G. Saidel, eds., *Sexual Violence against Jewish Women during the Holocaust* (Lebanon, NH: University Press of New England, 2010).

as a commodity with which to pay for the badly needed items that men were able to steal from the warehouses ... Detachments of male workers came into Camp C almost daily, to clean the latrines, build streets, and patch up leaking roofs. These men were trusted old prisoners who knew everything there was to know about camp life, had connections in the crematories and were masters at 'organizing'. Their full pockets make them the Don Juans of Camp C. They chose their women among the youngest, the prettiest, the least emaciated prisoners and in a few seconds the deal was closed. Openly, shamelessly, the dirty, diseased bodies clung together for a minute or two in the fetid atmosphere of the latrine – and the piece of bread, the comb, the little knife wandered from the pocket of the man into the greedy hands of the woman.[89]

Perl's evocative language and her not-entirely-sympathetic tone exemplify how women who bartered their bodies to survive were shamed by their fellow inmates both during and after the war. In the male blocks, such barter also took place between young boys and Kapos – the inmate-wardens of the prisoners' barracks. Most controversially, similar exchanges of sex for food and other necessities of survival were common between Jews in the ghettos or between Jews and their various protectors in partisan groups or in hiding.[90] Both the Nazi genocide and the struggle to survive it affected the circumstances under which sexual relationships of all kinds were formed and dramatically increased the vulnerability of some groups to sexual exploitation, violence and torture.[91]

These Nazi actions deeply affected European gender structures. Whereas in the First World War, mutual ground-level misogyny could be translated into mutual reinforcement of masculine ideas of protection at the national level, the Nazi conquest of the continent had revealed the military notion of masculine protection to be a mirage. Soldiers had failed to protect their own wives and children, and they increasingly came to believe that in order to win the war they would have to target women and children themselves. The initial military successes of the Nazis convinced state and military officials that defeating the German Reich would require an even greater 'totalization' of war than they had envisioned before, one that would entail direct assaults upon Axis civilians as legitimate and necessary war targets. In Great Britain at the start of the war, the 'terror' bombing of civilians was seen as immoral, but this judgement changed as the war progressed. By

---

[89] Quoted from Gisella Perl, *I Was a Doctor in Auschwitz* (New York: Ayer Company Publishers Inc., 1948), 57–8 in Goldenberg, 'Sex-Based Violence', 113–14.

[90] For accounts of sexual violence as a form of partisan reprisal, see Jeffrey Burds, 'Sexual Violence in Europe in World War II, 1939–1945', *Politics & Society* 37, no. 1 (1 March 2009): 35–73; and Myrna Goldenberg, 'Sex-Based Violence and the Politics and Ethics of Survival', in *Different Horrors/Same Hell: Gender and the Holocaust*, ed. Myrna Goldenberg and Amy Shapiro (Seattle: University of Washington Press, 2013), 112–16. This form of abuse was not confined to the Holocaust but was also common in Stalin's slave labour camps. See Wilson Bell, 'Sex, Pregnancy, and Power in the Late Stalinist Gulag', *Journal of the History of Sexuality* 24, no. 2 (2015): 198–224.

[91] Ronit Lentin, '"A Howl Unheard": Women Shoah Survivors Dis-Placed and Re-Silenced', in *When the War Was Over: Women, War and Peace in Europe, 1940–1956*, ed. Claire Duchen and Irene Bandhauer-Schöffmann (London and New York: Leicester University Press, 2000), 182.

1942, Churchill had approved a shift of Britain's strategic bombing plan from one that focused almost exclusively on the 'precision' bombing of key military and industrial sites to one that they called a 'de-housing' campaign. This was a euphemism grotesque even for a grotesque genre; in practice the idea was to 'break the spirit of the people' by killing civilians indiscriminately. By the summer of 1943, the strategy was being fully employed. A week of firebombing in Hamburg in July and August of that year left more than a million urban residents homeless, and it killed nearly as many people (about 50,000) as all German air raids in Britain did over the course of the entire war.[92]

The response of the targeted populations to these unprecedented assaults varied from place to place, but it had important implications for the gender order everywhere. In much of occupied Europe, the response was most obvious in underground movements. These movements responded to occupation and the assault on gender roles by both incorporating women into activities more extensively than had been envisioned or practised in earlier European wars and by urgently attempting to salvage some scraps of earlier gender identities.

The most extensive and unusual developments occurred in the Soviet Union, where the state and military both used the most traditional sorts of propaganda to energize Soviet masculinity and enlisted women into combat on a scale unseen either in Russian history or, for that matter, in the history of Europe as a whole. By 1943, roughly 8 per cent of total Soviet military personnel were women, about 800,000 women in all. When one includes partisan fighters in the mix, it is likely that more than a million Soviet women took an active military role, half of them at the front. For the most part, these women stayed in support services, but to a far greater extent than elsewhere they engaged in combat. Indeed, there were three entire female regiments in the Soviet Air Force between 1942 and 1945. Women flew more than 30,000 combat sorties.[93] Still, the iconic Soviet female war figure was not a combat soldier but the young partisan Zoya Kosmodemianskaia, who was executed by the Germans after she was caught setting fire to a stable filled with army horses. The Soviet press reported that she was tortured and undressed by her captors but went to the gallows bravely, saying 'Don't look glum, Comrades! Be brave, fight, kill the Germans, burn them, poison them! I am not afraid to die, Comrades. It is a great privilege to die for your people.' This model of belligerent sacrifice left a lasting impression. As one future dissident intellectual remembered, she was so taken by the Zoya tale that she 'modelled' her life upon her brave example.[94]

As Soviet women flew combat missions, as masses of women joined partisan units, and as millions of European men looked at the ravaged homes and ravaged families they had failed to defend, gendered practices and ideals across the continent lay in rubble. Gender ideals had been destroyed by the rise to power of the radical, aggressive,

---

[92] Gordon Wright, *The Ordeal of Total War, 1939–1945* (New York: Harper and Row, 1968), 176–9.

[93] Reina Pennington, *Wings, Women, and War: Soviet Airwomen in World War II Combat* (Lawrence, KS: University Press of Kansas, 2001), 1–2.

[94] Ludmilla Alekseeva and Paul Goldberg, *The Thaw Generation: Coming of Age in the Post-Stalin Era* (Pittsburgh, PA: University of Pittsburgh Press, 1993), 20.

misogynistic strand of masculinity that had crystallized in the First World War, had risen to prominence in the interwar period and had come to full power during the Second World War. The fascist movements had led the continent towards apocalypse, and Europe bathed in the blood that the fascists had sought and had revelled in. When their urge for destruction resulted in their own annihilation at the hands of Soviet men and women, and then finally in a wave of Allied assaults in 1944 and 1945, it remained an open question what would be left to salvage from the wreckage. Surely one of the major question marks was what sorts of masculinity and femininity would emerge.

## Conclusion: The recovery of masculine heroism

In contrast to the situation after the First World War, in which so many European soldiers, citizens and politicians felt more defeated than victorious at the end of the conflict, the Allied defeat of Nazi Germany and the elevation of anti-fascist politicians to national leadership allowed nearly every European nation (with the important exception of Germany) to feel that it had won the war, even though most states had seen at least part of their country occupied by foreign powers. It was everywhere a bitter victory, of course. In the Soviet Union, where the violence had raged unchecked for nearly four years, the celebrations that came with the Nazi surrender in May 1945 were muted by the destruction. Twenty-seven million Soviet citizens had died, and an additional twenty-five million were rendered homeless. About 1,700 towns and 70,000 villages had been destroyed, and major cities like Stalingrad and Sevastopol were so gutted that virtually no buildings remained standing. In Yugoslavia, a brutal civil war had accompanied the period of Nazi occupation; there too civilians had not been protected by their armies. In Paris, in Copenhagen and elsewhere, much of the war experience had been that of submission to foreign bureaucrats and soldiers. Men in occupied Europe were not masters of their own homes, their own cities or their own nations. By any of the measures of modern masculinity, most European men had failed this enormous test. Indeed, given that the atrocities of the war had resulted from the poisonous distillation of militarized national masculinity to its most brutal elements, the case could have been made that the very core of modern masculinity had been discredited by the experience of the Second World War. Perhaps it was not men but manhood that had failed.

As we have already seen, feminist peace activists had made this exact argument about the destructiveness of modern masculinity even prior to the world wars. It would be revived again a generation after the end of the Second World War, but it was not a popular stance while smoke still wafted from rubble across the continent. Instead Europeans did their best to salvage masculinity from the wreckage of fascism, total war and social apocalypse. A great deal of public attention was focused on incidents of masculine heroism rather than on masculine failure. In propaganda posters and in interpersonal exchanges alike, the fighting men of Europe were thanked for their service. The war was transformed into a Manichean battle between good and evil. There was a brief period of retribution right after the war's end that saw the girlfriends of German soldiers, particularly in France and

Norway, taunted and abused,[95] local quislings assaulted or killed, the cleansing of ethnic German populations in Poland and Czechoslovakia and the remnants of quasi-fascist paramilitary forces in places like Croatia and Ukraine annihilated. But within only a few years, the fascist sympathizers, the collaborators and the wise 'cowards' who kept their heads down during the catastrophe faded into the silent background. The trials of Nazi war criminals at Nuremberg, which placed blame directly at the top of the political and military chain while tacitly excusing the millions of men in the lower ranks, contributed to this post-war 'reconstruction'. It was as if a couple of potent icons like the swastika and Hitler's little moustache could be made to carry the enormous weight of Europe's sins.

It was perhaps understandable that the victorious nations should have accentuated the positive when they told themselves stories about the war. In these stories, the brave men of Europe saved civilization from barbarism. The defiant, stiff-backed resistance of men like France's Charles de Gaulle or Britain's Winston Churchill was taken to represent the honourable strength of their respective nations. The more lowly men in uniform were less personally recognizable, but they too got their share of the laurels. Idolized and idealized in print, the love affair with the Second World War combat soldier has been strong and shows little sign of waning, even as the survivors themselves are now succumbing to age.

More surprising was the speed with which this same generosity of memory and absolution was extended to Germany and other areas of Europe that had been ruled by fascist and dictatorial regimes. The first phase of forgiveness was rather personal. Allied occupation soldiers in Germany and in 'liberated' countries like France generally ignored their military's anti-fraternization rules and began relationships with local women. In Germany, these relationships actually helped to establish bonds of sympathy and understanding that were essential to the creation of the newly forming cross-Atlantic alliance.[96] In France, American soldiers tended to act as if 'France was a tremendous brothel', and their sexual fantasies were intertwined with their general lack of respect for a nation that had so quickly succumbed to Nazism and therefore clearly needed help to govern itself.[97] In both examples, however, the mere fact that an enormous number of American soldiers remained on European soil long after the war ended contributed to an intense discussion about the moral responsibilities for the war.

Americans, who had not experienced German occupation, were quicker to forgive than, say, citizens of the Soviet Union, where suspicion of Germans and German power lasted for another fifty years. We can see the key movements in this direction quite early.

---

[95] The punishment was usually a public head shaving. See Claire Duchen, 'Crime and Punishment in Liberated France: The Case of les femmes tondues', in *When the War Was Over: Women, War and Peace in Europe, 1940–1956*, ed. Claire Duchen and Irene Bandhauer-Schöffman (London and New York: Leicester University Press, 2000), 233–50; Kåre Olsen, *Schicksal Lebensborn: Die Kinder der Schande und ihrer Mütter* (Munich: Knauer Taschenbuch Verlag, 2004), 251–6; and Fabrice Virgili, *Shorn Women: Gender and Punishment in Liberation France*, trans. John Flower (Oxford and New York: Berg Publishers, 2002).

[96] Maria Höhn, *GIs and Fräuleins: The German-American Encounter in 1950s West Germany* (Chapel Hill & London: University of North Carolina Press, 2002); and Timothy L. Schroer, *Recasting Race after World War II: Germans and African Americans in American-Occupied Germany* (Boulder: University of Colorado Press, 2007).

[97] Mary Louise Roberts, *What Soldiers Do: Sex and the American GI in World War II France* (Chicago: University of Chicago Press, 2013).

In 1948, Edward Shils and Morris Janowitz, two young enterprising scholars (and former intelligence officers under General Dwight Eisenhower), wrote one of the most influential pieces in the entire history of the field of military sociology. Entitled 'Cohesion and Disintegration in the Wehrmacht', the article argued that the young conscripts in the German army had been so resolute during the war due to their loyalty to the 'primary group' of soldiers that surrounded them. The argument resurrected the notion of combat brotherhood and argued that it was precisely these 'positive' masculine attributes of loyalty, love for the men next to you and sense of duty that motivated the *Wehrmacht's* soldiers. They were not, in other words, really fascist: 'the unity of the German Army was in fact sustained only to a very slight extent by the National Socialist political convictions of its members.'[98] It was true that most of the soldiers were eventually to adopt a Nazi frame of mind and to revere Hitler personally, but this, in Shils and Janowitz's examination, was the result of sociological forces rather than ideological ones. Since many of their officers and junior officers had been part of the 'hard core' committed Nazis, who were 'imbued with the ideology of *Gemeinschaft* (community solidarity), were enthusiasts for the military life, had definite homo-erotic tendencies and accordingly placed a very high value on "toughness," manly comradeliness, and group solidarity',[99] they had been socialized into their roles rather than politically convinced. The article was important because it gave a systematic and compelling argument regarding the social dynamics of military units. This argument about the importance of small-scale socialization to military cohesion retains its vitality today, as our discussion of soldier society during the First World War indicated. But in this context and at this time, it also, intentionally or not, had the effect of 'rehabilitating' the millions of German men who had wielded weapons and actively destroyed the continent.

The logic of this line of reasoning reached its pinnacle in 1985, when US President Ronald Reagan agreed to visit a cemetery in Bitburg, West Germany, where forty-nine members of the Waffen SS (an elite Nazi corps responsible for many wartime atrocities) were buried. When challenged by many Holocaust survivors and by White House reporters, Reagan replied that he would not change his itinerary because the SS men and *Wehrmacht* soldiers were 'Victims of Nazism also … just as surely as the victims in the concentration camps'.[100] In case the point was missed, Reagan again made clear at Bitburg that the young men buried in the cemetery were victims of an 'ism'; and stated that 'today, freedom-loving people around the world must say, I am a Berliner, I am a Jew in a world still threatened by anti-Semitism. I am an Afghan, and I am a prisoner of the Gulag … I, too, am a potential victim of totalitarianism'.[101]

---

[98] Edward Shils and Morris Janowitz, 'Cohesion and Disintegration in the Wehrmacht in World War II', *The Public Opinion Quarterly* 12, no. 2 (1948): 281.

[99] Ibid.: 286.

[100] Ronald W. Reagan, 'Remarks and a Question-and-Answer Session with Regional Editors and Broadcasters'. Ronald Reagan Presidential Library and Museum: The Public Papers of President Ronald W. Reagan, 18 April 1985, available at http://www.reagan.utexas.edu/archives/speeches/1985/41885d.htm (accessed 10 July 2015).

[101] Ronald W. Reagan, 'Remarks at a Joint German-American Military Ceremony at Bitburg Air Base in the Federal Republic of Germany'. Ronald Reagan Presidential Library and Museum: The Public Papers of President Ronald W. Reagan, 5 May 1985, available at http://www.reagan.utexas.edu/archives/speeches/1985/50585b.htm (accessed 10 July 2015).

Reagan's comments (and the grateful welcome of them by German Chancellor Helmut Kohl) highlight two important post-war developments that help us conclude the discussion of war and gender in the twentieth century. In the first place, they show how effectively militarized masculinity had been resurrected after nearly destroying itself and the continent along with it. Soldiers were worth honouring just because they had been soldiers. While Europeans learned to look at fascists as strange and evil fanatics with whom they had nothing in common, when they looked at young men who died in uniform, they recognized them as their own. Courage, duty, hardness and valour were now the traits that marked those who 'fought for freedom', while Nazis were increasingly portrayed as social and sexual perverts.

The second point to make is how quickly and painlessly this form of masculinity was incorporated into the great conflict of post-war Europe, the Cold War. US President John F. Kennedy's proud 1963 'boast' that 'I am a Berliner' had stressed both that the Nazi past would be forgotten (or at least ignored) and that the young, virile fight for freedom was being joined once again, with true men taking sides in the contest. Reagan reminded his German listeners of Kennedy's speech in order to make the same point. By making the Holocaust and all the other atrocities of the Second World War simply episodes in the dramatic battle of freedom-loving men against totalitarianism, or, from the Soviet perspective, in the equally dramatic battle of freedom-loving men against capitalist aggression, it became possible to dust off those old uniforms and those old leather boots in order to fight the threat of the new enemy with a feeling of pride rather than painful guilt.

For better or worse, however, the conflict between the histories we would like and the histories we have is not so easily resolved in favour of the former. It was true that at least in the initial post-war period, the gender 'backlash' seemed to have succeeded. In France, a conservative focus on the traditional family was dominant, and women were urged to bear lots of children to replenish the nation.[102] But too much had happened and too much had changed for this revived gender structure to remain unchallenged. Many Europeans felt a deep unease about the similarities between the militarized dynamic of the first half of the century and the militarized dynamic of the second half. It turned out that not only the swastikas reminded people of the brutalities of the past, but those leather boots and warlike speeches did too. This unease played itself out in a variety of ways. The most important one to note here was that the cultural conflicts and the widespread rejection of the status quo by young people in the 1960s and 1970s included a powerful intellectual and political challenge by feminist movements. The final success of suffrage movements in the wake of the Second World War (Italy granted women the vote in 1945, and, anticipating liberation, the provisional government of France did so in 1944) had made possible this widespread political activism and had freed feminists to press ever harder on issues like social equality and peace. Scholars and organizers

---

[102] Sylvie Chaperon, 'Feminism Is Dead. Long Live Feminism! The Women's Movement in France at the Liberation', in *When the War Was Over: Women, War and Peace in Europe, 1940–1956*, ed. Claire Duchen and Irene Bandhauer-Schöffmann (London and New York: Leicester University Press, 2000), 157.

alike passionately criticized the dominant form of masculinity and the social order that nurtured and depended upon it. Society and gender may have been deeply militarized, but the process of total war had also helped develop the institutions and sentiments that would challenge the bellicose trend of the twentieth century.

Similarly, the rise of Holocaust studies, which emerged relatively late on the scene of Second World War scholarship, challenged both the normalization of German soldiers and the silence about fascist sympathy across the continent. New works of history convincingly rejected the view that German soldiers and women were unwilling accomplices of the Nazi project and that the rest of Europe had simply bowed to necessity. Most of these studies left readers with the unwelcome conclusion that fascism and genocide, far from being alien and exotic or the result of hypnotic brainwashing, were in fact an organic part of European history. 'Ordinary Men' had pulled the trigger on the civilian victims of the war, the Holocaust itself was a logical outcome of certain currents in European 'modernity', and not only Germans but also one's 'neighbours' could be the active agents of annihilation.[103] It was serendipitous but not perhaps totally coincidental that the culmination of these academic trends coincided with the end of the Cold War, which seemed to remove the necessity for the deep militarization of society. War certainly did not disappear after the Second World War, and one might expand the discussion of its effects on gender and sexual relations into the era of decolonization and the fierce conflicts it produced, such as the Algerian War of Independence against French colonial rule between 1954 and 1962. Still, Europeans at home were mostly shielded from the more violent aspects of the Cold War, and even the fact that we refer to the years after the Second World War as the 'post-war' period expresses the widespread hope that Europeans might eventually be free not only from the threat of war, but also from the harmful aspects of the militarized masculinity that accompanied that threat. This hope was not totally in vain, but neither was it fully borne out. European masculinity remains in a state of flux at the start of the twenty-first century, but the martial and fraternal form of masculinity that rose to prominence during the years of total war and that defined manhood across the continent for the duration of the bloody twentieth century remains alive and well today.

## Suggested readings

Albanese, Patrizia. *Mothers of the Nation: Women, Families and Nationalism in Twentieth-Century Europe*. Toronto: University of Toronto Press, 2006.
Crouthamel, Jason. *An Intimate History of the Front: Masculinity, Sexuality, and German Soldiers in the First World War*. New York: Palgrave MacMillan, 2014.

---

[103] Zygmunt Bauman, *Modernity and the Holocaust* (Ithaca, NY: Cornell University Press, 1989); Christopher R. Browning, *Ordinary Men: Reserve Police Battalion 101 and the Final Solution in Poland*, 1st edn (New York: HarperCollins, 1992); Jan Tomasz Gross, *Neighbors: The Destruction of the Jewish Community in Jedwabne, Poland* (Princeton: Princeton University Press, 2001).

Doan, Laura L. *Disturbing Practices: History, Sexuality, and Women's Experience of Modern War*. Chicago and London: University of Chicago Press, 2013.

Duchen, Claire, and Irene Bandhauer-Schöffmann, eds. *When the War Was Over Women, War and Peace in Europe, 1940–1956*. London and New York: Leicester University Press, 2000.

Goldman, Wendy Z. *Women, the State, and Revolution: Soviet Family Policy and Social Life, 1917–1936*. Cambridge, MA: Cambridge University Press, 1993.

Grayzel, Susan R. *Women's Identities at War: Gender, Motherhood, and Politics in Britain and France during the First World War*. Chapel Hill: University of North Carolina Press, 1999.

Harvey, Elizabeth. *Women and the Nazi East: Agents and Witnesses of Germanization*. New Haven, CT: Yale University Press, 2003.

Higonnet, Margaret R., Margaret C. Weitz, Jane Jenson and Sonya Michel, eds. *Behind the Lines: Gender and the Two World Wars*. New Haven, CT: Yale University Press, 1987.

Kent, Susan Kingsley. *Making Peace: The Reconstruction of Gender in Interwar Britain*. Princeton, NJ: Princeton University Press, 1993.

Mann, Michael. *Fascists*. Cambridge and New York: Cambridge University Press, 2004.

Pedersen, Susan. *Family, Dependence, and the Origins of the Welfare State: Britain and France, 1914–1945*. New York: Cambridge University Press, 1993.

Roberts, Mary Louise. *What Soldiers Do: Sex and the American GI in World War II France*. Chicago, IL: University of Chicago Press, 2013.

Sanborn, Joshua A. *Drafting the Russian Nation: Military Conscription, Total War, and Mass Politics, 1905–1925*. DeKalb: Northern Illinois University Press, 2003.

Whitaker, Elizabeth Dixon. *Measuring Mamma's Milk: Fascism and the Medicalization of Maternity in Italy*. Ann Arbor: University of Michigan Press, 2000.

# CHAPTER 5
# THE LONG SEXUAL REVOLUTION

In 1760, the Swiss physician Simon Auguste André David Tissot (1728–97) published a treatise, *L'Onanisme*, that reflected what many eighteenth- and nineteenth-century Europeans thought of the idea of sexual pleasure for its own sake. In that work, Tissot provided a particularly vivid description of the fate of one incurable masturbator L. D.***:

> L. D.***, watchmaker, had been good, and had enjoyed good health, up until the age of seventeen; at this period, he began to masturbate, an act which he reiterated daily, and often as many as three times a day. Before a year had passed, he began to notice a great weakness after each act; this warning was not sufficient to pull him from the mire; his soul, already given over to this filth was no longer capable of other ideas, and the repetitions of his crime became daily more frequent, until he found himself in a state where he feared death was imminent ... I learned of his state, I went to his home; what I found was less a living being than a cadaver lying on straw, thin, pale, exuding a loathsome stench, almost incapable of movement. A pale and watery blood often dripped from his nose, he drooled continually; subject to attacks of diarrhoea, he defecated in his bed without noticing it; there was a constant flow of semen; his eyes, sticky, blurry, dull, had lost all power of movement; his pulse was extremely weak and racing ... Mental disorder was equally evident; without ideas, without memory, incapable of linking two sentences ... Thus sunk below the level of the beast, a spectacle of unimaginable horror, it was difficult to believe that he had once belonged to the human race ... He died after several weeks, in June 1757, his entire body covered in edemas.[1]

Masturbation, Tissot argued, was not only a sinful but also a physically harmful act. Sexual acts performed solely for individual pleasure would be punished.

The authors of the *Encyclopedia* (the foundational text of the European Enlightenment) endorsed Tissot's arguments and ensured that they found acceptance across Europe well into the nineteenth century. Indeed, the hysteria about non-reproductive sex and the dangers of unbridled sexual passion reached a height in the late nineteenth century, an era that historians long characterized as an age of unparalleled sexual repression.

---

[1] Cited in Jean Stengers, *Masturbation: The History of a Great Terror*, trans. Kathryn Hoffmann (New York: Palgrave, 2001), 65–6.

Descriptions of sexuality in Victorian Britain included stories about how mothers of young brides sent them off to their wedding nights with the advice to 'close your eyes and think of England' and how middle-class housewives crafted lacy doilies to hide the sensual curves of piano legs, lest they provoke lascivious thoughts. Tracts like Tissot's lent credence to the historical argument that nineteenth-century Europeans considered sexual pleasure to be entirely sinful – an unwanted by-product of the reproductive act that needed to be countered with moral condemnation and strict rules of etiquette. Even at the beginning of the modern period, there was thus no clear divide between 'scientific' understandings of sexuality and moral/religious beliefs. The history of sexuality makes it abundantly clear that scientific understandings are as much a product of their social contexts as any other aspect of human knowledge.[2]

Two centuries after Tissot, it seemed clear to scholars and casual observers alike that a radical shift in the European approach to sex and its pleasures was occurring. Most believed that the key moment was a 'sexual revolution' in the 1960s, when cultural turbulence and the social impact of the birth control pill had created a new consensus that sexual pleasure was natural and that sexual 'liberation' was healthy. Since sex could be separated from reproduction, it could shed the moral strictures of past times. Sex seemed to be everywhere in the popular culture of these years. Movies became much more sexually explicit, premarital sex moved out of the shadows of taboo and became a subject of public debate, and self-proclaimed sexual revolutionaries advocated 'open' marriages and 'swinging' lifestyles as a path to self-knowledge and freedom. The British poet Philip Larkin eloquently summarized the atmosphere in his 1967 poem 'Annus Mirabilis'. 'Sexual intercourse began', the poem begins, 'In nineteen sixty-three'.[3] Larkin's poem joyously proclaims the end of the 'wrangling for the ring' that used to precede sexual contact and argues that new sexual freedoms made everyone happy. Everyone, that is, except for those who had already passed through the courtship stage of life and thus could only watch all the fun from the married sidelines, since, as he says, 1963 'was rather late for me'.

Larkin was not alone in feeling left out, and his poem nicely symbolizes the European social consensus that the boundaries of sexual behaviour had been radically altered. Soon songs like Serge Gainsbourg's sexually explicit 'Je T'aime … Moi Non Plus', sung in orgasmic moans with British actress Jane Birkin in 1969, were achieving massive commercial success across Europe and proving that there was an increased demand for frank discussions about sex. This did not occur without opposition. Gainsbourg's song was banned from radio in Italy, Sweden, Spain and the United Kingdom. But the argument that sexual activity needed to be contained within marriage to protect the interests of society had become less persuasive. Penicillin had been available as a cure for bacterial sexually transmitted diseases (syphilis, gonorrhoea and chancroids) since soon

---

[2] Crawford, *European Sexualities, 1400–1800*, 100–1.
[3] Philip Larkin, 'Annus Mirabilis' in *The Complete Poems of Philip Larkin*, ed. Archie Burnett (London: Faber & Faber, 2012).

after the Second World War.[4] With the arrival of the birth control pill in much of Europe after 1961, age-old arguments linking sexual behaviour, reproduction and the threat of disease and/or death were definitively buried. Or so it seemed.

While Jane Birkin's moans were indeed symbolic of a new era of public frankness about sex in the 1960s, it is misleading to argue, as many sexual revolutionaries have, that an increase in sexual satisfaction was the true core of this change. The youth of the 1960s generation may have been convinced that they were having more and better sex than their parents and that this would change the world, but their historical intervention had less to do with the quality of their orgasms than with their success in manipulating long-established political discussions about sex. From the perspective of the twentieth-century history of sexuality, focusing too much attention on the famous 1960s generation gap that pitted progressive youth against their supposedly conservative, prudish war-generation parents overemphasizes both the radicalism of the 1960s and the conservatism of the 1950s. The roots of the sexual revolution lie not in this generation gap, but in scientific, medical and political discourses and policies on sexual behaviour and gender that had developed at the beginning of the century and had even older precedents. In fact, the wishes of the sexual revolutionaries to make sex public and their conviction that sexuality and politics were intimately intertwined were actually far more compatible with previous discourses on sex than they were willing to admit.

The sexual revolutionaries of the 1960s were correct in identifying the politicization of sexual activity as a crucial sphere of social, cultural and indeed political life in twentieth-century European society. They were also correct to assume that the massive shift in the relationship between sex and politics came to full fruition in the 1960s and 1970s. They were wrong, however, in thinking that their 'revolution' would increase the influence of sexual pleasure on politics or social life. Rather than being the agents of something new, they were actually witnesses to the demise of something old. Sex played a less significant role in the political life of Europe after the intervention of the 1960s generation than it had before.[5] To demonstrate how this is true, it will first of all be necessary to explore how historians use the term 'sexuality'. Once we have established that the concept of 'sexuality' did not always exist, it will be easier to see how late nineteenth- and early twentieth-century scientific explorations of sexual behaviour combined with political

---

[4] Viral STDs, such as herpes, chlamydia and genital warts, only became prevalent after the 1960s and are significantly more difficult to diagnose and treat. This 'second generation' of STDs, as the World Health Organization calls them, now includes HIV/AIDS (to be discussed below). See Antoon de Schryver and André Z. Meheus, 'Epidemiology of Sexually Transmitted Diseases: The Global Picture', *Bulletin of the World Health Organization* 68, no. 5 (1990): 639–64.

[5] It should be noted that this way of viewing the 'long sexual revolution' differs from but does not contradict the argument made by Hera Cook in *The Long Sexual Revolution: English Women, Sex, and Contraception 1800–1975* (Oxford: Oxford University Press, 2004). We accept the argument that increased access to contraception was vital for the attainment of female sexual pleasure and, indeed, full political emancipation. But we concentrate here on how sexuality and politics were intertwined in the twentieth century for both men and women and on how this relationship shifted in the 1960s.

programmes to increase the birth rate and decisively affect attitudes towards sexuality during and after the two world wars.

## Defining sexuality

The account to follow relies on a definition of the term 'sexuality' that owes much to the late twentieth-century French philosopher Michel Foucault (1926–84). Foucault was and continues to be even after his death the most influential figure in the destruction of narratives of ever-increasing sexual liberation over the course of the modern period. In 1976, Foucault published a short introduction to a planned six-volume *History of Sexuality* (he completed only three volumes before his death in 1984). The first volume (originally published in English simply as *Volume One: Introduction*) riveted the attention of historians interested in the history of sexuality and made 'well-trodden terrain suddenly unfamiliar'.[6] The book reframed the relationship between sex and society and questioned the fundamental assumptions of the field. Foucault suggested that the supposed prudery of the Victorian period was a myth that obscured the fact that there was actually an expansion of the discussion of subjects related to sex in the nineteenth century.[7] He argued further that this concern with sex was deeply connected with changes in the larger structures of power in society, but he rejected the interpretation that the ultimate result was simply sexual repression.[8] What previous historians viewed as examples of social control (prohibitions on masturbation and calls for female chastity, for example) Foucault saw as indications that talk about sex so pervaded political culture that it took on an unprecedented importance, becoming a key conduit for relationships of power. When popularizing their own sexual norms and translating them into social policy, European property owners were less interested in controlling their inferiors than in solidifying their own growing political power. The middle classes, Foucault insisted, first examined their *own* sexual practices and made a science out of sexuality in the hopes of redefining their roles in society, setting themselves apart from previous ruling classes. In the process, a science of sexuality was created, a complex and multifaceted scientific exploration of sex that – unlike the erotic arts of other cultures – was less a search for truth in sexual pleasure than it was a quest for personal confessions about sexual experiences. Foucault argued that these confessions collectively created 'a complex machinery for producing true discourses on sex'.[9] In the

---

[6] Jan Goldstein, 'Foucault among the Sociologists: The "Disciplines" and the History of the Professions', *History and Theory* 23, no. 2 (1984): 171.

[7] Michel Foucault, *History of Sexuality*, reissue edition, vol. 1: *An Introduction* (New York: Vintage Books, 1990), 18–23.

[8] For a useful summary of both the impact of Foucault on the historiography of sexuality and of the historical impact of theories of 'perversity' upon nineteenth- and twentieth-century ideas about sex, see Stephen Garton, *Histories of Sexuality* (New York: Routledge, 2004), esp. chp. 9, 'Imagining Perversity'.

[9] Ibid., 68.

process of producing new forms of knowledge, a new and reciprocal relationship of power was formed between confessing individuals and the state.

While the search for truth about sex led to obsessions with masturbation and childhood sexuality, concerns about homosexuality and sexual perversion, the mysteries of women's bodies and the need to control reproductive behaviour, Foucault also believed that it created new forms of sexual pleasures and new identities. First under the auspices of Christianity and then in the doctor's office or on the psychiatrist's couch, teasing out sexual truth through confession incited desires. There was pleasure in the quest for truth about pleasure. Though this quest involved a relationship of power, this power did not quash sexual identities; it created them. 'L. D.***' had masturbated, but Doctor Tissot made him a 'Masturbator'. Foucault argues that it was in this confessional space that the very notion of sexual identity emerged. A search for the 'truth' of sexual experience that began in the West in the eighteenth century led to the conviction that sex constitutes our individuality and that individuals possess a core sexual essence, a natural and somewhat immutable sense of themselves that is tied to their sexual desires. As individuals confessed their sexual desires, medical experts categorized modes of sexual being, implicitly or explicitly labelling some 'normal' and others perverse. Foucault's insights have led others to explore how sexual behaviour became part of the consensus about a hierarchy of the human race as it had emerged with the growing acceptance of Darwin's theories at the turn of the century.[10] How someone's sexual desires expressed themselves came to be taken as a sign of their place on an evolutionary scale. As we saw in Chapter 3, part of the European imperial project involved the use of sexual categories and hierarchies of acceptable sexual behaviour to justify European dominance and reinforce beliefs in European racial superiority.

So what has been the effect of Foucault's intervention into the history of sexuality? Perhaps the best way to demonstrate the impact of *The History of Sexuality* is to look at how historical narratives have changed under its influence. The first generation of historians to seriously examine the history of sexual behaviour was motivated by their involvement in the liberation movements of the 1960s and 1970s: the women's liberation movement and the gay rights movement. Their books were written to uncover the 'lost' history of sexual minorities, and their arguments were formulated on the assumption that non-heterosexual sexual identities always existed. Books like John Boswell's path-breaking *Christianity, Social Tolerance and Homosexuality: Gay People in Western Europe from the Beginning of the Christian Era to the Fourteenth Century* (1980) tracked the history of homosexuality backwards into previous eras, looking for mechanisms of repression or, sometimes, modes of tolerance.[11] But his assumption that these same-sex sexual practices were identical to what we now call homosexuality has since been questioned by historians inspired by Foucault's undermining of the repressive hypothesis. In contrast to John Boswell, David

---

[10] Sander L. Gilman, *Difference and Pathology: Stereotypes of Sexuality, Race and Madness* (Ithaca, NY: Cornell University Press, 1985).

[11] For a summary of this historiography, see Duberman et al., *Hidden From History*.

Halperin's explorations of ancient Greece have led him to the conclusion that 'it is not immediately evident that patterns of sexual object-choice [choice of partner] are by their very nature more revealing about the temperament of individual human beings, more significant determinants of sexual *identity*, than for example, patterns of dietary choice'. Influenced by Foucault, Halperin insists that ancient cultures (not to mention many non-Western cultures of the present) simply did not share our belief that individuals could be separated into different 'sexualities' according to their choice of partner.[12]

Despite his destruction of the repressive hypothesis, many have read Foucault to be arguing that sexuality was created primarily through processes of discipline. As Scott Spector argues, there has been some conflation between Foucauldian theory and Marxist philosopher Louis Althusser's theory of ideology, which relied on a notion of 'interpellation' – the process through which ideological categories and structures create new identities. But Foucault always rejected the idea that individuals formed identities because they were somehow trapped by social or scientific categories imposed upon them from above.[13] The tendency to misread Foucault in this way has waned somewhat since scholars have begun to absorb the arguments of the second and third volumes of *The History of Sexuality*, published in English as *The Use of Pleasure* and *The Care of the Self*.[14] Abandoning the modern era and moving back to Ancient Greece and the early Christians, these later volumes place much more explicit emphasis on the construction of subjective identities through emotions and the influence of religious belief – what he called an 'aesthetics of the self'.[15] While his work, especially in its English translation, first prompted a rather obsessive search for mechanisms of discipline and repression in the history of sexuality, more recently historians have revisited his theories with an eye to emotions, subjectivities and the permanent plasticity (changeability) of human sexual desires and practices. As Helmut Puff summarizes it, 'wherever scholars have looked through this vaguely Foucauldian lens, the assumption of sexuality or homosexuality as a practically unchanging human experience did not stand up to close examination.'[16]

Despite the impact of Foucault's ideas, historians have generally been sceptical of his historical methods. They have criticized his periodization, his failure to delve very deeply into existing scholarship, his underemphasis of sexual difference (especially women's particular

---

[12] David M. Halperin, 'Is there a History of Sexuality?', *History and Theory* 28, no. 3 (1989): 270–71; see also his longer and very influential exploration in David M. Halperin, *How to Do the History of Homosexuality* (Chicago: University of Chicago Press, 2004).

[13] Scott Spector, 'Introduction: After *The History of Sexuality*? Periodicities, Subjectivities, Ethics', in *After The History of Sexuality: German Genealogies With and Beyond Foucault*, ed. Scott Spector, Helmut Puff and Dagmar Herzog (New York: Berghahn Books, 2012), 1–16, esp. 5.

[14] Michel Foucault, *The Use of Pleasure* (New York: Pantheon, 1985); Michel Foucault, *The Care of the Self*, trans. Robert Hurley (New York: Vintage Books, 1988).

[15] For a concise and useful summary of Foucault's entire body of work, see Gary Gutting, 'Michel Foucault', in *The Stanford Encyclopedia of Philosophy*, ed. Edward N. Zalta, 2014, available at http://plato.stanford.edu/archives/win2014/entries/foucault/ (accessed 10 July 2015).

[16] Helmut Puff, 'After the History of (Male) Homosexuality', in *After the History of Sexuality: German Genealogies with and beyond Foucault*, ed. Scott Spector, Helmut Puff and Dagmar Herzog (New York: Berghahn Books, 2012), 18.

experiences) and his tendency to make generalizations about massive social changes without specifically naming historical actors, events or causes.[17] Yet even as they make these critiques, historians like Halperin, Jeffrey Weeks and Joan Scott have drawn inspiration from Foucault's ideas to chart new territories of historical research. Foucault's arguments imply, even when he himself does not explain, that all forms of human sexuality – not simply those considered to be abnormal in a given time or place – are deeply conditioned by culture and society. His ideas suggest that culture also infuses 'normal' heterosexual practices. We take this suggestion seriously as we attempt to understand the history of the relationship between sexual practices and social forces in this chapter.

In this book, we have used 'sexuality' to denote something more than simply personal sexual desire, activity or fulfilment. Gender relations, we have argued, are invariably intertwined with social prescriptions on sexual behaviour and underlying assumptions about sexual propriety, the social meaning of sex and accepted standards of sexual behaviour for each gender. In other words, we have taken sexuality, like gender, to be a constructed, historically changing and socially malleable category, and we believe this to be a permanent condition. There will never be a time when the range of human sexual behaviours and desires will all be discovered and appropriately categorized. Even present-day debates about introducing gender-neutral pronouns into languages that lack them are revealing of this instability.[18] The thesis of permanent instability challenges the common-sense present-day usage of 'sexuality', which tends to assume that sexual desires are naturally and inherently present in each individual and that sex is (or at least should be) confined to the private sphere. As George Chauncey puts it, 'The belief that one's sexuality is centrally defined by one's homosexuality or heterosexuality is hegemonic in contemporary culture: it is so fundamental to the way people think about the world that it is taken for granted, assumed to be natural and timeless, and needs no defense,'[19] or, one might add, historical investigation. While it is common to acknowledge how social influences can cause sexual dysfunction or neurosis, there is a somewhat unacknowledged tendency to assume that each individual is born with a predetermined set of sexual desires. Society, in this definition of sexuality, acts only negatively: it represses or deforms our natural, healthy inclinations. Much of the discussion about 'sexual health' in popular culture and self-help books begins from the assumption that individuals must be protected from potential sexual dangers to ensure the healthy development of natural and pure sexual impulses.[20] But this popular understanding

---

[17] For general responses from historians, see Jeffrey Weeks, 'Foucault for Historians', *History Workshop Journal* 14 (1982): 106–19; Lynn Hunt, 'Foucault's Subject in the History of Sexuality', in *Discourses of Sexuality*, ed. Domna C. Stanton (Ann Arbor: University of Michigan Press, 1992), 78–93; and Goldstein, 'Foucault among the Sociologists'.

[18] The most prominent example of this is Sweden, where the word 'hen' is being popularized as a gender neutral pronoun. See 'Sweden Adds Gender-Neutral Pronoun to Dictionary', *The Guardian*, 24 March 2015, available at http://www.theguardian.com/world/2015/mar/24/sweden-adds-gender-neutral-pronoun-to-dictionary (accessed 28 July 2015).

[19] Chauncey, *Gay New York*, 13.

[20] For a brief account of 'the invention of sexuality', see Mottier, *Sexuality*, 25–48.

of sexuality looks less tenable once we start exploring sexuality as a historical subject. What does 'natural' actually mean when it comes to human sexual behaviour, and is our understanding of 'natural' also influenced by our particular cultural viewpoint? Once we ask these questions, our view of sexual behaviour in history changes.

## Sexual difference, politics and evolutionary theory

The nineteenth century saw an increasing emphasis on sexual dimorphism: the physical dissimilarity between male and female forms. The differences between men and women's bodies were taken as a given, while those who could not easily be classified under either definition were taken as exceptions.[21] In the case of intersexed individuals, then called hermaphrodites, medical scientists interpreted anomalous genital configurations in a way that actually reinforced binary divisions, placing emphasis on specific tissues (the ovaries and the testes) as signs of 'true' sex.[22] This view of physical difference did indeed generally translate into very different social roles for men and women. But historians are increasingly demonstrating that it is more instructive to explain rather than replicate this binary opposition. Historical accounts that focus solely on female experience have a tendency to repeat the very prejudices about female difference (about the importance of their bodily difference) that marginalized the historical actors under investigation.[23] They imply that masculinity is the default identity rather than unravelling how it too was constructed in relation to femininity. Scientific understandings of sexual differences between male and female bodies contributed to the tendency to understand sexual identities as innate natural qualities expressed to the outside world through bodies and gestures.

Several strands of political thought and scientific theory helped reinforce beliefs in sexual dimorphism in the mid-nineteenth century. The work of influential French historian Jules Michelet (1798–1874) provides an excellent example of how the science of sexual differences filtered down to political thinkers and influenced ideas about gender. In the late 1850s he wrote rhapsodies to women's reproductive organs, describing how they produced emotional effects equivalent to the painful/euphoric state of falling in love. Menstruation was for him a recurring wound that both proved women's weakness and allowed them insight into a higher emotional world.[24] Michelet accepted the value

---

[21] Robert A. Nye, 'Sexuality', in *A Companion to Gender History*, ed. Teresa A. Meade and Merry E. Wiesner-Hanks (Malden, MA, Oxford and Melbourne: Blackwell Publishing Ltd., 2004), 11.

[22] Alice Domurat Dreger, *Hermaphrodites and the Medical Invention of Sex* (Cambridge, MA: Harvard University Press, 1998). For earlier attitudes to hermaphrodites, see Lorraine Daston and Katherine Park, 'The Hermaphrodite and the Orders of Nature: Sexual Ambiguity in Early Modern France', *GLQ: A Journal of Gay & Lesbian Studies* 1, no. 4 (1995): 419–38.

[23] This case is made forcefully and convincingly in Jordanova, *Sexual Visions*. Jordanova argues that 'Retaining a belief in the validity of linking women and nature makes it excessively hard to be sufficiently critical in the process of unravelling its history' (p. 15).

[24] Jules Michelet, *L'Amour* (Paris: L. Hachette & Cie, 1858).

of women's sexual pleasure, but his main concern was to ensure that women would be encouraged to see their primary duty as childbearing. This was a political argument as well as a sexual one, since the French state was becoming increasingly worried about falling birth rates. Sex and politics were intertwined in other ways as well. When Michelet interpreted scientific reports about the little scars left on female ovaries when they release eggs as evidence that women were permanently wounded and therefore irrational, he was influenced by his political conviction that women's primary social task was childbirth. Like other nationalists and most medical scientists, Michelet was convinced that the declining birth rate could only be combated if sex (biological differentiation *and* social conventions about intercourse) determined how men and women interacted and how each individual viewed his or her role as a citizen.

The link between sex and citizenship was reinforced by evolutionary theory. In 1857, Bénédict-Augustin Morel (1809–73), a French asylum director, wrote his *Treatise on the Physical, Intellectual and Moral Degeneration of the Human Race*, which explained a huge array of physical, mental and social pathologies as evidence of 'the empire of the law of inheritance'.[25] Morel's theory that the bad behaviour of one generation (smoking, drinking and drugs) could permanently damage the quality of the next was well received all over Europe. It comprised an important part of the collection of evolutionary ideas that began to inform political thought on all sides of the political spectrum in the late nineteenth century. As we saw in Chapter 3, Charles Darwin's writings were especially influential in this regard. But Europeans quickly combined Darwin's explanations of evolutionary change in the plant and animal kingdoms with Morel and de Gobineau's theories about humankind. By the turn of the century a plethora of popularizers across Europe (particularly Herbert Spencer and Francis Galton in Britain) were emphasizing the possibility that the human race would decline in quality if science and public policy did not intervene. The theory of eugenics was born out of this combination of Darwin and theories of degeneration. Galton (who was Darwin's cousin) coined the word 'eugenics' in 1883 to describe public policies that encouraged selective breeding. He defined eugenics as 'the science of improving stock … to give the more suitable races or strains of blood a better chance of prevailing speedily over the less suitable than they otherwise would have had'.[26] He believed that only the most 'fit' should be allowed to have children and that the human races could be ranked in a hierarchy of value. These ideas spread rapidly through Europe, and in the early twentieth century, eugenics societies were formed not only in Great Britain, but also in Sweden, Norway, Russia, Switzerland, Germany, Poland, France, Spain and Italy. By the 1920s, eugenics had gained considerable prominence in North American social policy circles and had spread to Japan and Latin America.[27]

---

[25] Bénédict-Augustin Morel, *Traité des dégénéréscences physiques, intellectuelles et morales de l'espèce humaine* (Paris: Baillière, 1857).

[26] Francis Galton, *Inquiries into Human Faculty and Its Development* (London: Macmillan and Co., 1883), 24n.

[27] Daniel J. Kevles, *In the Name of Eugenics: Genetics and the Uses of Human Heredity* (New York: Knopf, 1985), 63.

Eugenics did not look the same everywhere. Benito Mussolini in Italy and Francisco Franco in Spain viewed a high birth rate as a path to national glory and colonial expansion.[28] These Catholic countries generally rejected the use of birth control and abortion and made the improvement of maternal and infant health care the centrepiece of their eugenic projects.[29] In many places, there was considerable debate between supporters of different versions of eugenics. In Romania, for example, proponents of a racially exclusionary eugenics that advocated forced sterilization argued with those whose view was more focused on educating lower- and middle-class people about their duties to the nation.[30] But in every variant, Social Darwinist thought (particularly when mixed with eugenic pronouncements on how the race as a whole could be improved through targeted social policy) provided a battle cry for those who sought to justify a variety of political programmes promising to improve European society and strengthen individual nations. As a result, evolutionary theory penetrated every sphere of medical science and social policy in the late nineteenth and early twentieth centuries. It provided the inspiration for the creation of new disciplines, particularly criminology, psychiatry and sexology, that sought to explore the social effects of sexual behaviour and choices.

## Sexology

The development of the discipline of sexology was a crucial precondition for the long sexual revolution, because it helped disseminate the idea that sexual desires are a core aspect of individual identity, personality and social motivation. The founders of the field of sexology placed themselves in competition with religion as arbiters of correct social behaviour. Like Christian moralists before them, late nineteenth- and early twentieth-century scientists of sex examined sexual behaviour for its moral content. While they avoided words like 'sin', their concern with the social effects of 'deviant' sexual behaviour had much in common with Christian concepts of social conformity and redemption.[31] Drawing inspiration from evolutionary theory, most sexologists viewed their task as the identification of sexual deviance for the protection of the larger social good. Categories of sexual behaviour were discovered, labelled and, when found to be abnormal (as they generally were), treated. This new strategy of treating sexual deviance as a medical issue seemed to make sex the problem of individuals rather than societies. Traditional community controls were replaced with the psychiatrist's couch and with specific laws

---

[28] Maria Sophia Quine, *Population Politics in Twentieth-Century Europe* (London and New York: Routledge, 1996), 88.

[29] Nancy Leys Stepan, 'Race, Gender and Nation in Argentina: The Influence of Italian Eugenics', *History of European Ideas* 15, no. 4–6 (1992): 749–56; David G. Horn, *Social Bodies: Science, Reproduction and Italian Modernity* (Princeton: Princeton University Press, 1994); and Mary Nash, 'Social Eugenics and Nationalist Race Hygiene in Early Twentieth Century Spain', *History of European Ideas* 15, no. 4–6 (1992): 741.

[30] Maria Bucur, 'Romania', in *Women, Gender, and Fascism in Europe, 1919–45*, ed. Kevin Passmore (New Brunswick: Rutgers University Press, 2003), 62.

[31] Robert A. Nye, *Sexuality* (Oxford: Oxford University Press, 1999), 115.

against specific acts. But the actual effect of this medicalization was to politicize sex. Particularly, though not exclusively, in the Protestant regions of Europe, the final arbiter of 'sinful' sexual behaviour was no longer one's terrestrial or heavenly confessor, but a doctor, psychiatrist or geneticist. These individuals were in turn the executors of public policies that were increasingly influenced by eugenic ideas. In the process, an entirely new public language of the social role of sex was developed, and the European understanding of sexuality was transformed.

The scientific study of sexual identities had its origins in the mid-nineteenth century. Austro-Hungarian doctor Heinrich Kaan produced a catalogue of sexual pathologies in 1844, and the Italian anthropologist Paolo Mantegazza (1831–1910) wrote a three-volume *Trilogy of Love* in the 1870s and 1880s.[32] The exploration of sex took on an even more scientific quality with the 1886 publication of Richard von Krafft-Ebing's (1840–1902) *Psychopathia Sexualis*, which was published in many editions and was a best-seller in many countries. Krafft-Ebing's definition of sexuality as a core aspect of individual identity is the foundation of today's common-sense understanding of what sexuality is. He argued that

> If the original constitution is favourable and normal, and factors injurious to the psycho-sexual personality exercise no adverse influence, then a psycho-sexual personality is developed which is unchangeable and corresponds so completely and harmoniously with the sex of the individual in question, that subsequent loss of generative organs (as by castration) or the climacterium [menopause] or senility, cannot essentially alter it.[33]

Krafft-Ebing epitomized the sexual essentialism of the nineteenth-century understanding of sexual identity; he relied on science to prove that each individual inherits an unchangeable sexual identity and set of sexual desires. But the actual scientific discipline of sexology did not actually exist until 1907, when the Berlin dermatologist Iwan Bloch coined the word *Sexualwissenschaft* (literally sexual science). His embrace of the overarching study of all forms of human sexuality represented a remarkable about-face and is an example of how quickly attitudes were changing in turn-of-the-century

---

[32] Kaan argued that the sexual instinct was natural, akin to hunger, but that several types of deviation were common, such as onanism (masturbation), pederasty (love of pre-pubescents), lesbian love (by which he meant both types of same-sex union), violation of corpses and bestiality. Michel Foucault has described the publication of Kaan's book as the 'date of birth … of sexuality and sexual aberrations in the psychiatric field'. Michel Foucault, *Abnormal: Lectures at the College de France, 1974–1975*, ed. Valerio Marchetti and Antonella Salomoni, trans. Graham Burchell (New York: Picador, 2004), 282. Mantegazza's anthropological approach helped bring about a general shift from viewing sex as primarily an erotic enterprise to studying it as an important sphere of human behaviour and culture. See also Gilman, *Difference and Pathology*, 73–4.

[33] Richard von Krafft-Ebing, *Psychopathia Sexualis, with Especial Reference to the Antipathic Sexual Instinct* (London: Staples Press, 1965), 187. It should be noted that Krafft-Ebing revised and expanded *Psychopathia Sexualis* twelve times. The first edition contained only 110 pages, while the last had 437. See Paul Kruntorad, 'Krafft-Ebing', in Richard von Krafft-Ebing, *Psycopathia Sexualis* (Munich: Matthes und Seitz Verlag, 1984), 7–13.

Berlin. In 1902, Bloch had argued that 'inborn' homosexuality did not exist and that such 'perversions' were the product of bourgeois decadence and idleness amongst the wealthy, who influenced the lower classes to follow primitive urges.[34] By 1907, he had come to believe that 'genuine homosexuality like heterosexuality has the character of an instinct rooted in the essential nature of the individual.'[35]

As Jeffrey Weeks has argued, early sexology's attempt 'to explain complex forms by means of an identifying inner force or truth' was wedded to Christian beliefs about the overpowering force of sexual desire in our lives and its negative impact on society and civilization.[36] The eagerness to determine the 'truth' about human sexuality in order to secure civilization led to a concentration on perversion and abnormality, rather than on 'normal' sexual pleasures. This tendency was particularly pronounced in Krafft-Ebing, whose reading of Darwin and other evolutionary theories persuaded him that sexology was part of a modern vanguard of scientific thought that would help to ensure that European social policy was based upon 'scientific' principles.[37] It is thus no accident that he employed the language of racialism, since terms like 'degeneration' implied the need for urgent action and the sovereignty of science to determine what was pathological and what was normal. As these and related ideas came to dominate European sexology into the early twentieth century, sexual identity – meaning, at this time, the labels that sexologists gave to specific spectra of sexual behaviour, but not yet the labels that individuals gave themselves – acquired increasing political importance.[38]

But Krafft-Ebing and other sexologists did not simply set out to punish sexually 'abnormal' individuals; they were also often activists for sexual rights. The Berlin physician Magnus Hirschfeld (1868–1935), for example, hoped that further research would lead to more justice and humanity. Hirschfeld's Scientific-Humanitarian Committee even began campaigning for the decriminalization of homosexual acts (which meant abolishing section 175 of the German criminal code) in 1897. Often called the 'Einstein of Sex',[39] Hirschfeld coined the word 'transvestism' and argued for the existence of an 'intermediate' sex between male and female. In 1919, the new Social Democratic government in Germany funded Hirschfeld's Institute for Sexual Science in Berlin's Tiergarten district, which housed a large library and museum and which provided sexual counselling for homosexuals and heterosexuals.[40] The institute became

---

[34] Edward Ross Dickinson, *Sex, Freedom, and Power in Imperial Germany, 1880–1914* (New York: Cambridge University Press, 2014), 164.

[35] Quoted from Iwan Bloch, *Das Sexualleben unserer Zeit in seinen Beziehungen zur modernen Kultur* (Berlin: Marcus, 1907) in Ibid., 165.

[36] Jeffrey Weeks, *Sexuality and Its Discontents: Meanings, Myths, and Modern Sexualities* (London and Boston: Routledge and Kegan Paul, 1985), 8.

[37] Ibid., 69.

[38] See Merl Storr, 'Transformations: Subjects, Categories and Cures in Krafft-Ebing's Sexology', in *Sexology in Culture: Labelling Bodies and Desires*, ed. Lucy Bland and Laura Doan (Cambridge: Polity Press, 1998), 11–25.

[39] See the 2001 documentary film of this title by Rosa von Praunheim.

[40] Atina Grossmann, *Reforming Sex: The German Movement for Birth Control and Abortion Reform, 1920–1950* (Oxford: Oxford University Press, 1995), 15.

a magnet for all those interested in sexual diversity, either out of personal or prurient interest. It was the first stop for poets and novelists like W. H. Auden and Christopher Isherwood, who were entranced by the 'young boys' who toured them around and who were surprised to find that the elderly women working at the institute were actually men in drag.[41] The latter attended various social evenings, lectures and performances. The institute was, in other words, not simply a place of research. It was also a social hub and a place of both physical and emotional refuge for individuals spanning the range of human sexual proclivities, comportments and desires.[42]

**Figure 5.1** A photograph taken at the Institute for Sexual Science. Hirschfeld is the man with glasses second from the right. He is holding the hand of Karl Giese, who was his lover. Giese's mother is sitting in the bottom left corner. Neither the context for the picture nor the reason for the costumes is known, but the atmosphere of friendship and conviviality is clear. Courtesy of the Magnus-Hirschfeld-Gesellschaft, Berlin.

---

[41] Beachy, *Gay Berlin*, ix–x.

[42] The founding members of the Magnus-Hirschfeld-Gesellschaft have explored this history in considerable detail. See Herrn, 'Magnus Hirschfeld (1868–1935)', 284–94; Rainer Herrn, *Schnittmuster des Geschlechts: Transvestitismus und Transsexualität in der Frühen Sexualwissenschaft* (Giessen: Psychosozial-Verlag, 2005); Ralf Dose, *Magnus Hirschfeld: Deutscher – Jude – Weltbürger* (Hentrich & Hentrich, 2005); and Manfred Herzer, *Magnus Hirschfeld: Leben und Werk eines jüdischen, schwulen und sozialistischen Sexologen* (Hamburg: MännerschwarmSkript-Verlag, 2001).

The concentration of thought about sexuality in Berlin was influenced by developments elsewhere. It was actually a non-medical activist, the Austrian-born Hungarian journalist Károly Mária Benkert (1824–82), who coined the word 'homosexual'. His campaigns against anti-homosexual laws were not motivated by the scientific compulsion with categorization but by a tragic personal experience (the suicide of a close friend) and general concern for human rights to privacy. Once Krafft-Ebing adopted Benkert's word in *Psychopathia Sexualis*, it came into general use, eventually replacing Karl-Heinrich Ulrichs's *Urning* and other words in use at the time, such as 'invert', 'pederast', 'sodomite' and their variations in other languages. The shifts in terminology reflected a diversity of attitudes towards homosexuality in sexology circles. Krafft-Ebing epitomized this ambivalence, since, like Bloch, over the course of his career, he moved from viewing homosexuality as a form of degeneracy to accepting the reality and legitimacy of homosexual love.[43] Along with the Swiss physician Auguste Forel (1848–1931) and the British psychologist Havelock Ellis (1859–1939), Krafft-Ebing joined with Hirschfeld to campaign against laws banning homosexual sex acts, an indication that science and social reform could be intertwined. These efforts culminated in the formation of the World League for Sexual Reform in 1928. The study of homosexuality and variations of human sexuality may have begun using the language of deviance, but it is difficult to imagine today's movements for the rights of sexual minorities without the contributions of these early pioneers and their close personal relationships with each other and with the objects of their study.

In other words, the medical language of these pioneers was often accompanied by very clear measures to help those emotionally and legally threatened by society's intolerance. Alongside efforts to repeal laws against sexual acts, Hirschfeld and his collaborators were also responsible for convincing the Berlin police to issue 'transvestite passes' to individuals (both men and women) who chose the clothing of a gender different from the ones on their birth certificates and who would otherwise have been subject to police harassment for crimes such as disturbing the peace or impersonation.[44] In cases of ambiguous genitalia, surgery was even performed, which sometimes resulted in a legal change of sex. As Geertje Mak has demonstrated, European doctors specializing in intersex conditions slowly began to relinquish their insistence that sex could be diagnosed – seen – in the body and started seeing themselves as surgeons who could help individuals transform their bodies to match the 'inner truth' of their self-perceptions.[45] The internationally recognized expert on what was called pseudo-hermaphroditism was Franz Ludwig von Neugebauer (born in Poland as Franciszek Ludwik Neugebauer), who published a survey of 1,100 cases from all over the world in 1908, and who developed surgical procedures to change appearance and improve function.[46]

---

[43] Harry Oosterhuis, *Stepchildren of Nature: Krafft-Ebing, Psychiatry and the Making of Sexual Identity* (Chicago: University of Chicago Press, 2000).

[44] Geertje Mak, '"Passing Women" in the Consulting Room of Magnus Hirschfeld. On Why the Term "Transvestite" Was Not Employed for Cross-Dressing Women', *Österreichische Zeitschrift für Geschichtswissenschaften* 9, no. 3 (1998): 384–99.

[45] Geertje Mak, *Doubting Sex: Inscriptions, Bodies and Selves in Nineteenth-Century Hermaphrodite Case Histories* (Manchester and New York: Manchester University Press, 2013), 232.

[46] Geertje Mak, 'Conflicting Heterosexualities. Hermaphroditism and the Emergence of Surgery Around 1900', *Journal of the History of Sexuality* 24, no. 3 (2015): 403.

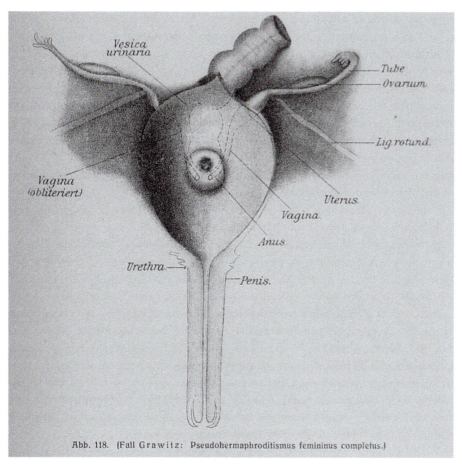

Abb. 118. (Fall Grawitz: Pseudohermaphroditismus femininus completus.)

**Figure 5.2** A diagram of intersexed genitalia reproduced in Franz Ludwig von Neugebauer, *Hermaphroditismus beim Menschen* (Leipzig: Werner Klinkhardt, 1908). (The book is in the public domain.)

Exactly how life-changing this could be is made clear in the anonymously published memoir of one of Hirschfeld's patients, describing his childhood as a girl, his early life as a very mannish woman and his great happiness after Hirschfeld's surgery made a legal change of sex possible, allowing him to marry his female lover.[47] Hirschfeld also supervised the first complete sexual reassignment surgery, performed on the Danish artist Einar Mogens Wegener, who thereafter called herself Lili Elbe and published her autobiography in 1931. She died during her fifth surgery shortly thereafter. Hirschfeld's primary role was to certify Elbe's transsexuality. In this and many other cases he provided scientific confirmation of individuals' deepest desires. That these stories still resonate with us today is demonstrated

---

[47] N. O. Body, *Memoirs of a Man's Maiden Years*, trans. Deborah Simon (Philadelphia: University of Pennsylvania Press, 2009).

by the fact that as we write this chapter images of Eddie Redmayne in his role as Lili Elbe in the 2015 film *The Danish Girl* are circulating on the Internet.[48]

Although both Krafft-Ebing and Hirschfeld paid attention to the emotional lives of their patients, it was the Viennese psychiatrist Sigmund Freud (1856–1939) who was most successful in disseminating the idea that sexuality stands at the core of human personality. Freud began his career as an anatomist, but in the late 1880s, he came under the influence of French neurologist Jean Charcot, who had used hypnotism to treat hysteria. Freud became increasingly interested in the unconscious and came to believe that humans were strongly motivated not only by observed reality, but also by their unconscious minds. While he insisted on the ability of science to be objective and rational, he stressed that irrational forces played a significant role in human behaviour. His arguments called moral conventions into question, since they suggested that individuals were not always making rational, self-conscious choices.

In three major books between 1900 and 1905, Freud developed the theory and techniques of psychoanalysis, a method of psychological treatment that relies on free association and dream interpretation to uncover the unconscious or repressed impulses at the heart of a patient's neurotic behaviours and psychic disorders.[49] While Freud's theories were initially rejected, a series of lectures he gave in the United States in 1909 greatly advanced his fame. By the mid-twentieth century his definition of psychological development as a rational process – something that can be scientifically understood according to the laws of cause and effect despite its basis in emotional conflict – was widely accepted. In the process of exploring how sexual urges and experiences caused psychological neuroses, Freud helped to define sexuality as an observable, definable and treatable aspect of the human character. More significantly, he argued for the first time that 'normal' heterosexuality was something that needed to be explained rather than simply taken for granted.[50]

We do not have space here to do justice to Freud's complex theories on sexuality.[51] For our purposes, it is important to emphasize three key areas. Although Freud had great respect for Darwin's evolutionary theory, he insisted that adult sexuality was not biologically predetermined but could be affected by experiences in early childhood and the conflicts that they produced. Humans, he argued, are sexually malleable; he used the term *Plastizität* – plasticity – to describe this condition, and his theories still influence research into what is now called neuroplasticity.[52] Freud argued that it is only social

---

[48] *The Danish Girl* (2015) [Film], Dir. Tom Hooper, United Kingdom: Benelux Film Distributors.

[49] Sigmund Freud, *The Interpretation of Dreams: The Complete and Definitive Text*, trans. James Strachey (New York: Basic Books, 1955 [original German 1900]); *The Psychopathology of Everyday Life*, trans. James Strachey (New York: W. W. Norton & Company, 1960 [original German 1901]); and *Three Essays on the Theory of Sexuality*, trans. James Strachey (New York: Basic Books, 1962 [original German 1905]).

[50] Sigmund Freud, 'Three Essays on the Theory of Sexuality [1905]' in *The Standard Edition of the Complete Psychological Works of Sigmund Freud*, ed. James Strachey, vol. 7 (London: Hogarth Press, 1953), 144–7.

[51] For a useful reference, see Edward Erwin, ed., *The Freud Encyclopedia: Theory, Therapy, and Culture* (New York: Routledge, 2001).

[52] For an accessible introduction to this concept, see Norman Doidge, *The Brain That Changes Itself: Stories of Personal Triumph from the Frontiers of Brain Science* (London: Penguin Books, 2007).

stricture that eventually stops a child from finding sexual pleasure in a wide range of bodily sensations, not just phallic (genital) but also oral and anal. This belief in 'polymorphous perversity' most famously led to Freud's Oedipus theory, which he developed at the end of the nineteenth century. Named after a Greek myth, the theory explained male sexual maturation as a process of identification with – and jealousy of – the father, and desire for the mother.[53] The Oedipus complex was part of Freud's larger seduction theory – the belief that hysteria (the name given to a wide variety of psychological neuroses at the time) was caused by a sexually traumatic experience in childhood. While Freud's theory, his evidence for developing it, and even the degree to which he himself was convinced by it have all been the subject of great controversy,[54] there is no doubting the fact that Freud's emphasis on childhood sexual development as a key to adult sexual and psychological health was extraordinarily influential and endures in some fundamental ways to this day. Freud moved beyond the study of perversion that preoccupied his contemporaries and sought to focus his scientific energies on the study of 'normal' sexuality.[55] The belief that any person's sexuality is conditioned by family relationships, childhood development and his or her not-entirely-controllable desires filtered down from elite investigations into public consciousness. Freudian allusions were ubiquitous in European literature, humour and even political discourse from the early twentieth century on. More than any other thinker, he changed public discourse about what sexuality means to individuals and to societies.

The most general way in which Freud's writing influenced European and North American views on the role of sex in society was his insistence that sexuality played a key role in civilization as a whole. Sexual drives, he argued, were fundamental to human behaviour and their healthy socialization is a necessary precondition for civilization. In *Civilization and Its Discontents* (1930), Freud even argued that civilization began when the first man restrained his primal, sexual urge to display sexual potency by putting out the fire with a stream of urine. Renouncing this instinct and allowing women (who lacked the appropriate equipment) to become guardians of the hearth ensured the conquest of culture.[56] Freud related libido, a strong sexual drive that he called Eros, to human inclinations towards aggressiveness and destructiveness, which he linked to the death instinct, or Thanatos. Civilization arose out of the struggle between these instincts. The 'pleasure principle' of human nature, Freud argued, leads to an egoistic drive to physically satisfy ourselves, but we are quickly forced to realize (through the 'reality principle') that society, our weak bodies and the natural world generally combine to frustrate the quest for physical pleasure. We learn to renounce our desires, control them and displace them into other activities. The result – civilization – promises to free us from conflict

---

[53] In the myth, Oedipus's parents abandoned him after hearing a prediction from the oracle. Later, as an adult, he unknowingly fulfilled the prediction by killing his real father and marrying his real mother.

[54] For summaries of the controversy about Freud's 'seduction theory', see Hall Triplett, 'The Misnomer of Freud's "Seduction Theory"', *Journal of the History of Ideas* 65, no. 4 (2004): 647–65; and Allen Esterson, 'Jeffrey Masson and Freud's Seduction Theory: A New Fable Based on Old Myths', *History of the Human Sciences* 11, no. 1 (1998): 1–21.

[55] Angus McLaren, *Twentieth-Century Sexuality: A History* (Oxford: Blackwell Publishers, 1999), 111.

[56] Freud, *Civilization and Its Discontents*. The book was originally published in German in 1930.

but actually ensures that we must forsake the satisfaction of our instinctual search for pleasure. We must sublimate our desires – suppress our quest for pleasure – in order to turn these energies into the actions necessary for our survival. This permanent sense of sexual dissatisfaction, Freud believed, helped to explain the inevitability of social conflict.

Finally, Freud developed a theory of female sexuality that dramatically reinforced the gendered norms of his day. He prized the penis as the most sexual and therefore important organ, argued that women had 'penis envy' and averred that 'probably no male human being is spared the fright of castration at the sight of a female genital'.[57] He denied the importance of the clitoris as a key site of sexual pleasure (at least for mature women) and insisted that only vaginal intercourse could provide true female sexual satisfaction. This rejection of centuries of anatomical knowledge was linked to Freud's belief that the sexual and marital norms of his day made European civilization possible.[58] The fact that he understood sexuality in primarily male terms (sexual pleasure, he argued, was best achieved through the 'discharge of sexual substances') made it clear that he was swayed by cultural norms that took men's experience as the standard of comparison, invalidating or pathologizing the experience of women.[59] Some women were also swayed by his logic. In 1932, French sexologist Marie Bonaparte extolled the virtues of surgery to move the clitoris closer to the vagina so as to eliminate the problem of women remaining immaturely fixated on the pleasure of its stimulation.[60] She was implying that Freud was right about the dangers of allowing women to focus on an organ of sexual pleasure (the clitoris) that had little to do with reproduction. Later feminists, particularly in the 1970s, were less convinced. They understood that Freud's definition of 'normal' female sexuality pathologized women who failed to live up to social stereotypes about mothers and who sought sexual pleasure for its own sake. (A more contemporary rejection of Freudian theories is the current wave of self-help books and web sites that teach women how to ejaculate.) But these feminist commentators did not notice Freud's most significant analytical weakness: the failure of his male-centred theory to define masculinity. While femininity and its 'normal' function garnered extensive treatment in Freud's writings, he generally took masculinity as a given. It was something that men had and that 'abnormal' women (particularly lesbians) could have too much of.[61]

Freud's contemporaries seemed to agree with his assessment of gender roles. For his eightieth birthday in May 1936, he received accolades from the most prominent cultural

---

[57] Sigmund Freud, 'Fetishism [1927]', in *The Standard Edition of the Complete Psychological Works of Sigmund Freud*, ed. James Strachey, vol. 21 (London: Hogarth Press, 1961), 154.

[58] Laqueur, *Making Sex*, 242.

[59] The view that female ejaculation was necessary for conception (which we discussed in the 'Introduction') had disappeared by this point. Krafft-Ebing was aware of the phenomenon but considered it a pathological result of 'intersexual gratification' between women, calling it 'sexually neurasthenic females [sic] ejaculation'. Krafft-Ebing, *Psychopathia Sexualis*, 265. Despite many claims to the contrary, Freud never mentioned female ejaculation. For a brief history of female orgasm that discusses how the promotion of female ejaculations as an empowering sexual practice complicates scientific understandings up to the present, see M.-H. Colson, 'Female Orgasm: Myths, Facts and Controversies', *Sexologies* 19, no. 1 (2010): 8–14.

[60] Cited from Marie Bonaparte, 'Les deux frigidités de la femme', *Bulletin de la societé de sexology* 1 (May 1932): 161–70 in McLaren, *Twentieth-Century Sexuality*, 110.

[61] McLaren, *Twentieth-Century Sexuality*, 117–20.

figures of his day, including James Joyce and Albert Einstein. Thomas Mann, the great German novelist, wrote that Freudian thought had long 'outgrown [its] purely medical implications and become a world movement which penetrated into every field of science and every domain of the intellect'.[62] Freud's theories, in other words, hit a very raw cultural nerve. His reinforcement of traditional gender norms (and their misogynistic tendencies) has to be understood in the context of the cultural politics of the time. Freud's emphasis on the productive power of male sexual desire and his insistence that female sexual pleasure was bound to reproductive function were views highly compatible with prevailing political concerns about population and civilization in Europe.

## Population policy, pronatalism and eugenics

In the late nineteenth century, as sexologists pioneered the investigation of individual sexual drives, social and political figures anxiously followed the dramatic shift in sexual reproduction and population growth that was taking place at the same time. Between 1860 and 1910, Austria-Hungary, Great Britain and Germany added between fifteen and twenty-nine million people to their populations.[63] Up to 1880, the increase was mainly due to rising birth rates made possible by earlier marriages as industrialization changed family patterns. After 1880, the increase in population was sustained by ever more successful strategies to combat the epidemic diseases (cholera, tuberculosis and typhoid) that had attacked European populations, particularly in rapidly growing urban centres. But the poorer parts of Europe and even some of the industrialized areas also experienced increasing rates of emigration. In the 1880s, 500,000 people left Europe each year. From 1906 to 1910, 1,300,000 were leaving yearly. In total, between 1846 and 1932, about sixty million people emigrated from Europe to the New World. In some cases (such as during the Irish Potato Famine of the late 1840s) emigration eased social burdens by allowing poor Europeans to escape grinding poverty. But emigration also represented a dramatic loss of potential strength, and politicians increasingly worried that slow population growth would mean weakness in the international arena. As we saw in the previous chapter, the requirements of total war placed a political premium on a growing population, and European governments (particularly in France and Germany) viewed their demographic statistics as a concrete indication of military strength. The massive loss of life in the First World War only intensified the relationship between population growth and war in the minds of European politicians and military leaders.[64] Policy-makers in Europe were also concerned that internal migration, particularly movement to increasingly overcrowded cities, was too quickly altering the social fabric and endangering health.

---

[62] Thomas Mann, 'Freud and the Future', in *Essays of Three Decades* (New York: Alfred A. Knopf, 1947), 411–28.
[63] Winks and Adams, *Europe, 1890–1945*, 2.
[64] This emphasis on population policy is well summarized in Quine's comparison of Germany, France and Italy. See Quine, *Population Politics in Twentieth-Century Europe*.

The first nation to experience an actual decline in birth rates was France. Marital fertility (the number of babies born to married couples) began to decline in 1800, about seventy years earlier than in other European countries. The population still grew but much less quickly than elsewhere in Europe. Between 1800 and 1900, the French population increased by 38 per cent compared with 252 per cent in England.[65] This caused great concern about France's ability to remain competitive both economically and militarily, and when other European nations began to experience similar, though far less dramatic, declines in marital fertility after about 1870, they also began to share French anxieties about the future. When Prussian forces decisively beat the French in 1870, those fears appeared to have been justified. The unification of the German Reich in 1871 only intensified concerns about demographic strength. Both countries developed pronatalist policies to combat the declining birth rate, and other European countries were pulled along by the tide of concern. Programmes such as the granting of baby bonuses and the creation of milk kitchens for infants generally called up images of a threatened nation, and they were not tied to any particular political affiliation. Policies intended to promote higher birth rates through support for families were equally prevalent in socially conservative France and more liberal states like Great Britain. Pronatalist policies even gained ground in Italy and Soviet Russia, where birth rates remained high.[66] The age of total war encouraged regimes with widely diverse ideologies to embrace the notion that a rising population would foster military and economic strength.

The slowing rates of population growth that so worried pronatalist politicians were in part the result of a dramatic increase in the use of various methods of contraception. While noble and middle-class families had begun limiting family size for financial reasons in the eighteenth century,[67] the pressures of urbanization over the course of the nineteenth century meant that even poor, formerly rural families changed their reproductive habits to conform to the economic realities they found in the cities. By the late nineteenth century, doctors and special clinics in Germany and the Netherlands were providing working-class women with cervical caps and various chemical spermicides. Douching with wall-mounted water devices or with substances like quinine was also common. Charles Goodyear's patent on the vulcanization of rubber in 1844 made the mass production of affordable condoms possible, although they remained beyond the budgets of most working-class families until after the First World War.[68] The use of diaphragms and sponges was widespread in France by the turn of the

---

[65] E. A. Wrigley, 'The Fall of Marital Fertility in Nineteenth-Century France: Exemplar or Exception? (Part 1)', *European Journal of Population/Revue europeenne de demographie* 1, no. 1 (1985): 33.

[66] On Italy, see Ipsen, *Dictating Demography*. On the Soviet Union, see David L. Hoffmann, 'Mothers in the Motherland: Stalinist Pronatalism in Its Pan-European Context', *Journal of Social History* 34, no. 1 (2000): 35.

[67] For an overview, see Smith, *Changing Lives*, 192–5.

[68] For a history of the condom in Germany, see Götz Aly and Michael Sontheimer, *Fromms: How Julius Fromm's Condom Fell to the Nazis* (Frankfurt am Main: Fischer Verlag, 2007).

century, and sex before marriage was becoming socially acceptable.[69] Most common of all, particularly in rural areas, were non-mechanical methods like withdrawal before ejaculation. Abortion rates also soared in the late nineteenth century. Over the course of the 1880s, 100,000 women had abortions in Paris alone.[70] This was the only method of limiting births that was absolutely effective at the time, though, given prevailing practices and standards of hygiene, it was also life-threatening for the woman. European countries' responses to these various efforts to limit family size varied. In some cases, contraception was viewed as an invaluable method of preventing the sick and the weak from reproducing. At other times, as in fascist Italy, it was viewed as a fundamentally anti-patriotic act.[71]

Given the ideological nature of European regimes in the first half of the twentieth century, it comes as no surprise that programmes to encourage higher birth rates varied dramatically across the continent. But these differences were not easy to predict on the basis of political system alone. Democracies, for instance, could be quite different in how they approached the problem of the birth rate. In Britain and to some degree in Weimar Germany, politicians espoused goals of progressive income distribution to poorer families. In France, in contrast, pronatalist policies were more explicitly conservative and aimed to support traditional family structures. These varying ideological goals did not equate to levels of effectiveness. Traditional France, for instance, more effectively directed aid to children than progressive Britain.[72] Even the Nazis used pronatalist policies to help families in need, though only those who passed strict racial criteria and fell in line with fascist ideology.[73] But while the Nazis were most likely to discriminate between the deserving and the undeserving, no European country in the early and mid-twentieth century was immune from new scientific ideas about the connection between evolutionary theory and politics.

The science of eugenics began to inform medical and political discussions about reproduction throughout the continent. After the turn of the century, eugenics societies cropped up all over Europe, and the argument that governments and doctors needed to actively intervene to improve the quality of the race (defined either broadly as the 'human race' or much more narrowly in nationalistic racist terms) came to dominate

---

[69] Anna Clark, *Desire: A History of European Sexuality* (New York: Routledge, 2008), 168; and Anne-Marie Sohn, 'French Catholics Between Abstinence and "Appeasement of Lust," 1930–50', in *Sexual Cultures in Europe: Themes in Sexuality*, ed. Gert Hekma, Franz Eder and Lesley A. Hall (Manchester and Vancouver: Manchester University Press, 1999), 233–54.

[70] Ibid., 345.

[71] Victoria de Grazia, *How Fascism Ruled Women: Italy, 1922–1945* (Berkeley and Oxford: University of California Press, 1992), 25.

[72] Susan Pedersen argues that French pronatalists, unlike their British counterparts, were uninterested in income distribution. Despite these characteristics of the 'parental welfare state', French programmes were more successful in delivering aid to children who needed it. Pedersen, *Family, Dependence and the Origins of the Welfare State*, 366, 420 and 417. See also Marie-Monique Huss, 'Pronatalism in the Inter-War Period in France', *Journal of Contemporary History* 25 (1990): 39.

[73] Annette F. Timm, *The Politics of Fertility in Twentieth-Century Berlin* (New York: Cambridge University Press, 2010), 118–56.

political discussions of social policy.[74] This had an immediate impact on public attitudes towards sexual behaviour, since the emphasis on race inevitably conjured up fears about the consequences of individual reproductive choices. These reproductive choices, the eugenicists argued, could only be made responsibly if the public were educated about their duties to conduct their sexual lives with the good of the society as a whole in mind. Eugenic theories encouraged pronatalists and social reformers to think not just in terms of quantity (numbers of babies being born) but also in terms of quality. From the turn of the century on, arguments made on the basis of eugenic thought ranged from socialist pronouncements about the need to prevent individual suffering by spreading knowledge about genetic and congenital diseases to extremely elitist (and sometimes racist) goals of carefully breeding a genetically superior human, weeding out inferiors either before or even after conception and birth. The most extreme variants of eugenics fed into justifications for forced sterilization, euthanasia and even genocide (the Holocaust). But this should not distract us from the fact that the basic argument of eugenics – that the government should attempt to influence reproductive behaviour in the interests of future generations – was almost universally accepted in Europe in the first half of the twentieth century. It was, for instance, particularly strong in Scandinavia, now generally thought of as a region of progressive gender and welfare politics.[75] Eugenics thus had a profound effect on the politicization of sexual behaviour, since its proponents argued that individual and sexual and reproductive choices were not private but extremely public matters.

One consequence of the prominence of pronatalist and eugenic rhetoric was to dramatically reinforce perceptions of gender difference. Posters extolling the female virtues of motherhood and the innate feminine ability to nurture not only valorized traditional roles for women but also linked female sexuality even more strongly to motherhood than it had been before. Even in predominantly Catholic countries, like Spain, a modern redefinition of gender occurred with eugenic logic and scientific argumentation replacing religious discourse in definitions of female (and male) gender roles.[76] Mothers who might formerly have been informed of their spiritual duties were now exhorted to contribute to the well-being and military strength of their nations by providing a future generation of soldiers. This was a direct admonishment that non-reproductive sex was immoral, not because it was sinful, but because it ran counter to the interests of the state. Particularly in the context of the dictatorial regimes and mass wars of the twentieth century, this helped intensify the phenomenon of what

---

[74] For overviews of how deeply entrenched eugenic and racial ideas were across Europe, see Marius Turda and Paul Weindling, eds, 'Blood and Homeland': Eugenics and Racial Nationalism in Central and Southeast Europe, 1900–1940 (Budapest and New York: Central European University Press, 2007); Alison Bashford and Philippa Levine eds., The Oxford Handbook of the History of Eugenics (New York: Oxford University Press, 2010); and the collection of essays on eugenics in East Central Europe 38, no. 1 (2011).

[75] Gunnar Broberg and Nils Roll-Hansen, eds, Eugenics and the Welfare State: Sterilization Policy in Denmark, Sweden, Norway, and Finland (East Lansing: Michigan State University Press, 1996).

[76] Nash, 'Un/Contested Identities', 32.

Judith Surkis describes as the 'sexed citizen' of the late nineteenth century.[77] Political pronatalism reinforced the distinction between female sexuality, which was connected to motherhood, and male sexuality, which was a much more free-floating and powerful force that could be harnessed and redirected into military efforts.

Pronatalist policies differed from country to country. In Germany, before but especially after the rise of the Nazis, mothers were the focus of most pronatalist social programmes and propaganda.[78] In France, fathers were much more prominent as recipients of government aid. In fascist Italy, a cultural tendency to prize male virility found expression not only in government statements about Italian superiority, but also in Benito Mussolini's rather public sexual conquests with a string of mistresses.[79] The practice of eugenics in both Spain and Portugal was fundamentally influenced by Catholicism. (Catholicism certainly also affected Italian eugenics, but Mussolini's personal atheism tempered this to some degree.) Spanish eugenic policy placed emphasis on female morality and was an attempt to recreate the model married woman, the *Perfecta Casada*, who had been destroyed when the Second Spanish Republic (1931–39) had granted women political rights, including the right to vote and to divorce. In keeping with Catholic values, the various subsidies and allowances for families were paid directly to the male head of the household.[80] Whereas Catholicism was reconciled with active eugenics in both Italy and Spain, it presented a more serious obstacle in Portugal.[81] Eugenics of all kind fell into disfavour under the dictator António Salazar. Portugal proved more willing than the other fascist dictatorships of Southern Europe to follow the dictates of Pope Pius XI's 1930 encyclical 'Casti Connubii' (which explicitly forbade Catholics from using birth control or seeking abortions), and Salazar's antipathy towards Hitler meant that news of Nazi forced sterilization programme and racial laws produced a quick condemnation of any kind of eugenic policy. Nevertheless, in 1934, Salazar instituted a pronatalist campaign of 'national regeneration' focused on convincing women of their reproductive duties to the state.

No matter what form eugenics took, however, public statements about birth rates and the need to increase them helped to entrench cultural perceptions about how one's reproductive function should determine one's social role. It was not uncommon, for instance, for European feminists to argue that women should gain the right to vote because their risk of death in childbirth was analogous to a soldier's risk of death on the

---

[77] Surkis, *Sexing the Citizen*.

[78] Timm, *The Politics of Fertility in Twentieth-Century Berlin*.

[79] Quine, *Population Politics in Twentieth-Century Europe*, 37. Mussolini's biographer reports that the *Duce* was reputed to have slept with 400 women. See R. J. B. Bosworth, *Mussolini* (New York: Oxford University Press, 2002), 74.

[80] Mary Nash, 'Pronatalism and Motherhood in Franco's Spain' in *Maternity and Gender Policies: Women and the Rise of the European Welfare States, 1880s–1950s*, ed. Gisela Bock and Pat Thane (London: Routledge, 1991), 161 and 172.

[81] Richard Cleminson, *Catholicism, Race and Empire: Eugenics in Portugal, 1900–1950* (Budapest: Central European University LLC, 2014); and Richard Cleminson, 'Eugenics in Portugal, 1900–1950: Setting a Research Agenda', *East Central Europe* 38, no. 1 (2011): 146–7.

battlefield. In each case full citizenship was to be gained through a specific contribution to the biological survival of the nation. Governments could rely on this logic when employing pronatalist policies that conveniently combined nationalistic goals with specific rewards for citizens. By mid-century, pronatalism had become a powerful tool for the legitimation of state projects.

The case of Soviet Russia is more complex in this regard. First of all, birth rates remained high in Eastern Europe, so pronatalist movements were not as strong, at least before the Second World War. Soviet ideology was also highly conflicted on the subject of sexuality and the family. After coming to power in 1917, the Bolsheviks originally set out to replace the institution of marriage with state support for families. Aleksandra Kollontai was the strongest proponent of the notion that the political revolution should also bring about a sexual revolution,[82] and she predicted that 'the family, in its bourgeois sense, will die out.'[83] There was a brief flowering of ideas about free love, cohabitation and the emancipation of women from family duties in the early Soviet years. Youth activists in the Communist Party preached sexual liberation as evidence of political liberation. Kollontai described this period of sexual experimentation in her collections of short stories *Love of the Worker Bees*, which detailed her hopes that communism and communal living arrangements would free women from domestic drudgery. But she came up against conservative opposition within the party and from Lenin himself, who told the German communist Clara Zetkin that he completely rejected these ideas:

In the sphere of sexual relations and marriage, a revolution is approaching – in keeping with the proletarian revolution. Of course, women and young people are taking a deep interest in the complex tangle of problems which have arisen as a result of this. Both the former and the latter suffer greatly from the present messy state of sex relations. Young people rebel against them with the vehemence of their years. This is only natural. Nothing could be falser than to preach monastic self-denial and the sanctity of the filthy bourgeois morals to young people. However, it is hardly a good thing that sex, already strongly felt in the physical sense should at such a time assume so much prominence in the psychology of young people ... Many people call it 'revolutionary' and 'communist.' They sincerely believe that this is so. I am an old man, and I do not like it. I may be a morose ascetic, but quite often this so-called 'new sex life' of young people – and frequently of the adults too – seems to me purely bourgeois and simply an extension of the good old bourgeois brothel. All this has nothing in common with free love as we Communists understand it. No doubt you have heard about the famous theory that in communist society satisfying sexual desire and the

---

[82] Sheila Fitzpatrick, *The Cultural Front: Power and Culture in Revolutionary Russia* (Ithaca, NY: Cornell University Press, 1992), 68. See also Eric Naiman, *Sex in Public: The Incarnation of Early Soviet Ideology* (Princeton: Princeton University Press, 1997).

[83] Quoted in Hoffmann, 'Mothers in the Motherland', 35. For a more extensive discussion, see Goldman, *Women, the State, and Revolution*.

craving for love is as simple and trivial as 'drinking a glass of water.' A section of our youth has gone made, absolutely mad, over this 'glass-of-water theory.' It has been fatal to many a young boy and girl. Its devotees assert that it is a Marxist theory. I want no part of the kind of Marxism which infers all phenomena and all changes in the ideological superstructure of society directly and blandly from its economic basis, for things are not as simple as all that … I consider the famous 'glass-of-water' theory as completely un-Marxist and, moreover, anti-social. It is not only what nature has given but also what has become culture, whether of a high or low level, that comes into play in sexual life.[84]

Lenin's rejection of the 'glass of water theory' and his belief that people with a 'personal abnormality … in sexual life' should keep it to themselves brought a quick end to a phase of experimentation, especially in the rapidly expanding universities.[85] Particularly given the ongoing battles that the Bolsheviks were waging to preserve their revolution against foreign and domestic military forces seeking to reverse it, the focus of gendered constructions shifted back towards military modes. With the rise of Joseph Stalin, Lenin's successor, the phase of tolerance towards premarital sex and freer access to divorce was definitively over. Concerns about youth delinquency in urban centres directed attention towards the family as a means of social stabilization. Women also argued that allowing freer divorce simply made it easier for men to abandon their families.[86] By the 1930s, the Soviets had recriminalized abortion, made divorce much more difficult and instituted family welfare policies that began to look much like those in other European countries, even though they rejected eugenics as fascist science.[87] As Russian losses mounted in the Second World War, pronatalist measures (such as medals for women with many children) were instituted to encourage citizens to produce future soldiers.

Pronatalist policies made sexual behaviour a matter of profound state interest and led to an intensification of social controls in the sexual sphere. Eugenic ideas helped to justify forced measures that often curtailed or limited individual choices. But this is only one aspect of a complex story. Eugenics could also justify programmes (such as making birth control available to economically needy or unhealthy mothers) that many people

---

[84] Clara Zetkin, 'My Recollections of Lenin', in *The Emancipation of Women. From the Writings of V.I. Lenin* (Lucknow: Rahul Foundation, 2010), 106–7.

[85] Dan Healey argues that although Lenin always viewed sex as a 'social act', since reproduction was crucial to the social system, he had no patience for much discussion of the subject. While insisting that he was not moralizing in a Western, middle-class fashion, he argued that there was an inherent unhealthiness in the contemplation of these issues by ordinary members of society. Dan Healey, *Homosexual Desire in Revolutionary Russia: The Regulation of Sexual and Gender Dissent* (University of Chicago Press, 2001), 113.

[86] On concerns about youth morality and the problem of pregnant women being abandoned, see Anne E. Gorsuch, '"A Woman Is Not a Man": The Culture of Gender and Generation in Soviet Russia, 1921–1928', *Slavic Review* 55, no. 3 (1996): 636–60.

[87] Fitzpatrick, *The Cultural Front*, 68. See also David L. Hoffmann and Annette F. Timm, 'Utopian Biopolitics: Reproductive Policies, Gender Roles, and Sexuality in Nazi Germany and the Soviet Union', in *Beyond Totalitarianism: Stalinism and Nazism Compared*, ed. Michael Geyer and Sheila Fitzpatrick (New York: Cambridge University Press, 2009), 87–129.

wanted and needed. A few specific examples will serve to illustrate the ambivalence of the politicization of sex and reproduction.

In an age before penicillin, the spread of venereal disease was viewed as a profound threat to the population (since these diseases could cause infertility and/or congenital defects), and many European nations, particularly France, Great Britain, Germany and the Scandinavian countries, implemented forced examinations not only for prostitutes, but also for anyone suspected of engaging in promiscuous behaviour. These measures disproportionately affected women, who were in far more danger of being accused of engaging in 'secret' prostitution and being forced to undergo medical examinations.[88] Throughout the late nineteenth and early twentieth centuries (right up until the post-Second World War period) it was quite possible for a completely innocent woman to be scooped up in a police raid and forcibly examined for venereal disease just because she was walking too slowly down a dubious street or was having a drink at a 'suspicious' bar. The effects on attitudes about women's public behaviour were incalculable. In this atmosphere, prostitution, as widespread as it was, took on a highly exaggerated role in public debates about social decline, family health and the ills of urbanization. Pronatalist and eugenic rhetoric only intensified the situation. Since prostitutes were universally identified as the primary source of venereal infection, and since unaccompanied women were in constant danger of being suspected of prostitution, all non-marital female sexual activity was stigmatized. This did not stop open displays of sexuality from flourishing in the cabarets and bars of the fin de siècle and the Roaring Twenties.[89] But the seductive nude dances of Josephine Baker in Paris and the androgynous and bisexual public displays of film actresses like Marlene Dietrich in Berlin were so remarked upon at the time precisely because they were so transgressive.

On the surface, at least, male sexual promiscuity seemed much less socially problematic. At a time when men were expected to be economically established before marriage, and when women were expected to be virgins at their weddings, male visits to prostitutes were socially tolerated. In satisfying the needs of men unlikely to remain chaste, the logic went, prostitutes helped to keep virtuous women pure.[90] Visiting a prostitute was virtually a rite of passage for many middle-class European men.[91] But there

---

[88] Judith Walkowitz, *Prostitution and Victorian Society: Women, Class and the State* (Cambridge and New York: Cambridge University Press, 1980); Abrams, 'Prostitutes in Imperial Germany, 1870–1918'; Corbin, *Women for Hire*; Roger Davidson and Lesley A. Hall, eds, *Sex, Sin and Suffering: Venereal Disease and European Society since 1870* (New York: Routledge, 2001).

[89] Carolyn J. Dean, *The Frail Social Body: Pornography, Homosexuality, and Other Fantasies in Interwar France* (Berkeley: University of California Press, 2000); Mary Louise Roberts, *Disruptive Acts: The New Woman in Fin-de-Siècle France* (Chicago: University of Chicago Press, 2002); Mary Louise Roberts, *Civilization without Sexes: Reconstructing Gender in Postwar France* (Chicago: University of Chicago Press, 1994); and Atina Grossmann, 'Girlkultur or Thoroughly Rationalized Female: A New Woman in Weimar Germany?', in *Women in Culture and Politics: A Century of Change*, ed. Judith Friedländer, Blanche Cook, Alice Kessler-Harris and Carroll Smith-Rosenberg (Bloomington: Indiana University Press, 1986), 62–80.

[90] Alain Corbin, 'Commercial Sexuality in Nineteenth-Century France: A System of Images and Regulations', in *The Making of the Modern Body: Sexuality and Society in the Nineteenth Century*, ed. Catherine Gallagher and Thomas Laqueur (Berkeley and Los Angeles: University of California Press, 1987), 213–14.

[91] Jarausch, 'Students, Sex and Politics in Imperial Germany'.

were unintended side effects to this acceptance of male promiscuity. The distribution of condoms to soldiers during wartime in some armies taught generations of men how to use them, increasing the odds that they would ignore pronatalist policies and employ condoms as birth control with their spouses.[92] Beliefs in the universally protean nature of male sexual desire also ran into conflict with the goal of improving national health. In some cases, such as in fascist Italy, masculine sexual energy embodied in the *Duce* was so critical to political symbolism that concerns about the health consequences were rarely voiced. But in Germany and elsewhere, where concerns about venereal disease ran high, policy-makers were concerned that men would bring the consequences of their indiscretions home to their wives, causing infertility. It thus became impossible to ignore the social effects of male sexual desire or its relationship to respectable female sexuality and reproduction.

The ambivalent effects of pronatalism and eugenics on the lives of everyday Europeans are also evident in the larger spectrum of social welfare programmes that they helped to justify. The First World War dramatically accelerated the creation of welfare states in all European countries. Increased attention to social welfare went hand in hand with nationalistic desires to strengthen the nation in the aftermath or in the expectation of war. These nationalistic impulses even influenced progressive sex reformers who, particularly in Germany, the Netherlands and Scandinavia, argued that access to birth control was not only a path to individual happiness, but also a way for the state to prevent abortion and ensure that fewer sickly and/or unwanted babies were born. In calling for tolerance for 'normal' sexuality and the production of only 'healthy' and wanted babies, these reformers often presumed (and helped create) categories of the abnormal and the unwanted. Helene Stöcker (1869–1943) in Germany, Marie Stopes (1880–1958) in Britain, Elise Ottesen-Jensen (1886–1973) and Alva Myrdal (1902–86) in Sweden and Aletta Jacobs (1854–1929) in the Netherlands all relied on such arguments in their campaigns for freer access to birth control. When Jacobs opened the world's first birth control clinic in 1885, American birth control advocate Margaret Sanger (1879–1966) gushed: 'So great were the results obtained that there has been a remarkable increase in the wealth, stamina, stature and longevity of the people, as well as a gradual increase in the population.'[93] But while such sentiments, based as they were on eugenic logic and the desire to increase the birth rate, might have influenced activists and convinced officials in cities like Berlin, London and Vienna to fund birth control clinics, those actually visiting the clinics were motivated by everyday struggles, poverty and the desire to control their material and bodily well-being. We cannot thus easily separate goals of preventing human suffering from nationalistic concerns about racial quality.

---

[92] James Woycke, *Birth Control in Germany, 1871–1933* (London: Routledge, 1988), 51.
[93] Margaret Sanger, *Woman and the New Race* (New York: Truth Publishing Company, 1920), 205.

**Figure 5.3** The exterior of the original Mothers' Clinic for constructive birth control, founded by Marie Stopes. Reprinted by permission of Mary Evans Picture Library.

Campaigns for birth control and eugenic health also contained widely divergent attitudes towards sexuality. While some birth control advocates, like radical feminist Helene Stöcker, placed emphasis on the importance of female sexual satisfaction, others, like the French socialist psychiatrist Madeleine Pelletier (1874–1939), emphasized that female sexuality was the primary tool that men used to oppress women. Pelletier was one of the first to insist that sexuality as a central core of human life was a cultural construct, and she viewed this construct as fundamentally misogynist.[94] In her 1912 book *L'Emancipation sexuelle de la femme* ('The Sexual Emancipation of Woman') Pelletier argued that 'woman is only an instrument man uses for his pleasure; he consumes her like a fruit.'[95] In her own personal life she chose chastity and often dressed in male clothing to protect herself from exploitation. She became more and more politically isolated and considered herself a political failure. In 1939, she was convicted

---

[94] Claudine Mitchell, 'Madeleine Pelletier (1874–1939): The Politics of Sexual Oppression', in *European Women's History Reader*, ed. Fiona Montgomery and Christine Collette (New York: Routledge, 2002), 256–71.

[95] Cited from Madeleine Pelletier, *L'Emancipation sexuelle de la femme* (Paris: M. Giard and E. Brière, 1911) in Offen, *European Feminisms*, 245.

and imprisoned for supervising abortions. Because she was already partially paralyzed by an earlier stroke, the judge decided that she would not fare well in prison and sent her to a mental hospital instead. She died there later the same year.[96] Her fate displays how controversial it was in her day to argue that sexuality was culturally constructed. While her views clearly countered conservative understandings of the family, they were no more welcome among feminists who saw more power in extolling the social importance of motherhood and employing the rhetoric of eugenics to achieve social benefits for women and families. Much more could be said about the relationship between feminist politics, pronatalism and eugenics.[97] But for our purposes here it is enough to point out that the prominence of these subjects in the political debates of early twentieth-century Europe helped politicize all subjects related to sexuality.

Fascist regimes were particularly adept at directing this attention to sexual matters towards political purposes. The emphasis in Italy was always on male sexual potency. The mayor of Bologna was rather explicit. Attempting to curb reliance on early withdrawal and its effects on the birth rate, he called on men to 'Screw and leave it in! Orders of the Party.'[98] While promoting higher birth rates in a country that many European observers viewed as overpopulated seemed to make little sense, pronatalism proved an effective tool of political mobilization. Mussolini's 'battle for births', first announced in a 1927 speech, was also linked to his colonial aspirations. 'Fertile people have a right to an Empire', he argued, and 'those with the will to propagate their race on the face of the earth' could rely on cheap labour to achieve world prominence.[99] He instituted various measures to try to achieve this aim, including social welfare programmes, family allowances, marriage and birth loans and health-care improvements, but also a 'tax on celibacy' for bachelors, crackdowns on prostitution and the criminalization of abortion, birth control and family planning advice. As later in Nazi Germany and Francoist Spain, even disseminating information about birth control or in any way 'impeding the fecundity of the Italian people' became a state crime after 1926. Of course, as Victoria de Grazia has pointed out, constant discussions about the 'horrible crime' of birth control may also have had the unintended effect of teaching Italians that such a thing was even possible.[100] On the whole, eugenics was not particularly strong in Italy, and truly racist measures were only instituted near the end of the regime as the association with Nazi Germany intensified.

If eugenic thinking made sex political, then no other regime provides a better example of the possible effects on individual lives than the Third Reich. When the National Socialists came to power in Germany in 1933, Helene Stöcker and other supporters of

---

[96] Scott, *Only Paradoxes to Offer* 155.
[97] For useful surveys, see Ann Taylor Allen, 'German Radical Feminism and Eugenics: 1900–1918', *German Studies Review* 11 (1988): 31–56; Karen Offen, 'Depopulation, Nationalism, and Feminism in Fin-de-Siècle France', *American Historical Review* 89, no. 3 (1984): 648–76; Diane B. Paul, 'What Was Wrong with Eugenics? Conflicting Narratives and Disputed Interpretations', *Science & Education* 23, no. 2 (2012): 259–71.
[98] de Grazia, *How Fascism Ruled Women*, 70.
[99] Quoted in Horn, *Social Bodies*, 59.
[100] de Grazia, *How Fascism Ruled Women*, 55. Similar campaigns against birth control were waged in the US, where laws against distributing obscenity were used to curtail the efforts of birth control crusader Margaret Sanger. See Jill Lepore, *The Secret History of Wonder Woman* (New York: Knopf, 2014).

progressive ideas about sexuality were forced into exile. (Magnus Hirschfeld was already in Paris and chose not to come back.) The Nazis initially sought to project an image of extreme sexual propriety, and their propaganda campaigns extolling the virtues of motherhood and the family, not to mention their persecution of homosexuals and their categorization of prostitutes as 'asocials', seemed to suggest that only reproductive, heterosexual sex within the context of marriage would be tolerated. Laws prohibiting sexual relationships between Jews and 'Aryan' Germans explicitly linked definitions of acceptable sexual behaviour to the racist goals of the regime. Forced abortions and sterilization of the 'unfit' were justified with the same logic as euthanasia of the 'feeble-minded' and the murder of millions of Jews. Historians of sexuality have been rather quick to suggest that the Nazi case provides an extreme example of the effects of sexually repressive ideas on social policy.[101] But this is an oversimplification of Nazi policies on sex. While Nazi propagandists certainly stressed that traditional family values would be reinstated and supported by the state, and they never tired of associating the sexual decadence of the Weimar years with economic turmoil and social distress, life in the Third Reich actually provided citizens with more opportunities for pre- and extramarital sex than ever before. It was well known that the massive gatherings staged by the Hitler Youth were inevitably followed, nine months later, by hundreds of illegitimate births.[102] SS leader Heinrich Himmler's call to unmarried girls to provide the Führer with babies before the war also had a public effect. Maternity and increasing the birth rate might have been the goal, but the ingenious intertwining of nationalism and sexual allure provided seductive rewards for those who supported the regime. Men who did not meet the ideal of soldierly masculinity were treated with hormones to enhance their virility.[103] The Nazis even set up brothels for slave labourers and concentration camp inmates in the hopes of exacting more labour with the promise of sexual rewards.[104] The depiction of the Third Reich as an entirely sexually repressive regime thus requires some rethinking.[105]

All this demonstrates that by the mid-twentieth century sexual behaviour had become an extremely political affair. Rhetorical links between individual sexual and reproductive choices and the fate of nations encouraged citizens to relate their individual decisions in this sphere to their roles as citizens of a nation. But the dramatic failure of the fascist projects of the twentieth century changed the context for such debates. In the aftermath of

---

[101] See the otherwise very convincing arguments of Nye, 'Sexuality', 21; and McLaren, *Twentieth-Century Sexuality*, 136–42.

[102] Kater, *Hitler Youth*. 108.

[103] In the year 1943 alone, 700,000 ampoules of the testosterone-based 'Testoviron' were sold in Nazi Germany. See Hans-Georg Hofer, 'Wenn Männer altern. Ein Projekt zur Geschichte der "männlichen Wechseljahre"', *L'Homme. Europäische Zeitschrift für Feministische Geschichtswissenschaft* 17, no. 1 (2006): 101–8.

[104] Christa Paul, *Zwangsprostitution: Staatlich Errichtete Bordelle Im Nationalsozialismus* (Berlin: Edition Hentrich, 1995); and Robert Sommer, 'Camp Brothels: Forced Sex Labour in Nazi Concentration Camps', in *Brutality and Desire: War and Sexuality in Europe's Twentieth Century*, ed. Dagmar Herzog (New York: Palgrave Macmillan, 2011), 168–96. Sommer makes clear that the brothels were staffed only with non-Jewish inmates.

[105] See Dagmar Herzog, *Sex after Fascism: Memory and Morality in Twentieth-Century Germany* (Princeton: Princeton University Press, 2005. For the larger European context, see Dagmar Herzog, 'Syncopated Sex: Transforming European Sexual Cultures', *American Historical Review* 114, no. 5 (2009): 1287–1308.

the Holocaust and the massive displacement of people caused by the Second World War, eugenic language became more guarded (particularly in West Germany, where it moved into the realm of taboo), even though it did not entirely disappear. In all European (and North American) nations, the trauma of the war led to a fierce search for normality that involved a certain amnesia about the character of pre-war regimes in the interests of a focus on rebuilding families and regenerating the broken spirits of men.[106] In Hungary and Eastern Germany, the experience of mass rape made it particularly likely that political language about sex and reproduction that might call up too many painful memories should be temporarily silenced.[107] A generational shift also played an important role in changing the terms of discourse. Estimates of the number of people killed as a direct result of the Second World War range from 50 million to over 63 million. The majority of those killed were in the prime of life. The post-war period offered many challenges in economically struggling Europe, but it also provided opportunities for the young to take advantage of the absence of an entire generation and move into positions of responsibility very quickly. For widowed women and young family fathers, the late 1940s and early 1950s were focused on survival, recovery and material improvements in living conditions. After an initial explosion of sexual activity during the period of demobilization and occupation (and the resulting baby boom and epidemic of sexually transmitted diseases) sex retreated from public view.[108]

## Sexual revolution: Scientific and philosophical origins

Historians have long commented on the prudery of the 1950s. But this view is now being challenged, and our periodization of the 1960s and the sexual revolution is being revised backwards.[109] The most influential voice in the scientific study of sex was the American scientist named Alfred C. Kinsey, who published the findings of a massive research project in *Sexual Behavior in the Human Male* in 1948 and *Sexual Behavior in the Human Female* in 1953. Kinsey mobilized a large research team to administer questionnaires about sexual behaviour across the United States, and his findings about

---

[106] See Elizabeth D. Heineman, *What Difference Does a Husband Make? Woman and Marital Status in Nazi and Postwar Germany* (Berkeley: University of California, 1999), esp. 108–75; and Frank Biess, 'Survivors of Totalitarianism: Returning POWs and the Reconstruction of Masculine Citizenship in West Germany, 1945–1955', in *The Miracle Years: A Cultural History of West Germany, 1949–1968*, ed. Hanna Schissler (Princeton: Princeton University Press, 2000), 57–82. For an account of similar themes in East Germany, see Donna Harsch, *Revenge of the Domestic: Women, the Family, and Communism in the German Democratic Republic* (Princeton: Princeton University Press, 2001).

[107] See Andrea Peto, 'Memory and the Narrative of Rape in Budapest and Vienna', in *Life after Death. Approaches to a Cultural and Social History of Europe*, ed. Richard Bessel and Dirk Schumann (New York: Cambridge University Press, 2003), 129–49; Naimark, *The Russians in Germany*, 73–116; Jennifer V. Evans, *Life among the Ruins: Cityscape and Sexuality in Cold War Berlin* (Houndmills, Basingstoke and New York: Palgrave Macmillan, 2011).

[108] This explosion seems to have been particularly intense in occupied Germany. See Timm, *The Politics of Fertility in Twentieth-Century Berlin*, 187–226.

[109] For a very strong argument about the United States that has comparative relevance for Europe, see Alan Petigny, 'Illegitimacy, Postwar Psychology, and the Reperiodization of the Sexual Revolutionary', *Journal of Social History* 38, no. 1 (2004): 63–79.

the prevalence of homosexuality, premarital sex, masturbation and other adventurous and non-procreative acts caused a media sensation around the world.[110] His research had an immediate impact in Europe, causing marriage counsellors in both East and West Germany, for instance, to rethink their attitudes towards sexuality and place more emphasis on sexual counselling as a means of preserving marriages.

American sexology continued to influence European psychologists, scientists and doctors into the 1950s and 1960s. William H. Masters and Virginia Johnson built upon Kinsey's research in *Human Sexual Response* in 1966 and *Human Sexual Inadequacy* in 1970. Masters and Johnson observed sexual behaviour in a clinical setting, developing comprehensive treatment programmes for sexual dysfunction and sophisticated equipment to measure and track human sexual response. Their research subjects performed sexual intercourse in a laboratory, with wires and cameras attached to track vaginal lubrication, heart rates and blood pressure, and the rhythmic contractions and other physiological effects of orgasm. In 1966, they 'discovered' the female ability to reach multiple orgasms and tracked various other gender differences in male and female sexual response. As had Kinsey before them, Masters and Johnson gained immediate worldwide attention for their research, and they helped to transform the landscape for medical, psychological and sociological research into sexual behaviour. Underlying each project was the conviction that medical science could increase human happiness by helping individuals to recognize and counteract the negative influence of modern, Western culture upon their innate ability to achieve sexual pleasure. Masters and Johnson became the iconic representatives of an international scientific and social movement that sought to demystify sex, employing scientific observation along with political and philosophical debate to liberate human sexual pleasure from the shackles of political, religious and social conventions. This was the scientific side of the 1960s sexual revolution.

Scientific observations of 'natural' sexual responses were not always compatible with euphoric calls for 'free love' and the arguments of student activists that sexual repression facilitated political oppression. New sexual therapies and medicalised forms of birth control ensured the continuing authority of experts in these matters, much to the chagrin of Europe's youth. While marriage counsellors and psychologists in Europe read Masters and Johnson, student activists on the battle front of the sexual revolution were more likely to turn to literary and philosophical sources of inspiration.

Because we do not have the kind of sociological data for European populations that Kinsey collected in America, we must use cultural and philosophical signposts to understand the origins of sexual revolution in Europe.[111] Shifting from the scientific data about sexual acts to the realm of cultural analysis intensifies the impression that the

---

[110] Donna J. Drucker, *The Classification of Sex: Alfred Kinsey and the Organization of Knowledge* (Pittsburgh: University of Pittsburgh Press, 2014).

[111] There were a couple of pioneering surveys. A radical social science group in Britain carried out 'Little Kinsey' in 1949. But its authors were dissatisfied with their analysis and did not immediately publish their research. See Liz Stanley, *Sex Surveyed, 1949–1994: From Mass Observation's 'Little Kinsey' to the National Survey and the Hite Reports* (London and Bristol, PA: Taylor & Francis Ltd., 1995).

war experience was crucial to post-Second World War attitudes towards sexuality. But this was true in different ways for different countries, as a comparison between France and West Germany will make clear. In the Federal Republic of Germany, the tone was set by Wilhelm Reich's anti-fascist conviction that 'sexual satisfaction and sadism were mutually exclusive'.[112] The French response to the horrors of the Holocaust was quite the opposite. Key literary and philosophical texts of the 1940s and 1950s returned to the teachings of the Marquis de Sade in an effort to understand the allure of fascism and the human psychology of its crimes.

The primary guru of the sexual revolution in West Germany was Austrian-American psychoanalyst and sexologist Wilhelm Reich. In fact, it was the 1945 English translation of theories that Reich had developed in the 1930s, *The Sexual Revolution: Toward a Self-Governing Character Structure*, that first brought the term 'sexual revolution' into widespread use.[113] In *The Mass Psychology of Fascism*, he relied on Marxist theory to argue that economic forces had produced a form of family life in which authoritarian fathers created an atmosphere of sexual repression that encouraged submission and created the personality types likely to support fascism. An end to social constraints on sexual expression, Reich insisted, would revolutionize political life by producing happier citizens who would not so easily fall victim to the rhetoric of demagogues eager to perpetrate violence and war.

Reich's elaborations of this theory are rather difficult to take seriously today. For instance, he invented a machine that he called the Orgone Energy Accumulator, which he believed could collect energy from orgasms to be used to cure various psychological and physical illnesses.[114] But after languishing in obscurity for decades, his theories became enormously influential when they were rediscovered in the 1960s, affecting the activism of sexual radicals and even the theories of serious scientists.[115] For progressive young intellectuals coming of age at the height of the Cold War, Reich provided both an explanation for the violence and oppression of the past – particularly its fascist

---

[112] Herzog, *Sex after Fascism*, 159. This is not to say that German philosophers of this era ignored sadism and its links to totalitarianism and fascism. An analysis of de Sade's *Juliette* formed a significant part of Theodor Adorno and Max Horkheimer's argument that the crimes of the Holocaust had undermined the Enlightenment project. See Theodor Adorno and Max Horkheimer, *Dialectic of Enlightenment: Philosophical Fragments* (New York: Verso, 2002).

[113] His theory was originally published in 1930 in *Geschlechtsreife, Enthaltsamkeit, Ehemoral*. But the English version (Wilhelm Reich, *The Sexual Revolution: Toward a Self-Governing Character Structure*, 1st English edn. (New York: Orgon Institute Press, 1945)) was a translation of Wilhelm Reich, *Die Sexualität Im Kulturkampf: Zur Sozialistischen Umstrukturierung Des Menschenmacher*, 2nd revised edn. (Copenhagen: Sexpol-Verlag, 1936). Nicolaus Sombart argues, however, that the Austrian anarchist (later communist) psychoanalyst Otto Gross had developed this meaning of the term 'sexual revolution' (to describe how social or political emancipation could be achieved through the freeing of individual erotic potential) twenty years before Reich. See Nicolaus Sombart, *Die Deutschen Männer und Ihre Feinde. Carl Schmitt – Ein Deutsches Schicksal Zwischen Männerbund und Matriarchmythos* (Munich and Vienna: Carl Hanser, 1991), 109–10.

[114] This theory still has adherents. See: www.orgonics.com, www.orgone.org and http://www.wilhelmreichmuseum.org (accessed 10 July 2015).

[115] Weeks, *Sexuality and Its Discontents*, 164.

variant – and a welcome prescription for the future. Immersed in what they viewed as a critical political conflict with the generation that had conducted the Second World War, European youth found Reich's arguments convincing and enticing. Particularly in Germany, his writings provided the blueprint for the political manifestos, patterns of sexual behaviour and communal-living projects that have since become almost clichéd under the slogans 'free love', 'the summer of love' and 'make love, not war'. 'Read Wilhelm Reich and act accordingly' read an inspirational slogan that appeared in Frankfurt graffiti as early as 1968.[116] Reich's disciples truly believed that love could change the world by defeating the forces of dictatorship and authoritarian power.

The popularity of Reich's argument that sexual pleasure could provide an antidote to the abuse of power was less convincing to the French. One telling indication of this difference is the popularity of *Histoire d'O* (the *Story of O*), a novel written in 1954 by Anne Desclos under the pseudonym Pauline Réage. (She also used the pseudonym Dominique Aury and was well known under this name as an editor and judge of literary prizes.)[117] Her true identity was not revealed until forty years after the novel's publication. In elegant prose, the novel tells the story of a young woman, known only as O, who is initiated into a sex cult by her lover René. Taken to a chateau in a French suburb, she is forced to don bondage-style clothing, cannot speak to any other woman and must obey the commands of the men who come to violate her. O is a willing participant in these ritualized sex acts and views her submission as evidence of her love for René. The *Story of O* was immediately banned in other countries but won the French literature prize Priz des Deux Magots in 1955. Feminists still debate its themes of female objectification. But this novel was written in a pre-feminist mode and its author initially intended it as a private seduction of her lover and employer Jean Paulhan, whom she feared losing and who did not believe that women could write erotic literature. The fact that the public initially assumed that the novel must have been penned by a man indicates exactly how revolutionary the book was. It has never gone out of print and, despite censorship measures, was read more widely outside of France in the 1960s than any other French novel.

Looking back with some historical distance, one might also view *Story of O* as a way of returning to the lessons of the eighteenth-century author Marquis de Sade (1740–1814), whose erotic literature inspired the word 'sadism' – the practice of achieving sexual pleasure through the infliction of pain on someone else. In an era still wracked by the images of the victims of concentration camps and still reeling with each new piece of information about Nazi tortures, there was an urgent need to make sense of evil and explain the human ability to inflict torture. French intellectuals looked to sex as a path to understanding the most perplexing philosophical questions of the day.[118] While this enterprise risked extreme disrespect to the victims of the Holocaust (in one scene O

---

[116] Herzog, *Sex after Fascism*, 159.

[117] Geraldine Bedell, 'I Wrote the Story of O', *The Guardian*, 25 July 2004, available at http://www.theguardian.com/books/2004/jul/25/fiction.features3 (accessed 10 July 2015).

[118] Nancy Huston, 'Erotic Literature in Postwar France', *Raritan* 12, no. 1 (1992): 29–46.

hopes that the 'gas chambers' will never open so that René will never leave her), it can also be viewed as a somewhat courageous acceptance of the universality of the human qualities that made the crimes of the previous decades possible. It is perhaps significant that in the post-Second World War period it was often women who explored these themes. Along with Réage, Marguerite Duras's (1914–96) writings also played with the theme of female sacrifice. The fact that both women had been members of the French Resistance against the Nazi occupation of France, and that Duras's husband had been interned in a concentration camp, makes it plausible to assume that memories of the war were at least subconsciously present in their writings.

But the most prominent French writer to explore the issue of violence and sexuality in the post-Second World War period was Simone de Beauvoir (1908–86). Her path-breaking 1949 book *Le Deuxième Sexe* (translated as *The Second Sex*) helped fuel what came to be called 'second-wave' feminism (the first wave having been the women's rights movements of the late nineteenth and early twentieth centuries that fought for the right to vote) and continues to influence feminist thinkers today. De Beauvoir argued that women have to have the right to choose with whom they spend their lives, and she described the history of male oppression of women through an analysis of history, literature and myth. Men, she insisted, had always been taken as the positive norm to which women – as the 'other' – had been compared. De Beauvoir argued that one is not born but becomes a woman. She was certainly influenced by her lifelong relationship with the philosopher Jean-Paul Sartre (1905–80), but she added a significant gender dimension to his existentialist view that human action, not the natural order, creates meaning.[119] De Beauvoir later explored the ethical implications of sexual choices in more detail in her 1951 essay entitled 'Must we Burn Sade?' She argued that one had to take de Sade's position on freedom seriously, suspending judgement on the tortures he inflicted on others in order to understand what humans are capable of.[120] The metaphor of burning in de Beauvoir's title called to mind the burning of books, heretics, Joan of Arc and, not least, only six years after the war, Jews.[121] Yet de Beauvoir refused to associate de Sade with fascism, attempting instead to understand the Marquis's bizarre sexual 'ethics' in their own terms. Moving beyond Freud's emphasis on childhood experience, she suggested that all aspects of a person's life must be understood in order to comprehend their sexuality and that sexuality is more than an unconscious drive.[122] We must understand de Sade, she implied, because he was the product not just of an upbringing but of a society too. As Judith Butler has argued, de Beauvoir found it necessary to explore de Sade's cruelty, because she saw him 'as a definite

---

[119] The two were engaged in a lifelong intimate relationship that involved bisexual and 'shared' relationships. Recent biographical accounts suggest that Sartre was more enamoured of this 'open' arrangement than de Beauvoir. For an overview see Louis Menand, 'Stand by Your Man: The Strange Liaison of Sartre and Beauvoir', *New Yorker*, 26 September 2005.

[120] Simone de Beauvoir, 'Must We Burn Sade?', in *The Marquis de Sade: The 120 Days of Sodom and Other Writings*, ed. and trans. Austryn Wainhouse and Richard Seaver (New York: Grove, 1966), 3–64.

[121] Judith Butler, 'Beauvoir on Sade: Making Sexuality into an Ethic', in *The Cambridge Companion to Simone de Beauvoir*, ed. Claudia Card (Cambridge and New York: Cambridge University Press, 2003), 168–88.

[122] Ibid., 178.

human possibility, one that is, therefore, at least potentially ours'.[123] De Beauvoir rejected de Sade's insistence on the primacy of individual sensations and feelings, arguing instead that 'the only sure bonds among men are those they create in transcending themselves within a common world by means of a common project.'[124] In other words, sexuality may be a primary component of human interaction, but it is not outside of individual choice and it is not the foundation of all human action. In her quest to assert woman's right to avoid being simply the object of male desire, de Beauvoir rejected both de Sade and Freud's tendency to argue that drives are more powerful than choice. She also believed that Freud was painting a picture of an amoral world when he argued that civilization was simply the product of repressed (sublimated) drives. 'To paint, to write, to engage in politics – these are not merely "sublimations"; here we have aims that are willed for their own sakes. To deny it is to falsify all human history.'[125] The power of de Beauvoir's theories derives from her success at revealing how these arguments about sexuality and civilization were themselves gendered; they relied on a specific understanding of male sexuality and its role in civilization and thus justified male domination.

A similar interest in the relationship between Eros and civilization motivated the work of the German philosopher Herbert Marcuse (1898–1979). In fact, Marcuse's work provides an interesting bridge between Reich and de Beauvoir, since he began his philosophical writing in the 1920s with the conscious intention of fusing Marxism and existentialism. He established himself as an academic in the US with a book, *Eros and Civilization* (1955), that drew inspiration from both Marx and Freud. Like Reich, Marcuse believed that sexual liberation was related to political liberation. But, like de Beauvoir, he was also aware of the possibility that sexual pleasures could be manipulated for the purposes of exercising power.

Celebrated in the 1960s as the 'father of the New Left', Marcuse was one of the founders of the Institute for Social Research in Frankfurt, famous for its critical theory and later known simply as the Frankfurt School. Marcuse's Jewish heritage forced him into exile from Nazi Germany in 1934. He joined his colleagues Theodor Adorno and Max Horkheimer at Columbia University but spent most of his first ten years in the US working as an intelligence analyst, first for the Office of War Information and later for the Office of Secret Services (OSS). In the meantime, he continued to develop his philosophical critique of 'one-dimensional' societies – both capitalist and communist. He has been called the 'cornerstone' of the sexual revolution in the US,[126] but he continued to influence thought on sex and society in Europe as well.[127] In *Eros and Civilization* he criticized Reich for missing how sexual instincts had been fused with

---

[123] Ibid., 183.

[124] Cited in Ibid.

[125] Simone de Beauvoir, *The Second Sex* (New York: Vintage Books, 1989 [1952]), 51.

[126] David Allyn, *Make Love, Not War: The Sexual Revolution, an Unfettered History* (New York: Routledge, 2001), 196.

[127] *One-Dimensional Man* was widely read by those who participated in the student rebellions in Paris in 1968 (discussed below). Kristin Ross, *May '68 and Its Afterlives* (Chicago: University of Chicago Press, 2002), 193.

violence and destructive impulses in history. Marcuse was drawing on his wartime analysis of German fascism for the OSS. He had argued in the 1940s that the Nazis had skilfully manipulated the public by promising sexual pleasures in return for political compliance.[128] Marcuse rejected the idea that sexual freedom could be an end in itself, and he accepted Freud's theory of the need for some repression of sexual urges in civilized society. But he argued that the 'performance principle' in capitalist societies produced a surplus of sexual repression, because it forced people into unfulfilling work that required a subordination of physical pleasures. Countering Freud (and echoing de Beauvoir) he argued that 'Civilization arises from pleasure, we must hold fast to this thesis, in all its provocativeness.'[129] He believed that non-procreative sexual acts contained revolutionary potential that could be used to counter the regimentation of capitalist life. By the time he wrote *One-Dimensional Man*, however, Marcuse was much more pessimistic about how far sexual liberation by itself could achieve change in a capitalist society that had learned to use pleasure in a repressive way.[130] Although Marcuse gave lectures on university campuses all over the United States and in Europe and is sometimes credited with having coined the most ubiquitous slogan of the sexual revolution – 'make love, not war' – he was somewhat uncomfortable with his status as the darling of sexual revolutionaries, who often underplayed his more complex Marxist critique of capitalist and consumerist society and perverted his message in order to justify sexual satisfaction at any cost and as an end in itself.

Few at the time noted the complete absence of gender analysis in Marcuse's theories or the fact that he painted feminine sexuality simply as a passive form of masculine sexuality. In constructing a total critique of capitalist theory that included (unlike Marx) an analysis of sexuality, Marcuse and Reich before him overemphasized the significance of sexual liberation without actually explaining the processes of sexual repression, including the repression of female and homosexual sexualities.[131] As feminists across Europe noted in the 1960s and 1970s, there were deficiencies in the argument that freer access to sexual pleasure was universally liberating. Indeed, what later became known as second-wave feminism began in part as a very personal reaction to sexual dynamics within European student movements and the new place of sex in European popular culture.

## Sexual revolution: Politics and popular culture

The sexual revolution in Europe cannot be separated from the history of student activism. While a detailed description of European student rebellion is beyond the scope of this chapter, we must note the prominence of socialist student activism and youth protest on

---

[128] Herbert Marcuse, 'The New German Mentality', in *Technology, War and Fascism. Collected Papers of Herbert Marcuse*, vol. 1, ed. Douglas Kellner (New York: Routledge, 1998), 139–90.
[129] Quoted from a 1955 lecture in Weeks, *Sexuality and its Discontents*, 166.
[130] Herbert Marcuse, *One-Dimensional Man: Studies in the Ideology of Advanced Industrial Society* (London: Routledge and Kegan Paul Ltd., 1964).
[131] Weeks, *Sexuality and Its Discontents*, 169.

European university campuses and in the large cities of Europe. In the 1960s, left-wing students across Europe staged increasingly well-organized protests against what they saw as the primary crimes of capitalist societies: the war in Vietnam, police repression of left-wing movements, colonialism, and Western ties to Third World dictators, like the Shah of Iran. These protests had strong international currents and were fed by events like the Soviet invasion of Czechoslovakia (to put down the reform efforts of Alexander Dubček's 'Prague Spring') in January 1968 and the assassination of American civil rights activist Martin Luther King in April of the same year. In April 1968, Rudi Dutschke, the head of a nationwide, socialist organization of student activists, the Socialist German Student Union (SDS), was shot at a political demonstration. Protest exploded across the country. In May 1968, the West German government issued emergency laws, giving police the power to suspend civil liberties. Meanwhile, in Paris, conflicts between right-wing groups and students campaigning against the war in Vietnam had grown increasingly violent. On 3 May, a group of students met at Sorbonne University to protest the closing of Nanterre University. The protest quickly escalated, and police used tear gas to try to disperse the growing crowds. During the week that followed, students joined with union organizers and agricultural groups in anti-government protests, and a wave of strikes, student walkouts and political demonstrations swept the country.

These protests vastly strengthened the self-confidence of student groups across Europe and fed an atmosphere of generational revolt that soon assumed mythic proportions. With some historical distance, we can now see that the importance of this generational divide has been vastly overrated. As Kristin Ross has argued for the French case, overemphasizing the role played by student leaders distorts the historical record, because the actions of union organizers and members of agricultural movements produced more lasting effects on French society.[132] But the students' enduring success at highlighting the importance of their historical role is instructive in itself. Having linked their cause in the public mind to earlier protests against repressive European societies, youth activists masterfully manipulated media images to strengthen their message. Their primary weapon in this endeavour was sex.

Already before the riots of 1968, sexual revolutionaries were using sex to deliver political messages. In West Berlin in 1967, the group 'Commune One' advertised their anti-bourgeois lifestyle with a picture, taken from behind, of all the commune members (four men, three women and one child) standing naked and spreadeagled up against a wall. Students across the country flocked to West Berlin as the centre of the 'happenings' and as the city where, due to its unique four-power status, men could avoid conscription. That same year, the Swedish film *I am Curious – Yellow* caused a sensation and was censored in Europe and North America due to its explicit conflation of sexual and political themes, its critique of the Swedish class system and its steamy sex scenes. These were of course extreme expressions of changing social attitudes towards sex outside of marriage, but while meant to provoke, they were a symptom of larger changes.

---

[132] Ross, *May '68 and Its Afterlives*, 6, 121–2, and 199–200.

Sociological data from the period suggests that a transformation of social values about sex was indeed taking place. In 1967, a public opinion poll asked Germans: 'When a young man and a young woman live together, without being married, do you think that this is going too far or do you think it doesn't matter?' Forty-three per cent of unmarried men and 65 per cent of unmarried women said that this was going too far. By 1973, when the same question was posed, only 5 per cent of men and 2 per cent of women thought that premarital cohabitation was unacceptable.[133] Divorce rates in Britain doubled after 1969, and, by 1977, 44 per cent of French couples had lived together before marriage (up from 17 per cent in 1968).[134] These statistics represented a widespread and international social change of attitudes and behaviours.[135]

It is common to argue that the main cause of these changes was the introduction of the birth control pill, which was invented by the American medical researcher Gregory Pincus at the urging of birth control activist Margaret Sanger. It first received US government approval in May 1960, but its legality was not confirmed for the whole country until the Supreme Court overturned the 1879 ban on birth control in their landmark Griswold vs Connecticut decision in 1965.[136] While 'the pill' became available in West Germany and Britain in the early 1960s,[137] its introduction in other European countries was delayed by religious and political objections. We do not have the space here to track the complexities of birth control policies in the various European countries. Briefly: laws limiting access to all types of birth control had remained in force in Austria until the 1950s, in West Germany and the Netherlands up until the 1960s, and in Belgium until 1973.[138] Catholic countries were influenced by the Pope's 1951 pronouncement that even unreliable techniques of birth control like the rhythm method should be used only in cases of 'serious' threats to the woman's health and never to entirely prevent births. In the Netherlands in the 1950s, this prompted doctors to require a note from a married woman's priest before she could receive instructions on how the rhythm method worked.[139] Birth control remained illegal in France until 1967, until 1971 in Italy and until 1980 in the Republic of Ireland. In Spain and Portugal, freer access to birth control

---

[133] Werner Hülsberg, *The German Greens: A Social and Political Profile* (London and New York: Verso, 1988), 71–3.

[134] McLaren, *Twentieth-Century Sexuality*, 172 and 174.

[135] For an examination of equivalent events in the United States, see Allyn, *Make Love, Not War*.

[136] For a detailed account of the politics and scientific wrangling around the invention of the pill, see Matthew Connelly, *Fatal Misconception: The Struggle to Control World Population* (Cambridge: Belknap Press of Harvard University Press, 2010).

[137] On West Germany, see Timm, *The Politics of Fertility in Twentieth-Century Berlin*, 227–256, and 292–318. On Britain, see Kate Fisher, *Birth Control, Sex, and Marriage in Britain 1918–1960* (Oxford and New York: Oxford University Press, 2008); and Simon Szreter and Kate Fisher, *Sex Before the Sexual Revolution: Intimate Life in England 1918–1963* (Cambridge, UK and New York: Cambridge University Press, 2010).

[138] For overviews of the politics of birth control in this period see Ann Taylor Allen, *Women in Twentieth-Century Europe* (Houndmills, Basingstoke, Hampshire and New York: Palgrave Macmillan, 2008), 86–7; and Matthew Connelly, *Fatal Misconception*.

[139] Dagmar Herzog, *Sexuality in Europe: A Twentieth-Century History* (Cambridge and New York: Cambridge University Press, 2011), 113–14.

came only years after the collapse of dictatorship: 1976 in Portugal and 1978 in Spain. But the existence of the pill – extremely easy to prescribe and much more reliable than mechanical methods – changed everything. Even in countries like Francoist Spain, which otherwise restricted birth control, it could be prescribed for health reasons after 1965.

In every country where it was introduced, the pill received immediate and intense media attention. But it is easy to exaggerate how widespread use of the pill was in Europe and underestimate the emotional and social restrictions on acquiring the precious prescription. Some women certainly did find sympathetic doctors willing to prescribe birth control to the unmarried. In Italy, for instance, one in ten women were using the pill to treat 'menstrual disorders' in 1969 even though it would not become legal for all until 1971.[140] Still, three years after the pill was legalized in France, it was still only being used by 6 per cent of women.[141] And not all women viewed the pill as a panacea. Extremely high doses of hormones in the early formulations produced severe side effects for some women. In West Germany, feminist groups actively campaigned against the medicalization of reproductive choices represented by a pill that could only be obtained with a prescription from a doctor, who at the time was almost always male. Despite its obvious benefits, feminists argued, the pill shifted responsibility for birth control exclusively to women while also forcing them to carry any of the associated physical side effects of hormonal intake. Female members of the German SDS began to note that the pro-sex slogans of their male counterparts failed to take these factors into consideration. They complained that men were using the theory of sexual liberation along with the existence of the pill and penicillin to coerce women into bed. When, at a September 1968 meeting of the SDS in Frankfurt, female members called upon the organization to support better access to day care and more attention to issues directly facing women, they were met with bemusement and belittlement. In response, Sigrid Röger, the token woman in the SDS leadership, pelted a male leader with tomatoes. This was the end of the presumption that male socialist student activists were also speaking for their female counterparts. Separate women's groups (calling themselves *Weiberräten* – or broads' councils) quickly multiplied across the country. The first, in Frankfurt, published a leaflet with the slogan 'Liberate the socialist pricks from their bourgeois dicks' and graphic drawings depicting the act of chopping off a penis.[142] Similar disillusionment with socialist student movements across Europe led to the formation of separate feminist groups (the contemporary term was 'women's liberation') in Italy, France and Great Britain.[143] In the West, European women's

---

[140] Ibid., 137.

[141] McLaren, *Twentieth-Century Sexuality*, 170.

[142] Dagmar Herzog, "'Pleasure, Sex and Politics Belong Together": Post-Holocaust Memory and the Sexual Revolution in West Germany', *Critical Inquiry* 24, no. 2 (1998): 419.

[143] Good overviews of the development of second-wave women's liberation movements in Europe can be found in Arthur Marwick, *The Sixties: Cultural Revolution in Britain, France, Italy and the United States* (Oxford and New York: Oxford University Press, 1998), 679–70; Geoff Eley, *Forging Democracy: The History of the Left in Europe, 1850–2000* (New York: Oxford University Press, 2002), 366–83; and Allen, *Women in Twentieth-Century Europe.*

movements gradually expanded their demands to include abortion rights, pay equity, equal access to education and training and expanded day-care services. Meanwhile, in the Eastern Bloc, communist governments argued (somewhat disingenuously) that they had already liberated women by providing them with all these things. Abortion laws varied in Eastern European countries, though they were generally much more liberal than in the West (except in Romania, where both abortion and birth control were strictly prohibited).

But Eastern Bloc countries were less open to the cultural drivers of the sexual revolution, viewing, for instance, the rock music anthems of the 1960s as symbols of Western imperialism. Even in the 1950s, East German authorities argued that the West was a place where 'American non-culture, nationalist-supremacist race hatred, gangster movies, trash novels, boogie-woogie, etc. are supposed to prepare the adolescents for murder, killings, and war.'[144] In 1959, party bureaucrats even recruited musicians and dance instructors to develop a 'modern' dance style to compete with decadent and overly sexualized rock 'n' roll dancing. It is not surprising that the Lipsi, a modified waltz, never really caught on with the East German public. Meanwhile, in the Soviet Union, rock 'n' roll was perceived as a direct capitalist assault on the communist system and an attempt to undermine socialist society. These official attitudes only fed the popularity of music as a weapon of cultural, generational and political revolt. A huge black market for Western rock music existed in all Eastern European countries, and occasional loosening of controls in favour of popular demand was followed in waves by harsh repressions.[145] The appeal of Elvis, the Beatles and later the Rolling Stones was at least partially sexual. When the Stones played in Warsaw in April 1967, fans hoped to hear, among other things, the song 'Let's Spend the Night Together'. But they were prevented from buying tickets, which mostly went to Communist Party members, and 3,000 of them rioted and damaged the interior of the Palace of Culture. During the mid-1960s, the Czech underground band the Plastic People of the Universe sang songs influenced by the experimental musician Frank Zappa, the 'pop art' artist Andy Warhol, and the American beat poet Allen Ginsberg. Particularly after their arrest and the conviction of four band members on charges of 'organized disturbance of the peace' in 1976, the Plastic People became a focal point for political dissidents. Under the leadership of playwright Václev Havel, a group of Plastic People supporters formed Charter 77, an underground political organization later instrumental in the fall of communism. Politics, sex and rock 'n' roll were never so intimate.

Rock music also produced concerns about sexual propriety in the West. Female fans swooning in front of popular singers was not an invention of rock 'n' roll, but nothing

---

[144] Quoted in Uta G. Poiger, 'Rebels with a Cause? American Popular Culture, the 1956 Youth Riots, and New Conceptions of Masculinity in East and West Germany', in *The American Impact on Postwar Germany*, ed. Reiner Pommerin (Providence, RI and Oxford: Berghahn Books, 1995), 99.
[145] Timothy W. Ryback, *Rock around the Bloc: A History of Rock Music in Eastern Europe and the Soviet Union* (New York: Oxford University Press, 1990).

before (or even since) quite matched the orgiastic moans that greeted the Beatles wherever they performed. Something in the cultural atmosphere of the 1960s induced youth to display their sexual longings more openly and loudly. University attendance reached unprecedented levels across Europe in these years, so it is certainly possible that young people were reading and being influenced by the theories we discussed above. But it is far more likely that popular and high culture were both circling around sexual themes independently; the two spheres fed off each other but did not necessarily act as cause or sole inspiration.

One final aspect of sexual liberation must be mentioned. Even before the pill encouraged people to separate sexuality from reproduction in their attitudes and behaviours and to accept the notions of private sexual freedom, attitudes towards homosexuality were beginning to liberalize. Laws against homosexuality had reached their most severe level of repression between the 1930s and 1950s. During the Cold War, sexual deviance was viewed as a sign of moral decay or a flaw that could leave one vulnerable to persuasion or blackmail by political enemies.[146] This attitude was so ingrained that it could even bring down prominent figures, as the case of Alan Turing makes clear. One of the founders of computer science, Turing worked with British intelligence during World War II and helped to develop the Enigma machine, which cracked the code of German military communications, thus helping to win the Battle of the Atlantic. His service to his country did not prevent his prosecution for homosexual acts in 1952, and to avoid prison, he consented to chemical castration. The precise circumstances of his death from cyanide poisoning in 1954 are still debated,[147] but Turing's fate illustrates the degree to which homosexuality was still vilified in 1950s Britain. Yet even as prosecutions of homosexuality remained common across Europe, Kinsey's data on widespread homosexual activity influenced European attitudes. The Netherlands decriminalized homosexuality in 1946. In September 1957, a British government commission, the Committee on Homosexual Offences and Prostitution, published the Wolfenden Report, which declared homosexuality a medical rather than a criminal problem. Laws to this effect were eventually passed in 1968. Homosexuality was decriminalized in Hungary, Poland, Czechoslovakia and East Germany in the mid- to late 1960s. In 1968 and 1969, first East and then West Germany repealed section 175 of the German criminal code, which had made homosexual acts illegal. Conservative and repressive attitudes and practices persisted in France, prompting the formation, in 1968, of Guy Hocquenghem's Front d'Action Révolutionnaire to fight for gay rights. Following in the footsteps of women's liberation movements, this organization and others like it across Europe

---

[146] McLaren, *Twentieth-Century Sexuality*, 187. See also the story of a gay American soldier who defected to the GDR: Jürgen Dahlkamp, 'Agents: No Country more Beautiful', *Spiegel Online*, 14 July 2003, available at http://www.spiegel.de/international/spiegel/agents-no-country-more-beautiful-a-257041.html (accessed 10 July 2015).

[147] Andrew Hodges, *Alan Turing: The Enigma* (Princeton and Oxford: Princeton University Press, 2014 [1983]). In a new preface to the 2014 printing of this book, Hodges discusses how much easier it has become to discuss Turing's homosexuality, a subject that critics criticized him for raising in 1983. See p. xix.

fought for an end to discriminatory practices. Europeans drew inspiration from their counterparts in the US, where the New York Stonewall riots of 1969 provided symbolic encouragement to actively resist police repression. France was one of the last European countries to decriminalize homosexuality in 1982. In the process of legal liberalization, gay culture also changed. Casual sex in bathhouses and other pickup venues became less common, though it did not disappear, and the political movement turned to fighting battles for the kinds of benefits (like the right to adopt children, to be the beneficiary of a partner's pension or insurance policy and the right to marry) that still occupy it today.[148] But in the 1980s, these struggles experienced a serious setback and were refocused as the world became aware of the existence of Human Immunodeficiency Virus (HIV) and its physical manifestation Acquired Immune Deficiency Syndrome (AIDS).

The collection of illnesses identified as AIDS and later associated with underlying HIV (Human Immunodeficiency Virus) infection was first noticed by doctors in the parts of San Francisco that had a thriving gay subculture. It was first thought of as an exclusively 'gay' (meaning, in this context, homosexual male) disease. This impression invigorated both the gay rights movement and its enemies and still lingers today. But by 1983, it had become clear that the disease could also be passed through blood and through heterosexual sexual contact. In Europe, the disease only appeared to be primarily homosexual in West Germany, Denmark and the United Kingdom. In France and Belgium, it was more common among those with links to Central Africa, where doctors were beginning to notice a massive spread of diseases associated with AIDS.[149] Very quickly, however, intravenous drug use was recognized as a primary transmission path for the disease in Europe. After the fall of communism in 1989, drug use soared in Eastern Europe, and countries that had considered themselves relatively immune from the disease had to face its consequences.[150] By 2005, the UN was estimating that there were 1.6 million cases of HIV in Eastern Europe. By 2011, 20 million people had died of the disease worldwide.[151] While intravenous drug use continues to be a primary source of contagion, in May 2006, delegates to an Eastern European and Central Asian AIDS conference in Moscow admitted that heterosexual contact, particularly through prostitution, was growing in importance as a means of transmission of the disease.[152]

---

[148] McLaren, *Twentieth-Century Sexuality*, 197. It should be noted that the shift in emphasis towards gaining family rights has neither been uncontroversial nor complete within gay rights movements in Europe. Many gays and lesbians would still agree with Guy Hocquenghem that 'homosexual love [outside of family ties] is immensely superior' and that 'Family heterosexuality dominates the whole of civilized sexuality; it is certainly no liberation to have to go through it'. See Guy Hocquenghem, *Homosexual Desire*, trans. Daniella Dangoor (Durham and London: Duke University Press, 1993), 131 and 139. Current legal changes, by now too extensive to summarize here, have only fuelled this debate.

[149] I. Weller et al. 'Homosexual Men in London: Lymphadenopathy, Immune Status, and Epstein-Barr Virus Infection', *Annals of the New York Academy of Science* 437, no. 1 (1984): 248–9.

[150] Francoise F. Hamers and Angela M. Downs, 'HIV in Central and Eastern Europe', *Lancet* 361 (2003): 1035–44.

[151] Jacques Pépin, *The Origins of AIDS* (Cambridge and New York: Cambridge University Press, 2011), 2.

[152] 'Moscow Hosts Key AIDS Conference', *BBC News*, 15 May 2006, available at http://news.bbc.co.uk/2/hi/europe/4771409.stm (accessed 10 July 2015).

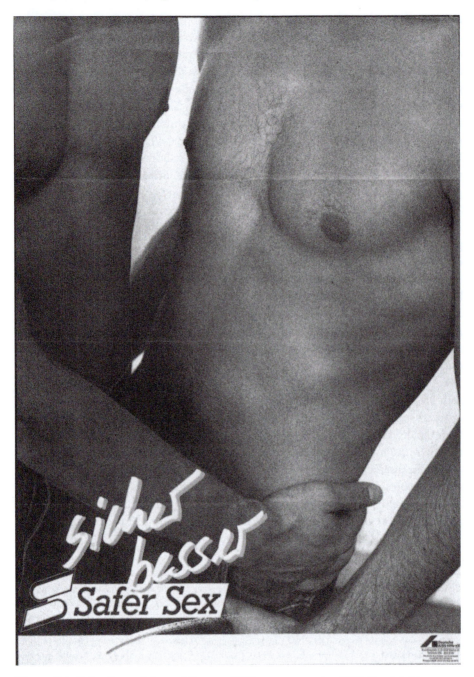

**Figure 5.4** 'Safe = Better. Safer sex.' German AIDS awareness poster, 1986. Reprinted by permission of the Bundesarchiv Berlin.

But how big an effect has the AIDS epidemic had on social attitudes towards sexuality in Europe? The ultimate analysis of this question will have to await future historians and sociologists. It is, however, already certain that AIDS has powerfully influenced rhetoric, behaviours and laws. As with venereal disease in the twentieth century, knowingly infecting someone with the HIV virus that causes AIDS can lead to legal prosecution, though many European countries (Germany, France, Hungary, Italy, Finland, Estonia, Switzerland and the United Kingdom) rely on general laws against inflicting bodily harm or assault. In many cases, this approach replaced earlier specific laws that targeted venereal diseases. Other European countries (such as Austria, Belgium, Bosnia and Herzegovina, the Czech Republic, Estonia and the Scandinavian countries) rely on laws against purposely passing on incurable or contagious diseases. Poland, Portugal, Russia, Serbia and Montenegro, and the Netherlands specifically name HIV in more general laws, with punishments ranging from three (Poland) to fifteen (the Netherlands) years' imprisonment.[153] Only Georgia, Latvia, Moldova, Slovakia and Ukraine have specific HIV laws. Ukraine's 1992 law 'On preventing AIDS and social protection of the population' is by far the most detailed in Europe and looks most like measures that Great Britain and Germany took against venereal disease in the late nineteenth and early twentieth centuries. AIDS activists argue that these laws simply stigmatize the afflicted without providing any social benefit. But the rates of convictions are, in comparison with measures taken in the past against victims of venereal disease, extremely low. While AIDS has certainly once again raised the spectre of disease as a punishment for promiscuity, most Europeans have moved well beyond allowing these fears to turn the clock back on the liberalization of sexual norms.

A final irony about AIDS in Europe concerns its origins. Most experts in epidemiological history now agree that the original virus was transmitted to humans from chimpanzees and gorillas in Africa. How it spread across the planet from there is more controversial, but epidemiologists from Oxford University in England and the University of Leuven in Belgium have used both historical sources and DNA samples to convincingly argue that a particularly set of historical circumstances in 1920s West Africa produced a perfect storm for the generation of disease. Both the Congo river and the building of an extensive railway network in the Belgian Congo created rapid industrialization in cities like Kinshasa – then called Leopoldville – and attracted labourers to the area. The resulting gender imbalance produced an explosion of prostitution so that a virus that had previously died out in other parts of Africa quickly spread. Tragically, modern health care programmes then transmitted the disease through imperfectly sterilized syringes to the population at large, and it spread across Africa, to Haiti, and eventually across the world.[154] There are various theories about how the disease spread after this, but epidemiologist Jacques Pépin notes

---

[153] See the informative website of the Terrence Higgins Trust, a leading HIV and AIDS charity in the United Kingdom: 'Criminalisation of HIV Transmission in Europe', Global Network of People Living with HIV/AIDS, available at http://criminalisation.gnpplus.net/site/index.shtml (accessed 10 July 2015).

[154] Pépin, *The Origins of AIDS*; and Nuno R. Faria et al., 'The Early Spread and Epidemic Ignition of HIV-1 in Human Populations', *Science* 346, no. 6205 (2014): 56–61

that ties to Zaire (formerly the Belgian Congo and now the Democratic Republic of the Congo) were present in almost half of the first hundred cases of AIDS in Europe. We now know that patients were dying of AIDS in Europe by the mid-1970s if not earlier, but their illnesses were poorly understood until the HIV virus was discovered and named by French and German virologists in 1983.[155] The circuitous route that HIV took from Africa to other parts of the world provides a striking example of the inextricability of sex, gender, economics and politics. It was not homosexuality that produced the AIDS epidemic; it was European colonial greed and its production of sexual exploitation in Africa. Yet enduring moral prejudices about sex tend to produce irrational existential fears about sexually transmitted diseases that dramatically complicate efforts to curtail their spread and that in some cases are still used to justify the repression of sexual freedoms.

## Birth control and abortion after the sexual revolution

From today's vantage point, the changes wrought by the sexual revolution have been significant. Change has by no means been uniform across the continent, but a quick survey of abortion and birth control demonstrates that the trajectory, with some exceptions, has generally moved towards liberalization. Access to birth control is now easiest in Western Europe and expanding in Eastern Europe and Greece (where it was illegal until 1980). New forms of birth control, like the 'morning-after pill', digital instruments to track ovulation and hormone-releasing intra-uterine devices have been developed and made widely available. Where birth control is hard to get or culturally spurned, such as in Ireland and Poland, teen pregnancy and abortion rates remain high (though often, as in the Irish case, women must go abroad to obtain them).[156] Between the 1950s and 1990s, Western European countries like Sweden, the Netherlands, Great Britain and (to a somewhat lesser degree) West Germany liberalized their abortion laws while also providing easier access to birth control. Where birth control and abortion are both accessible, abortion rates tend to be low. The Netherlands, which provides free birth control under state-funded medical insurance, has the lowest rate of induced abortion in the world. Such policies do not necessarily mean a low birth rate. Despite its liberal birth control laws (including the legalization of the French 'abortion pill' RU 486) Sweden's fertility rate increased in the 1990s, dipped in the early 2000s and has risen again since 2009. Maintaining a tradition that began with the influence of Gunnar and Alva Myrdal in the 1930s, Sweden has found a formula of universality in the provision of good-quality day care and generous maternity leaves for both genders that makes it easier for families to balance child care and work.[157]

---

[155] Pépin, *The Origin of AIDS*, 6.
[156] Caroline O'Doherty, 'Birth Control Use Here among EU Lowest', 18 November 2014, available at http://www.irishexaminer.com/ireland/birth-control-use-here-among-eu-lowest-298253.html (accessed 10 July 2015). O'Doherty cites the United Nations Population Fund report *State of World Population 2014*, available at http://www.unfpa.org/swop (accessed 10 July 2015).
[157] Steven Philip Kramer, *The Other Population Crisis: What Governments Can Do about Falling Birth Rates* (Washington, DC and Baltimore: Woodrow Wilson Center Press, 2013).

Despite strong rhetorical support for large families, Catholic countries like Spain and Portugal have been less amenable to these strategies. They have restricted abortion to extreme cases, where the life of the woman is threatened. In Italy, fierce opposition from the Catholic Church and the refusal of many doctors to terminate a pregnancy makes access to abortion difficult, though it remains legal.

The situation is more complex in Eastern Europe, where decades of extremely limited access to birth control made abortion the most common means of limiting family size. The Soviet Union overturned Stalinist restrictions on abortion in 1955, and many Eastern European countries followed suit. Bulgaria, Albania and Romania recriminalized abortion in the mid- to late 1960s in an attempt to increase the birth rate. Combined with limited access to birth control, this resulted in high rates of illegal abortions, maternal mortality and, particularly in Romania, disastrous conditions in overcrowded orphanages. East Germany, in contrast, re-*legalized* abortion in 1972, primarily as a political means of highlighting a stronger record on women's rights compared to West Germany. The unification of Germany in 1990 meant that East German women lost some of these freedoms, since they now fell under more restrictive West German laws, which allowed abortion only in cases of medical necessity or extreme emotional distress (such as in the case of rape). A unified Germany sought a compromise, and in 1992 first-trimester abortion on demand was legalized but only after mandatory counselling and a waiting period. Most Eastern European countries have greatly expanded access to abortion but have had a more difficult time countering strong prejudices in the population against birth control. According to the World Health Organization, this has led to some of the highest abortion rates in the world even in countries like Poland, where abortion is still illegal except in cases where it is necessary to save the life of the mother.[158]

The birth control pill was not the panacea that Margaret Sanger had hoped.[159] Struggles over funding, access to abortion and the moral questions surrounding premarital sex and teenage pregnancy continue to make news in Europe. But with a few exceptions, Europeans now generally accept that sex and reproduction do not have to go together.

## Conclusion

Despite dramatic changes in attitudes towards premarital sex in the late twentieth century, the optimistic hopes of the '68ers' (as those involved in the student revolts of the late 1960s and early 1970s now call themselves) that sexual liberation would bring about a dramatic change in family relationships, an end to sexual violence, world peace and an

---

[158] World Health Organization Regional Office for Europe, 'Facts and Figures about Abortion in the European Region', available at http://www.euro.who.int/en/health-topics/Life-stages/sexual-and-reproductive-health/activities/abortion/facts-and-figures-about-abortion-in-the-european-region (accessed 10 July 2015).
[159] Connelly, *Fatal Misconception*, 10.

increase in individual sensual pleasure proved illusory. Families with double careers and childcare responsibilities are simply too weighed down by daily responsibilities to follow the dictates of the make-love-not-war generation. Even the claims of the 68ers that they had more and better sex are being called into question. Historical data are demonstrating that changes in sexual behaviour (such as increases in premarital sex) were initiated by the previous generation in the 1940s and 1950s and that the popular culture of the 1960s followed rather than led social trends in this sphere.[160]

Perhaps more significantly, sex in the late twentieth century played a different role in public discourse than it did before the sexual revolution. Whereas it was extremely common for European politicians in the first half of the twentieth century to discuss why it was important for the government to influence people's decisions about with whom they slept and when and how they used birth control, by the second half of the century doing so would have prompted (and still would prompt) public outcry about unjustifiable government interference in people's private lives. While concern about falling birth rates continued to grow in many European countries, discussions about how to combat this problem began focusing on economic and social incentives, such as support for childcare and tax breaks, rather than on teaching individuals to make sexual decisions with the good of the state in mind. The more ubiquitous sex became – in the media, on television and on the Internet – the less political power it seemed to carry. This is not to say, of course, that the social power of sex disappeared in European society. Advertising and popular entertainment continued to rely on sexual stereotypes and to perpetuate gendered understandings of the meaning of sexual pleasure. But it became less rather than more likely that a politician would address the issue of sexual pleasure to make a political point. Even in discussions about legalizing same-sex marriage, it became extremely rare for either side of the debate to mention sexual acts that these couples might engage in. Having gained the legal right to engage in sexual acts of their choice, most European homosexuals began focusing their attention on gaining social, familial and economic rights. The interest in engaging in a political discourse on sex as an act, let alone making sexual pleasure the centrepiece of political change, had all but disappeared.

The story that we have told here is not one of a simple end to repression from above, nor a story of how the private finally became political in the 1960s. The repression did not always come from above, and it was generally the result of a complex negotiation between citizens and states. Sometimes the most repressive states even used sex to seduce new followers. Similarly, the private (the sexual) had long become political by the time the 68ers started chanting their slogans. Indeed, those slogans were only possible because sexuality – in its political and cultural sense – already existed in social discourse, and the connection between society and individual sexual desires had been carefully, scientifically and sociologically analysed. The sexual revolution began long before the communards in Berlin decided to pose naked and long before European teenagers

---

[160] Petigny, 'Illegitimacy, Postwar Psychology, and the Reperiodization of the Sexual Revolutionary'.

discovered the Rolling Stones. As soon as the biological mechanisms of reproduction began to be understood, the question of how to control them and who should decide how became burning political issues. The proliferation of laws dealing with reproduction and sexual behaviour, the vast expansion of scientific discourse about sex, and the close relationship between social policies in this sphere and the larger geopolitical projects of European regimes set the stage for the battles that reached their peak – but did not begin – in the 1960s.

## Suggested readings

Allyn, David. *Make Love, Not War: The Sexual Revolution, an Unfettered History*. New York: Routledge, 2001.

Cook, Hera. *The Long Sexual Revolution English Women, Sex, and Contraception, 1800–1975*. Oxford: Oxford University Press, 2004.

Crawford, Katherine. *European Sexualities, 1400–1800*. Cambridge, MA: Cambridge University Press, 2007.

Dickinson, Edward Ross. *Sex, Freedom, and Power in Imperial Germany, 1880–1914*. New York: Cambridge University Press, 2014.

Eley, Geoff. *Forging Democracy: The History of the Left in Europe, 1850–2000*. New York: Oxford University Press, 2002.

Fitzpatrick, Sheila. *The Cultural Front: Power and Culture in Revolutionary Russia*. Ithaca, NY: Cornell University Press, 1992.

Garton, Stephen. *Histories of Sexuality*. New York: Routledge, 2004.

Harsch, Donna. *Revenge of the Domestic: Women, the Family, and Communism in the German Democratic Republic*. Princeton, NJ and Oxford: Princeton University Press, 2007.

Herzog, Dagmar. *Sexuality in Europe: A Twentieth-Century History*. Cambridge, UK and New York: Cambridge University Press, 2011.

Marwick, Arthur. *The Sixties: Cultural Revolution in Britain, France, Italy and the United States*. Oxford and New York: Oxford University Press, 1998.

McLaren, Angus. *Twentieth-Century Sexuality: A History*. Oxford: Blackwell Publishers, 1999.

Mottier, Véronique. *Sexuality: A Very Short Introduction*. Oxford and New York: Oxford University Press, 2008.

Pépin, Jacques. *The Origins of AIDS*. Cambridge, UK and New York: Cambridge University Press, 2011.

Quine, Maria Sophia. *Population Politics in Twentieth-Century Europe*. London and New York: Routledge, 1996.

Szreter, Simon, and Kate Fisher. *Sex Before the Sexual Revolution: Intimate Life in England 1918–1963*. Cambridge, UK and New York: Cambridge University Press, 2010.

Timm, Annette F. *The Politics of Fertility in Twentieth-Century Berlin*. New York: Cambridge University Press, 2010.

Turda, Marius, and Paul Weindling. *'Blood and Homeland': Eugenics and Racial Nationalism in Central and Southeast Europe, 1900–1940*. Budapest and New York: Central European University Press, 2007.

Weeks, Jeffrey. *Sexuality and Its Discontents: Meanings, Myths, and Modern Sexualities*. London and Boston: Routledge and K. Paul, 1985.

# CHAPTER 6
## SEX, GENDER AND POLITICS IN TWENTY-FIRST-CENTURY EUROPE

In the spring of 2008, a new movement appeared on the streets of Kyiv, Ukraine that grabbed media attention from around the world. A group of young Ukrainian feminists calling themselves 'Femen' launched a series of protests against sex trafficking, sexual harassment at Ukrainian universities and the oppression of Ukrainian women more generally. Feminists in Ukraine, including some of the women who would join Femen, had raised these issues in previous years, but they had been ignored both domestically and internationally. Femen's major innovation in the Ukrainian context was to adopt a different style of street action, one both theatrical and risqué, on the premise that public attention had to be seized before public policy could be changed. Most notably, they decided to conduct their protests topless, often with slogans painted across their bare chests. The strategy was not without risk, including physical risk, as bystanders and police attacked them both in the midst of the protests and behind closed doors, but they quickly achieved at least one of their key goals. Young female breasts did generate global and domestic coverage both in traditional media and on more explicit Internet news sites. Femen used this platform for many causes, but their most important early campaign was to protest sex trafficking in Ukraine and to warn that the upcoming 2012 European football championships in Poland and Ukraine would make the situation much worse.

Radical street art and radical street protest invite passion and controversy, and Femen experienced its share of both. Even the most casual observer (as most initially were) found the disjuncture between public sexual exhibitionism and a sharp critique of commercial sex jarring. But the particular juncture of sex, gender and politics that Femen explored proved much richer and more complicated than this one apparent paradox. Indeed, we suggest that an investigation of the Femen phenomenon can help us tie together many of the themes we have traced in the previous five chapters: the challenge to patriarchy posed by the democratic and industrial revolutions; the intersection of empire and Europe in the realms of sex, gender and power; the effects of war; the complicated relationship between 'Eastern' and 'Western' Europe; and the multiple outcomes of the century-long sexual revolution.

### Sex trafficking

Femen's decision to target sex trafficking and sex tourism in Ukraine tapped directly into many of the core anxieties present in twenty-first-century Europe. As at the turn of the last century, the combined impact of a wave of international migration, the growth of large metropolitan cities and a laissez-faire capitalist ethos led many social observers to fear the emergence of a new 'White Slave Trade'. 'White' is (and was) not exactly the right term to use, as many migrants in the contemporary European sex trade have come from outside of Europe and are women (and men) of colour, but public attention has been especially gripped by the plight of young women from the economically devastated areas of Eastern Europe. The figure of the Eastern European prostitute raises questions about the nature and desirability of European integration, highlights the diversity of European living conditions in the new gilded age and reveals yet again the centrality of sexual and racial thinking to political and social imagination.[1] She was the guilty shame (and, for some, guilty pleasure) of the 'New Europe', a warning counterbalance to the happy tales of continental peace and prosperity that the softening of European national borders had also produced.

As in the other periods covered in this book, however, the prostitute was not simply a symbol. The rise in sexual migration was real. In part, it was facilitated by the changes in immigration and labour laws that were at the centre of the creation of the European Union, but there was also increasing migration from parts of Europe that were (and are) not part of the EU.[2] Estimates of the number of trafficked individuals vary widely, and none have solved the methodological problem of how to effectively count the number of migrants and the number of those who move under coercion, but most settle on a number between 100,000 and 500,000 per year within Europe alone, most of them from Eastern Europe.[3] Activists and authors researching the sex trade have had little difficulty discovering the geographical origins of women in some key sex markets in Western Europe. Siddarth Kara spent an evening in southern Italy interviewing thirty street prostitutes, where he found that twenty-seven of them were under the age of eighteen and that all of them came from the former Soviet bloc, some from EU countries but many not.[4] Some of these young women told him the story that has become paradigmatic in the European imagination. One Ukrainian told Kara that

---

[1] Loretta Ihme, 'Victims, Villains, Saviors: On the Discursive Constructions of Trafficking in Women', in *Violence and Gender in the Globalized World: The Intimate and the Extimate*, ed. Sanja Bahun-Radunović and V. G. Julie Rajan (Aldershot: Ashgate Publishing, 2008), 157–74.

[2] The EU expanded over the time period covered in this chapter, as did the so-called Schengen Zone, within which border posts and travel restrictions between the states involved were dismantled. These zones do not precisely overlap. Romania, Bulgaria, Croatia, the United Kingdom and Ireland are all in the EU but outside of the Schengen Zone. Norway and Switzerland are within the Schengen Zone but not in the EU. For the purposes of this chapter, it is important to be aware that Ukraine, Belarus and Russia are outside of both of these zones. Migrating for work from these states requires a visa; failing to acquire one makes a migrant an illegal immigrant.

[3] D. Scharie Tavcer, 'The Trafficking of Women for Sexual Exploitation: The Situation from the Republic of Moldova to Western Europe', *Police Practice & Research* 7, no. 2 (May 2006): 135–6.

[4] Siddharth Kara, *Sex Trafficking: Inside the Business of Modern Slavery* (New York: Columbia University Press, 2009), 84.

she was seduced by promises of a better life in 'rich' Western Europe and willingly went with a man who took her to Serbia (a non-EU state), forced her into the sex trade at a night club in Belgrade and then re-trafficked her to Italy.[5] It is a tale that is told often, of young women living in crumbling towns with few good economic or marital prospects being persuaded that emigration is their only choice. Particularly for those women living outside of the EU, emigration to Western Europe poses large difficulties, and they accept the assistance of migration brokers to smuggle them across borders or to forge documents. This, in turn, puts them in debt to the traffickers, which they are told they have to repay through prostitution. With their documents held by the traffickers, they are deprived of their possibility of return and do as they are told. Their debts are then continually (and fraudulently) increased, leaving them in a condition approaching slavery.[6]

The figure of the East European sex slave proved irresistible for cultural producers. Television shows, movies and novels repeated this story (and the correlated story of the male Eastern European gangster) so often that it became a staple theme of contemporary European mass culture. There are too many of these films and television shows to list here, but some of the more prominent ones, such as the Golden Globe-nominated *Eastern Promises* (2007), achieved critical success. Viggo Mortensen, the lead actor, was nominated for many awards (including an Oscar for best performance in a leading role) and won several (including best actor in the British Independent Film Awards and the 'best depiction of nudity or sexuality' from the Alliance of Women Film Journalists).[7] The discourse extended well beyond Europe. The figure of the (Eastern European) prostitute held in bondage by the (Eastern European) gangster has been a staple of American popular culture as well, from the weekly potboilers on *Law & Order* to more highbrow series like *The Wire*.

Sex trafficking is a real phenomenon in contemporary Europe. But the relationship between migration and sex work, poverty and wealth, East and West, cannot be reduced to enslavement. Some researchers have found, in contrast to Kara and Hughes, that most of the women they studied migrated without any interaction with organized crime and with the full knowledge that they would be working in the sex trade.[8] Just as tellingly, in recent years a noticeable change has occurred in both scholarly and (to a lesser extent) media discussions of prostitution, with more and more authors talking about 'sex workers'. There are good reasons for this shift in

---

[5] Ibid., 85.

[6] Donna Hughes, 'The "Natasha" Trade: The Transnational Shadow Market of Trafficking in Women', *Journal of International Affairs* 53, no. 2 (2000): 625–51; Helga Konrad, 'Trafficking in Human Beings – the Ugly Face of Europe', *Helsinki Monitor* 13, no. 3 (July 2002): 260–71; Gail Kligman and Stephanie Limoncelli, 'Trafficking Women after Socialism: To, through, and from Eastern Europe', *Social Politics: International Studies in Gender, State & Society* 12, no. 1 (Spring 2005): 118–40; and Paola Monzini, *Sex Traffic: Prostitution, Crime and Exploitation*, trans. Patrick Camiller (London: Zed, 2005).

[7] *Eastern Promises* (2007), [Film] Dir. David Cronenberg, United States: Universal Studios.

[8] Dina Siegel, 'Human Trafficking and Legalized Prostitution in the Netherlands', *Temida* 12, no. 1 (2009): 7.

terminology. In the first place, discussing sex 'work' allows for useful comparisons between sexual labour and other forms of (both free and coerced) labour. Indeed, seeing sexual migrants as part of a broader 'traffic' in exploited female labour is one of the most productive lines of analysis in the recent literature on 'trafficking'.[9] In the second place, it is the result of an attempt by sex workers themselves to speak for themselves in the roiling debates about prostitution. Those current and past sex workers do not, of course, speak with a single voice. In terms of policy prescriptions, there is no unanimity regarding the desirability and/or forms of the criminalization of prostitution (though those who remain in the sex industry usually argue for decriminalization). But the fact that some sex workers openly argue against seeing all prostitutes as victims and against the demonization of the sex trade has had a noticeable effect.

This collision of developing narratives – the new white slave trade on the one hand and the tale of the sexual entrepreneur on the other – has led to several different strands of analysis. On the one hand, there is a clear move on the part of some sexuality researchers to refrain from moralizing judgements regarding sex work. This has often put them in an uncomfortable situation. One scholar who thought it might be useful to inquire as to the motivations, thoughts and emotions of sexual clients encountered hostility from her colleagues and found that the disgust many felt towards men who purchase sex was transferred onto her.[10] On the other hand, the descriptions of enslaved women have energized (or re-energized) many across the political and intellectual spectrum. Cracking down on sex trafficking turns out to have appeal both to those who see sex work as inherently dehumanizing and misogynistic and to those whose larger goals include restricting migration of all sorts.

There is no point in belabouring the obvious conclusion – that the intersection between sex and commerce is vast and that men and women participate in sexual markets across the spectrum from liberty to coercion. Most European policy-makers have come to this conclusion as well. As a result, many states have turned away from arresting sex workers and have sought ways to prosecute coercion and abuse rather than all forms of paid sex. This path has not been easy or straightforward. Places that chose the path of decriminalization and regulation, such as the Netherlands, discovered that neither trafficking nor abuses came to an end. High-profile cases that exposed mafia involvement in Dutch prostitution and sex trafficking may have been 'exaggerated in the media', but they nevertheless proved that decriminalization of prostitution did not, in itself, eliminate criminality in the sex work sector.[11] Sweden (soon followed by Norway and Iceland) took the innovative step of criminalizing the purchase of sex while decriminalizing the sale of it, but there too little evidence suggests that the scale either

---

[9] Anca Parvulescu, *The Traffic in Women's Work: East European Migration and the Making of Europe* (Chicago and London: University of Chicago Press, 2014).

[10] Teela Sanders, *Paying for Pleasure: Men Who Buy Sex* (Cullom: Willan, 2008), 6.

[11] Siegel, 'Human Trafficking and Legalized Prostitution in the Netherlands', 9.

of prostitution or the abuses surrounding it has lessened.[12] England and Wales sought to tackle the issue by passing a law that placed 'strict liability' upon purchasers of sex. A client was subject to prosecution if he paid for sexual services and if the prostitute he hired was being 'exploited' by another party. Furthermore, under 'strict liability', there was no need to prove that the consumer had any knowledge of this exploitation. The stated purpose of the law was both to combat sex trafficking and to reduce demand for prostitution nationwide. The first comprehensive study of the application of this law demonstrated that the statute is rarely used by police, though in one jurisdiction it has been used so often as to suggest that the police there used it in an 'inappropriate manner'.[13] In Ukraine, prostitution remains officially criminalized but unofficially tolerated. Sex workers advertise both in print and on the web, and they ply their trade relatively openly. This too is a common state of affairs in twenty-first-century Europe. Prostitutes remain in a legal limbo, vulnerable to coercion from the police, their pimps and their clients. At the same time, Ukraine, like many other cities in the former Eastern Bloc, became a new destination for 'sex tourists' and their foreign currency. Local officials have done little to discourage this boost to their economy.

## Femen's challenge to European feminism

Femen made these hypocrisies the theme of a series of protest actions in 2008 and 2009. They would appear suddenly, usually at some significant or symbolic location (such as the prosecutor's office, a prominent church or a football stadium), strip to the waist and show slogans painted on their bodies and on handheld placards with a simple message for a given 'action'. These messages were typically in Ukrainian, Russian or English, often a combination of the three, with words like 'Death to Sadists!' or 'Save the Woman'. Their overall message was always clear. As one participant put it, 'we protest against patriarchy in all its forms, against anything that infringes upon the rights of women.'[14] Initially, their energy was largely devoted to protests against the sex trade. Prostitution was a social evil, and Ukraine's position as a destination for sex tourism was humiliating. 'Ukraine', one shouted as she was being dragged to a police van, 'should be ashamed'.[15] The Ukrainian government, desperate to promote a good image of the country to those who might invest in it, visit it or attend football matches there, was unsurprisingly hostile to Femen.

---

[12] Jay Levy and Pye Jakobsson, 'Sweden's Abolitionist Discourse and Law: Effects on the Dynamics of Swedish Sex Work and on the Lives of Sweden's Sex Workers', *Criminology and Criminal Justice* 14, no. 5 (2014): 593–607; see also Don Kulick, 'Four Hundred Thousand Swedish Perverts', *GLQ: A Journal of Lesbian and Gay Studies* 11, no. 2 (2005), 205–35.

[13] Sarah Kingston and Terry Thomas, 'The Police, Sex Work, and Section 14 of the Policing and Crime Act 2009', *The Howard Journal* 53, no. 3 (2014): 255–69.

[14] *Ukraine Is Not a Brothel* (2013), [Film] Dir. Kitty Green, Australia: Film Platform.

[15] Ibid.

**Figure 6.1** Russian President Vladimir Putin (L) is attacked by an activist of the Ukrainian women rights group 'Femen' as German Chancellor Angela Merkel (R) looks on during their visit to the industrial exhibition 'Hannover Messe' on 8 April 2013 in Hannover Germany. Reprinted by permission of Getty Images.

Not all of Femen's critics came from conservative state bureaucracies. Some of those complaining about Femen did so from a self-described 'radical' position. The Krasnals, a Polish experimental art collective, created a pictorial, 'Krasnals contra Femen Diversity Parade', in which they defended the position of 'prostitutes who want to earn some extra money on Euro 2012'. Attacking Femen as a symptom of the same Orange Revolution that had descended into a corrupt 'symbiosis between government and business elites',[16] they showed women in orange jumpsuits, many of them open to the waist to expose their chests. They carried a huge pink penis above their heads while some bore placards saying 'I love Poznan' (a Polish site of the Euro 2012 games) and 'Femen! Get the Fuck Out of Our Business.' In the text of the website itself, the Krasnals wrote in bold that 'Femen pseudo-feminism has nothing to do with the clever, intelligent, systematic, persistent work on behalf of women.' Moreover, they hinted, Femen was both intolerant to other views and likely sponsored by some secret force.[17] Similar accusations were made by others across the political spectrum.

---

[16] The 'Orange Revolution' was one of several 'colour' revolutions that occurred in the first years of the twenty-first century. Launched in Kyiv in late 2004 to protest contested election results, it succeeded in forcing the seemingly elected Viktor Yanukovych to surrender the presidency to Viktor Yushchenko. Yushchenko's popular mandate soon dissipated amidst economic decline and charges of continuing state corruption.

[17] 'The Krasnals Contra Femen/Diversity Parade', available at http://thekrasnals.blogspot.com/2012/06 /krasnals-contra-femen-diversity-parade.html (accessed 10 July 2015).

Indeed, some of the most strident criticisms of Femen have come from other feminists. Theresa O'Keefe, writing in the *Feminist Review*, has argued that Femen is an example of a broader, 'femmenist' strand of political action that has become popular in recent years and that deserves condemnation. The extra 'men' in her term is meant to highlight how the 'shared space occupied by third-wave and postfeminism ... [is producing] the uncritical embodiment of hegemonic, heteronormative corporealities that are unquestionably rooted within patriarchal and capitalist values. It is an emphasis on bodies as free, fun and playful, celebratory'. Far from critiquing capitalism, 'postfeminism' is in fact a manifestation of neo-liberalism and 'carves out a distinct space to encourage consumption'.[18] The tactic of protesting topless is particularly counterproductive in O'Keefe's reading. Even if the intent is to create a parody, 'if parody is not exaggerated, then it is not always read as parody and thus ceases to be subversive'.[19] And O'Keefe doubts that parody is what Femen aims for: 'Femen need the male gaze; they explicitly seek to capture it. They take the commodification and objectification of women's bodies and use it to sell a message'. O'Keefe reinforces her point that Femen simply conflate performance and commodification by quoting one of the group's founders, Anna Hutsol: 'I think if you can sell cookies in this way [through mass appeal] why not also push for social issues using the same method? I don't see anything wrong with that'.[20] O'Keefe's answer is that self-commodification is not liberation; it is simply another means to inscribe oneself within the dominant patriarchal and capitalist systems.

Other feminists, while noting this strand of critique, see something more, both in Femen and in their style of protest. Marian Rubchak, in an article that places Femen within the context of Ukrainian social and political protest in the twenty-first century, observes that Femen succeeded in raising the profile of 'small and fragile' feminist 'micro-publics' in two short years. Equally importantly, she witnessed significant evolution in the organization as it 'evolved from a woman's rights oriented organization into a radical opposition'.[21]

The most substantial engagement, however, came from within the Ukrainian feminist movement itself in the form of a sympathetic but critical essay by Mariia Maerchik and Ol'ga Plakhotnik.[22] They noted at the outset that the tactic of topless feminist protest in fact has had a long history, both in Eastern Europe and in 'the West'. Femen, however, did not only bare their breasts, but did so from the beginning by 'creating their own new style, intentionally sexualized' and modelled on the form of the 'glamorous blond post-Soviet model of femininity'. In essence, they had 'armed themselves with the marketing principle that you can sell anything with tits'. But Femen did more than just expose themselves.

---

[18] Theresa O'Keefe, 'My Body Is My Manifesto! Slutwalk, Femen and Femmenist Protest', *Feminist Review* 107 (2014): 5.

[19] Ibid., 4.

[20] Ibid., 10.

[21] Marian Rubchak, 'Seeing Pink: Searching for Gender Justice through Opposition in Ukraine', *European Journal of Women's Studies* 19, no. 1 (2012): 67.

[22] Mariia Maerchik and Ol'ga Plakhotnik, '"Femen" na trope protesta', *Zerkalo nedeli*, 30 December 2010.

They then sought to 'develop' their protests. For example, soon after their demonstrations regarding sex tourism, they created and distributed flyers both to foreign tourists and to young Ukrainian women, they lobbied the Ukrainian government and they pushed to have the Ukrainian parliament adopt a Swedish-style criminalization of sexual clients. But as Maerchik and Plakhotnik observe, 'all of these efforts went unnoticed and were almost useless.' Only costumed topless protests caught the media's attention. Within this 'economy of protest', Femen (a group with few financial resources) decided that they achieved maximum impact for the least investment with their radical approach. Put in terms of 'high theory', Maerchik and Plakhotnik argue, Femen 'has created an attempt to decolonize the female body, usurped for the purpose of profit (in neoliberal discourse) or reproduction (in neo-right discourse)'. They 'bravely threw themselves into an experiment, making their bodies their own and "unusable" for the other roles, which creates stress and dissonance in mass consciousness … raises new questions and stimulates new solutions'.

But Femen's weak spots were also evident as early as 2010. The flip side of their focus on action (pithily expressed in the title of their blog: 'I Came, I Stripped, I Conquered') was a 'strategic indifference to complicated political/feminist theories'. This left them exposed to criticism when, for instance, they used homophobic slurs to describe the Ukrainian Cabinet of Ministers.[23] Femen, wrote one Indian critic, too frequently 'gets a big F in intersectionality'.[24] 'Intersectionality' is the term used by contemporary theorists to signal the claim that social oppression cannot be broken into discrete categories such as 'race', 'class' or 'gender'. Instead, these hierarchical orders are intimately interrelated, and this interrelation calls for more complex analysis and a more holistic political strategy for social justice. It is not totally fair to claim that Femen gets an 'F', though like many academic terms, 'intersectionality' is perhaps difficult to paint on one's torso. They are certainly aware of the ways that gender discrimination and sexual abuse are linked to other socio-cultural systems. What has landed them in trouble has been their 'strategic indifference' to the people they target. If there was little complaint about 'intersectionality' from potential feminist allies when they protested against the Ukrainian government, against Ukrainian professors who demanded sex from their students or against European punters (johns), that all changed when they took up the cause of Muslim women persecuted by their governments.

The first Femen action of this type took the form of an action in front of the Iranian Embassy in Kyiv on 3 November 2010 to protest the death penalty handed down to Sakineh Mohammadi-Ashtiani, a mother of two from Tabriz who was convicted of adultery and sentenced to be stoned to death. A worldwide (and ultimately successful) campaign to stay the sentence was undertaken by several NGOs, and Femen's actions fit broadly within that framework. At the protest itself, the women carried a number of banners, some of them unobjectionable to the left, such as 'Save the Woman' (in English), but some that implied that Islamic states (or even entire Islamic societies) were inferior, such

---

[23] Ibid.

[24] Swatinair, 'The Tactics and Critical Analysis of Femen', *Nirmukta: Promoting Science, Freethought and Secular Humanism in India*, available at http://nirmukta.com/2013/05/10/the-tactics-and-critical-analysis-of -Femen/ (accessed 10 July 2015).

as the simple placard 'каменный век' ('Stone Age') in the centre of the ring of women.[25] This campaign broadened the scope of Femen's actions considerably. Where they had once focused on Ukrainian issues, they now consciously became a more internationally minded group. Their early criticisms of the Orthodox Church in Ukraine now expanded into a criticism of other religious institutions, such as the papacy, but especially into a denunciation of Islam. They rushed to support Alia al-Mahdi, an Egyptian blogger who posted a nude photo of herself on the Internet in November 2011. Al-Mahdi was hounded out of Egypt the following year by repeated death threats, and once abroad she collaborated with Femen in 2012 to publish even more provocative photos, including one in which she held a paper bearing the word 'Coran' over her genitals.[26] In November 2013, Femen staged a 'topless jihad' in Paris, Brussels, Milan, Kyiv and Stockholm to support Amina Tyler, a Tunisian activist who had adopted Femen's strategy and had published an image of herself naked with the words 'I own my body; it's not the source of anyone's honor' written across her breasts. The body art of many of the women at the Femen demonstrations was direct – 'Fuck Your Morals!' – and the action provoked violence from onlookers near the mosques they picketed.[27]

The outrage at their actions was not limited to Internet trolls (e.g. 'Whores, who gave you the right to demand the change of another people's traditions and culture?')[28] or the men who tried to kick them during their day of topless jihad. Their assault upon Islam also sparked criticism that they were repeating the 'neocolonial' mistakes that earlier feminists had made. One scholar wrote that

> [f]eminism has the potential to be greatly emancipatory by adopting an anti-racist, anti-homophobic, anti-transphobic and anti-Islamophobic rhetoric [but] … Femen is using colonial feminist rhetoric that defines Arab women as oppressed by culture and religion, while no mention is made of capitalism, racism, or global imperialism …. Yet again, the lives of Muslim women are to be judged by European feminists.[29]

O'Keefe, in her *Feminist Review* article, concurred, attacking Femen's 'racist overtones': 'Their opposition to veiling routinely slips into uncomplicated derision of Islam, Islamophobia, and the universalisation of Muslim women as "Other" to be saved by Western, "enlightened" women.'[30]

Femen initially brushed these criticisms aside. In part, this is because they had designed their protests to provoke impassioned responses, and they have accepted from the start

---

[25] See a brief clip of this protest at Anna Hutsol, 'Femen Pod Posol'stvom Irana', available at https://www.youtube.com/watch?v=87plsqkW1SE (accessed 10 July 2015).

[26] Sara M. Salem, 'Femen's Neocolonial Feminism: When Nudity Becomes a Uniform', *Alakhbar*, 26 December 2012.

[27] Alan Taylor, 'Femen Stages a "Topless Jihad"', in *In Focus with Alan Taylor* (The Atlantic, 2013).http://www.theatlantic.com/photo/2013/04/femen-stages-a-topless-jihad/100487/, accessed 15 January 2015.

[28] Hutsol, 'Femen Pod Posol'stvom Irana'.

[29] Salem, 'Femen's Neocolonial Feminism'.

[30] O'Keefe, 'My Body Is My Manifesto!', 12, 14.

that some, perhaps most, of these responses would be negative.[31] But their refusal to engage with unimpressed feminists and other hostile observers goes beyond thick skins. It is also based on the idea that excessive theorizing has left the feminist movement paralyzed and unable to act. Inna Shevchenko, one of the leaders of Femen, told a reporter from *The Guardian* in 2011, 'we didn't want to be traditional feminists ... Women's organisations and groups here only write papers and nothing more. We need activists who will scream and leave their clothes in the street.'[32] Shevchenko went further in an interview with *The Atlantic* in 2014. In response to a question about one of her tweets that read 'Islam is ugly and disgusting. Islam oppresses, cripples and kills', she told the reporter:

> Call me an Islamophobe, but I hate Islam! The masses cannot tolerate bold political announcements. If you say what you really think and ignore the rules of political correctness, people reject you. But such 'tolerance' is not for us. Repression against women always comes back in some way to religion, whether it's Catholicism or Islam.

Given such statements, it is unsurprising that critics continue to condemn Femen for being 'neo-colonialist'.

## Queerness in twenty-first-century multicultural Europe

The issue of the relationship between sexual activists and Islamic communities goes well beyond Femen's pronouncements. The questions raised by the emergence of large Muslim communities in Europe have shaken traditional political coalitions of 'the left' more broadly, in particular in regard to sexual issues. This political realignment can be seen in even more acute form in discussions surrounding homosexuality. Plainly, the most remarkable shift in terms of the legal regulation of sexuality since the end of the Cold War has been the rapid acquisition of a set of civil rights by the gay and lesbian community across large swathes of Europe. The process of decriminalizing gay sex has a long history in Europe. Revolutionary France led the way, and then Napoleon spread it through his civil code to several other Northern European countries. As a result, gay sex has been legal in a handful of European states throughout the modern era. Additional waves of decriminalization in the twentieth century culminated in one large push of twelve European countries in the five years following the 1991 dismemberment of the Soviet Union. Finally, in 2001, Bosnia-Herzegovina became the final European country to legalize sexual relations between members of the same sex.[33] Same-sex marriage and civil unions are a much more recent development. The first country to create civil unions in Europe was Denmark in 1989, and the first to legalize gay marriage was the Netherlands in 2001. Eleven countries now recognize gay marriage and an additional

---

[31] Maerchik and Plakhotnik, '"Femen" na trope protesta'.

[32] Homa Khaleeli, 'The Nude Radicals: Feminism Ukrainian Style', *The Guardian*, 15 April 2011.

[33] Achim Hildebrand, 'Routes to Decriminalization: A Comparative Analysis of the Legalization of Same-Sex Sexual Acts', *Sexualities* 17, no. 1/2 (2014): 230–53.

thirteen have civil union legislation. In Southern Europe, this transformation was primarily the result of a quickly mobilized and effective LGBT (lesbian, gay, bisexual and transgender) movement that overcame religious objections to make a case for the normalization of homosexuality in otherwise traditional societies.[34]

This legal shift has moved in tandem with greater representation and cultural sympathy for gays and lesbians in mainstream European cultures. In 2014, one of Britain's most popular actors (Benedict Cumberbatch) played the leading role in a biopic about Alan Turing, the 'father' of computer science in the twentieth century and wartime code-breaker described in Chapter 5.[35] The film ends not with Turing's wartime victories but with his 1952 arrest for 'gross indecency' and his death the following year. In at least one (full) London theatre in November 2014, the audience was snuffling and sobbing by the end of the film, and the conversations on the way to the street centred on the idea of great injustice. The filmmakers had achieved their goal (despite multiple criticisms about the liberties they took with the histories of computers, code-breaking and Turing's life).[36] More to the point for our purposes, they had accurately judged the willingness of the public to purchase tickets for a film about a wronged gay man and to savour the empathy they felt for him. The success of the film gave further weight to a campaign (quickly joined by Cumberbatch) to pardon all of the nearly 50,000 British men convicted of 'gross indecency' for homosexual acts.[37]

The sympathy is present in other arenas as well, most notably perhaps in the wild popularity of Eurovision. Eurovision is a song competition in which one performer or musical group from each nation competes live on stage (and on television) to win the grand prize and glory for themselves and their nation. It has also become a gay-themed and gay-friendly event. As Julie Cassiday puts it:

> The combination of a capacious definition of Europe, cutthroat competition between syrupy love ballads and up-beat youth anthems, and a simultaneously broad and LGBT-focused fan base fosters a peculiar form of identity politics at Eurovision. Whether straight viewers know it or not, the 1990s and 2000s, when Western Europe's LGBT citizens gained important civil rights, saw Eurovision come out of the closet as an annual media event with special significance for gays and the ability to articulate a queer European identity.[38]

---

[34] Ana Cristina Santos, *Social Movements and Sexual Citizenship in Southern Europe* (Houndmills, Basingstoke, Hampshire and New York: Palgrave Macmillan, 2012); Ana Cristina Santos, 'Are We There Yet? Queer Sexual Encounters, Legal Recognition and Homonormativity', *Journal of Gender Studies* 22, no. 1 (2013): 54–64.

[35] *The Imitation Game* (2014), [Film] Dir. Morten Tyldum, United Kingdom: StudioCanal.

[36] Christian Caryl, 'Saving Alan Turing from His Friends', *The New York Review of Books* LXII, no. 2 (5 February 2015): 19–21.

[37] Helen Nianias, 'Benedict Cumberbatch and Stephen Fry Campaign to Pardon Gay Men Convicted with Imitation Game Codebreaker Alan Turing', *The Independent*, 27 January 2015, available at http://www.independent.co.uk/news/people/benedict-cumberbatch-and-stephen-fry-campaign-to-pardon-gay-men-convicted-with-imitation-game-codebreaker-alan-turing-10005530.html (accessed 10 July 2015).

[38] Julie A. Cassiday, 'Post-Soviet Pop Goes Gay: Russia's Trajectory to Eurovision Victory', *Russian Review* 73, no. 1 (2014): 2.

Legally, socially and culturally, the acceptance of homosexual acts and of homosexual identities has never been greater.

Still, anxiety persists. Some of this unease comes from within the homosexual community itself, where more than a few activists feel that the legal 'mainstreaming' of the movement has dulled its radical edge. What sort of 'queer' politics claims assimilation to the conservative bourgeois institution of marriage as a victory? What happened to the ideals of transgression, rebellion and hedonism? Likewise, the emergence of gay districts in major European cities – taken in one reading as a mark of tolerance and acceptance into European urban cultures – can be taken another way, as a sign of gentrification, not just of neighbourhoods but of the 'gay' movement itself, increasingly seen as prosperous, white and male. This tension, broadly speaking, between 'gay' and 'queer' expresses itself in different ways in different cities, but it is a political fact of life throughout the continent.[39]

More troubling, for many, is the sense that these shifts towards tolerance and acceptance are neither complete nor necessarily permanent. It is in the context of this concern that the problems regarding intersectionality have emerged in discussions of the politics of homosexuality. The most obvious expression of this anxiety is the development of 'homonationalism' – the articulation of 'right-wing' projects of restricted immigration and racial exclusion for the purpose of protecting 'left-wing' achievements in the realm of sexual liberty, sexual equality and sexual tolerance.[40] The most famous proponent of homonationalism was the Dutch politician Pim Fortuyn. The Netherlands had established a reputation for sexual liberation in the second half of the twentieth century, and many Dutch people had correspondingly incorporated the notion of sexual tolerance into their own conceptions of their national identity. Fortuyn leveraged this pride in a radical new way by divorcing the promotion of sexual tolerance from the political left, where it had long resided. He was openly, even flamboyantly gay, but he pursued an extremely anti-Islamic agenda, calling for an end to Muslim immigration, a racially based crackdown on crime, and finally for a repeal of Article One of the Dutch Constitution, which prohibits discrimination.[41] He was assassinated in 2002 by an environmental activist named Volkert van der Graaf, who stated at his trial that he had shot Fortuyn to prevent him from making Muslims the 'scapegoats' of the Netherlands' problems.[42]

Most gay activists did not support these extreme policies. Nevertheless, some did express misgivings about the growing strength of a Muslim community that appeared

---

[39] See for instance the excellent work in Lisa Downing and Robert Gillett, eds, *Queer in Europe: Contemporary Case Studies* (Farnham, Surrey: Ashgate, 2011); and Matt Cook and Jennifer V. Evans, eds, *Queer Cities, Queer Cultures: Europe since 1945* (London: Bloomsbury, 2014).

[40] Jasbir K. Puar, *Terrorist Assemblages: Homonationalism in Queer Times* (Durham: Duke University Press, 2007).

[41] 'Obituary: Pim Fortuyn', BBC, available at http://news.bbc.co.uk/1/hi/world/europe/1971462.stm (accessed 10 July 2015).

[42] Ambrose Evans-Pritchard and Joan Clements, 'Fortuyn Killed "to Protect Muslims"', *The Telegraph*, 28 March 2003, available at http://www.telegraph.co.uk/news/worldnews/europe/netherlands/1425944/Fortuyn-killed-to-protect-Muslims.html (accessed 10 July 2015).

to be hostile to their newly won liberties. Just as Femen attacked Islam as inherently oppressive in its treatment of women, so too did some gay activists decry Muslims as homophobic. In one particularly memorable exchange at the closing panel of a prominent conference on 'Sexual Nationalisms' held in Amsterdam in 2011, Gert Hekma opined (in the record of one hostile observer) that 'I prefer a defense of these white secular ideas above a muslim [sic] ideology that has no good record when it comes to these rights – not in Holland, Europe, or the Middle East.'[43] The heated debate that followed displayed deep generational divisions between LGBT activists seeking appropriate responses to sexually conservative immigrant cultures. What seemed a self-evident statement about encroaching fundamentalism to Hekma was met with fury from queer participants of colour and their supporters. Even before the final panel, two of the speakers had walked out, both highly critical of what they described as the excessively white focus of the conference and of the marginalization of scholars and communities of colour embedded in the programme. It is not necessary to take sides in this debate to understand how it exemplifies the new political fissures within movements for sexual rights in Europe today.

This was a debate about 'intersectionality' at its most robust. Those critical of the programme committee argued that even the very name of the conference – 'Sexual Nationalisms' – robbed the term 'Homonationalism' of its critical edge. Those who truly understand the importance of intersectionality, these younger gay activists argued, can easily see that those who express concern about the impact of Muslim immigration upon sexual cultures are simply 'homonationalists'. On the other hand, the conference revealed the danger of validating the position of anti-immigrant positions, as concerns about attitudes towards sexual equality could quickly slip into inflammatory diatribes.

Recent sociological research suggests that the attitudes of European Muslim communities towards issues of sexuality and sexual equality are more complicated – and more fluid – than the two positions articulated at the 'Sexual Nationalisms' conference might indicate. Polling data has consistently shown that Muslim communities in Europe are on balance more resistant to ideas of gender and sexual egalitarianism than their neighbours are, but researchers have begun conducting more fine-tuned analyses of these questions. Most now agree that Muslim women, particularly in the second and third generations, are increasingly 'decoupling religiosity from gender traditionalism the longer they remain in the host society'.[44] The situation is less clear in regard to Muslim men. Some researchers argue that Muslim identity in itself provides a source of gender traditionalism, since second-generation immigrants from Muslim countries show much greater conservatism than similarly religious second-generation immigrants from non-

---

[43] Mikki Stelder, 'Start with Amsterdam! An Alternative Statement on the Sexual Nationalisms Conference', blog post, 16 February 2011, available at https://queerintersectional.wordpress.com/2011/02/16/start-with -amsterdam-2/ (accessed 10 July 2015).

[44] Antje Röder, 'Explaining Religious Differences in Immigrants' Gender Role Attitudes: The Changing Impact of Origin Country and Individual Religiosity', *Ethnic and Racial Studies* 37, no. 14 (2014): 2632.

Muslim countries.[45] Others observe a similar correlation between Muslim identity and opposition to gender egalitarianism but suggest that this relationship is relatively weak.[46] Studies in the UK also show that though social conservatism more broadly is almost entirely the result of levels of religiosity, 'on some social issues (specifically gender roles in the home and the morality of homosexuality and premarital sex) being a Muslim independently predicts being more conservative than other Britons.'[47]

What these data mean politically is far from clear. Certainly, notions that the Islamic community is uniformly and unchangingly hostile to sexual rights and liberties are not sustainable. The 'conservative' poll data from the UK used by sociologists indicates, for instance, that 73 per cent of Muslims believe homosexuality is always wrong and that 33 per cent support legalizing gay marriage or civil unions. While this is much lower than the percentages for the British population as a whole (among non-Muslims, 38 per cent believe that homosexuality is always wrong and 70 per cent believe that gay marriage and civil unions should be allowed), one out of every three British Muslims actually supports the legal enactment of gay rights – far from an insignificant portion of that community.[48] By the same token, the notion that it is racist to point out these attitudinal differences seems not simply morally questionable but also politically problematic. If intersectional politics are to have any chance of working, they must surely be based on the premise that friction and disagreement will be central parts of that process. Finally, we should note that not all Muslim communities in Europe are composed of recent migrants. Many areas of settlement, largely but not exclusively in south-eastern Europe, have been predominantly Muslim for centuries. These historically based Muslim communities have struggled with some of the same dilemmas of new immigrants and Islamic identification that other European regions contend with, and many place a good deal of importance on identifying themselves (and their more liberal ideas about sexual equality) as 'European' and the new immigrants from elsewhere as alien. For instance, the long beards worn by immigrant men and the *burqas* (full-body covering) worn by immigrant women in Macedonia have become 'a subject of critique among Muslims, who see it as a symbol of backwardness and intolerance.'[49]

Thus, perhaps oddly, but certainly importantly, twenty-first-century Europe is linked decisively to feminism and gay rights, not just for its own citizens, but also for those who wish to define themselves against it. This has become especially relevant to continental politics in the period since the first edition of this book was published in 2007. It has

---

[45] Ibid., 2631.
[46] Jana A. Scheible and Fenella Fleischmann, 'Gendering Islamic Religiosity in the Second Generation: Gender Differences in Religious Practices and the Association with Gender Ideology among Moroccan- and Turkish-Belgian Muslims', *Gender & Society* 27, no. 3 (2013): 372–95.
[47] Valerie A. Lewis and Ridhi Kashyap, 'Are Muslims a Distinctive Minority? An Empirical Analysis of Religiosity, Social Attitudes and Islam', *Journal for the Scientific Study of Religion* 52, no. 3 (2013): 621.
[48] Ibid.
[49] Anna Zadrożna, '"I Am Muslim but I Am the European One": Contextual Identities among Muslims from Western Macedonia in Everyday Practices and Narratives', *Anthropological Journal of European Cultures* 22, no. 2 (2013): 35–52.

long been evident that the countries of the former Soviet bloc held a much dimmer view of feminism and homosexual freedoms than the countries located on the other side of the former 'iron curtain'. Opinion polls have consistently shown that policies aimed at female equality and sexual equality are less popular in Eastern Europe than in the countries of Western Europe. One of the most interesting political dynamics in the states that sought to join the major European institutions such as the EU and NATO was the gender politics surrounding accession, as socially conservative countries such as Poland first protested and then accepted the demand that they harmonize their social legislation with those of the more liberal countries to their west. Despite fears that this process would harden the opposition, there is instead some evidence to suggest that this precocious policy-making actually helped to strengthen an atmosphere of tolerance and led to greater support for egalitarian measures.[50]

Outside of the EU accession zone, however, the political dynamic has been much different. In Ukraine, as we have seen, mainstream European feminism has led a precarious existence, attacked by politicians and rejected even by many of the women it wishes to support. The situation is even worse for the LGBT community. As one of the most recent studies notes, 'The results of public opinion surveys demonstrate that the population is not ready to accept lesbian, gay, bisexual, and transgender (LGBT) people as citizens of Ukraine with human and civil rights, even though Ukraine – in transition to democracy, an open society, and equality officially declares that all people have human rights.'[51] Even more worryingly, Ukrainians of all generations became 'more homophobic between 2002 and 2007', a development the author links to a backlash against greater LGBT activism in the country and to the 'hate speech' against gays that intensified among politicians, within a newly re-energized church, and within the mass media.[52]

This phenomenon was even more pronounced in Russia. Though Ukrainians and Russians were roughly equal (and both at the bottom of Europe-wide measures) in their lack of support for the statement that 'gay men and lesbians should be free to live their own life as they wish',[53] it was the Russian government that launched a striking anti-gay campaign between 2011 and 2013.[54] In some respects, the campaign was a bit surprising. Though gay sex was decriminalized in Russia in 1993, there was little pressure on the political system to expand civil liberties for homosexuals any further than that. Most Russians opposed measures like gay marriage or civil unions, a conservative and popular president firmly controlled the legislative agenda and there

---

[50] Judit Takacs and Ivett Szalma, 'Homophobia and Same-Sex Partnership Legislation in Europe', *Equality, Diversity & Inclusion* 30, no. 5 (October 2011): 356–78.

[51] Tamara Martsenyuk, 'The State of the LGBT Community and Homophobia in Ukraine', *Problems of Post-Communism* 59, no. 2 (2012): 51.

[52] Ibid., 54.

[53] Data from the European Social Survey cited in Takacs and Szalma, 'Homophobia and Same-Sex Partnership Legislation in Europe', 362.

[54] See the analysis in Eric Allen Engle, 'Gay Rights in Russia? Russia's Ban on Gay Pride Parades and the General Principle of Proportionality in International Law', *The Journal of Eurasian Law* 6, no. 2 (2013): 165–86.

was no prospect of accession to the EU to prod liberalization. With the 2014 Sochi Winter Olympics approaching, there seemed to be no reason for the government to bring up gay issues at all. Those issues could, and would, have stayed safely in the closet for the duration of the international festival. Why then did President Putin invite international hostility by publicly targeting the gay community with a series of restrictive new laws?

Understanding this campaign requires a deeper analysis of the relationship between gender, sexuality and politics of the type that we have pursued throughout this volume. The reasons given by the Russian government for the new bans on 'gay propaganda', on the adoption of Russian children by gay parents and on pro-gay protests were remarkably flimsy. The laws were justified with arguments for the "'prevention of riots and protection of health, morals and the rights and freedoms of others,'" i.e. to maintain public order and/or to protect children and foster reproduction'.[55] However, this framing of the legal initiatives as a defensive device made little sense. There was no crisis of children seduced into 'gayness', no reasonable way to explain how the relatively small number of foreign adoptions might affect Russia's long-term demographic trends, and no riots, unless one includes the frequent beatings of Russian Gay Pride marchers by counter-demonstrators as gay-sponsored riots. So why launch this campaign?

The answer lies in the broader sphere of geopolitics. Putin, in his third term, had two major goals: to fend off threats to his position generated by local dissent and the activity of non-governmental organizations and to establish Russia as an independent force in world politics. His enemy in both endeavours, broadly speaking, was 'the West'. He believed that all of the major political demonstrations in the former Soviet bloc in recent years had been the work of American 'soft power' initiatives, funded by the CIA and designed to oust him and the regional heads of state friendly to him. Thus the 'Colour Revolutions', especially the 2004–5 Orange Revolution in Ukraine, were best seen, in his view, as Western plots using duped local partners. When political demonstrations blossomed in Russia in late 2011, Putin understood them in the same way. Finally, the huge Maidan protests in Ukraine in late 2013 and early 2014, where activists protested Russia's attempt to veto the growing integration between Ukraine and Europe and ousted Putin's ally Viktor Yanukovich from office, led to further anxiety about encroaching Western powers.

What, one might reasonably ask, does feminism or gay rights have to do with this? The answer was viscerally clear to Eastern European authoritarians, and they deployed it immediately. In order to steer their populations away from the elements of the 'West' that were attractive, they had to stress the elements that held negative associations. Almost immediately, these politicians brought forward the series of anti-gay measures described above, as a repeated reminder of the decadence and unmanliness of the 'West', and they persistently deployed traditional homophobia and misogyny in

---

[55] Ibid., 166.

their analysis of current events. The defence of tradition – and thus of traditional persecutions – was strengthened as a marker of identity, the thing that made Russia different from Sweden. It provided popular rallying cries, and it further strengthened Putin's conscious and successful strategy to leverage a particular form of masculinity into significant political capital.

The most substantial gendered protest against this intensified masculinist regime within Russia was launched by a women's radical punk collective calling itself Pussy Riot, which formed as an offshoot of the older Russian radical art group Война ('War') in 2011. In contrast to Femen, they chose not nudity but the anonymity of balaclavas as their stage costume. They released songs on the Internet, beginning with the song 'Убей сексиста' ('Kill the Sexist'). Soon, however, they began appearing at prominent public places such as railway stations and detention centres. Then, they showed up in the midst of the turmoil surrounding the disputed Russian parliamentary elections, in January 2012 in Red Square itself, where they performed the song 'Путин зассал' ('Putin pissed himself'). Some members of the group were detained, and two were fined for violation of the rules regarding rallies. Their next performance was even more consequential. On 21 February 2012, the band performed 'Панк-молебен "Богородица, Путин прогони"' ('Punk Prayer: Mother of God, Put Putin Away') at the Cathedral of Christ the Saviour in Moscow. The performance was quickly broken up, and the Russian Orthodox Church reacted violently, asking for new legislation to criminalize blasphemy and pushing for the punishment of Pussy Riot. Less than two weeks later, three members of the group were arrested, and later in 2012 they were sentenced to two years in prison for 'hooliganism motivated by religious hatred'.

Both Femen and Pussy Riot are important politically and important to understand as we contemplate gender and power in the twenty-first century. Both groups lie at the radical fringe. Neither enjoys 'majority' support in the societies from which they emerged, but this was neither their goal nor the point of their protest. Each, in their own way, exposed the unspoken, uncomfortable and frequently unconscious relationships between gender, religion, sexuality, authority, violence and power. They did not necessarily expose 'the truth', and there has been plenty of thoughtful criticism of their messages and the media in which they chose to express it. But there is no denying that they have succeeded in laying bare certain aspects of European politics and life that many would prefer to keep modestly hidden.

The campaigns of the Putin Administration in Russia and the Yanukovich Administration in Ukraine against Pussy Riot and Femen were saturated with the same themes of anti-westernism and anti-feminism that had marked much of their recent discourse. Feminist groups, in this reading, were sponsored by the West, supported by the West or working for Western interests. In a crude sense, there was some truth to these allegations, at least in Femen's case. Anna Hutsol, one of their leaders, had spent time at a workshop in Bethlehem, Pennsylvania, sponsored by the Open World Leadership Center, an organization funded by the United States Congress to support civil society initiatives in Eastern Europe. 'The main lesson I have learned in the U. S.', she wrote, 'while watching the work of American NGOs, [is] never to wait till the problem resolves itself or the government starts solving it …. You should yourself initiate change.'[56] While this fact of participation in programmes sponsored by the United States government seems to some like conclusive proof of 'Western' destabilization of traditionalist authoritarian regimes, in truth it reveals the complicated lineaments of political power in the contemporary world. 'Non-governmental' organizations are (and have traditionally been) engaged with and occasionally even directly or indirectly funded by governments. This does not mean that they are the clandestine arms of national power. Instead, most of these groups and the people who work within them take a broad view of their jobs, reaching beyond (or below) the constraints of national states to undertake global projects or to perform tasks that governments cannot or will not perform. They are in meaningful ways separate from the state, and it is in this gelatinous medium of global civil society that both Femen and Pussy Riot have operated, globally aware but locally focused.

This permeability of boundaries can be seen in other ways as well. In 2013 and 2014, Femen migrated. As with most migrations, there were both push-and-pull factors at play. On the 'pull' side, Femen's protests had demonstrated significant appeal among feminists elsewhere in Europe looking to tackle the issues Femen was addressing and eager to do so using Femen's brash tactics. 'Branch' operations of the group opened in other major European cities, and many members of Femen's Ukrainian core left to help those new branches establish themselves. Femen-France became the largest of these offshoots, and activists there maintained a steady drumbeat of protest against such institutions as the Catholic Church, the French National Assembly and the famous Moulin Rouge cabaret in Paris, despite conflicts from within the organization and increasing displeasure from the authorities.[57]

Conditions within Ukraine were also changing. As dissatisfaction grew surrounding issues of Ukrainian poverty and of political corruption, the political opposition expanded as well. That opposition exploded in late 2013 in an extended demonstration at the 'Maidan' (Independence Square) in Kyiv, where the Orange Revolution had taken place nine years before. President Yanukovich responded by attacking the protestors, which led in short order to riots in the streets and eventually to a panicked flight by Yanukovich to Russia. The turmoil did not stop there, as President Putin took advantage of the chaos to denounce the Maidan demonstrators as Western agents and as neo-fascists. Leveraging that interpretation, he then proceeded to throw Russian military support towards separatists on the Crimean Peninsula (who quickly voted to separate from Ukraine and to join the Russian Federation) and to insurgents along the Russian border in Eastern Ukraine. Armed conflict erupted in these eastern provinces and the entire region remains destabilized as of this writing. In these conditions, Femen's leadership decided to pause their activities in Ukraine.

---

[56] *Open World 2008 Annual Report* (Washington, DC: Open World Leadership Center, 2008), 7.

[57] Jeffrey Tayler, 'Is Femen Dying? The Radical Feminist Movement Struggles to Survive in France', *The Atlantic*, 22 August 2014, available at http://www.theatlantic.com/international/archive/2014/08/is-femen-dying/378992/ (accessed 10 July 2015).

Finally, Femen suffered from internal conflict in 2013 and 2014. The Australian documentary filmmaker Kitty Green, who filmed and lived with the women founders of Femen for a long period of time, revealed that for much of its existence, Femen had been under the hidden thumb of a man named Viktor Svyatski. When Green asked Sasha Shevchenko, one of the activists, 'In your opinion, who is the leader of Femen?' her friend fidgeted and said 'Uh oh. Oh Kitty … If I'm speaking honestly … right? And people have seen Viktor in the film, right? … It's such a difficult question to answer.' Sasha admits that Viktor has directed much of the action and compares her position to that of a hostage sympathetic to her captor in a 'Stockholm Syndrome', to that of the dependency that Ukraine has in its relationship with Russia and to that of a wife suffering under a drunken and abusive husband. According to Sasha, Femen as a whole was both 'psychologically' and pathologically dependent on him. In a separate interview, Svyatski also paused initially when confronted with questions about his leadership before confessing: 'Yes … my participation in the organization can be seen as a patriarchal influence. My influence on the girls is the very same as the patriarchal influence against which we are protesting. I understand this.'[58] 'But', he continued haltingly, 'I very much hope that my behaviour towards the girls will help them reject that … that product which … the product of which I am also a result. I hope that in my swinish behaviour they see a swine.' Patriarchy, Svyatski argues in conclusion, takes everything from women, but 'I too am a slave to that system.'

By the end of the film, the leading activists have tired of Svyatski's authoritarian influence and move to take control of the organization, in part by moving the centre of their activity to another country. Inna Shevchenko (no relation to Sasha), while explaining this strategy to Green, is packing a Paris guidebook into her suitcase. Here too porous boundaries, not just in Europe, but in the very notions of political activity and identity, became evident. Just as questions were raised as to whether Anna Hutsol could be an authentic Ukrainian feminist because she had learned at least some of her tradecraft from American NGOs, so too could questions about the legitimacy of feminist actions led by a man be raised. Some of those concerns are apparently overblown. As Inna Shevchenko was forced to point out 'in response to journalists who have not yet seen the film', though Svyatski had been part of Femen, he was 'not a founder of Femen, nor a creator of our topless strategy and ideology. But he did lead the movement some time ago.'[59] Should Femen be totally discredited as a result? Is it truly 'Western' rather than Ukrainian? Is it a male fantasy of feminism rather than 'authentic' feminism? These are questions that go to the heart of the nature of political claims in contemporary Europe, and they are difficult to resolve.

As 2014 ended, however, the authenticity of Anna Hutsol and Inna Shevchenko was not the largest political problem facing Ukraine or Europe. People were dying every day

---

[58] *Ukraine is Not a Brothel.*
[59] Inna Shevchenko, 'Femen Let Victor Svyatski Take Over Because We Didn't Know How To Fight It', *The Guardian*, 5 September 2013.

in the separatist conflict in Eastern Ukraine, and happy thoughts about the peacefulness of the contemporary European order were dying along with them. But this does not mean that the actions of Femen or of Pussy Riot have become irrelevant. On the contrary, we have tried to show in this chapter that European political imagination continues to be centred around deeply gendered ideas. The big issues of the day – migration, social equality, the economy and war – are all inflected by ideas of sexuality and gender in very specific ways. Why else would the hugely important phenomenon of intra-European labour migration in the era of the European Union continue to be represented most often through the figure of the Eastern European sex slave? Why else would states take the challenge of sensationalist feminist groups so seriously that they beat them (as in Ukraine), jail them (as in Russia) or threaten them with execution and then dump them bound in the woods (as in Belarus)?[60]

## Internationalism and multiculturalism

The Femen phenomenon shows one more thing: despite the legacies of the Cold War, Eastern and Western Europe are integrated and interrelated as never before in their history. Moreover, the movement of people, products and ideas continues to go both ways. The existence of a 'Femen-France' organization highlights the fact that Ukrainian and French feminists confront similar (though not identical) problems and that they can take inspiration from one another as they do so. And not just feminists. On 7 January 2015, there was an attack on the offices of the French satirical magazine *Charlie Hebdo*. Members of an Islamic terrorist group linked to Al-Qaeda in Yemen claimed responsibility and proclaimed that the murders were retaliation for cartoons that had mocked Islam. All over Europe, and indeed all over the world, those shocked by the crime proclaimed 'Je suis Charlie' on social media sites and placards. In this wave of reactions, it emerged that one of the more recent friends and collaborators with this old and very French journal was none other than Inna Shevchenko. She had been interviewed by the magazine soon after her departure from Ukraine and continued to collaborate and socialize with the editors thereafter. And why not? They shared a taste for the provocative, an attitude towards Islam that even many of their potential sympathizers felt was not just negative but self-destructive and an inclination for direct action. Both had been attacked in the past (most recently when arsonists had targeted Femen offices in the summer of 2014), and they had laughed nervously together about the prospect of attacks in the future.

---

[60] 'Ukrainian Activists Allegedly Kidnapped, Terrorized in Belarus Found', available at http://www.rferl.org /content/femen_activists_detained_by_belarus_kgb/24428304.html (accessed 10 July 2015); see also the video of a shaken but defiant Inna Shevchenko the following day, 'Femen Activists Describe Their Alleged Ordeal in Belarus', Radio Free Europe/Radio Liberty, 21 December 2011, available at http://www.rferl.org/media /video/24429634.html (accessed 10 July 2015).

**Figure 6.2** Je suis Charlie – Republican march in Paris, 11 January 2015. Reprinted by permission of Shutterstock.

Their collaboration was not the only kind of European-ness imaginable in the early twenty-first century, but it was a poignant one. When Shevchenko (who was one year old when the Soviet Union collapsed) met *Charlie Hebdo's* editor-in-chief, Stéphane Charbonnier, for the first time, he hearkened back to an (Eastern) European past they did not share by calling her comrade and flashing her the salute of the young communist Pioneers, a gesture that charmed and heartened her.[61] Female and male, Eastern and Western, young and old, there was much they did not have in common, and yet they found shared grounds of memory, of action and of visions of the future.

Sadly, this newfound feeling of European unity came at the expense of Europe's minorities. The reaction to the *Charlie Hebdo* attacks can only be understood in the context of decades of fierce debate about the integration of very large Muslim minorities into France, Germany, the Netherlands and Scandinavia. Often, these debates have arisen from arguments that conservative Islamic restrictions on the behaviour and comportment of girls and women are incompatible with Western ideals of female emancipation. This debate has centred around the headscarf, which, according to Bronwyn Winter, has become

the most discussed, and fought over, item of women's clothing (or any clothing) ever. It has come to be the primary globalized symbol, for Muslims and non-Muslims

---

[61] Inna Shevchenko, 'Charlie Hebdo Paris Massacre: Everyone Says "Je suis Charlie" Now, But Where Were They When My Friends Were Alive?', *International Business Times*, 12 January 2015, available at http://www.ibtimes.co.uk /charlie-hebdo-paris-massacre-je-suis-charlie-demos-are-too-late-save-my-friends-1483003 (accessed 10 July 2015).

alike, of a feminized and often fetishized Muslim identity, and it is brandished as a political weapon in the supposed confrontation between Islam and the West.[62]

The debates over the headscarf in its various forms (including the *hijab*, the *niqab* and the *burqa*) have been particularly fierce in France, not least because of the universalist ideas of the French Revolution that we described in Chapter 1. They first surfaced in 1989 when two teenage girls in Creil were expelled from school for refusing to remove their headscarves. The furore that resulted eventually led to the government to officially ban all 'conspicuous signs' of religious belief in schools in 2004. Those against the headscarf argue that it is a symbol of the subjection of women. But as Joan Scott counters, the very public shaming of wearers of headscarves in France demonstrates how 'French universalism' equates sameness and equality so that 'assimilation means the eradication of difference'. Both Winter and Scott convincingly argue that women tend to be merely the symbols of these debates, which hide fears about multiculturalism behind a disingenuous concern for female equality.[63] For one thing, they have overstated the scale of the phenomenon. In France in 2004, only 14 per cent of Muslim women wore it. When a law proposed outlawing the *burqa* in the Netherlands, there were probably only fifty to a hundred women in the country wearing them.[64] But Winter argues that the fact that all sides of the debate tend to make their claims in terms of feminism (the wearers of the headscarf argue that their clothing choice is a sign of their own agency) is an indication of 'how easily feminist history is rewritten and the principles of feminism distorted and put to the service of other ends that many not only be nonfeminist but even anathema to the longer-term protection of all women's rights.'[65] Not only have the debates about women's rights not disappeared in the twenty-first century, they have become considerably more complex.

Conflicts over multiculturalism in Europe today are evidence that the scars of the colonial era and of twentieth-century political and ideological division still hang over Europeans today. These tensions were glaringly revealed when the numbers of anti-Islamic protesters organized by a group calling itself 'Patriotic Europeans Against the Islamization of the West' (Pegida, following the German acronym) reached as high as 25,000 in Dresden on 12 January 2015.[66] The choice of Mondays for Pegida's weekly marches (which began in October 2014) and the fact that the crowds often spontaneously broke into a chant of the phrase '*Wir sind das Volk*' (we are the people),[67] were both conscious allusions to the

---

[62] Bronwyn Winter, *Hijab & The Republic: Uncovering the French Headscarf Debate* (Syracuse, NY: Syracuse University Press, 2008), 2–3.

[63] Joan Wallach Scott, *The Politics of the Veil* (Princeton, NJ: Princeton University Press, 2010), 4.

[64] Ibid., 3.

[65] Winter, *Hijab & The Republic*, 337.

[66] 'Numbers Drop as PEGIDA Rally Returns to Dresden', *Deutsche Welle*, 25 January 2015, available at http://www.dw.de/numbers-drop-as-pegida-rally-returns-to-dresden/a-18213834 (accessed 10 July 2015). Related organizations have formed under acronyms like Legida and Begida, with the first initial referring to specific cities, Leipzig and Bonn in these cases.

[67] See for example the video of the PEGIDA rally in Dresden on 24 November 2014, available at https://www.youtube.com/watch?v=CvqoRfmfBEw (accessed 10 July 2015). Please note that any crowd statistics cited here are from individual journalistic sources, which are by their nature fairly subjective.

Monday demonstrations of the autumn of 1989, where protestors in Dresden, Leipzig and other East German cities gathered in ever greater numbers to protest communist rule and its injustices. After the *Charlie Hebdo* attacks, Pegida protestors also adopted the 'Je suis Charlie' slogan to further assert their devotion to democratic 'Western' values while alluding to Islamic terrorism. Pegida's rejection of the 'neo-Nazi' label rings rather hollow, however. Lutz Bachmann, one of the group's leaders, was forced to resign in January 2015 after pictures of him dressed as Hitler surfaced. More ominously, Pegida mimicked fascist practices when group members attacked a camp of refugees in Dresden in March 2015. There are lessons here about the continued existence of fiercely racist attitudes and how new political movements are seeking to reframe old prejudices through allusions to the political transformations of twentieth-century European history.

But for our purposes, it is also important that discussions of sexual identity have cropped up in the conflict between Pegida demonstrators and the (often much larger) counter-demonstrations that picked up steam across Germany in the winter of 2014/15. Two incidents will serve as examples. On 6 November 2014, the controversial Turkish-German author Akif Pirinçci spoke to Pegida supporters in Dresden about his recently published book, whose title might be translated as *Germany Gone Mad: The Crazy Cult Around Women, Homosexuals, and Immigrants*.[68] The talk was advertised as a

> settling of accounts with … [all] those who don't want to hear anything about family and homeland, with a confused public discussion that sanctifies every sexual abnormality, with feminism and gender mainstreaming, with the ever-more aggressively expanding Islam and its German supporters, and with functionaries and politicians who burn our taxes like play money.[69]

Pirinçci and his Muslim-baiting, sexist, racist and anti-environmentalist rants have become hugely popular in right-wing circles in Germany (possibly not least because of the jarring fact of his Turkish heritage), and the news magazine *Der Spiegel* credits this talk with giving a boost to the Pegida demonstrations, which up until this point had had only hundreds rather than thousands of participants.[70]

The intertwining of notions of national identity and insecurities about sexual and gender identity could not be more clear. Recognizing the link, a small anonymous group joined the approximately 7,500 Pegida demonstrators marching in Dresden on 1 December 2014. Nobody really noticed them or thought much about what their sign – which read 'Home-Oriented [people] March Openly FOR Saxon-Teutonic ENgagement'

---

[68] Akif Pirincci, *Deutschland von Sinnen: Der irre Kult um Frauen, Homosexuelle und Zuwanderer* (Waltrop: Manuscriptum, 2014).

[69] This is from the announcement of the talk on the website of the Wilhelm Külz Foundation, available at http://www.wks-sachsen.de/?p=1899 (accessed 10 July 2015).

[70] Maximilian Popp and Andreas Wassermann, 'Origins of German Anti-Muslim Group Pegida', *Spiegel Online*, 1 December 2015, available at http://www.spiegel.de/international/germany/origins-of-german-anti-muslim -group-pegida-a-1012522.html (accessed 10 July 2015).

**Figure 6.3** 'Homofürsten' – banner by Die PARTEI in a Pegida march on 2 December 2014. Reprinted by permission of Die PARTEI.

(capitalization intentional) – might mean. It was later revealed that the sign was devised by the satirical political party known as Die PARTEI – the party – and that its capitalized letters spelled out the word *Homofürsten* or 'gaylords'.

The pranksters were hoping to point out that Pegida members are rather selective in the kind of democratic rights that they support. Denunciations of Pegida rhetoric multiplied in Germany and elsewhere, and counter-demonstrations quickly grew larger than the Pegida marches, particularly in Western Germany. Anti-Pegida demonstrators claim that they outnumbered Pegida marchers by 20,000 to 200 at the rallies in Cologne on 5 January 2015, and the city turned out the lights of its famous cathedral to symbolically protest Pegida's anti-foreigner hatred.[71] Although Pegida announced in July 2015 that it would begin running candidates in Land (provincial) elections, as we write this chapter, it is difficult to predict whether this xenophobic movement will continue to gain ground.

## Conclusion

This is the Europe of today. It is diverse, disputatious and troubled by problems that have no clear solutions. We mention these very recent events not to suggest that the clock is

---

[71] Rahel Gebreyes, 'This German Anti-Islamic Group Is Using the Charlie Hebdo Attack to Its Advantage', *The Huffington Post*, 14 January 2015, available at http://www.huffingtonpost.com/2015/01/14/germany-pegida -paris-terror_n_6463226.html (accessed 10 July 2015).

starting to move backwards but to point out that power, gender and sexuality continue to combine to create potent political forces that affect the everyday lives of all Europeans. The two centuries of history that we have tracked reveal how difficult it has been for Europeans to conceive of themselves in terms beyond race, gender or kinship. Even so, Europe is changing, with new connections across the continent that make the categories of 'East and West' seem increasingly quaint. Men and women now work together in ways that previous generations would have found difficult to envisage.

## Suggested readings

Downing, Lisa, and Robert Gillett, eds. *Queer in Europe: Contemporary Case Studies*. Farnham, Surrey: Ashgate Publishing, 2011.

Evans, Jennifer V., and Matt Cook, eds. *Queer Cities, Queer Cultures: Europe Since 1945*. London: Bloomsbury, 2014.

O'Keefe, Theresa. 'My Body Is My Manifesto! Slutwalk, Femen and Femmenist Protest', *Feminist Review* 107, no. 1 (2014): 1–19.

Parvulescu, Anca. *The Traffic in Women's Work: East European Migration and the Making of Europe*. Chicago and London: University of Chicago Press, 2014.

Rubchak, Marian. 'Seeing Pink: Searching for Gender Justice through Opposition in Ukraine', *European Journal of Women's Studies* 19, no. 1 (2012): 55–72.

Santos, Ana Cristina. *Social Movements and Sexual Citizenship in Southern Europe*. Houndsmills, Basingstoke, Hampshire and New York: Palgrave MacMillan, 2013.

Scott, Joan Wallach. *The Politics of the Veil*. Princeton, NJ: Princeton University Press, 2010.

Takács, Judit, and Ivett Szalma. 'Homophobia and Same-Sex Partnership Legislation in Europe', *Equality, Diversity and Inclusion: An International Journal* 30, no. 5 (2011): 356–78.

Winter, Bronwyn. *Hijab & the Republic Uncovering the French Headscarf Debate*. Syracuse, NY: Syracuse University Press, 2008.

# CONCLUSION

In 1991, as Europe was being wholly transformed by the massive political and demographic changes associated with the end of the Cold War, an anthropologist named Miguel Vale de Almeida travelled to Pardais, a village of 659 people in the Alentejo province of Portugal, searching for 'a place where *ancien régime* structures would meet "modernity"'.[1] It was a region of significant economic change. The marble quarries in the area had been expanding, destroying much of the agricultural land in the area, and new housing developments were filling the spaces between previously separate small towns and villages, making them a single urban area. It was, in many ways, a familiar landscape in late twentieth-century Europe, one important to understand as we conclude our discussion of the gender revolution of the past 200 years.

One of the men de Almeida spoke with during his fieldwork was Beto, the 25-year-old son of a sharecropper, who worked in the local quarries. He and his wife had four children, all of them under six years of age, and when he had finished working for the day he frequented local watering holes with his friends

> Beto often went out in the evenings. As with most men, he was hardly ever at home. When he came back from work, he would go home to wash and change his clothes, only to go straight out to the café to have his afternoon *aperitifs*. He would interrupt this activity to go home for dinner, and once this was done, be back at the café where he remained until 11 p.m. or even later. Once or twice a week and always at weekends, he would leave the village for a [larger party].

When with male companions, Beto liked to drink, to talk about women and to boast of his own sexual prowess. Alone with the anthropologist, he discussed his 'dreams and nightmares, states of soul, melancholy and sadness, dissatisfaction and impotence'. In all company, he was proud of being a good provider for his family and proclaimed his love for them.[2]

Women in Pardais had developed their own form of single-sex sociability. When de Almeida asked Beto's wife what she thought about the fact that he spent nearly all his free time drinking with his male friends, she replied that 'it was all right with her, provided that he came back home every night and shared the bed with her, since she actually preferred to have her man outside the house: men "get in our way", "make things a mess", "do not know how to behave at home" and "their place is in the streets"'.[3] The

---

[1] Miguel Vale de Almeida, *The Hegemonic Male: Masculinity in a Portugese Town* (Providence, RI and Oxford: Berghahn Books, 1996), 11.
[2] Ibid., 40.
[3] Ibid.

men and women of Pardais had truly built a society of separate spheres, one in which the idea that sexual difference was natural and biologically based was strong and in which proper gender behaviour was taught at a very tender age. Young boys were encouraged to play games that combined conflict and public performance, while young women were taught passivity and modesty and played games that 'reproduce[d] family life and motherhood by imitation'.[4] It was a fraternal system in which many nineteenth-century men (and women) would have felt quite comfortable but which came under enormous strain throughout Europe as the result of the world wars and the sexual revolutions of the twentieth century.

But this does not mean that the citizens of Pardais were somehow 'unmodern'. On the contrary, as we have endeavoured to show throughout this book, 'modern' gender relations were built not by replacing earlier beliefs about sexual difference but by layering on new interpretations and new possibilities for behaviour, a process that frequently resulted in contestation but never in total victory for one gendered ideal over another. The sort of gender ideals seen in Pardais has been present in one form or another throughout the modern era, and despite the changes that occurred in many locations during the twentieth century, they are widespread today. Change has certainly occurred. Trendlines have clearly been moving towards greater equality for women, but there are many families across the continent in which systematic male domination is alive and well. These trends, however, are not inexorable or direct. History moves in crooked ways. For most of the nineteenth and twentieth centuries, Marxists were sure that historical 'progress' was inevitable and that the workers of the world would unite to throw off their capitalist chains and build a world of justice, prosperity and harmony. Free-market ideologues were similarly convinced that unfettered capitalism would mean democracy, wealth, peace and happiness. In the wake of the collapse of the Soviet system and the devastation of Yugoslav civil wars, during which ethnic cleansing, mass rape and bloody retribution were daily fare during the 1990s, and in view of the significant cultural and political tensions that have arisen throughout the continent in the past twenty-five years, these visions now seem impossibly utopian.

The potential of Europeans, both positive and negative, is determined not by logic but by historical conditions, by the remnants of the failed and successful experiments of their predecessors, and by the institutions and languages of power developed over the past two and a half centuries. As knowledge spreads more easily, and as humans move more quickly, those historical conditions are now global in scope. Historians and biologists alike now regularly read the scholarship of colleagues across the world. Immigrants from Morocco now live in Paris, share the metro with American tourists and send their children to school with the descendants of traditional French peasants. This global context increases the fund of potential views and potential behaviours, and it complicates the model of social interaction to such a degree that it is impossible to predict the outcome of these historical processes with confidence. It is entirely possible

---

[4] Ibid., 50.

that those who would like the system of separate spheres that is present in Pardais to reassert itself more broadly across the continent will succeed.

But such a retrenchment seems unlikely. Pockets of patriarchy will likely persist in Europe for some time, perhaps even indefinitely. Even in the most cosmopolitan and liberalized cities, there are many families who live 'traditionally', who believe that the honour of their daughters and their families depends upon chastity and who grant the eldest male the authority to make decisions for the entire household. Fraternalist ideology is even stronger. In contrast to earlier eras, however, the institutional, cultural and legal contexts of the 'New Europe' work to undermine these traditional gender systems rather than support them. Few powerful Europeans would now publically make derogatory comments about women or would suggest that they are unfit to participate in the public sphere. Just as importantly, state institutions now affirm the right of individuals to choose their own family circumstances, to leave unhappy situations or to move to a new village, a new city or even a new country. These legal guarantees do not protect all vulnerable individuals from abuse, but they do make a difference. In Pardais, for example, de Almeida met a young woman named Manuela, who was forthright and autonomous. She was a high-school graduate and was living outside of marriage with her boyfriend. She was a census official, and de Almeida joined her for pleasant trips around the countryside as he interviewed her. Soon, the tongues of the young men in the village were wagging, and they suggested to de Almeida that he could have his way with Manuela since she was easy. He ignored them, and so, apparently, did Manuela, who married her boyfriend on her own terms the following year and had a baby.[5] It was much harder for independent women in earlier eras to deal with efforts to force them into roles they did not wish to occupy.

The statistics demonstrate that the scale of change may be even greater than this sketch of Pardais suggests. Portugal remains one of the least urban of European countries, with just 61 per cent of the population living in cities, compared to over 80 per cent in the Scandinavian countries and 99 per cent in Belgium. Still, literacy rates for both men and women are virtually 100 per cent, the infant mortality rate is only 3 per 1,000 live births and fully 27 per cent of parliament is made up of women. By virtually every statistical measure, Portugal has rapidly caught up to European standards since we published the first edition of this book. While still not quite matching Sweden's numbers for female members of parliament (46 per cent) or Finland's infant mortality rate of only 1.3 per 1,000, Portugal has now moved ahead of France (19 per cent) for the former and Germany (3.3 per 1,000) for the latter statistic. If we look at things from a global perspective, these achievements are even more impressive. In the United States, where 79 per cent of the population lives in cities, the infant mortality rate is almost double Portugal's (at 5.4 per 1,000) and only 17 per cent of Congress is female. African and Asian countries compare much less favourably.[6]

---

[5] Ibid., 130.

[6] *PRB Country Profiles* (Population Reference Bureau, 2014), available from www.prb.org (accessed 10 July 2015). See also: Therborn, *Between Sex and Power.*

Europeans now live in societies that have many different family forms, ideas of proper gender roles and opportunities for men and women. We have seen over the course of this book how that variety developed. Our story began in the Enlightenment, when European scholars offered new ways of thinking about the natural world and eventually about human beings and their place in that world. These investigations were based on the supposition that one could discover natural patterns through disciplined and rational scientific enquiry and also that human beings and human societies should seek to make their own behaviour congruent with the natural order. As we saw with our discussion of Rousseau, this scientific literature tended to emphasize rather than downplay the notion of sexual difference, a tendency that only strengthened in the nineteenth century under the influence of Darwin's writings.

Still, the shift had consequences. In the first place, the very idea that 'tradition' should serve as the basis for social order came into question. In the second, placing humans in a biological context led many to assert that there was a fundamental human equality in nature that was thwarted only by ignorant and oppressive political systems. As Rousseau famously wrote in 1762, 'Man is born free, but he is everywhere in chains.'[7] The radical philosopher Thomas Paine, who was born in England and would take part in both the American and French Revolutions, made the point even more clearly in his incendiary 1776 pamphlet *Common Sense*:

> Mankind being originally equals in the order of creation, the equality could only be destroyed by some subsequent circumstance ... But there is ... [a] distinction for which no truly natural or religious reason can be assigned, and that is, the distinction of men into kings and subjects. Male and female are the distinctions of nature, good and bad the distinctions of heaven; but ... exalting one man so greatly above the rest cannot be justified on the equal rights of nature.[8]

We can see here in Paine that the conviction that sexual difference was based in nature and ought to have social and political implications meant that the rights to equality and freedom were limited to men in the minds of many Enlightenment philosophers. As our discussion of Olympe de Gouges and Mary Wollstonecraft indicated, however, the logical implication that women were also naturally equal by virtue of membership in the human species was taken up at once. Those who pressed for women's equality lost in the revolutionary era, as political figures across the continent sought stability amidst the upheaval by reaffirming the principle of male superiority within the family and society. But the logical contradiction at the heart of revolutionary political ideology remained as an irritant and a spur to action from that point forwards.

---

[7] Jean-Jacques Rousseau, *The Social Contract*, trans. Maurice Cranston (New York: Penguin, 1968), 49.
[8] Thomas Paine, 'Selections from Common Sense', in *Reading the American Past: Selected Historical Documents*, ed. Michael P. Johnson (Boston: Bedford Books, 1998), 95.

The other major gendered challenge to the old order that occurred in the revolutionary era was the elaboration of the concept of 'fraternity', which was based on the idea that young men, being equal to older men, deserved a larger share of power and authority in European political and social systems. This impetus was clear in the passage from Paine, as was the implication that republican forms of governance were more likely to assure male equality than monarchies were. The initial victories of fraternal republicans in France were short-lived, as monarchy and patriarchy returned with the rise of Napoleon to the throne, but both the idea of fraternity and its most powerful state form – the establishment of universal military service for young men – would remain powerful forces throughout the nineteenth century. Nationalism, the political form that most clearly expressed the fraternal ideal, developed rapidly in Europe in that time period and soon posed a challenge to monarchies and indeed empires across the continent.

The nineteenth century saw other important political and social developments that were intimately linked with the question of gender. The two we focused on here were the social changes brought about by the new modes of work and production established by the Industrial Revolution and the cultural and political changes that occurred as the result of Europe's intensive colonization of the rest of the world. As we saw in Chapter 2, the economic changes of the nineteenth century crippled the traditional family economy. In the first place, a great many Europeans left rural villages for work and residence in the booming cities of the era. The process of urbanization definitively changed social interactions wherever it occurred, including interactions between men and women. In the second place, the nature of labour was transformed. European economies, which had previously operated largely on a non-cash basis, now re-centred themselves around wage labour.

More precisely, the trends of the era led to a situation in which only those activities that produced cash were considered economically valuable. For most women, this meant a further devaluation of the sorts of labour they performed, from cooking to cleaning to child-rearing, which they did 'for free' in their own households. For wealthy women, it meant an opportunity to further reinforce their own superior class position by hiring lower-class women to do these sorts of chores for them, right down to breastfeeding their children. Proper domestic behaviour now centred not on labour but on providing emotional support to one's husband, who was, it was thought, buffeted during the day by the storms of modern economic life and who needed a safe, gentle harbour at night. Sexual relations were part of this emotional support, but here too the 'cash nexus' of the capitalist economy made itself felt. Prostitution was not new, of course, but it expanded in scope and in visibility over the course of the nineteenth century, fitting nicely with the hierarchies of sex and class that solidified over the course of the industrial era. There was ample cause for women and lower-class men to suspect that the new modern Europe was no improvement over the old and, in terms of social security, might even have represented a decline.

European imperialism left an even more ambiguous legacy in terms of gender. On the one hand, as we saw in Chapter 3, the exposure to other societies allowed for even greater criticism of European cultural and political practices, including sexual ones. In addition, the very opening of new colonies allowed those who felt hemmed in by life in European countries to explore alternative paths. This was true for ambitious young men trying to get away from their fathers. It was also true for those who sought new erotic experiences with members of the opposite sex, with members of the same sex and with any number of combinations of the two. As we saw in our discussion of concubinage, European men frequently adopted polygamous practices, keeping a wife at home and a concubine in the colonies. Women too found different sorts of adventures abroad. Wives of missionaries on the frontier often lived dangerous but personally fulfilling lives, and even those white women who stayed near the governor's mansion were important participants in the affairs of their homeland, not simply by being active colonizers, but also by forwarding ambitious moral reform programmes that affected life in the colonies and in the metropole alike.

On the other hand, the fundamental organizing principle of empire was that of European superiority. This superiority required ideological work to maintain, and the core of that work was the establishment of scientifically based 'natural' hierarchies. The two main axes were those of race and sex. Both women and men worked hard to establish these distinctions, and all parties took advantage of developments in the science of biology, especially that of genetics, to substantiate their claims of difference. The principle of separate spheres was reinforced both by scientific research and by the languages used by men and women to forward political programmes. Female activists became more visible when they claimed the right to moral superiority that was central to the definition of womanhood in the nineteenth century. The principle of racial division was also sustained by scholars like Joseph-Arthur de Gobineau and Charles Darwin, both of whom also reasserted that sexual difference and sexual competition were natural facts of life. A great many European women and men were convinced by this social and scientific research, and they sought (and not infrequently found) fulfilment by working within the context of these racial and sexual hierarchies.

This increasingly cosmopolitan, hierarchical and imperial European system proved both durable and powerful. By the beginning of the twentieth century, indeed, Europeans had established it (with some local variation) across the globe. But this political order was vulnerable, both because it was based on competitive and powerful individual states that were coming into more frequent conflict with one another and because it had spawned socially disaffected groups and a political language that could articulate that unrest and mobilize people to oppose the European Great Powers. Fraternal, anti-colonial nationalists increasingly opposed patriarchal imperialists, and feminists opposed the male domination at the heart of both the patriarchal and fraternal forms. The First World War began as a revolt against imperialism within Europe, as Serbia contested the claims of the Habsburg Empire to assert hegemony on the Balkan peninsula. Given that European military systems traced their organizational and ideological roots back to the fraternalism of the revolutionary, the Napoleonic and the anti-Napoleonic military systems of the period from 1792 to 1815, the outbreak of war strengthened the hand of the fraternal nationalists. This time, fraternity would not be dislodged. The great land empires of Eastern and Central Europe broke apart, and new national states dominated by young war veterans took their place. At the same time, the social pressures of the war itself had required women to break out of their 'sphere' and assume important roles in both the war effort and in the symbolic construction of the nation itself. In practical terms, as we saw in Chapter 4, this meant not only increased participation in the industrial sector, but also the establishment of state-run social welfare systems that gave assistance to women and children not on the principle of charity but on the principle that they were deserving citizens. Europe in the 1920s and 1930s thus saw the development of highly militarized and masculine states with welfare systems and public programmes that included women as civic actors. The degree of actual political influence that women were able to wield varied widely from country to country; however, the idea of 'separate spheres' had come into question, ironically, through a war marked by a physical separation of the sexes unprecedented in European history.

The Second World War would do still more to break down the idea of separate spheres. Whereas women had been granted the vote in many places in Europe after the First World War, it happened across the continent in the wake of the Second World War. While the fiction of a separation between front and home front could reasonably be maintained in many places in Europe during the Great War, the devastation and widespread occupation of the continent by foreign armies during the Second World War made such a neat division impossible. Indeed, as the experience of the Holocaust and other less drastic assaults on civilians would demonstrate, women and children became primary rather than secondary targets in a conflict that took the principle of total war to its logical, apocalyptic conclusion. The suffering and chaos of the war years led to two contradictory impulses. On the one hand, the desire for normality led to intensive and initially successful efforts to stabilize society by re-establishing traditional and comfortable family and gender roles. On the other hand, the connection between modern European masculinity and the great catastrophes of the twentieth century was now only too evident. Those who wished to avoid a repetition of the carnage began systematically examining ways that they might transform European social structures, gender norms and political practices.

There were many ways in which this process developed, and it is still too early to say how extensive the results of this social reappraisal might be, but it is indisputable that the change has been very significant. The area we focused on in this book was the realm of sexual relations. As we argued in Chapter 5, sex was not transformed overnight in the 1960s by a group of longhaired, freedom-seeking rebels. The 'sexual revolution' had a much longer history, going all the way back to the sexologists of the late nineteenth and early twentieth centuries who insisted that sexual practices had political implications. If Freud had paraphrased Rousseau, he might have claimed that men and women could only be free if they were sexually in chains. Sexual revolutionaries, conscious as a result of the wars and experiences of military authoritarianism that the path of European 'civilization' did not always run through freedom, challenged Freud's premise. As early as 1936, Wilhelm Reich and his followers argued instead that the mechanisms of sexual control, oppression and repression in fact encouraged fascism and war. This view found even more fertile ground after the experience of the Second World War, which saw a grotesque sort of sexual 'liberation' through the destruction of the local communities that had previously policed sexual practices, through the privations of civilian flight, poverty and existential desperation, and finally through the normalization of various forms of coerced sex. These were experiences few wanted to repeat, but they had broken up long-standing patterns of sexual behaviour across the continent. The sexual order that would follow the war would have to be constructed rather than simply maintained.

These transformations in sexual thought and sexual practice coincided in the 1960s with technological developments like the birth control pill and with widespread social unrest based on the rejection of the 'old Europe' of colonies, capitalism and war. This conjunction of forces resulted in the social and political phenomenon we today call 'The Sixties'. 'The Sixties' began long before the decade did, reached their peak in many ways in the 1970s and continue to exert influence today. The rebels of 'The Sixties' failed to attain their goals in many respects. War is still around, and so is imperialism, though both exist now in different forms. In terms of sexual liberation, however, those rebels can rightly claim victory. Most Europeans, to the great dismay of conservatives, especially in older generations, can now have sex how they please and with whom they please without fear of legal action (as long as it is between consenting adults). This is true not only for married and unmarried heterosexual couples, but for homosexual couples as well. The victory of sexual revolutionaries was not, of course, complete. Social norms, which are in any case almost always stronger than legal ones, continue to limit sexual liberty in many areas of the continent. Homosexual practices are still viewed with suspicion and denounced in many places, but homophobia too seems to be in sharp decline across Europe. As the sexologists realized decades ago, this change in sexual tolerance and sexual practices has political consequences. In particular, male dominance in its patriarchal and fraternal forms has been based upon the sexual control of women. Today's European feminists are now trying to see whether the significant gains that women have made in the realms of equality and liberty might be extended by undercutting fraternity once and for all. That is a social transformation that will occur, if it does, as much in the bedroom as in the boardroom.

In the long run, feminists who seek this change have good reason to be optimistic. In the short term, affairs can seem much more muddled. As women have successfully asserted their right to take a place in the public sphere in Western Europe, they have discovered what their sisters in Eastern Europe could have told them much earlier: that entering the workforce and the political world means taking on the 'double burden' of paid work outside the home and continuing to do much of the unpaid work within it.

Trying to balance career and family is a precarious act, and this struggle has rapidly come to occupy a central role in discussions of what earlier commentators would have called the European 'woman question'. For couples with children in the European Union at the start of the twenty-first century, it remains the case that men spend more time in paid labour, and women more time in unpaid household labour. Beyond that, significant differences exist. In the two countries to have most recently joined the EU in 2007, Bulgaria and Romania, men who marry continue to see a reduction in their total labour (paid labour combined with domestic labour). In all countries that joined the EU prior to 2007, however, both men and women see an increase in total work after marriage and children. In most of these countries, women work more overall than men, because they do more work in the home, but this difference is rapidly declining in many areas. In all European countries except for France, Luxembourg and Romania, at least a bare majority of women (in other words over 50 per cent) now believe that they do no more than their fair share of the housework.[9]

This evidence that men are now joining women in shouldering the 'double burden' alerts us to the presence of what we might call the contemporary 'man question'. Most European men now take it as a personal, even a masculine, duty to play a role in household affairs. This is particularly true in Sweden, where close to 90 per cent of fathers take advantage of their right to parental leave to take care of young children.[10] But in most countries it remains the case that when couples have children, women tend to reduce the amount of time they spend working outside the home and men tend to increase that time to compensate for lost income. As a result, men have become increasingly anxious about their domestic shortcomings. In the 'old' fifteen countries of the EU, 32 per cent of surveyed men in couples with children reported that they have found it 'difficult ... to fulfil my family responsibilities because of the amount of time I spend on the job'. In the ten member states that joined in 2004, that number jumps to 50 per cent. Both figures are higher than that reported by women (27 per cent and 35 per cent respectively). Only in the candidate states do women report that they experience difficulty more than men, and there both the numbers are high (50 per cent for women and 48 per cent for men).[11] For most Europeans, the argument that men and women should occupy separate spheres is unpersuasive. But no one appears sure what a new, equitable family model, and with it a new and equitable gender order, might look like. Most now agree that men and women should be equal, but that only goes so far. Many young Europeans are troubled by questions about how to be a good mother or a good father, to be a good partner to one's lover or to be a responsible member of one's community. Worse, they are not even sure that they will know when they have stumbled upon the answer. European gender structures are in the midst of a major realignment. It is too soon to tell, for instance, what the effect of gay marriage and liberalized adoption policies for same-sex couples will have on the politics and policies of childcare. What is clear is that this transition period will continue to be marked by enormous stress and uncertainty.

And what of the villagers of Pardais? Does clinging to the fraternal family form mean that they are able to avoid this anxiety, to live in harmony and to find refuge in a model they believe brought stability and happiness to their forebears? De Almeida thinks not:

> It is quite common to say that men are also victims of masculine domination. Many women may feel this statement to be dishonest ... [But women] seem to be able

---

[9] See the statistics of the European Union's Agency, The European Foundation for the Improvement of Living and Working Conditions (Eurofund), at http://eurofound.europa.eu/ (accessed 10 July 2015).
[10] 'Why Swedish Men Take so Much Paternity Leave', *The Economist*, 22 July 2014, available at http://www.economist.com/blogs/economist-explains/2014/07/economist-explains-15 (accessed on 10 July 2015).
[11] Ibid., 39.

to appropriate for themselves symbols and practices that are labeled as masculine, thanks precisely to the hierarchy that defines these as 'superior' and closer to the moral standards of personhood. Also, a process of relative 'feminisation' of social values has been occurring in the society at large, and women in Pardais are not unaware of the growing social salience of sentiments, introspection, self-reflexivity and so on. For men, however, it is rather more difficult to invent new identity forms since – following the dichotomous thought – the alternative is manifestly 'inferior.' They are like aristocrats who have 'lost everything' and no longer know who and what they are. Acknowledging that the hegemonic model probably is just a paper tiger might be the first step for the invention of new social relations and new identities relating to gender.[12]

The comparison with aristocrats is apt. The nobles and other patriarchs of the old regime did not lose power immediately as a result of the revolutionary era, but they did lose hegemony, or the capacity to completely dominate the ideological conditions in which they lived. The same is true for those who want to maintain a system of male domination based in biology and tradition today. Their days of power look to be coming to a close, and they know it.

But we have not reached the 'End of History' in gendered terms. We still think about our world both literally and metaphorically in terms of sexual difference. It would be difficult even to create meaning through language today, much less understand political or social developments, without recourse to the long and rich history of gender associations left to us by language, by literature and by our cultures as a whole. If gender has a history, it probably has a future too. Only those unaware of the past will expect that future to unfold logically according to 'Equality', 'Justice' or 'Nature'. Women and men will create it in their family rooms and their bedrooms as surely as they do in their offices and legislative chambers. And, as always, they will create it together.

---

[12] De Almeida, *The Hegemonic Male*, 168.

# WORKS CITED

Abrams, Lynn. 'Prostitutes in Imperial Germany, 1870–1918: Working Girls or Social Outcasts?' In *The German Underworld: Deviants and Outcasts in German History*. Edited by Richard Evans, 189–209. London and New York: Routledge, 1991.

Adorno, Theodor, and Max Horkheimer. *Dialectic of Enlightenment: Philosophical Fragments*. Edited by Gunzelin Schmid Noerr. Translated by Edmund Jephcott. Palo Alto: Stanford University Press, 1987.

Ågren, Maria, and Amy Louise Erickson, eds. *The Marital Economy in Scandinavia and Britain, 1400– 1900*. Aldershot, UK: Ashgate, 2005.

Albanese, Patrizia. *Mothers of the Nation: Women, Families and Nationalism in Twentieth-Century Europe*. Toronto: University of Toronto Press, 2006.

Aldrich, Robert. *Colonialism and Homosexuality*. London and New York: Routledge, 2002.

Aldrich, Robert, ed. *Gay Life & Culture: A World History*. New York: Universe, 2006.

Alexeyeva, Ludmilla, and Paul Goldberg. *The Thaw Generation: Coming of Age in the Post-Stalin Era*. Pittsburgh, PA: University of Pittsburgh Press, 1993.

Allen, Ann Taylor. 'German Radical Feminism and Eugenics: 1900–1918'. *German Studies Review* 11 (1988): 31–56.

Allen, Ann Taylor. *Women in Twentieth-Century Europe*. New York: Palgrave Macmillan, 2008.

Allen, Robert C. 'Tracking the Agricultural Revolution in England'. *The Economic History Review*, New Series, 52, no. 2 (May 1999): 209–35.

Aly, Götz, and Michael Sontheimer. *Fromms: How Julius Fromm's Condom Fell to the Nazis*. Frankfurt a. M.: S. Fischer, 2007.

Allyn, David. *Make Love, Not War: The Sexual Revolution, an Unfettered History*. New York: Routledge, 2001.

Anderson, Bonnie S. 'The Lid Comes off: International Radical Feminism and the Revolutions of 1848'. *NWSA Journal* 10, no. 2 (July 1998): 1–12.

Andress, David. *The Terror: The Merciless War for Freedom in Revolutionary France*. Reprint edn. New York: Farrar Straus & Giroux, 2006.

Anonymous. *A Woman in Berlin: Eight Weeks in the Conquered City*. New York: Metropolitan Books, 2005.

Arendt, Hannah. *The Human Condition*. Chicago and London: University of Chicago Press, 1958.

Arendt, Hannah. *On Revolution*. London: Penguin Books, 1963.

Auricchio, Laura. *The Marquis: Lafayette Reconsidered*. New York: Knopf, 2014.

Auslander, Leora. *Taste and Power: Furnishing Modern France*. Berkeley: University of California Press, 1996.

Bailey, Charles E. 'The British Protestant Theologians in the First World War: Germanophobia Unleashed'. *Harvard Theological Review* 77, no. 2 (April 1984): 195–221.

Bailey, Joanne. *Unquiet Lives: Marriage and Marriage Breakdown in England, 1660–1800*. Cambridge: Cambridge University Press, 2003.

Ballhatchet, Kenneth. *Race, Sex and Class Under the Raj: Imperial Attitudes and Policies and Their Critics, 1793–1905*. London: Weidenfeld and Nicolson, 1980.

Barclay, Paul D. 'Cultural Brokerage and Interethnic Marriage in Colonial Taiwan: Japanese Subalterns and Their Aborigine Wives, 1895–1930'. *The Journal of Asian Studies* 64, no. 2 (May 2005): 323–60.

Barrett, Michelle, and Mary McIntosh. 'The "Family Wage": Some Problems for Socialists and Feminists'. *Capital and Class* 11 (1980): 51–72.

Barry, Ursula. 'Abortion in the Republic of Ireland'. *Feminist Review*, no. 29 (1988): 57–63.

Bartov, Omer. *The Eastern Front, 1941–45: German Troops and the Barbarisation of Warfare*. New York: St. Martin's Press, 1986.

Bashford, Alison, and Philippa Levine, eds. *The Oxford Handbook of the History of Eugenics*. New York: Oxford University Press, 2010.

Bauer, Heike. 'Theorizing Female Inversion: Sexology, Discipline, and Gender at the Fin de Siècle'. *Journal of the History of Sexuality* 18, no. 1 (2009): 84–102.

Bauman, Zygmunt. *Modernity and the Holocaust*. Ithaca, NY: Cornell University Press, 1989.

Bäumer, Gertrud. *Die Frau Im Deutschen Staat*. Berlin: Junker & Dünnhaupt Verlag, 1932.

Beachy, Robert. 'Business Was a Family Affair: Women of Commerce in Central Europe, 1650–1880'. *Histoire Sociale/Social History* 34, no. 68 (November 2001): 307–30.

Beachy, Robert. *Gay Berlin: Birthplace of a Modern Identity*. New York: Knopf, 2014.

Beck, Birgit. 'Wehrmacht und sexuelle Gewalt: Sexualverbrechen vor deutschen Militärgerichten 1939–1945'. Dissertation. Paderborn: Ferdinand Schöningh, 2004.

Bedell, Geraldine. 'I Wrote the Story of O'. *The Guardian*, 25 July 2004. http://www.theguardian.com/books/2004/jul/25/fiction.features3, accessed 10 July 2015.

Beevor, Antony. *The Fall of Berlin, 1945*. New York: Viking, 2002.

Bell, John D. *Peasants in Power: Alexander Stamboliski and the Bulgarian Agrarian National Union, 1899–1923*. Princeton, NJ: Princeton University Press, 1977.

Bell, Susan Groag, and Karen Offen, eds. *Women, the Family and Freedom: The Debate in Documents*. Stanford: Stanford University Press, 1983.

Bell, Wilson T. 'Sex, Pregnancy, and Power in the Late Stalinist Gulag'. *Journal of the History of Sexuality* 24, no. 2 (2015): 198–224.

Belmessous, Saliha. 'Assimilation and Racialism in Seventeenth and Eighteenth-Century French Colonial Policy'. *American Historical Review* 110, no. 2 (2005): 322–49.

Bender, Daniel E. '"Too Much of Distasteful Masculinity": Historicizing Sexual Harassment in the Garment Sweatshop and Factory'. *Journal of Women's History* 15, no. 4 (2004): 91–116.

Berend, Ivan T. *History Derailed: Central and Eastern Europe in the Long Nineteenth Century*. New edn. Berkeley: University of California Press, 2005.

Berg, Maxine. *The Age of Manufactures: Industry, Innovation, and Work in Britain, 1700–1820*. Totowa, NJ: Fontana, 1985.

Bergen, Doris L. 'Sexual Violence in the Holocaust: Unique and Typical?' In *Lessons and Legacies VII: The Holocaust in International Perspective*. Edited by Peter Hayes and Dagmar Herzog, 179–200. Evanston, IL: Northwestern University Press, 2006.

Berkhoff, Karel C. *Harvest of Despair: Life and Death in Ukraine Under Nazi Rule*. Cambridge, MA: Belknap Press of Harvard University Press, 2004.

Biess, Frank. 'Survivors of Totalitarianism: Returning POWs and the Reconstruction of Masculine Citizenship in West Germany, 1945–1955'. In *The Miracle Years: A Cultural History of West Germany, 1949–1968*. Edited by Hanna Schissler, 57–82. Princeton, NJ: Princeton University Press, 2000.

Birkenhead, Lord. *Rudyard Kipling*. New York: Random House, 1978.

Bland, Lucy. *Banishing the Beast: English Feminism and Sexual Morality, 1885–1914*. London: Penguin, 1995.

Bland, Lucy. 'White Women and Men of Colour: Miscegenation Fears in Britain after the Great War'. *Gender & History* 17, no. 1 (2005): 29–61.

Bleys, Rudi C. *The Geography of Perversion: Male-To-Male Sexual Behavior Outside the West and the Ethnographic Imagination, 1750–1918*. New York: New York University Press, 1995.

Bloch, Ivan Stanislavovich. *The Future of War in Its Technical, Economic, and Political Relations: Is War Now Impossible?* Translated by R. C. Long. New York: Garland Publishing, 1899.

Bloch, Iwan. *Das Sexualleben unserer Zeit in seinen Beziehungen zur modernen Kultur*. Berlin: L. Marcus, 1907.

Bochkareva, Mariia, and Isaac Don Levine. *Yashka, My Life as Peasant, Officer and Exile*. New York: Frederick A. Stokes Co., 1919.

Bock, Gisela. 'Die Frauen und der Nationalsozialismus. Bemerkungen zu einem Buch von Claudia Koonz'. *Geschichte und Gesellschaft* 15, no. 4 (1989): 563–79.

Bock, Gisela. 'Racism and Sexism in Nazi Germany: Motherhood, Compulsory Sterilization, and the State'. *Signs: Journal of Women in Culture & Society* 8, no. 3 (1983): 400–21.

Body, N. O. *Memoirs of a Man's Maiden Years*. Translated by Deborah Simon. Philadelphia: University of Pennsylvania Press, 2009.

Boittin, Jennifer Anne. *Colonial Metropolis: The Urban Grounds of Anti-Imperialism and Feminism in Interwar Paris*. Lincoln: University of Nebraska Press, 2010.

Bonaparte, Marie. 'Les Deux Frigidities de La Femme'. *Bulletin de La Societé de Sexology* 1, (May 1932): 161–70.

Boone, Joseph A. *The Homoerotics of Orientalism*. New York: Columbia University Press, 2014.

Bos, Pascale R. 'Feminists Interpreting the Politics of Wartime Rape: Berlin, 1945; Yugoslavia, 1992–1993'. *Signs: Journal of Women in Culture & Society* 31, no. 4 (2006): 995–1025.

Bosworth, R. J. B. *Mussolini*. New York: Oxford University Press, 2002.

Brake, Wayne Ph. te, Rudolf M. Dekker, and Lottee C. van de Pol. 'Women and Political Culture in the Dutch Revolutions'. In *Women and Politics in the Age of the Democratic Revolution*. Edited by Harriet B. Applewhite and Darline G. Levy, 109–46. Ann Arbor: University of Michigan Press, 1990.

Brand, Adolf. 'What We Want (1925)'. In *Homosexuality and Male Bonding in Pre-Nazi Germany: The Youth Movement, the Gay Movement, and Male Bonding Before Hitler's Rise: Original Transcripts from Der Eigene, the First Gay Journal in the World*. Edited by Harry Oosterhuis and Hubert Kennedy, 155–66. New York: Haworth Press, 1991.

Brauner, Sigrid. *Fearless Wives and Frightened Shrews: The Construction of the Witch in Early Modern Germany*. Amherst: University of Massachusetts Press, 1995.

Bray, Alan. *Homosexuality in Renaissance England*. 2nd edn. New York: Columbia University Press, 1996.

Breuer, Karin. 'Competing Masculinities: Fraternities, Gender and Nationality in the German Confederation, 1815–30'. *Gender & History* 20, no. 2 (August 2008): 270–87.

Broberg, Gunnar, and Nils Roll-Hansen. *Eugenics and the Welfare State Sterilization Policy in Denmark, Sweden, Norway, and Finland*. East Lansing: Michigan State University Press, 1996.

Browning, Christopher R. *Ordinary Men: Reserve Police Battalion 101 and the Final Solution in Poland*. New York: HarperCollins, 1992.

Bruns, Claudia. 'The Politics of Masculinity in the (Homo-)Sexual Discourse (1880 to 1920)'. *German History* 23, no. 3 (2005): 306–20.

Bruns, Claudia. *Politik des Eros: der Männerbund in Wissenschaft, Politik und Jugendkultur (1880–1934)*. Köln: Böhlau, 2008.

Buci-Glucksmann, Christine. 'Catastrophic Utopia: The Feminine as Allegory of the Modern'. *Representations*, no. 14 (1986): 220–29.

Bucur, Maria. 'Romania'. In *Women, Gender, and Fascism in Europe, 1919–45*. Edited by Kevin Passmore, 56–78. New Brunswick: Rutgers University Press, 2003.

Buikema, Rosemarie. 'The Arena of Imaginings: Sarah Bartmann and the Ethics of Representation'. In *Doing Gender in Media, Art and Culture*. Edited by Iris van der Tuin, 70–84. London and New York: Routledge, 2009.

Burds, Jeffrey. 'Sexual Violence in Europe in World War II, 1939—1945'. *Politics & Society* 37, no. 1 (2009): 35–73.

Burrow, J. W. *The Crisis of Reason: European Thought, 1848-1914*. New Haven, CT and London: Yale University Press, 2000.

Burrows, Simon, Jonathan Conlin, Russell Goulbourne, and Valerie Mainz, eds. *The Chevalier d'Eon and His Worlds: Gender, Espionage and Politics in the Eighteenth Century*. London and New York: Bloomsbury Academic, 2010.

Butler, Judith. 'Beauvoir on Sade: Making Sexuality into an Ethic'. In *The Cambridge Companion to Simone de Beauvoir*. Edited by Claudia Card, 168–88. Cambridge and New York: Cambridge University Press, 2003.

Butler, Judith. *Gender Trouble: Feminism and the Subversion of Identity*. New York: Routledge, 1990.

Callaway, Helen. *Gender, Culture, and Empire: European Women in Colonial Nigeria*. Urbana and Chicago: University of Illinois Press, 1987.

Canning, Kathleen. *Gender History in Practice: Historical Perspectives on Bodies, Class and Citizenship*. Ithaca, NY: Cornell University Press, 2006.

Carpenter, Roger M. 'Womanish Men and Manlike Women: The Native American Two-Spirit as Warrior'. In *Gender and Sexuality in Indigenous North America, 1400–1850*. Edited by Sandra Slater and Fay A. Yarbrough, 146–64. Columbia: University of South Carolina Press, 2011.

Carter, Paul. 'Enclosure, Waged Labour and the Formation of Class Consciousness: Rural Middlesex C. 1700–1835'. *Labour History Review: Bulletin of the Society for the Study of Labour History* 66, no. 3 (2001): 269–93.

Carter, Sarah. *Capturing Women: The Manipulation of Cultural Imagery in Canada's Prairie West*. Montreal and Buffalo: Mcgill Queens University Press, 1997.

Caryl, Christian. 'Saving Alan Turing from His Friends'. *The New York Review of Books*, 5 February 2015.

Cassiday, Julie A. 'Post-Soviet Pop Goes Gay: Russia's Trajectory to Eurovision Victory'. *Russian Review* 73, no. 1 (2014): 1–23.

Cayton, Andrew R. L. *Love in the Time of Revolution: Transatlantic Literary Radicalism and Historical Change, 1793–1818*. Chapel Hill: University of North Carolina Press, 2013.

Chaperon, Sylvie. 'Feminism Is Dead. Long Live Feminism! The Women's Movement in France at the Liberation'. In *When the War Was Over Women, War and Peace in Europe, 1940–1956*. Edited by Claire Duchen and Irene Bandhauer-Schöffmann, 146–60. London and New York: Leicester University Press, 2000.

Chastain, John. 'Encyclopedia of 1848 Revolutions'. http://www.ohiou.edu/~chastain/index.htm, accessed 10 January 2015.

Chauncey Jr., George. *Gay New York: Gender, Urban Culture, and the Making of the Gay Male World, 1890–1940*. New York: Basic Books, 1994.

Cherry, Deborah. 'Going Places: Women Artists in Central London in the Mid-Nineteenth Century'. *The London Journal* 28, no. 1 (2003): 73–96.

Choquette, Leslie. 'Degenerate or Degendered? Images of Prostitution and Homosexuality in the French Third Republic'. *Historical Reflections/Réflexions Historiques* 23, no. 2 (1997): 205.

Choquette, Leslie. 'Paris-Lesbos: Lesbian Social Space in the Modern City, 1870–1940'. *Proceedings of the Western Society for French History* 26 (1999): 122.

Clark, Alice. *The Working Life of Women in the Seventeenth Century*. New Impression edn. London: Routledge, 2013.

Clark, Anna. *Desire: A History of European Sexuality*. New York: Routledge, 2008.

Clark, Anna. *The Struggle for the Breeches: Gender and the Making of the British Working Class*. Berkeley: University of California Press, 1995.

Cleminson, Richard. *Catholicism, Race and Empire: Eugenics in Portugal, 1900–1950*. Budapest: Central European University Press, 2014.

Cleminson, Richard. 'Eugenics in Portugal, 1900–1950: Setting a Research Agenda'. *East Central Europe* 38, no. 1 (2011): 133–54.

Clifford, Dale L. 'Can the Uniform Make the Citizen? Paris, 1789–1791'. *Eighteenth-Century Studies* 34, no. 3 (2001): 363–82.

Colpitts, George W. *Game in the Garden: A Human History of Wildlife in Western Canada to 1940*. Vancouver, BC: UBC Press, 2003.

Colson, M. H. 'Female Orgasm: Myths, Facts and Controversies'. *Sexologies* 19, no. 1 (2010): 8–14.

Combs, William. 'Fatal Attraction: Duelling and the SS'. *History Today* 47, no. 6 (June 1997): 11–16.

Conlin, Jonathan. 'The Strange Case of the Chevalier d'Eon'. *History Today* 60, no. 4 (2010): 45–51.

Connelly, Matthew. *Fatal Misconception: The Struggle to Control World Population*. Cambridge, MA: Belknap Press of Harvard University Press, 2010.

Cook, Hera. *The Long Sexual Revolution: English Women, Sex, and Contraception, 1800–1975*. Oxford: Oxford University Press, 2004.

Cook, Matt. 'Queer Conflicts: Love, Sex and War, 1914-1967'. In *A Gay History of Britain: Love and Sex Between Men Since the Middle Ages*. Edited by Matt Cook, Robert Mills, Randolph Trumbach, and Harry Cocks, 145–78. Oxford and Westport, CT: Praeger, 2007.

Corbin, Alain. 'Commercial Sexuality in Nineteenth-Century France: A System of Images and Regulations'. In *The Making of the Modern Body: Sexuality and Society in the Nineteenth Century*. Edited by Catherine Gallagher and Thomas Laqueur, 209–19. Berkeley and Los Angeles: University of California Press, 1987.

Corbin, Alain. *Women for Hire: Prostitution and Sexuality in France after 1850*. Cambridge, MA: Harvard University Press, 1990.

Corsini, Carlo A., and Pier Paolo Viazzo. *The Decline of Infant and Child Mortality: The European Experience, 1750–1990*. The Hague: Kluwer Law International (UNICEF), 1997.

Costlow, Jane. 'Compassion and the Hero: Women in *A Hero of Our Time*'. In *Lermontov's 'A Hero of Our Time': A Critical Companion*. Edited by Lewis Bagby, 85–108. Evanston, IL: Northwestern University Press, 2002.

Crais, Clifton, and Pamela Scully. *Sara Baartman and the Hottentot Venus: A Ghost Story and a Biography*. Reprint edn. Princeton, NJ: Princeton University Press, 2010.

Crawford, Katherine. *European Sexualities, 1400–1800*. Cambridge, MA: Cambridge University Press, 2007.

Crawford, Katherine. *The Sexual Culture of the French Renaissance*. Cambridge, MA: Cambridge University Press, 2010.

Crouthamel, Jason. *An Intimate History of the Front: Masculinity, Sexuality, and German Soldiers in the First World War*. New York: Palgrave MacMillan, 2014.

D'Cruze, Shani. 'Sexual Violence Since 1750'. In *The Routledge History of Sex and the Body: 1500 to the Present*. Edited by Sarah Toulalan and Kate Fisher, 444–59. Abingdon, Oxon, and New York: Routledge, 2013.

Dahlkamp, Jürgen. 'Agents: No Country More Beautiful'. *Spiegel Online*, 14 July 2003. http://www.spiegel.de/international/spiegel/agents-no-country-more-beautiful-a-257041.html, accessed 10 July 2015.

*The Danish Girl* (2015). [Film] Dir. Tom Hooper, United Kingdom: Benelux Film Distributors.

Darwin, Charles. *Charles Darwin's Letters: A Selection, 1825–1859*. Edited by Frederick Burkhardt. Cambridge and New York: Cambridge University Press, 1996.

Darwin, Charles. *Descent of Man, and Selection in Relation to Sex*. New York: D. Appleton Co., 1875.

## Works Cited

Darwin, Charles. *The Origin of Species: By Means of Natural Selection, or the Preservation of Favoured Races in the Struggle for Life*. New York: Penguin, 1958.

Daskalova, Krassimira. 'Bulgarian Women in Movements, Laws, Discourses (1840s–1940s)'. *Bulgarian Historical Review* 27, no. 1 (1999): 180–96.

Daston, Lorraine, and Katharine Park. 'The Hermaphrodite and the Orders of Nature: Sexual Ambiguity in Early Modern France'. *GLQ: A Journal of Gay & Lesbian Studies* 1, no. 4 (2004): 419–38.

Davidoff, Leonore. 'Class and Gender in Victorian England: The Diaries of Arthur J. Munby and Hannah Cullwick'. *Feminist Studies* 5 (1979): 86–141.

Davidoff, Leonore, and Catherine Hall. *Family Fortunes: Men and Women of the English Middle Class, 1780–1850*. Chicago: University of Chicago Press, 1987.

Davidson, Roger, and Lesley A. Hall. *Sex, Sin and Suffering: Venereal Disease and European Society since 1870*. New York: Routledge, 2001.

Davies, Norman. *Europe: A History*. Oxford & New York: Oxford University Press, 1996.

Davis, Belinda J. *Home Fires Burning: Food, Politics, and Everyday Life in World War I Berlin*. Chapel Hill: University of North Carolina Press, 2000.

de Almeida, Miguel Vale. *The Hegemonic Male: Masculinity in a Portuguese Town*. Providence, RI, and Oxford: Berghahn Books, 1996.

de Baecque, Antoine. *The Body Politic: Corporeal Metaphor in Revolutionary France, 1770–1800*. Translated by Charlotte Mandell. Stanford, CA: Stanford University Press, 1997.

de Baecque, Antoine. *Glory and Terror: Seven Deaths Under the French Revolution*. New York: Routledge, 2013.

de Beauvoir, Simone. 'Must We Burn Sade?' In *The Marquis de Sade: An Essay by Simone de Beauvoir*, 3–64. New York: Grove, 1953.

de Beauvoir, Simone. *The Second Sex*. New York: Vintage Books, 1989.

de Gobineau, Arthur. *Selected Political Writings*. Edited by Michael D. Biddiss. New edn. London: Jonathan Cape Ltd, 1971.

de Grazia, Victoria. *How Fascism Ruled Women: Italy, 1922–1945*. Berkeley and Oxford: University of California Press, 1992.

de Groot, Gertjan, and Marlou Schrover. 'Between Men and Machines: Women Workers in New Industries, 1870–1940'. *Social History* 20, no. 3 (October 1995): 279–96.

de Madariaga, Isabel. *Russia in the Age of Catherine the Great*. New Haven and London: Yale University Press, 1981.

de Montaigne, Michel. *Essays*. Translated by John Michael Cohen. New York and London: Penguin Books, 1958.

de Schryver, Antoon, and André Z. Meheus. 'Epidemiology of Sexually Transmitted Diseases: The Global Picture'. *Bulletin of the World Health Organization* 68, no. 5 (1990): 639–64.

de Vries, Jan. *European Urbanization, 1500–1800*. Cambridge: Harvard University Press, 1984.

Deak, Istvan. 'Latter-Day Knights: Officers' Honor and Duelling in the Austro-Hungarian Army'. *Österreichische Osthefte* 28, no. 3 (1986): 311–27.

Dean, Carolyn J. *The Frail Social Body: Pornography, Homosexuality, and Other Fantasies in Interwar France*. Berkeley: University of California Press, 2000.

Dean, Carolyn J. 'Lesbian Sexuality in Interwar France'. In *Connecting Spheres: Women in the Western World, 1500 to the Present*. 2nd edn. Edited by Marilyn J. Boxer and Jean H. Quataert, 289–94. Oxford and New York: Oxford University Press, 1999.

DeGroat, Judith. 'Working-Class Women and Republicanism in the French Revolution of 1848'. *History of European Ideas* 38, no. 3 (September 2012): 399–407.

Des Jardins, Julie. *Women and the Historical Enterprise in America: Gender, Race, and the Politics of Memory, 1880–1945*. Chapel Hill: University of North Carolina Press, 2003.

Desan, Suzanne. *The Family on Trial in Revolutionary France*. Berkeley: University of California Press, 2006.

Deslanes, Paul R. 'Exposing, Adorning, and Dressing the Body in the Modern Era'. In *The Routledge History of Sex and the Body: 1500 to the Present*. Edited by Sarah Toulalan and Kate Fisher, 179–203. New York: Routledge, 2013.

Desmond, Adrian J., and James Moore. *Darwin*. Reprint edn. London: Michael Joseph, 1991.

Dickinson, Edward Ross. *Sex, Freedom, and Power in Imperial Germany, 1880–1914*. New York: Cambridge University Press, 2014.

Dixon, Joy. *Gender, Politics, and Culture in Modern Europe*. Vancouver: Access Guided Independent Study, University of British Columbia, [n.d.].

Doan, Laura L. *Disturbing Practices: History, Sexuality, and Women's Experience of Modern War*. Chicago and London: University of Chicago Press, 2013.

Doan, Laura L. *Fashioning Sapphism: The Origins of a Modern English Lesbian Culture*. New York: Columbia University Press, 2001.

Doan, Laura. 'Passing Fashions: Reading Female Masculinities in the 1920s'. *Feminist Studies* 24, no. 3 (1998): 663–700.

Doidge, Norman. *The Brain That Changes Itself: Stories of Personal Triumph from the Frontiers of Brain Science*. London: Penguin Books, 2007.

Domansky, Elisabeth. 'Militarization and Reproduction in World War I Germany'. In *Society, Culture, and the State in Germany, 1870–1930*. Edited by Geoff Eley, 427–63. Ann Arbor, MI: University of Michigan Press, 1996.

Dose, Ralf. *Magnus Hirschfeld: Deutscher, Jude, Weltbürger*. Teetz: Hentrich & Hentrich, 2005.

Downing, Lisa, and Robert Gillett, eds. *Queer in Europe: Contemporary Case Studies*. Farnham, Surrey: Ashgate Publishing, 2011.

Downs, Laura Lee. *Writing Gender History*. 2nd edn. London and New York: Bloomsbury Academic, 2010.

Dreger, Alice Domurat. *Hermaphrodites and the Medical Invention of Sex*. Cambridge, MA: Harvard University Press, 1998.

Drucker, Donna J. *The Classification of Sex: Alfred Kinsey and the Organization of Knowledge*. Pittsburgh: University of Pittsburgh Press, 2014.

Duberman, Martin Bauml. 'Reclaiming the Gay Past'. *Reviews in American History* 16, no. 4 (1988): 515–25.

Duberman, Martin, Martha Vicinus, and George Chauncey Jr., eds. *Hidden From History: Reclaiming the Gay and Lesbian Past*. New York: Meridian, 1989.

Duchen, Claire. 'Crime and Punishment in Liberated France: The Case of Les Femmes Tondues'. In *When the War Was Over: Women, War and Peace in Europe, 1940–1956*. Edited by Irene Bandhauer-Schöffmann and Claire Duchen, 233–50. London and New York: Leicester University Press, 2000.

Duchen, Claire, and Irene Bandhauer-Schöffmann, eds. *When the War Was Over Women, War and Peace in Europe, 1940–1956*. London and New York: Leicester University Press, 2000.

Durkheim, Emile. 'The Conjugal Family'. In *Emile Durkheim on Institutional Analysis*. Edited by Mark Traugott, 229–39. Chicago: University of Chicago Press, 1994.

*Eastern Promises*. (2007). [Film] Dir. David Cronenburg, United States: Universal Studios.

*The Einstein of Sex* (2002). [Film] Dir. Rosa von Praunheim, United States: TLA Releasing.

Eley, Geoff. *Forging Democracy: The History of the Left in Europe, 1850–2000*. New York: Oxford University Press, 2002.

Ellis, John, and Michael Cox. *The World War I Databook: The Essential Facts and Figures for All the Combatants*. London: Aurum, 2001.

Elshtain, Jean Bethke. *Women and War*. Chicago: University Of Chicago Press, 1987.

Embacher, Helga. 'Unwelcome in Austria: Returnees and Concentration Camp Survivors'. In *When the War Was Over Women, War and Peace in Europe, 1940–1956*. Edited by Claire

Duchen and Irene Bandhauer-Schöffmann, 194–206. London and New York: Leicester University Press, 2000.

Engel, Barbara Alpern. *Breaking the Ties That Bound: The Politics of Marital Strife in Late Imperial Russia*. Ithaca, NY: Cornell University Press, 2011.

Engle, Eric Allen. 'Gay Rights in Russia? Russia's Ban on Gay Pride Parades and the General Principle of Proportionality in International Law'. *The Journal of Eurasian Law* 6, no. 2 (2013): 165–86.

Erickson, Amy Louise. *Women and Property in Early Modern England*. London and New York: Routledge, 1993.

Erskine, Fiona. '*The Origin of Species* and the Science of Female Inferiority'. In *Charles Darwin's the Origin of Species: New Interdisciplinary Essays*. Edited by David Amigoni and Jeff Wallace, 95–121. Manchester and New York: Manchester University Press, 1995.

Erwin, Edward, ed. *The Freud Encyclopedia: Theory, Therapy, and Culture*. New York: Routledge, 2001.

Esterson, Allen. 'Jeffrey Masson and Freud's Seduction Theory: A New Fable Based on Old Myths'. *History of the Human Sciences* 11, no. 1 (1998): 1–21.

*The European Foundation for the Improvement of Living and Working Conditions (Eurofund)*. http://eurofound.europa.eu, accessed 10 July 2015.

Evans-Pritchard, Ambrose, and Joan Clements. 'Fortuyn Killed 'to Protect Muslims''. *The Telegraph*, 28 March 2003. http://www.telegraph.co.uk/news/worldnews/europe/netherlands/1425944/Fortuyn-killed-to-protect-Muslims.html, accessed 10 July 2015.

Evans, Jennifer V. *Life Among the Ruins: Cityscape and Sexuality in Cold War Berlin*. Houndmills, Basingstoke and New York: Palgrave Macmillan, 2011.

Evans, Jennifer V., and Matt Cook, eds. *Queer Cities, Queer Cultures: Europe Since 1945*. London: Bloomsbury, 2014.

Evans, Richard J. *Comrades & Sisters: Feminism, Socialism & Pacifism in Europe, 1870–1945*. St. Martin's Press: New York, 1987.

Evans, Richard J. 'The Concept of Feminism: Notes for Practicing Historians'. In *German Women in the Eighteenth and Nineteenth Centuries*. Edited by Ruth-Ellen B. Joeres and Mary Jo Maynes. Bloomington: Indiana University Press, 1986.

Evans, Richard J. 'German Women and the Triumph of Hitler'. *The Journal of Modern History* 48, no. 1 (1976): 123–75.

Evans, Richard J. 'Prostitution, State, and Society in Imperial Germany'. *Past and Present* 70 (1976): 129.

'Event Invitation Wilhelm Kütz Foundation'. 29 October 2014. http://www.wks-sachsen.de/?p=1899, accessed 10 July 2015.

Faderman, Lillian. *Surpassing the Love of Men: Romantic Friendship and Love between Women from the Renaissance to the Present*. New York: William Morrow and Company, Inc., 1981.

Fahrmeir, Andreas. *Citizenship: The Rise and Fall of a Modern Concept*. New Haven and London: Yale University Press, 2007.

Faria, N. R. et al. 'The Early Spread and Epidemic Ignition of Hiv-1 in Human Populations'. *Science* 346, no. 6205 (2014): 56–61.

'Femen Activists Describe Their Alleged Ordeal in Belarus'. *Radio Free Europe/Radio Liberty*, 21 December 2011. http://www.rferl.org/media/video/24429634.html, accessed 10 July 2015.

Ferguson, Eliza Earle. *Gender and Justice: Violence, Intimacy and Community in Fin-de Siècle Paris*. Baltimore: Johns Hopkins University Press, 2010.

Fest, Joachim C. *The Face of the Third Reich: Portraits of the Nazi Leadership*. Harmondsworth: Penguin, 1972.

Firmin, Anténor. *The Equality of the Human Races*. Translated by Asselin Charles. Urbana: University of Illinois Press, 2002.

Fischer, Klaus P. *Nazi Germany: A New History*. New York: Continuum, 1995.

Fisher, Kate. *Birth Control, Sex and Marriage in Britain, 1918–1960*. Oxford and New York: Oxford University Press, 2008.

Fitzpatrick, Sheila. *The Cultural Front: Power and Culture in Revolutionary Russia*. Ithaca, NY: Cornell University Press, 1992.

'Forced Labor – Background'. *Forced Labor 1939–1945: Memory and History*, 7 May 2008. http://www.zwangsarbeit-archiv.de/en/zwangsarbeit/zwangsarbeit/zwangsarbeit-2/index.html, accessed 10 July 2015.

Forrest, Alan. 'Conscription as Ideology: Revolutionary France and the Nation in Arms'. In *The Comparative Study of Conscription in the Armed Forces*. Edited by Lars Mjøset and Stephen van Holde, 95–115. Bingley, UK: Emerald Group, 2002.

Foucault, Michel. *Abnormal: Lectures at the Collège De France, 1974–1975*. Edited by Valerio Marchetti and Antonella Salomoni. Translated by Graham Burchell. New York: Picador, 2004.

Foucault, Michel. *The Care of the Self*. Translated by Robert Hurley. New York: Vintage Books, 1988.

Foucault, Michel. *History of Sexuality. Vol. 1: An Introduction*. Reissue edn. New York: Vintage Books, 1990.

Foucault, Michel. 'Is There a History of Sexuality?' *History and Theory* 28, no. 3 (1989): 257–74.

Foucault, Michel. *Reforming Sex: The German Movement for Birth Control and Abortion Reform, 1920–1950*. Oxford: Oxford University Press, 1995.

Foucault, Michel. *The Use of Pleasure*. New York: Pantheon Books, 1985.

Frader, Laura L. 'Doing Capitalism's Work: Women in the Western European Industrial Economy'. In *Becoming Visible: Women in European History*. Edited by Renate Bridenthal, Susan Mosher Stuard and Merry E. Wiesner, 3rd edn., 295–335. Boston: Houghton Mifflin, 1998.

Frader, Laura L. 'Labor History after the Gender Turn: Transatlantic Cross Currents and Research Agendas'. *International Labor and Working-Class History* 63 (April 2003): 21–31.

Fraisse, Geneviève. *Reason's Muse: Sexual Difference and the Birth of Democracy*. Translated by Jane Marie Todd. Chicago: University Of Chicago Press, 1994.

Frantzen, Allen J. *Bloody Good: Chivalry, Sacrifice, and the Great War*. Chicago: University of Chicago Press, 2004.

Frederiksen, Bodil Folke. 'Jomo Kenyatta, Marie Bonaparte and Bronislaw Malinowski on Clitoridectomy and Female Sexuality'. In *The History of Sexuality in Europe: A Sourcebook and Reader*. Edited by Anna Clark, 236–37. New York: Routledge, 2011.

Freud, Sigmund. *Civilization and Its Discontents*. Reprint edn. New York: W. W. Norton & Company, 2010.

Freud, Sigmund. *The Standard Edition of the Complete Psychological Works of Sigmund Freud*. Edited by James Strachey, 24 vols. London: Hogarth Press, 1961.

Frevert, Ute. *Men of Honour: A Social and Cultural History of the Duel*. Cambridge, England: Polity Press, 1995.

Frevert, Ute. 'The Taming of the Nobel Ruffian: Male Violence and Dueling in Early Modern and Modern Germany'. In *Men and Violence: Gender, Honor, and Rituals in Modern Europe and America*. Edited by Pieter Spierenburg, 37–63. Columbus: Ohio State University Press, 1998.

Friedman, Rebecca. *Masculinity, Autocracy and the Russian University, 1804–1863*. Houndmills, Basingstoke and New York: Palgrave Macmillan, 2005.

Friedrich, O. *Before the Deluge: A Portrait of Berlin in the 1920s*. New York: HarperPerennial, 1995.

Friedrichs, Christopher R. 'The City: The Early Modern Period'. In *Encyclopedia of European Social History from 1350–2000*. Edited by Peter N. Stearns, 2: 249–62. New York: Charles Scribner's Sons, 2001.

# Works Cited

Frykman, Jonas, and Orvar Lofgren. *Culture Builders: A Historical Anthropology of Middle-Class Life*. Translated by John Crozier. New Brunswick: Rutgers University Press 1987.

Fussell, Paul. *The Great War and Modern Memory*. New York: Oxford University Press, 1975.

Galton, Francis. *Inquiries Into Human Faculty and Its Development*. London: Macmillan and Co., 1883.

Garton, Stephen. *Histories of Sexuality*. New York: Routledge, 2004.

Gatrell, Peter. *A Whole Empire Walking: Refugees in Russia during World War I*. Bloomington: Indiana University Press, 1999.

Gay, Peter. 'Mensur–the Cherished Scar'. In *The Bourgeois Experience, Victoria to Freud, Vol. III: The Cultivation of Hatred*, 9–33. New York and London: W.W. Norton & Company, 1993.

Gebreyes, Rahel. 'This German Anti-Islamic Group Is Using The Charlie Hebdo Attack To Its Advantage'. *The Huffington Post*, 14 January 2015. http://www.huffingtonpost.com/2015/01/14/germany-pegida-paris-terror_n_6463226.html, accessed 10 July 2015.

Gibbon, Edward. *The History of the Decline and Fall of the Roman Empire*. Edited by David Womersley. London and New York: Penguin, 1994.

Gibson, Craig. *Behind the Front: British Soldiers and French Civilians, 1914–1918*. Cambridge and New York: Cambridge University Press, 2014.

Gibson, Mary. *Prostitution and the State in Italy, 1860–1915*. 2nd edn. Columbus: Ohio State University Press, 2000.

Gilbert, Sandra M. 'Soldier's Heart: Literary Men, Literary Women, and the Great War'. In *Behind the Lines: Gender and the Two World Wars*. Edited by Margaret R. Higonnet, Jane Jenson, Sonya Michel and Margaret C. Weitz, 197–226. New Haven: Yale University Press, 1987.

Gilfoyle, Timothy J. 'Prostitutes in History: From Parables of Pornography to Metaphors of Modernity'. *The American Historical Review* 104, no. 1 (February 1999): 117–41.

Gillis, John R. *For Better, for Worse: British Marriages, 1600 to the Present*. New York: Oxford University Press, 1985.

Gilman, Sander. *Difference and Pathology: Stereotypes of Sexuality, Race and Madness*. Ithaca, NY: Cornell University Press, 1985.

Glenny, Misha. *The Balkans: Nationalism, War, and the Great Powers, 1804–1999*. New York: Penguin Books, 1999.

Godineau, Dominique. *The Women of Paris and Their French Revolution*. Translated by Katherine Streip. Berkeley: University of California Press, 1998.

Goldenberg, Myrna. 'Sex-Based Violence and the Politics and Ethics of Survival'. In *Different Horrors, Same Hell: Gender and the Holocaust*. Edited by Myrna Goldenberg and Amy H. Shapiro, 112–16. Seattle: University of Washington Press, 2013.

Goldman, Wendy Z. *Women, the State, and Revolution: Soviet Family Policy and Social Life, 1917–1936*. Cambridge, MA: Cambridge University Press, 1993.

Goldstein, Jan. 'Foucault Among the Sociologists: The "Disciplines" and the History of the Professions'. *History and Theory* 23, no. 2 (1984): 170–92.

Goldstein, Joshua S. *War and Gender: How Gender Shapes the War System and Vice Versa*. Cambridge: Cambridge University Press, 2001.

Goode, William J. *The Family*. 2nd revised edn. Englewood Cliffs, NJ: Prentice Hall, 1982.

Goodman, Dena. *The Republic of Letters: A Cultural History of the French Enlightenment*. 1st New edn. Ithaca, NY: Cornell University Press, 1996.

Gordon, Daniel. *Citizens without Sovereignty: Equality and Sociability in French Thought, 1670–1789*. Princeton, NJ: Princeton University Press, 1994.

Gordon, Daniel, David A. Bell and Sarah Maza. 'Forum: The Public Sphere in the Eighteenth Century'. *French Historical Studies* 17, no. 4 (1992): 882–956.

Gorsuch, Anne E. '"A Woman Is Not a Man": The Culture of Gender and Generation in Soviet Russia, 1921–1928'. *Slavic Review* 55, no. 3 (1996): 636–60.

Gould, Jenny. 'Women's Military Services in First World War Britain'. In *Behind the Lines: Gender and the Two World Wars*. Edited by Margaret R. Higonnet, Sonya Michel, Jane Jenson and Margaret C. Weitz, 114–25. New Haven, CT and London: Yale University Press, 1987.

Grayzel, Susan R. *Women's Identities at War: Gender, Motherhood, and Politics in Britain and France during the First World War*. Chapel Hill: University of North Carolina Press, 1999.

Gross, Jan T. *Neighbors: The Destruction of the Jewish Community in Jedwabne, Poland*. Princeton, NJ: Princeton University Press, 2001.

Gross, Raphael. '"Loyalty" in National Socialism: A Contribution to the Moral History of the National Socialist Period'. *History of European Ideas* 33, no. 4 (2007): 488–503.

Grossmann, Atina. 'The "Big Rape": Sex and Sexual Violence, War, and Occupation in German Post-World War II Memory and Imagination'. In *Gender and the Long Postwar: The United States and the Two Germanys, 1945–1989*. Edited by Karen Hagemann and Sonya Michel, 31–50. Washington, DC, and Baltimore: Woodrow Wilson Center Press and Johns Hopkins University Press, 2014.

Grossmann, Atina. 'Girlkultur or Thoroughly Rationalized Female: A New Woman in Weimar Germany?' In *Women in Culture and Politics: A Century of Change*. Edited by Judith Friedländer, Blanche Cook, Alice Kessler-Harris and Carroll Smith-Rosenberg, 62–80. Bloomington: Indiana University Press, 1986.

Grossmann, Atina. 'A Question of Silence: The Rape of German Women by Occupation Soldiers'. In *West Germany Under Construction: Politics, Society, and Culture in the Adenauer Era*. Edited by Robert G. Moeller, 33–52. Ann Arbor: University of Michigan Press, 1997.

Grunberger, Richard. *A Social History of the Third Reich*. Harmondsworth: Penguin, 1974.

Guinnane, Timothy. 'Coming of Age in Rural Ireland at the Turn of the Twentieth Century'. *Continuity and Change* 5, no. 3 (1990): 443–72.

Gullace, Nicoletta F. *The Blood of Our Sons: Men, Women, and the Renegotiation of British Citizenship During the Great War*. New York: Palgrave Macmillan, 2004.

Gutting, Gary. 'Michel Foucault'. In *The Stanford Encyclopedia of Philosophy*. Edited by Edward N. Zalta, 2014. http://plato.stanford.edu/archives/win2014/entries/foucault/.

Habermas, Jürgen. *The Structural Transformation of the Public Sphere: An Inquiry into a Category of Bourgeois Society*. Cambridge: The MIT Press, 1991.

Hagemann, Karen. 'Female Patriots: Women, War and the Nation in the Period of the Prussian-German Anti-Napoleonic Wars'. *Gender & History* 16, no. 2 (2004): 397–424.

Hall, Catherine. 'The Early Formation of Victorian Domestic Ideology'. In *Gender and History in Western Europe*. Edited by Robert Shoemaker and Mary Vincent, 181–96. London: Arnold, 1998.

Hall, Catherine. 'Of Gender and Empire: Reflections on the Nineteenth Century'. In *Gender and Empire*. Edited by Philippa Levine, 46–76. Oxford and New York: Oxford University Press, 2007.

Halperin, David M. *How to Do the History of Homosexuality*. Chicago: University of Chicago Press, 2004.

Hamers, Françoise F., and Angela M. Downs. 'HIV in Central and Eastern Europe'. *The Lancet* 361, no. 9362 (March 2003): 1035–44.

Harper, Marjory. 'British Migration and the Peopling of the Empire'. In *The Oxford History of the British Empire: Volume III: The Nineteenth Century*. Edited by Andrew Porter, 75–87. Oxford and New York: Oxford University Press, 1999.

Harsch, Donna. *Revenge of the Domestic: Women, the Family, and Communism in the German Democratic Republic*. Princeton and Oxford: Princeton University Press, 2007.

Harsin, Jill. *Policing Prostitution in Nineteenth Century Paris*. Princeton, NJ: Princeton University Press, 1985.

# Works Cited

Harvey, A. D. 'Homosexuality and the British Army During the First World War'. *Journal of the Society for Army Historical Research* 79, no. 320 (2001): 313–19.

Harvey, Elizabeth. *Women and the Nazi East: Agents and Witnesses of Germanization*. New Haven, CT: Yale University Press, 2003.

Harvey, Karen, and Alexandra Shepard. 'What Have Historians Done with Masculinity? Reflections on Five Centuries of British History, circa 1500–1950'. *Journal of British Studies* 44, no. 2 (April 2005): 274–80.

Hause, Stephen C., and Anne R. Kenney. 'The Limits of Suffragist Behavior: Legalism and Militancy in France, 1876–1922'. *American Historical Review* 86, no. 4 (1981): 781–806.

Hausen, Karin. 'Patriarchat: Vom Nutzen Und Nachteil Eines Konzepts Für Frauengeschichte Und Frauenpolitik'. *Journal Für Geschichte* 5 (1986): 12–58.

Healey, Dan. *Homosexual Desire in Revolutionary Russia: The Regulation of Sexual and Gender Dissent*. Chicago: University of Chicago Press, 2001.

Healy, Maureen. *Vienna and the Fall of the Habsburg Empire: Total War and Everyday Life in World War I*. Cambridge and New York: Cambridge University Press, 2004.

Hedgepeth, Sonja M., and Rochelle G. Saidel, eds. *Sexual Violence Against Jewish Women During the Holocaust*. Lebanon: University Press of New England, 2010.

Heineman, Elizabeth D. *What Difference Does a Husband Make? Women and Marital Status in Nazi and Postwar Germany*. Berkeley: University of California Press, 1999.

Herrn, Rainer. 'Magnus Hirschfeld (1868–1935)'. In *Personenlexikon der Sexualforschung*. Edited by Volkmar Sigusch and Günter Grau, 284–94. Frankfurt a. M.: Campus, 2009.

Herrn, Rainer. *Schnittmuster des Geschlechts: Transvestitismus und Transsexualität in der frühen Sexualwissenschaft*. Giessen: Psychosozial-Verlag, 2005.

Herrup, Cynthia B. *A House in Gross Disorder: Sex, Law, and the 2nd Earl of Castlehaven*. New York: Oxford University Press, 2001.

Herzer, Manfred. *Magnus Hirschfeld: Leben und Werk eines jüdischen, schwulen und sozialistischen Sexologen*. Hamburg: MännerschwarmSkript-Verlag, 2001.

Herzog, Dagmar. '"Pleasure, Sex and Politics Belong Together": Post-Holocaust Memory and the Sexual Revolution in West Germany'. *Critical Inquiry* 24, no. 2 (1998): 393–444.

Herzog, Dagmar. *Sex after Fascism: Memory and Morality in Twentieth-Century Germany*. Princeton, NJ: Princeton University Press, 2005.

Herzog, Dagmar. *Sexuality in Europe: A Twentieth-Century History*. Cambridge, UK, and New York: Cambridge University Press, 2011.

Herzog, Dagmar. 'Syncopated Sex: Transforming European Sexual Cultures'. *American Historical Review* 114, no. 5 (2009): 1287–1308.

Hetherington, Philippa Leslie. 'Victims of the Social Temperament: Migration and the Traffic in Women from Late Imperial Russia and the Soviet Union, 1870–1935'. Ph.D. dissertation, Harvard University, 2014.

Heuer, Jennifer Ngaire. *The Family and the Nation: Gender and Citizenship in Revolutionary France, 1789–1830*. Ithaca, NY and London: Cornell University Press, 2005.

Hildebrand, Achim. 'Routes to Decriminalization: A Comparative Analysis of the Legalization of Same-Sex Sexual Acts'. *Sexualities* 17, no. 1/2 (2014): 230–53.

Hirschfeld, Magnus. *Berlins Drittes Geschlecht*. Berlin: Rosa Winkel, 1991.

Hirschfeld, Magnus. *Geschlechtskunde*. Vol. 4. Bilderteil. Stuttgart: Julius Puttmann, 1930.

Hitler, Adolf. 'Hitler's Speech to the National Socialist Women's League, 8 September 1934'. In *Nazism 1919–1945. Volume 2: State, Economy and Society 1933–39: A Documentary Reader*. Edited by Jeremy Noakes and Geoffrey Pridham, 255–6. Exeter: University of Exeter Press, 2000.

Hobsbawm, E. J. *The Age of Capital 1848–1875*. New York: Charles Scribner's Sons, 1975.

Hocquenghem, Guy. *Homosexual Desire*. Translated by Daniella Dangoor. Durham, NC, and London: Duke University Press, 1993.

Hodges, Andrew. *Alan Turing: The Enigma.* Princeton and Oxford: Princeton University Press, 2014.

Hofer, Hans-Georg. 'Wenn Männer altern. Ein Projekt zur Geschichte der "männlichen Wechseljahre"'. *L'Homme. Europäische Zeitschrift für Feministische Geschichtswissenschaft* 17, no. 1 (2006): 101–8.

Hoffmann, David L. 'Mothers in the Motherland: Stalinist Pronatalism in Its Pan-European Context'. *Journal of Social History* 34, no. 1 (2000): 35–54.

Hoffmann, David L., and Annette F. Timm. 'Utopian Biopolitics: Reproductive Policies, Gender Roles, and Sexuality in Nazi Germany and the Soviet Union'. In *Beyond Totalitarianism: Stalinism and Nazism Compared.* Edited by Michael Geyer and Sheila Fitzpatrick, 87–129. New York: Cambridge University Press, 2009.

Hoffmann, Stefan-Ludwig. 'Civility, Male Friendship, and Masonic Sociability in Nineteenth-Century Germany'. *Gender & History* 13, no. 2 (August 2001): 224–48.

Höhn, Maria. *GIs and Fräuleins the German-American Encounter in 1950s West Germany.* Chapel Hill: University of North Carolina Press, 2002.

Holland, Kenneth. 'The European Labor Service'. *The ANNALS of the American Academy of Political and Social Science* 194, no. 1 (November 1937): 152–64.

Honeycutt, Karen. 'Clara Zetkin: A Socialist Approach to the Problem of Women's Oppression'. *Signs* 3, no. 3/4 (1976): 131–44.

Hopkin, David M. 'Sons and Lovers: Popular Images of the Conscript, 1798–1870'. *Modern & Contemporary France* 9, no. 1 (February 2001): 19–36.

Horn, David G. *Social Bodies: Science, Reproduction and Italian Modernity.* Princeton Studies in Culture/Power/History. Princeton, NJ: Princeton University Press, 1994.

Horne, John, and Alan Kramer. *German Atrocities, 1914: A History of Denial.* New Haven, CT: Yale University Press, 2001.

Houlbrook, Matt. 'Toward a Historical Geography of Sexuality'. *Journal of Urban History* 27, no. 4 (May 2001): 497–504.

Hufton, Olwen H. *Poor of Eighteenth-Century France, 1750–89.* New edn. Oxford England: Oxford University Press, 1974.

Hufton, Olwen H. *Women and the Limits of Citizenship in the French Revolution.* Toronto: University of Toronto Press, 1992.

Hughes, Donna M. 'The "Natasha" Trade: The Transnational Shadow Market of Trafficking in Women'. *Journal of International Affairs* 53, no. 2 (2000): 625–51.

Hugo, Victor. *Les Misérables.* Translated by Norman Denny. Reprint edn. London: Penguin Classics, 1982.

Hull, Isabel V. *Absolute Destruction: Military Culture and the Practices of War in Imperial Germany.* Ithaca, NY: Cornell University Press, 2005.

Hull, Isabel V. *Sexuality, State, and Civil Society in Germany, 1700–1815.* Ithaca, NY: Cornell University Press, 1996.

Hülsberg, Werner. *The German Greens: A Social and Political Profile.* London and New York: Verso, 1988.

Hunt, Karen. 'The Politics of Food and Women's Neighborhood Activism in First World War Britain'. *International Labor and Working Class History* 77, no. 1 (2010): 8–26.

Hunt, Lynn. *The Family Romance of the French Revolution.* Berkeley and Los Angeles: University of California Press, 1992.

Hunt, Lynn. 'Foucault's Subject in the History of Sexuality'. In *Discourses of Sexuality: From Aristotle to Aids.* Edited by Domna C. Stanton, 78–93. Ann Arbor: University of Michigan Press, 1992.

Hunt, Nancy Rose. 'Le Bébé En Brousse: European Women, African Birth Spacing, and Colonial Intervention in Breast Feeding in the Belgian Congo'. In *Tensions of Empire: Colonial Cultures in a Bourgeois World*. Edited by Frederick Cooper and Ann Laura Stoler, 287–321. Berkeley: University of California Press, 1997.

Hunt, Margaret R. *The Middling Sort: Commerce, Gender, and the Family in England, 1680–1780*. Berkeley: University of California Press, 1996.

Hunt, Margaret R. *Women in Eighteenth-Century Europe*. Harlow: Pearson Longman, 2010.

Hurd, Madeleine. 'Class, Masculinity, Manners, and Mores: Public Space and Public Sphere in Nineteenth-Century Europe'. *Social Science History* 24, no. 1 (2000): 75–110.

Huss, Marie-Monique. 'Pronatalism in the Inter-War Period in France'. *Journal of Contemporary History* 25, no. 1 (1990): 39–68.

Huston, Nancy. 'Erotic Literature in Postwar France'. *Raritan* 12, no. 1 (1992): 29–46.

Hutsol, Anna. 'Femen Pod Posol'stvom Irana'. https://www.youtube.com/watch?v=87plsqkW1SE, accessed 10 July 2015.

Hutton, Marcelline J. *Russian and West European Women, 1860–1939: Dreams, Struggles, and Nightmares*. Lanham, MD: Rowman & Littlefield, 2001.

Ihme, Loretta. 'Victims, Saviors: On the Discursive Constructions of Trafficking in Women'. In *Violence and Gender in the Globalized World: The Intimate and the Extimate*. Edited by Sanja Bahun and V. G. Julie Rajan, 157–74. Aldershot: Ashgate Publishing, 2008.

*The Imitation Game* (2014). [Film] Dir. Morten Tyldum, United Kingdom: StudioCanal.

Ipsen, Carl. *Dictating Demography: The Problem of Population in Fascist Italy*. Cambridge and New York: Cambridge University Press, 1996.

James, William. 'The Moral Equivalent of War'. In *The Moral Equivalent of War and Other Essays*. Edited by John K. Roth, 3–16. New York: Harper and Row, 1971.

Jarausch, Konrad H. 'Students, Sex and Politics in Imperial Germany'. *Journal of Contemporary History* 17 (1982): 285–303.

Jasanoff, Maya. *Edge of Empire: Lives, Culture, and Conquest in the East, 1750–1850*. New York: Alfred A. Knopf, 2005.

Jolluck, Katherine R. *Exile and Identity: Polish Women in the Soviet Union During World War II*. Pittsburgh, PA: University of Pittsburgh Press, 2002.

Jordanova, Ludmilla. *Sexual Visions: Images of Gender in Science and Medicine between the Eighteenth and Twentieth Centuries*. Madison: University of Wisconsin Press, 1989.

Kara, Siddharth. *Sex Trafficking: Inside the Business of Modern Slavery*. New York: Columbia University Press, 2009.

Kater, Michael H. *Hitler Youth*. Cambridge, MA: Harvard University Press, 2004.

Kates, Gary. *The Cercle Social, the Girondins, and the French Revolution*. Princeton, NJ: Princeton University Press, 1985.

Keane, John. *Civil Society and the State: New European Perspectives*. London and New York: Verso, 1988.

Kelly, James. *That Damn'd Thing Called 'Honour': Duelling in Ireland, 1570–1860*. Cork: Cork University Press, 1995.

Kent, Susan Kingsley. *Gender and Power in Britain, 1640–1990*. New York: Routledge, 1999.

Kent, Susan Kingsley. *Making Peace: The Reconstruction of Gender in Interwar Britain*. Princeton, NJ: Princeton University Press, 1993.

Kent, Susan Kingsley. *Sex and Suffrage in Britain 1860–1914*. Princeton, NJ: Princeton University Press, 1987.

Kerber, Linda K. *Toward an Intellectual History of Women: Essays by Linda K. Kerber*. Chapel Hill: University of North Carolina Press, 2002.

Kerber, Linda K. *Women of the Republic: Intellect and Ideology in Revolutionary America*. Chapel Hill: University of North Carolina Press, 1980.

Kessel, Martina. 'The "Whole Man": The Longing for a Masculine World in Nineteenth–Century Germany'. *Gender & History* 15, no. 1 (April 2003): 1–31.

Kestnbaum, Meyer. 'Citizenship and Compulsory Military Service: The Revolutionary Origins of Conscription in the United States'. *Armed Forces & Society* 27, no. 1 (October 2000): 7–36.

Kevles, Daniel J. *In the Name of Eugenics: Genetics and the Uses of Human Heredity*. New York: Knopf, 1985.

Khaleeli, Homa. 'The Nude Radicals: Feminism Ukrainian Style'. *The Guardian*, 15 April 2011.

Kingston, Sarah, and Terry Thomas. 'The Police, Sex Work, and Section 14 of the Policing and Crime Act 2009'. *The Howard Journal* 53, no. 3 (2014): 255–69.

Kipling, Rudyard. *Rudyard Kipling: Complete Verse: Definitive Edition*. Garden City, NY: Doubleday and Co., 1946.

Kligman, G., and S. Limoncelli. 'Trafficking Women After Socialism: To, Through, and from Eastern Europe'. *Social Politics: International Studies in Gender, State & Society* 12, no. 1 (Spring 2005): 118–40.

Kocka, Jürgen. 'Problems of Working-Class Formation in Germany'. In *Working-Class Formation: Nineteenth-Century Patterns in Western Europe and the United States*. Edited by Ira Katznelson and Aristide R. Zolberg, 279–351. Princeton, NJ: Princeton University Press, 1986.

Komlos, John. 'Stature and Nutrition in the Habsburg Monarchy: The Standard of Living and Economic Development in the Eighteenth Century'. *The American Historical Review* 90, no. 5 (1986): 1149–61.

Konrad, Helga. 'Trafficking in Human Beings - the Ugly Face of Europe'. *Helsinki Monitor* 13, no. 3 (July 2002): 260–71.

Koonz, Claudia. *Mothers in the Fatherland: Women, the Family, and Nazi Politics*. New York: St. Martin's Press, 1987.

Koonz, Claudia. 'A Tributary and a Mainstream: Gender, Public Memory, and Historiography of Nazi Germany'. In *Gendering Modern German History: Rewriting Historiography*. Edited by Karen Hagemann and Jean H. Quataert, 147–68. New York and Oxford: Berghahn Books, 2007.

Koven, Seth. *Slumming: Sexual and Social Politics in Victorian London*. Princeton: Princeton University Press, 2004.

Krafft-Ebing, Richard von. *Psychopathia Sexualis, with Especial Reference to Contrary Sexual Instinct*. London: Staples Press, 1965.

Kramer, Steven Philip. *The Other Population Crisis: What Governments Can Do About Falling Birth Rates*. Washington, DC, and Baltimore: Woodrow Wilson Center Press, 2013.

'The Krasnals Contra Femen/Diversity Parade'. n.d. http://thekrasnals.blogspot.com/2012/06/krasnals-contra-femen-diversity-parade.html, accessed 10 July 2015.

Kruntorad, Paul. 'Krafft-Ebing'. In *Psycopathia Sexualis*. Edited by Richard von Krafft-Ebing, 7–13. Munich: Matthes und Seitz Verlag, 1984.

Kühne, Thomas. 'Comradeship: Gender Confusion and Gender Order in the German Military, 1918–1945'. In *Home/Front: The Military, War, and Gender in Twentieth-Century Germany*. Edited by Karen Hagemann and Stefanie Schüler-Springorum, 233–54. Oxford: Berg Publishers, 2002.

Kühne, Thomas. *Kameradschaft: Die Soldaten des Nationalsozialistischen Krieges und das 20. Jahrhundert*. Göttingen: Vandenhoeck & Ruprecht, 2006.

Kulick, Don. 'Four Hundred Thousand Swedish Perverts'. *GLQ: A Journal of Lesbian and Gay Studies* 11, no. 2 (2005): 205–35.

Kuper, Adam. 'Incest, Cousin Marriage, and the Origin of the Human Sciences in Nineteenth-Century England'. *Past & Present* 174, no. 1 (2002): 158–83.

Landes, David S. *The Unbound Prometheus: Technological Change and Industrial Development in Western Europe from 1750 to Present*. 2nd edn. Cambridge: Cambridge University Press, 1969.

Landes, Joan B. *Visualizing the Nation: Gender, Representation, and Revolution in Eighteenth-Century France*. Ithaca, NY: Cornell University Press, 2001.

Landes, Joan B. *Women in the Public Sphere in the Age of the French Revolution*. Ithaca, NY and London: Cornell University Press, 1988.

Lanser, Susan S. *The Sexuality of History: Modernity and the Sapphic, 1565–1830*. Chicago and London: University Of Chicago Press, 2014.

Laqueur, Thomas. *Making Sex: Body and Gender from the Greeks to Freud*. Cambridge, MA, and London: Harvard University Press, 1990.

Laqueur, Thomas. 'Orgasm, Generation, and the Politics of Reproductive Biology'. *Representations*, no. 14 (1986): 1–41.

Laqueur, Thomas W. 'Sex in the Flesh'. *Isis; an International Review Devoted to the History of Science and Its Cultural Influences* 94, no. 2 (June 2003): 300–6.

Larkin, Philip. 'Annus Mirabilis'. *Poetry Connection*, 1967. http://www.poetryconnection.net/poets/Philip_Larkin/4761, accessed 10 July 2015.

Larkin, Philip. *The Complete Poems of Philip Larkin*. Edited by Archie Burnett. London: Faber & Faber, 2012.

Lasch, Christopher. 'The Family and History'. *The New York Review of Books*, 13 November 1975.

Layton, Susan. *Russian Literature and Empire: Conquest of the Caucasus from Pushkin to Tolstoy*. Cambridge and New York: Cambridge University Press, 1994.

Leck, Ralph M. 'Conservative Empowerment and the Gender of Nazism: Paradigms of Power and Complicity in German Women's History'. *Journal of Women's History* 12, no. 2 (2000): 147–69.

Lee, Robert. 'Demography, Urbanization, and Migration'. In *A Companion to Nineteenth-Century Europe: 1789–1914*. Edited by Stefan Berger, 56–69. Malden, MA: Wiley-Blackwell, 2006.

Lefebvre, Georges. *The French Revolution*. Translated by Elizabeth M. Evanson. New York: Columbia University Press, 1962.

Lefebvre, Georges. *The Great Fear of 1789: Rural Panic in Revolutionary France*. Translated by John Albert White. New York: Schocken Books, 1973.

Lefort, Claude. *The Political Forms of Modern Society: Bureaucracy, Democracy, Totalitarianism*. Cambridge: Polity, 1986.

LeGates, Marlene. *In Their Time: A History of Feminism in Western Society*. New York and Abingdon: Routledge, 2001.

Lemire, Beverly. *The Business of Everyday Life: Gender, Practice and Social Politics in England, c.1600–1900*. Manchester: Manchester University Press, 2006.

Lentin, Ronit. '"A Howl Unheard": Women Shoah Survivors Dis-Placed and Re-Silenced'. In *When the War Was Over Women, War and Peace in Europe, 1940–1956*. Edited by Claire Duchen and Irene Bandhauer-Schöffmann, 179–93. London and New York: Leicester University Press, 2000.

Lepore, Jill. *The Secret History of Wonder Woman*. New York: Knopf, 2014.

Lermontov, Mikhail. *A Hero of Our Time*. Translated by Vladimir Nabokov and Dmitri Nabokov. Ann Arbor, MI: Ardis, 1988.

Levine, David. 'The Population of Europe: Early Modern Demographic Patterns'. In *Encyclopedia of European Social History*. Edited by Peter N. Stearns, vol. 2. New York: Charles Scribner's Sons, 2001.

Levine, Philippa. *Prostitution, Race and Politics: Policing Venereal Disease in the British Empire*. New York: Routledge, 2003.

Levine, Philippa. 'Sexuality, Gender and Empire'. In *Gender and Empire*. Edited by Philippa Levine, 134–55. Oxford and New York: Oxford University Press, 2004.

Levy, Darline Gay, and Harriet B. Applewhite. 'A Political Revolution for Women? The Case of Paris'. In *Becoming Visible: Women in European History*. Edited by Renate Bridenthal, Susan Mosher Stuard and Merry E. Wiesner, 3rd edn., 265–92. Boston: Houghton Mifflin, 1998.

Levy, Darlene Gay, Harriet B. Applewhite, and Mary Durham Johnson. *Women in Revolutionary Paris, 1789–1795: Selected Documents.* Urbana: University of Illinois Press, 1979.

Levy, J., and P. Jakobsson. 'Sweden's Abolitionist Discourse and Law: Effects on the Dynamics of Swedish Sex Work and on the Lives of Sweden's Sex Workers'. *Criminology and Criminal Justice* 14, no. 5 (2014): 593–607.

Lewis, Jane. 'The Working-Class Wife and Mother and State Intervention 1870–1940'. In *Labour and Love: Women's Experience of Home and Family 1850–1940.* Edited by Jane Lewis, 99–122. London and New York: Basil Blackwell, 1986.

Lewis, Valerie A., and Ridhi Kashyap. 'Are Muslims a Distinctive Minority? An Empirical Analysis of Religiosity, Social Attitudes, and Islam'. *Journal for the Scientific Study of Religion* 52, no. 3 (2013): 617–26.

Lieven, D. C. B. *Russia and the Origins of the First World War.* New York: St. Martin's Press, 1983.

Linton, Marisa. *Choosing Terror: Virtue, Friendship, and Authenticity in the French Revolution.* Oxford and New York: Oxford University Press, 2013.

Linton, Marisa. 'Robespierre and the Terror'. *History Today* 56, no. 8 (August 2006): 23–29.

Liu, Tessie P. 'What Price a Weaver's Dignity? Gender Inequality and the Survival of Home-Based Production in Industrial France'. In *Gender and Class in Modern Europe.* Edited by Laura L. Frader and Sonya O. Rose, 57–76. Ithaca, NY and London: Cornell University Press, 1996.

Loudon, Irvine. *The Tragedy of Childbed Fever.* Oxford and New York: Oxford University Press, 2000.

Lucas, Colin. 'The Theory and Practice of Denunciation in the French Revolution'. *Journal of Modern History* 68, no. 4 (December 1996): 768–85.

Lukas, Richard C. *Did the Children Cry? Hitler's War Against Jewish and Polish Children, 1939–1945.* New York: Hippocrene Books, 1994.

Lutz, Rolland Ray. 'The Burschenschaft: Reformist Movement or Conformist Movement?' *Consortium on Revolutionary Europe 1750–1850* 19, part 1 (1989): 357–77.

Maerchik, Mariia and Ol'ga Plakhotnik. '"Femen" Na Trope Protesta'. *Zerkalo nedeli*, 30 December 2010.

Mahood, Linda. *The Magdalones. Prostitution in the Nineteenth Century.* New York: Routledge, 1990.

Mailänder, Elissa. *Female SS Guards and Workaday Violence: The Majdanek Concentration Camp, 1942–1944.* Translated by Patricia Szobar. East Lansing: Michigan State University Press, 2015.

Mailänder Koslov, Elissa. *Gewalt im Dienstalltag: die SS-Aufseherinnen des Konzentrations- und Vernichtungslagers Majdanek, 1942–1944.* Hamburg: Hamburger Edition, 2009.

Mak, Geertje. 'Conflicting Heterosexualities. Hermaphroditism and the Emergence of Surgery Around 1900'. *Journal of the History of Sexuality* 24, no. 3 (2015): 402–27.

Mak, Geertje. *Doubting Sex: Inscriptions, Bodies and Selves in Nineteenth-Century Hermaphrodite Case Histories.* Manchester and New York: Manchester University Press, 2013.

Mak, Geertje and Mirjam Hausmann. '"Passing Women" in the Consulting Room of Magnus Hirschfeld. On Why the Term "Transvestite" Was Not Employed for Cross-Dressing Women'. *Österreichische Zeitschrift für Geschichtswissenschaften* 9, no. 3 (1998): 384–99.

Makdisi, Saree. *Romantic Imperialism: Universal Empire and the Culture of Modernity.* Cambridge: Cambridge University Press, 1998.

Makepeace, Clare. 'Male Heterosexuality and Prostitution during the Great War: British Soldiers' Encounters with Maisons Tolérées'. *Cultural and Social History* 9, no. 1 (2012): 65–83.

Mani, Lata. *Contentious Traditions: The Debate on Sati in Colonial India.* Berkeley: University of California Press, 1998.

Mann, Michael. *Fascists.* Cambridge and New York: Cambridge University Press, 2004.

## Works Cited

Mann, Thomas. 'Freud and the Future'. In *Essays of Three Decades*, 411–28. New York: Random House Inc, 1947.

Marcuse, Herbert. 'The New German Mentality'. In *Technology, War and Fascism: Collected Papers of Herbert Marcuse*. Edited by Douglas Kellner, 1:139–90. London: Routledge, 1998.

Marcuse, Herbert. *One-Dimensional Man: Studies in the Ideology of Advanced Industrial Society*. London: Routledge & Kegan Paul Ltd., 1964.

Mark, James. 'Remembering Rape: Divided Social Memory and the Red Army in Hungary 1944–1945'. *Past & Present* 188, no. 1 (2005): 133–61.

Marrese, Michelle Lamarche. *A Woman's Kingdom: Noblewomen and the Control of Property in Russia, 1700–1861*. Ithaca, NY and London: Cornell University Press, 2002.

Martin, Terry. 'Modernization or Neo-Traditionalism? Ascribed Nationality and Soviet Primordialism'. In *Stalinism: New Directions*. Edited by Sheila Fitzpatrick, 348–67. London and New York: Routledge, 1999.

Martsenyuk, Tamara. 'The State of the LGBT Community and Homophobia in Ukraine'. *Problems of Post-Communism* 59, no. 2 (2012): 51–62.

Marwick, Arthur. *The Sixties: Cultural Revolution in Britain, France, Italy and the United States*. Oxford and New York: Oxford University Press, 1998.

Marx, Karl. *Karl Marx Selected Writings In Sociology and Social Philosophy*. Translated by T. B. Bottomore. London: McGraw-Hill, 1964.

Marx, Karl, and Friedrich Engels. *Manifesto of the Communist Party*. 2nd revised edn. Moscow: Progress Publishers, 1977.

Mascuch, Michael. 'Continuity and Change in a Patronage Society: The Social Mobility of British Autobiographers, 1600–1750'. *Journal of Historical Sociology* 7, no. 2 (1994): 177–97.

Maubach, Franka. 'Die Stellung halten: Kriegserfahrungen und Lebensgeschichten von Wehrmachthelferinnen'. Dissertation. Göttingen: Vandenhoeck & Ruprecht, 2009.

Mayer, Arno J. *The Furies: Violence and Terror in the French and Russian Revolutions*. Princeton, NJ: Princeton University Press, 2000.

McAleer, Kevin. *Dueling: The Cult of Honor in Fin-de-Siecle Germany*. Princeton, NJ: Princeton University Press, 1994.

McCormick, Richard W. 'From Caligari to Dietrich: Sexual, Social, and Cinematic Discourses in Weimar Film'. *Signs* 18, no. 3 (1993): 640–68.

McLaren, Angus. *Twentieth Century Sexuality: A History*. Oxford: Blackwell Publishers, 1999.

Menand, Louis. 'Stand By Your Man'. *The New Yorker*, 19 September 2005. http://www.newyorker.com/magazine/2005/09/26/stand-by-your-man, accessed 10 July 2015.

Meyer, Alfred G. *The Feminism and Socialism of Lily Braun*. Bloomington: Indiana University Press, 1985.

Michelet, Jules. *L'Amour*. Paris: L. Hachette, 1858.

Midgley, Claire, ed. 'Anti-Slavery and the Roots of 'Imperial Feminism''. In *Gender and Imperialism*, 161–79. New York and Vancouver: Manchester University Press, 1998.

Mill, John Stuart. *Mill: Texts, Commentaries*. Edited by Alan Ryan. New York: W. W. Norton, 1997.

Mill, John Stuart. *Utilitarianism, on Liberty*. London and Rutland, VT: Everyman Paperbacks, 1993.

Miller, Pavla. *Transformations of Patriarchy in the West, 1500–1900*. Bloomington: Indiana University Press, 1998.

Millet, Kate. *Sexual Politics*. New York: Ballantine Books, 1969.

Mitchell, Claudine. 'Madeleine Pelletier (1874–1939): The Politics of Sexual Oppression'. In *European Women's History Reader*. Edited by Fiona Montgomery and Christine Collette, 256–71. New York: Routledge, 2002.

Möding, Nori. "'Ich muß irgendwo engagiert sein – fragen Sie mich bloß nicht, warum" Überlegungen zu Sozialisationserfahrungen von Mädchen in NS-Organisationen'.

In '*Wir kriegen jetzt andere Zeiten': auf der Suche nach der Erfahrung des Volkes in nachfaschistischen Ländern*. Edited by Lutz Niethammer and Alexander von Plato, 256–304. Berlin: J.H.W. Dietz, 1985.

Montefiore, Simon Sebag. *The Prince of Princes: The Life of Potemkin*. New York: St. Martin's Press, 2000.

Monzini, Paola. *Sex Traffic: Prostitution, Crime, and Exploitation*. Translated by Patrick Camiller. London: Zed, 2005.

Moran, Daniel, and Arthur Waldron, eds. *The People in Arms: Military Myth and National Mobilization since the French Revolution*. Cambridge: Cambridge University Press, 2006.

Morel, Bénédict Auguste, *Traité des dégénérescences physiques, intellectuelles, et morales de l'espèce humaine et des causes qui produisent ces variétés maladives*. Paris: Baillière, 1857.

Moring, Beatrice. 'Marriage and Social Change in Southwestern Finland, 1700–1870'. *Continuity and Change* 11, no. 1 (May 1996): 91–113.

Morris, Marilyn. 'Identity, Gender, Genre and Truth in The Maiden of Tonnerre: The Vicissitudes of the Chevalier and Chevalière d'Eon'. In *The Chevalier d'Eon and His Worlds: Gender, Espionage and Politics in the Eighteenth Century*. Edited by Simon Burrows, Jonathan Conlin, Russell Goulbourne and Valerie Mainz, 147–60. London and New York: Bloomsbury Academic, 2010.

Morris, Marilyn. *Sex, Money and Personal Character in Eighteenth-Century British Politics*. New Haven, CT: Yale University Press, 2014.

Mort, Frank. *Dangerous Sexualities: Medico-Moral Politics in England since 1830*. London and New York: Routledge and Kegan Paul, 1987.

Moruzzi, Norma Claire. *Speaking Through the Mask: Hannah Arendt and the Politics of Social Identity*. Ithaca, NY: Cornell University Press, 2000.

'Moscow Hosts Key Aids Conference'. *BBC*, 15 May 2006, sec. Europe. http://news.bbc.co.uk/2/hi/europe/4771409.stm, accessed 10 July 2015.

Moses, Claire. 'Saint Simonian Men/Saint Simonian Women: The Transformation of Feminist Thought in 1830s' France'. *Journal of Modern History* 54, no. 2 (1982): 240–67.

Mosse, George. 'Masculinity and Decadence'. In *Sexual Knowledge: Sexual Science: The History of Attitudes to Sexuality*. Edited by Roy Porter and Mikulas Teich, 251–66. Cambridge and New York: Cambridge University Press, 1994.

Mosse, George L. *Toward the Final Solution: A History of European Racism*. New York: Fertig, 1978.

Mottier, Véronique. *Sexuality: A Very Short Introduction*. Oxford and New York: Oxford University Press, 2008.

Mühlhäuser, Regina. *Eroberungen. Sexuelle Gewalttaten und intime Beziehungen deutscher Soldaten in der Sowjetunion 1941–1945*. Hamburg: Hamburger Edition, 2010.

Mühlhäuser, Regina. 'The Unquestioned Crime: Sexual Violence by German Soldiers During the War of Annihilation in the Soviet Union, 1941–45'. In *Rape in Wartime*. Edited by Raphaelle Branche and Fabrice Virgili, 34–46. London and New York: Palgrave Macmillan, 2012.

Munform, Clarence J. 'Conscription and the Peasants of the Morvan District of Chateau-Chinon, 1792–1794'. *Canadian Journal of History/Annales Candiennes D'histoire* 4, no. 2 (August 1969): 1–18.

Naiman, Eric. *Sex in Public: The Incarnation of Early Soviet Ideology*. Princeton, NJ: Princeton University Press, 1997.

Naimark, Norman M. 'The Russians and Germans: Rape during the War and Post-Soviet Memories'. In *Rape in Wartime*. Edited by Raphaëlle Branche and Fabrice Virgili, 201–19. London and New York: Palgrave Macmillan, 2012.

Naimark, Norman M. *The Russians in Germany: A History of the Soviet Zone of Occupation, 1945–1949*. Cambridge, MA: Belknap Press of Harvard University Press, 1995.

Nash, Mary. 'Pronatalism and Motherhood in Franco's Spain'. In *Maternity and Gender Policies: Women and the Rise of the European Welfare States, 1880s–1950s*. Edited by Gisela Bock and Pat Thane, 160–77. London: Routledge, 1991.

Nash, Mary. 'Social Eugenics and Nationalist Race Hygiene in Early Twentieth-Century Spain'. *History of European Ideas* 15, no. 4/6 (1992): 741–48.

Nash, Mary. 'Un/Contested Identities: Motherhood, Sex Reform and the Modernization of Gender Identity in Early Twentieth-Century Spain'. In *Constructing Spanish Womanhood: Female Identity in Modern Spain*. Edited by Victoria Lorée Enders and Pamela Beth Radcliff, 25–49. Albany: State University of New York Press, 1998.

Nash, Stanley D. 'Marriage'. In *Britain in the Hanoverian Age, 1714–1837: An Encyclopedia*. Edited by Gerald Newman and Leslie Ellen Brown, 439–40. New York and London: Garland, 1997.

Nelson, Robert L. *German Soldier Newspapers of the First World War*. Cambridge and New York: Cambridge University Press, 2011.

Nemes, Robert. 'Women in the 1848–1849 Hungarian Revolution'. *Journal of Women's History* 13, no. 3 (2001): 193–207.

Netting, Robert McC. *Smallholders, Householders: Farm Families and the Ecology of Intensive, Sustainable Agriculture*. Stanford, CA: Stanford University Press, 1993.

Nianias, Helen. 'Benedict Cumberbatch and Stephen Fry Campaign to Pardon Gay Men Convicted with Imitation Game Codebreaker Alan Turing'. *The Independent*, 27 January 2015. http://www.independent.co.uk/news/people/benedict-cumberbatch-and-stephen-fry-campaign-to-pardon-gay-men-convicted-with-imitation-game-codebreaker-alan-turing-10005530.html, accessed 10 July 2015.

'Numbers Drop as PEGIDA Rally Returns to Dresden'. *Deutsche Welle*, 25 January 2015. http://www.dw.de/numbers-drop-as-pegida-rally-returns-to-dresden/a-18213834, accessed 10 July 2015.

Nussbaum, Martha C. *Political Emotions: Why Love Matters for Justice*. Cambridge, MA: Belknap Press, 2013.

Nye, Robert A. 'Sexuality'. In *A Companion to Gender History*. Edited by Teresa A. Meade and Merry E. Wiesner, 11–25. Malden, MA: Blackwell Publishing Ltd., 2004.

Nye, Robert A., ed. *Sexuality*. Oxford: Oxford University Press, 1999.

'Obituary: Pim Fortuyn'. *BBC News Europe*, 6 May 2002. http://news.bbc.co.uk/1/hi/world/europe/1971462.stm, accessed 10 July 2015.

O'Conner, D. J. 'Representations of Women Workers: Tobacco Strikers in the 1890s'. In *Constructing Spanish Womanhood: Female Identity in Modern Spain*. Edited by Victoria Lorée Enders and Pamela Beth Radcliff, 151–72. Albany: State University of New York Press, 1998.

O'Doherty, Caroline. 'Birth Control Use Here among EU Lowest'. 18 November 2014. http://www.irishexaminer.com/ireland/birth-control-use-here-among-eu-lowest-298253.html, accessed 10 July 2015.

O'Keefe, Theresa. 'My Body Is My Manifesto! Slutwalk, Femen and Femmenist Protest'. *Feminist Review* 107, no. 1 (2014): 1–19.

Offen, Karen. 'Defining Feminism: A Comparative Historical Approach'. *Signs* 14, no. 1 (1988): 119–57.

Offen, Karen. 'Depopulation, Nationalism, and Feminism in Fin-de-Siecle France'. *American Historical Review* 89, no. 3 (1984): 648–76.

Offen, Karen. *European Feminisms, 1700–1950: A Political History*. Palo Alto: Stanford University Press, 1999.

Offen, Karen. 'The New Sexual Politics of French Revolutionary Historiography'. *French Historical Studies* 16, no. 4 (October 1990): 909–22.

Olsen, Kåre. *Schicksal Lebensborn: die Kinder der Schande und ihre Mütter*. Munich: Knaur Taschenbuch Verlag, 2004.

Oosterhuis, Harry. 'General Introduction: Homosexual Emancipation in Germany Before 1933: Two Traditions'. In *Homosexuality and Male Bonding in Pre-Nazi Germany: The Youth Movement, the Gay Movement, and Male Bonding Before Hitler's Rise: Original Transcripts from* Der Eigene, *the First Gay Journal in the World*. Edited by Harry Oosterhuis and Hubert Kennedy, 1–27. New York: Haworth Press, 1991.

Oosterhuis, Harry. *Stepchildren of Nature: Krafft-Ebing, Psychiatry and the Making of Sexual Identity*. Chicago: University of Chicago Press, 2000.

'Open World 2008 Annual Report'. Washington, DC: Open World Leadership Center, 2008.

Opitz, Reinhard. *Der deutsche Sozial-Liberalismus: 1917–1933*. Cologne: Pahl-Rugenstein, 1973.

'Orgonics'. *Orgonics*, accessed 16 January 2015. http://www.orgonics.com/.

Outram, Dorinda. *The Body and the French Revolution: Sex, Class and Political Culture*. New Haven, CT: Yale University Press, 1989.

Pagden, Anthony. *Lords of All the World: Ideologies of Empire in Spain, Britain and France c.1500-c.1800*. New Haven, CT: Yale University Press, 1995.

Paine, Thomas. 'Selections from Common Sense'. In *Reading the American Past, Volume I: To 1877: Selected Historical Documents*. Edited by Michael P. Johnson, 94–9. Boston: Bedford Books, 1998.

Paret, Peter. *Understanding War: Essays on Clausewitz and the History of Military Power*. Princeton, NJ: Princeton University Press, 1992.

Parr, Joy. 'Gender History and Historical Practice'. In *Gender and History in Canada*. Edited by Joy Parr and Mark Rosenfeld, 8–27. Toronto: Copp Clark, 1996.

Parvulescu, Anca. *The Traffic in Women's Work: East European Migration and the Making of Europe*. Chicago and London: University Of Chicago Press, 2014.

Pateman, Carol. *The Sexual Contract*. Stanford, CA: Stanford University Press, 1988.

Paul, Christa. *Zwangsprostitution: Staatlich Errichtete Bordelle Im Nationalsozialismus*. Reihe Deutsche Vergangenheit. Berlin: Edition Hentrich, 1995.

Paul, Diane B. 'What Was Wrong with Eugenics? Conflicting Narratives and Disputed Interpretations'. *Science & Education* 23, no. 2 (2014): 259–71.

Pedersen, Susan. *Family, Dependence and the Origins of the Welfare State: Britain and France 1914–1945*. New York: Cambridge University Press, 1993.

Pedersen, Susan. 'National Bodies, Unspeakable Acts: The Sexual Politics of Colonial Policy-Making'. *Journal of Modern History* 63, no. 4 (1991): 647–80.

'PEGIDA Dresden 24.11.2014 Wir Sind Das Volk'. 2014. https://www.youtube.com/watch?v=CvqoRfmfBEw, accessed 10 July 2015.

Pelletier, Madeleine. *L'Emancipation sexuelle de la femme*. Paris: M. Giard and E. Brière, 1911.

Pennington, Reina. *Wings, Women, and War: Soviet Airwomen in World War II Combat*. Lawrence: University Press of Kansas, 2001.

Pépin, Jacques. *The Origins of AIDS*. Cambridge, UK, and New York: Cambridge University Press, 2011.

'PRB Country Profiles'. *Population Reference Bureau*, 2014. http://www.prb.org, accessed 10 July 2015.

Perry, Adele. *On the Edge of Empire: Gender, Race, and the Making of British Columbia, 1849–1871*. Toronto: University of Toronto Press, 2001.

Petigny, Alan. 'Illegitimacy, Postwar Psychology, and the Reperiodization of the Sexual Revolutionary'. *Journal of Social History* 38, no. 1 (2004): 63–79.

'Petition of Women of the Third Estate to the King (1 January 1789)'. *Liberty, Equality, Fraternity: Exploring the French Revolution. City University of New York and George Mason University*, 1789. http://chnm.gmu.edu/revolution/d/472/, accessed 28 July 2015.

Peto, Andrea. 'Memory and the Narrative of Rape in Budapest and Vienna'. In *Life after Death: Approaches to a Cultural and Social History of Europe During the 1940s and 1950s*. Edited by Richard Bessel and Dirk Schumann, 129–49. New York: Cambridge University Press, 2003.

Phillips, Anne, and Barbara Taylor. 'Sex and Skill: Notes Towards a Feminist Economics'. In *Feminism and History*. Edited by Joan Wallach Scott, 317–30. New York: Oxford University Press, 1996.

Pirincci, Akif. *Deutschland von Sinnen Der irre Kult um Frauen, Homosexuelle und Zuwanderer*. Waltrop: Manuscriptum, 2014.

Plakans, Andrejs. 'Agrarian Reform and the Family in Eastern Europe'. In *The History of the European Family*. Edited by David I. Kertzer and Marzio Barbagli, 3 vols., 2: 73–105. New Haven: Yale University Press, 2002.

Plakans, Andrejs. 'Peasant Farmsteads and Households in the Baltic Littoral, 1797'. *Comparative Studies in Society and History* 17, no. 1 (January 1975): 2–35.

Pocock, J. G. A. *The Machiavellian Moment: Florentine Political Thought and the Atlantic Republican Tradition*. Revised edn. Princeton, NJ: Princeton University Press, 1975.

Poiger, Uta G. 'Rebels with a Cause? American Popular Culture, the 1956 Youth Riots, and New Conceptions of Masculinity in East and West Germany'. In *The American Impact on Postwar Germany*. Edited by Reiner Pommerin, 93–123. Providence, RI, and Oxford: Berghahn Books, 1995.

Ponzanesi, Sandra. 'Beyond the Black Venus: Colonial Sexual Politics and Contemporary Visual Practices'. In *Italian Colonialism: Legacy and Memory*. Edited by Jacqueline Andall and Derek Duncan, 165–89. Bern and New York: Peter Lang, 2005.

Popp, Maximilian, and Andreas Wassermann. 'Origins of German Anti-Muslim Group Pegida'. *Spiegel Online*, 1 December 2014. http://www.spiegel.de/international/germany/origins-of-german-anti-muslim-group-pegida-a-1012522.html, accessed 10 July 2015.

Porter, Laurence M. *Emmeline Pankhurst: A Biography*. New edn. London and New York: Routledge, 2002.

Porter, Laurence M. *A Gustave Flaubert Encyclopedia*. Westport, CT: Greenwood Publishing Group, 2001.

Puar, Jasbir K. *Terrorist Assemblages: Homonationalism in Queer Times*. Durham: Duke University Press, 2007.

Puff, Helmut. 'After the History of (Male) Homosexuality'. In *After the History of Sexuality: German Genealogies with and Beyond Foucault*. Edited by Scott Spector, Helmut Puff and Dagmar Herzog, 17–30. New York: Berghahn Books, 2012.

Purvis, June. 'Deeds Not Words'. *History Today* 52, no. 5 (2005): 56–63.

Pyecroft, Susan. 'British Working Women and the First World War'. *The Historian* 56, no. 4 (1994): 699–710.

Quataert, Jean H. 'The Shaping of Women's Work in Manufacturing: Guilds, Households, and the State in Central Europe, 1648–1870'. *The American Historical Review* 90, no. 5 (December 1985): 1122–48.

Quataert, Jean H. 'Unequal Partners in an Uneasy Alliance: Women and the Working Class in Imperial Germany'. In *Socialist Women: European Socialist Feminism in Nineteenth and Early Twentieth Century Europe*, 112–40. New York: Elsevier, 1978.

Quine, Maria Sophia. *Population Politics in Twentieth-Century Europe*. London and New York: Routledge, 1996.

Ragab, Ahmed. 'One, Two, or Many Sexes: Sex Differentiation in Medieval Islamicate Medical Thought'. *Journal of the History of Sexuality* 24, no. 3 (2015): 428–54.

Ramsey, Glenn. 'The Rites of Artgenossen: Contesting Homosexual Political Culture in Weimar Germany'. *Journal of the History of Sexuality* 17, no. 1 (2008): 85–109.

Rauschning, Hermann. *Hitler Speaks. A Series of Political Conversations with Adolf Hitler on His Real Aims*. London: Thornton Butterworth, 1939.

Reagan, Ronald W. 'Remarks and a Question-and-Answer Session With Regional Editors and Broadcasters'. *Ronald Reagan Presidential Library and Museum: The Public Papers*

*of President Ronald W. Reagan*, 18 April 1985. http://www.reagan.utexas.edu/archives/
speeches/1985/41885d.htm, accessed 10 July 2015.

Reagan, Ronald W. 'Remarks at a Joint German-American Military Ceremony at Bitburg Air
Base in the Federal Republic of Germany'. *Ronald Reagan Presidential Library and Museum:
The Public Papers of President Ronald W. Reagan*, 5 May 1985. http://www.reagan.utexas.edu/
archives/speeches/1985/50585b.htm, accessed 10 July 2015.

Reese, Dagmar. 'Bund Deutscher Mädel - Zur Geschichte der weiblichen deutschen Jugend im
Dritten Reich'. In *Mutterkreuz und Arbeitsbuch: zur Geschichte der Frauen in der Weimarer
Republik und im Nationalsozialismus*. Edited by Frauengruppe Faschismusforschung, 163–83.
Frankfurt a. M.: Fischer, 1981.

Reich, Wilhelm. *Die Sexualität im Kulturkampf: Zur sozialistischen Umstrukturierung des
Menschen*. Copenhagen: Sexpol-Verlag, 1936.

Reich, Wilhelm. *Geschlechtsreife, Enthaltsamkeit, Ehemoral: eine Kritik der bürgerlichen
Sexualreform*, Vienna: Münster-Verlag 1930.

Reich, Wilhelm. *The Sexual Revolution: Toward a Self-Governing Character Structure*. 1st English
edn. New York: Orgon Institute Press, 1945.

Reid, Robert. *Lermontov's* A Hero of Our Time. London: Bristol Classical Press, 1997.

Reis, Elizabeth. 'Divergence or Disorder?: The Politics of Naming Intersex'. *Perspectives in Biology
and Medicine* 50, no. 4 (2007): 535–43.

Rendall, Jane. *The Origins of Modern Feminism: Women in Britain, France, and the United States
1780–1860*. Basingstoke: Macmillan, 1984.

Reyfman, Irina. *Ritualized Violence Russian Style: The Duel in Russian Culture and Literature*.
Palo Alto, CA: Stanford University Press, 1999.

Reynolds, Siân. 'Marianne's Citizen? The Republic and Universal Suffrage in France'. In *Gender
and History in Western Europe*. Edited by Robert Shoemaker and Mary Vincent, 306–218.
London: Arnold, 1998.

Richie, Alexandra. *Faust's Metropolis: A History of Berlin*. London: HarperCollins, 1998.

Riley, Denise. *Am I That Name? Feminism and the Category of 'Women' in History*. London and
Minneapolis: Macmillan and University of Minnesota Press, 1988.

Ritvo, Harriet. 'Classification and Continuity in the Origin of Species'. In *Charles Darwin's* The
Origin of Species: *New Interdisciplinary Essays*. Edited by David Amigoni and Jeff Wallace,
47–67. Manchester and New York: Manchester University Press, 1995.

Roberts, Mary Louise. *Civilization Without Sexes: Reconstructing Gender in Postwar France,
1917–1927*. Chicago: University of Chicago Press, 1994.

Roberts, Mary Louise. *Disruptive Acts: The New Woman in Fin-de-Siècle France*. Chicago:
University of Chicago Press, 2002.

Roberts, Mary Louise. *What Soldiers Do: Sex and the American GI in World War II France*.
Chicago, IL: University of Chicago Press, 2013.

Röder, Antje. 'Explaining Religious Differences in Immigrants' Gender Role Attitudes: The
Changing Impact of Origin Country and Individual Religiosity'. *Ethnic and Racial Studies* 37,
no. 14 (2014): 2615–35.

Rodriguez-Ruiz, Blanca and Ruth Rubio-Marín. *The Struggle for Female Suffrage in Europe:
Voting to Become Citizens*. Leiden and Boston: Brill, 2012.

Roper, Lyndal. *Oedipus and the Devil: Witchcraft, Religion and Sexuality in Early Modern Europe*.
London and New York: Routledge, 1994.

Rose, Sonya O. 'Gender Antagonism and Class Conflict: Exclusionary Strategies of Male Trade
Unionists in Nineteenth-Century Britain'. *Social History* 13, no. 2 (1988): 191–208.

Ross, Andrew Israel. 'Serving Sex: Playing with Prostitution in the Brasseries à Femmes of Late
Nineteenth-Century Paris'. *Journal of the History of Sexuality* 24, no. 2 (2015): 288–313.

Ross, Kristin. *May '68 and Its Afterlives*. Chicago: University Of Chicago Press, 2002.

## Works Cited

Rousseau, Jean-Jacques. *The Collected Writings of Rousseau*. Edited by Roger D. Masters and Christopher Kelly. 9 vols. Hanover, CT: Published for Dartmouth College by University Press of New England, 1990.

Rousseau, Jean Jacques. *The Social Contract*. Translated by Maurice Cranston. New York: Penguin, 1968.

Rowbotham, Sheila. *Hidden from History: 300 Years of Women's Oppression and the Fight Against It*. London: Pluto, 1973.

Rubchak, Marian. 'Seeing Pink: Searching for Gender Justice Through Opposition in Ukraine'. *European Journal of Women's Studies* 19, no. 1 (2012): 55–72.

Ruskin, John. *Sesame and Lilies*. Edited by Deborah Epstein Nord. New Haven, CT: Yale University Press, 2002.

Ryback, Timothy W. *Rock around the Bloc: A History of Rock Music in Eastern Europe and the Soviet Union*. New York: Oxford University Press, 1990.

Rydström, Jens. 'From Sodomy to Homosexuality: Rural Sex and the Inclusion of Lesbians in Criminal Discourse'. *NORA – Nordic Journal of Feminist and Gender Research* 13, no. 1 (April 2005): 20–35.

Sabean, David Warren. *Property, Production, and Family in Neckarhausen, 1700–1870*. Cambridge: Cambridge University Press, 1991.

Said, Edward W. *Orientalism*. New York: Vintage Books, 1979.

Saldern, Adelheid von. 'Victims or Perpetrators? Controversies About the Role of Women in the Nazi State'. In *Nazism and German Society, 1933–1945*. Edited by David F. Crew, 141–65. London and New York: Routledge, 1994.

Salem, Sara M. 'Femen's Neocolonial Feminism: When Nudity Becomes a Uniform'. *Alakhbar*, 26 December 2012. http://english.al-akhbar.com/node/14494

Sanborn, Geoffrey. *The Sign of the Cannibal: Melville and the Making of a Postcolonial Reader*. Durham, NC: Duke University Press, 1998.

Sanborn, Joshua A. *Drafting the Russian Nation: Military Conscription, Total War, and Mass Politics, 1905–1925*. DeKalb: Northern Illinois University Press, 2003.

Sanders, Teela. *Paying for Pleasure: Men Who Buy Sex*. Cullompton: Willan, 2008.

Sanger, Margaret. *Woman and the New Race*. New York: Truth Publishing Company, 1920.

Santos, Ana Cristina. 'Are We There Yet? Queer Sexual Encounters, Legal Recognition and Homonormativity'. *Journal of Gender Studies* 22, no. 1 (2013): 54–64.

Santos, Ana Cristina. *Social Movements and Sexual Citizenship in Southern Europe*. Houndsmills, Basingstoke, Hampshire and New York: Palgrave MacMillan, 2013.

Sauer, Edith. *Liebe und Arbeit: Geschlechterbeziehungen im 19. und 20. Jahrhundert*. Vienna: Böhlau, 2014.

Sauerteig, Lutz. 'Militär, Medizin und Moral: Sexualität im Ersten Weltkrieg'. In *Die Medizin und der Erste Weltkrieg*. Edited by Wolfgang Uwe Eckart and Christoph Gradmann, 197–226. Pfaffenweiler: Centaurus-Verlagsgesellschaft, 1996.

Schama, Simon. *Citizens: A Chronicle of the French Revolution*. Toronto: Vintage Canada, 1990.

Scheible, J. A. and F. Fleischmann. 'Gendering Islamic Religiosity in the Second Generation: Gender Differences in Religious Practices and the Association with Gender Ideology Among Moroccan- and Turkish-Belgian Muslims'. *Gender & Society* 27, no. 3 (2013): 372–95.

Schivelbusch, Wolfgang. *The Culture of Defeat: On National Trauma, Mourning and Recovery*. New York: Picador, 2003.

Schmitt, Bernadotte E. *The Annexation of Bosnia, 1908–1909*. New York: Howard Fertig, 1970.

Schroer, Timothy L. *Recasting Race After World War II: Germans and African Americans in American-Occupied Germany*. Boulder: University Press of Colorado, 2007.

Scott, Joan Wallach. *The Fantasy of Feminist History*. Durham: Duke University Press, 2012.

Scott, Joan Wallach. 'Gender: A Useful Category of Historical Analysis'. *American Historical Review* 91, no. 5 (1986): 1053–75.

Scott, Joan Wallach. *Only Paradoxes to Offer: French Feminists and the Rights of Man*. Cambridge, MA: Harvard University Press, 1996.

Scott, Joan Wallach. *The Politics of the Veil*. Princeton, NJ: Princeton University Press, 2010.

Scotto, Peter. 'Prisoners of the Caucasus: Ideologies of Imperialism in Lermontov's "Bela."' *PMLA* 107, no. 2 (March 1992): 246–60.

Seeley, John Robert. *The Expansion of England*. Chicago: University of Chicago Press, 1971.

Sepinwall, Alyssa Goldstein. 'Robespierre, Old Regime Feminist? Gender, the Late Eighteenth Century, and the French Revolution Revisited'. *Journal of Modern History* 82, no. 1 (March 2010): 1–29.

Sewell, William H. 'Artisans and Factory Workers, 1789–1848'. In *Working-Class Formation: Nineteenth-Century Patterns in Western Europe and the United States*. Edited by Ira Katznelson and Aristide R. Zolberg, 45–70. Princeton, NJ: Princeton University Press, 1986.

Sewell, William H. 'Le Citoyen/La Citoyenne: Activity, Passivity, and the Revolutionary Concept of Citizenship'. In *The French Revolution and the Creation of Modern Political Culture: The Political Culture of the Old Regime*. Edited by Colin Lucas, 2. Political Culture of the French Revolution:105–25. New York: Pergamon Press, 1987.

Sharpe, James A. *Instruments of Darkness: Witchcraft in Early Modern England*. Philadelphia: University of Pennsylvania Press, 1997.

Shcherbatov, Prince M. M. *On the Corruption of Morals in Russia*. Translated by A. Lentin. Cambridge: Cambridge University Press, 1969.

Sher, Richard B. 'Adam Ferguson, Adam Smith, and the Problem of National Defense'. *The Journal of Modern History* 61, no. 2 (June 1989): 240–68.

Shevchenko, Inna. 'Charlie Hebdo Paris Massacre: Everyone Says "Je Suis Charlie" Now, but Where Were They When My Friends Were Alive?'. *International Business Times*, 12 January 2015. http://www.ibtimes.co.uk/charlie-hebdo-paris-massacre-je-suis-charlie-demos-are-too-late-save-my-friends-1483003, accessed 10 July 2015.

Shevchenko, Inna. 'Femen Let Victor Svyatski Take over Because we Didn't Know How to Fight It'. *The Guardian*, 5 September 2013.

Shik, Na'ama. 'Sexual Abuse of Jewish Women in Auschwitz-Birkenau'. In *Brutality and Desire: War and Sexuality in Europe's Twentieth Century*. Edited by Dagmar Herzog, 211–46. London and New York: Palgrave Macmillan, 2011.

Shils, Edward A., and Morris Janowitz. 'Cohesion and Disintegration in the Wehrmacht in World War II'. *The Public Opinion Quarterly* 12, no. 2 (1948): 280–315.

Shoemaker, Robert B. *Gender in English Society, 1650–1850: The Emergence of Separate Spheres*. London and New York: Longman, 1998.

Shoemaker, Robert B. 'The Taming of the Duel: Masculinity, Honour and Ritual Violence in London, 1660–1800'. *The Historical Journal* 45, no. 3 (2002): 525–45.

Sibalis, Michael David. 'The Regulation of Male Homosexuality in Revolutionary and Napoleonic France, 1789–1815'. In *Homosexuality in Modern France*. Edited by Jeffrey Merrick and Bryant T. Ragan, 80–101. New York: Oxford University Press, 1989.

Siegel, Dina. 'Human Trafficking and Legalized Prostitution in the Netherlands'. *Temida* 12, no. 1 (2009): 5–16.

Simonton, Deborah. 'Women Workers; Working Women'. In *The Routledge History of Women in Europe since 1700*. Edited by Deborah Simonton, 134–76. London and New York: Routledge, 2006.

Sinha, Mrinalini. *Colonial Masculinity: The 'Manly Englishman' and the 'Effeminate Bengali' in the Late Nineteenth Century*. Manchester: Manchester University Press, 1995.

# Works Cited

Smart, Annie K. *Citoyennes: Women and the Ideal of Citizenship in Eighteenth-Century France*. Newark, NJ: University of Delaware Press, 2011.

Smith, Bonnie G. *Changing Lives Women in European History since 1700*. Boston: Houghton Mifflin Company, 1989.

Smith, Bonnie G. *The Gender of History: Men, Women, and Historical Practice*. Cambridge, MA: Harvard University Press, 1998.

Smith, Bonnie G. *Ladies of the Leisure Class: The Bourgeoises of Northern France in the Nineteenth Century*. Princeton, NJ: Princeton University Press, 1981.

Smith, Douglas, ed. *Love and Conquest: Personal Correspondence of Catherine the Great and Prince Grigory Potemkin*. Princeton, NJ: Princeston University Press, 2004.

Sneeringer, Julia. *Winning Women's Votes: Propaganda and Politics in Weimar Germany*. Chapel Hill: The University of North Carolina Press, 2002.

Snyder, Louis Leo. *The Blood and Iron Chancellor: A Documentary-Biography of Otto von Bismarck*. Princeton, NJ: D. Van Nostrand, 1967.

Snyder, Timothy. *Bloodlands: Europe between Hitler and Stalin*. New York: Basic Books, 2010.

Sohn, Anne-Marie. 'French Catholics Between Abstinence and "Appeasement of Lust"'. In *Sexual Cultures in Europe: Themes in Sexuality*. Edited by Gert Hekma, Franz Eder and Lesley A. Hall, 233–54. Manchester and Vancouver: Manchester University Press, 1999.

Sombart, Nicolas. *Die Deutschen Männer Und Ihre Feinde. Carl Schmitt – Ein Deutsches Schicksal Zwischen Männerbund Und Matriarchmythos*. Munich and Vienna: Carl Hanser, 1991.

Sommer, Robert. 'Camp Brothels: Forced Sex Labour in Nazi Concentration Camps'. In *Brutality and Desire: War and Sexuality in Europe's Twentieth Century*. Edited by Dagmar Herzog, 168–96. New York: Palgrave Macmillan, 2011.

Sowerwine, Charles. *Sisters or Citizens?: Women and Socialism in France Since 1876*. Cambridge and New York: Cambridge University Press, 1982.

Sowerwine, Charles. 'Socialism, Feminism, and the Socialist Women's Movement from the French Revolutionary to World War II'. In *Becoming Visible: Women in European History*. Edited by Renate Bridenthal, Susan Mosher Stuard and Merry E. Wiesner, 3rd edn., 357–87. Boston: Houghton Mifflin, 1998.

Spector, Scott. 'Introduction: After The History of Sexuality? Periodicities, Subjectivities, Ethics'. In *After the History of Sexuality: German Genealogies with and Beyond Foucault*. Edited by Scott Spector, Helmut Puff and Dagmar Herzog, 1–16. New York: Berghahn Books, 2012.

Sperber, Jonathan. *The European Revolutions, 1848–1851*. Cambridge: Cambridge University Press, 1984.

Sperber, Jonathan. *Karl Marx: A Nineteenth-Century Life*. New York: Liveright Pub. Corp., 2013.

Spivak, Gayatri Chakravorty. 'Can the Subaltern Speak?' In *Marxism and the Interpretation of Culture*. Edited by Cary Nelson and Lawrence Grossberg. Urbana: University of Illinois Press, 1988.

Stanley, Liz, *Sex Surveyed, 1949–1994: From Mass-Observation's 'Little Kinsey' to the National Survey and the Hite Reports*. London and Bristol, PA: Taylor & Francis, 1995.

Stark, Gary D. 'The Ideology of the German Burschenschaft Generation'. *European History Quarterly* 8, no. 3 (1978): 323–48.

Stauter-Halsted, Keely. 'The Physician and the Fallen Woman: Medicalizing Prostitution in the Polish Lands'. *Journal of the History of Sexuality* 20, no. 2 (May 2011): 270–90.

Stearns, Peter N. *Gender in World History*. London and New York: Routledge, 2000.

Stearns, Peter N. *Sexuality in World History*. London and New York: Routledge, 2009.

Steedman, Carolyn. *An Everyday Life of the English Working Class: Work, Self and Sociability in the Early Nineteenth Century*. Cambridge and New York: Cambridge University Press, 2014.

Steedman, Carolyn. *Master and Servant: Love and Labour in the English Industrial Age*. Cambridge and New York: Cambridge University Press, 2007.

Steinbach, Susie. *Women in England 1760–1914: A Social History*. New York: Palgrave Macmillan, 2004.

Steinbacher, Sybille, *Volksgenossinnen: Frauen in der NS-Volksgemeinschaft*. Göttingen: Wallstein Verlag, 2007.

Steinbrügge, Lieselotte. *The Moral Sex: Woman's Nature in the French Enlightenment*. Translated by Pamela E. Selwyn. Oxford and New York: Oxford University Press, 1995.

Stelder, Mikki. 'Start with Amsterdam! An Alternative Statement on the Sexual Nationalisms Conference'. *Queer Intersectional*, 16 February 2011. https://queerintersectional.wordpress.com/2011/02/16/start-with-amsterdam-2, accessed 10 July 2015.

Stengers, Jean. *Masturbation: The History of a Great Terror*. Translated by Kathryn Hoffmann. New York: Palgrave, 2001.

Stepan, Nancy Leys. 'Race, Gender and Nation in Argentina: The Influence of Italian Eugenics'. *History of European Ideas* 15, no. 4–6 (1992): 749–56.

Stepan, Nancy Leys. 'Race, Gender, Science and Citizenship'. In *Cultures of Empire: Colonisers in Britain and the Empire in the Nineteenth and Twentieth Centuries: A Reader*. Edited by Catherine Hall, 61–86. New York: Routledge, 2000.

Stewart, William Kilborne. 'The Mentors of Mussolini'. *The American Political Science Review* 22, no. 4 (1928): 843–69.

Stocking, George W. Jr. *Victorian Anthropology*. New York and London: Free Press, 1987.

Stolberg, Michael. 'A Woman Down to Her Bones: The Anatomy of Sexual Difference in the Sixteenth and Early Seventeenth Centuries'. *Isis* 94, no. 2 (2003): 274–99.

Stoler, Ann Laura. *Carnal Knowledge and Imperial Power: Race and the Intimate in Colonial Rule*. Berkeley and Los Angeles: University of California Press, 2002.

Stone, Judith F. 'Republican Ideology, Gender and Class: France, 1860s–1914'. In *Gender and Class in Modern Europe*. Edited by Laura L. Frader and Sonya O. Rose, 238–59. Ithaca, NY and London: Cornell University Press, 1996.

Stone, Lawrence. *The Family, Sex, and Marriage in England, 1500–1800*. New York: Harper and Row, 1977.

Storr, Merl. 'Transformations: Subjects, Categories and Cures in Krafft-Ebing's Sexology'. In *Sexology in Culture: Labelling Bodies and Desires*. Edited by Lucy Bland and Laura Doan, 11–25. Cambridge: Polity Press, 1998.

Stuurman, Siep. 'The Deconstruction of Gender: Seventeenth-Century Feminism and Modern Equality'. In *Women, Gender, and Enlightenment*. Edited by Sarah Knott and Barbara Taylor, 371–88. New York: Palgrave Macmillan, 2005.

Sundin, Jan. 'Sinful Sex: Legal Prosecution of Extramarital Sex in Preindustrial Sweden'. *Social Science History* 16, no. 1 (1992): 99–128.

Surkis, Judith. *Sexing the Citizen: Morality and Masculinity in France, 1870–1920*. Ithaca, NY: Cornell University Press, 2006.

Swatinair. 'The Tactics and Critical Analysis of Femen'. *Nirmukta: Promoting Science, Free Thought and Secular Humanism in India*, http://nirmukta.com/2013/05/10/the-tactics-and-critical-analysis-of-Femen/, accessed 10 July 2015.

'Sweden Adds Gender-Neutral Pronoun to Dictionary'. *The Guardian*, accessed 28 July 2015.

Szreter, Simon, and Kate Fisher. *Sex Before the Sexual Revolution: Intimate Life in England 1918–1963*. Cambridge and New York: Cambridge University Press, 2010.

Tabili, Laura. 'Empire Is the Enemy of Love: Edith Noor's Progress and Other Stories'. *Gender & History* 17, no. 1 (2005): 5–28.

Tackett, Timothy. *The Coming of the Terror in the French Revolution*. Cambridge: Belknap Press, 2015.

Takács, Judit, and Ivett Szalma. 'Homophobia and Same-Sex Partnership Legislation in Europe'. *Equality, Diversity and Inclusion: An International Journal* 30, no. 5 (2011): 356–78.

Tamagne, Florence. *A History of Homosexuality in Europe: Berlin, London, Paris, 1919–1939*. New York: Algora Publishing, 2004.

Tavcer, D. Scharie. 'The Trafficking of Women for Sexual Exploitation: The Situation from the Republic of Moldova to Western Europe'. *Police Practice & Research* 7, no. 2 (2006): 135–47.

Taylor, Alan. 'Femen Stages a "Topless Jihad"'. *The Atlantic*, 2013. http://www.theatlantic.com/photo/2013/04/femen-stages-a-topless-jihad/100487/

Taylor, Barbara. *Eve and the New Jerusalem: Socialism and Feminism in the Nineteenth Century*. New York: Pantheon Books, 1983.

Taylor, Barbara. '"The Men Are as Bad as Their Masters.": Socialism, Feminism and Sexual Antagonism in the London Tailoring Trade in the Early 1830's'. *Feminist Studies* 5 (1979): 7–40.

Tayler, Jeffrey. 'Is Femen Dying? The Radical Feminist Movement Struggles to Survive in France'. *The Atlantic*, 22 August 2014. http://www.theatlantic.com/international/archive/2014/08/is-femen-dying/378992, accessed 10 July 2015.

Terrence Higgins Trust. 'Criminalisation of HIV Transmission in Europe'. *Global Network of People Living with HIV/AIDS*. http://criminalisation.gnpplus.net/site/index.shtml, accessed 15 January 2015.

Tester, Keith, ed. *The Flaneur*. London and New York: Routledge, 1994.

Therborn, Göran. *Between Sex and Power: Family in the World, 1900–2000*. London and New York: Routledge, 2004.

Thompson, Christopher. 'Un troisième sexe? Les bourgeoises et la bicyclette dans la France fin de siècle'. *Le Mouvement Social* 192, no. 3 (2000): 9–40.

Thompson, Dorothy. 'Women and Nineteenth-Century Radical Politics: A Lost Dimension'. In *The Rights and Wrongs of Women*. Edited by Juliet Mitchell and Ann Oakley, 112–38. New York: Penguin Books, 1976.

Thompson, E. P. 'Time, Work-, Discipline, and Industrial Capitalism'. *Past and Present* 38 (1967): 56–97.

Tilly, Louise, and Joan W. Scott. *Women, Work and Family*. New York: Holt Rinehart and Winston, 1978.

Tilly, Louise, and Joan W. Scott. 'Women's Work and the Family in Nineteenth Century'. *Comparative Studies in Society and History* 17, no. 1 (1975): 36–64.

Timm, Annette F. 'Mothers, Whores or Sentimental Dupes? Emotion and Race in Historiographical Debates about Women in the Third Reich'. In *Beyond the Racial State*. Edited by Mark Roseman, Devin Pendas and Richard F. Wetzell. Princeton, NJ: Princeton University Press, forthcoming.

Timm, Annette F. *The Politics of Fertility in Twentieth-Century Berlin*. New York: Cambridge University Press, 2010.

Tolstoy, Leo. *Tolstoy's Writings on Civil Disobedience and Non-Violence*. Philadelphia: New Society Publishers, 1987.

Tomlinson, B. R. 'Economics and Empire: The Periphery and the Imperial Economy'. In *The Oxford History of the British Empire: Volume III: The Nineteenth Century*. Edited by Andrew Porter. Oxford and New York: Oxford University Press, 1999.

Tone, John Lawrence. 'A Dangerous Amazon: Agustina Zaragoza and the Spanish Revolutionary War, 1808—1814'. *European History Quarterly* 37, no. 4 (October 2007): 548–61.

Tone, John Lawrence. 'Spanish Women in the Resistance to Napoleon, 1808–1814'. In *Constructing Spanish Womanhood: Female Identity in Modern Spain*. Edited by Victoria Lorée Enders and Pamela Beth Radcliff, 259–82. Albany, NY: State University of New York Press, 1998.

Tosh, John. 'Domesticity and Manliness in the Victorian Middle Class: The Family of Edward White Benson'. In *Manful Assertions: Masculinities in Britain since 1800*, 44–73. London and New York: Routledge, 1991.

Treitschke, Heinrich von. *Treitschke's History of Germany in the Nineteenth Century*. Edited by Eden Paul and Cedar Paul. Vol. 1. New York: McBride Nast, 1915.

Trexler, Richard C. *Sex and Conquest: Gendered Violence, Political Order, and the European Conquest of the Americas*. Ithaca, NY: Cornell University Press, 1999.

Triplett, Hall. 'The Misnomer of Freud's "Seduction Theory"'. *Journal of the History of Ideas* 65, no. 4 (2004): 647–65.

Trouille, Mary Seidman. *Sexual Politics in the Enlightenment: Women Writers Read Rousseau*. Albany, NY: State University of New York Press, 1997.

Trumbach, Randolph. 'The Birth of the Queen: Sodomy and the Emergence of Gender Equality in Modern Culture 1660–1750'. In *Hidden From History: Reclaiming the Gay and Lesbian Past*. Edited by Martin Duberman, Martha Vicinus and George Chauncey Jr., 129–40. New York: Meridian, 1989.

Trumbach, Randolph. 'Modern Sodomy: The Origins of Homosexuality, 1700–1800'. In *A Gay History of Britain: Love and Sex Between Men Since the Middle Ages*. Edited by Matt Cook, Robert Mills, Randolph Trumbach and H. G. Cocks, 77–106. Oxford and Westport, CT: Praeger, 2007.

Turda, Marius, and Paul Weindling. *'Blood and Homeland': Eugenics and Racial Nationalism in Central and Southeast Europe, 1900–1940*. Budapest and New York: Central European University Press, 2007.

Tuson, Penelope. 'Mutiny Narratives and the Imperial Feminine: European Women's Accounts of the Rebellion in India in 1857'. *Women's Studies International Forum* 21, no. 3 (1998): 291–303.

*Ukraine Is Not a Brothel* (2013). [Film] Dir. Kitty Green, Australia: Film Platform.

'Ukrainian Activists Allegedly Kidnapped, Terrorized in Belarus Found'. 20 December 2012. http://www.rferl.org/content/femen_activists_detained_by_belarus_kgb/24428304.html, accessed 10 July 2015.

Ulrichs, Karl Heinrich. *Prometheus*. Leipzig: Gerbe'sche Verlagsbuchhandlung, 1870.

Ulrichs, Karl Heinrich. 'The Urning and His Rights'. In *Sodomites and Urnings: Homosexual Representations in Classic German Journals*. Edited by Michael A. Lombardi-Nash, 21–24. Binghamton, NY: Harrington Park Press, 2006.

United Nations Department of Economic and Social Affairs (Population Division). *World Urbanization Prospects: The 2003 Revision*. New York: United Nations, 2004.

United Nations Population Fund. 'State of World Population 2014'. http://www.unfpa.org/swop, accessed 10 July 2015.

Valenze, Deborah M. *Prophetic Sons and Daughters: Popular Religion and Social Change in England 1790–1850*. Princeton NJ: Princeton University Press, 1985.

van Leeuwen, Marco H. D. 'Partner Choice and Homogamy in the Nineteenth Century: Was There a Sexual Revolution in Europe?' *Journal of Social History* 36, no. 1 (2002): 101–23.

Vertinsky, Patricia. *The Eternally Wounded Woman: Women, Exercise and Doctors in the Late Nineteenth Century*. Manchester: Manchester University Press, 1990.

Vervenioti, Tasoula. 'The Adventure of Women's Suffrage in Greece'. In *When the War Was Over: Women, War and Peace in Europe, 1940–1956*. Edited by Claire Duchen and Irene Bandhauer-Schöffmann, 103–118. London and New York: Leicester University Press, 2000.

Vickery, Amanda. 'Golden Age to Separate Spheres? A Review of the Categories and Chronology of English Women's History'. In *Gender and History in Western Europe*. Edited by Robert Shoemaker and Mary Vincent, 197–225. New York and London: Arnold, 1998.

'Vintage Video: Death of Suffragette at Epsom Derby, 1913'. *FirstWorldWar.com*, accessed 16 January 2015. http://www.firstworldwar.com/video/epsomsuffragette.htm.

Virgili, Fabrice. *Shorn Women: Gender and Punishment in Liberation France*. Translated by John Flower. Oxford and New York: Berg Publishers, 2002.

# Works Cited

W.W.P. (pseudo). 'Woman as She Is and as She Ought to Be'. *New Moral World* 5, no. 13 (January 1839): 210.

Walkowitz, Judith. *City of Dreadful Delight: Narratives of Sexual Danger in Late-Victorian London*. Chicago: Chicago University Press, 1992.

Walkowitz, Judith. 'Male Vice and Female Virtue: Feminism and the Politics of Prostitution in Nineteenth Century Britain'. In *Powers of Desire: The Politics of Sexuality*. Edited by Ann Snitow, Christine Stansell and Sharon Thompson, 419–38. New York: Monthly Review Press, 1983.

Walkowitz, Judith. *Nights Out – Life in Cosmopolitan London*. New Haven: Yale University Press, 2012.

Walkowitz, Judith. *Prostitution and Victorian Society: Women, Class and the State*. Cambridge and New York: Cambridge University Press, 1980.

Wallerstein, Immanuel. 'Citizens All? Citizens Some! The Making of the Citizen'. *Comparative Studies in Society and History* 45, no. 4 (October 2003): 650–79.

Watson, Alexander. '"Unheard-of Brutality": Russian Atrocities against Civilians in East Prussia, 1914–1915'. *The Journal of Modern History* 86, no. 4 (December 2014): 780–825.

Weber, Max. 'National Character and the Junkers'. In *From Max Weber: Essays in Sociology*. Edited by H. H. Gerth and C. Wright Mills, 386–95. Oxford and New York: Oxford University Press, 1946.

Weeks, Jeffrey. 'Foucault for Historians'. *History Workshop Journal* 14, no. 1 (1982): 106–19.

Weeks, Jeffrey. 'Inverts, Perverts, and Mary-Annes: Male Prostitution and the Regulation of Homosexuality in England in the Nineteenth and Early Twentieth Centuries'. In *Hidden From History: Reclaiming the Gay and Lesbian Past*, 195–211. New York: New American Library, 1989.

Weeks, Jeffrey. 'Queer(y)ing the "Modern Homosexual."' *Journal of British Studies* 51, no. 3 (2012): 523–39.

Weeks, Jeffrey. *Sexuality and Its Discontents: Meanings, Myths, and Modern Sexualities*. London and Boston: Routledge and K. Paul, 1985.

Weitz, Eric D. 'The Heroic Man and the Ever-Changing Woman: Gender and Politics in European Communism, 1917–1950'. In *Gender and Class in Modern Europe*. Edited by Laura L. Frader and Sonya O. Rose, 311–52. Ithaca, NY and London: Cornell University Press, 1996.

Weller, I., D. H., Crawford, V. Iliescu, K. MacLennan, S. Sutherland, R. S. Tedder and M. W. Adler. 'Homosexual Men in London: Lymphadenopathy, Immune Status, and Epstein-Barr Virus Infection'. *Annals of the New York Academy of Sciences* 437 (1984): 238–53.

Wesseling, H. L. *Divide and Rule: The Partition of Africa, 1880–1914*. Westport, CT: Praeger, 1996.

Wette, Wolfram. *The Wehrmacht. History, Myth, Reality*. Cambridge, MA: Harvard University Press, 2006.

Whisnant, Clayton J. 'Gay German History: Future Directions?' *Journal of the History of Sexuality* 17, no. 1 (2008): 1–10.

Whitaker, Elizabeth Dixon. *Measuring Mamma's Milk: Fascism and the Medicalization of Maternity in Italy*. Ann Arbor: University of Michigan Press, 2000.

Whittam, John. *Fascist Italy*. Manchester, UK, and New York: Manchester University Press, 1995.

'Why Swedish Men Take So Much Paternity Leave'. *The Economist*, 22 July 2014. http://www.economist.com/blogs/economist-explains/2014/07/economist-explains-15, accessed 10 July 2015.

Wiesner, Merry E. *Women and Gender in Early Modern Europe*. 3rd edn. (New Approaches to European History; 41). Cambridge and New York: Cambridge University Press, 2008.

Wiesner-Hanks, Merry E. *Gender in History: Global Perspectives*. 2nd edn. Chichester and Malden, MA: Wiley-Blackwell, 2011.

'The Wilhelm Reich Museum'. http://www.wilhelmreichmuseum.org, accessed 16 January 2015.

Wilson, Kathleen. 'Empire, Gender, and Modernity in the Eighteenth Century'. In *Gender and Empire*. Edited by Philippa Levine, 14–45. Oxford and New York: Oxford University Press, 2004.

Wingfield, Nancy M. 'Destination: Alexandria, Buenos Aires, Constantinople; "White Slavers" in Late Imperial Austria'. *Journal of the History of Sexuality* 20, no. 2 (May 2011): 291–311.

Winks, Robin W., and R. J. Q. Adams. *Europe, 1890–1945: Crisis and Conflict*. New York: Oxford University Press, 2003.

Winter, Bronwyn. *Hijab & the Republic Uncovering the French Headscarf Debate*. Syracuse, NY: Syracuse University Press, 2008.

Woloch, Isser. *The New Regime: Transformations of the French Civic Order, 1789–1820s*. New York and London: W. W. Norton & Company, 1994.

Woolf, Virginia. *A Room of One's Own*. New York: Harcourt, Brace and Co., 1929.

World Health Organization Regional Office for Europe. 'Facts and Figures about Abortion in European Region'. http://www.euro.who.int/en/health-topics/Life-stages/sexual-and-reproductive-health/activities/abortion/facts-and-figures-about-abortion-in-the-european-region, accessed 10 July 2015.

Woycke, James. *Birth Control in Germany, 1871–1933*. Wellcome Institute Series in the History of Medicine. London and New York: Routledge, 1988.

Wright, Gordon. *The Ordeal of Total War, 1939–1945*. New York: Harper and Row, 1968.

Wrigley, E. A. 'The Fall of Marital Fertility in Nineteenth-Century France: Exemplar or Exception? (Part I)'. *European Journal of Population/Revue Européenne de Démographie* 1, no. 1 (1985): 31–60.

Wunder, Heide. *He Is the Sun, She Is the Moon: Women in Early Modern Germany*. Translated by Thomas Dunlap. Cambridge and London: Harvard University Press, 1998.

Zabus, Chantal. *Out in Africa: Same-Sex Desire in Sub-Saharan Literatures & Cultures*. Woodbridge, Suffolk England: James Currey, 2013.

Zadrozna, Anna. '"I Am Muslim but I Am the European One": Contextual Identities Among Muslims from Western Macedonia in Everyday Practices and Narratives'. *Anthropological Journal of European Cultures* 22, no. 2 (2013): 35–52.

Zetkin, Clara. *Clara Zetkin: Selected Writings*. Edited by Philip S. Foner and Angela Davis. New York: International Publishers, 1984.

Zetkin, Clara, and V. I. Lenin. 'My Recollections of Lenin'. In *The Emancipation of Women. From the Writings of V..I. Lenin*, 97–123. Lucknow: Rahul Foundation, 2010.

Zinsser, Judith P., ed. *Men, Women, and the Birthing of Modern Science*. DeKalb: Northern Illinois University Press, 2005.

Zola, Émile. *The Ladies' Paradise*. Translated by Brian Nelson. Berkeley: University of California Press, 1992.

# INDEX

# Index

# Index

# Index

# Index

# Index